LEARNING

PRINCIPLES AND APPLICATIONS

SECOND EDITION

Stephen B. Klein

Mississippi State University

McGRAW-HILL, INC.

New York   St. Louis   San Francisco   Auckland   Bogotá
Caracas   Hamburg   Lisbon   London   Madrid   Mexico   Milan   Montreal
New Delhi   Paris   San Juan   São Paulo   Singapore   Sydney   Tokyo   Toronto

This book was set in Times Roman by Waldman Graphics, Inc.
The editors were Christopher Rogers and Scott Amerman;
the production supervisor was Kathryn Porzio.
The cover was designed by Carla Bauer.
R. R. Donnelley & Sons Company was printer and binder.

LEARNING

Principles and Applications

1 2 3 4 5 6 7 8 9 0   DOC DOC   9 0 9 8 7 6 5 4 3 2 1

ISBN 0-07-035094-9

Library of Congress Cataloging-in-Publication Data

Klein, Stephen B.
  Learning: principles and applications / Stephen B. Klein.—2nd ed.
    p.   cm.
  Includes bibliographical references and index.
  ISBN 0-07-035094-9
  1. Learning.   2. Conditioned response.   I. Title.
  LB1060.K59   1991
  370.15'23—dc20   90-48081

ABOUT
THE AUTHOR

STEPHEN B. KLEIN is professor and head of the Psychology Department at Mississippi State University. He received the Ph.D. degree in psychology in 1971 from Rutgers University. Professor Klein taught at Old Dominion University for twelve years and at Fort Hays State University for seven years prior to coming to Mississippi State University last year. He is author of many publications in psychological journals, *Motivation: Biosocial Approaches*, published by McGraw-Hill in 1982, and *Learning: Principles and Applications*, published by McGraw-Hill in 1987. Dr. Klein coedited the two-volume text *Contemporary Learning Theories* which was published in 1989 by Lawrence Erlbaum and Associates. His family includes his wife, Marie, and three children, Dora, David, and Jason.

In Memory of
My Grandparents
Selma and Arthur Golden
and
Dora and Joseph Klein
Who gave me their love
and showed me
the importance of knowledge

CONTENTS

PREFACE

The first edition of *Learning: Principles and Applications* was published by McGraw-Hill in 1987. One goal of this text was to provide the student with an up-to-date presentation of the current knowledge in learning and memory. [Basic principles were described and were supplemented by research studies to provide validation of those principles.] Both classic experiments and important contemporary studies were incorporated into the text.

A second aim of this text was to show the student the relevance of basic processes. This was accomplished in several ways: First, each chapter opened with a vignette. The short story gave the student an idea of the material to be presented in the chapter. Next, real-world examples of abstract concepts were provided throughout the text. The examples not only showed the operation of abstract ideas but also allowed the student to gain a better understanding of the principles being discussed. Finally, each chapter presented at least one application of these learning principles. [It is my belief that a student's knowledge of learning and memory principles is enhanced by the use of chapter-opening vignettes, real-world examples, and applications.]

This revision retains the engaging character of the first edition. The pedagogy remains a central feature of this new version, but approaches have been reworked to enhance their impact. Vignettes have been rewritten to provide a stronger focal person for each story; new real-world examples have been added involving situations relevant to student life; and applications are now more closely tied to principles and theories from which each application evolved.

Several pedagogical features have been added. Each chapter now contains section reviews, which allow the student to appreciate the main points being covered. Each review provides continuity between major discussions and guides the student to the material in the next section. The chapter-ending summaries now bring all of the main points together to enable the student to understand the central ideas presented in each chapter. There are many new terms introduced in a learning text. To ease the difficulty in incorporating and understanding the new terms, this edition contains a glossary.

Psychologists have spent most of this century intensively studying the learning process. They have uncovered many important aspects concerning how we acquire information about the structure of our environment and how we use this understanding to interact effectively with that environment. The aim of this textbook is to describe what psychologists have discovered about the nature of the learning process.

The solid current presentation of basic principles and description of new research studies found in the first edition is retained in the revision. To this end, a major change in the second edition is the incorporation of recent research into the text. There has been much exciting new research in learning and memory in the last few years, and I have described these new ideas here.

The text presents the important contributions of both animal and human research, since both are crucial to our understanding of the learning process. In many instances, animal studies and human experimentation have yielded identical results, indicating the generality of the processes governing learning. While there are many general laws of learning, there are also instances where species differ in their ability to learn a particular behavior. The use of different animals has shown that biological character affects learning. Furthermore, in some situations, only animal research can be ethically conducted, while in other cases, only human research can identify the learning process that is unique to people. The text describes the research necessary to illustrate a specific learning process.

This edition contains 13 chapters. Chapter 1 gives an introduction to learning as well as a discussion of how experience can alter instinctive behavior. A brief presentation of the ethics of conducting research is included.

Chapter 2 provides a description of learning theory. The student will see the changes that have taken place in learning theory during this century and how contemporary views of the learning process have been shaped by the ideas expressed by previous generations of psychologists.

Chapters 3 and 4 detail Pavlovian conditioning, a process that involves learning when events will or will not occur. Chapter 3 discusses the factors that govern the acquisition or elimination of conditioned responses. A detailed presentation of theories and applications of Pavlovian conditioning can be found in Chapter 4.

Chapters 5 and 6 describe instrumental/operant conditioning, a process that involves learning how to behave in order to obtain the positive aspects (reinforcers) and avoid the negative aspects (punishers) which exist in our environment. The variables influencing the development or extinction of appetitive or reinforcer-seeking behavior are described in Chapter 5, while Chapter 6 presents the determinants of avoidance behavior.

Chapter 7 discusses the environmental control of behavior and how the stimulus environment can exert a powerful influence on how we act. Cognitions can also have an important influence on our actions. Chapter 8 describes the cognitive processes that affect how and when we behave.

Chapter 9 details four cognitive learning processes and shows how we identify concepts, solve problems, make decisions, and learn to use language.

Chapters 10, 11, and 12 discuss memory, the process that allows us to retain our present experience into the future. The nature of memory storage is described in Chapter 10, while the encoding or organization of our experiences is described in Chapter 11. The processes that allow us to retrieve some experiences or forget others are detailed in Chapter 12. Further, the biological basis of memory storage and retrieval is presented in these chapters.

Chapter 13 provides a discussion of the biological processes that influence learning. In some instances, learning is enhanced by instinctive systems, while in others, learning is impaired by our biological character. Chapter 13 also describes the biological processes that provide the pleasurable aspects of reinforcement and the negative aspects of punishment.

The textbook has had input from many people. I thank the students in my learning classes who read drafts of the chapters and pointed out which sections they liked, which they disliked, and which were unclear. I am especially grateful to Patricia Ault-Duel, Traci Belden, Jacalyn Johnson, Nancy Sellers, and Betty Stamper.

The staff at McGraw-Hill played an important role in the creation of this edition. The psychology editors, James Anker, Maria Chiappetta, and Christopher Rogers, guided the development of the text from its inception to this final product. The editing supervisor, Scott Amerman, ensured that the text was not only easy to read but also aesthetically appealing.

I also thank my colleagues who reviewed chapters of the second edition. I am especially grateful to Dr. Monnie Louise Bittle, Virginia Polytechnic Institute and State University; Dr. Michael Boivin, Spring Arbor College; Dr. Robert Gelhart, Pepperdine University; Dr. Roger Mellgren, University of Texas at Arlington; Dr. Ralph Miller, State University of New York at Binghamton; Dr. Jack Nation, Texas A&M University; and Dr. Michael Scavio, California State University, Fullerton, for their detailed and constructive comments.

My family has been very supportive of my work on this edition. I am very appreciative of their support.

Stephen B. Klein

1

AN INTRODUCTION
TO LEARNING

DO YOU HAVE A LIGHT?

For 2 days, Greg has resisted the urge to smoke. Having attempted to quit on
more occasions than he can count, he's determined not to let his extreme
nervousness and irritability keep him from succeeding this time. His family
tries to distract his thoughts from cigarettes, but these attempts work only
temporarily. Anticipating tonight's televised championship boxing match helped
him for a while, but even this cannot prevent his recurrent, intense impulses
to smoke.

Greg began smoking cigarettes when he was 15. All his friends had started
the habit, so it seemed like the natural thing to do. At first, he did not enjoy
smoking, for it made him cough and sometimes feel slightly nauseated. Greg
smoked only with his friends and, to feel part of the group, pretended to inhale.
However, as the unpleasant effects began to disappear, he learned to inhale
and began to smoke more often. By the age of 18, Greg smoked two or three
packs of cigarettes a day. He never thought about stopping until he met Paula.
A nonsmoker, she tried to convince him to quit. Finding himself unable to
break the habit, he simply did not smoke while with Paula.

After they married, Paula continued to plead with Greg to stop smoking. He
has tried every now and then over the past 10 years to resist cigarettes, usually
stopping for a day or two. This time had to be different. At 35, Greg thought
that he was in perfect health, but a routine checkup with the family physician
2 days ago proved him wrong. Greg learned that his extremely high blood
pressure made him a prime candidate for a heart attack. The doctor told Greg
that the pressure could be lowered through special diet, medication, and cessation
of smoking. Continued smoking would undoubtedly interfere with the other
treatments. The threat of a heart attack frightened Greg; he had seen his father

suffer the consequences of an attack several years ago. Determined now to quit, he only hopes that he can endure his withdrawal symptoms.

Greg's intense desire to smoke, as well as his record of repeated attempts to stop, is shared by millions of people. Their addiction, stemming from dependence on the effects of cigarettes, motivates their behavior. Evidence of this dependence is the aversive withdrawal symptoms which many people experience when they attempt to stop smoking. When strong enough, the withdrawal state motivates them to resume smoking.

Cigarette smoking is just one example of addictive behavior. People become addicted to many drugs which have quite different effects. For example, the pain-inhibiting effects of heroin contrast sharply with the arousing effects of amphetamines. Although the effects of drugs may differ, the cycle of drug effects, withdrawal symptoms, and resumption of addictive behavior characterizes all addictive behaviors.

Addiction illustrates how experience affects people's behavior. In this text, we will examine the learning process, or the behavior changes that occur as a result of experience. We begin our explanation by identifying what we mean by learning.

A DEFINITION OF LEARNING

What do we mean by the term *learning?* Learning can be defined as *an experiential process resulting in a relatively permanent change in behavior that cannot be explained by temporary states, maturation, or innate response tendencies.* This definition of learning has three important components: First, learning reflects a change in the *potential* for a behavior, it does not automatically lead to a change in behavior. We must be sufficiently motivated to translate learning into behavior. For example, although you may know the location of the campus cafeteria, you will not be motivated to go there until you are hungry. Also, we might be unable to exhibit a particular behavior even though we have learned it and are sufficiently motivated to exhibit it. For example, you may learn from friends that a good movie is playing but not see it because you cannot afford to go.

Second, behavior changes caused by learning are not always permanent. As a result of new experiences, previously learned behavior is no longer exhibited. For example, you may learn a new and faster route to work and no longer take the old route. Also, there are times when we forget a previously learned behavior and therefore are no longer able to exhibit it. Forgetting the story line of a movie is one instance of the transient aspect of learning.

Third, changes in behavior can be due to processes other than learning. Our behavior can change as the result of motivation rather than learning. For example, you eat when you are hungry or study when you are worried about an upcoming exam. However, eating or studying may not necessarily be due to learning. Motivational changes rather than learning could trigger eating or studying. You may have already learned to eat, and your hunger motivates your eating behavior. Likewise, you may have learned to study to prevent failure, and your fear motivates studying behavior. These behavior changes are temporary; when the motivational state changes again, the behavior will also change. Therefore, you will stop eating when you are no longer hungry and quit studying when you no longer fear failing the examination. Stopping eating or studying is another instance where a temporary state rather than learning leads to a change in behavior.

Many changes in behavior reflect the result of maturational developments. For example, a young child may fear darkness, while an adult does not show an emotional reaction to being in the dark. This change in emotionality reflects a maturational process and is not dependent on experiences with darkness. Another example of the impact of maturation is a child who cannot open a door at age 1 but can do so when 2 years old. The change in the child's behavior reflects physical growth which allows the child to reach the doorknob.

Also, behavior changes can be due to instinctive processes rather than learning. A person who experiences a painful event becomes angry and strikes out. This change in behavior reflects an instinctive reaction and is not learned.

We begin our exploration of learning by examining the nature of instinctive systems. We first consider the simplest form of learning, which involves changes in an animal's or a person's instinctive reactions to environmental events. Later in the chapter we discuss changes in instinctive reactions that occur as a result of experience.

THE INSTINCTIVE BASIS OF BEHAVIOR

Konrad Lorenz (1969) suggested that instinctive systems enhance an animal's or a human's ability to adapt to the environment. Adaptation sometimes involves internal energy (or tension) aroused by a specific environmental stimulus that motivates a predetermined sequence of behaviors. In these cases, experience affects neither the eliciting stimuli nor the behavior. However, in other cases, experience can alter the eliciting environmental stimulus, the instinctive action motivated by internal tension, or both.

According to Lorenz, the ability to learn from experience and respond differentially to varied environmental circumstances is programmed into the genetic structure of a species and provides the flexibility needed to adapt to changing conditions. Sometimes experience alters the ability of environmental events to elicit behavior, the efficiency of instinctive behavior elicited by a particular stimulus, or both. Under other conditions, learning provides new eliciting stimuli, new behaviors, or both, which enhance survival. Lorenz contends that learning facilitates adaptation to the environment and that the ability to learn is innate.

The Search for Knowledge

The evolutionary process is central to an animal's or a person's capacity to adapt (see Lorenz, 1969). *Evolution* represents changes in the behavioral and physical characteristics that a species undergoes in order to survive in a new environment. The environment contains much information, and knowledge of this information provides an animal or a person with adaptive capacity. Lorenz asserts that knowledge represents an increased sensitivity to particular aspects of the environment. A species' ability to adapt increases as, through natural selection, it incorporates knowledge about its environment into its genetic programming. According to Lorenz, evolution occurs when a species incorporates into its genetic structure the ability to absorb environmental knowledge.

The Interaction of Energy and Environment

The instinctive theory of Lorenz and his colleague Niko Tinbergen developed from years of observing animal behavior. To illustrate their model, one of Lorenz and Tinbergen's classic observations is presented, followed by their analysis of the systems controlling this observed behavior.

In 1938, Lorenz and Tinbergen reported their observations of the egg-rolling behavior of the greylag goose. This species builds a shallow nest on the ground to incubate its eggs. When an egg rolls to the side of the nest, the goose reacts by stretching toward the egg and bending its neck, so that its bill is brought toward its breast. This action causes the egg to roll to the center of the nest. If during transit the egg begins to veer to one side, the goose adjusts the position of its bill to reverse the direction of the egg. What causes the goose to react to the rolling egg? Lorenz's energy model addresses this important question.

Energy Model   According to Lorenz (1950), *action-specific energy* constantly accumulates (see Figure 1-1). This accumulation of energy resembles the concept of filling a reservoir with water; the more liquid in the reservoir, the greater the internal pressure for its release. In behavioral terms, the relationship is that the greater the pressure, the more motivated the animal is to behave. The internal pressure (action-specific energy) motivates *appetitive behavior,* which enables an animal to reach an environment containing a distinctive event, a *sign stimulus*. The presence of the sign stimulus releases the accumulated energy. In terms of our example, the stretching movement and adjustment reaction are appetitive behaviors directed toward the rolling egg or sign stimulus.

The goose does not exhibit the retrieving behavior until it has reached the egg. The retrieving behavior is an example of a *fixed action pattern,* an instinctive behavior triggered by the presence of a specific environmental cue, the sign stimulus. An internal block exists for each fixed action pattern, preventing the occurrence of the behavior until the appropriate time. The animal's appetitive behavior, motivated by the buildup of action-specific energy, produces the appropriate releasing stimulus. According to Lorenz and Tinbergen, the sign stimulus acts to remove the block by stimulating an internal *innate releasing mechanism* (IRM). The IRM removes the block, thereby releasing the fixed action pattern. The sight of the egg stimulates the appropriate IRM, which triggers the retrieving response in the goose. After the greylag goose has retrieved one egg and its energy reserve

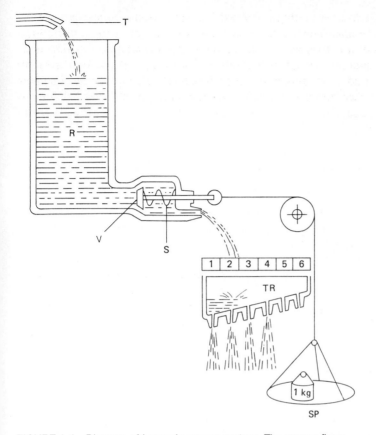

FIGURE 1-1 Diagram of Lorenz's energy system. The energy flows constantly from the tap T into the reservoir R. The cone valve V represents the releasing mechanism, which is open when the sign stimulus exerts pressure on the scale pan SP. The weight on the pan corresponds to the intensity of stimulation. The spring S represents inhibition from higher centers. Energy released from the reservoir R flows into the reservoirs for lower instinctive levels TR. The diagram shows the interaction of internal pressure that occurs from the accumulation of action-specific energy and the external stimulation of the sign stimulation; both act to release the stored energy. Adapted from Lorenz, K. (1950). The comparative method of studying innate behavior patterns. In J. F. Danelli & R. Brown, *Symposia of the Society for Experimental Biology: Physiological mechanisms in animal behavior.* New York: Academic.

is dissipated, the bird will allow another egg to remain at the side of the nest until sufficient action-specific energy has accumulated to motivate the bird to return the second egg to the middle of the nest.

In some situations, a chain of fixed action patterns occurs (see Figure 1-1). In this case, a block exists for each specific fixed action pattern in the sequence, and the appropriate releasing mechanism must be activated for each behavior.

For example, a male Siamese fighting fish exhibits a ritualistic aggressive display when he sees another male or even when he sees a reflection of himself in a mirror. However, no actual physical aggressive behavior occurs until one male intrudes on the other's territory. The second fixed action pattern is blocked until the two males come into close proximity. If neither fish retreats after the ritualistic display, the fish approach each other (an appetitive act) and fighting behavior is released.

Environmental Release   In some cases, the sign stimulus for a particular fixed action pattern is a simple environmental stimulus. For example, Tinbergen (1951) observed that the red belly of the male stickleback is the sign stimulus that releases fighting behavior between two male sticklebacks. Evidence supporting this conclusion is the demonstration that an experimental dummy stickleback, which resembles the stickleback only in color, releases aggressive behavior in a real male stickleback.

The releasing sign stimulus can be quite complex for other fixed action patterns; the sexual pursuit of the male grayling butterfly (see Tinbergen, 1951) is an example. Tinbergen found that a female grayling flying past a male was pursued by the male. Although the color and shape of a model grayling did not influence the male's flight behavior, pursuit was influenced by the darkness of the females, the distance from the male, and the pattern of movement that stimulated the male's forward and backward flight. Tinbergen noticed that the absence of one female characteristic could be compensated for by an increased value of another component. For instance, if the model did not pass near the male, no flight reaction was elicited. However, with the presentation of a darker model at the same distance, male pursuit occurred.

The likelihood of eliciting a sign stimulus depends upon both the accumulated level of action-specific energy and the intensity of the sign stimulus. Research (see Lorenz, 1950; Tinbergen, 1951) indicates that the greater the level of accumulated energy, the weaker the sign stimulus that can still release a particular fixed action pattern. For example, Baerends, Brouwer, and Waterbolk (1955) examined the relationship between a male guppie's readiness to respond and the size of the female. They found that a large female model released courtship behavior even in a male that was typically unresponsive.

Why does reliance on external stimulation for the release of a fixed action pattern decrease as the time increases since the last response? Lorenz (1950) envisioned an IRM as a gate blocking the release of stored energy. The gate is opened either by pulling from external stimulation or by pushing from within. As the internal pressure increases, the amount of external pull needed to open the gate and release the behavior decreases. Another view, proposed by Tinbergen (1951), suggested that sensitivity to the sign stimulus changes as a function of time since the occurrence of the specific behavior. According to Tinbergen, the sensitivity of the innate releasing mechanism to the sign stimulus increases when there has been no recent fixed action pattern.

Conflicting Motives An often observed phenomenon occurs when two in-compatible sign stimuli are encountered; the response is different from the fixed action patterns typically released by either sign stimuli acting alone. According to Tinbergen (1951), when an animal or a human is experiencing conflict due to the presence of two antagonistic sign stimuli, energy overflows into another motivational instinct system and releases a behavior from this other system. The process of activating a third instinct system, which is different from the two involved in the conflict, is called *displacement*.

Naturalistic settings are ideal for observing displacement behaviors. Tinbergen and Van Iersel (1947) reported that the stickleback, when between its own territory and the territory of another stickleback, often displays nest-building behavior. This "out-of-context" nest building is presumably due to the fish's conflict between attacking the neighbor's territory and escaping into its own territory. A person who whistles nervously before a date may be exhibiting displaced activity resulting from the conflict between anticipation of dating an attractive person and fear of acting inappropriately.

It is important to distinguish the instinctive approach from the hypothetical energy system. Our understanding of the factors that govern a wide range of behaviors has benefited from the instinctive approach. Further, the hypothetical energy system is an excellent way to conceptualize the processes motivating instinctive behavior. Environmental stimuli do release instinctive behaviors, and the likelihood of environmental release is dependent upon both the time since the last occurrence of the behavior and the intensity of the releaser. Animals do approach environmental releasers and the intensity of their approach is influenced by the animal's motivation level. However, recent physiological research has raised questions concerning certain aspects of Lorenz and Tinbergen's theory. Although scientists have identified brain systems responsible for the release of both appetitive behavior and fixed action patterns, there is no physiological system that operates according to the structure of the energy model. Energy does not appear to accumulate in any identified brain systems, nor does it appear to flow from one system to another. Brain structures do communicate and interact, but not in accordance with Lorenz and Tinbergen's energy model.

The Importance of Experience

You might have the impression that an instinctive response is inflexible or that the releasing sign stimulus cannot be altered. Although this view is often an accurate concept of the instinctive processes, there are some circumstances in which experience can modify instinctive systems. Lorenz suggested that the instinctive processes of lower animals and human beings are programmed to change as the result of experience. An experience, referred to as learning, or *conditioning*, provides additional knowledge about the environment.

According to Lorenz, a conditioning experience can alter instinctive behavior, the releasing mechanism for instinctive behavior, or both. Only the consummatory response at the end of the behavior chain, according to Lorenz, is resistant to

modification. Conditioning can alter the effectiveness of existing appetitive behavior or change the sensitivity of the releasing mechanism to the sign stimulus.
Depending on the nature of the conditioning experience, this change can be either
increased or decreased sensitivity. In addition, new behaviors or new releasing
stimuli can be developed through conditioning. All of these modifications increase
ability to adapt to the environment.

Lorenz's observations of the jackdaw's nest building illustrates his view of the
importance of learning in adaptation. He discovered that the jackdaw does not
instinctively know the best type of twigs to use as nesting material. This bird
displays an instinctive nest-building response—stuffing twigs into a foundation—
but must try different twigs until it finds one that lodges firmly and does not
break. Having discovered a successful type of twig, the bird then selects only
that type. According to Lorenz, the twig gained the ability to release instinctive
behavior as the result of the bird's success.

Section Review

Lorenz and Tinbergen stress the instinctive aspects of behavior. According to
these ethologists, a specific internal tension (or action-specific energy) exists for
each major instinct. The accumulation of internal energy motivates appetitive
behavior, which continues until a specific environmental cue called a sign stimulus is encountered. This sign stimulus can activate an innate releasing mechanism
(IRM), which releases the stored energy and activates the appropriate fixed action
pattern.

The instinctive system is not inflexible; the releasing stimuli or the instinctive
behavior (or both) can sometimes be altered by experience. In some cases, the
modification involves altering the effectiveness of the existing instinctive actions.
At other times, new releasing stimuli, new behaviors, or both, enable an animal
or a human to adapt. According to Lorenz, this adaptability is programmed into
the genetic structure.

Lorenz assumed that conditioning enhanced a species' adaptation to its environment and that the ability to learn is programmed into each species' genetic
structure. However, Lorenz did not detail the mechanism responsible for translation of learning into behavior. In addition, the factors determining the effectiveness of conditioning were not investigated by the ethologists. We begin by
examining the changes in instinctive behavior that occur with experience. In later
chapters, we will discuss how new releasing stimuli or new behaviors are acquired
as a result of experience.

HABITUATION AND SENSITIZATION

Students who have to give speeches in a class show different reactions to their
experience. Some students become less nervous with experience; yet, for others,
the anxiety increases rather than declines with experience. Why do some students
experience less distress after several speeches while others find the experience

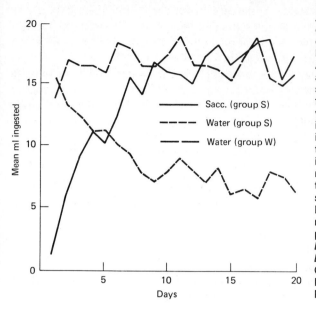

FIGURE 1-2
Animals show a reluctance to consume novel foods. Repeated exposure to food will lead to habituation of neophobia. Animals in group S were given access each day to a 2% saccharin solution for 30 minutes followed by 30 minutes of tap water. Over a 20-day period, the intake of saccharin in group S increased while consumption of tap water declined. The animals in group W received only 30 minutes of tap water each day, their intake of water remained steady. From Domjan, M. (1976). Determinants of the enhancement of flavored-water intake by prior exposure. *Journal of Experimental Psychology: Animal Behavior Processes, 2,* 17–27. Copyright 1976 by the American Psychological Association. Reprinted by permission.

more distressing? The habituation and sensitization phenomena provide one reason for the different reactions to giving a speech.

With *habituation,* responsiveness to a specific stimulus declines with repeated experiences with that stimulus. In our example, the lessened anxiety shown by students when giving a speech may be due to habituation. *Sensitization* refers to an increased reaction to environmental events. The greater nervousness shown by students when giving a speech may be due to sensitization. It also is possible that Pavlovian conditioning leads to the increased or decreased reactions to giving a speech. For example, a change in nervousness may be the result of negative or positive consequences associated with giving the speech. (We will look at Pavlovian conditioning in Chapters 2, 3, and 4.) There are many examples of habituation and sensitization; we will examine these phenomena next.

Suppose an animal is given a new food. Most animals would eat only a little of this novel food. The avoidance of novel food is referred to as *ingestional neophobia.* This neophobic response has considerable adaptive significance. Many foods in the natural environment contain poisons. If the animal eats too much of a poisoned food, it will die. To determine if the food can be safely consumed, the animal eats only a small quantity of the food on the first exposure. With repeated experiences of a nonpoisoned food, the neophobic response habituates and the animal consumes greater amounts of the novel food.

Domjan's 1976 study documents the habituation of ingestional neophobia. Rats received either a 2% saccharin and water solution or just water. Figure 1-2 shows that the rats drank very little saccharin solution when first exposed to this novel flavor. However, intake of saccharin increased with each subsequent experience with this flavor. Eventually, the animals drank as much as rats given only water. These results indicated that the habituation of the animals neophobic response led to the greater consumption of saccharin.

Animals also can show an increased neophobic response. Suppose that an animal is sick. Under this illness condition, the animal will exhibit an increased ingestional neophobia (see Domjan, 1977). The greater neophobic response when animals are ill is due to the sensitization process.

The Nature of Habituation and Sensitization

Why do animals show a decreased (habituated) or increased (sensitized) reaction to environmental events? Groves and Thompson (1970) suggested that habituation reflects a decreased responsiveness of innate reflexes; that is, a stimulus becomes less able to elicit a response as a result of repeated exposure to that stimulus. In contrast, sensitization reflects an increased readiness to react to all stimuli. This increased reactivity operates in the animal's central nervous system. According to Groves and Thompson, drugs that stimulate the central nervous system increase an animal's overall readiness to respond, while reactivity is suppressed by depressant drugs. Emotional distress can also affect responsivity: Anxiety increases reactivity; depression decreases responsiveness.

Research on the startle response provides support for Groves and Thompson's view (see Davis, 1974). When animals are exposed to an unexpected stimulus, they show a sudden jump reaction due to tensing of muscles. A variety of stimuli, such as a brief tone or light, will elicit the startle response. As an example, imagine your reaction when you are working on a project and someone talks to you unexpectedly. In all likelihood, you would exhibit the startle reaction to the unexpected conversation.

Repeated presentations of unexpected stimuli can lead to either a decreased or an increased intensity of the startle reaction. Davis (1974) investigated habituation and sensitization of the startle reaction in rats. A brief 90-millisecond, 110-decibel (dB) tone was presented to two groups of rats. For one group of rats, the unexpected tone was presented against a relatively quiet 60-dB noise background. Davis noted that repeated presentation of the tone in this condition produced a decreased startle response (see Figure 1-3). The other group of rats experienced the unexpected tone against a louder 80-dB noise background. In contrast to the habituation observed with the quiet background, repeated experiences with the tone against the louder background intensified the startle reaction (refer to Figure 1-3).

Why is habituation of the startle response observed with a quiet background but sensitization with a loud background? A loud background is arousing and should lead to enhanced reactivity. This greater reactivity should lead to a greater startle reaction (sensitization). In contrast, in a quiet background, arousal of the central nervous system would be minimal and should lead to a reduced ability of the unexpected stimulus to elicit the startle reaction (habituation).

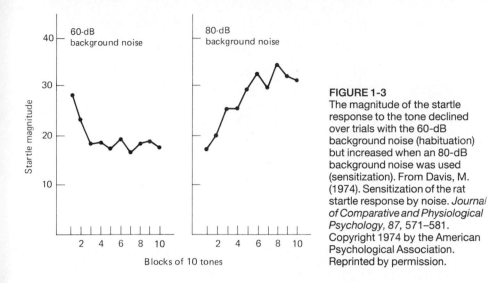

FIGURE 1-3
The magnitude of the startle response to the tone declined over trials with the 60-dB background noise (habituation) but increased when an 80-dB background noise was used (sensitization). From Davis, M. (1974). Sensitization of the rat startle response by noise. *Journal of Comparative and Physiological Psychology, 87,* 571–581. Copyright 1974 by the American Psychological Association. Reprinted by permission.

John Garcia and his associates (see Garcia, 1988; Garcia, Brett, & Rusiniak, 1989) suggested that changes in animal's innate reactions to environmental events have considerable adaptiveness. For example, the reduced neophobia to safe foods allows the animal to consume nutritionally valuable foods. We will discuss the modification of innate feeding responses furthur when we look at biological influences on learning in Chapter 13.

The Likelihood of Habituation and Sensitization

Habituation or sensitization does not always occur with repeated experience. A number of variables affect the occurrence of habituation or sensitization; we will look at several important ones next.

First, research (see Groves, Lee, & Thompson, 1969) indicates that more intense stimuli produce stronger sensitization than do weaker ones. Further, greater sensitization occurs when a strong stimulus is experienced more frequently. In contrast, habituation to a stimulus does not appear to be affected by either intensity or frequency.

Second, habituation to a stimulus appears to depend upon the specific characteristics of the stimulus (refer to Thompson & Spencer, 1966). A change in a salient characteristic of the stimulus will result in an absence of habituation. For example, many birds become alarmed when seeing a hawklike object flying overhead (see Tinbergen, 1951). This alarm reaction can be elicited by any novel object flying overhead, but the reaction will habituate when the stimulus is repeatedly experienced.

In one study, Schleidt (1961) reported habituation of the alarm reaction in young turkeys when either a circular or a rectangular silhouette flew overhead. However, if the shape of the stimulus is changed, the alarm reaction returns.

What is the significance of these observations? There appears to be no specific sign-stimulus eliciting alarm in young turkeys. In the natural environment, the birds will habituate their alarm reaction to members of their species. When a hawk approaches (or the shape changes), the turkeys experience a new shape and their alarm reaction is elicited.

A change in the properties of the stimulus typically does not affect sensitization. The effect of stimulus specificity on habituation but not sensitization provides further support for the view that habituation reflects changes in an innate response to a specific stimulus while sensitization represents an increased responsiveness to many stimuli.

Finally, both habituation and sensitization can be relatively transient phenomena. When a delay intervenes between stimulus presentations, habituation weakens (see Thompson & Spencer, 1966). In some instances, habituation is lost if several seconds or minutes intervene between stimuli. Yet, at other times, delay does not lead to a loss of habituation. This long-term habituation does not appear to reflect a change in an innate response to a stimulus. Instead, it seems to represent a more complex type of learning. We will look at the long-term habituation of responding to a stimulus in Chapter 4.

Sensitization also is affected by time and is lost shortly after the sensitizing event ends. For example, Davis (1974) noted that sensitization of the startle response to a tone was absent 10 to 15 minutes after a loud noise was terminated. Unlike the long-term habituation effect, sensitization always is a temporary effect. This result also points to a nonspecific increased responsivity as the cause of sensitization.

Section Review

Habituation is a decreased response to a stimulus following repeated experiences with that stimulus. In contrast, an increased reaction to a stimulus reflects sensitization. Groves and Thompson suggest that habituation is the result of decreased ability of the stimulus to elicit the response (innate reflexes), while sensitization represents an increased reactivity to all stimuli (central nervous system).

Animals exposed to a novel food show ingestional neophobia, or an avoidance of the food. With repeated experience, the ingestional neophobia habituates and the animal eats more of the food. When an animal is ill, it becomes sensitized and shows enhanced ingestional neophobia.

We have learned that experience can lead to either an intensification (sensitization) or a diminution (habituation) of reaction to environmental events. Our discussion has focused on the response produced *during* exposure to a situation. However, responses also occur *following* an experience. Solomon and Corbit examined this aspect of the innate reaction to events. We now turn our attention to their *opponent process theory*.

OPPONENT PROCESS THEORY

Recall Greg's addiction to cigarettes described in the chapter-opening vignette. Why does Greg crave cigarettes and find it so difficult to stop smoking? Opponent process theory provides us with an answer to this question.

Our Initial Reaction

Solomon and Corbit (1974) observed that all experiences (both biological and psychological) produce an initial affective reaction, the *A state* (see Figure 1-4). This A state can be either pleasant or unpleasant. For example, drinking alcohol produces a pleasurable A state, while taking an exam produces an unpleasant A state. According to Solomon and Corbit's view, the strength of the A state depends upon the intensity of the experience; the stronger the event, the more intense the A state.

The A state arouses a second affective reaction, the *B state*. The B state is the opposite of the A state; if the A state is positive, then the B state will be negative, and vice versa. Thus, the pleasurable A state aroused by drinking initiates an opposing, or opponent, aversive affective state. Similarly, the pain produced during the examination creates a pleasurable relief response. In Solomon and Corbit's

FIGURE 1-4 Schematic diagram of the affective changes during and after an environmental event. (a) Changes for the first few presentations. Notice the large initial A state reaction and the small opponent B state reaction that occurred after termination of the event. (b) Affective responses after many presentations. There is a small A state response (tolerance) and a large and long B state reaction (withdrawal). Adapted from Solomon, R. L., & Corbit, J. D. (1974). An opponent-process theory of motivation: Temporal dynamics of affect. *Psychological Review, 81,* 119–145. Copyright 1974 by the American Psychological Association. Reprinted by permission.

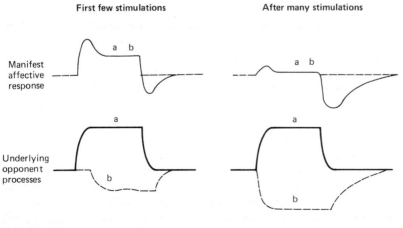

view, our biological systems automatically initiate an opposite, or opponent, response to counter the initial effect of all events.

Several important aspects of the opponent process must be described in order to understand the system depicted in Figure 1-4. First, the B state is initially less intense than the A state. Second, the B state intensifies more slowly than the A state. Finally, after an event has terminated, the strength of the B state diminishes more slowly than the A state. As a result of the slower decline of the B state than the A state, the B state will be experienced when the event ends.

Consider Greg's addiction to smoking to illustrate the operation of these rules. Smoking a cigarette activates a pleasant A state—pleasure. Automatic arousal of the opponent B state—pain or withdrawal—causes his initial A state (pleasure) to diminish after several puffs of the cigarette. When Greg stops smoking, the A state declines quickly, and he experiences the B state (pain or withdrawal), which will slowly diminish with time.

The Intensification of the Opponent B State

Solomon and Corbit discovered that repeated experience with a certain event often increases the strength of the opponent B state (refer to Figure 1-4), which in turn reduces the affective reaction (the A state) experienced during the event. Thus, the strengthening of the opponent B state is thought to be responsible for the development of *tolerance*. Tolerance represents a decreased reactivity to an event with repeated experience (see Chapter 4). Furthermore, when the event ends, an intense B state is experienced. The strong opponent B state which is experienced in the absence of the event is called *withdrawal*.

Let's return to our example of Greg's cigarette smoking to illustrate this intensification of the B state process. Greg has smoked for many years, causing him to experience only a mild A state of pleasure. However, he feels intense prolonged pain or withdrawal when he stops smoking.

A study by Katcher and associates (1969) demonstrates this process. The experimenters observed physiological reactions in dogs during and after the termination of electric shock. After the termination of shock, physiological response (for example, heart rate) declined below preshock levels for several minutes before returning to baseline. After many presentations, the decline was greater and lasted longer. These observations show (1) a strong A state and a weak opponent B state during the first presentations of shock and (2) a diminished A state (tolerance) and an intensified B state (withdrawal) after many experiences.

The opponent process operates in many different situations (see Solomon & Corbit, 1974). Epstein's (1967) description of the emotional reactions of military parachutists is one real-world example of the opponent process. He reported that during the first free-fall, all the parachutists showed an intense aversive A state (terror). This A state diminished after they had landed, and they looked stunned for several minutes. Then, the parachutists began to talk enthusiastically with friends. This opponent B state (relief) lasted for about 10 minutes.

The affective response of experienced parachutists is quite different. During the free-fall, experienced parachutists seemed tense, eager, or excited, reporting only a mildly aversive A state. Their opponent B state was exhilaration. Having landed safely, experienced parachutists showed (1) a high level of activity, (2) euphoria, and (3) intense social interaction. This opponent B state (exhilaration) decreased slowly, lasting for several hours.

The Addictive Process

Opponent process theory (see Solomon, 1977, 1980) offers an explanation for the development of addiction. In Solomon's view, addictive behavior is a coping response to an aversive opponent B state; it is an example of behavior motivated to terminate (or prevent) the unpleasant withdrawal state.

Most people who are heavy drinkers do not become alcoholics. Similarly, people who consume other drugs do not always become drug addicts. Solomon suggests that in order for addiction to develop, people must recognize that abstinence causes withdrawal symptoms and that the resumption of the addictive behavior after abstinence eliminates or prevents aversive feelings. People who think that the discomfort they experience with abstinence is caused by factors other than the absence of the substance or event are not motivated to resume the addictive behavior. Under these circumstances, addiction does not develop.

There is another reason why addiction may not occur following repeated exposure. The number of exposures to a substance or event alone does not determine the intensification of the B state. If sufficient time intervenes between experiences, the opponent state does not intensify. And without the aversive withdrawal B state, the motivation for addiction does not exist. In support of Solomon's view, Starr (1978) discovered that young ducklings showed no distress to the absence of the mother when a 5-minute interval lapsed between separations. In contrast, with a 1- or 2-minute interval, strong withdrawal symptoms occurred. The importance of frequency in strengthening the opponent state suggests why some people can take a drug infrequently and never experience intense withdrawal symptoms after its effect has ended.

Once an addiction is established, an addict is motivated to prevent or terminate withdrawal symptoms. One consequence of addiction is the sacrifice of potential rewards (for example, friends or a job). Most addicts recognize the serious consequences of their addiction and try to stop their self-destructive behavior. Now let's examine why it is so difficult for addicts to break their habits.

The Influence of Other Adversive Events

Why is it so difficult for addicts to be cured? The adversive withdrawal reaction is a nonspecific unpleasant affective state. Therefore, any event that arouses the adversive state will motivate the addictive behavior. For example, multiple problems face alcoholics who attempt to stop drinking. Inhibiting drinking while experiencing the B state is only part of the problem. Many daily stressors, such as problems at work or home, can activate the adversive motivational state, which can motivate the habitual addictive behavior.

Suppose an alcoholic's mother-in-law arrives and her presence is a very adversive event. Under these conditions, the mother-in-law's presence will activate the adversive state, thus intensifying the pressure to drink. Solomon believes that all potential adversive events must be prevented in order for addicts to break their habits. Other reasons for the difficulty of eliminating addictive behavior will be described in Chapter 4.

The Search for Pleasure

Most of us equate addictive behavior with situations in which people are motivated to terminate the adversive withdrawal state and reinstate a pleasant initial state. However, there are also occasions in which people deliberately expose themselves to an adversive A state in order to experience the pleasant opponent B state (Solomon, 1977, 1980). The behavior of experienced parachutists exemplifies this process. Most people anticipating parachuting from an aircraft never jump at all or quit after one jump. However, those who do jump and experience a strong pleasurable B state are often quite motivated to jump again. Epstein reported that some experienced jumpers become extremely depressed when bad weather cancels a jump. The behavior of these parachutists when denied the opportunity to jump resembles that of drug addicts who cannot obtain the desired drug. Other behaviors in which the positive opponent state may lead to addiction include running in marathons (Milvy, 1977) and jogging (Booth, 1980).

Craig and Siegel (1980) discovered that introductory psychology students taking a test felt apprehensive and experienced a positive euphoric feeling when the test ended. However, it is unlikely that students' level of positive feeling after having taken a test is as strong as that of experienced parachutists after jumping. Perhaps most students are not tested often enough to develop a strong opponent pleasurable B state. You might suggest that your instructor test you more frequently to decrease your initial aversive apprehension and to intensify your positive affective relief when the test ends.

THE ETHICS OF CONDUCTING RESEARCH

We will discuss many studies using both animals and humans in this text. There are limits to the type of research that can be conducted. Research that violates principles of ethical conduct is prohibited. This chapter ends by examining the research that is permissible with animals and humans.

Conducting Research with Humans

Psychological research with human subjects must be conducted in accordance with the ethical principles published by the American Psychological Association in the book entitled *Ethical Principles in the Conduct of Research with Human Participants*. Let's briefly discuss what ethical principles must be followed by a psychologist conducting research with humans.

When a psychologist plans to conduct research using human subjects, an ethics committee decides if that research is permissible under the guidelines provided by the American Psychological Association. The main principle determining whether or not the ethics committee approves the research project is the demonstration that the planned study maximizes potential gain in knowledge and minimizes the costs and potential risks to human subjects. In conducting human research, the psychologist typically enters into an agreement with the subject. The general purpose of the study and potential risks of participating are explained to subjects. It also is essential that subjects are not coerced into participation in the study. For example, it used to be true at many schools that students were required to participate in psychological experiments as a course requirement in general psychology. This requirement is a form of coercion and is no longer permissible. Students can volunteer to participate, but failing to volunteer cannot be counted against the student. The subjects must also be free to withdraw from the study at any time.

As part of the agreement between the researcher and each subject, the subject is informed that he or she will receive some tangible rewards (that is, money), personal help (that is, counseling), or information regarding the study (that is, results). The researcher must live up to this agreement, as it is a contract between the researcher and participant. After the study is completed, the subject must be provided with information about the results of the study. Further, the anonymity and confidentiality of the subject's behavior in the study must be maintained. All of this information must be explained to the individual in a written agreement, and the subject must sign this agreement to indicate that he or she consents to participate in the study.

The Use of Animals in Research

Many of the studies that will be described in this text used nonhumans as subjects. Some of the nonhumans included mice, rats, birds, cats, dogs, and monkeys. Why do psychologists use animals in their research? There are several reasons. One reason is the problem of documenting causal relationships. People differ greatly in terms of their behavior, which makes it difficult to obtain a representative sample. Because the behavior of animals is less variable, it is easier to show causal relationships in animals than in humans.

Another reason for using animals is that some types of research cannot be ethically conducted with humans. For example, suppose a psychologist suspects that damage to a certain area of the brain impairs memory storage. This idea comes from case histories of individuals with memory disorders who have a tumor in this brain area. But these case histories cannot be used to infer causality. The only way to demonstrate causality is to damage this area of the brain and see if memory storage problems result. Obviously, we cannot do this type of research with humans; it would be unethical to expose a person to any treatment that would lead to a behavior pathology. The use of animals provides the means of showing that this brain area controls memory storage and that damage to it leads to memory disorders.

Some individuals object to the use of animals for demonstrating that a certain area of the brain controls memory storage, or for any other reason. However, several arguments have been offered in defense of the use of animals for psychological research. Humans suffer from many different behavior disorders, and animal research can provide us with the knowledge concerning the causes of these disorders, as well as the treatments that can prevent or cure behavioral problems. As the noted psychologist Neal Miller (1985) points out, animal research has led to a variety of programs, including rehabilitation treatments of neuromuscular disorders and the development of drugs and behavioral treatments of phobias, depression, schizophrenia, and other behavior pathologies. Certainly animals should not be tortured and any discomfort should be minimized. Yet, when a great deal of human suffering may be prevented, the use of animals in studies seems appropriate (see Feeney, 1987).

SUMMARY

1 We have defined learning as an experiential process resulting in a relatively permanent change in behavior that cannot be explained by temporary states, maturation, or innate response tendencies.

2 Lorenz and Tinbergen stress the instinctive aspects of behavior. According to these ethologists, a specific internal tension (or action-specific energy) exists for each major instinct. The accumulation of internal energy motivates appetitive behavior, which continues until a specific environmental cue called a sign stimulus is encountered. This sign stimulus can activate an innate releasing mechanism (IRM), which releases the stored energy and activates the appropriate fixed action pattern.

3 The instinctive system is not inflexible; the releasing stimuli or the instinctive behavior (or both) can sometimes be altered by experience. In some cases, the modification involves altering the effectiveness of the existing instinctive actions. At other times, new releasing stimuli, new behaviors, or both enable an animal or human to adapt. According to Lorenz, this adaptability is programmed into the genetic structure.

4 Habituation is a decreased response to a stimulus following repeated experiences with that stimulus. In contrast, an increased reaction to a stimulus reflects sensitization. Groves and Thompson suggest that habituation is the result of decreased ability of the stimulus to elicit the response (innate reflex), while sensitization represents an increased reactivity to all stimuli (central nervous system).

5 Animals exposed to a novel food show ingestional neophobia, or an avoidance of the food. With repeated experience, the ingestional neophobia habituates and the animal eats more of the food. When an animal is ill, it becomes sensitized and shows enhanced ingestional neophobia.

6 Solomon and Corbit observed that all experiences produce an initial affective reaction, called the A state. The A state can be either pleasant or unpleasant. The A state arouses a second affective reaction, called the B state. The B state is the opposite of the A state; if the A state is positive, then the B state will be negative, and vice versa. The

B state is initially less intense, develops more slowly, and declines more slowly than the A state.

7 When an event is experienced often, the strength of the B state increases. This increased B state reduces the affective reaction (A state) experienced during the event. Further, after the event ends, the increased B state leads to the experience of a strong opponent B state. The reduced A response to the event is called tolerance, and the intensified opponent reaction in the absence of the event is called withdrawal.

8 Some people become addicted to pleasurable experiences even though arousal decreases with repeated experience. Addiction develops when these people learn that withdrawal occurs when the event ends, and that their addictive behavior terminates the adversive opponent withdrawal state.

9 A second form of addiction occurs when a person learns that an intense pleasurable opponent state can be produced following exposure to an initial adversive state. Although early experience with the event was unpleasant, "the pleasure addict" now finds the initial affective response only mildly adversive and the opponent state very pleasurable. The anticipated pleasure motivates the addict to experience the adversive event.

10 Ethical principles established by the American Psychological Association govern what kind of research is permissible with humans. A researcher must demonstrate to an ethics committee that the planned study maximizes the potential gain in psychological knowledge and minimizes the costs and potential risks to human subjects.

11 Many psychologists use animals as subjects in their research. One reason for using animal subjects is that causal relationships can be demonstrated in animals in certain types of studies that cannot be ethically conducted in humans. The discomfort experienced by the animals should be minimized; however, a great deal of human suffering can be prevented by conducting research with animals.

2

THEORETICAL APPROACHES TO LEARNING

THE OLDIES BUT GOODIES

Justin went to the movies every Friday night. He was a regular at the Cinema Theater, which showed classic movies like *On the Waterfront* and *To Kill a Mockingbird*. Although he had not missed a show in almost a year, Justin had not always been a fan of the classics. Before going to college, his favorite movies were science fiction and adventure films. He especially enjoyed the *Star Wars* series; he had seen each movie at least three times.

Justin's new interest in classic films developed in his first semester at college. During enrollment he had met with his advisor to discuss the courses that he should take. Four courses were required, but he could enroll in one of his choosing. His advisor had given him a list of courses that would fulfill the university's General Education program requirements. As he looked over the list, he spotted a course entitled "Introduction to Motion Pictures," which was offered by the theater department. Since he liked movies so much, he had decided to take the course.

When Justin went to the first class, he was given a list of 15 movies that would be covered that semester. Justin had not seen most of the films on the list and several were not familiar to him. The instructor informed the class that they would discuss each movie's strengths and weaknesses after viewing it.

The first film that the class saw was *High Noon*. Justin had seen many Westerns, but none compared with this movie. It was action packed yet revealed well-defined characters. The next week, he saw *Grapes of Wrath*. He could not believe that he would like a black-and-white movie, but it was wonderful. Every week was a new and exciting experience.

Justin started going to the theater in town around the middle of the term. The theater was sponsoring a Humphrey Bogart film festival and several students in the class asked Justin to go with them. The Bogart movies were great and Justin had a super time. He was now hooked on classics.

Why does Justin go to the movie theater every Friday night? His past enjoyable experiences with movies are responsible for his present behavior. Yet, how have Justin's experiences been translated into actions? Many psychologists have speculated on the nature of the learning process. Some theories have attempted to explain the basis of all human actions, while others have focused on specific aspects of the learning process. Some theories would attempt to describe both why Justin liked movies and why he went to the theater every Friday. In contrast, other theories would tell us either why Justin enjoyed movies or why he went on Friday night.

In this chapter, we will examine several different global theories of learning, that is, several views that attempt to explain all aspects of behavior. Global theories of learning emerged in the 1930s and were especially popular into the late 1960s. These global views have provided us with considerable knowledge concerning the nature of learning. Recently, psychologists have focused on more specific aspects of the learning process. At the end of this chapter, we will describe the reasons for the shift from global to more specific learning theories.

HISTORICAL ORIGINS OF LEARNING THEORY

Psychology was not always interested in the role of experience in governing human behavior. Early thinking in the field focused on the importance of instincts in human activity.

Functionalism

Functionalism was an early school of psychology that emphasized the instinctive origins and adaptive function of behavior. According to its proponents, the function of behavior is to promote survival, and behaviors that are adaptive allow an animal to survive. However, the functionalists expressed various ideas concerning the mechanisms controlling human behavior. John Dewey (1886) suggested that the reflexive behaviors of the lower animals have been replaced in humans by the mind, which has evolved as the primary mechanism for human survival. The brain enables the individual to adapt to the environment. The main aspect of Dewey's functionalism was his idea that the manner of human survival differed from that of lower animals.

In contrast to Dewey, William James, a fellow 19th-century psychologist, argued that the major difference between humans and lower animals lies in the character of their respective inborn or instinctual motives. According to James

(1890), human beings possess a greater range of instincts which guide behavior (for example, rivalry, sympathy, fear, sociability, cleanliness, modesty, and love) than do lower animals. These social instincts directly enhance (or reduce) our successful interaction with our environment and thus our survival. William James also proposed that all instincts, both human and animal, have a mentalistic quality, possessing both purpose and direction. Unlike Dewey, James assumed that instincts similarly motivated the behavior of humans and lower animals.

Some psychologists (see Troland, 1928), who opposed a mentalistic concept of instinct, argued that internal biochemical forces motivate behavior in all species. Concepts developed in physics and chemistry during the second half of the 19th century provided a framework for this mechanistic approach to motivation. Ernst Brucke stated in 1874 that "the living organism is a dynamic system in which the laws of chemistry and physics apply"—a view that led to great advances in physiology. Troland and others used a physiochemical approach to explain the motivation for human and animal behavior.

A number of psychologists strongly criticized the instinct concept proposed by the functionalists on several grounds. First, anthropologists pointed to a variety of values, beliefs, and behaviors among different cultures, an observation inconsistent with the idea of universal human instincts. Second, Watson and Morgan's (1917) observations of human infants led them to conclude that only three innate emotional responses—fear, rage, and love—existed, and that these could be elicited by only a small number of stimuli. Third, the widespread and uncritical use of the instinct concept did not advance an understanding of the nature of human behavior. Bernard's (1924) analysis illustrates the weaknesses of the instinct theories of the 1920s. Bernard identified several thousand, often conflicting, instincts proposed by the functionalists. For example, he described one instinct as "with a glance of the eye we can estimate instinctively the age of a passerby" (page 132). With this type of instinct, it is not surprising that many psychologists reacted so negatively to the instinctive concept.

In the 1920s American psychology moved away from the instinct explanation of human behavior and began to emphasize the learning process. The psychologists who view experience as the major determinant of actions are called behaviorists. Contemporary views suggest that behavior is controlled both by instinctive and experiental processes. In the last chapter, we looked at instinctive processes and how experience affects instinctive reactions. In this chapter, we examine the behaviorists' ideas concerning the nature of the learning process. The influence of instincts on learning will be addressed in Chapter 13.

Behaviorism

Behaviorism is a school of thought that emphasizes the role of experience in governing behavior. According to behaviorists, the important processes governing behavior are learned. Both the drives that initiate behavior and the specific behaviors motivated by these drives are learned through our interaction with the environment. A major goal of the behaviorists is to determine the laws governing learning. This concern about the nature of learning has dominated academic psychology for most of this century. A number of ideas contributed to the behavioral view. The Greek philosopher Aristotle's concept of the association of ideas is one important origin of behaviorism.

Associationism   Suppose that a friend approaches you after class and remarks that your party last week was terrific. This remark causes you to recall meeting a very attractive person at your party, which in turn reminds you to ask this person for a date. This whole thought process reflects the concept of association of ideas: Two events can become associated with each other; thus, when you think of one event, you automatically recall the other. Aristotle proposed that, in order for an association to develop, the two events must be *contiguous* (temporally paired) and either similar to or opposite each other.

During the 18th century, British empiricists described the association process in great detail. David Hume (1739) hypothesized that another factor—causal events—might be capable of producing associations. For example, if you overslept and missed breakfast, you would become hungry by 10 o'clock. Your learned association might be that oversleeping causes you to be hungry before lunch.

Thorndike   The work of Edward Thorndike was another important influence on the behaviorist view. Thorndike's 1898 publication of his studies established that animal behavior could change as a consequence of experience. Thorndike's ideas on learning and motivation developed from his research with his famous puzzle box (see Figure 2-1). In these studies, he placed a hungry cat in a locked box and put food outside the box. The cat could escape from the box to obtain food by exhibiting one of a number of possible behaviors. For example, two effective behaviors were pulling on a string and pressing a pedal. Not only did the cat escape, but also, with each successive trial, the time needed for escape slowly decreased. It appears that the cat's escape from the box progressed from a chance act to a learned behavior.

Thorndike proposed that the cat formed an association between the stimulus (the box) and the effective response. Learning, according to Thorndike, reflects the development of an S-R (stimulus-response) association. As the result of learning, when the animal reexperiences the specific stimulus, the appropriate response is elicited. Thorndike asserted that the animal is not conscious of this association but is instead exhibiting a mechanistic habit in response to a particular stimulus. The S-R association developed because the cat was *rewarded:* When the cat was hungry, the appropriate response was followed by the presentation of food, which produced a satisfying state and strengthened the S-R bond. Thorndike labeled this strengthening of an association by a satisfying event or reward the *law of effect*.

Thorndike did not think that the law of effect applied only to animal behavior; he argued that it also describes the human learning process. Thorndike (1932)

FIGURE 2-1   Thorndike's famous puzzle box: The hungry cat can escape by exhibiting one of three potential responses and thereby obtain food. From Swenson, L. C. (1980). *Theories of learning.* Belmont, CA: Wadsworth.

presented his human subjects with a concept to learn. Telling his subjects that they had responded correctly enabled the subjects to learn the appropriate response.

Reward is not the only process strengthening a stimulus-response association. According to Thorndike's *law of exercise,* the strength of a stimulus-response connection can be increased by use. Further, he asserted that the connection is weakened with disuse.

Although Thorndike's views concerning the nature of the learning process were quite specific, his ideas on the motivational process which determines behavior were more vague. According to Thorndike, learning occurs or previously learned behavior is exhibited only if the animal or human is "ready." Thorndike's *law of readiness* proposes that the animal or human must be motivated to develop an association or to exhibit a previously established habit. Thorndike did not hypothesize about the nature of the motivation mechanism, leaving such endeavors to future psychologists. Indeed, the motivational basis of behavior became of critical concern to later generations of behaviorists.

Pavlov   How did the cat initially choose the correct response in Thorndike's puzzle box studies? Thorndike explained the process as one of trial and error; the cat simply performed various behaviors until it discovered a correct one. Reward then functioned to strengthen that correct response. However, the research of Ivan Pavlov (1927) suggested that the learning process is anything but trial and error. According to Pavlov, definite rules determine which behavior occurs in the learning situation.

Behaviorists were profoundly influenced by Pavlov's work. His description of the conditioning process first appeared in English when his Huxley lecture, delivered at Charing Cross Hospital, was published in *Science* in 1906. The translation into English of his work, *Conditioned Reflexes,* in 1927 provided a comprehensive description of his research. Pavlov was a physiologist, not a psychologist; his initial plan was to uncover the laws governing digestion. He observed that animals exhibit numerous reflexive responses when food is placed in their mouths (for example, salivation, gastric secretion). The function of these responses is to aid in the digestion process.

Pavlov observed during the course of his research, that his dogs began to secrete stomach juices when they saw food or when it was placed in their food dishes. He concluded that the dogs had learned a new behavior, because he had not observed this response during their first exposure to the food. To explain his observation, he suggested that both animals and humans possess innate or *unconditioned reflexes.* An unconditioned reflex consists of two components—an *unconditioned stimulus* (UCS, for example, food), which involuntarily elicits the second component, the *unconditioned response* (UCR, for example, release of saliva). A new or *conditioned reflex* develops when a neutral environmental event occurs with the unconditioned stimulus. As conditioning progresses, the neutral stimulus becomes the *conditioned stimulus* (CS, for example, the sight of food) and is able to elicit the learned, or *conditioned response* (CR). The conditioned response (for example, salivating to sight of food) is strengthened by increasing the number of pairings of the conditioned stimulus with the unconditioned stimulus.

The demonstration of a learned reflex in animals was an important discovery, illustrating not only an animal's ability to learn but also the mechanism responsible for the learned behavior. According to Pavlov, any neutral stimulus paired with the unconditioned stimulus could, through conditioning, develop the capacity to elicit a CR. In his classic demonstration of the conditioning process, he first implanted a tube, called a fistula, in a dog's salivary glands to collect saliva (see Figure 2-2). He then presented the conditioned stimulus, the sound of a metronome, and shortly thereafter placed the unconditioned stimulus, meat powder, in the dog's mouth. On the first presentation, only the meat powder produced saliva (UCR). However, with repeated pairings of the tone with food, the tone (CS) began to elicit saliva (CR); the strength of the conditioned response increased with increased pairings of the conditioned and unconditioned stimuli. Figure 2-3 presents a diagram of Pavlov's classical conditioning process.

Pavlov conducted an extensive investigation of the conditioning process, identifying many procedures that influence an animal's learned behaviors; many of his ideas are still accepted today. Pavlov showed that if, after conditioning, the conditioned stimulus is presented without the unconditioned stimulus, the strength of the conditioned response diminishes. Pavlov named this process of eliminating an established conditioned response *extinction.* A conditioned response also can

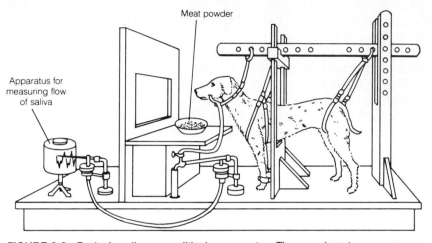

Meat powder

Apparatus for measuring flow of saliva

FIGURE 2-2 Pavlov's salivary-conditioning apparatus. The experimenter can measure saliva output when either a conditioned stimulus (for example, a bell) or an unconditioned stimulus (for example, meat powder) is presented to the dog. The dog is placed in a harness to minimize movement, thus ensuring an accurate measure of the salivary response. Adapted from Yerkes, R. M., & Margulis, S. (1909). The method of Pavlov in animal psychology. *Psychological Bulletin,* 6, 257–273. Copyright 1909 by the American Psychological Association. Reprinted by permission.

be eliminated through the counterconditioning process. In *counterconditioning,* the conditioned stimulus is paired with an opponent or antagonistic unconditioned stimulus. The conditioning of the opponent response causes the conditioned stimulus no longer to elicit the original conditioned response.

Pavlov's observations have profoundly influenced psychology. His conditioning process, often called Pavlovian conditioning, has been demonstrated in various animals, including humans. Conditioned responses also have been established to many different unconditioned stimuli, and psychologists have shown that most environmental stimuli can become conditioned ones.

Pavlov and Thorndike described two different learning processes—classical conditioning and instrumental conditioning. In the past, especially during the two decades following the publication of Pavlov's work, the classical conditioning process was emphasized. Later, during the 1940s and 1950s, researchers focused on the instrumental conditioning process initially described by Thorndike. A renewed interest in Pavlovian conditioning has occurred during the past decade. We will discuss in greater detail the Pavlovian conditioning process in Chapters 3 and 4 and the instrumental conditioning process in Chapters 5 and 6.

Watson Neither Thorndike nor Pavlov was a behaviorist. Each merely described the learning process. It was John B. Watson who demonstrated its importance in human behavior. Although Pavlov's research excited Watson, the work of another Russian, Vladimir Bechterev, was an even greater influence.

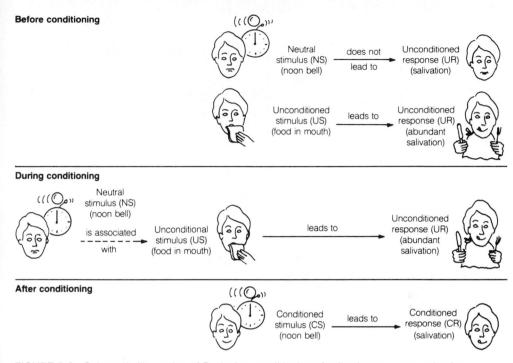

Before conditioning

Neutral stimulus (NS) (noon bell) — does not lead to → Unconditioned response (UR) (salivation)

Unconditioned stimulus (US) (food in mouth) — leads to → Unconditioned response (UR) (abundant salivation)

During conditioning

Neutral stimulus (NS) (noon bell) is associated with ------→ Unconditional stimulus (US) (food in mouth) — leads to → Unconditioned response (UR) (abundant salivation)

After conditioning

Conditioned stimulus (CS) (noon bell) — leads to → Conditioned response (CR) (salivation)

FIGURE 2-3 Schematic illustration of Pavlovian conditioning of salivation to a noon stimulus. Before conditioning, the presentation of the noon stimulus elicits no response when presented alone. During conditioning, the noon stimulus is followed by the unconditioned stimulus, food, which can produce the physiological response of salivation, the UCR. After conditioning, the presentation of the noon stimulus elicits the conditioned salivation response. Adapted from Davidoff, L. (1980). *Introduction to psychology* (2d ed.). New York: McGraw-Hill.

Bechterev and Pavlov conducted their research at the same time, and the 1913 American publication of Bechterev's work also contributed greatly to the popularity of behaviorism.

Whereas Pavlov used positive or pleasant UCSs, Bechterev employed aversive or unpleasant ones (for example, shock) to study the conditioning process. Bechterev found that a conditioned leg withdrawal response could be established in dogs by the pairing of a neutral stimuli with the shock. In his duplication of Bechterev's studies, Watson showed that after several pairings with electric shock, a previously neutral stimulus elicited not only a finger withdrawal response but also an emotional arousal (revealed by increased heart rate) as the conditioned response.

Watson assumed that abnormal, as well as normal, behavior is learned. He was particularly concerned with demonstrating that human fears are acquired through Pavlovian conditioning. To illustrate this point, Watson and Rayner (1920) showed a white rat to Albert, a healthy infant attending a day-care center. As the child reached for the rat, he heard a loud sound (UCS) produced by

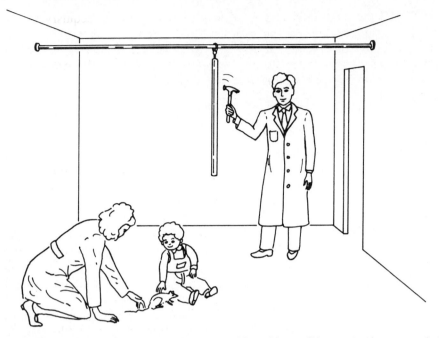

FIGURE 2-4 While "little Albert" was playing with a white rat, Watson struck a suspended steel bar with a hammer. The loud sound disturbed the child, causing him to develop a conditioned fear of the white rat. Rosalie Rayner, Watson's assistant, distracted "little Albert" while Watson approached the bar. From Swenson, L. C. (1980). *Theories of learning*. Belmont, CA: Wadsworth.

Watson's hitting a heavy iron rail with a hammer (see Figure 2-4). After three CS-UCS pairings, Watson and Rayner observed that presentation of the rat (CS) alone produced a fear response in the child. The rat elicited strong emotional arousal, demonstrated by the child's attempts to escape from it, after six CS-UCS pairings. The authors observed a strong emotional response to similar objects: The child also showed fear of a white rabbit and a white fur coat.

Although Watson had intended to extinguish Albert's fear, Albert's mother withdrew him from the day-care center before Watson could eliminate the infant's fear. Mary Cover Jones, a student working with Watson, in 1924 developed an effective technique for eliminating conditioned fears. A young child served as the subject. Jones paired a white rabbit with a loud noise often enough for the rabbit to elicit a fear response on its own. Once the fear was well established, she brought the rabbit into the same room with the child while the child was eating, keeping enough distance between the rabbit and child so that the child was not alarmed. She then moved the rabbit closer and closer to the child, allowing the child to grow accustomed to it in gradual steps. Eventually the child was able to touch and hold the formerly fear-inducing animal. According to Jones, this procedure had eliminated fear by conditioning a positive emotional response, produced by eating, to the rabbit. The elimination of fear by the acquisition of a fear-inhibiting emotional response occurs through the counterconditoning process. Approximately 30 years later, Jones's study played an important role in the development of an effective treatment of human phobic behavior. We will discuss this treatment, systematic desensitization, in Chapter 4.

Section Review

This century began with the functionalist emphasis on the instinctive character of human behavior. However, the functionalists could not agree on the nature of instinctive processes or the number of instincts. Many psychologists adopted the behavioral view, or the belief that most human behavior is learned.

Thorndike observed that hungry cats could learn a new behavior to obtain food. He placed the cats in a puzzle box and found that the behavior which enabled the cat to escape from the puzzle box was increasingly used when the cats later were returned to the box. Thorndike assumed that the effect of the food reward was to strengthen the association between the stimulus of the puzzle box and the effective behavior.

Pavlov demonstrated the conditioning of a new reflex. He paired a novel stimulus (the conditioned stimulus) with a biologically significant event (the unconditioned stimulus). Pavlov observed that prior to conditioning, only the unconditioned stimulus elicited the unconditioned response. After the pairing of the conditioned and unconditioned stimuli, the conditioned stimulus was able to elicit the conditioned response.

Watson showed that an emotional fear response could be conditioned in humans. He discovered that a young child would become frightened of a rat paired with a loud noise. The child also showed fear to other white objects.

TRADITIONAL LEARNING THEORY

Two major theoretical approaches have been proposed to explain the nature of the learning process. The S-R theorists advocate a mechanistic view of the learning process. Learning, according to the S-R approach, consists of an originally neutral environmental stimulus developing the ability to elicit a specific response through association with a stimulus which innately elicits the response. In contrast, the cognitive theorists advocate a mentalistic view of the learning process. Learning, according to the cognitive approach, involves the recognition of when important events, such as reward and punishment, are likely to occur and the understanding of how to attain reward and avoid punishment. A flexible view of behavior is advocated by the cognitive theorists, which contrasts with the inflexible approach of the S-R theorists. Perhaps you feel that only one of these approaches is correct; however, according to the literature, both mechanistic and cognitive processes influence our behavior. We begin by describing the S-R theories and follow with a discussion of the cognitive approach.

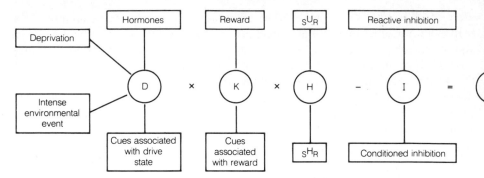

FIGURE 2-5 Diagram of Hull's theory. The terms in the circles show the major variables influencing the likelihood of behavior in Hull's view. Drive (D), habit strength (H), and incentive (K) increase the excitatory potential ($_sE_R$), thereby enhancing the likelihood that the stimulus will elicit a particular response. In contrast, inhibition (I) decreases excitatory potential. The terms in the rectangles represent the processes that influence each major process. From Klein, S. B. (1982). *Motivation: Biosocial approaches.* New York: McGraw-Hill.

S-R Views

The Concept of Drive In 1918, Robert S. Woodworth introduced the concept of *drive* to psychology. He defined drive as an intense internal force that motivates behavior. How is drive translated into behavior? Clark Hull (1943, 1952) provided us with some important insights into the nature of the drive process.

Hull's Drive Theory Clark Hull developed the most influential drive theory. His view asserts that the combined influence of several factors determines the intensity of instrumental activity. According to Hull, the relationship is represented as behavioral potential ($_sE_R$) = drive (D) × incentive (K) × habit strength (H) − inhibition (I). The factors influencing each aspect of the theory are presented in Figure 2-5. In Hull's view, accurate prediction of behavior is possible only when each factor in the mathematical relationship is known.

Imagine the "butterflies" that you experience before taking a test. The scheduled exam creates this arousal or nervousness; the prior scheduling of the exam is the antecedent condition producing the internal drive state. Your nervousness motivates the behavior which in the past produced drive reduction; it is hoped that this behavior includes studying. We begin by examining the antecedent conditions inducing drive and motivating behavior.

Unconditioned Sources of Drive Hull (1943) proposed that events which threaten survival (for example, failure to obtain food) create the internal drive state. Survival requires that internal biological systems operate effectively. A deficit in these internal systems threatens survival and thus represents, according to Hull, an antecedent condition that will motivate behavior designed to restore biological systems to normal. In some cases, normal functioning may be restored through an internal adjustment. For instance, in the absence of food, an individual will use stored energy to maintain normal functioning. However, if the deficiency persists, behavior will be initiated to resolve the deficiency. Thus, using too much stored energy motivates action to obtain food.

In 1952, Hull acknowledged that events which do not threaten survival can also motivate behavior. Several types of studies forced Hull to acknowledge that an internal drive state can appear even in the absence of deprivation. First, animals show a strong preference for saccharin, consuming large quantities even when they are not hungry. Although saccharin has no caloric value, deprived animals will eat it rather than a more nutritionally valuable food. In addition, hungry rats can learn an instrumental behavior to secure saccharin (Sheffield & Roby, 1950). Thus, instrumental behavior can occur in the absence of a biologically induced deficiency. Several classes of nondeprivation events can induce drive and motivate behavior.

Hull assumed that intense environmental events motivate behavior by activating the internal drive state. Electrical shock is one external stimulus that can induce internal arousal. The shock may be aversive, but it does not necessarily threaten survival. Yet, the presentation of electrical shock is one antecedent condition motivating defensive behavior.

The internal drive state which motivates behavior can be produced by a number of circumstances, including deprivation and intense environmental events. These events instinctively produce drive. However, many stimuli in our environment acquire the capacity to induce the internal drive state. Let's next examine how external cues develop the capacity to motivate behavior.

Acquired Drives   In the classical conditioning process, Hull (1943) suggested that environmental stimuli can acquire the ability to produce an internal drive state. From this view, the association of environmental cues with the antecedent conditions which produce an unconditioned drive state causes the development of a conditioned drive state. Once this conditioned drive state has developed, these cues can induce internal arousal and motivate behavior on subsequent occasions, even in the absence of the stimuli that induce the unconditioned drive state.

Consider the following example to illustrate Hull's acquired-drive concept: A person goes to the ballpark late in the afternoon. Hunger, produced by the long time since lunch, motivates going to the concession stand and consuming several hot dogs. The hot dogs reduce the hunger, and because of this experience, even early in the afternoon, the person will feel hunger when walking past the concession stand at the ballpark and purchase several hot dogs.

The Reinforcing Function of Drive Reduction   From the Hullian view, drive motivates behavior, but each specific behavior depends on the environment; that is, environmental events direct behavior. Which behavior does a specific stimulus elicit? Hull thought that when an animal or human is motivated (drive exists), the environmental cue present automatically elicits a specific response—the response with the strongest habit strength. The strength of the habit can either be innate ($_sU_R$) and/or be acquired through experience ($_sH_R$).

How does habit strength develop? If that response reduces the drive state, the bond between the stimulus and response is strengthened; thus, habit strength can be increased as the result of drive reduction. The habit strength increases each time the behavior produces drive reduction.

Let's examine how the Hullian view of reinforcement would explain a person's eating a hot dog at the ballpark. This person's primary drive initially motivated behavior to reduce hunger. After eating the hot dog, his or her hunger was eliminated. Hull would assert that the drive reduction strengthened the bond between the concession stand and eating a hot dog. Each subsequent experience strengthened the bond until the behavior became habitual.

The Elimination of Unsuccessful Behavior   According to Hull, unsuccessful behavior causes drive to persist. If drive persists, all behavior is temporarily inhibited—a process referred to as *reactive inhibition*. When the reactive inhibition declines, this habitual behavior will occur again. The continued failure of the response to reduce drive leads to a permanent *conditioned inhibition*.

Conditioned inhibition is specific to a particular response and acts to reduce the excitatory strength of the habit. The continued failure of one behavior to reduce drive causes the second strongest response in the *habit hierarchy* to be elicited. If this behavior is successful in producing drive reduction, the habit strength of this response increases. This effective habit will become the dominant habit and the response is again elicited when the animal is motivated. If the second habit in the hierarchy is ineffective, the animal will continue down the habit hierarchy until a successful response occurs.

Incentive Motivation   To suggest that the person would continue to visit the concession stand if it no longer stocked hot dogs is probably inaccurate; the behavior does reflect to some degree a desire to eat hot dogs. Hull's 1943 theory assumed that drive reduction or reward only influences the strength of the S-R bond; a more valuable reward produces greater drive reduction and, therefore, a stronger habit. Once the habit is established, motivation depends on the drive level but not the reward value.

However, various studies showed that the value of the reinforcer has an important influence on motivational level. For example, Crespi (1942) found that shifts in reward magnitude produced a rapid change in rats' runway performance for food. When he increased reward magnitude from 1 to 16 pellets on the 20th trial, performance after just two or three trials equaled that of animals that always received the higher reward. If reward magnitude influenced only learning level, as Hull had suggested, the change in runway speed should have been gradual. The rapid shift in the rats' behavior indicates that reward magnitude influenced their motivation; the use of a larger reward increased the rats' motivational level. A similar rapid change in behavior occurred when the reward was decreased from 256 to 16 pellets. These rats quickly decreased their running speed to a level equal to that of rats receiving the lower reward on each trial. Figure 2-6 presents the results of Crespi's study.

The results of these experiments convinced Hull (1952) that reward magnitude affects the intensity of the motivation producing instrumental behavior. According

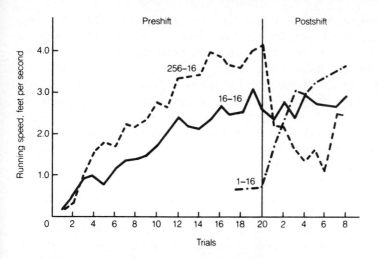

FIGURE 2-6   Speed in the runway was a function of the magnitude of reinforcement. The rats received 1, 16, or 256 pellets of food. (The acquisition data for the 1-pellet group are not presented.) Sixteen pellets were given to each rat after trial 20. A shift from 1 to 16 pellets produced a rapid increase in performance, while a rapid decline in speed was noted when reward magnitude was lowered from 25 to 16 pellets. Adapted from Crespi, L. P. (1942). Quantitative variation of incentive and performance in white rats. *American Journal of Psychology, 55,* 467–517.

to Hull, a large reward produces a greater arousal level and thereby more motivation to act than does a small reward. Furthermore, he theorized that environmental stimuli associated with reward acquire incentive motivation properties and that the cues present with a large reward will produce a greater conditioned incentive motivation than stimuli associated with a small reward. The importance of these acquired incentive cues is most evident when reward cannot be seen; the cues associated with large reward elicit a greater approach to reward than do cues associated with a small reward.

Hull's drive view represented the dominant behavioral theory during the period from the 1930s to the 1960s. Many of Hull's ideas do accurately reflect an important aspect of human behavior: (1) intense arousal can motivate behavior; (2) environmental stimuli can develop the ability to produce arousal, thereby motivating behavior; and (3) the value of reward influences the intensity of instrumental behavior. Evidence of the validity of these aspects of Hull's drive theory will be discussed throughout the text. Although Hull's drive theory developed from research with animals, psychologists have used it to explain the basis of many human behaviors.

However, Hull's drive concept has encountered some difficulties. His concept of reward has proved to be inaccurate; that is, reward and drive reduction are not synonymous. Two types of evidence challenge the drive-reduction view of reward. First, numerous experiments—the initial study by Olds and Milner in 1954 is classic—demonstrate that direct stimulation of the brain is reinforcing. Olds and Milner placed a small wire, an *electrode,* into a rat's brain and passed an electrical current through the electrode. They noted that their rats learned to bar press to obtain brain stimulation. Other studies have reported that rats will learn the correct path in a maze for this reward (see Mendelson & Chorover, 1965). The rewarding property of brain stimulation argues against a drive-reduction interpretation.

Sheffield (1966) argued that drive induction rather than reduction strengthens instrumental behavior. In addition, according to Sheffield, rewards produce excitement or arousal, which motivates subsequent behavior. For example, it is the excitement produced by the presentation of food that motivates approach behavior; the food subsequently motivates eating. This interpretation of reward explains how secondary rewards acquire the ability to elicit behavior through association with primary rewards; this characteristic of secondary or learned rewards was an enigma to the Hullian view. A secondary reward (for example, money) not only rewards behavior but also motivates future behavior. The drive-induction interpretation also explains the observation that sensory-deprived animals are motivated to obtain stimulation. For example, Butler and Harlow (1954) discovered that monkeys learned an instrumental response so that they could view a normal laboratory environment from their isolation chamber.

Hull's drive theory focused on the acquisition of habitual reactions. Although he did indicate that environmental stimuli associated with reward could acquire the ability to motivate behavior, he did not specify the mechanism responsible for the motivational influence of these environmental stimuli. Following Hull's death in 1952, Kenneth Spence described the process responsible for the acquisition of incentive motivation. Other psychologists subsequently used the system detailed by Spence to describe the conditioning of other motives. We will briefly examine their views next; their contribution will be evident throughout the text.

Acquired Motive Approach

The Anticipation of Reward   To explain the influence of reward value on behavior, Hull (1952) introduced the concept of incentive motivation, or K. Although Hull indicated that an animal or a human would be more motivated after receiving a large reward rather than a small one, Kenneth Spence (1956), Hull's colleague, detailed the transformation of K into behavior. Let's use the behavior of the person who orders a hot dog at the ballpark to describe Spence's view.

Spence suggested that when a reward (hot dog) is obtained in a goal environment, this reward elicits an unconditioned goal response (R_G). For example, when the hungry person smells and tastes the hot dog, the hot dog initiates an internal response. This internal response (for example, salivation, gastric secretion) produces an internal stimulus state (S_G), which motivates the person to eat the hot dog. The characteristics of S_G resemble those of Hull's drive state (D): They represent an internal arousal that motivates behavior. The internal response is intensified as the person eats. Until eating is inhibited, the hot dog will continue to elicit the internal goal response. The intensity of the goal response is determined by the reward value; the greater the reward magnitude, the stronger the goal response.

Spence thought that during the first few experiences, the environmental cues present during reward (for example, the concession stand) become associated with reward, and subsequently produce a conditioned or anticipatory goal response (r_G). This conditioned goal response then causes internal stimulus changes (S_G) that motivate approach behavior. Thus, the person becomes aroused when going to the ballpark and seeing the concession stand. The arousal motivates the person to go to the concession stand and buy a hot dog.

The reward magnitude used during conditioning determines the maximum level of responding. Since a large reward creates a more intense r_G than does a smaller reward, Spence assumed that the environmental cues associated with the large reward produce a stronger r_G than if paired with a small reward. This idea conforms to basic Pavlovian conditioning principles: The strength of a CR depends on UCS intensity; the stronger the UCS, the greater the CR. Spence's incentive motivation concept is supported by observations that performance level improves with greater reward (for example, Crespi, 1942). As noted earlier, Crespi found that rats ran down an alley faster for a larger reward than for a smaller one.

Spence's theory suggests that Pavlovian conditioning was responsible for approaching reward. Other psychologists have adopted this acquired motive view to explain motivation to avoid frustrating or painful circumstances (for example, Amsel, 1958; D'Amato, 1970).

Avoidance of Frustrating Events   According to Hull (1943), the absence of reward acts to inhibit behavior. Hull suggested that by inhibiting habitual behavior, nonreward allows the strengthening of other behaviors. However, this view does not completely describe the influence of nonreward on behavior. Abram Amsel's frustration theory (1958) asserts that frustration both motivates avoidance behavior and suppresses approach behavior. Amsel proposed that the frustration state differs from the approach state. Nonreward presented in a situation in which reward previously occurred produces an unconditioned frustration response (R_F). This frustration response has motivational properties: The stimulus aftereffects (S_F) energize escape behavior. The cues present during the frustration (R_F) become conditioned to produce an anticipatory frustration response (r_F). The anticipatory frustration response also produces distinctive internal stimuli (s_F); these stimuli (s_F) motivate an animal or human to avoid a potentially frustrating situation.

The following example illustrates the central aspects of Amsel's frustration model. Suppose you have 10 minutes to reach the theater before the movie begins. You get into your car, but it will not start. The failure of your car to start produces nonreward, which in turn produces frustration (R_F). The stimulus aftereffects of frustration (S_F) motivate escape behavior; that is, you leave the car and return home. According to Amsel's view, the car becomes associated with nonreward and, therefore, produces an anticipatory frustration response (r_F). If your car continues not to start, you probably will sell it to avoid future frustration.

Avoidance of Painful Events Michael D'Amato (1970) has used this acquired motive approach to explain our avoidance of painful events. According to D'Amato, an adversive event (for example, shock) elicits an unconditioned pain response (R_p); the unconditioned stimulus of painful shock (S_p) motivates escape behavior. Through Pavlovian conditioning, the environmental cues present during shock acquire the ability to produce an anticipatory pain response (r_p) whose stimulus aftereffects (s_p) also motivate escape behavior. D'Amato's r_p-s_p mechanism motivates escape from the conditioned stimulus, just as Amsel's r_F-s_F system caused an animal to escape from a situation associated with frustration.

D'Amato suggested that the termination of an adversive event (UCS; for example, the shock) produces an unconditioned relief response (R_R). The stimulus consequences (S_R) of the relief response are rewarding. In addition, according to D'Amato, the stimuli associated with the termination of the adversive event become capable of producing an anticipatory relief response (r_R); the stimulus consequences (s_R) of this anticipatory response (r_R) are also rewarding. In addition, the sight of the cues associated with anticipatory relief produces approach behavior in a manner closely resembling Spence's description of the approach response to anticipatory-goal-related cues. This idea suggests a second motivational basis of avoidance responding: The animal or human is not only escaping from an aversive situation but is also approaching a rewarding one.

Let's consider how D'Amato's theory would explain some people's avoidance of dogs. Being bitten by a dog is an adversive event that produces an unconditioned pain response and causes the dog to be associated with being bitten. Through this conditioning, the dog produces an anticipatory pain response (r_p). The r_p-s_p mechanism motivates a person who has been bitten to get away from a dog when he or she sees one; this produces an unconditioned relief response. Suppose such a person runs into a house to escape the dog. The house then becomes associated with relief and is able to produce an anticipatory relief response. Thus, if the dog is seen again, the sight of the house produces the r_R-s_R complex, which motivates the person to run into the house. Therefore, the anticipation of both pain and relief motivates the person to avoid the dog.

Nature of Anticipatory Behavior Rescorla and Solomon (1967) pointed to a serious problem with the r_G-s_G mechanism proposed by Kenneth Spence. Although incentive value does influence motivation level, there are no peripheral physiological changes (for example, salivation) that are always related to instrumental behavior. Psychologists who attempted to observe r_G directly and evaluate its influence on behavior have found that salivation might precede or follow instrumental behavior; other times an animal might salivate without responding or respond without salivating (Kintsch & Witte, 1962; Lewis, 1959). Rescorla and Solomon suggested that r_G is a central rather than a peripheral event. This central process is classically conditioned; its strength is determined by reward magnitude and its effect is to motivate behavior. As we will discover in Chapter

7, Rescorla and Solomon also suggested that fear, frustration, and relief are central rather than peripheral events.

A Contiguity View   Hull's drive theory assumed that reward was responsible for the establishment of S-R associations. Although most psychologists during the 1930s and 1940s accepted this S-R approach, Edwin Guthrie (1935, 1942, 1959) rejected the view that reward strengthened the bond between a stimulus and a response. Instead, Guthrie proposed that contiguity was sufficient to establish an S-R association. According to Guthrie, if a response occurs when a particular stimulus is present, the stimulus and response will automatically become associated.

According to Guthrie, learning is a simple process governed entirely by the contiguity principle: Whenever a particular stimulus and response occur simultaneously, an animal or person reencountering that stimulus will exhibit that response. Guthrie provided many real-life examples of how a behavior could be changed based on his theory. Consider the following example to illustrate Guthrie's view of learning:

> The mother of a ten-year-old girl complained to a psychologist that for two years her daughter had annoyed her by a habit of tossing her coat and hat on the floor as she entered the house. On a hundred occasions the mother had insisted that the girl pick up the clothing and hang it in its place. These wild ways were changed only after the mother, on advice, began to insist not only that the girl pick up the fallen garments from the floor, but that she also put them on, return to the street, and re-enter the house, this time removing the coat and hanging it properly. (Guthrie, 1935, page 21).

Why was this technique effective? According to Guthrie, the desired response is for the child to hang up her clothes directly when entering the house; that is, to associate hanging up her clothes with entering the house. Having the child hang up the clothes after being in the house will not establish the correct association; learning, in Guthrie's view, will occur only when stimulus (entering the house) and response (hanging up the coat and hat) occur together.

Impact of Reward   Guthrie assumed that reward has an important effect on the response to a specific environmental circumstance; however, he did not believe that reward strengthens S-R associations. According to Guthrie, many responses can become conditioned to a stimulus, and the response exhibited just prior to reward will be associated with the stimulus and will be produced when the stimulus is reinstated again. For example, a child may draw, put together a puzzle, and study at the same desk. If her parents reward the child by allowing her to play outside after she studies but not after she draws or works on the puzzle, the next time the child sits down at the desk she will study rather than draw or play with a puzzle. In Guthrie's view, an animal or a person must respond in a particular way (to study) in the presence of a specific stimulus (the desk) to obtain reward (playing outside).

Once the animal or person exhibits the appropriate response, the obtained reward acts to change the stimulus context (internal and/or external) that was present prior to reward. For example, the child is no longer sitting at the desk but is outside riding her bike. Any new actions will be conditioned to this new stimulus circumstance (being outside), therefore allowing the appropriate response (studying) to be produced by the stimulus context (desk) when it is experienced again. Thus, reward functions to prevent further conditioning and not to strengthen an S-R association. In the example of the studying child, the reward of going outside prevents her from doing anything else at the desk; the reward does not per se strengthen the child's association between studying and the desk.

Guthrie assumed that reward must be presented immediately after the appropriate response if that response is to occur on the next stimulus exposure. If the reward is delayed, the actions occurring between the appropriate response and reward will be exhibited when the stimulus is encountered again. For example, if the child did not go outside immediately after studying but instead watched television at the desk and then went outside, the child would watch television at the desk rather than study.

The Function of Punishment   How did Guthrie explain the influence of punishment? Guthrie assumed that punishment is an unconditioned stimulus capable of eliciting a number of responses, such as crying, pouting, or fleeing. If the response terminates the adversity, the response will become conditioned to the stimulus context in which punishment occurred. When this stimulus circumstance is encountered again, the conditioned response will be elicited. If this anticipatory response is effective, punishment will not occur. However, if the response that terminates punishment does not prevent punishment, punishment cannot be avoided, only escaped.

Guthrie suggested that punishment may not always eliminate the undesired, punished behavior. Punishment will work only if the response elicited by punishment and, therefore, conditioned to the punishment situation is incompatible with the inappropriate response. For example, suppose a child is punished for hitting a younger sibling. Punishment often acts to elicit aggression. Because the punished response (hitting a younger sibling) is not incompatible with the response elicited by punishment (aggression), punishing the child may not suppress the inappropriate behavior.

Importance of Practice   According to Guthrie, learning occurs in a single trial; that is, the strength of an S-R association reaches its maximum value following a single pairing of the stimulus and a response. You might wonder why Guthrie believed that learning occurred on a single trial when it is obvious that the efficiency and strength of behavior improves with experience. Guthrie did not deny that behavior improves with experience; however, he rejected the Hullian view that the strength of the S-R bond slowly increases with experience.

According to Guthrie, performance gradually improves for three reasons. First, *although many potential stimuli are present during the initial conditioning, only some of these stimuli will be active (or attended to)*. The stimuli present when an animal or person responds vary from trial to trial. For a stimulus active on the particular trial to produce a response, this stimulus must also have been active during a previous response. For example, suppose that in an instrumental conditioning situation, a rat is rewarded in the black compartment of a T-maze but is not attending to the color of the goal box. On a future trial, the rat does not go the black side, even though it was rewarded in that environment on the previous trial. Although the rat's behavior may change from trial to trial, change reflects an attentional process rather than a learning process. Second, *many different stimuli can become conditioned to produce a particular response.* As more stimuli become able to elicit a response, the strength of the response will increase. However, this increased intensity of a response is not caused by an increased S-R association but rather by the increased number of stimuli able to produce the response. Third, *a complex behavior consists of many separate responses.* For the behavior to be efficient, each response element must be conditioned to the stimulus. As each element is conditioned to the stimulus, the efficiency of behavior will improve. According to Guthrie, the more varied the stimuli and/or the responses that must be associated to produce effective performance, the more practice is needed to make behavior efficient.

An Evaluation of Contiguity Theory   The S-R contiguity view proposed by Guthrie during the 1930s and 1940s was not accepted by many psychologists. During his career as a professor at the University of Washington, he conducted few studies to validate his approach. The lack of empirical evaluation meant that Guthrie's theory remained unrevised from its original proposal in 1935 until his final writings in 1959. Recent experiments to test Guthrie's theory have found some ideas accurate and others inaccurate.

Some parts of Guthrie's theory have been shown to accurately describe certain aspects of the learning process. First, punishment can intensify an inappropriate behavior when the response elicited by punishment is compatible with the punished response; however, the impact of this facilitatory influence of punishment is limited. Chapter 6 will more closely examine the impact of punishment on behavior. Second, contiguity between a response and reward is critical to prevent the acquisition of competing associations. (The child must go outside immediately after studying; if she watches television first, she will associate her desk with watching television rather than with studying.) Third, only a portion of the environmental stimuli are active at a particular moment; therefore, only some of the potential conditioned stimuli can become associated with the response. Later chapters will examine evidence supporting these aspects of Guthrie's view.

Some aspects of Guthrie's theory, however, do not accurately describe the learning process. First, Guthrie rejected the law of effect, suggesting instead that reward functions to change the stimulus situation. However, numerous experiments (see Bower & Hilgard, 1981) have disproved his reward concept. An experimenter can arrange for many changes (for example, jiggling the box or having the floor drop out from under the box) to occur after a response, but these actions do not act like a reward and the response will not be conditioned, even though substantial stimulus change followed the response. Second, Guthrie believed that recency and frequency determined which response a particular stimulus would produce. However, Noble's (1966) extensive research indicated that reward predicted responding significantly better than did either frequency or recency. Third,

Guthrie assumed that learning occurs on a single trial; that is, a single, simultaneous pairing of a stimulus and response results in the development of the maximum S-R associative strength. Many studies have evaluated Guthrie's view that learning occurs after a single S-R pairing. To test this view, the conditioning situation must be simple, and the trial-to-trial behavior of each subject must be assessed. In an eye-blink conditioning study using humans, Voeks (1954) conducted a well-controlled evaluation of Guthrie's view. Voeks observed that most subjects showed all-or-none learning; that is, they showed no CR on one trial and an intense CR on the next trial. However, other studies have not reported single-trial learning for individual subjects; instead, they have found a gradual conditioning of a response (see Bower & Hilgard, 1981).

Spence (1956), accepting that rapid changes in responding do occur in some circumstances, indicated how an incremental learning approach could explain these results. (An incremental view assumes that the strength of learned behavior increases slowly over trials.) According to Spence, although S-R habit strength increases slowly over trials, the response will not be elicited until its strength exceeds the threshold of response evocation. According to Spence, if the threshold is near maximum strength, the learning process will appear to be of the all-or-none type. Spence's analysis allowed an incremental theory to explain the apparent single-trial learning, but recent theories suggest that some aspects of learning can develop on a single trial, while others develop slowly. We will discuss this idea in greater detail in Chapter 7.

Section Review

Two mechanistic S-R views were presented during the 1930s: Hull's approach emphasized the importance of reward in the learning process; Guthrie's approach proposed that contiguity was sufficient for learning. The Hullian drive view was the dominant behavioral approach from the 1930s to the mid-1960s, and only recently have some of Guthrie's views been recognized as playing an important role in learning.

Hull theorized that a nonspecific intense internal arousal—drive—motivates behavior. Several classes of stimuli (deprivation and intense environmental events) are inherently capable of initiating drive, and any stimuli associated with these innate-drive stimuli develop the capacity to produce drive through the classical conditioning process. Also, reward, and those stimuli associated with reward, are able to produce arousal and motivate behavior. According to Hull, behavior is then directed by the specific prevailing stimulus conditions. A specific stimulus is capable of eliciting several behaviors, and the behavior with the strongest bond (or habit strength) will be repeated; the bond strengthens if the behavior produces drive reduction.

Spence suggested that the presentation of reward elicits an unconditioned emotional response (R_G). The association of environmental events with reward causes the development of a conditioned anticipatory goal response (r_G). The stimuli (S_G) produced by this conditioned response motivate the approach to reward.

Amsel proposed that nonreward in a situation previously associated with reward produces an unconditioned frustration response (R_F). The anticipatory-frustration-response mechanism (r_F-s_F) motivates avoidance of a potentially frustrating situation. According to D'Amato, the classical conditioning of the anticipatory-pain-response mechanism (r_p-s_p) to the environmental cues associated with an aversive event motivates escape from these cues. Furthermore, the termination of pain produces an unconditioned relief response (R_R). The establishment of the anticipatory-relief-response mechanism (r_R-s_R) provides motivation to approach the cues associated with unconditioned relief.

Guthrie advocated a contiguity approach to S-R learning. According to Guthrie, when a stimulus and response occur together, they automatically become associated, and when encountered again, that stimulus will produce the response. Guthrie assumed that reward alters the stimulus environment, thereby precluding the acquisition of any new competing S-R associations. Furthermore, Guthrie asserted that punishment suppresses an inappropriate behavior only if the response produced by punishment is incompatible with the punished response; in contrast, punishment can actually increase responding if the response elicited by punishment is compatible with the punished response. Practice increases the number of stimuli associated with a response and thereby the intensity of that response.

The S-R theories assume that a mechanistic process governs behavior. In contrast, the cognitive approach suggests that actions are guided by purpose rather than by internal and external forces. Furthermore, the cognitive approach asserts that behavior is a flexible reaction rather than a habitual response. Next, we will briefly examine the cognitive view of learning. Chapter 8 discusses this approach to learning in greater detail.

Cognitive Approaches

Tolman's Purposive Behaviorism   Edward Tolman (1932, 1959) proposed a cognitive view of learning during the 1930s and 1940s that was not accepted by most psychologists. Instead, Hull's mechanistic drive theory represented the accepted view of learning during that period. During the 1950s the cognitive view gained some acceptance and other psychologists expanded Tolman's original approach. In the last two decades, the cognitive approach has become an important theory of learning. Our discussion begins with Tolman's work. Later in the chapter, we'll study contemporary cognitive theories.

Flexibility of Behavior   Tolman's view conflicted with Hull's drive theory described earlier in this chapter. Tolman did not believe that behavior was an automatic response to an environmental event. Instead, he proposed that behavior had both direction and purpose. Tolman assumed that behavior is goal-oriented; that is, we are motivated either to achieve a desired condition or to avoid an aversive situation. According to Tolman, there are paths leading to our goals as well as tools which we can use to obtain these goals. In Tolman's view, through experience we can understand the structure of our environment. This knowledge allows us to reach desired goals.

Not only is our behavior goal-oriented, but also we expect specific outcomes to follow specific behaviors. For example, you may expect to receive an A for working hard in this class. If you do not receive an A, you will continue to work hard for the reward and will not be satisfied with a less-valued goal object. Thus, if you received a B on your first test, you would not be satisfied with the B and would work even harder for an A on the next test.

Tolman also believed that certain events in the environment convey information about where our goals are located. We can reach our goals only after we have learned the signs leading to reward or punishment in our environment. For example, you must learn the signs leading to the cafeteria to obtain food. It is important to recognize that although Tolman believed that behavior is purposeful, he did not mean that we are aware of either the purpose or the direction of our behavior. Tolman assumed only that we act *as if* we expect a particular behavior to lead to a specific goal.

Motivation Processes According to Tolman, there are two types of motivations. Deprivation is one source of motivation. In Tolman's view, deprivation produces an internal drive state that increases demand for the goal object. Tolman (1959) also suggested that environmental events can acquire motivational properties through association with either a primary drive or a reward. The following example illustrates Tolman's view. A thirsty child sees a soda. According to Tolman, the ability of thirst to motivate behavior transfers to the soda. Tolman called this transference process *cathexis,* a term he borrowed from psychoanalytic theory. As a result of cathexis, the soda is now a preferred goal object, and in the future this child, even when not thirsty, will be motivated to obtain a soda. The preference for the soda is a positive cathexis. In contrast, avoiding a certain place could reflect a negative cathexis. In Tolman's opinion, if we associate a certain place with an unpleasant experience, we will think of the place as an aversive object.

You might remember that Hull suggested that drives could be conditioned. Tolman's cathexis concept is very similar to Hull's view of acquired drive. And Tolman's *equivalence belief principle* is comparable to Spence's anticipatory goal concept. Animals or people react to a secondary reward (or subgoal) as they do to an original goal object; for instance, our motivation to obtain money reflects our identification of money with a desired goal object such as food.

Is Reward Necessary for Learning? We learned earlier in this chapter that Thorndike assumed that S-R associations are learned when the response leads to a satisfying state of affairs. Hull (1943) adopted Thorndike's law of effect concept and suggested that habit strength increases when a particular response decreases the drive state. In contrast to these views, Tolman (1932) proposed that reward is not necessary for learning to occur and that the simultaneous experiencing of two events is sufficient for learning. Thus, according to Tolman, an understanding of when events will occur can develop without reward. What is the influence of reward in Tolman's view? Tolman proposed that reward affects performance but not learning. The presence of a reward will motivate an animal or person to exhibit a previously learned behavior. For example, a child may have learned how to mow the yard but needs to be rewarded to do the job.

An Evaluation of Purposive Behaviorism   Tolman proposed that the expectation of future reward or punishment motivates instrumental activities. Furthermore, knowledge of the paths and/or the tools which enable us to obtain reward or avoid punishment guides our behavior. Although the research designed by Tolman and his students did not provide conclusive evidence for his cognitive approach, his work caused Hull to make major changes in his theory to accommodate Tolman's observation. For example, the idea that a conditioned anticipation of reward (r_G) motivates us to approach reward is clearly similar to Tolman's view that the expectation of reward motivates behavior intended to produce reward. Furthermore, the view that frustration can motivate both the avoidance of a less-preferred reward and the continued search for the desired reward represents the drive explanation of the observation that not any reward will be acceptable. However, once Tolman's observations were incorporated into drive theory, most psychologists ignored Tolman's cognitive view, and the drive view of learning continued to be generally accepted. When problems developed with the drive approach during the 1960s and 1970s, the cognitive view gained wider approval. Psychologists began to use a cognitive approach to explain how behavior is learned. In the next section we will look at a more recent cognitive approach.

Expectancy-Value Theory   Tolman's cognitive approach is the foundation of Julian Rotter's (1954) expectancy-value theory. Rotter expanded Tolman's view by describing the types of expectancies we develop.

Basic Tenets   There are three main ideas expressed in Rotter's expectancy theory. First, Rotter suggested that our preference for a particular event is determined by its reward value. According to Rotter, the value of a particular event is relative; its value reflects a comparison with other events. Thus, some of us may find an event highly rewarding because we have not experienced many rewarding events, while others who have experienced many rewarding events may not find this event as rewarding. Rotter also suggested that a reward can change its value when new rewards are introduced. A restaurant you have valued may lose its appeal when compared to a new restaurant.

The second component of Rotter's expectancy-value theory is that each person has a subjective expectation concerning the likelihood of obtaining a particular reward. We believe that there is a specific probability of reaching a desired goal; these beliefs may or may not reflect reality. For example, you may feel that someone whom you like will not accept your dinner invitation, even though he or she would, in fact, come if you extend an invitation. The actual probability that an event will occur does not influence your behavior; you simply will not ask because your expected probability is low. Thus, in Rotter's view, even if you are motivated, you will not behave if you do not expect reward.

That our expectation of obtaining reward is determined by the situation is the third aspect of expectancy-value theory. We may expect to receive reward in one setting but not in another. Our past experiences determine this situational dependence; we acquire the expectation that a particular goal is more likely to occur under some circumstances than others. For example, suppose that you have a

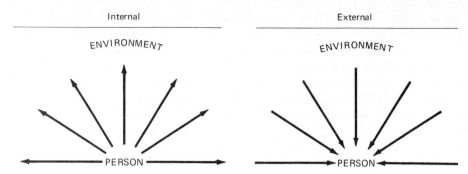

FIGURE 2-7   An internal expectancy reflects a belief that obtaining a goal depends upon one's own actions. In contrast, an external expectancy is a belief that events are determined by the environment and are beyond one's control.

strong preference for Italian food. You would then be more likely to expect reward in an Italian restaurant than in a French cafe. Your relative expectations act to guide your behavior: If you have to choose between these two restaurants, you are more likely to choose the Italian restaurant than the French one.

Yet, sometimes we encounter new situations. How do we respond to new events? According to Rotter, our generalized expectations from past experiences guide our actions. Recall your initial feelings when you were a college freshman. You had never attended college and therefore had no direct experience upon which to base your expectations. Under these circumstances, your past expectations governed your behavior.

Finally, Rotter's theory proposes that our behavior potential determines the likelihood that we will act in a particular way. Our behavioral potential represents our expectation of obtaining reward in a particular situation as well as the value of that reward. In Rotter's view, we can predict behavior if we multiply expectation of reward by value of the reward. This mathematical formula has proved useful in describing and predicting behavior. See Atkinson's (1964) research on achievement motivation as one example of its use.

Locus of Control   Rotter (1966) is most noted for his concept of locus of control. According to Rotter, there are two significant generalized expectancies—internal and external expectancies. An *internal expectancy* represents a belief that obtaining a goal depends upon one's own actions (see Figure 2-7). Suppose that you would like to receive a high grade on an exam next week. An internal expectancy in this situation would be that hard work will lead you to get the good grade, and your expectancy that hard work brings success will cause you to spend long hours studying for this next exam.

However, you will not exert much effort studying if you believe that luck will determine your grade on the exam. Rotter refers to this type of cognition as an *external expectancy*. An external expectation reflects a belief that events are beyond your control (refer to Figure 2-7). Examples of external expectancies include beliefs that luck, or chance, or the power of others is responsible for your attaining a desired reward. Since you believe that little connection exists between your behavior and reward, you will make little or no effort to obtain reward.

There are environmental situations in which each type of expectancy is appropriate. In skill tasks, you can obtain reward by exhibiting the appropriate ability. Two examples of rewards obtained in skill tasks are a goal by a hockey player and a standing ovation for an actor. Chance tasks, in contrast, do not rely on any specific behavior for reward. A blackjack in gambling or a star player in a pack of baseball cards are two examples of rewards on chance tasks.

Many of us are aware of the distinction between external and internal expectancys and exhibit different expectancies in each type of setting. We assume in skill situations that our behavior can enable us to obtain reward. When we are successful in skill tasks, we increase our expectancy of future success, while failure often causes us to decrease our expectancy of future reward. Our response during chance situations is quite different: Since we assume that reward occurs independently of our actions in chance tasks, we are not likely to change our expectancies of future reward following either success or failure.

It is most appropriate for us to perceive each situation separately. We should attempt to obtain reward in skill settings but either avoid or merely cope with those situations in which success or failure occurs independently of our actions. However, many people show a generalized expectancy by treating all situations as being either skill or chance. In Rotter's view, internally oriented persons believe that success or failure is caused by their own actions. Externally oriented individuals, on the other hand, assume that they have no control over their fate. Rotter coined the term *locus of control* to refer to our generalized expectation that either internal or external factors control our behavior.

Skinner's Behaviorist Methodology

The work of B. F. Skinner, a noted American behaviorist, spans more than half a century and has contributed greatly to our understanding of the learning process. Skinner's behaviorism, often referred to as *behaviorist methodology,* is quite different from theories advocated by the other behaviorists we have discussed in this chapter. In his 1938 text, *The Behavior of Organisms,* Skinner asserted that the goal of behaviorism should be to identify and isolate the environmental factors that govern behavior. Skinner stated that we will understand a particular behavior only after we have learned how to predict and control the behavior. Also, Skinner suggested that the ability to predict and control a behavior depends on understanding the circumstances governing the occurrence of the behavior.

Skinner designed many studies to examine the factors that govern behavior. He first studied the variables responsible for a rat's behavior—pressing a lever for food reinforcement—in an operant chamber. Much of his research focused on the influence of reinforcement on operant responding. Skinner defined a *reinforcer* as an event whose occurrence increases the frequency of behavior that preceded the event. According to Skinner, the environment identified the operant response necessary to produce reinforcement. Skinner referred to the specified relationship between the operant response and reinforcement as a *contingency*. Contingencies have an important impact on an animal's behavior. An animal is sensitive to contingencies and behaves according to the specified behavior needed to produce reinforcement. We will look more closely at the influence of behavior reinforcement contingencies in Chapter 5.

Skinner then expanded his analysis of behavior to include other animals, humans, and situations and behaviors that differed greatly from operant chambers and bar pressing. For example, in his 1957 text, *Verbal Behavior,* he argued that people do not have an instinctive capacity for expressing ideas. Instead, he believed that verbal behavior, like any other operant behavior, is controlled by differential reinforcement and punishment administered by significant others, such as parents and friends. Skinner's methodology led to the development of behavior modification, an effective approach to treating behavior pathology. Evidence of Skinner's contribution to the establishment of desired and elimination of undesired behavior can be seen in Chapter 5.

How does Skinner's view differ from those of the other behaviorists described in this chapter? Skinner (1938) asserted that the use of "hypothetical constructs" does not contribute to our understanding of behavior. In Skinner's view, the search for evidence to validate a particular hypothetical construct interferes with the functional analysis of the variables controlling the behavior and thereby limits understanding of the circumstances governing behavior.

Consider the following example to illustrate Skinner's approach. Many psychologists have speculated that stimulus-response associations are strengthened as the result of reinforcement, and years of research have been devoted to validating this view. According to Skinner, understanding the theoretical construct underlying the effect of reinforcement on stimulus-response associations is useful only in that it points out that reinforcement is one environmental variable which can control how frequently a specific behavior occurs in a particular context.

Many psychologists do not agree with Skinner's view. These psychologists argue that theory guides research, which in turn identifies the variables controlling behavior as well as explains similar results of various experiments. The work of psychologists who use theory to guide their research has contributed greatly to our understanding of learning and has increased our ability to predict and control behavior. For example, Hull's drive theory, discussed earlier, greatly influenced the development of systematic desensitization, a behavior therapy that effectively modifies phobic behavior (we will describe systematic desensitization in Chapter 4). The contribution of Hull and other theorists also will be evident throughout the text.

CONTEMPORARY DIRECTIONS FOR LEARNING THEORIES

One significant change in learning theory since the late 1960s has been the shift away from global theories of learning to a focus on more specific aspects of the learning process. For example, a contemporary learning theorist might attempt to describe the nature of the conditioned response or the mechanism responsible for the impact of conditioned stimuli on operant behavior.

Why have psychologists abandoned their search for a global explanation of the learning process? Mowrer and Klein (1989) identified three main reasons for the current emphasis on specific learning principles. First, global theories of learning primarily dealt with the instrumental conditioning process. Global learning theories assumed that Pavlovian conditioning is a simple reflexive type of learning which is applicable to only a few situations. Also, they assumed that most responses are not classically conditioned. However, contemporary research has shown that Pavlovian conditioning is not a simple reflexive form of learning, and that conditioned responses have a wide impact on human behavior. Further, the study of Pavlovian conditioning has revealed different processes than those involved in instrumental conditioning. The recognition of two distinct learning processes makes it difficult to develop a single, unitary theory to explain all behavior.

Traditional learning theory assumes that there are some general laws of learning which are applicable to all species. This view has led to generalization of results of studies using animals as subjects. However, considerable research indicates that an animal's biological character influences whether or not it will learn as well as how rapidly it learns a specific behavior. The recognition that biological character affects learning has led to the development of psychobiological accounts of learning. This increased examination of the psychobiology of learning has been a second reason for the shift away from global theories of learning.

Finally, the greater acceptance of cognitive views of learning also has resulted in a greater focus on specific learning principles. For example, the relative contribution of associative and cognitive processes in Pavlovian conditioning has been the topic of much research. The realization that both cognitive and associative principles may be involved in learning has made it difficult to develop a single global learning theory.

The work of contemporary learning theorists can be found throughout the remainder of the text. Their ideas and research have expanded our understanding of learning. However, the global theories should not be ignored. The value of these theories is not merely historical. Instead, important principles of learning remain from the global theories. This text incorporates traditional and contemporary learning theories; we have learned much from both approaches.

SUMMARY

1 Many psychologists have speculated on the nature of the learning process, and two opposing viewpoints have characterized the debate about the mechanism that underlies the development or the elimination of behavior. For most of this century, the majority of psychologists advocated a mechanistic view or the view that the environment automatically produces a response. In contrast, a few psychologists suggested that learning

reflects a mental process in which behavior is flexible and goal-oriented. Contemporary learning theory assumes that a complex interaction of mechanistic and cognitive processes underlies learning.

2 This century began with the functionalist emphasis on the instinctive character of human behavior. However, the functionalists could not agree on the nature of instinctive processes or the number of instincts. Many psychologists adopted the behavioral view, or the belief that most human behavior is learned.

3 Thorndike observed that hungry cats could learn a new behavior to obtain food. He placed the cats in a puzzle box and found that the behavior which enabled the cats to escape from the puzzle box was increasingly used when the cats later were returned to the box. Thorndike assumed that the effect of the food reward was to strengthen the association between the stimulus of the puzzle box and the effective behavior.

4 Pavlov demonstrated the conditioning of a new reflex. He paired a neutral stimulus (the conditioned stimulus) with a biologically significant event (the unconditioned stimulus). Pavlov observed that prior to conditioning, only the unconditioned stimulus elicited the unconditioned response. After the pairing of the conditioned and unconditioned stimuli, the conditioned stimulus was able to elicit the conditioned response.

5 Watson showed that an emotional fear response could be conditioned in humans. He discovered that a young child would become frightened of a rat paired with a loud noise. The child also feared other white objects.

6 Hull theorized that a nonspecific intense internal arousal—drive— motivates behavior. Several classes of stimuli (deprivation and intense environmental events) are inherently capable of initiating drive, and any stimuli associated with these innate-drive stimuli develop the capacity to produce drive through the classical conditioning process. Also, reward, and those stimuli associated with reward, are able to produce arousal and motivate behavior. According to Hull, behavior is then directed by the specific prevailing stimulus conditions. A specific stimulus is capable of eliciting several behaviors, and the behavior with the strongest bond (or habit strength) will be repeated; the bond strengthens if the behavior produces drive reduction.

7 Spence suggested that the presentation of reward elicits an unconditioned emotional response (R_G). The association of environmental events with reward causes the development of a conditioned anticipatory goal response (r_G). The stimuli (S_G) produced by this conditioned response motivate the approach to reward. Amsel proposed that nonreward in a situation previously associated with reward produces an unconditioned frustration response (R_F). The anticipatory-frustration-response mechanism (r_F-s_F) motivates avoidance of a potentially frustrating situation. According to D'Amato, the classical conditioning of the anticipatory-pain-response mechanism (r_p-s_p) to the environmental cues associated with an adversive event motivates escape from these cues. Furthermore, the termination of pain produces an unconditioned relief response (R_R). The establishment of the anticipatory-relief-response mechanism (r_R-s_R) provides the motivation to approach the cues associated with unconditioned relief.

8 Guthrie advocated a contiguity approach to S-R learning. According to Guthrie, when a stimulus and a response occur together, they automatically become associated, and when encountered again, that stimulus will produce the response. Guthrie assumed that reward alters the stimulus environment, thereby precluding the acquisition of any new competing S-R associations. Furthermore, Guthrie asserted that punishment suppresses an inappropriate behavior only if the response produced by punishment is incompatible with the punished response; in contrast, punishment can actually increase

responding if the response elicited by punishment is compatible with the punished response. Practice increases the number of stimuli associated with a response and thereby the intensity of that response.

9 Tolman proposed a cognitive explanation of behavior. He maintained that our behavior is goal-oriented: We are motivated to reach specific goals and continue to search until we obtain them. Tolman further argued that expectations determine the specific behavior we perform to obtain reward or avoid punishment.

10 Rotter's expectancy-value theory proposed that the likelihood that a person will act in a particular way is determined jointly by the perceived expectancy of reaching a goal and the perceived value of that reward. According to Rotter, behavior may be inconsistent due to perceived differences in the expectancies of obtaining reward between situations, or generalized expectancies may cause a person to behave in the same way in different settings. An internal expectancy is a belief that one's actions entirely determine the likelihood of success or failure. In contrast, an external expectancy reflects the view that events are beyond one's control. Locus of control refers to the extent to which either internal or external expectancies guide all of one's actions.

11 B. F. Skinner argued that attempting to explain the theoretical basis of behavior interferes with the discovery of the causes of behavior. He believed that psychologists should seek to identify the environmental factors governing behavior. Once these variables have been discovered, Skinner assumed that we would be able to predict and control behavior. Skinner defined a reinforcer as any event that increases the frequency of behavior that preceded the reinforcer. The relationship between behavior and reinforcement is called a contingency. He found that the rate of responding increased with reinforcement, while discontinuance of reinforcement leads to a decrease in the operant behavior. According to Skinner, reinforcement can be programmed either on the numbers of responses needed to produce reinforcement or on the time between available reinforcement.

12 Skinner's investigations have increased the understanding of the circumstances that influence responding and contributed to a methodology which allows reliable prediction and effective control of behavior. However, the theoretical emphasis criticized by Skinner has also produced important research—research that has contributed to our understanding of the common elements of various situations and behaviors, and has produced effective procedures for controlling behaviors. Throughout the text, we will see the importance of both theoretical and experimental analysis of behavior.

3

PRINCIPLES OF PAVLOVIAN CONDITIONING

A LINGERING FEAR

Diane is an attorney for a prestigious law firm. Although her coworkers often ask her to socialize after work, Diane always rejects their requests; instead, driving home, she proceeds hurriedly from her car to her apartment. Once inside, Diane locks the door and refuses to leave until the next morning.

On weekends, Diane will shop with her sister who lives with their parents several blocks away. However, once darkness approaches, Diane compulsively returns to her apartment. Although her sister, her parents, and close friends sometimes visit during the evening, Diane refuses any of their invitations to go out after dark.

Several men—all seemingly pleasant, sociable, and handsome—have asked Diane for dates during the past year. Diane has desperately wanted to socialize with them, but she has been unable to agree to accept any of their invitations.

Diane's fear of going out at night and her inability to accept dates began 13 months ago. She had dined with her parents at their home and had left about 9:30 P.M. Because it was a very pleasant fall evening, she decided to walk the several blocks to her apartment. Within a block of her apartment, a man grabbed her, dragging her to a nearby alley. He gagged her with a handkerchief, preventing her from screaming, and raped her. Because she did not see her assailant, the police doubted that they could apprehend him. The few friends and relatives whom Diane had told about the attack tried to support her, but, she found no solace from their efforts.

Diane still has nightmares about the rape and often wakes up terrified. During the few occasions after the attack that Diane did go out after dark, she felt very uncomfortable; she was frightened by even the sight of any man.

This intense reaction forced her to return home. The one date that she had accepted after her rape had caused her to become intensely anxious and to terminate the evening by claiming that she had become ill. Diane wants to overcome her fears but does not know how.

Diane's fears reflect two separate classically conditioned emotional reactions which she acquired from being raped: She is now afraid of darkness and of men. These fears motivate Diane to avoid both going out at night and dating men. In this chapter, we will describe the classical conditioning process responsible for Diane's intense internal reactions. The learning mechanism that causes Diane to avoid men and darkness will be discussed in Chapter 6. Two effective behavior therapies, systematic desensitization and flooding, which employ the classical conditioning process in order to eliminate conditioned fear reactions like Diane's, will be presented in Chapters 4 and 6.

ACQUISITION OF THE CONDITIONED RESPONSE

The Conditioning Procedure

Basic Components   There are four basic components of the conditioning procedure: (1) the *unconditioned stimulus* (UCS), (2) the *unconditioned response* (UCR), (3) the *conditioned stimulus* (CS), and (4) the *conditioned response* (CR). Prior to conditioning, the UCS elicits the UCR, but the CS cannot elicit the CR. During conditioning, the CS is paired with the UCS. Following conditioning, the CS is able to elicit the CR. The strength (or intensity) of the CR increases steadily during acquisition until a maximum or *asymptotic level* is reached (see Figure 3-1). The UCS-UCR complex is referred to as the *unconditioned reflex;* the CS-CR complex is called the *conditioned reflex.*

FIGURE 3-1   Acquisition and extinction of a conditioned response. The strength of the conditioned response increases during acquisition when the CS and UCS are paired, while presentation of the CS without the UCS during extinction results in a lowered strength of the conditioned response. The strength of the conditioned response will spontaneously recover when a short interval follows extinction, but it will decline again with additional CS-alone presentations.

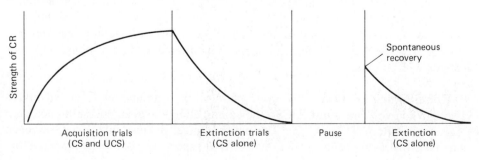

Although the pairing of the CS and UCS is essential to the development of the CR, other factors determine whether or not conditioning occurs and what the final asymptotic level of the CR is. We will detail the conditions that influence the ability of the CS to elicit the CR later in the chapter. Let's now use two examples to illustrate the basic elements of conditioning.

Conditioning of Hunger   Suppose you become hungry when arriving home after class; the home environment at this time of day is the CS eliciting the hunger reaction (CR). This conditioned hunger is assumed to reflect the association of arriving home (CS) with deprivation-induced hunger: Deprivation is the UCS; hunger, the UCR (see Hull, 1943). One probable cause of this conditioning is that very often you arrive home later in the day, have not eaten for a while, and are hungry.

Your hunger undoubtedly intensifies when you go into the kitchen and see the refrigerator. Opening the refrigerator, you notice the milk and pie. Why does the sight of the refrigerator and the food increase your hunger and motivation to obtain food? The answer lies in the association of the kitchen, the refrigerator, and the sight of the food (CSs) with the taste and the smell of the food (UCSs).

When animals or people are exposed to food, they exhibit a set of unconditioned responses which prepare them to digest, metabolize, and store ingested food. These unconditioned feeding responses include the secretion of saliva, gastric juices, pancreatic enzymes, and insulin. One important action of insulin is to lower blood glucose, which in turn stimulates hunger and motivates eating (see Mayer, 1953). Thus, we become hungry when we taste or smell food. The intensity of these unconditioned feeding responses is directly related to the palatability of food. The more attractive the food, the greater the unconditioned feeding responses and the larger the meal that is subsequently eaten.

These unconditioned feeding responses to food can be conditioned (see Powley, 1977). The conditioning of these feeding responses to environmental cues plays an important role in your motivation to eat when you arrive home. Since the cues such as the kitchen and the refrigerator have been associated with food, they are capable of eliciting these feeding responses. As a result of this conditioning experience, when you go to the kitchen and see the refrigerator, your body reflexively releases insulin, which lowers your blood glucose level and thus makes you hungry. As we will discover shortly, the strength of the conditioned response (CR) is dependent upon the intensity of the unconditioned stimulus (UCS). If you have associated the environment of the kitchen with highly palatable foods capable of eliciting an intense unconditioned feeding reaction, the stimuli in the kitchen will elicit an intense conditioned feeding response and your hunger will be great.

Conditioning of Fear   For most people, an examination is an adversive event. When you take a test (UCS), the examination elicits an unconditioned pain reaction (UCR; see Chapter 2). The psychological distress that you experience when an instructor hands you a test is one aspect of your pain reaction; the increased physiological arousal is another part of your response to receiving an examination. Although the adversity may lessen while you are taking a test, you will not experience relief until you complete it.

Examinations differ considerably in their degree of adversiveness. You respond intensely to some tests; others elicit only a mild pain reaction. Many factors determine the adversiveness of an examination. The severity of the test is one factor influencing how intensely you will respond; a difficult test eliciting a stronger pain reaction than an easy exam is one example of the influence of the severity of the test (UCS) on the intensity of the pain reaction (UCR). Another factor often affecting the adversiveness of a test is the number of examinations experienced. You probably experience more distress while taking the first test in a course than during subsequent examinations. Your experience with prior tests may cause the development of tolerance and thereby a reduced pain reaction to a later test (see Chapter 1).

Through past experiences, the cues that predict an examination become able to elicit an anticipatory pain reaction (CR; see Chapter 2). We typically call this anticipatory pain reaction *fear*. One stimulus associated with an examination is the announcement of an impending test. Thus, you become frightened (CR) when an instructor announces (CS) that an examination will be given during the next class period. As the time of the test approaches, you become more aroused. This arousal motivates you to study to prevent failure.

Psychologists have consistently observed that fear is conditioned when a novel stimulus (CS) is associated with an aversive event. The Russian physiologist Vladimir Bechterev's 1913 observation that a conditioned response (for example, withdrawal of the leg) can be established by pairing a neutral stimulus with shock was the first experimental demonstration of fear conditioning. In 1916, John Watson showed that emotional arousal was conditioned during the pairing of a novel stimulus with shock. Other researchers have consistently reported the development of fear through classical conditioning in animals (Miller, 1948) and humans (Staats & Staats, 1957).

Fear also motivates an instrumental escape response to an aversive event. Neal Miller's classic 1948 study demonstrates the motivational properties of fear. Miller first conditioned fear in rats by presenting electric shock in the white compartment of a shuttle box apparatus (see Figure 3-2). Having administered shock, Miller allowed the rats to escape into the black compartment. After the initial pairings of the white compartment with shock, he confined the animals in the white compartment without any additional shock. However, each rat could escape the white chamber by turning a wheel to open the door to the black compartment. Miller found that about half of the rats learned to turn the wheel to escape the adversive white chamber; the other half "froze" and did not learn the required response. The results show that the association of an environment (white chamber) with an unconditioned adversive event (shock) can cause the environment to acquire motivational properties.

We learned earlier that the degree of hunger induced by environmental events is dependent upon the UCS intensity; the stronger the UCS, the more intense our

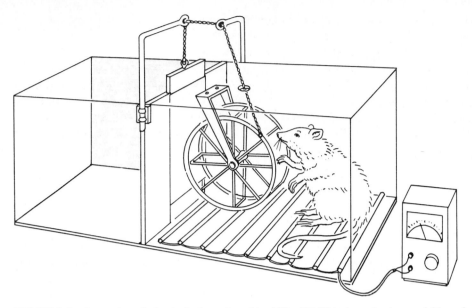

FIGURE 3-2 Apparatus similar to that employed by Miller (1948) to investigate acquisition of a fear response. The rat's emotional response to the white chamber, previously paired with shock, motivates the rat to learn to turn the wheel, which raises the gate and allows escape. From Swenson, L. C. (1980). *Theories of learning.* Belmont, CA: Wadsworth.

conditioned hunger reaction. Our conditioned fear reaction is also influenced by the strength of the adversive unconditioned event. We are more fearful of a difficult test than of an easy one. Similarly, more fear will be elicited by an important test than by an unimportant test.

Not all students become frightened by an impending examination, and some do not learn that studying represents an effective way of reducing fear and preventing failure. This chapter describes the conditions that influence the development of a conditioned fear response. Chapter 6 will detail the factors governing avoidance acquisition.

Other Examples of Conditioned Responses Hunger and fear are not the only responses that can be conditioned. Other examples include feeling nauseous when seeing a type of food that had previously made you ill, becoming thirsty at a ballgame as a result of having previously consumed drinks in that setting, and experiencing sexual arousal during a candlelight dinner because of the association of a romantic evening with sexual activity. The above examples not only demonstrate conditioned responses—nausea, thirst, and sexual arousal—but also show that stimuli other than food or shock can be involved in the conditioning process. The unconditioned stimuli in the above examples are rotten food, fluid, and sexual activity. There are many more conditioned responses and unconditioned stimuli that people encounter in the real world, other examples are presented in the remainder of this chapter.

Most of the experiments on classical conditioning have investigated the conditioning of only a single conditioned response. In most cases, several responses are conditioned during CS-UCS pairings. The conditioning of several responses has an obvious adaptive value. For example, when a CS is experienced with food, several different digestive responses occur: The conditioned salivary reflex aids in swallowing, the conditioned gastric secretion response facilitates digestion, and the conditioned insulin release enhances food storage.

Conditioning Paradigms

Five different paradigms have been used in conditioning studies (see Figure 3-3). These procedures, representing the varied ways in which a CS can be paired with the UCS, are not equally effective (see Keith-Lucas & Guttman, 1975; Sherman, 1978). The delayed conditioning paradigm usually is the most effective; the back-

FIGURE 3-3   Schematic drawing of the five major classical conditioning paradigms. The CS occurs prior to the UCS but remains on until UCS is presented in delayed conditioning; the CS occurs and ends prior to the UCS in trace conditioning; the CS and UCS occur together in simultaneous conditioning; and the CS occurs after the UCS in backward conditioning. There is no explicit CS in temporal conditioning.

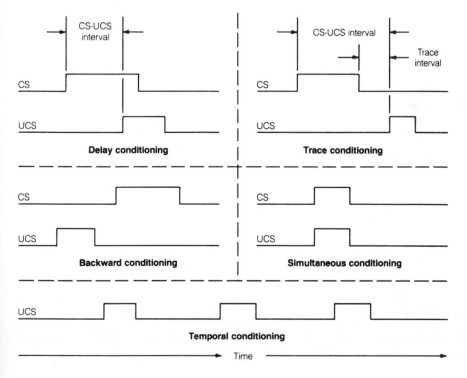

ward conditioning, the least effective. The other three paradigms typically have an intermediate level of effectiveness.

Delayed Conditioning In delayed conditioning, CS onset precedes UCS onset. The termination of the CS occurs either with UCS onset or during UCS presentation. If, for instance, a darkening sky precedes a severe storm, this situation is an example of delayed conditioning. The darkening sky is the CS; its occurrence precedes the storm and it remains present until the storm occurs. Having experienced this type of conditioning, a person will be quite frightened whenever he or she sees a darkened sky.

Trace Conditioning With this conditioning paradigm, the CS is presented and terminated prior to UCS onset. A parent who calls a child to dinner is using a trace conditioning procedure. In this example, the announcement of dinner (CS) terminates prior to the presentation of food (UCS). As we will discover in the next section, hunger developed with this paradigm can be quite weak unless the interval between CS termination and UCS onset is very short.

Simultaneous Conditioning The CS and UCS are presented together when the simultaneous conditioning paradigm is used. An example of simultaneous conditioning would be walking into a fast food restaurant. In this setting, the restaurant (CS) and food (UCS) occur at the same time. The simultaneous conditioning paradigm in this case probably would lead to weak hunger conditioned to the restaurant.

Backward Conditioning In the backward conditioning paradigm, the UCS is presented and terminated prior to the CS. Suppose a candlelight dinner follows sexual activity. In this example, the candlelight dinner (CS) follows the sexual activity (UCS). With this example of backward conditioning, sexual arousal to the candlelight dinner may not develop. In fact, contemporary research (see Tait & Saladin, 1986) indicates that the backward conditioning paradigm often results in the development of another type of CR. The backward conditioning paradigm is also a conditioned inhibition procedure; that is, the CS is paired with the absence of the UCS. In some instances, a person would experience conditioned inhibition rather than conditioned excitation when exposed to the CS. We will look at the factors that determine whether excitation or inhibition is conditioned by a backward conditioning paradigm in the next chapter.

Temporal Conditioning There is no distinctive CS in temporal conditioning. Instead, the UCS is presented at regular intervals, and over time the CR will be exhibited just prior to the onset of the UCS. To show that conditioning has occurred, the UCS is omitted and the strength of the CR assessed. What mechanism allows for temporal conditioning? In temporal conditioning, a biological state provides the CS. When the same internal state precedes each UCS exposure, that state will be conditioned to elicit the CR.

Consider the following example to illustrate the temporal conditioning procedure. You set your alarm to awaken you at 7:00 A.M. for an 8:00 A.M. class. After several months, you awaken just prior to the alarm's sounding. The reason for your actions lies in the temporal conditioning process. The alarm (UCS) produces an arousal reaction (UCR) that awakens you. Your internal state present every day just before the alarm rings (CS) becomes conditioned to produce arousal; this arousal (CR) awakens you prior to the alarm's sounding.

Section Review

Many environmental stimuli can produce internal reactions; these emotional responses often act to motivate our behavior. The hunger you experience while watching a commercial about food on television, or the fear you experience when told of an impending examination, are two examples of our emotional reaction to environmental stimuli. Furthermore, the hunger response may be sufficiently intense to motivate you to get a sandwich from the refrigerator, or the fear response may be intense enough to motivate you to open your book and study for the test.

The ability of these environmental events to produce internal emotional reactions, which, in turn, motivate instrumental behavior, develops through the classical conditioning process. Conditioning involves the pairing of a neutral environmental cue with a biologically important event. Prior to conditioning, only the biologically important stimulus, called an unconditioned stimulus, can elicit a response. This response, called the unconditioned response, consists of both an overt behavioral reaction and an internal emotional response. As the result of conditioning, the neutral environmental stimulus, now a conditioned stimulus, can also elicit a response, called the conditioned response.

There are five conditioning paradigms. With delayed conditioning, the CS remains present until the UCS begins. The CS ends prior to the onset of the UCS with trace conditioning. With simultaneous conditioning, the CS and UCS occur at the same time, while backward conditioning involves the CS following the presentation of the UCS. Temporal conditioning takes place when the UCS is presented at regular intervals of time. The most efficient conditioning usually occurs with delayed conditioning and the least efficient with backward conditioning.

How Readily Is a Conditioned Response Learned?

In the last section we discovered that a conditioned response developed when a novel stimulus is paired with an unconditioned stimulus. However, the pairing of a CS and a UCS does not automatically insure that a conditioned response will be acquired. A number of factors determine whether a CR will develop following CS-UCS pairings. First, *the CS and UCS must be contiguous; that is, the conditioned stimulus must precede the unconditioned stimulus by only a brief period of time.* As we will learn shortly, the longer the delay between the CS and the UCS, the weaker the CR. Second, *the strength of the CR is affected by the intensity of the CS, the UCS, or both.* Increases in the UCS intensity typically lead to faster conditioning and a higher level of the conditioned response. In contrast, a stronger CS does not always produce a stronger CR. Under some conditions, a higher CS intensity leads to a greater CR; under others, there is little difference in CR strength as a function of CS intensity. Context determines the influence of CS intensity on the strength of the CR. The comparison of a weak CS to a strong CS causes a more intense response to the strong than to the weak CS. Without a comparison, there is little difference between the response to a weak CS and a strong CS. Third, *the nature of the CS affects the strength of the CR acquired following CS-UCS pairing.* Although Pavlov (1927) suggested that any neutral stimulus paired with the unconditioned stimulus could, through conditioning, develop the capacity to elicit a CR, contemporary research shows that some stimuli are readily associated with a specific unconditioned stimulus. Fourth, *the CS must consistently precede the occurrence of the UCS.* Even though the CS and UCS may be frequently paired, no CR will develop if the UCS occurs without the CS as often as with it. Also, little or no conditioning of the CR will develop if the CS occurs frequently in the absence of the UCS. Thus, the greater the predictive value of the CS, the stronger the CR elicited by the CS. Finally, *the CS must provide more reliable information about the occurrence of the UCS than do other cues in the environment.* The presence of another predictive cue will prevent, or *block,* the development of the CR to a second stimulus. Although the second cue predicts the occurrence of the UCS, it does not provide new information; thus, no CR develops.

We have learned that many factors affect the classical conditioning process. Let us now look at the evidence indicating that these factors play an important role in classical conditioning.

Contiguity   Consider the following example to illustrate the importance of contiguity on the development of a conditioned response. An 8-year-old boy hits his 6-year-old brother. The mother informs her aggressive son that his father will punish him when he gets home from work. Even though this father frequently punishes his older son for aggression toward his younger brother, the mother's threat instills no fear. The failure of her threat to elicit fear renders the mother unable to curb her son's inappropriate behavior.

Why doesn't the boy fear his mother's threat, since it has been consistently paired with his father's punishment? The answer to this question is in the significance of the close temporal pairing, or *contiguity,* of the CS and the UCS in classical conditioning. A threat (CS) provides information concerning future punishment and elicits the emotional state which motivates avoidance behavior. Although the mother's threat does predict future punishment, the child becoming frightened when the threat is given is not adaptive since the punishment will not occur for several hours. Instead of being frightened from the time that the threat is made until the father's arrival, the boy becomes afraid only when his father arrives. This boy's fear now motivates him to avoid punishment, perhaps by crying and promising not to hit his little brother again.

The Optimal CS-UCS Interval   Many studies document the importance of contiguity in the acquisition of a conditioned response. Experiments designed to evaluate the influence of contiguity on classical conditioning have varied the interval between the CS and the UCS, then evaluated the strength of the CR. The results of these studies show that the optimal CS-UCS interval, or interstimulus interval (ISI), is very short. Intervals even shorter than the optimal ISI produce weaker conditioning, with the strength of the CR increasing as the ISI becomes longer until the optimal CS-UCS interval is reached. Further, an ISI longer than the optimal CS-UCS interval leads to weaker conditioning, with the intensity of the CR decreasing as the ISI increases beyond the optimal ISI.

The optimal CS-UCS interval is different for different responses. For example, the optimal conditioning interval is 450 milliseconds for eye-blink conditioning. This 450 millisecond ISI for the conditioning of the eyelid closure reflex has been observed in both animals (see Frey & Ross, 1968; Smith, Coleman, & Gormezano, 1969) and humans (see Kimble & Reynolds, 1967). Figure 3-4 presents the CS-UCS interval gradient for eye-blink conditioning in humans. Some other optimal ISIs include 2.0 seconds for skeletal movements (see Noble & Harding, 1963), 4.0 seconds for salivary reflexes (see Gormezano, 1972), and 20 seconds for heart rate responses (see Church & Black, 1958).

Why does the optimal CS-UCS interval vary between responses? The optimal ISI is thought to reflect the latency to respond in a particular reflex system (see Hilgard & Marquis, 1940). Hilgard and Marquis suggested that the different optimal CS-UCS intervals occur because the response latency of the autonomic nervous system is longer than that of the eye-blink closure reflex. Wagner and Brandon (1989) tell us why response latency affects the optimal ISI; we will look at their view in the next chapter.

A Bridge between the CS and the UCS   We have learned that the acquisition of the CR is impaired when the CS-UCS interval is longer than a few seconds. Several studies (see Bolles, Collier, Bouton, & Marlin, 1978; Kaplan, 1984; Kaplan & Hearst, 1982; Kehoe, Gibbs, Garcia, & Gormezano, 1979; Pearce, Nicholas, & Dickinson, 1981; Rescorla, 1982) have reported that the attenuation of conditioning produced by a temporal gap between the CS and UCS can be reduced if a second stimulus is presented between the CS and UCS.

Consider the Rescorla (1982) study to illustrate this phenomenon. Rescorla's subjects, pigeons, were shown a colored light followed by food 10 seconds later. On the trials when one color (for example, red) was presented, a second stimulus, either a white light or a tone, was presented during the 10 seconds between the colored light and the food. The white light or tone was not presented on trials in which a different colored light, (for example, green) was used. Rescorla found that the level of conditioning was significantly greater to the color (in this case, the red light) paired with the white light or tone than to the color (in this case, the green light) which was not followed by the intermediate stimulus.

Why does the intermediate stimulus produce conditioning despite a delay between the CS and the UCS? According to Rescorla (1982), the intermediate stimulus acts as a catalyst, enhancing the association of the CS and the UCS. This observation

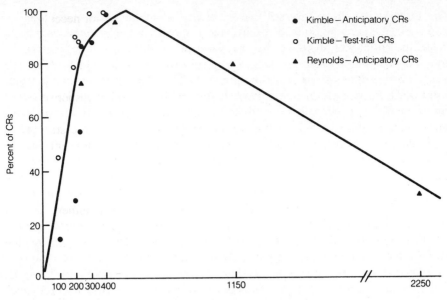

FIGURE 3-4 An idealized interstimulus interval (ISI) gradient obtained from eye-blink conditioning data in humans. The graph shows that the level of conditioning increases with CS-UCS delays up to the optimal interval, then declines with greater CS-UCS intervals. From Kimble, G. A., & Reynolds, B. (1967). Eyelid conditioning as a function of the interval between conditioned and unconditioned stimuli. In G. A. Kimble (Ed.), *Foundations of conditioning and learning.* New York: Appleton-Century Crofts.

suggests that with appropriate procedures, a high level of conditioning can develop even though there is a significant delay between the CS and the UCS.

Long-Delay Learning There is one noteworthy exception to the contiguity principle. Animals and humans are capable of associating a flavor stimulus (CS) with an illness experience (UCS) that occurs several hours after the taste cue exposure. The association of taste with illness, called *flavor-aversion learning,* contrasts sharply with the other forms of classical conditioning, in which no conditioning occurs if the CS-UCS interval is longer than several minutes. While flavor-aversion learning can occur with long delays, there is a CS-UCS interval gradient, with the strongest conditioning occurring when the flavor and illness are separated by 30 minutes (see Garcia, Clark, & Hankins, 1973). We will take a more detailed look at flavor-aversion learning in Chapter 13.

The Influence of Intensity

CS Intensity Suppose you were bitten by a dog. Would you be more afraid of the dog if it were large or small? If we assume that the pain induced by bites (UCS) from each are equivalent, research on the intensity of the CS and the strength of conditioning indicates your fear would be equivalent only if one dog bites you. However, if you were bitten by both sizes of dogs (not necessarily at the same time), you would be afraid of the more intense CS, the large dog. Let's now look at research examining the influence of CS intensity on CR strength.

Initial research indicated that the intensity of the CS does not affect CR strength. For example, Grant and Schneider (1948, 1949) reported that CS intensity did not influence the classical conditioning of the eye-blink response in humans. Carter (1941) and Wilcott (1953) showed similar results. However, more recent research clearly demonstrates that CS intensity can affect the strength of the conditioned response. A greater CR strength produced by a more intense CS has been shown in dogs (Barnes, 1956), rabbits (Frey, 1969), rats (Kamin & Schaub, 1963), and humans (Beck, 1963; Grice & Hunter, 1964).

Why does an intense CS only sometimes elicit a stronger CR than a weak CS? When an animal or person experiences only a single stimulus (either weak or intense), an intense CS does not produce an appreciably greater CR than a weak CS. However, if both the intense and the weak CS are experienced, the intense CS will produce a significantly greater CR than the weak CS will.

A study by Grice and Hunter (1964) shows the important influence of the type of training procedure on the magnitude of CS intensity effect. In Grice and Hunter's study, one group of human subjects received 100 eyelid conditioning trials of a loud (100-dB) tone CS paired with an air puff UCS. A second group of subjects had a soft (50-dB) tone CS paired with the air puff for 100 trials. The third group of subjects was given 50 trials with the loud tone and 50 with the soft tone. Grice and Hunter's results, presented in Figure 3-5, show that CS intensity (loudness of tone) had a much greater effect on conditioning when a subject experienced both stimuli than when a subject was exposed to only the soft or the loud tone.

UCS Intensity Recall Diane's intense fear of darkness and men described in the chapter-opening vignette. The intensity of the rape was a critical factor in causing Diane to be extremely frightened of darkness and men. Yet, all experiences are not as aversive as Diane's rape. Suppose you have the misfortune of being in an automobile accident. How much fear will be elicited the next time you get into a car? Research on UCS intensity and CR strength indicates that your level of fear will depend upon the intensity of the accident; the more severe the accident, the greater your fear of automobiles. Thus, if the accident was a minor one causing only slight discomfort, your subsequent fear will be minimal. However, a severe accident will cause an intense fear.

The literature provides conclusive documentation that the strength of the CR increases with higher UCS intensity. To show the influence of UCS on eyelid response conditioning, Prokasy, Grant, and Myers (1958) gave their human subjects either a 50-, 120-, 190-, or 260-mm intensity air puff UCS paired with a light CS. They found that the strength of the CR was directly related to the UCS intensity; that is, the more intense the air puff, the stronger the eye-blink CR (see Figure 3-6).

The Salience of the CS Seligman (1970) suggested that animals or humans have an evolutionary predisposition or *preparedness* to associate a particular

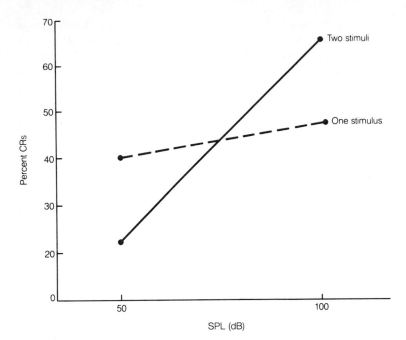

FIGURE 3-5 The percentage of conditioned responses during the last 60 trials is greater to a loud (100-dB), tone than to a soft (50-dB) tone in the two stimuli condition but not in the one-stimulus condition. From Grice, G. R., & Hunter, J. J. (1964). Stimulus intensity effects depend upon the type of experimental design. *Psychological Review, 71,* 247–256. Copyright 1964 by the American Psychological Association. Reprinted by permission.

stimulus with a specific unconditioned stimulus, but that other CS-UCS associations cannot be learned. The concept of *contrapreparedness* suggests that stimuli, despite repeated CS-UCS pairings, cannot become associated with a particular UCS. The likelihood that a particular neutral stimulus will become able to elicit a conditioned response after pairing with an unconditioned stimulus reflects the *salience* of the neutral stimulus. Salient stimuli rapidly become associated with a particular unconditioned stimulus, while nonsalient stimuli do not, despite repeated CS-UCS pairings. Many, perhaps most, stimuli are not particularly salient or nonsalient; instead, these stimuli will gradually develop the ability to elicit a conditioned response as the result of conditioning experiences. It is also important to recognize that salience is species-dependent; that is, a stimulus may be salient to one species but not to another. Chapter 13 discusses the biological significance of stimulus salience in Pavlovian conditioning; we will examine the influence of species-specific stimulus salience on the acquisition of a conditioned response in that chapter.

The Overshadowing of a Less Salient CS There are many occasions when two or more cues are presented together with the UCS, a procedure called *com-*

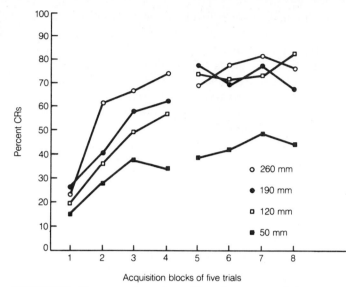

FIGURE 3-6   The percentage of conditioned responses during acquisition increases with greater UCS intensities. Adapted from Prokasy, W. P., Jr., Grant, D. A., & Myers, N. A. (1958). Eyelid conditioning as a function of unconditioned stimulus intensity and intertrial interval. *Journal of Experimental Psychology, 55,* 242–246. Copyright 1958 by the American Psychological Association. Reprinted by permission.

pound conditioning. Which cue will become associated with the UCS? Most of the time, a greater CR will develop to the more salient (or intense) CS than to the less salient (or intense) CS. Also, the larger the difference in salience (or intensity), the greater the difference in CR strength elicited by the cues. Thus, the presence of a more salient (or intense) cue interferes with, or overshadows, the association of the less salient (or intense) cue with the UCS. This phenomena, called *overshadowing,* was originally observed by Pavlov (1927). Pavlov found that a more intense tone overshadowed the association of a less intense tone with the UCS.

Overshadowing is readily observed in flavor-aversion experiments. For example, Lindsey and Best (1973) presented two novel fluids (saccharin and casein hydrosylate) prior to illness, finding that a strong aversion developed to the salient saccharin flavor but only a weak aversion was established to the less salient casein hydrosylate solution. Similar overshadowing by a salient flavor cue of the development of an aversion to a less salient cue was observed by Green and Churchill (1970), Kalat and Rozin (1970), and Klein and associates (1984).

The Potentiation of a Less Salient Cue   Overshadowing does not always occur when two cues of different salience are paired with a UCS; in fact, there are some circumstances in which the presence of a salient cue leads to a stronger CR than would have occurred had the nonsalient cue been presented alone with the UCS. The increased conditioned response to a nonsalient stimulus as the result of also presenting a salient cue during conditioning was first described by John Garcia and his associates (see Garcia & Rusiniak, 1980; Palmerino, Rusiniak, & Garcia, 1980; Rusiniak, Palmerino, & Garcia, 1982). They observed that the presence of a salient flavor *potentiated* rather than overshadowed the establishment of an aversion to a nonsalient odor cue paired with illness.

Rusiniak, Palmerino, and Garcia (1982) presented one group of rats a relatively nonsalient odor cue (either almond or vanilla) and a salient saccharin taste cue prior to lithium chloride-induced illness; other subjects received only the odor cue before experiencing illness. Tests showed that a strong aversion to almond or vanilla developed when the odor cue was presented with the saccharin taste cue, but only a weak aversion to the odor cue was established when this cue alone occurred prior to illness. Other researchers (see Best, Batson, Meachum, Brown, & Ringer; 1985; Klein, Freda, & Mikulka, 1985; Rescorla & Holland, 1982) have reported that a flavor stimulus potentiated the formation of an aversion to a place as well as to an odor. What process determines whether overshadowing or potentiation of a nonsalient stimulus is produced by the presence of a more salient stimulus? An answer to this question can be found in the next chapter.

The Predictiveness of the CS   Robert Bolles (1972, 1979) proposed that contiguity alone is not sufficient for the development of a conditioned response. In Bolles's view, events must consistently occur together before we can acquire a conditioned response. A neutral stimulus may be simultaneously paired with a UCS, but unless the neutral stimulus reliably predicts the occurrence of the UCS, the CR will not be elicited by the neutral stimulus. Additionally, when two or more stimuli are presented with the UCS, only the most reliable predictor of the UCS will become associated with the UCS.

The following example illustrates the important influence of *cue predictiveness* on the development of a conditioned response. Many parents threaten their children prior to punishment; yet, their threats instill no fear, despite repeated threat-punishment (CS-UCS) pairings. Why is parental threat ineffective? One likely reason is that these parents may often threaten their children without punishing them. Under these circumstances, the threat is not a reliable predictor of punishment and its presentation will elicit little or no fear, even though the threat and punishment have been frequently experienced together. We first examine evidence showing that the acquisition of the CR is impaired if the UCS is often presented without the CS, and follow this with a description of research which shows that presentations of the CS alone decrease the development of the CR.

UCS-Alone Presentations   Robert Rescorla's (1968) research demonstrates the influence of cue predictiveness in classical conditioning. After his rats learned to bar press for food, Rescorla divided the 2-hour training sessions into 2-minute segments. One of three events occurred in each segment: (1) a distinctive cue (CS; tone) was paired with a shock (UCS), (2) shock was presented without the distinctive cue, or (3) neither tone nor shock occurred during the interval. Res-

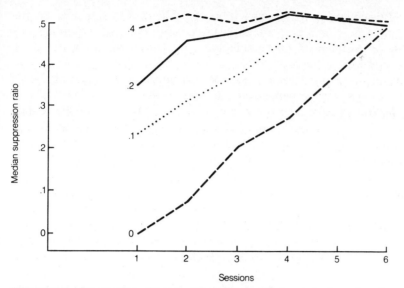

FIGURE 3-7 Suppression of bar-pressing behavior during six test sessions (a low value indicates that the CS elicits fear and thereby suppresses bar pressing for food). The probability of the UCS occurring with the CS is 0.4 for all groups, and the values shown in the graph represent the probability that the UCS will occur alone in a 2-minute segment. When the two probabilities are equal, the CS does not elicit fear and, therefore, does not suppress responding. Only when the UCS occurs more frequently with than without the CS will the CS elicit fear and suppress bar pressing. Adapted from Rescorla, R. A. (1968). Probability of shock in the presence and absence of CS in fear conditioning. *Journal of Comparative and Physiological Psychology, 68,* 1–5. Copyright 1968 by the American Psychological Association. Reprinted by permission.

corla varied the likelihood that the shock would occur with (or without) the tone in each 2-minute segment. He found that the tone suppressed bar-press responding for food when the tone reliably predicted shock, indicating that an association is formed between the tone and the shock. However, the influence of the tone on the rats' behavior diminished as the frequency of shock occurring without the tone increased. The tone had no effect on behavior when the shock occurred as frequently in the absence of the tone as it did when the tone was present. Figure 3-7 presents the results of the subjects who received a 0.4 UCS-alone probability (or UCS alone on 40 percent of the 2-minute segments).

One important aspect of Rescorla's data is that even with only a few pairings, the presentation of the tone produced intense fear and suppressed bar pressing if the shock was applied only with the tone. However, when the shock occurred without the tone as frequently as it did with it, no conditioning resulted even with a large number of tone-shock pairings. Apparently, the predictablility of a stimulus, not the number of CS-UCS pairings, determines an environmental event's ability to elicit a CR.

CS-Alone Presentations The acquisition of a CR is also impaired or prevented when the CS is presented alone during conditioning. Many studies (see Hall, 1976) have documented the attenuation of conditioning when the CS is presented alone as well as with the UCS.

The level of conditioning depends upon the percentage of trials pairing the CS with the UCS; the greater the percentage, the greater the conditioning. Hartman and Grant's (1960) study provides one example of the influence of the percentage of paired CS-UCS presentations on the CR strength. All of Hartman and Grant's human subjects received 40 light (CS) and air puff (UCS) pairings. For subjects in the 25 percent group, the UCS occurred following 40 of the 160 CS presentations; for subjects in the 50 percent group, the air puff followed the tone on 40 of 80 CS presentations; for subjects in the 75 percent group, the UCS followed the CS on 40 of 54 trials; for subjects in the 100 percent group, the air puff was presented after the light on 40 of 40 trials. Hartman and Grant's results showed that the strength of conditioning was an increasing function of the percentage of trials which paired the CS with the UCS (see Figure 3-8).

The Redundancy of the CS Recall from the last section the example of the failure of parental threat to instill fear. In addition to a lack of predictiveness, another possible explanation for this lack of fear is that the child is already afraid when the threat is presented. Perhaps the child is afraid of his or her parents; if so, parental presence (CS) will interfere with the acquisition of fear to the threat, despite repeated threat-punishment pairings.

The Blocking Paradigm In order for a cue to elicit a CR, and thereby influence behavior, Bolles (1978) suggested that the cue must not only predict the

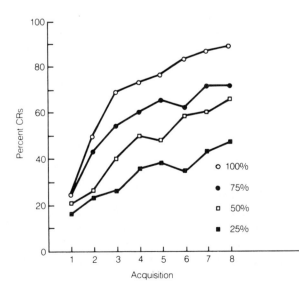

FIGURE 3-8
The percentage of conditioned responses during each block of acquisition trials decreases with a lower percentage of trials in which the UCS follows the CS. Adapted from Hartman, T. F., & Grant, D. A. (1960). Effect of intermittent reinforcement on acquisition, extinction, and spontaneous recovery of the conditioned eyelid response. *Journal of Experimental Psychology, 60,* 89–96. Copyright 1960 by the American Psychological Association. Reprinted by permission.

occurrence of the UCS but also provide information not signaled by the other cues present in the environment. The research of Leon Kamin (1968) demonstrates that the presence of a predictive cue (CS$_1$) will prevent, or *block,* the development of an association between a second cue (CS$_2$) also paired with the UCS. To demonstrate the importance of relative cue predictability, Kamin presented all of his subjects a distinctive cue (CS$_1$, a light) paired with a shock (UCS) eight times during the first phase of the study (see Figure 3-9). In the second phase of the study, the experimental-group subjects received eight pairings of the light (CS$_1$), a new cue (CS$_2$, a tone), and shock (UCS). Kamin observed that while presentation of the light (CS$_1$) suppressed bar-press responding, the tone cue (CS$_2$) when presented alone had no influence on bar pressing. The light had become associated with the shock, while tone apparently had not. Kamin's results are not due to the tone being unable to be associated with shock. Control-group animals that received only tone-shock pairings during the second phase of study showed strong suppression caused by the tone (CS$_2$).

The Nature of Blocking Why did the tone suppress bar pressing in the control animals but not in the experimental subjects? Kamin (1969) offered two possible explanations for the blocking phenomenon. One view is that the presence of the predictive light cue (CS$_1$) caused the experimental-group animals to not attend to the tone (CS$_2$). In the absence of the light, the control-group rats paid attention to the tone and associated its presence with shock.

A study by Wagner (1969) shows that animals in the blocking condition were aware of the presence of the tone but did not use this information. Wagner reported that when the light and tone cues together predicted no shock, the tone cue developed the ability to inhibit avoidance behavior. His observations

FIGURE 3-9 The design of Kamin's blocking study. In phase 1, the CS$_1$ (light) is paired with the UCS (shock); in the second phase, both the CS$_1$ and CS$_2$ (tone) are paired with the UCS (shock). The ability of the CS$_2$ (tone) to elicit fear is assessed during phase 3.

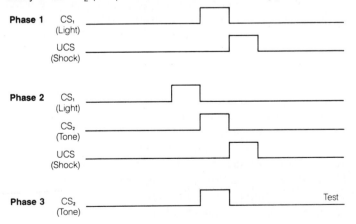

demonstrated that the rats were attending to the tone; otherwise, there would have been no inhibition conditioned with light and tone pairings.

Kamin's second view assumes that when the animals first experience shock they are surprised by this unanticipated event. The surprise causes the rats to associate a light cue with shock; learning, according to Kamin, takes place only when surprising events occur. Following conditioning, encountering the light cue causes no surprise. Since the light produced an anticipation of shock in the experimental group, the rats were not surprised when the tone was experienced. As a result of a lack of surprise, the tone did not develop the ability to produce fear.

Mackintosh and his associates (see Dickinson, Hall, & Mackintosh, 1976; Mackintosh, Bygrave, & Picton, 1977) showed that a surprising event can prevent the CS_1 from blocking the CS_2-CR association. In the first phase of their studies, animals received CS_1-UCS-UCS pairings until CS_1 suppressed bar pressing. Following the acquisition of fear to CS_1, some subjects were given CS_1-CS_2-UCS pairings, while others received CS_1-CS_2-UCS-UCS pairings. Mackintosh and his associates observed that when they omitted the second UCS, creating a surprising event, no blocking occurred and fear was conditioned to the CS_2. In contrast, the development of fear was blocked in those subjects who received the anticipated second UCS. These results indicate that the omission of the UCS can diminish the blocking effect.

Why is surprise necessary for conditioning? Why can surprise eliminate the blocking phenomenon? Two theories (Mackintosh, 1975; Rescorla & Wagner, 1972) have proposed answers to these questions. According to Rescorla and Wagner (1972), only surprising or unpredicted UCSs are reinforcing; that is, surprise enables the UCS to be effective. In contrast, Mackintosh (1975) asserted that surprising UCSs serve to maintain the associability of the CS; that is, a CS is relevant only when the UCS is unpredictable. Although a large number of studies (for example, Dickinson, Colwill, & Pearce, 1980; Dickinson, Hall, & Mackintosh, 1976; Kremer, Specht, & Allen, 1980; Mackintosh, Dickinson, & Cotton, 1980; Maleske & Frey, 1979; Neely & Wagner, 1974; Randich & LoLordo, 1979) have attempted to discover the underlying mechanism responsible for the influence of surprise in conditioning, the reason why a surprising UCS is necessary for the acquisition of a conditioned response is unclear (refer to Dickinson, 1980, for a discussion of the issue).

Section Review

Although pairing of the conditioned and unconditioned stimuli is essential for the development of a conditioned response, it is not sufficient to insure the acquisition of a conditioned response. There are five factors, in addition to its presentation with the unconditioned stimulus, that determine whether or not a stimulus develops the ability to elicit a conditioned response. One factor affecting the strength of conditioning is temporal contiguity: Contiguity must exist between the CS and the UCS for conditioning to occur. An intermediate stimulus between the CS and the UCS can act to facilitate the development of a conditioned response, while an aversion to a flavor cue paired with illness can develop despite a lack of contiguity.

The intensity of the CS and the UCS is a second factor affecting the intensity of the CR. An intense stimulus typically leads to a stronger CR than a weak stimulus. A third variable influencing conditioning is salience. Some stimuli are more salient than others and therefore are more likely to elicit a CR following pairing with a specific UCS. The stimulus must also be a reliable predictor of the UCS. The more often the CS occurs without the UCS, or the UCS is presented without the CS, the weaker the CR. Redundancy is the final factor affecting the strength of the conditioned response. The presence of a conditioned stimulus can prevent or block the development of a conditioned response to a new stimulus when both stimuli are paired with the UCS. Blocking occurs due to a lack of surprise when the UCS follows the new stimulus in the presence of the original conditioned stimulus.

EXTINCTION OF THE CONDITIONED RESPONSE

Earlier in the chapter, you were given examples of conditioned hunger and fear. From them, you learned that environmental stimuli, through their association with deprivation, reward, or both, can acquire the ability to elicit hunger. Similarly, we can become afraid of examinations by associating them with their adversive consequences. Our conditioned responses typically have an adaptive function; the development of a conditioned hunger or fear reaction enables us to eat at regularly scheduled times or study for scheduled examinations. However, the conditioning of hunger and fear can also be harmful. People can eat too much and become obese or become too fearful to perform effectively. Clinical research (see Rimm & Masters, 1979) has revealed that overweight people eat in many situations (for example, while watching television, driving, or at the movies). In order to lose weight, overweight people must restrict their food intake to the dining room (or the room where they usually eat), a process called *stimulus narrowing*. Yet, how can those who are overweight control their intake in varied environmental circumstances? One answer is *extinction,* a method of eliminating a conditioned response. As the person's hunger response to varied environmental circumstances has developed through the classical conditioning process, the extinction of the conditioned hunger reaction represents one approach to losing weight.

Extinction can also be effective therapy for the many people who are extremely fearful of examinations. Their test anxiety motivates such people to avoid tests rather than to study. Since an intense fear of examinations is acquired through the classical conditioning process, extinction again represents a potentially effective method of eliminating an intense fear reaction.

Next, we describe the extinction process and indicate how extinction might eliminate a person's hunger reaction to an environmental event or reduce someone's fear reaction to a scheduled examination. The reason that extinction is not always an effective method of eliminating a conditioned response will also be explored in this section. Let's begin by looking at the extinction procedure.

Extinction Procedure

The extinction of a conditioned response will occur when the conditioned stimulus is presented without the unconditioned stimulus. The strength of the CR decreases as the number of CS-alone experiences increases, until eventually no CR is elicited by the CS (refer to Figure 3-1).

Pavlov (1927) reported that a classically conditioned salivation response in dogs could be rapidly extinguished by presenting the CS (tone) without the UCS (meat powder). Since Pavlov's initial observations, many psychologists have documented the extinction of a CR by using CS-alone presentations; the extinction procedure is definitely one of the most reliable conditioning phenomenon.

Extinction is one way by which a person's hunger reaction to environmental stimuli such as watching television can be eliminated. In this case, the hunger response can be eliminated by repeatedly watching television without eating food (UCS). However, people experiencing hunger-inducing circumstances are not always able to refrain from eating. Other behavioral techniques (for example, aversive counterconditioning, reinforcement therapy) are often necessary to inhibit eating and thereby the extinction of the conditioned hunger response. The use of reinforcement is examined in Chapter 5; the use of punishment is discussed in Chapter 6.

An extreme fear of examinations can also be eliminated by extinction. If a person takes an examination and failure does not occur, this person's fear will be diminished. However, fear is not only an extremely aversive emotion but also an intense motivator of avoidance behavior. Thus, persons having test anxiety may not be able to withstand the fear and inhibit avoidance of taking the test. Other techniques (for example, desensitization, response prevention, and participant modeling) also are available to eliminate fear and enable the person to take an examination. Desensitization is discussed in the next chapter; response prevention will be addressed in Chapter 6, and participant modeling is examined in Chapter 8.

We have learned that many factors facilitate or hinder the acquisition of the CR; we now discuss those variables that determine the rate of extinction of the CR.

How Rapidly Does a Conditioned Response Extinguish?

Three factors influence the extinction of a conditioned response. First, *the strength of the CR can affect the extinction of the conditioned response.* Under most circumstances, the stronger the CR at the end of acquisition, the longer it will take to extinguish the CR. Second, *the percentage of trials in which the UCS follows the CS can influence the extinction of a conditioned response.* The literature shows that presenting the UCS without (as well as with) the CS during acquisition usually results in a slower extinction of the CR than presenting the UCS only with the CS. Third, *the length of exposure to the CS during extinction affects the level of extinction.* Empirical investigation reveals that the longer the CS-alone exposure, the greater the reduction in CR strength.

The Strength of the CR.   Hull (1943) envisioned the extinction process as a mirror image of acquisition; that is, the stronger the CS-CR bond, the more difficult it is to extinguish the association. Thus, Hull assumed that the stronger the CR, the slower the extinction of that response. Although many studies have found that acquisition level does influence resistance to extinction, other research has not observed a perfect relationship between the strength of the CR during acquisition and the rate of the extinction of that response. As Hall (1976) stated, one reason for this discrepancy is that the omission of the UCS during extinction changes the subject's motivational level from that which existed during acquisition. This altered motivation level makes extinction differ from acquisition and thereby decreases the correlation between the CR acquisition level and the resistance to extinction.

The Influence of Predictiveness   In 1939, Humphreys examined how the percentage of trials in which the UCS followed the CS during acquisition influenced the resistance to extinction. To study this effect, an eye-blink response was conditioned in humans. During acquisition, subjects in group 1 received 96 CS-UCS pairings and no CS-alone presentations; subjects in group 2 received 48 CS-UCS pairings and 48 CS-alone presentations; subjects in group 3 were given 48 CS-UCS pairings and no CS-alone presentations. Humphreys discovered that in the subjects who received CS-UCS pairings on 50 percent of the trials (group 2), the conditioned eye-blink response extinguished significantly more slowly than in those subjects given CS-UCS pairings on 100 percent of the trials (groups 1 and 3). Humphreys' results are presented in Figure 3-10.

Duration of CS Exposure   We have discovered that the strength of the conditioned response declines as the CS-alone experience increases. You might have the impression that the number of CS-alone presentations determines the level of extinction; that is, as the number of extinction trials increases, the strength of the CR declines. However, research (see Berman & Katzev, 1972; Monti & Smith, 1976; Shipley, 1974) clearly shows that the total duration of CS-alone exposure, not the number of extinction trials, determines the rate of extinction. These studies demonstrate that as the duration of CS exposure increases, the strength of the CR weakens. Let's briefly look at Shipley's study to see the influence of CS-alone duration on the extinction of a CR.

Shipley (1974) initially trained water-deprived rats to lick a water tube to obtain liquid reinforcement. Following lick training, the animals received 20 exposures to a tone paired with electric shock. Extinction occurred following fear

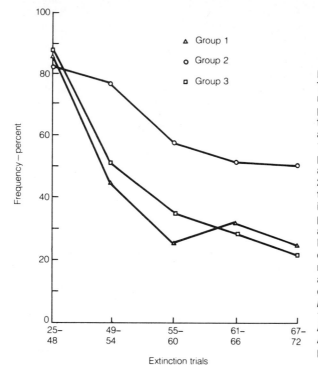

FIGURE 3-10
The extinction of the conditioned response as a function of the percentage of trials where UCS followed the CS during acquisition. Subjects in groups 1 and 3 received CS-UCS pairings on 100 percent of the acquisition trials; those in group 2, on 50 percent. Resistance to extinction is greater with intermittent than with continuous pairings of CS and UCS in acquisition. Adapted from Humphreys, L. G. (1939). The effect of random alternation of reinforcement on the acquisition and extinction of conditioned eyelid reactions. *Journal of Experimental Psychology, 25,* 141–158. Copyright 1939 by the American Psychological Association. Reprinted by permission.

conditioning. Half of the animals were given 25-second CS-alone exposures during extinction; the other half received a 100-second and CS-alone experience during extinction. One-third of the animals in both the 25-second and the 100-second CS-duration groups were given sufficient extinction experience so that they received a total of 200 seconds of CS exposure, another third received 400 seconds, and the last third 800 seconds of exposure. For example, to have 200 total seconds of CS exposure, the animals given 25 seconds on each trial received eight trials compared to two trials for subjects receiving 100 seconds on each trial. Shipley reported that the suppression of licking produced by the CS was not affected by either the number of CS-alone exposures or the duration of each exposure. Only the total duration of CS exposure during extinction determined the rate of extinction of the CR; the greater the length of the total CS exposure during extinction, the less suppression produced by the tone (see Figure 3-11). We have examined the variables that affect extinction rate; let's next look at the process responsible for the extinction of a CR.

The Nature of the Extinction

Pavlov (1927) proposed that the extinction of a CR is caused by the *inhibition* of the CR. This inhibition develops as the result of the activation of a central

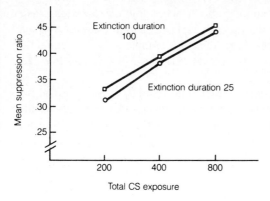

FIGURE 3-11
The suppression of licking for water response to the conditioned stimulus increases with greater duration of CS exposure during extinction. Adapted from Shipley, R. H. (1974). Extinction of conditioned fear in rats as a function of several parameters of CS exposure. *Journal of Comparative and Physiological Psychology, 87,* 699–707. Copyright 1974 by the American Psychological Association. Reprinted by permission.

inhibitory state which occurs when the CS is presented without the UCS. This inhibitory state is strengthened by the continued presentation of the CS without the UCS and acts to prevent the occurrence of the CR.

The initial inhibition of the CR which occurs as the result of extinction is only temporary. According to Pavlov, the arousal of the inhibitory state declines following the initial extinction. As the strength of the inhibitory state diminishes, the ability of the CS to elicit the CR returns (see Figure 3-1). The return of the CR following extinction is called *spontaneous recovery.* The continued presentation of the CS without the UCS eventually leads to the long-term suppression of the CR. The inhibition of a CR can become permanent as the result of conditioned inhibition; we will discuss the conditioned inhibition process shortly.

Guthrie (1935) suggested a different explanation for the extinction of a conditioned response. According to Guthrie, the presentation of the CS without the UCS causes the conditioning of another response to the CS, which will interfere with the ability of the CS to elicit the CR. As the strength of the interfering response increases, the CR will decrease in strength. A number of types of studies have evaluated Pavlov's inhibitory view and Guthrie's response competition view of extinction. This research generally supports Pavlov's approach; let's now examine some of this evidence (see Hall, 1976, for a more detailed review of this literature).

Evidence supporting Pavlov's view of extinction is provided by comparisons of massed versus spaced extinction. According to Pavlov, during spaced extinction trials the level of inhibition declines during the interval between trials, thereby slowing the development of the inhibitory state. In contrast, the level of inhibition does not decline during the interval between trials during massed extinction, and therefore the inhibitory state develops quickly. Massed extinction, producing a more rapid increase of the inhibitory state than spaced extinction, should thus lead to faster extinction than does spaced extinction. Guthrie's approach makes the opposite prediction. Since he assumed that extinction is due to the conditioning of a competing response and spaced practice produces faster acquisition of the CR than does massed practice, spaced practice should also lead to faster extinction. The research, however, clearly demonstrates that extinction is faster with massed extinction than with spaced extinction (see Hilgard & Marquis, 1940).

Further evidence that Pavlov's theory, rather than Guthrie's, is correct is provided by a number of studies which show that acquisition and extinction are also affected by various drugs (see Hilgard & Marquis, 1940). For example, both caffeine and benzedrine (two stimulants) increase the rate of acquisition but interfere with extinction. In contrast, sodium bromide (a depressant) retards the rate of acquisition but enhances extinction of a CR. Since Pavlov assumed that acquisition and extinction were due to different processes while Guthrie suggested that acquisition and extinction reflected the same process, the observation that stimulant and depressant drugs have opposite effects on the acquisition and extinction of a CR supports Pavlov's view of extinction.

Rescorla (1969) presented evidence suggesting that extinction may not be due to inhibition. Two types of inquiry support his view. The first support comes from studies using the *summation test*. The summation test involves presentation of the extinguished CS with another CS. If the extinguished CS has inhibitory properties, it should act to suppress responding to the other CS. Rescorla found that an extinguished CS failed the summation test; that is, the extinguished CS did not suppress responding to the other CS. The second type of research involves the *retardation test*. In the retardation test, the CS is again paired with the UCS. If the extinguished CS has inhibitory properties, reacquisition of the CR should be impaired. However, Rescorla found that an extinguished CS also failed the retardation test; that is, reacquisition of a CR was not slower after extinction than had been the original acquisition.

While these results suggest that extinction is not due to inhibition, Mackintosh (1983) argued against this conclusion. According to Mackintosh, extinction involves not only inhibition but other processes as well; the omission of the UCS may change the stimulus context from that experienced during acquisition, as well as lead to a decline in motivational state. Several studies (see Frey & Butler, 1973; Rescorla & Skucy, 1969) have tried to determine if extinction involves processes other than inhibition. In these studies, an extinction procedure in which the UCS is omitted is compared to a procedure where both the CS and the UCS are presented but not paired. This second procedure produces a decline in responding, yet not as rapid a decline as that caused by the traditional extinction procedure. Since the rate of extinction differed depending on the type of extinction process used, it is probable that extinction involves more than just one process. Further, the influence of these other processes may also hinder the detection of the inhibitory aspects of extinction when using the summation and retardation tests, whereas the observation that stimulants impair extinction while depressants facilitate extinction provides support for the view that at least one process involved in extinction is inhibition.

Other Inhibitory Processes

We have learned that a temporary internal inhibition is one process involved in the extinction of a conditioned response. The inhibition of the CR can become permanent, a process which Pavlov called conditioned inhibition. There are also several other types of inhibitions: external inhibition, latent inhibition, and inhibition of delay. Inhibition can be eliminated through a process called disinhibition.

Conditioned Inhibition   The initial inhibition of a CR can become permanent. If a new stimulus (CS−) similar to the conditioned stimulus (CS+) is presented in the absence of the unconditioned stimulus, the CS− will act to inhibit a CR to the CS+. The process of developing a permanent inhibitor is called *conditioned inhibition*. Conditioned inhibition is assumed to reflect the ability of the CS− to activate the inhibitory state, which can suppress the CR.

Consider the following example to illustrate the conditioned inhibition phenomenon. Recall our discussion of conditioned hunger; because of past experiences, you became hungry when arriving home after your classes. Suppose when you open the refrigerator, you find no food. In all likelihood, the empty refrigerator would act to inhibit your hunger. This inhibitory property of the empty refrigerator developed as a result of past pairings of the empty refrigerator with an absence of food. Many studies have shown that associating new stimuli with the absence of the UCS causes these stimuli to develop permanent inhibitory properties; let's examine one of these studies.

Rescorla and LoLordo (1965) initially trained their dogs to avoid electric shock using a Sidman avoidance schedule. With this procedure, the dogs received a shock every 10 seconds unless they jumped over a hurdle dividing the two compartments of a shuttle box (see Chapter 2). If a dog avoided a shock, the next shock was postponed for 30 seconds. The advantage of this technique is twofold: No external CS is employed during Sidman avoidance conditioning, and the influence of fear-inducing cues (CS+) and fear-inhibiting cues (CS−) can be assessed. After three days of avoidance conditioning, the dogs were locked in one compartment of the shuttle box and exposed on some trials to a 1200-hertz (Hz) tone (CS+) and shock (UCS) and other trials to a 400-Hz tone (CS−) without shock. Following conditioned inhibition training, the CS+ aroused fear and thereby increased avoidance responding. In contrast, the CS− inhibited fear, causing the dogs to stop responding. These results indicate that the CS+ elicited fear and the CS− inhibited fear, and that conditioned stimuli have an important motivational influence on instrumental behavior; we will examine that influence in Chapter 7.

External Inhibition   Pavlov (1927) suggested that inhibition could occur in situations other than extinction. In support of his theory, he observed that the presentation of a novel stimulus during conditioning reduces the strength of the conditioned response. Pavlov labeled this temporary activation of the inhibitory state *external inhibition*. The inhibition of the CR will not occur on a subsequent trial unless the novel stimulus is presented again; if the novel stimulus is not presented during the next trial, the strength of the conditioned response will return to its previous level.

Latent Inhibition   Preexposure to the CS impairs conditioning of the CR when the CS and the UCS are later presented together. Lubow and Moore (1959) suggested the effect of CS preexposure was due to *latent inhibition;* that is, exposure to the CS prior to conditioning caused the CS to acquire inhibitory properties which subsequently interfered with excitatory conditioning when the CS and the UCS were paired.

Mackintosh (1983) believes that CS preexposure leads to learned irrelevance— the subject learns that a stimulus does not predict any significant event and therefore has difficulty recognizing the correlation between the stimulus and the UCS. We will now examine evidence that inhibition is not involved in the CS preexposure effect.

A number of studies (see Baker & Mackintosh, 1977; Halgren, 1974; Rescorla, 1971) have examined the effect of CS preexposure on the acquisition of conditioned inhibition. If the impact of CS preexposure resulted from inhibition, then the CS preexposure should enhance conditioned-inhibition training. However, these studies showed that preexposure to a stimulus not only retards excitatory conditioning but also interferes with inhibitory conditioning. Thus, it appears that CS preexposure does not lead to the development of latent inhibition. We will look more closely at the influence of CS preexposure on classical conditioning in the next chapter.

Inhibition of Delay   There are many occasions when a short delay separates the CS and the UCS. For example, several minutes elapse from the time that we enter a restaurant until we receive our food. Under these conditions, we inhibit our responding until just prior to receiving the food. (If we did begin to salivate as soon as we entered the restaurant, our mouths would be dry when we were served our food and our digestive process would be impaired.) Further, the ability to inhibit responding until the end of the CS-UCS interval improves with experience. At first we respond immediately when a CS is presented; our ability to withhold the CR improves with increased CS-UCS pairings.

Pavlov's classic research (1927) with dogs demonstrated the development of the ability to suppress the CR until the end of the CS-UCS interval, a phenomenon he labeled *inhibition of delay*. Other experimenters (see Ellison, 1964; Kimmel, 1965; Sheffield, 1965) have also shown that animals and humans can inhibit the CR until just before the UCS presentation. For example, Kimmel (1965) gave human subjects 50 trials of red light (CS) and shock pairings (UCS). The red light was presented 7.5 seconds prior to shock, and both terminated simultaneously. Kimmel reported that the latency of the galvanic skin response (GSR) increased with increased training trials (see Figure 3-12).

Disinhibition   We have learned that the presentation of a novel stimulus during conditioning causes the CS to inhibit the elicitation of the CR. Presenting a

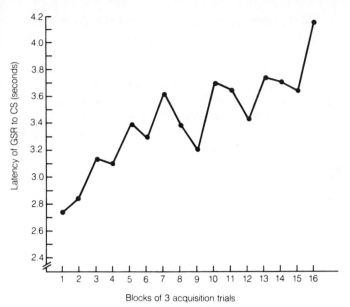

FIGURE 3-12 The average latency of GSR response to a conditioned stimulus, which preceded the unconditioned stimulus by 7.5 seconds, increases with greater pairings of the CS and the UCS. From Kimmel, H. D. (1965). Instrumental inhibitory factors in classical conditioning. In W. F. Prokasy (Ed.), *Classical conditioning: A symposium.* New York: Irvington.

novel stimulus during extinction also causes disruption; however, in this case the novel stimulus causes an increase in the strength of the conditioned response. The extinction process will proceed normally on the next trial if the novel stimulus is not presented. Pavlov labeled the process of increased strength of the CR *disinhibition.*

Kimmel's (1965) study shows the disinhibition phenomenon in an inhibition of delay paradigm. Kimmel observed that a novel tone presented with the CS disrupted the ability of the subjects to withhold the CR during the 7.5-second CS-UCS interval. Whereas the CR was exhibited approximately 4.0 seconds after the CS was presented following 50 acquisition trials, the CR latency dropped to 2.3 seconds when the novel stimulus was presented with the CS. These results indicate that a novel stimulus can disrupt the inhibition of a CR and also that inhibition is responsible for the suppression of the CR observed in the inhibition of delay phenomenon.

Section Review

Stimuli sometimes produce undesired conditioned emotional reactions. Extinction represents an effective method of eliminating the ability of the conditioned stimulus to elicit the conditioned response; the presentation of the CS without the UCS will cause a reduction in CR strength. With continued CS-alone presentations, eventually the conditioned stimulus will not elicit any response.

Extinction of a conditioned response is thought to reflect an inhibitory process as well as changes either in motivational state or in the stimulus context present during conditioning. Other inhibitory processes that suppress conditioned responses include conditioned inhibition, external inhibition, and inhibition of delay. Conditioned inhibition develops when the CS + is paired with the UCS and the CS − with the absence of the UCS; external inhibition occurs when a novel stimulus is experienced prior to the CS during extinction; and inhibition of delay reflects the suppression of the CR until the UCS is presented in a trace conditioning procedure. These inhibitory processes can be disrupted by presentation of a novel stimulus, causing a disinhibition effect and resulting in an increased CR strength.

A CR WITHOUT A CS-UCS PAIRING?

Although many conditioned responses are acquired through direct experiences, many stimuli develop the ability to elicit a conditioned response indirectly; that is, a stimulus that is never directly paired with the UCS nevertheless elicits a CR. For example, although many people with test anxiety have developed their fear because of the direct pairing of a test and failure, many others fear tests, even though they have never failed an examination.

There are four ways in which a stimulus can indirectly acquire the ability to elicit a CR. First, *a stimulus never paired with the UCS can elicit the CR through the stimulus generalization process.* Generalization causes stimuli similar to the CS to elicit the CR. In terms of our example, a person with test anxiety may have failed similar events (for example, homework assignments). Second, *a stimulus never directly paired with the UCS can produce the CR through the higher-order conditioning process.* In higher-order conditioning, following the direct pairing of a conditioning stimulus (CS; for example, a tone) with the UCS (for example, food), the conditioned stimulus is then paired with another stimulus (for example, a light). After several tone-light pairings, an animal or a person will exhibit the CR when presented with the light, even though the light was never paired directly with the food. Let's see how test anxiety could be acquired through higher-order conditioning. Leaving home to go to school is very distressing to some children. The association of this distress with school could cause the children to fear the school itself. Since schools give examinations, tests (CS_2) become associated with school (CS_1); thus, as the result of higher-order conditioning, examinations elicit fear.

Third, *sensory preconditioning can cause the development of a CR to a stimulus never paired directly with the UCS.* Sensory preconditioning is similar to higher-order conditioning except that during sensory preconditioning, the CS_1 and CS_2 are paired prior to conditioning instead of presented after CS-UCS pairing. Let's use the test anxiety example to illustrate the sensory preconditioning process. Examinations are a typical school activity, and as the result of attending school, students will associate school (CS_1) with examinations (CS_2). Aversive experiences sometimes occur at school; for example, a child may be teased by other children during recess. This abuse causes the child to dislike school. Because the child associates school with tests, this child now fears tests even though examinations have never been directly paired with adversity. Fourth, *the ability of a stimulus to elicit a CR can be acquired vicariously.* Observing the pairing of a CS with a UCS in other people can cause us to respond to the CS as if we had experienced the CS-UCS presentation. Suppose a child observed another child fail an examination. As the result of this experience, the observer associates an examination with failure and is now afraid of tests. Thus, a stimulus can develop the ability to elicit a CR indirectly, through generalization, higher-order conditioning, sensory preconditioning, and/or vicarious conditioning.

Several sources may contribute to the intensity of the conditioned response. For example, the combined influence of vicarious conditioning and sensory preconditioning may cause an intense conditioned reaction to the CS. Chapter 7 examines generalization process; we will discuss it in that chapter. This section will examine the higher-order conditioning, sensory preconditioning, and the vicarious conditioning processes.

Higher-Order Conditioning

The Higher-Order Conditioning Paradigm   Pavlov (1927) observed that following CS-UCS pairings, presenting the CS with another neutral stimulus (CS_2) enabled the CS_2 to elicit the CR. In one of Pavlov's studies using dogs, a tone (the beat of a metronome) was paired with meat powder. After this first-order conditioning, the tone was presented with a black square, but the meat powder was omitted. Following the tone–black square pairings, the black square (CS_2) alone was able to elicit salivation. Pavlov called this conditioning process *higher-order conditioning.* (In this particular study, the conditioning was of the second order.) Figure 3-13 presents a diagram of the higher-order conditioning process.

The strength of a CR acquired through higher-order conditioning is weaker than that developed through first-order conditioning. Pavlov discovered a second-order CR to be approximately 50 percent as strong as a first-order CR, and a third-order CR to be very weak. He found it impossible to develop a fourth-order CR.

Psychologists since the time of Pavlov's original studies have not always been successful in producing a CR through higher-order conditioning. Rescorla's (see Holland & Rescorla, 1975; Rescorla, 1973, 1978; Rizley & Rescorla, 1972) elegant analysis of the higher-order conditioning process demonstrated the reason for these failures. According to Rescorla, the problem with higher-order conditioning is that the pairing of CS_2-CS_1 without the UCS during the second phase of conditioning also represents a conditioned inhibition paradigm. Thus, not only is the excitation of the CR being conditioned to the CS_2 during CS_2-CS_1 pairings,

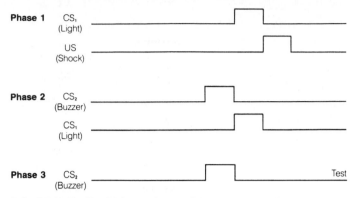

FIGURE 3-13 The higher-order conditioning process. In phase 1, the CS₁ (light) is paired with the UCS; in phase 2, the CS₁ (light) and the CS₂ (buzzer) are presented together. The ability of the CS₂ to elicit the CR is evaluated in phase 3.

but the inhibition of the CR is also being conditioned as the result of the pairing of the compound stimulus (CS₂ and CS₁) in the absence of the UCS.

When will higher-order conditioning occur? Rescorla and his associates have discovered that conditioned excitation develops more rapidly than the acquisition of conditioned inhibition. Thus, with only a few pairings, CS₂ will elicit the CR. However, as conditioned inhibition develops, CR strength in response to the CS₂ declines until the CS₂ can no longer elicit the CR. At this time, the conditioned inhibition equals the conditioned excitation produced by the CS₂ and the presentation of CS₂ will not elicit the CR.

Rizley and Rescorla's (1972) study illustrates the influence of the number of CS₂-CS₁ pairings on the strength of a higher-order conditioned fear. Rizley and Rescorla gave rats eight pairings of a 10-second flashing light (CS₁) paired with a 1-ma 0.5-second electric shock (USC). Following first-order conditioning, the light (CS₁) was paired with an 1800-Hz tone (CS₂). Rizley and Rescorla discovered that the strength of fear to the CS₂ increased with initial CS₂-CS₁ pairings, reaching a maximum strength after four pairings (see Figure 3-14). However, the intensity of fear elicited by the CS₂ declined with each additional pairing until the CS₂ produced no fear after 15 CS₂-CS₁ presentations. Holland and Rescorla (1975) observed a similar influence of the amount of higher-order conditioning on the development of a conditioned appetitive response. In summary, the work of Rescorla and his colleagues demonstrates that higher-order conditioning will occur after a few but not after many CS₂-CS₁ presentations.

The observation that the strength of a second-order CR diminishes after the presentation of more than a few CS₂-CS₁ pairings does not indicate that higher-order conditioning has no role in real-world settings. For example, once a CR, such as fear, is conditioned to the CS₂, such as high places, the fear produced by the CS₂ will motivate avoidance behavior, resulting in only a brief exposure to the CS₂. A rapid avoidance response will produce a short exposure to the CS₂

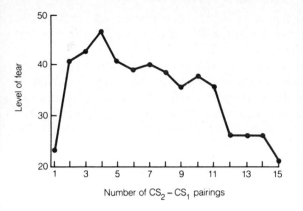

FIGURE 3-14
The fear response to CS_2 increases with a few CS_1 and CS_2 pairings but decreases with greater pairings of CS_1 and CS_2. Adapted from Rizley, R. C., & Rescorla, R. A. (1972). Associations in second-order conditioning and sensory preconditioning. *Journal of Comparative and Physiological Psychology, 81,* 1–11. Copyright 1972 by the American Psychological Association. Reprinted by permission.

and result in slow development of conditioned inhibition. The slow acquisition of conditioned inhibition to the CS_2 permits CS_2 to elicit fear for a very long, possibly indefinite, period of time.

The Nature of Higher-Order Conditioning   What mechanism is responsible for the CS_2 elicitation of the CR? Rescorla (1973, 1978) suggested three possibilities: (1) the CS_2 causes recall of the CS_1, which, in turn, elicits the CR; (2) during CS_2 and CS_1 pairings, the presence of CS_1 elicits the memory of the UCS, which then elicits the CR. The CS_2 is then associated with the memory of the UCS; or (3) the CS_2 directly elicits the CR. Rescorla and his associates' research (Holland & Rescorla, 1975; Rizley & Rescorla, 1972) indicates that the CS_2 directly elicits the CR. Let's see how they arrived at this conclusion.

To test the first alternative, Rizley and Rescorla (1972) presented the CS_1 alone after second-order conditioning of fear to the CS_2. If the ability of the CS_2 to elicit fear reflects the aversiveness of the CS_1, then extinguishing the CR to the CS_1 should also eliminate the fear-eliciting ability of the CS_2. Rizley and Rescorla discovered that the CS_2 continued to produce fear, even after the CS_1 no longer did. Apparently, the ability of CS_2 to elicit fear does not depend upon the aversiveness of the CS_1. Holland and Rescorla (1975) observed similar results with an appetitive conditioned response.

Rizley and Rescorla (1972) evaluated the second alternative by eliminating the adversiveness of the UCS after higher-order conditioning. To do this, they used a 2-second 112-dB noise as the UCS. (Unlike a shock UCS, continued presentation of a loud noise results in its reduced adversiveness until it is no longer considered to be adversive.) In the first phase of the study, a light (CS_1) was paired with the loud noise, followed by tone-light (CS_2-CS_1) pairings in the second phase. Following higher-order conditioning, the animals received 36 UCS exposures; this procedure eliminated the adversiveness of the loud noise. Rizley and Rescorla reported that the CS_2 continued to elicit fear even though the UCS was no longer an adversive event. Thus, it appears that the ability of the CS_2 to elicit fear does not depend upon the adversiveness of either the CS_1 or the UCS. However, Rizley and Rescorla found that the CS_1 was no longer able to elicit the CR when the UCS was no longer adversive.

Rizley and Rescorla's observations may enhance our understanding of the etiology of people's phobias, the origins of which are often quite difficult to uncover. It is possible that phobias develop through higher-order conditioning; if so, the original source of the phobia may no longer be aversive, but the phobic object still elicits fear due to its independence from the CS_1 and the UCS. Recall our example of test anxiety used to explain higher-order conditioning. The adversiveness of leaving home to attend school typically declines with repeated experiences. While the loss of the UCS adversiveness causes the child to no longer fear school (CS_1), tests (CS_2) continue to elicit fear. Rizley and Rescorla's findings also suggest that there is no need to search for the origins of a phobia; the only method of eliminating a higher-order CR is to present the CS_2 alone. The applicability of the animal research conducted by Rescorla and his associates to the higher-order conditioned responses of humans awaits future investigation.

Sensory Preconditioning

Consider the following example to illustrate the sensory preconditioning process. Your neighbor owns a large German shepherd; you associate the neighbor with his dog. As you are walking down the street, the dog bites you, causing you to become afraid of the dog. You will also develop a disliking for your neighbor as the result of your previous association of the neighbor with the dog.

The Sensory Preconditioning Paradigm   In sensory preconditioning, two neutral stimuli, CS_1 and CS_2, are paired (see Figure 3-15). Following the association of CS_1 and CS_2 (neighbor and dog), CS_1 is presented with an unconditioned stimulus (bite). The CS_1-UCS pairings result in the ability of the CS_2, as well as the CS_1, to elicit the CR (fear). Thus, as a result of the initial CS_2-CS_1 association, the CS_2 is able to produce the CR even though it is not directly paired with the UCS.

Research on Sensory Preconditioning   Brogden's (1939) classic research represents an early successful sensory preconditioning study. In the first phase of Brogden's experiment, dogs in the experimental condition received 200 simultaneous pairings of a light and buzzer. Control animals did not receive light-buzzer pairings. Following this initial conditioning, one of the cues (either the light or the buzzer) was presented with an electric shock to the dog's foot. Brogden reported that presentation of the cue not paired with shock elicited the CR (leg flexion) in experimental but not in control condition animals. Although Brogden's results showed that a cue can develop the ability to elicit a CR through the sensory preconditioning process, the leg flexion CR to the CS_2 was weaker than the CR to the CS_1. Other researchers (see Kimble, 1961) during the 1940s and

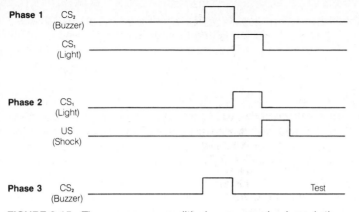

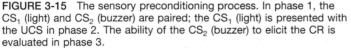

FIGURE 3-15 The sensory preconditioning process. In phase 1, the CS_1 (light) and CS_2 (buzzer) are paired; the CS_1 (light) is presented with the UCS in phase 2. The ability of the CS_2 (buzzer) to elicit the CR is evaluated in phase 3.

1950s also observed that the magnitude of the sensory preconditioning effect was small.

Recent studies (Prewitt, 1967; Rizley & Rescorla, 1972; Tait, Marquis, Williams, Weinstein, & Suboski, 1969) indicate that the early studies did not employ the best procedures to produce a strong, reliable sensory preconditioning effect. These studies found that the CS_2 will elicit a strong CR if, during the initial conditioning, (1) the CS_2 precedes the CS_1 by several seconds and (2) only a few CS_2-CS_1 pairings are used in order to prevent the development of learned irrelevance. Recall that when the CS is presented without the UCS prior to conditioning, there is a diminished conditioning of a CR when the CS and UCS are paired during training.

The Nature of Sensory Preconditioning   Mediation appears to be responsible for the sensory preconditioning effect. According to this view, the presentation of the CS_2 causes recall of the CS_1, which results in the elicitation of the CR. Thus, the memory of the CS_1 mediates the ability of the CS_2 to elicit the CR. Rizley and Rescorla's (1972) study provides support for a mediation view.

Rizley and Rescorla (1972) presented their standard sensory preconditioning treatment to two groups of rats. After CS_2-CS_1 pairings and CS_1-UCS (shock) pairings, one group of rats was given repeated CS_1-alone presentations until the CS_1 no longer elicited the CR. The other group of animals did not receive CS_1-CR extinction trials. Both groups of rats were then exposed to the CS_2. Rizley and Rescorla found that animals given CS_1-alone experience (extinction) did not respond to the CS_2, while the CS_2 did suppress behavior in animals that had not received CS_1-alone presentations. These observations indicate that the ability of the CS_2 to elicit the CR depends upon the continued ability of the CS_1

to elicit the CR. Therefore, unlike higher-order conditioning, an animal's response to CS_2 acquired through sensory preconditioning is not independent of its reaction to CS_1.

Vicarious Conditioning

A person can develop an emotional response to a specific stimulus through direct experience; a person can also learn to respond to a particular stimulus as a result of observing the experiences of others. For example, a person can become afraid of dogs after being bitten or can learn to fear dogs after seeing another person being bitten. The development of a CS's ability to elicit a CR following such an observation is called *vicarious conditioning*. Although it is clear that many emotional responses are developed through direct conditioning experience, the research (see Bandura, 1977) also demonstrates that CS-CR associations can be acquired through vicarious conditioning experiences; let's now examine several studies that show the vicarious conditioning of a CR.

Research on Vicarious Conditioning Berger's study (1962) demonstrates the vicarious conditioning of a conditioned fear reaction to a neutral stimulus. Berger's subjects listened to a neutral tone, then saw another person receiving an electric shock and exhibiting pain reactions (this other person, a confederate, pretended to be shocked and hurt). Berger found that subjects who repeatedly witnessed the scene, which was preceded by the tone, developed an emotional response to the tone. Bandura and Rosenthal (1966) also observed that vicarious conditioning of fear occurred when a subject observed another person being shocked.

An emotional reaction can develop by observing people fail a task as well as by watching individuals receiving electric shock (see Bandura, Blanchard, & Ritter, 1969; Craig & Weinstein, 1965). In the Craig and Weinstein study, subjects watched another person either succeed or fail a motor task. The subjects who witnessed the other person fail showed a stronger conditioned stress reaction to the task than those subjects who saw the other person succeed at the task. Furthermore, subjects who were told that shock was contingent upon the person's failure did not show a stronger conditioned affective reaction than subjects who only witnessed failure. Apparently, we can learn to fear a task merely by watching others fail it.

Vicarious conditioning is not unique to humans. Crooks (1967) reported that monkeys can develop a fear of certain objects after viewing the experience of another monkey with these objects. In Crooks's study, the subjects heard a tape-recorded distress when a model monkey touched some particular objects; they did not hear the emotional reaction when the model touched other objects. Crooks discovered that subjects subsequently played with those objects not associated with distress but would not touch the objects which appeared to have hurt the other monkey. In a more recent, study, Mineka and associates (1984) found that monkeys learned to fear snakes after exposure to another monkey reacting fearfully to a snake. In the absence of this experience, the monkeys showed no evidence of a fear of snakes.

The Importance of Arousal   We do not always develop a CR after watching the experiences of others. In order for vicarious conditioning to occur, we must respond emotionally to the scene we witness. Bandura and Rosenthal (1966) evaluated the level of vicarious CR conditioning as a function of the subjects' arousal level during conditioning. They found that observers moderately aroused by seeing a confederate being shocked subsequently showed strong autonomic reaction to the tone that had been paired with the scene; subjects either minimally distressed or intensely upset by viewing the confederate being shocked displayed only weak vicarious conditioning. The highly aroused subjects stopped attending to the person receiving the shock; Bandura and Rosenthal suggested that the altered attention of these subjects reduced the association of the tone with shock. Apparently, we must be aroused—but not too aroused—if we are to develop conditioned responses from observing the experiences of others.

SUMMARY

1 The ability of environmental events to produce internal emotional reactions, which, in turn, motivate instrumental behavior, develops through the classical conditioning process. Conditioning involves the pairing of a neutral environmental cue with a biologically important event. Prior to conditioning, only the biologically important stimulus, called an unconditioned stimulus, can elicit a response. This response, called the unconditioned response, consists of both an overt skeletal reaction and an internal emotional response. As the result of conditioning, the neutral environmental stimulus, now a conditioned stimulus, can also elicit a response, called the conditioned response.

2 There are five conditioning paradigms. With delayed conditioning, the CS remains on until the UCS begins. The CS ends prior to the onset of the UCS with trace conditioning. The CS and the UCS occur at the same time with simultaneous conditioning, while backward conditioning involves the CS following the presentation of the UCS. Temporal conditioning takes place when the UCS is presented at regular intervals of time. The most efficient conditioning usually occurs with delayed conditioning and the least with backward conditioning.

3 There are five factors that determine whether or not a stimulus develops the ability to elicit a conditioned response—in addition to its presentation with the unconditioned stimulus. One factor affecting the strength of conditioning is temporal contiguity. Under most conditions, temporal contiguity must exist between the CS and the UCS for conditioning to occur. An intermediate stimulus between the CS and the UCS can facilitate the development of a conditioned response. One exception involves flavor-aversion conditioning; an aversion to a flavor cue paired with illness can develop despite a lack of contiguity.

4 The intensity of the CS and the UCS is a second factor affecting the intensity of the CR. An intense CS and/or UCS typically leads to a stronger CR than a weak CS and/or UCS. A third variable influencing conditioning is salience. Some stimuli are more salient than others and therefore are more likely to develop a CR when paired with a specific UCS. The stimulus must also be a reliable predictor of the UCS. The more

often the CS occurs without the UCS or the UCS is presented without the CS, the weaker will be the CR. Redundancy is the final factor affecting the strength of conditioning. The presence of a conditioned stimulus can prevent or block the development of a conditioned response to a new stimulus when both stimuli are paired with the UCS. Blocking occurs due to a lack of surprise when the UCS follows the new stimulus in the presence of the original conditioned stimulus.

5 Sometimes stimuli produce undesired conditioned emotional reactions. Extinction represents an effective method of eliminating the ability of the conditioned stimulus to elicit the conditioned response; the presentation of the CS without the UCS will cause a reduction in CR strength. With continued CS-alone presentations, eventually the conditioned stimulus will not elicit any response.

6 Extinction of a conditioned response is thought to reflect an inhibitory process as well as changes either in the motivational state or in the stimulus context present during conditioning. Other inhibitory processes that suppress conditioned responses include conditioned inhibition, external inhibition, and inhibition of delay. Conditioned inhibition develops when CS+ is paired with the UCS and CS− with the absence of the UCS; external inhibition occurs when a novel stimulus is experienced prior to the CS during extinction; and inhibition of delay is the supression of the CR until the UCS is presented in a delayed conditioning procedure. These inhibitory processes can be disrupted by presentation of a novel stimulus, causing a disinhibition effect and resulting in an increased CR strength.

7 A conditioned stimulus can develop the ability to elicit the conditioned response indirectly, that is, without being directly associated with the UCS. Generalization represents one way that a CR can be acquired indirectly; stimuli that are similar to the CS also are able to elicit the CR. Other methods include higher-order conditioning, sensory preconditioning, and vicarious conditioning.

8 Higher-order conditioning occurs when, after CS_1 and UCS pairings, a new stimulus (CS_2) is presented with CS_1. In contrast, CS_1 and CS_2 occur together prior to CS_1 and UCS pairings with sensory preconditioning. In both higher-order conditioning and sensory preconditioning, the CS_2 elicits the CR despite never having been directly paired with the UCS. Higher-order conditioning involves the establishment of an autonomous CS_2-CR association, whereas a CS_2-CS_1 association mediates sensory preconditioning. A CR can be established through vicarious conditioning when a person observes the pairing of CS and UCS in another individual. In order for vicarious conditioning to occur, the observer must be sufficiently aroused while witnessing the other person's conditioning experience.

4

THEORIES AND APPLICATIONS OF PAVLOVIAN CONDITIONING

HE NEVER SAW IT COMING

Kevin started dating Tricia several weeks ago. Their different personalities—
Kevin was quiet and shy and Tricia was outgoing and very social— did not
keep them from becoming very close. Tricia introduced Kevin to a social life
that he had never experienced. There were romantic dinners and exciting parties.
Tricia was an excellent dancer, which made dancing fun. Kevin was not used
to partying until very late. He had to get up early for work and felt drained the
entire day. Yet, the late nights did not seem to bother Tricia, and she was
wide awake the next day even with only a few hours' sleep.

   Last week, Tricia started to drink a lot of alcohol. Kevin rarely drank more
than a beer or two, and he was quite concerned about Tricia's drinking. She
called him a lightweight for having only one or two drinks. Kevin did not
mind the teasing but really did not like to drink very much. He thought that he
was in love with Tricia; however, he was troubled by some of her actions
toward him. The last several times that they were out, Tricia had become very
angry and verbally abusive toward him for no apparent reason. The verbal
comments were harsh and Kevin was very hurt by them. The next day, Tricia
would apologize for her behavior and promise not to be nasty again. Yet, the
next time that they went out, Tricia again became angry and abusive toward him.

   Kevin could not figure out why Tricia became hostile, and he considered
breaking off their relationship. He mentioned his concerns to his friend John.
To Kevin's surprise, John said he knew why Tricia became hostile. He felt that
the alcohol made her nasty. Kevin was not sure that John was right but decided
that he would pay close attention to the amount she drank and whether or
not she became hostile. He was hopeful that this was the reason for her hostility,
but he was not sure what he would do if it was.

Why did Kevin fail to see the relationship between Tricia's drinking and her hostility? The answer to this question may lie in a phenomenon called the CS preexposure effect. When a stimulus is first presented without a UCS, subsequent conditioning is impaired when that stimulus is presented with the UCS. Kevin had seen people drinking without becoming aggressive, and this experience may have caused him to fail to recognize the relationship between Tricia's drinking and her hostility. We examine the CS preexposure effect later in the chapter; our discussion may tell us what caused Kevin to fail to associate the sight of Tricia's drinking (CS) and her hostility toward him (UCS).

THE NATURE OF PAVLOVIAN CONDITIONING

Pavlov (1927) conducted an extensive investigation of the principles governing the acquisition and extinction of a conditioned response. During the past 20 years, there have been many studies examining both how conditioned responses are acquired and whether or not the CR is similar to or different from the UCR. This research has challenged Pavlov's assumptions regarding both the nature of conditioning and the conditioned response. New theories have emerged to explain these recent research findings.

The Character of the Conditioned Response

One important question in Pavlovian conditioning concerns the nature of the conditioned response. Is the CR just the UCR elicited by the CS? Or is the CR a behavior distinctively different from the UCR?

The Stimulus Substitution Model   Pavlov (1927) suggested that as a result of conditioning, the conditioned stimulus becomes able to elicit the same response as the unconditioned stimulus. Why would Pavlov assume that the CR and the UCR were the same response? Pavlov was observing the same digestive responses (for example, saliva, gastric juices, insulin) as both the CR and the UCR. The fact that both the CS and the UCS elicit similar responses logically leads to the conclusion that the CR and the UCR are the same.

How does the CS become able to elicit the same response as the UCS? According to Pavlov, the presentation of the UCS activates one area of the brain. Stimulation of the neural area responsible for processing the UCS leads to the activation of a brain center responsible for generating the UCR. In Pavlov's view, there is an innate, direct connection between the UCS brain center and the brain center controlling the UCR; this neural connection allows the UCS to elicit the UCR.

When the conditioned stimulus is presented, it excites a distinct brain area. When the UCS follows the CS, the brain centers responsible for processing the CS and the UCS are active at the same time. According to Pavlov, the simultaneous activity in two neural centers leads to a new functional neural pathway between the active neural centers. The establishment of this neural connection

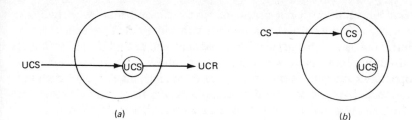

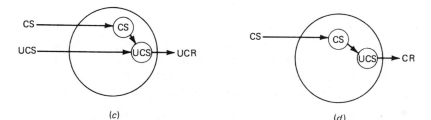

FIGURE 4-1 Pavlov's stimulus-substitution view of classical conditioning. (a) The UCS activates the UCS brain center, which elicits the UCR; (b) the CS arouses the area of the brain responsible for processing it; (c) a connection between CS and UCS brain centers develops with contiguous presentation of CS and UCS; and (d) the CS elicits the CR as a result of its ability to activate the UCS brain center.

causes the CS to activate the neural center processing the CS, which then arouses the UCS neural center. Activity in the UCS center leads to activation in the response center for the UCR, which then allows the CS to elicit the CR. In other words, Pavlov is suggesting that the CS becomes a substitute for the UCS and elicits the same response as the UCS; that is, the CR is the UCR elicited by the CS instead of the UCS. Figure 4-1 provides an illustration of Pavlov's stimulus-substitution view of conditioning.

The Conditioning of an Opponent Response While the conditioned and unconditioned responses are often similar, there are many cases where the CR and the UCR seem dissimilar. These dissimilarities have been noted for many years. For example, the conditioned response of fear differs in many ways from the unconditioned response of pain. While both involve internal arousal, the sensory aspects of the two responses are not the same. Warner's 1932 statement that "whatever response is grafted onto the CS, it is not snipped from the UCS" indicates a recognition of CR and UCR differences. The research of Shepard Siegel and his colleagues (Siegel, 1975, 1976, 1979, 1981; Siegel, Hinson, & Krank, 1978; Siegel, Hinson, Krank, & McCully, 1982; Siegel, Sherman, & Mitchell, 1980) represents the most impressive accumulation of evidence that the conditioned and unconditioned responses may be different; their work will be briefly described to illustrate the observation of CR and UCR differences.

In several of their studies, Siegel and his associates (Siegel, 1976, 1978; Siegel et al., 1978) used morphine as the unconditioned stimulus. *Analgesia,* or reduced sensitivity to pain, is one unconditioned response to morphine. Siegel reported that the conditioned response to stimuli that have been paired with morphine is *hypoalgesia,* or increased sensitivity to a painful event.

How did Siegel know that a conditioned stimulus associated with morphine makes an event more unpleasant? To illustrate both the analgesic effect of morphine and the hypoalgesic effect of a stimulus paired with morphine, Siegel placed a rat's paw on a hot plate and measured how long it took the rat to remove its paw. He observed that rats injected with morphine (UCS) took longer to remove the paw from the heated plate than did animals not receiving the morphine injection. In contrast to the analgesia produced by the morphine, presentation of the CS (light or tone) resulted in the rat removing its paw more quickly than animals that had been presented a stimulus not paired with the UCS. Similar results have been observed by others; see Tiffany and Baker (1981) for another example.

Siegel (1975) also found that while the UCR to insulin is hypoglycemia, the CR to a stimulus paired with insulin is hyperglycemia. Additional studies (refer to Crowell, Hinson, & Siegel, 1981; Le, Poulos, & Cappell, 1979) reported that the UCR to alcohol is hypothermia, while the CR to a stimulus associated with alcohol is hyperthermia.

Siegel's research suggests not only that the CR can be opposite of the UCR, but also that conditioning is responsible at least in part for the phenomenon of drug tolerance. Tolerance to a drug develops when, with repeated use, the effectiveness of the drug declines and thus larger doses are necessary to achieve the same pharmacological effect (see Chapter 1). According to Siegel, tolerance represents the conditioning of a response, which is opposite the unconditioned drug effects. Thus, the environmental cues present during drug administration antagonize the drug's action and result in a lower pharmacological reaction to the drug.

Two lines of evidence support a role of conditioning in drug tolerance. First, Siegel (1977) found that exposure to the CS (environment) without the UCS (drug), once the association has been conditioned, results in the extinction of the opponent CR; the elimination of the response to the CS produces a stronger reaction to the drug itself (see Figure 4-2). Second, Siegel et al. (1978) reported that an increased response to the drug can also be induced by changing the stimulus context in which the drug is administered. The novel environment does not elicit a CR opposite to the drug's unconditioned effect; the absence of the opposing CR results in a stronger unconditioned drug effect. Other researchers (see Tiffany & Baker, 1981) have also discovered that a change in context leads to reduced drug tolerance. A heightened drug reponse in a new environment is not limited to animals. Siegel et al. (1982) observed that a drug overdose typically occurs when an addict takes his or her usual drug dose, but in an unfamiliar

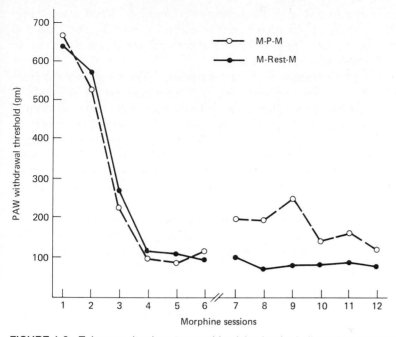

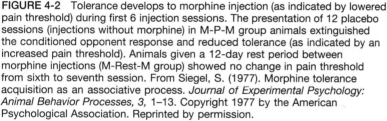

FIGURE 4-2 Tolerance develops to morphine injection (as indicated by lowered pain threshold) during first 6 injection sessions. The presentation of 12 placebo sessions (injections without morphine) in M-P-M group animals extinguished the conditioned opponent response and reduced tolerance (as indicated by an increased pain threshold). Animals given a 12-day rest period between morphine injections (M-Rest-M group) showed no change in pain threshold from sixth to seventh session. From Siegel, S. (1977). Morphine tolerance acquisition as an associative process. *Journal of Experimental Psychology: Animal Behavior Processes, 3,* 1–13. Copyright 1977 by the American Psychological Association. Reprinted by permission.

environment. Without the protective opposing response, the effect of the drug is increased, resulting in the overdose.

Why is the CR sometimes similar to the UCR and sometimes dissimilar to the UCR? Allan Wagner's *Sometimes Opponent Process (SOP) theory* provides one answer to this question; we will look at his view next.

Sometimes Opponent Process (SOP) Theory   Recall our discussion of Solomon and Corbit's opponent process theory in Chapter 1. We learned that an event not only elicits a primary affective response but also a secondary opponent affective reaction. Wagner's SOP theory (see Donegan & Wagner, 1987; Mazur & Wagner, 1982; Wagner, 1981; Wagner & Brandon, 1989) is an extension of opponent process theory and can explain why the CR sometimes appears the same as and sometimes different from the UCR. According to Wagner, the UCS elicits two unconditioned responses—a primary A1 component and a secondary A2 component. The primary A1 component is elicited rapidly by the UCS and decays quickly after the UCS ends. In contrast, both the onset and the decay of the secondary A2 component is very gradual.

The Importance of the Nature of the A2 Response The secondary A2 component of the UCR can be the same as the A1 component, or the A1 and A2 components can be different. Whether or not A1 and A2 are the same or different is important. A key aspect of Wagner's view is that conditioning occurs only to the secondary A2 component; that is, the CR is always the secondary A2 reaction (see Figure 4-3). The CR and the UCR will appear to be the same when the A1 and A2 components are the same. Different A1 and A2 components will yield a CR and UCR that look different; however, the CR and the UCS are really the same in this case. This is true because the A1 component is the response we associate with the UCR. When the A2 reaction is opponent to the A1, it looks as if the CR (A2) and the UCR (A1 and A2) are different. Yet, the CR is merely the secondary A2 component of the UCR. Perhaps several examples would clarify this aspect of the SOP theory.

Suppose an animal is exposed to a brief electric shock. The initial reaction to shock is agitated hyperactivity. This increased reactivity is followed by a long-lasting hypoactivity or "freezing" response (see Blanchard & Blanchard, 1969;

FIGURE 4-3 Wagner's SOP theory. (a) The continuous pairing of CS and UCS leads to establishment of a connecting path between CS and UCS. (b) The path connection leads to the association of the CS and the A2 component of the UCR. From Wagner, A. R., & Brandon, S. E. (1989). Evolution of a structured connectionist model of Pavlovian conditioning (AESOP). In S. B. Klein & R. R. Mowrer (Eds.), *Contemporary learning theory: Pavlovian conditioning and the status of traditional learning theory.* Hillsdale, N. J.: Erlbaum.

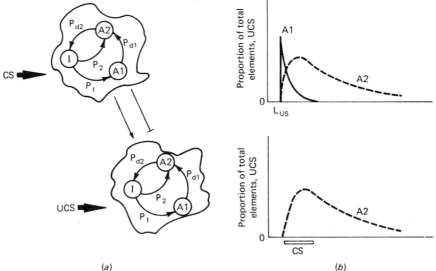

(a)   (b)

Bolles & Riley, 1973). The freezing response or *conditioned emotional reaction* is recognized as the response conditioned to a stimulus paired with electric shock.

Paletta and Wagner (1986) demonstrated the two-phase reaction of an animal to a morphine injection. The initial A1 reaction to morphine is sedation or hypoactivity. Figure 4-4 shows that the activity level is lower initially in rats given morphine rather than saline. However, 2 hours after the injection, the morphine rats are significantly more active than the control saline animals.

What is the conditioned reaction to an environmental stimulus paired with morphine? As seen in Figure 4-4, the morphine animals were hyperactive when tested in the environment where they received morphine. Testing the morphine animals in their home cages produced a level of activity comparable to that of control animals not receiving morphine injections. These observations indicate that the conditioned reaction produced by morphine is hyperactivity, or the A2 secondary component of the UCR.

We have looked at two examples in which A1 and A2 components were opposite. There are other cases in which A1 and A2 are the same. Grau (1987) observed that the unconditioned response to radiant heat consisted of an initial short-duration hypoalgesia followed by a more persistent hypoalgesia. How do we know that both A1 and A2 reactions to a painful stimulus such as radiant heat are hypoalgesia? The use of the opiate antagonist naloxone can demonstrate

FIGURE 4-4   Illustration of the activity following injections of morphine or saline. Activity first decreases, then increases above normal after morphine injections. Animals given morphine in a distinctive environment show increased activity or conditioned A2 response when placed in that environment without morphine (shown in bar graph). From Paletta, M. S., & Wagner, A. R. (1986). Development of context-specific tolerance to morphine: Support for a dual-process interpretation. *Behavioral Neuroscience, 100*, 611–623. Copyright 1986 by the American Psychological Association. Reprinted by permission.

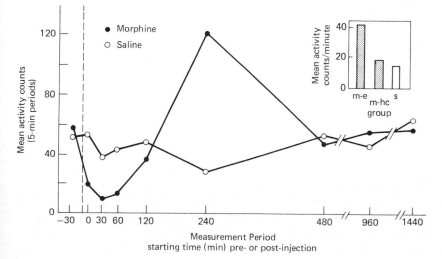

this similarity of A1 and A2 response. Naloxone blocks the long-term persistant hypoalgesia (A2) but has no effect on the short-term immediate hypoalgesia (A1). This effect of naloxone means that the A1 hypoalgesic response is nonopoid while the A2 hypoalgesia involves the opoid system. Furthermore, Fanselow and his colleagues (see Fanselow & Baackes, 1982; Fanselow & Bolles, 1979) showed that it is the A2 opoid hypoalgesia reaction that is conditioned to environmental stimuli paired with a painful unconditioned stimulus. These researchers observed that showed that naloxone prevented the conditioning of the hypoalgesic response to environmental cues paired with painful events.

A study by Thompson and colleagues (1984) provides perhaps the most impressive support for SOP theory. These researchers investigated the conditioning of an eye-blink response to a tone paired with a corneal air puff to a rabbit's eye. They found that two neural circuits mediate a rabbit's unconditioned eye-blink response. A fast-acting A1 response is controlled by a relatively direct path from the area of UCS application on the 5th sensory nucleus to the 6th and 7th motor nuclei controlling the eye-blink response. Stimulation of this neural circuit produces a fast-acting and rapidly decaying eye-blink response. A secondary A2 circuit begins at the 5th nucleus and goes through the inferior olive, cerebellar structures, red nucleus before reaching the motor nuclei. Activation of this A2 circuit produces a slow-acting eye-blink response. Thompson et al. also found that destruction of the indirect pathway eliminated a previously conditioned eye-blink response but did not affect the short-latency unconditioned eye-blink response. Also, with the indirect A2 pathways no longer intact, any reconditioning of the eye-blink response was not possible.

Backward Conditioning of an Excitatory CR   We learned in the last chapter that a forward conditioning paradigm produces a more reliable acquisition of the CR than does a backward conditioning paradigm. While this statement is generally correct, Wagner's SOP theory indicates that backward conditioning can yield an excitatory CR if the CS is presented just prior to the peak of the A2 unconditioned response.

Larew (1986) provided strong support for this aspect of Wagner's SOP theory. In this study, rats received a 2-second foot shock UCS followed by a 30-second tone. The tone occurred either 1 second, 31 seconds, or 60 seconds after the UCS. Control rats received no UCS-CS pairings. Larew observed an excitatory conditioned response with the 31-second UCS-CS backward conditioning procedure but no excitatory conditioning with either a 1-second UCS-CS interval or a 60-second UCS-CS interval. These results show excitatory conditioning occurs with a backward procedure when the CS just precedes A2 reaction.

Problems with SOP Theory   Wagner and Brandon (1989) commented that despite the strong support for SOP theory, some research seems to be inconsistent with this view. One significant problem concerns divergent results obtained from different measures of conditioning. SOP theory assumes that all response measures should yield a comparable indication of conditioning and that variations in the conditions of training should have a similar effect on all response measures. Suppose that heart rate and eye-blink response are recorded during conditioning. Since both responses are assumed to be due to A2 neural activity, the optimal

CS-UCS interval should be equal for both response measures. Yet, Vandercar and Schneiderman (1967) found maximum heart rate conditioning with a 2.25-second CS-UCS interval, while the strongest eye-blink response occurred with a 7.5-second CS-UCS interval.

Recall our earlier discussion of the Thompson et al. (1984) study. We learned that destruction of the indirect inferior olive-cerebellar-red nucleus pathway eliminated the conditioned eye-blink response. However, the authors reported that this same surgical procedure had no effect on a conditioned heart rate response. To address these inconsistent findings, Wagner and Brandon (1989) recently introduced a modification of the SOP theory; we will look at this revision next.

Affective Extension of SOP (AESOP)   Wagner and Brandon (1989) suggested that there are two distinct unconditioned response sequences—a sensory sequence and an emotive one. The sensory and emotive attributes of an unconditioned stimulus activate separate sequences of A1 and A2 activity. Further, the latency of the sensory and emotive activity sequence (A1 and A2) can differ; that is, A2 may take longer to develop for one component than for the other. This difference leads to diverse optimal CS-UCS intervals for the emotive or sensory components. For example, a shorter latency A2 activity for the sensory rather than the emotive component of a UCS causes a shorter optimal CS-UCS interval for the sensory rather than the emotive CR. The difference in latency of sensory and emotive A2 responses can lead one CS to elicit an emotive CR and another CS to elicit a sensory CR (see Figure 4-5).

There are several additional aspects of Wagner's AESOP theory. A conditioned stimulus may activate a strong sensory conditioned response but only a weak emotive CR, or vice versa. This difference would lead to the lack of correspondence between response measures of conditioning. Further, while the sensory A2 neural activity elicits a discrete response, the emotive A2 neural activity produces a diffuse reaction. For example, the sensory CR might be an eye-blink response while the emotive CR could be an increase in general activity. Finally, two unconditioned stimuli might activate the same emotive A2 activity but different sensory A2 activities. This fact would lead to both similarities and differences in the responses conditioned by separate UCSs.

AESOP is a relatively new theory that has just begun to be evaluated. Tait and Saladin (1986) provide support for AESOP. These authors trained rabbits to respond to a 1000-millisecond tone CS by presenting the tone 5000 milliseconds after a 100-millisecond shock UCS to the rabbits' eyes. Two conditioned response measures were taken in this study: the tendency of the CS (1) to suppress ongoing drinking behavior (conditioned emotional response) and (2) to elicit the eye-blink response (sensory CR). Tait and Saladin found a strong emotive CR; that is, the CS suppressed drinking. In contrast, the CS did not elicit the eye-blink response. In fact, the CS was capable of inhibiting an eye-blink response to another CS, a result often seen with backward conditioning. These results show a divergence of the conditioning of the sensory and emotive components of an unconditioned stimulus. Why was an emotive CR but not a sensory CR acquired in the Tait and Saladin study? AESOP theory assumes that the CS occurred prior to the emotive A2 response but after the sensory A2 reaction.

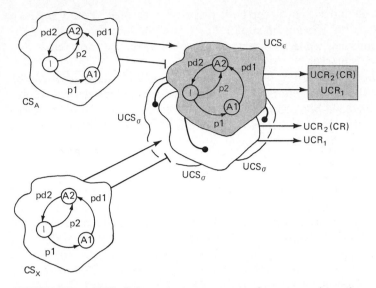

FIGURE 4-5   A UCS elicits separate sequences of sensory and emotive reactions. The differential optimal CS-UCS intervals for sensory and emotive A2 UCR can lead one stimulus (CS_A) to elicit an emotive CR and another stimulus (CS_X) to produce the sensory CR. From Wagner, A. R., & Brandon, S. E. (1989). Evolution of a structured connectionist model of Pavlovian conditioning (AESOP). In S. B. Klein & R. R. Mowrer (Eds.), *Contemporary learning and the status of traditional learning theory* (pp. 149–189). Hillsdale, N. J.: Erlbaum.

Section Review

Pavlov suggested that the presentation of the UCS activates the brain area responsible for processing the UCS, which leads to the stimulation of the neural area generating the UCR. The CS also excites a neural area and if the UCS follows the CS, the brain centers for processing the CS and UCS are active at the same time. This simultaneous activity results in a neural pathway developing between the CS and UCS brain centers. Following conditioning, the CS elicits the UCR as a result of its ability to arouse the UCS and UCR brain areas.

The CR and the UCR often are the same, but there are instances when these two responses appear to be different. The most vivid example of this difference is Siegel's work on the conditioning of an opponent drug response. Siegel noted that while the unconditioned reaction to morphine is analgesia, or reduced sensitivity to pain, the conditioned response is hypoalgesia, or an increased sensitivity to pain. Other examples of conditioned opposing responses include hypoglycemia with an insulin UCS and hypothermia with an alcohol UCS.

Wagner's Sometimes Opponent Process (SOP) theory assumes that the UCS elicits two unconditioned responses—a primary A1 component and a secondary A2 component. The primary A1 component is elicited rapidly by the UCS and

TABLE 4-1
EXPLANATION OF THREE CONDITIONING PHENOMENA BY FOUR MODELS
OF PAVLOVIAN CONDITIONING

	Overshadowing	Blocking	Predictiveness
Rescorla-Wagner Model	Salient stimulus acquires associative strength more readily than nonsalient stimulus	Associative strength to blocking stimulus prevents conditioning to blocked stimulus	Context associations prevent conditioning to conditioned stimulus
Comparator Theory	Conditioning to salient stimulus is stronger than nonsalient stimulus	Conditioning stronger for blocking stimulus than for blocked stimulus	Context associations stronger than conditioning to conditioned stimulus
Attentional Theory	Salient stimulus is more associable than nonsalient stimulus	Absence of surprise prevents conditioning to the blocked stimulus	Animals learn that conditioned stimulus does not reliably predict unconditioned stimulus
Retrospective Processing Theory	Animals recognize the salience of different stimuli	Animals recognize greater contingency between blocking and unconditioned stimuli	Animals recognize the lack of contingency between conditioned stimulus and unconditioned stimulus

decays quickly after the UCS ends. In contrast, the onset and decay of the secondary A2 component are very gradual. Sometimes the A1 and A2 UCR components are different, at other times, they are similar. According to Wagner, the secondary A2 UCR becomes the CR. If the A1 and A2 components are dissimilar, the CR will seem different from the UCR, if the A1 and A2 components are alike, the CR will appear to be similar to the UCR. AESOP, or a revision of the SOP theory, assumes that the UCS elicits separate emotive and sensory unconditioned responses. The emotive and sensory UCRs can have different time courses, which can lead to divergent conditioning outcomes for sensory and emotive CRs.

The Nature of the Conditioning Process

In the last chapter we learned that the predictiveness of the conditioned stimulus influences how readily a conditioned response is acquired. We also discovered that the predictive value of other stimuli also affects the conditioning to the CS. How does an animal or person judge the relative predictiveness of a stimulus? Several different views have been developed to explain the mechanism by which predictiveness affects classical conditioning (see Table 4-1). The Rescorla-Wagner associative view suggests that the availability of associative strength determines whether or not a CR develops to a CS paired with the UCS; comparator theory assumes that performance of a conditioned response involves a comparison of the response strength to the CS and competing stimuli; Mackintosh's attentional theory proposes that the relevance of and attention to a stimulus determines whether or not that stimulus will become associated with the UCS; and Baker's retrospective processing approach suggests that conditioning involving continuous monitoring of contingencies between a CS and UCS, with the recognition of a lack of predictiveness diminishing the value of the CS.

The Rescorla-Wagner theory was developed to explain the influence of predictiveness on conditioning. We begin our influence of the nature of classical conditioning with a description of this theory. We will examine several Pavlovian conditioning phenomena that have been used to test the validity of the Rescorla-Wagner model. Some of this research has supported this theory, while other studies have pointed to its weaknesses. We will then look at alternatives to the Rescorla-Wagner associative model of conditioning.

Rescorla-Wagner Associative Model The associative model of classical conditioning developed by Robert Rescorla and Allen Wagner (1972) expresses four main ideas. First, *there is a maximum associative strength that can develop between a CS and a UCS*. The limit of associative strength, or asymptote level of conditioning, is determined by the UCS; different UCSs support different maximum levels of conditioning, and therefore have different asymptotic values. Second, *while the associative strength increases with each training trial, the amount of associative strength gained on a particular training trial is affected by the level of prior training.* Since the typical learning curve in Pavlovian conditioning is negatively accelerating (refer to Figure 4-6), more associative strength will accrue on early training trials than on later trials. In fact, as can be seen in Figure 4-6, the increment on each conditioning trial declines with each CS-UCS pairing. Third, *the rate of conditioning varies depending on the CS and the UCS used.* Associative strength accrues quickly to some stimuli, but slowly to others. Figure 4-6 shows the learning curve of two stimuli: One stimulus readily gains associative strength, while conditioning to the other stimulus occurs slowly. Further, some UCSs produce more rapid learning than other UCSs. Fourth, *the level of conditioning on a particular trial is influenced not only by the amount of prior conditioning to the stimulus but also by the level of previous conditioning to other stimuli associated with the UCS.* A particular UCS can only support a certain amount of conditioning, even when more than one stimulus is paired with the UCS. When two (or more) stimuli are presented, these stimuli must share the associative strength that can be supported by the UCS. Thus, associative strength that accrues to one stimulus is not available to be conditioned to the other stimuli. For example, suppose two stimuli are paired with a UCS and the maximum associative strength which can be supported by that UCS is 10. If 7 units are conditioned to one cue paired with the UCS, only 3 units can develop to the other cue.

Rescorla and Wagner (1972) developed a mathematical equation based on the four ideas outlined above. Their mathematical model of Pavlovian conditioning

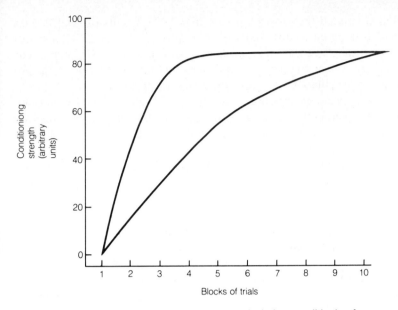

FIGURE 4-6 The change in associative strength during conditioning for two different stimuli. One stimulus rapidly develops associative strength; the other acquires associative strength more slowly.

is $\Delta V_A = K (\lambda - V_{AX})$. In this formula, V_A is associative strength between the conditioned stimulus A and the UCS, and ΔV_A is the change in associative strength that develops on a specific trial when the CS_A and the UCS are paired. K refers to the rate of conditioning that is determined by the nature of the CS_A and the intensity of the UCS. (The K value can be separated into α, or alpha, which refers to the power of CS_A, and β, or beta, which reflects the intensity of the UCS.) The symbol λ defines the maximum level of conditioning supported by the UCS. The term V_{AX} indicates the level of conditioning that has already accrued to the conditioned stimulus (A) as well as to other stimuli (X) present during conditioning. Thus, $V_{AX} = V_A + V_X$.

To see how this mathematical model works, suppose a light stimulus is paired with shock on five trials. Prior to training, the value of K is 0.50, λ is 90, and $V_A = 0$. When we apply these values to the Rescorla-Wagner model, we get:

> Trial 1: $\Delta V_A = 0.50 (90 - 0) = 45$
> Trial 2: $\Delta V_A = 0.50 (90 - 45) = 22.5$
> Trial 3: $\Delta V_A = 0.50 (90 - 67.5) = 11.3$
> Trial 4: $\Delta V_A = 0.50 (90 - 78.8) = 5.6$
> Trial 5: $\Delta V_A = 0.50 (90 - 84.4) = 2.8$
> Total associative strengths after five trials = 87.2

The data provided by the above equation show that conditioning to CS_A occurs rapidly; associative strength grows 45 units on trial 1, 22.5 units on trial 2, 11.3 units on trial 3, 5.6 units on trial 4, and 2.8 units on trial 5. Thus, 87.2 units of associative strength accrued to the CS_A after just five trials of conditioning. The rapid development of associative strength indicates that CS_A is an intense and/or a salient stimulus or that the UCS is a strong stimulus, or both.

The Rescorla-Wagner model has been used to explain a number of conditioning phenomena. Let's see how it explains blocking (see Chapter 3). Suppose we pair a light with a shock for five trials. The K value for the light is 0.5 and the maximum level of conditioning, or λ, is 90 units of associative strength. As we learned earlier, 87.2 units of associative strength would accrue to the light after five pairings with the shock. Next, we pair the light, tone, and shock for five more trials. The K value for the tone is 0.5, and we would expect that five pairings of the tone and shock would yield strong conditioning. However, only 2.8 units of associative strength are still available to be conditioned, according to the Rescorla-Wagner model, and the tone must share this associative strength with the light cue. Because strong conditioning has already occurred to the light, the Rescorla-Wagner equation predicts little conditioning to the tone. The weak conditioning to the tone due to prior accrued associative strength to light can be seen below.

Trial 1: $\Delta V_{light} = 0.5 (90 - 87.2) = 1.4$ $\Delta V_{tone} = 0.5 (90 - 87.2) = 1.4$
Trial 2: $\Delta V_{light} = 0.5 (90 - 90) = 0$ $\Delta V_{tone} = 0.5 (90 - 90) = 0$
Trial 3: $\Delta V_{light} = 0.5 (90 - 90) = 0$ $\Delta V_{tone} = 0.5 (90 - 90) = 0$
Trial 4: $\Delta V_{light} = 0.5 (90 - 90) = 0$ $\Delta V_{tone} = 0.5 (90 - 90) = 0$
Trial 5: $\Delta V_{light} = 0.5 (90 - 90) = 0$ $\Delta V_{tone} = 0.5 (90 - 90) = 0$
Total associative strength light $= 88.6$ tone $= 1.4$

We learned earlier that blocking occurs when a stimulus previously paired with a UCS is presented with a new stimulus and the UCS. The Rescorla-Wagner model suggests that blocking occurs because the initial CS has already accrued most or all of the associative strength and little is left to condition to the other stimulus. As shown in the above equations, little conditioning occurred to the tone because most of the associative strength had been conditioned to the light prior to the compound pairing of the light, tone, and shock. Based on this explanation, the equation generated by the Rescorla-Wagner model predicts cue blocking.

An Evaluation of the Rescorla-Wagner Model   A number of studies have evaluated the validity of the Rescorla-Wagner model of Pavlovian conditioning. While many of these studies have supported this view, other observations have not been consistent with the Rescorla-Wagner model. We will first discuss one area of research—the UCS preexposure effect—which has provided data supportive of the Rescorla-Wagner view. Next, we will look at four areas of research—potentiation, CS preexposure, cue predictiveness, and cue deflation—which provide findings that are not predicted by the Rescorla-Wagner model. Finally, we will consider several alternative views of Pavlovian conditioning.

The UCS Preexposure Effect   Suppose you have had several bouts of the flu recently and again become sick after eating a distinctive food. Would you develop an aversion to this food? Your previous experiences with sickness, independent of the particular food, probably would prevent the conditioning of an association between eating this food and being sick.

The previous example illustrates the effect of preexposure to the UCS (illness) without the CS (food) on the acquisition of a CR (aversion) when the CS is later presented with the UCS. Psychologists (see Baker & Mackintosh, 1979, Randich & Ross, 1985) refer to this phenomenon as the *UCS preexposure effect.* Many studies have consistently observed that preexposure to the UCS impairs subsequent conditioning; for example, several researchers (Best & Domjan, 1979; Cannon, Berman, Baker, & Atkinson, 1975; Domjan & Gemberling, 1980; Mikulka, Leard, & Klein, 1977) have demonstrated that the presentation of a drug that induces illness (UCS) prior to conditioning impairs the subsequent association of a distinctive food (CS) with illness. Similar preexposure interference has been reported with other UCSs (for example, shock: Baker & Mackintosh, 1979; Baker, Mercier, Gabel, & Baker, 1981; Randich & LoLordo, 1979; Rescorla, 1974; food: Balsam & Schwartz, 1981; Engberg, Hanson, Welker, & Thomas, 1973; Tomie, Murphy, & Fath, 1980).

Why does preexposure to the UCS impair subsequent conditioning? The Rescorla-Wagner model provides an explanation: The presentation of the UCS without the CS occurs in a specific environment or context, which results in the development of associative strength to the context. Since the UCS can only support a limited amount of associative strength, conditioning of associative strength to stimulus context reduces the level of possible conditioning to the CS. Thus, the presence of the stimulus context will block the acquisition of a CR to the CS when the CS is presented with the UCS in the stimulus context. (Referring back to the blocking phenomenon described in Chapter 3, it would be helpful to think of the context as CS_1 and the new stimulus as CS_2.)

How can the context blocking explanation of the UCS preexposure effect be validated? One method is to change the context when the CS is paired with the UCS. A number of studies (see Baker et al., 1981; Balsam & Schwartz, 1981; Randich & Ross, 1985; Rescorla, Durlach, & Grau, 1985; Tomie et al., 1980) have shown that the UCS preexposure effect was attenuated when the preexposure context was different from the conditioning context. As a result of the change in context, no stimuli were present during conditioning that can compete with the association of the CS and the UCS. Therefore, the CR was readily conditioned to the CS when paired with the UCS in the new context. We will briefly discuss the Randich and Ross (1985) study to illustrate the effect of context change on the impact of the UCS preexposure effect.

Randich and Ross (1985) placed four groups of rats in context 1 during the first phase of the study. Context 1 was characterized by noise from a fan but did not have a light, painted walls, or the odor of Pine-Sol. Two of these groups—

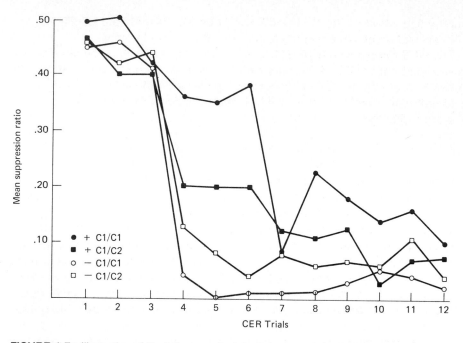

FIGURE 4-7 Illustration of the influence of context change on the UCS preexposure effect. Animals in the +C1/C1 experimental group receiving preexposure and conditioning in context 1 showed significantly slower acquisition of a conditional emotional response than did animals in the +C1/C2 experimental group given preexposure in context 1 and conditioning in context 2. Control animals in −C1/C1 and −C1/C2 groups who did not receive UCS preexposure readily conditioned fear to either context 1 or 2. From Randich, A., & Ross, R. T. (1985). Contextual stimuli mediate the effects of pre- and postexposure to the unconditioned stimulus on conditioned suppression. In P. D. Balsam & A. Tomie (Eds.), *Context and learning.* Hillsdale, N. J: Erlbaum.

the +C1/C1 and +C1/C2 experimental groups—received a 10-second unsignaled shock (UCS) in context 1; the other two groups—the C1/C1 and −C1/C2 control groups—did not receive the shock in context 1. After 10 trials in context 1, animals in the +C1/C1 group were placed again in context 1 and received pairings of a 3-minute noise CS and shock. The −C1/C1 group animals also were given noise CS-shock (UCS) pairings in context 1. Randich and Ross observed that the rats that had been preexposed to the shock in context 1 and then conditioned in context 1 showed much less fear of the noise CS than did the control group animals that had not been preexposed to shock. The second experimental group (+C1/C2) of animals received noise CS and shock pairings in context 2. The other control (−C1/C2) group also were given noise-shock pairings in context 2. Context 2 was quite different from context 1; it had a light, black-and-white striped walls, and Pine-Sol odor but no fan. Strong fear of the noise CS was exhibited by animals given UCS preexposure in context 1 and then conditioned in context 2 (see Figure 4-7). These results suggest that context associations formed during UCS preexposure are responsible for the decrease in the conditioning to the CS when paired with the UCS.

Our discussion provides support for the context blocking explanation of the UCS preexposure effect. This view is also consistent with and predicted by the Rescorla-Wagner model. Even so, there are several processes in Pavlovian conditioning that are not consistent with the Rescorla-Wagner model. Next, we examine four of these processes.

Problems with the Rescorla-Wagner Model   In this section, we will discuss several observations that are not predicted by the Rescorla-Wagner model. The first problem area is the potentiation effect.

The Potentiation of a Conditioned Response   As we stated earlier, the Rescorla-Wagner model predicts that when a salient and a nonsalient cue are presented together with the UCS, the salient cue will accrue more associative strength than the nonsalient cue. However, *overshadowing* does not always occur when both a salient and a nonsalient stimulus are presented together with the unconditioned stimulus. We learned in the last chapter that the presence of a salient flavor *potentiated* rather than overshadowed an aversion to a less salient odor cue; that is, a stronger aversion to an odor was conditioned when a flavor was present rather than absent.

Why does the presence of a salient taste cue potentiate rather than overshadow the acquisition of an odor aversion? According to Garcia and Rusiniak (1980), the taste stimulus "indexes" the odor stimulus as a food cue and thereby mediates the establishment of a strong odor aversion. This indexing process has considerable adaptive significance. The potentiation of the odor aversion by the taste cue enables an animal to recognize a potentially poisonous food early in the ingestive sequence. Thus, an odor aversion causes animals to avoid dangerous foods even without tasting them.

Rescorla (1982) presents a different view of the potentiation effect, a view consistent with the Rescorla-Wagner model. According to Rescorla, potentiation occurs because the animal perceives the compound stimuli (taste and odor) as a single unitary event and then mistakes the individual elements for the compound. If Rescorla's view is accurate, the potentiation effect should depend upon the strength of the taste-illness association: Potentiation should occur with a strong taste aversion, and weakening the taste-illness association should result in an elimination of the potentiation. Rescorla (1981) presented evidence to support his view; that is, he found that extinction of the taste aversion also attenuated the animal's aversion to an odor cue. However, Lett (1982) observed that taste-alone exposures eliminated the taste aversion but not the odor aversion. The cause of potentiation remains unclear; we will discuss this phenomenon again when we look at Rescorla's within-compound view later in the chapter.

The Influence of CS Preexposure   Recall our discussion in the chapter-opening vignette of Kevin's failure to associate Tricia's drinking and aggression. The *CS preexposure effect* provides an explanation of his failure to develop an apprehension of Tricia's drinking. Many studies (see Hall & Honey, 1989) have reported that preexposure to a specific stimulus (drinking) subsequently retarded the development of a CR (apprehension) to that stimulus when paired with a UCS (hostility). The CS preexposure effect has been reported in a variety of Pavlovian conditioning situations, including conditioned licking of water in rats (see Baker & Mackintosh, 1979), conditioned fear in rats (for example, Dickinson, 1976; Hall & Pearce, 1979; Pearce, Kaye, & Hall, 1982; Rescorla, 1971), eyelid conditioning in rabbits (Siegel, 1969), leg-flexion conditioning in sheep and goats (Lubow & Moore, 1959), and flavor-aversion learning in rats (for example, Best & Gemberling, 1977; Fenwick, Mikulka, & Klein, 1975; Revusky & Bedarf, 1967).

Why is the CS preexposure effect a problem for the Rescorla-Wagner model? According to Rescorla and Wagner (1972), exposure to the CS prior to conditioning should have no effect on its subsequent association with the UCS. This prediction is based on the assumption that readiness of a stimulus to be associated with a UCS depends only on the intensity and salience of the CS; these values are represented by the parameter K in the Rescorla-Wagner model. Although neither the intensity nor the salience of the CS is changed as the result of CS preexposure, the subsequent interference with conditioning indicates that the associability of the CS changes when the CS is experienced without the UCS prior to conditioning.

How can the influence of CS preexposure on subsequent conditioning be explained? One explanation involves modifying the Rescorla-Wagner model to allow for a change in the value of K as the result of experience. Yet, the effect of CS preexposure on the acquisition of a CR appears to involve more than just a reduction in the value of K. Instead, Mackintosh (1983) argues that animals learn that a particular stimulus is irrelevant because it predicts no significant event; the recognition of stimulus irrelevance causes the animal to ignore that stimulus in the future. This failure to attend to the CS and the events that follow the CS is suggested to be responsible for the interference with conditioning produced by CS preexposure. We will look more closely at this attentional view of CS preexposure when we describe Mackintosh's attentional model of conditioning.

A Better Predictor of the Future   We discovered in the last chapter that conditioning is impaired when a CS is not predictive of the UCS; that is, when a UCS occurs both with and without the CS during conditioning. According to the Rescorla-Wagner model, context blocking is responsible for the reduced conditioning observed when the UCS occurs more without the UCS than with it. While the UCS can occur with or without the CS, the UCS is always presented in a specific environment or context. The pairing of the stimulus context with the UCS will result in the development of associative strength to the context. As the context develops associative strength, it will block the conditioning to the CS.

Whereas the Rescorla-Wagner model assumes that context blocking is responsible for the decreased conditioning when the CS is not predictive of the UCS, a study by Klein et al. (1984) suggests that predictiveness involves more than context blocking; this research indicates that an animal plays an active role in determining whether or not a cue is predictive, rather than the passive role as-

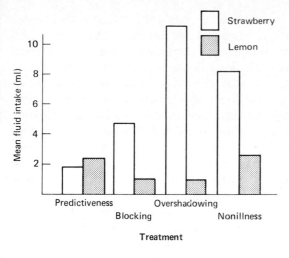

FIGURE 4-8
The impact of predictiveness on conditioning. A strong aversion to a nonsalient strawberry flavor developed in the predictiveness group but not in blocking or overshadowing conditions. In contrast, a weaker aversion to the salient lemon flavor was seen in the blocking and overshadowing treatments than in the predictive treatment. From Klein, S. B., McGee-Davis, T., Cohen, L., & Weston, D. (1984). Relative influence of cue predictiveness and salience on flavor aversion learning. *Learning and Motivation, 15,* 188–202.

sumed by the Rescorla-Wagner associative model of conditioning. In Klein and colleagues' study, one group of animals received four trials of a nonsalient strawberry flavor prior to illness. On each trial, a different but more salient flavor was also paired with illness. Thus, the strawberry flavor was more predictive of illness than any of the other flavors. Although no aversion was established to the nonsalient strawberry flavor after a single pairing with illness, a strong aversion to the strawberry flavor was present after the fourth flavor was paired with illness.

It is possible that the aversion to strawberry was merely due to four pairings of strawberry and illness. To assess this possibility, a second group of animals received only strawberry paired with illness on the first three trails and strawberry, lemon, and illness on the fourth trial. If four pairings are responsible for the strong aversion to strawberry in the predictiveness treatment, similar results should be seen in the blocking group. However, a modest aversion to strawberry was conditioned with a blocking treatment (refer to Figure 4-8). Further, a stronger aversion to lemon developed in the blocking than in the predictive treatment. This result indicates that associative blocking is not solely responsible for the influence of cue predictiveness on the development of a conditioned response. The impact of predictiveness on conditioning appears to involve more than associative blocking. Baker's retrospective processing theory presents an account of Pavlovian conditioning that can explain the results of Klein et al.; we will look at his view shortly.

The Effect of Cue Deflation   The Rescorla-Wagner model suggests that the overshadowing phenomenon involves the greater conditioning to a more salient than a less salient stimulus; that is, greater associative strength accrues to the more salient cue than to the less salient cue. What do you suppose would happen to an animal's response to the less salient stimulus if the conditioned response to the more salient stimulus were extinguished? The Rescorla-Wagner model does not suggest any change in the reaction to the less salient cue. However, a number of studies (Kaufman & Bolles, 1981; Matzel, Schachtman, & Miller, 1985) reported that extinction of the more salient (or overshadowing) stimulus increased responding to the less salient (or overshadowed) stimulus. It is important to note that not all studies report increased responding to a less salient stimulus following extinction to a more salient cue; instead, these articles report decreased responding to both the overshadowing and overshadowed stimuli (see Durlach, 1989).

Another example of increased responding to a CS without additional experience occurs with extinction of context associations acquired with UCS preexposure. Recall that exposure to the UCS prior to CS-UCS pairings produces a weaker response to the CS than is observed when no UCS preexposure is given. We learned earlier that context-UCS associations acquired during UCS preexposure blocks strong conditioning to the CS. Several studies (see Matzel, Brown, & Miller, 1987; Timberlake, 1986) show that postconditioning extinction of the response to the training context results in an enhanced responding to the CS. Again, not all studies that extinguished the response to the training context have noted an increased responding to the CS (refer to Durlach, 1989). What process is responsible for the change in response to one stimulus following extinction of a response to another stimulus? Why do some studies report that diminished responding to one stimulus increased responding to the CS, while other studies find that this same procedure decreased the reaction to the CS? The next two sections address these questions.

The Importance of Within-Compound Associations   Suppose a tone and a light are paired together with food. According to the Rescorla-Wagner model, the light and tone will compete for associative strength. Recently, Robert Rescorla and his associates (see Durlach & Rescorla, 1980; Rescorla & Cunningham, 1978; Rescorla & Durlach, 1981; Speers, Gillan, & Rescorla, 1980) have suggested that rather than two stimuli competing for associative strength, a within-compound association between the light and the tone can be established during conditioning. This within-compound association will result in a single level of conditioning to both stimuli. One procedure facilitating a within-compound association is the simultaneous experience of both stimuli. As a result of the development of a within-compound association, any change in the value of one stimulus will have a similar impact on the other stimulus.

We saw earlier that the concept of within-compound associations can be used to explain the potentiation phenomena. Rescorla suggested that the within-compound association of a salient flavor cue and a nonsalient odor cue led to a strong aversion (potentiation) when both cues were paired with illness. The within-compound conditioning view asserts that potentiation is dependent upon the establishment of an association between the odor and flavor cues. According to this view, the failure to form a within-compound association between odor and flavor should eliminate potentiation. One procedure used to prevent within-compound associations is pairing the odor and taste cues sequentially rather than simultaneously. This procedure eliminates potentiation of the odor cue by the flavor stimulus (see Holder & Garcia, 1987; Kucharski & Spear, 1985; Rescorla & Durlach, 1981).

While within-compound conditioning may contribute to potentiation, it is not the entire story. As we learned earlier, Lett (1982) did not find that extinction of the flavor aversion eliminated the odor aversion. Further, a number of studies (see Bouton, Jones, McPhillips, & Swartzentruber, 1986; Westbrook, Homewood, Horn, & Clarke, 1983) have found overshadowing rather than potentiation of an odor aversion by a flavor cue. In these studies, overshadowing was found under conditions that were favorable to within-compound associations. We introduced a stimulus indexing explanation of potentiation earlier; we will take a further look at this idea in Chapter 13.

Recall our discussion of the deflation effect presented in the last section. We learned that several studies showed that extinction of responding to one component of a compound stimulus enhanced responding to the other component. Yet, other experiments reported that extinction to one component also reduced responding to the other component. The latter result is consistent with the within-compound analysis; that is, a within-compound association is established to both components and reducing responding to one has a comparable effect on the other. However, the former studies are not consistent with the within-compound analysis. Comparator theory can explain why extinction of responding to one component should increase responding to the other.

A Comparator Theory of Pavlovian Conditioning   Several psychologists (see Balsam, 1984; Gibbon & Balsam, 1981; Miller & Matzel, 1989; Miller & Schachtman, 1985) have proposed that animals learn about all CS-UCS relationships. However, a particular association may not be evident in an animal's behavior. A strong CS-UCS association may exist but not be expressed in behavior if compared with a CS that is more strongly associated with the UCS. Thus, the ability of a particular stimulus to elicit a CR is determined by a comparison to various other stimuli's level of conditioning. Only when the level of conditioning to that stimulus exceeds that to other stimuli will the CS elicit the CR.

Consider the blocking phenomenon to illustrate the comparator view. This approach assumes that an association does exist between the CS_2 and the UCS but is not evident because of the expression of a stronger CS_1-UCS association. (Recall that the Rescorla-Wagner model assumes that the presence of the CS_1 blocks or prevents the establishment of the CS_2-UCS association.) The comparator theory suggests that there is one condition in which the CS_2 can elicit the CR in a blocking paradigm. The extinction of the conditioned response to CS_1 can allow the CS_2 to now elicit the CR. The reason that extinction of the response to CS_1 results in responding to the CS_2 is that the comparison now favors the CS_2-UCS association. Prior to extinction, the CS_1-UCS association was stronger than the CS_2-UCS association. After extinction, the CS_2-UCS association is stronger than the CS_1-UCS association.

We learned in an earlier section that extinction of responding to the training context may eliminate the UCS preexposure effect. Some studies (see Matzel et al., 1987; Timberlake, 1986) show that deflation of responding to the training context leads to an increased responding to the CS. This greater responding occurred even though no additional CS-UCS pairings were given. Additional support for the comparator theory comes from experiments in which devaluation of the overshadowing (more salient) stimulus caused increased responding to the overshadowed (less salient) stimulus (see Kaufman & Bolles, 1981; Matzel et al., 1985). This observation suggests that an association between the overshadowed stimulus and the UCS was formed but was not evident because of its comparison with overshadowing stimulus.

While these observations provide support for the comparator theory, not all studies have found that deflation of one stimulus increases responding to another stimulus. In fact, most studies have reported that extinguishing responding to one stimulus produces a comparable reduction in the other stimulus, a result that favors the within-compound association view presented in the last section (see Durlach, 1989, for a discussion of this literature).

What is responsible for this discrepancy of deflation results? Durlach (1989) suggests that the presence of strong within-compound associations might overwhelm the comparator effect. In her view, the comparator effect would only be evident when within-compound associations are weak. Evidence supporting this view, or any other explanation, awaits future investigation.

Mackintosh's Attentional View   Nicholas Mackintosh (1975) suggested that animals seek information from their environment which predicts the occurrence of biologically significant events (UCSs). Once an animal has identified a cue that reliably predicts a specific event, it ignores other stimuli that also provide information about the event. According to Mackintosh, animals attend to stimuli that are predictive and ignore those that are not essential. Thus, an animal plays an active role in the conditioning process; that is, conditioning depends not only on the physical characteristics of stimuli but also on the animal's recognition of the correlation (or lack of correlation) between events (CS and UCS).

Mackintosh's view of Pavlovian conditioning can explain the CS preexposure effect, which poses a problem for the Rescorla-Wagner model. We discovered earlier in the chapter that CS preexposure impairs the acquisition of the CR when the CS and the UCS are later paired. According to Mackintosh, an animal learns that the CS is irrelevant as the result of preexposure to the CS. In Mackintosh's view, once the animal discovers that a stimulus is irrelevant, it will stop attending to that stimulus and therefore will have difficulty learning that the CS is correlated with the UCS.

Support for a *learned irrelevance* view of CS preexposure is provided by studies in which uncorrelated presentations of the CS and the UCS prior to conditioning led to substantial interference with the acquisition of the CR. In fact, Baker and Mackintosh (1977) found that significantly greater interference is produced by uncorrelated presentations of the CS and the UCS than is caused by only CS preexposure or UCS preexposure. In their study, water licking to a tone was significantly less in animals receiving prior unpaired presentations of the tone

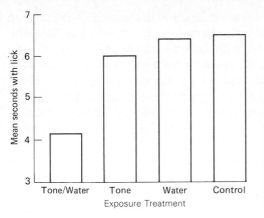

FIGURE 4-9
The amount of licking to tone (CS) paired with water (UCS) is significantly less in animals preexposed to both the tone or water than only water, only tone, or no preexposure. Adapted from Baker, A. G., & Mackintosh, N. J. (1979). Preexposure to the CS alone, US alone, or CS and US uncorrelated: Latent inhibition, blocking by context or learned irrelevance. *Learning and Motivation, 10*, 278–294.

(CS) and water (UCS) than either tone alone, water alone, or no preexposure (refer to Figure 4-9). This greater impairment of subsequent conditioning when the CS and the UCS are unpaired also has been demonstrated in studies of conditioning fear in rats (Baker, 1976; Kremer, 1971) and the eyelid conditioning in rabbits (Siegel & Domjan, 1971).

Several recent studies by Geoffrey Hall and his associates (see Hall & Channell, 1985; Hall & Honey, 1989; Hall & Schachtman, 1987) provide additional evidence for an attentional view of the CS preexposure effect. Animals exposed to a novel stimulus exhibit an orienting response to that stimulus. Hall and Channell (1985) showed that repeated exposure to light (CS) leads to habituation of the orienting response to that stimulus (see Chapter 1). They also found that later pairings of the light (CS) with milk (UCS) yield a reduced CR compared with control animals that did not experience preexposure to the light. These results suggest that habituation of an orienting response to a stimulus is associated with the later failure of conditioning to that stimulus.

What if the orienting response could be reinstated to the conditioned stimulus? Would this procedure restore conditionability to the stimulus? Hall and Channell (1985) reported that the presentation of the conditioned stimulus in a novel context reinstated the orienting response. They also found that pairing of the CS and UCS in the new context led to a strong CR. These results indicate that a reinstatement of the orienting response eliminated the CS preexposure effect; that is, the CS now elicits a strong CR.

Why would reinstatement of the orienting response lead to a return of CS conditionability? An orienting response indicates that an animal is attending to the stimulus, and attention allows the stimulus to be associated with the UCS. These observations provide further support for the view that learned irrelevance is responsible for the CS preexposure effect.

The Retrospective Processing View   Theories of Pavlovian conditioning have traditionally held that learning occurs at the time of training and that responding is based upon the level of training. Baker and Mercier (1989) refer to these models of Pavlovian conditioning as ''input-based'' theories. The Rescorla-Wagner associative theory, Rescorla's within-compound association view, and Mackintosh's attentional prospective are input-based theories of Pavlovian conditioning. In contrast, Miller's comparative theory is an output-based model because it assumes that performance is determined by comparing the level of prior conditioning of stimuli at the time of testing. However, all of these theories assume that unless further conditioning is provided, the level of learning remains constant after training.

Baker and Mercier (1989) present a very different view of Pavlovian conditioning. They contend that the level of conditioning to a CS can change even with no additional CS-UCS pairings. According to these researchers, animals are constantly assessing the contingency between events in their environment. Rather than viewing learning as a static representation of the degree of correlation between events, they suggest that learning changes over time as new information about the degree of contingency between a CS and a UCS is encountered. For example, what may seem to be two highly correlated events may later be viewed as having little correlation at all. This change in learning would occur if initial CS-UCS pairings were followed by many UCS-alone experiences. Baker and Mercier refer to the idea that animals are constantly assessing contingencies as *retrospective processing*. New data may cause an animal to reassess past experiences and form a new representation of the relationship between the CS and the UCS.

Retrospective processing requires an ability to remember past experiences. It also assumes that an animal has a representation of past encounters that can be modified. In this section, we will look at several studies supportive of retrospective processing.

Suppose that after a tone and a light were paired with shock, the tone was presented alone prior to shock. How would the animal respond to the light? Baker and Baker (1985) performed such a study and found that fear of the light was reduced compared to a control group that did not receive tone-shock pairings. This study is similar to the blocking paradigm described in the last chapter. In fact, the only difference between the procedures is the order of tone-light-shock and tone-shock pairings. Baker and Mercier (1989) refer to a procedure in which the tone-shock follows rather than precedes tone-light-shock pairing as *backward blocking*.

What causes backward blocking? Baker and Mercier argue that when animals receive tone-shock after tone-light-shock pairings, they discover that the tone is a better predictor of shock than the light. Through retrospective processing, the animals decide that the light is not an adequate predictor of shock. This decision causes the animals to no longer fear the light. We should note that several studies (see Rescorla & Durlach, 1981; Schweitzer & Green, 1982) have failed to observe backward blocking, and the validity of this finding needs to be more clearly established.

Recall our discussion of the UCS preexposure effect. We learned that exposure to the UCS impaired later conditioning of the CS and the UCS. A similar impairment of conditioning occurs when UCS-alone experiences are intermixed with CS-UCS pairings (see Jenkins, Barnes, & Barrera, 1981). According to Baker and Mercier (1989), the animal revises its view of the contingency between the CS and the UCS as a result of UCS-alone experience. In other words, the animal retrospectively examines its earlier view of the CS-UCS contingency and decides that the CS is no longer well correlated with the UCS.

Other theories of Pavlovian conditioning can explain the effects of UCS-alone exposure intermixed with CS-UCS pairings. The Rescorla-Wagner associative model assumes that contextual associations block the establishment of strong CS-UCS associations. Yet, the retrospective processing theory is very new and will undoubtedly generate further evaluation. We will look again at this view when we examine cognitive control of behavior in Chapter 8.

Section Review

The Rescorla-Wagner associative theory of conditioning assumes (1) that there is a maximum level of conditioning supported by the UCS, (2) that the associative strength increases readily early in training but more slowly later in conditioning as associative strength approaches asymptote, (3) that the rate of conditioning is more rapid with some CSs or UCSs than others, and (4) that the level of conditioning on a particular trial is dependent upon the level of prior conditioning to the CS and to the other stimuli present during conditioning. The Rescorla-Wagner model assumes that overshadowing occurs due to the rapid accumulation of associative strength to a more salient stimuli, which leaves little conditioning possible to the less salient stimulus. Blocking occurs as a result of conditioning of associative strength to one stimulus, preventing the conditioning to a second stimulus due to a lack of available associative strength.

Under some conditions, Rescorla suggests that two stimuli paired with a UCS develop a within-compound association instead of competing for associative strength. According to Rescorla, potentiation reflects the establishment of a within-compound associated between salient flavor and nonsalient odor cues. This within-compound association will be observed with simultaneous but not sequential pairings of odor and flavor stimuli.

The comparator theory assumes that animals learn about all CS-UCS relationships. According to the comparator theory, blocking occurs when the animal does not respond to the CS_2, because the CS_2-UCS association is weaker than the CS_1-UCS association. Deflation of the value of the CS_1 by extinction results in an increased responding to CS_2.

Mackintosh's attentional view suggests that animals seek information that predicts the occurrence of biologically significant events (UCSs). According to Mackintosh, preexposure to a stimulus prior to conditioning impairs the later acquisition of the CR when that stimulus (CS) and the UCS are paired. In Mackintosh's view, the animal learns that the CS is irrelevant as the result of pre-exposure to the CS. Once an animal discovers that a CS is irrelevant, it has difficulty learning that the CS is correlated with the UCS.

Baker's retrospective processing theory assumes that animals are continuously monitoring the contingency between CS and UCS. Subsequent experience with CS or UCS alone can lead the animal to reevaluate the predictive value of the CS. Exposure to other CS-UCS contingencies can also result in a reevaluation of the original CS-UCS association. The backward blocking phenomenon refers to reduced responding to CS_2 when CS_1-UCS pairings follow CS_1-CS_2-UCS pairings and provides support for the retrospective processing theory.

We have examined five different views of Pavlovian conditioning. As we discovered in the last chapter, Pavlovian conditioning is a complex process. Each of the approaches described in this chapter has added to our understanding of how CRs are acquired. These views will undoubtedly be modified and new ones added as the investigation into the nature of Pavlovian conditioning continues.

APPLICATIONS OF PAVLOVIAN CONDITIONING

We will discuss three applications of Pavlovian conditioning in this chapter. The first application involves the use of Pavlovian conditioning principles to modify phobic behavior. This procedure, called systematic desensitization, has been used to eliminate fear in phobic individuals for over 30 years. The second application involves extinction of a person's craving for a drug and has only been recently used to treat drug addiction. The last application has not been clinically tested but may represent a possible use of Pavlovian conditioning to correct immune system dysfunction in patients with lupus and other diseases of the immune system.

Systematic Desensitization

Suppose a person is extremely frightened of taking examinations. This fear could cause the individual to do poorly in college. What can be done to allow this person to take examinations with minimal or no fear? Systematic desensitization is a therapy developed by Joseph Wolpe to inhibit fear and suppress phobic behavior (a phobia is an unrealistic fear of an object or situation). Wolpe's therapy can help people with extreme test anxiety. His treatment is based on Pavlovian conditioning principles and represents an important application of classical conditioning. Let's now examine this technique to discover how Pavlovian conditioning has been used to alter extreme fear.

Original Animal Studies   Wolpe's therapy evolved from his animal research. In an initial study (see Wolpe, 1958), he shocked one group of cats in their home cages after they heard a buzzer. For the other cats, he paired the buzzer with food in the home cages and then shocked them. Both groups of cats later showed extreme fear of the buzzer. One indication of their fear was their refusal to eat when hearing the buzzer.

Since fear inhibited eating, Wolpe reasoned that eating could—if sufficiently intense—suppress fear. Also, Wolpe proposed that the repeated pairing of the reinforcing aspects of eating with the feared stimulus would cause the fear of the stimuli to become a permanent inhibitor rather than an elicitor of fear. The process of establishing a response that competes with a previously acquired response is called *counterconditioning* (see Chapter 2). Wolpe suggested that counterconditioning represented a potentially effective way of treating human phobic behavior. He based this idea on three lines of evidence: (1) Sherrington's statement (1906) that an animal can only experience one emotional state at a time—a process Wolpe termed *reciprocal inhibition,* (2) Jones's report (1924) that she had successfully eliminated a young boy's conditioned fear of rabbits by presenting the feared stimulus (a rabbit) while the boy was eating (see Chapter 2), and (3) Wolpe's own research using cats.

Wolpe initially placed his phobic cats in a cage with food; this cage was quite dissimilar to their home cage. He used the dissimilar cage (which produced only a low fear level due to little generalization) because use of the home cage would produce too intense a fear and therefore inhibit eating. Wolpe observed that his cats ate in the dissimilar cage and did not appear afraid after eating. Wolpe concluded that in the dissimilar environment, the eating response had replaced the fear response. Once the fear in the dissimilar cage was eliminated, the cats were less fearful in another cage more closely resembling the home cage. The reason for this reduced fear is that the inhibition of fear conditioned to the dissimilar cage generalized to the second cage. The counterconditioning process was now employed with this second cage, and Wolpe found that presentation of food in this cage quickly reversed the cats' fear. Wolpe continued the gradual counterconditioning treatment by slowly changing the characteristics of the test cage until the cats were able to eat in their home cage without any evidence of fear. Wolpe also found that a gradual exposure of the buzzer paired with food modified the cats' anxiety of the buzzer.

Clinical Treatment   Wolpe (1958) asserted that human phobias could be eliminated in a manner similar to that which he used with his cats. Wolpe chose not to use eating to inhibit human fears but instead used three classes of inhibitors: relaxation, assertion, and sexual responses. We will limit our discussion in this chapter to the use of relaxation.

Wolpe's therapy using relaxation to counter human phobic behavior is called *systematic desensitization.* Basically, desensitization involves relaxing while imagining anxiety-inducing scenes. To promote relaxation, Wolpe used a series of muscle exercises developed by Jacobson in 1938. These exercises involve tensing a particular muscle and then releasing this tension. It is assumed that tension is related to anxiety and that tension reduction is relaxing (or reinforcing). The patient tenses and relaxes each major muscle group in a specific sequence.

TABLE 4-2
THEMATIC HIERARCHY OF ANXIETY

Level	Scene
1	You are in your office with an agent, R. C., discussing a prospective interview. The client in question is stalling on his payment, and you must tell R. C. what to do.
2	It is Monday morning and you are at your office. In a few minutes you will attend the regularly scheduled sales meeting. You are prepared for the meeting.
3	Conducting an exploratory interview with a prospective client.
4	Sitting at home. The telephone rings.
5	Anticipating returning a call from the district director.
6	Anticipating returning a call from a stranger.
7	Entering the Monday sales meeting unprepared.
8	Anticipating a visit from the regional director.
9	A fellow agent requests a joint visit with a client.
10	On a joint visit with a fellow agent.
11	Attempting to close a sale.
12	Thinking about attending an agents' and managers' meeting.
13	Thinking of contacting a client who should have been contacted earlier.
14	Thinking about calling a prospective client.
15	Thinking about the regional directors' request for names of prospective agents.
16	Alone, driving to prospective client's home.
17	Calling a prospective client.

Note: In the anxiety hierarchy, a higher level represents greater anxiety.
Source: Rimm, D. C., & Masters, J. C. (1979). Behavior therapy: Techniques and empirical findings (2d ed.). New York: Academic.

Rimm and Masters (1979) indicated that relaxation is most effective when the tension phase lasts approximately 10 seconds and is followed by 10 to 15 seconds of relaxation for each muscle group. The typical procedure requires about 30 to 40 minutes to complete; however, less time is needed later in therapy as the patient becomes more readily able to experience relaxation. Once relaxed, the patient is asked to concentrate on a specific word (for example, *calm*). This procedure, labeled *cue-controlled relaxation* by Russell and Sipich (1973), promotes the development of a conditioned relaxation response which enables relaxation to be elicited promptly by a specific stimulus; the patient then uses the cue to inhibit any anxiety occurring during therapy.

The desensitization treatment consists of four separate phases: (1) construction of the anxiety hierarchy; (2) relaxation training; (3) actual counterconditioning, or the pairing of relaxation with the feared stimulus; and (4) assessment of whether the patient can successfully interact with the phobic object. In the first stage, the patients are instructed to construct a graded series of anxiety-inducing scenes related to their phobia. A 10-to-15-item list of low-, moderate-, and high-anxiety scenes is typically employed. Using index cards, a patient writes descriptions of the scenes, then ranks them in a hierarchy from low to high anxiety.

Paul (1969) identified two major types of hierarchies: *thematic* and *spatial-temporal*. In thematic hierarchies, the scenes are related to a basic theme. Table 4-2

TABLE 4-3
SPATIAL-TEMPORAL HIERARCHY OF ANXIETY

Level	Scene
1	Four days before an examination.
2	Three days before an examination.
3	Two days before an examination.
4	One day before an examination.
5	The night before an examination.
6	The examination paper lies face down before the student.
7	Awaiting the distribution of examination papers.
8	Before the unopened doors of the examination room.
9	In the process of answering an examination paper.
10	On the way to the university on the day of an examination.

Note: In the anxiety hierarchy, a higher level represents greater anxiety.
Source: Wolpe, J. (1982). *The practice of behavior therapy* (3d ed.). Oxford: Pergamon.

presents a hierarchy detailing the anxiety experienced by an insurance agent when anticipating interactions with coworkers or clients. Each scene in the hierarchy is somewhat different, but all are related to the agent's fear of possible failure in professional situations. In contrast, a spatial-temporal hierarchy is based on phobic behavior in which intensity of fear is determined by distance (either physical or temporal) to the phobic object. The test anxiety hierarchy shown in Table 4-3 indicates that the level of anxiety is related to the proximity to exam time.

One important aspect of the hierarchy presented in Table 4-3 needs to be mentioned. Perhaps contrary to your intuition, this patient experienced more anxiety while on the way than actually at the test area. Others have a different hierarchy; when taking the exam, they experience the most fear. These observations indicate that each individual's phobic response is highly idiosyncratic and dependent on one person's unique learning experience. Therefore, a hierarchy must be specially constructed for each patient. Some phobias require a combination of thematic and spatial-temporal hierarchies. For example, a person with a height phobia can experience varying levels of anxiety— at different places and at different distances from the edge of these places.

After the hierarchy is constructed, the patient learns to relax. Relaxation training follows the establishment of the hierarchy to prevent the generalization of relaxation to the hierarchical stimuli and thereby precluding an accurate assessment of the level of fear to each stimulus. The counterconditioning phase of treatment begins following relaxation training. The patient is instructed to relax and imagine as clearly as possible the lowest scene on the hierarchy. Since even this scene elicits some anxiety, Rimm and Masters (1979) suggested that the first exposure be quite brief (5 seconds). The duration of the imagined scene can then be slowly increased as counterconditioning progresses.

It is crucial that the patient not become anxious while picturing the scene; otherwise, additional anxiety rather than relaxation will be conditioned. The therapist instructs the patient to signal when experiencing anxiety, and the therapist terminates the scene. After a scene has ended, the patient is instructed to relax. The scene can again be visualized when relaxation has been reinstated. If the individual can imagine the first scene without any discomfort, the next highest scene in the hierarchy is imagined. The process of slowly counterconditioning each level of the hierarchy continues until the patient can imagine the most aversive scene without becoming anxious.

Clinical Effectiveness The last phase of desensitization evaluates the therapy's success. To test the effectiveness of desensitization, the individual is required to encounter the phobic object. The success of desensitization as a treatment of phobic behavior is quite impressive. Wolpe (1958) reported that 90 percent of 210 patients showed significant improvement with desensitization, compared to the 60 percent success rate when psychoanalysis was used. The comparison is more striking because desensitization produced a rapid extinction of phobic behavior (according to Wolpe, 1976, a range of 12 to 29 sessions was most effective) compared to the longer length of treatment (3 to 5 years) necessary for psychoanalysis to cure phobic behavior. Although Lazarus (1971) reported that some patients showed a relapse 1 to 3 years after therapy, the renewed anxiety could be readily reversed with additional desensitization. The types of phobias successfully treated or extinguished by desensitization are quite extensive: fears of height, driving, snakes, dogs, insects, tests, water, flying, rejection by others, crowds, enclosed places, and injections, to name a few. In addition, desensitization apparently can be used with any behavior disorder initiated by anxiety. For instance, desensitization should be able to be used to treat an alcoholic whose drinking occurs in response to anxiety.

In addition to evaluating the effectiveness of desensitization, clinical research has assessed whether relaxation or graded exposure is a necessary step in the desensitization process. Some studies (for example, Davison, 1968) found no clinical improvement when relaxation was not part of the desensitization process, while other experiments (for example, Miller & Nowas, 1970) indicated that relaxation was not essential. Schubot (1966) reported that only extremely phobic individuals needed the relaxation phase. Rimm and Masters (1979) suggested that because only severely phobic people seek treatment, relaxation should be included in desensitization therapy.

Additionally, Krapft (1967) discovered that the presentation of the scenes in descending order was approximately as effective as the typically employed ascending order. The reduction in phobic behavior with the use of descending order is not surprising; the flooding technique (or forced exposure to the CS; see Chapter 6) shows that exposure to the feared stimulus is sufficient to eliminate phobic behavior. However, Rimm and Masters (1979) pointed out that intense fear is experienced if the items at the top of the hierarchy are presented first. In contrast, the generalization of relaxation occurring during the standard desensitization procedure reduces the anxiety level exhibited when the patient reaches the items at the top of the hierarchy. Thus, the graded ascending exposure is preferred because it reduces the aversiveness of the therapy. Perhaps the most positive aspect of desensitization treatment is that it represents a relatively painless method of suppressing phobic behavior.

Explorations for the Future

Desensitization is a well-established application of Pavlovian conditioning. New applications based on current research are presently being developed; we will look at two of these new applications in this section.

An Intense Craving   In Chapter 1 we discovered that animals and people experience withdrawal following a drug exposure. The withdrawal from the drug can be quite intense and can act to motivate continued use of the drug. Our discussion of Siegel's work earlier in this chapter indicated that the opponent withdrawal state could be conditioned to the environmental cues surrounding drug administration. Exposure to these cues can produce withdrawal as a conditioned response. The conditioned withdrawal response in turn produces a drug craving which then motivates the person to take the drug. Further, the greater the intensity of the withdrawal response, the greater the craving and the higher the likelihood of continued drug use.

Can an environmental stimulus produce withdrawal symptoms? Wikler and Pescor (1967) demonstrated that the *conditioned withdrawal reaction* can be elicited even after months of abstinence. They repeatedly injected dogs with morphine when the animals were in a distinctive cage. The addicted dogs were then allowed to overcome their unconditioned withdrawal reaction in their home cages and were not injected for several months. When placed in the distinctive cages again, these dogs showed a strong withdrawal reaction, including excessive shaking, hypothermia, loss of appetite, and increased emotionality.

Why is it so difficult for an addict to stop using drugs? Whenever an addict encounters the cues associated with a drug (for example, the end of a meal for a smoker), a conditioned withdrawal will be elicited. The experience of this withdrawal may motivate the person to resume taking the drug. According to Solomon (1980), it is this conditioned withdrawal reaction that makes eliminating addictions so difficult.

Any treatment of substance abuse needs to pay attention to conditioned withdrawal reactions. To ensure a permanent cure, an addict must not only stop "cold turkey" and withstand the pain of withdrawal but also extinguish the conditioned withdrawal reactions produced by all of the cues associated with the addictive behavior. Ignoring these conditioned withdrawal reactions increases the likelihood that addicts will eventually return to their addictive behavior. Consider the alcoholic who goes to a bar just to socialize. Even though the individual may have abstained for weeks, the environment of the bar can produce a conditioned withdrawal reaction and motivate him or her to resume drinking.

Can exposure to drug-related stimuli enhance an addict's ability to avoid relapse? Charles O'Brien and his colleagues (see Childress, Ehrman, McLellan, &

O'Brien, 1986) have addressed this issue. These researchers repeatedly exposed cocaine addicts to the stimuli associated with their drug taking. Extinction experiences for these cocaine abusers involved watching videotapes of the "cook-up" procedure, listening to audiotapes of cocaine talk, and handling drug paraphernalia. The researchers reported that their patients' withdrawal responses and craving for drugs decreased as a result of exposure to drug-related cues. Further, the extinction treatment significantly reduced the resumption of drug use. Their results indicate the important role of the environment in motivating addictive behavior. We can expect greater application in the future of this extinction procedure in the treatment of addictive disorders.

The Conditioning of Immune System Suppression   Robert Ader and Nathan Cohen (see Ader & Cohen, 1981, 1982, 1985) discovered that environmental events could suppress the functioning of the immune system. Interestingly, they made this discovery by accident. Following the pairing of saccharin-flavored water (CS) with cyclophosphamide (UCS), a drug that produces nausea, Ader and Cohen extinguished the aversion to the saccharin-flavored water. They reported that some of the test animals died as a result of the presentation of the CS without the UCS.

Why would presentation of saccharin-flavored water kill some of the animals? Ader and Cohen (1981) recognized that cyclophosphamide not only produces nausea but also suppresses the immune system. Perhaps the association of saccharin and cyclophosphamide resulted in the conditioning of immune system suppression as well as nausea.

Ader and Cohen (1981) tested the idea that conditioned immune system suppression was responsible for the death of animals exposed to the saccharin-flavored water. They first injected animals with red blood cells from sheep. This alien substance normally activates the animals' immune system and produces high levels of antibodies. Following injection of the red blood cells, some animals were presented saccharin paired with cyclophosphamide. Other animals did not experience the saccharin-cyclophosphamide pairing. All animals then were given several extinction trials in which saccharin was presented alone. Ader and Cohen reported that the presence of saccharin during extinction produced significantly fewer antibodies in those animals that received saccharin paired with cyclophosphamide than in animals that had not experienced saccharin as the CS. These results indicate that exposure to an environmental event (saccharin) associated with the drug cyclophosphamide produced immune system suppression as a CR.

The conditioning of the immune system could be used to treat diseases of the immune system. The drug cyclophosphamide is used to suppress the immune system as part of the treatment for lupus, a disorder in which the immune system turns the body against itself. Yet, cyclophosphamide has some seriously disabling side effects. Perhaps the dose of cyclophosphamide could be reduced and supplemented with a psychological treatment to suppress the immune system. Ader and Cohen (1982) provided support of this view by showing that conditioning of immune system suppression delayed the development of systemic lupus erythe-

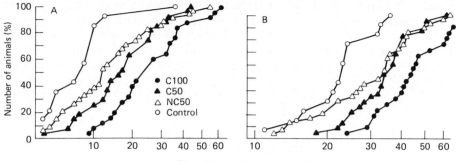

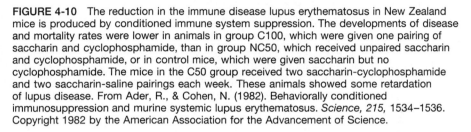

Time after conditioning (weeks)

FIGURE 4-10 The reduction in the immune disease lupus erythematosus in New Zealand mice is produced by conditioned immune system suppression. The developments of disease and mortality rates were lower in animals in group C100, which were given one pairing of saccharin and cyclophosphamide, than in group NC50, which received unpaired saccharin and cyclophosphamide, or in control mice, which were given saccharin but no cyclophosphamide. The mice in the C50 group received two saccharin-cyclophosphamide and two saccharin-saline pairings each week. These animals showed some retardation of lupus disease. From Ader, R., & Cohen, N. (1982). Behaviorally conditioned immunosuppression and murine systemic lupus erythematosus. *Science, 215,* 1534–1536. Copyright 1982 by the American Association for the Advancement of Science.

matosus in New Zealand mice. The experimental (C100) group female mice received one saccharin-cyclophosphamide pairing each week. Ader and Cohen found that experimental animals showed a slower rate of development of lupus disease and lower mortality than animals that did not have saccharin paired with cyclophosphamide (NC50 group) or who received saccharin but not cyclophosphamide (control animals). Some retardation was seen in animals given an equal number of saccharin-cyclosphosphamide and saccharin-saline pairings (C50 group). Figure 4-10 shows the results of Ader and Cohen's study. The possible applications of conditioned immune system suppression will undoubtedly be explored further in the future.

SUMMARY

1 Pavlov suggested that the presentation of the UCS activates the brain area responsible for processing the UCS, which leads to the stimulation of the neural area that generates the UCR. The CS also excites a neural area and if the UCS follows the CS, the brain centers for processing the CS and the UCS are active at the same time. This simultaneous activity results in the establishment of a new neural pathway between the CS and the UCS brain centers. Following conditioning, the CS elicits the UCR as a result of its ability to arouse the UCS brain area.

2 The CR and the UCR often are the same, but there are instances when these two responses appear to differ. The most vivid example of this difference is Siegel's work on the conditioning of a response that appears to be the opposite of a drug's unconditioned effects. Siegel noted that while the unconditioned reaction to morphine is analgesia, or reduced sensitivity to pain, the conditioned response is hypoalgesia, or increased sensitivity to pain. Other examples of conditioned opposing responses include hypoglycemia with insulin UCS and hypothermia with alcohol UCS.

3 Wagner's Sometimes Opponent Process (SOP) theory assumes that the UCS elicits two unconditioned responses—a primary A1 component and a secondary A2 component. The primary A1 component is elicited rapidly by the UCS and decays quickly after the UCS ends. In contrast, the onset and decay of the secondary A2 component are very gradual. Sometimes the A1 and A2 UCR components differ. Yet, at other times, the A1 and A2 components are similar reactions. According to Wagner, it is the secondary A2 UCR that becomes the CR. If the A1 and A2 components are dissimilar, the CR will seem different from the UCR, while the CR will appear to be like the UCR when A1 and A2 components are similar.

4 AESOP, a revision of the SOP theory, assumes that the UCS elicits separate emotive and sensory A1 and A2 unconditioned responses. The emotive and sensory UCRs can have different time courses, which can lead to divergent conditioning outcomes for sensory and emotive CRs.

5 The Rescorla-Wagner associative theory of conditioning assumes that (1) there is a maximum level of conditioning that can be supported by the UCS, (2) the associative strength increases more readily early in training but more slowly later in conditioning as associative strength approaches asymptote, (3) the rate of conditioning is more rapid with some CSs or UCSs than with others, and (4) the level of conditioning on a particular trial is dependent upon the level of conditioning to both the CS and other stimuli present during conditioning. According to the Rescorla-Wagner model, overshadowing occurs due to the rapid accumulation of associative strength to a more salient stimuli, which leaves little conditioning possible to the less salient stimulus. The prior conditioning of associative strength to one stimulus can block the conditioning to a second stimulus because of a lack of available strength, when both stimuli are paired with the UCS.

6 Rescorla suggested that two stimuli paired with a UCS sometimes develop a within-compound association instead of competing for associative strength. The simultaneous experience of the two stimuli is one procedure that can facilitate the formation of within-compound associations. According to Rescorla, potentiation is the result of the establishment of a within-compound association between the salient flavor and non-salient odor cues. Potentiation has been found with simultaneous but not with sequential pairings of odor and flavor stimuli.

7 The comparator theory assumes that animals learn about all CS-UCS relationships. According to the comparator theory, blocking, or failure to respond to the CS_2, occurs because the CS_2-UCS association is weaker than the CS_1-UCS association. Deflation of the value of the CS_1 by extinction results in increased responding to CS_2. Comparator theory assumes that devaluation of CS_1 leads to a comparison more favorable to the CS_2-UCS association.

8 Mackintosh's attentional view suggests that animals seek information that predicts the occurrence of biologically significant events (UCSs). According to Mackintosh, exposure to a stimulus prior to conditioning impairs the later acquisition of the CR when the CS and the UCS are paired. In Mackintosh's view, the animal learns that the CS is irrelevant as the result of preexposure to the CS. Once an animal discovers that a CS is irrelevant, it has difficulty learning that the CS is correlated with the UCS. A change in context has been found to eliminate the CS preexposure effect. This new

context reinstates the orienting response, which leads the animal to attend to the CS and discover its predictive value.

9 Baker's retrospective processing theory assumes that animals are continuously monitoring the contingency between the CS and the UCS. Subsequent experience with CS or UCS alone can lead to reevaluation of the predictive value of the CS. Exposure to other CS-UCS contingencies can also result in a reevaluation of the original CS-UCS association.

10 Pavlovian conditioning principles have been used successfully to modify undesired conditioned responses. Wolpe developed a technique called systematic desensitization, a graduated counterconditioning procedure, to eliminate phobias. The patient first constructs a hierarchy of feared stimuli; relaxation is then paired with the feared stimuli. The counterconditioning process begins with imagining the least feared stimulus for a brief time. The time this stimulus is imagined is increased until the patient can concentrate on this stimulus without any discomfort. The next stimulus on the hierarchy is then associated with relaxation. The process of slowly counterconditioning each level continues until the patient can imagine the most aversive stimulus without becoming anxious. The effectiveness of desensitization is determined by the patient's ability to encounter the actual phobic object. The success of desensitization is considerable; fears of heights, driving, tests, flying, and enclosed places are only a few examples of phobias that have been eliminated using this procedure.

11 The stimuli paired with the use of drugs can elicit a conditioned withdrawal state. This withdrawal state produces a craving for a drug and motivates resumption of drug use. As part of a treatment program for addiction, exposure to the stimuli associated with drug use can extinguish the conditioned craving and reduce the likelihood of continued use.

12 A flavor stimulus presented prior to administration of cyclophosphamide, a drug that suppresses the immune system, can become able to elicit a conditioned suppression of the immune system. Conditioned immune system suppression can help explain the increased likelihood of disease associated with exposure to stressful events. It also represents a potential application of Pavlovian conditioning in the treatment of lupus and other diseases of the immune system.

5

PRINCIPLES AND
APPLICATIONS OF
APPETITIVE
CONDITIONING

A LOSS OF CONTROL

Traci and her husband, Sidney, moved to Las Vegas last month. Sidney had been asked to relocate by the accounting firm for which he worked; the new position would pay more and would be more challenging. The couple discussed the move for several weeks before they agreed to the transfer.

At first, Traci was quite upset about the move. She was a sophomore in college and would have to transfer to a new school. She was also concerned about being so far from home, but Sidney promised that they would visit her family several times each year.

The company took care of all the moving details, and Traci and Sidney were able to find a great apartment near the office. As the time approached, Traci became excited. She had never been to Las Vegas and was especially looking forward to visiting the casinos. Her friends asked her if she was going to do any gambling. Traci enjoyed playing the state lottery and thought that gambling in a casino would be fun.

Traci and Sidney arrived in Las Vegas several days early and decided to stay at one of the large casino hotels. Traci was struck by the glitter of the casino. She could hardly wait to unpack and go down to the gaming floor. Sidney did not seem interested in gambling. He was tired and wanted to take a nap. He suggested she go by herself to the casino. When he awoke, he would come down and meet her for dinner.

Traci decided to play the $5 blackjack table. To her surprise, she got blackjack on her first hand and won $7.50. The thrill of winning was fantastic and she bet another $5 on the next hand. She lost that hand and was disappointed. She continued to play for the next two hours until Sidney came down to meet her. Traci did not want to leave. She was down $25 but felt that her luck was changing. Reluctantly, she agreed to go to dinner. Throughout the meal she could think of nothing else but getting back to blackjack.

Afterwards, Traci and Sidney returned to the casino. Sidney wanted to tour the town, but Traci was insistent upon gambling. Had she not been self-conscious, she would have run back to the blackjack tables. She decided to try her luck at the $10 table and became quite excited when the first card she was dealt was an ace.

Why was Traci so anxious about returning to the blackjack table? Winning a hand of blackjack can be a very powerful reinforcer. Traci's excitement was due to the reinforcing power of winning. In this chapter, we will examine the influence of reinforcement on behavior. Gambling can be a seriously impairing behavior. Unless Traci can limit her gambling activities, she might be headed for serious trouble. The use of reinforcement to alter undesired behavior will be described later.

THE ACQUISITION OF AN APPETITIVE RESPONSE

Skinner's Contribution

In 1938, B. F. Skinner conducted an extensive investigation of the influence of reinforcement on behavior (see Chapter 2). His work showed that reinforcement has a significant impact on our actions. The concept of contingency is a central aspect of Skinner's theory. A *contingency* is a specified relationship between behavior and reinforcement. According to Skinner, the environment determines contingencies, and people must perform the appropriate behavior to obtain a reinforcer.

What is a *reinforcer?* We discovered in Chapter 2 that Thorndike thought of a reinforcer as a satisfying state, while Hull equated reinforcement with drive reduction. Skinner rejected such internal explanations of reinforcement; instead, he proposed that an event is reinforcing if it increases the frequency of behavior that precedes the event. Thus, Skinner defined reinforcement by the degree of influence on future behavior. In Skinner's view, any event that increases behavioral probability is a reinforcer.

You might wonder why Skinner defined reinforcement in terms of its influence on behavior. One reason is that the same event may be reinforcing to one person but not to another. Rather than using one's own perspective on what is satisfying or drive reducing, a psychologist can select a reinforcer based on its observed effect on behavior. This definition forces the psychologist to ignore preconceptions about what might be an effective reinforcer and to select one that actually works. We will have more to say about the use of reinforcement to modify behavior.

The Distinction between Instrumental and Operant Conditioning

Psychologists have used many different procedures to study the impact of reinforcement on behavior. Some psychologists have examined learning in a setting where the opportunity to respond is constrained; that is, the animal or person being studied has limited opportunity to behave. For example, suppose a psychologist is rewarding an animal for running down an alley or turning right in a T-maze (see Figure 5-1). In both of these situations, the animal has a limited opportunity to gain reward. The rat can run down the alley or turn right in the maze and be rewarded, but future opportunities are determined by whether or not the researcher puts the rat back in the alley or maze. Thus, the rat has no control over how often it has the opportunity to obtain reward.

When the environment constrains the opportunity for reward, the researcher is investigating *instrumental conditioning*. Evidence of the acquisition of an instrumental response could be how rapidly the rat runs down the alley or how many errors the rat makes in the maze.

Consider the following example to illustrate the instrumental conditioning process: A parent is concerned about his or her child's failure to do required homework. The child could be rewarded each evening following the completion of assigned homework. The child can obtain reward by doing homework; however, the child has only a single opportunity to gain reward each evening.

Operant conditioning involves situations in which there is no constraint on the amount of reinforcement that can be obtained. In an *operant conditioning situation,* an animal or a person is able to control the frequency of responding and thereby determine the amount of reinforcement obtained. The lack of response constraint allows the behavior to be repeated, and evidence of learning is the frequency and consistency of responding. (There often is some limit on the length of time that reinforcement is available, but within that time period, the animal or person controls the amount of reinforcement received.)

B. F. Skinner needed a simple structured environment in order to study operant behavior, so he invented his own. This apparatus, called an *operant chamber,* is an enclosed environment with a small bar on the inside wall. There is a dispenser for presenting either food or liquid reinforcement when the bar is pressed. (A more elaborate version of an operant chamber has the capacity to present tones or lights in order to study generalization and discrimination.) The operant chamber has been modified to accommodate many different animal species. Figure 5-2 presents a basic operant chamber, for use with pigeons, in which a pecking key replaces the bar press used for rats and some other species.

Skinner also developed his own methodology to study behavior. More interested in observing the rate of a behavior than the intensity of a specific response, he developed the cumulative recorder (refer to Figure 5.2). The pen attached to the recorder moves at a specific rate across the page; at the same time, each bar-press response produces an upward movement on the pen, thus enabling the experimenter to determine the rate of behavior. Modern technology has replaced

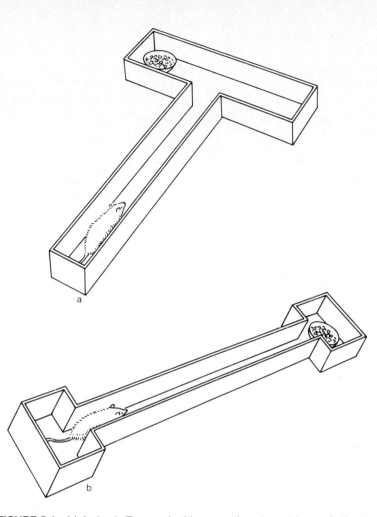

FIGURE 5-1   (a) A simple T-maze. In this maze, the rat must learn whether to turn left or right to obtain reward. (b) A runway. In this apparatus, the rat receives reward when it reaches the goal box; latency to run down the alley is the index of performance. By Edmund Fantino and Cheryl A. Logan. *The experimental analysis of behavior: A biological perspective.* Copyright © 1979 by W. H. Freeman and Company. Reprinted by permission.

the cumulative recorder with a computer that generates sophisticated graphics showing the animal's behavior.

There are many real-world examples of operant conditioning. In the chapter-opening vignette, Traci was being reinforced in an operant conditioning situation. There were no constraints on the number of reinforcers that she could earn, and the amount of reinforcement was partly determined by the number of times she played blackjack. Other instances of operant conditioning include fishing (when

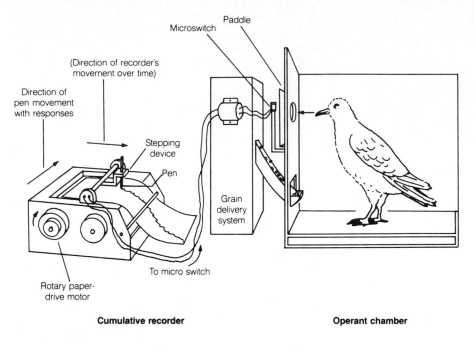

FIGURE 5-2 Operant chamber designed for pigeons. When the pigeon pecks the key, reinforcement (a pellet) is delivered. Each peck produces an upward deflection on the cumulative recorder, providing a permanent record of the pigeon's behavior. From Swenson, L. C. (1980). *Theories of learning.* Belmont, CA: Wadsworth.

a person can freely cast) and dating (when the individual can ask out as many people as he or she wants).

Skinner felt that operant behavior is not elicited by a stimulus. Instead, he believed that an animal or a person voluntarily emits a specific behavior in order to receive reinforcement. Yet, environmental stimuli do affect operant responding. According to Skinner, environmental events set the occasion for operant behavior; that is, they inform the animal or the person when reinforcement is available and thus act to motivate operant responding. (The occasion-setting function of environmental stimuli will be examined in Chapter 7.)

Instrumental behavior is also influenced by environmental circumstance. Thorndike assumed that stimulus-response connections developed as a result of reward (see Chapter 2). Hull also proposed that S-R associations were developed during instrumental conditioning. Conditioned stimuli have a powerful influence over instrumental activity; we will see this influence in Chapter 7.

In the next three sections we will examine several processes that affect instrumental and operant behavior. We will discover that these processes have a comparable influence on both instrumental and operant conditioning.

One further point deserves mentioning at this time. Reward and reinforcer are two frequently used concepts in psychology. For our purposes, there is no distinction between the two concepts. The concept of reward is typically used in instrumental conditioning situations, while a reinforcer usually is used in operant conditioning. We will maintain this distinction between reward and reinforcer to help distinguish instrumental and operant conditioning.

Types of Reinforcers

Skinner (1938) identified several different categories of reinforcers. A *primary reinforcer* has innate reinforcing properties; a *secondary reinforcer* has developed its reinforcing properties through its association with primary reinforcers. For example, food is a primary reinforcer, whereas money is a secondary reinforcer.

A number of variables affect the strength of a secondary reinforcer. First, *the magnitude of the primary reinforcer paired with the secondary reinforcing stimulus influences the reinforcing power of the secondary reinforcer.* Butter and Thomas (1958) presented a click prior to either an 8 percent sucrose solution or a 24 percent solution. These investigators found that rats made significantly more responses to the cue associated with the larger than with the smaller reinforcer. These results indicate that a stimulus paired with a large reinforcer acquires more reinforcing properties than a cue associated with a small reinforcer.

Second, *the number of pairings of the secondary stimulus and primary reinforcer affects the strength of the secondary reinforcer.* Many experiments (see Bersh, 1951; Hall, 1951; Miles, 1956) have found that the greater the number of secondary reinforcing stimulus–primary reinforcer pairings, the stronger the reinforcing power of the secondary reinforcer. For example, Bersh (1951) presented a 3-second light cue prior to 10, 20, 40, 80, or 120 reinforcements (food) for bar pressing. After training, primary reinforcement was discontinued and the bar-press response extinguished; this procedure reduced the bar-press response strength for all subjects. The testing phase consisted of the presentation of the light following a bar-press response. As seen in Figure 5-3, the number of responses to produce the light increased as a function of light-food pairings; these results point out that the reinforcing power of a secondary reinforcer increases with greater numbers of pairings of the secondary reinforcing stimulus and the primary reinforcer.

Third, *the time elapsing between the presentation of a secondary reinforcing stimulus and the primary reinforcer affects the strength of the secondary reinforcer.* Bersh (1951) varied the interval between light and food reinforcement in an operant chamber; the food followed the light stimulus by either 0.5, 1.0, 2.0, 4.0, or 10.0 seconds. Bersh observed that the number of responses emitted to obtain the light cue decreased as the interval between the secondary and the primary reinforcers increased. Bersh's results indicate that the power of a secondary reinforcer decreases as the interval between the secondary reinforcer stimulus and the primary reinforcer increases.

We have discovered that the value of the primary reinforcer, the number of pairings, and the temporal delay affect the reinforcing strength of a secondary reinforcer. The influence of these variables is not surprising: Secondary reinfor-

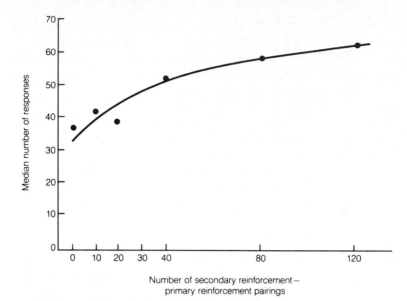

FIGURE 5-3 The strength of a secondary reinforcer increases as a function of the number of secondary and primary reinforcer pairings during acquisition. The measure of the power of the secondary reinforcer is the number of responses emitted during the first 10 minutes of testing. Adapted from Bersh, P. J. (1951). The influence of two variables upon the establishment of a secondary reinforcer for operant responses. *Journal of Experimental Psychology, 41,* 62–73. Copyright 1951 by the American Psychological Association. Reprinted by permission.

cers acquire their reinforcing ability through the Pavlovian conditioning process. As we learned in Chapter 3, these variables influence the association of a conditioned stimulus and an unconditioned stimulus.

Skinner also distinguished between positive and negative reinforcers. A *positive reinforcer* is an event added to the environment that increases the frequency of the behavior that produced it. Examples of positive reinforcers include food and money. The termination of an aversive event can also be reinforcing. When the reinforcer is the termination of adversity, the reinforcer is referred to as a *negative reinforcer.*

In an experimental demonstration of a negative reinforcer, Skinner (1938) observed that rats learned to bar press to turn off electric shock. As a real-world example, suppose a teacher is standing over a child doing schoolwork, encouraging the child to complete the assignment. As a result of the teacher's presence, the child rapidly finishes the work. When the child completes the homework, the teacher leaves. In our example, the teacher's presence is considered aversive, and the child's finishing his or her homework is reinforced by the teacher's leaving.

Shaping

The environment specifies the behavior necessary to obtain reinforcement. However, many operant behaviors occur infrequently or not at all, making it unlikely that the behavior-reinforcement contingency will be experienced. Under such conditions, the result is either no change or a slow change in the frequency of the behavior. Skinner (1938) developed *shaping* or the *successive approximation procedure* to increase the rate at which an operant behavior is learned. During shaping, a behavior with a higher baseline rate of responding than the desired behavior is selected and reinforced. When this behavior increases in frequency, the contingency is then changed and another behavior which is a closer approximation to the desired final behavior is reinforced. The contingency is slowly changed until the only way that the animal can obtain reinforcement is by performing the appropriate behavior.

Training a Rat to Bar Press Many scientists have demonstrated that the successive approximation technique effectively and quickly modifies behavior. This technique has been used, for example, to train a rat to bar press to obtain reinforcement. A rat's operant rate of bar pressing is not necessarily zero, since an animal exploring a small operant chamber may occasionally hit the bar. Therefore, the rat on its own might learn the association between pressing the bar and obtaining food. However, this self-training procedure is often slow, and the rate of learning varies considerably between animals. Shaping of bar pressing is used to ensure a rapid acquisition of desired behavior.

The first stage of the shaping procedure involves reinforcing the rat for eating out of the food dispenser. When this feeding response occurs consistently (which will be only a short time after training begins), the contingency must be changed to a closer approximation of the final bar-press response. The second stage of shaping consists of reinforcing the rat when it is moving away from the food dispenser (refer to Figure 5-4). The moving-away response continues to be reinforced until this behavior occurs consistently; then the contingency is changed again.

In the third phase of shaping, the rat is reinforced only for moving away from the dispenser in the direction of the bar. The change in contingency at first causes the rat to move in a number of directions. The experiemnter must wait, reinforcing only movement toward the bar. The shaping procedure is continued, with closer and closer approximations reinforced until the rat presses the bar. At this point, shaping is complete. The use of shaping to develop a bar-press response is a reliable technique and can be used to train most rats to bar press in approximately an hour. Let's next consider a real-world application of the shaping technique.

Shaping Social Discourse Many parents struggle to teach their children social skills. Even simple social skills like talking with company can be difficult for many children. Many parents undoubtedly use reinforcement (probably praise)

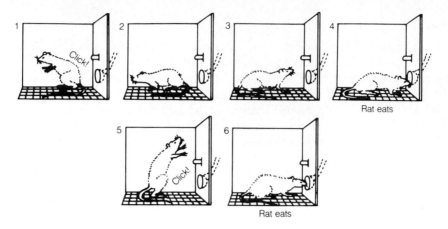

FIGURE 5-4   Shaping a bar-press response in rats. In the initial phase, the rat is reinforced for eating out of the pellet dispenser (not pictured). During the second phase of shaping (scenes 1, 2, 3, and 4), the rat must move away from the dispenser to receive reinforcement. Later in the shaping process (scenes 5 and 6), the rat must move toward the bar for food. From *Psychology* (2d ed.), by Camille Wortman and Elizabeth F. Loftus. Copyright 1985 by Alfred A. Knopf, Inc. Reprinted by permission of the publisher.

and punishment (probably scolding) to try to teach their children social skills. Yet, parents typically reinforce only the final response. Because children need considerable practice to learn effective social skills, children may experience much frustration and give up.

Parents can employ the shaping technique to teach social skills to their children. Beginning by reinforcing a behavior that their children can readily perform (for example, opening the door for company), parents should then gradually change the contingencies to train more complex behaviors. Now the child must say hello to company in order to be reinforced. Next, a question such as "How are you today?" or "Would you like something to drink?" would yield reinforcement. By successively reinforcing behaviors that more and more closely resemble the final desired behavior, parents can quickly teach their children to converse with others.

Section Review

Reinforcers have a powerful influence on human behavior. According to Skinner, a reinforcer is an event whose occurrence increases the frequency of behavior that produces it. A contingency specifies the behavior needed to produce reinforcement. Instrumental conditioning refers to situations in which there are constraints on the opportunity to gain reward; operant conditioning has no constraints and the animal or person can freely respond to obtain reinforcement.

Primary reinforcers possess innate reinforcing ability, whereas secondary reinforcers develop the capacity to reinforce operant or instrumental behavior. The reinforcing property of a secondary reinforcer is determined by (1) the amount of primary reinforcement associated with the secondary reinforcer, (2) the number of pairings of the primary and secondary reinforcers, and (3) the delay between primary and secondary reinforcement. A positive reinforcer is an event, such as food or money, the occurrence of which has reinforcing properties; in contrast, a negative reinforcer is the termination of an aversive event.

The environment specifies the relationship between the appropriate response and reinforcement; however, when the level of responding is zero, the operant response will not increase in frequency despite the contingency between reinforcement and the operant response. Furthermore, learning is slow if the rate of responding is low. The shaping procedure can be used to ensure rapid conditioning. Shaping involves reinforcing a response that occurs at a high rate and then changing the contingency so that closer and closer approximations to the final behavior are necessary to produce reinforcement.

We have learned that the contingency between behavior and reinforcement influences how we act. Our discussion has focused on situations in which a single behavior produces reinforcement. However, reinforcement typically is not programmed to occur like this; usually, we must not only learn how to act to be reinforced, but also how often and/or when to behave. Skinner's research (see Ferster & Skinner, 1957; Skinner, 1938) called this aspect of the contingency the *schedule of reinforcement,* which specifies how often or when we must act to receive reinforcement.

Schedules of Reinforcement

Reinforcement can be programmed using two basic methods. First, reinforcement can be provided on the basis of the number of responses emitted. A situation in which the contingency specifies that a certain number of responses are necessary to produce reinforcement was labeled a *ratio schedule of reinforcement* by Skinner (1938).

Reinforcement also can be scheduled on a time basis; Skinner called the programming of reinforcement on the basis of time an *interval schedule of reinforcement.* In an interval schedule, reinforcement becomes available at a certain period of time after the last reinforcement. Any behavior occurring during the interval receives no reinforcement, with the first response occurring at the end of the interval being reinforced. It should be noted that in an interval schedule, reinforcement must be obtained before another interval begins.

There are two classes of ratio and interval schedules: fixed and variable reinforcement. In a fixed-ratio (FR) schedule, a constant number of responses is necessary to produce reinforcement. In contrast, in a variable-ratio (VR) schedule, an average number of responses produces reinforcement; that is, the number of responses needed to obtain reinforcement varies from one reinforcer to the next. Reinforcement can be programmed on a fixed-interval (FI) schedule of reinforcement, in which the same interval always separates available reinforcements. Also, reinforcement can become available after a varying interval of time. With a var-

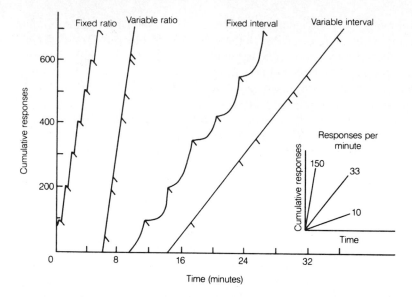

FIGURE 5-5 Samples of cumulative records of bar-press responding under the simple schedules of reinforcement. The slash marks on the response records indicate the presentations of reinforcement. The steeper the cumulative response gradient, the higher the animal's rate of responding.

iable-interval (VI) schedule, there is an average interval between available reinforcements, but the exact interval between each reinforcement differs.

We have discussed four types of reinforcement schedules. These schedules of reinforcement have an important influence on our behavior. The pattern and rate of behavior are very different depending on the type of reinforcement schedule. Let's now briefly examine the behavioral characteristics of these reinforcement schedules. The interested reader should refer to Ferster and Skinner (1957) for a detailed discussion of schedules of reinforcement.

Fixed-Ratio Schedule   On a fixed ratio schedule, a specific number of responses are necessary to produce reinforcement. In an FR-1 (or continuous) schedule, reinforcement is given after a single response. Likewise, 10 responses must occur to receive reinforcement on an FR-10 schedule. As an example of a fixed-ratio schedule, a rat may be reinforced after every 10 bar presses. This would be a case of an FR-10 schedule. Two real-world examples of a fixed-ratio schedule are an adult getting a dollar for every five telephone books delivered and a child receiving a toy from a company for sending in five cereal box tops.

Fixed-ratio schedules produce a consistent response rate; that is, an animal or a person responds at a steady rate during the entire time that reinforcement is possible or until satiation occurs (refer to Figure 5-5). Furthermore, the rate of responding increases with higher FR schedules. For example, Collier, Hirsch, and

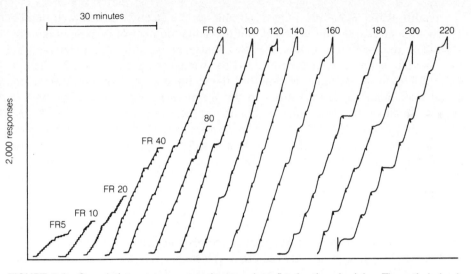

FIGURE 5-6 Cumulative response records on various fixed-ratio schedules. The rat's behavior is affected by the fixed ratio used during conditioning. The rate of responding increases with higher FR ratios, and the postreinforcement pause occurs only at highest FR schedules. From Collier, G., Hirsch, E., & Hamlin, P. H. (1972). The ecological determinants of reinforcement in the rat. *Physiology and Behavior, 9,* 705–716. Copyright 1972, Pergamon Press, Ltd.

Hamlin (1972) noted that rats bar press at a higher rate on an FR-20 schedule than on an FR-10 schedule and higher still on an FR-60 schedule than on an FR-40 schedule (see Figure 5-6). Similar results were obtained with pigeons (Felton & Lyon, 1966), cats (Kanarek, 1974), prairie dogs (Todd & Cogan, 1978), and children (Stephens, Pear, Wray, & Jackson, 1975).

Fixed-ratio schedules have another distinctive characteristic. Following reinforcement, responding will temporarily stop. The pause after reinforcement is called a *postreinforcement pause*. After the pause, responding resumes at the rate present before reinforcement. Therefore, the animal or person on a fixed-ratio schedule either responds at the intensity characteristic of that ratio or does not respond at all.

A postreinforcement pause is not observed with all fixed-ratio schedules. The higher the number of responses needed to obtain reinforcement, the more likely it is that a pause will follow reinforcement. As seen in Figure 5-6, there is no pause after reinforcement on an FR-100 schedule, but a pause does follow reward on an FR-200 schedule. The length of the pause also varies; the higher the ratio schedule, the longer the pause (see Felton & Lyon, 1966; Todd & Cogan, 1978). Other researchers (for example, Collier et al., 1972) have noted that the greater the effort necessary to obtain reinforcement, the longer the pause after receiving reinforcement. The length of the pause also depends upon satiation (Sidman & Stebbins, 1954). Sidman and Stebbins found that the greater the satiation, the longer the pause following reinforcement.

Variable-Ratio Schedule   On a variable-ratio schedule, an average number of responses produces reinforcement, but the actual number of responses required to produce reinforcement varies over the course of training. To understand the VR schedule, suppose a rat is reinforced for bar pressing on a VR-20 schedule. While the rat must bar press 20 times on the average to receive a reinforcement, the rat may press the bar 10 times to get the reinforcer one time, but have to respond 30 times the next time to obtain the next reinforcer. Two real-world examples of a variable ratio schedule are a door-to-door salesperson who makes two consecutive sales and then has to knock on 50 doors before making another sale, and a person at a social gathering who may successfully ask two people in a row for a dance, but then may have to ask five people before finding another dance partner.

Like the FR schedules, VR schedules produce a consistent response rate (refer to Figure 5-5). Furthermore, the greater the average number of responses necessary to produce reinforcement, the higher the response rate. For example, Felton and Lyon (1966) found that rats bar press at a higher rate on a VR-200 schedule than on a VR-50 schedule. Similarly, Ferster and Skinner (1957) observed that pigeons' rate of key pecking was higher on a VR-100 schedule than on a VR-50 schedule and still higher on a VR-200 schedule of reinforcement.

In contrast to the pause after reinforcement on a fixed-ratio schedule, post-reinforcement pauses occur only occasionally on variable-ratio schedules (see Felton & Lyon, 1966, Ferster & Skinner, 1957). The relative absence of pause behavior after reinforcement on VR schedules results in a higher response rate on a VR schedule than on a comparable FR schedule. Thus, rats bar press more times during an hour session on a VR-50 schedule than on an FR-50 schedule (see Figure 5-5).

The high response rate occurring with VR schedules can explain the persistent and vigorous behavior characteristic of gambling. For example, a slot machine is programmed to pay off after an average number of operations. However, the exact number of operations necessary to obtain reinforcement is unpredictable. The behavior of people who play a slot machine for hours, constantly putting money into it, occurs because of the variable-ratio programming of slot machines.

Fixed-Interval Schedule   On an FI schedule, the occurrence of reinforcement depends upon both the passage of time and the exhibition of the appropriate behavior. Reinforcement is available only after a specified period of time, and the first response emitted after the interval has elapsed is reinforced. Therefore, a rat on an FI 1-minute schedule is reinforced for the first bar press after the minute interval has elapsed; in contrast, a rat on an FI 2-minute schedule must wait 2 minutes before its response in reinforced.

One example of a fixed-interval schedule is having the mail delivered at about the same time every day. Making gelatin is another real-world example of a fixed-interval schedule. After cooking, the gelatin is placed in the refrigerator to set. After a few hours, the gelatin is ready to be eaten. However, while the person may eat the gelatin as soon as it is ready, a few hours or even a few days may elapse before the cook actually goes to the refrigerator and obtains the gelatin reinforcement.

Have you ever seen the behavior of a child waiting for gelatin to set? The child will go to the refrigerator, shake the dish, recognize that it is not ready, and place it back in the refrigerator. The child will repeat this action every once in a while. A similar checking behavior occurs when waiting for the mail. With each check, the gelatin is closer to being ready or the mail nearer to being delivered. These behaviors illustrate one aspect of a fixed-interval schedule. After receiving reinforcement on a fixed-interval schedule, an animal or a person stops responding, then slowly increases responding as the time approaches when reinforcement will once more become available (refer to Figure 5.5). This characteristic pattern of responding produced by an FI schedule was referred to as the *scallop effect* by Ferster and Skinner. The scallop effect has been observed with a number of species including pigeons (Catania & Reynolds, 1968, Dews, 1962), rats (Innis, 1979; Madigan, 1978), and humans (Shimoff, Catania, & Matthews, 1981).

Two variables affect the length of the pause seen on FI schedules. First, the ability to withhold responding until close to the end of the interval increases with experience (see Cruser & Klein, 1984; Schneider, 1969). Second, the pause is longer with longer FI schedules (refer to Gentry, Weiss, & Laties, 1983; Schneider, 1969).

While a considerable amount of research has investigated fixed-interval schedules, it is important to note that there are not many real-world situations in which behavior is rewarded on a fixed-interval schedule. Consider the example of a person being paid once a week, a situation often used to illustrate behavior rewarded on a fixed-interval schedule. In reality, being paid weekly is not an example of a fixed-interval schedule; instead, a weekly paycheck reflects the operation of response-cost or negative punishment (refer to Chapter 6). In a response-cost situation, a person receives reinforcement (money) without having to perform a specific behavior but can lose money or be fired for failing to perform the appropriate behavior.

Variable-Interval Schedule   On a VI schedule, there is an average interval of time between available reinforcements; however, the interval of time varies from one reinforcement to the next. For example, the average interval is 2 minutes on a VI 2-minute schedule; yet, one time, the rat may wait only 1 minute between reinforcements and the next time, 5 minutes. Consider the following example to illustrate a variable-interval schedule. Suppose you go fishing. How successful will your fishing trip be? The number of times that you cast is not important. Instead, how often a fish swims by the bait is critical. You may have to wait only a few minutes between catches on one occasion but have to wait many minutes on another.

VI schedules are characterized by a steady rate of responding (see Figure 5-5). Furthermore, the rate of responding is affected by VI length; the longer the average interval between reinforcements, the lower the response rate. For example, Catania and Reynolds (1968) discovered that pigeons responded 60 to 100 times per minute on a VI two-minute schedule, but only 20 to 70 times per minute on a VI 7.1-minute schedule. Similar results were obtained by Nevin (1973) in rats and by Todd and Cogan (1978) in prairie dogs.

The scallop effect which is characteristic of FI schedules does not occur on VI schedules; there is no pause following reinforcement on a VI schedule. However, Catania and Reynolds (1968) reported that the maximum rate of responding on VI schedules occurred just prior to reinforcement.

Compound Schedule The contingency between behavior and reinforcement sometimes involves more than one schedule. In a *compound schedule,* two or more schedules are combined. As an example, consider the rat who must bar press 10 times (FR 10) and wait 1 minute after the last bar press (FI 1 minute) until bar pressing produces reinforcement. The rat must complete both schedules in the appropriate sequence in order to obtain reinforcement. Animals and humans are sensitive to the complexities of schedules and can learn to respond appropriately. An extensive discussion of compound schedules of reinforcement is beyond the scope of this text. Interested readers should consult D'Amato (1970) for a more detailed discussion of the varied compound schedules of reinforcement.

We have learned that in order to obtain reinforcement, animals or people must discover the contingency that exists between behavior and reinforcement. A number of variables affect the acquisition of instrumental behavior. Let's now turn our attention to the factors that influence whether or not we respond according to the contingency and thus obtain reinforcement.

How Readily Is an Instrumental Response Learned?

Although many variables affect the development of instrumental behavior, we will look at two factors in particular that play a significant role in determining the strength of conditioning. First, *the delay of reward affects the level of conditioning.* Contiguity has a dramatic impact on instrumental behavior; the closer in time the response and the reward, the greater the conditioning of the instrumental response. Second, *the strength of conditioning is affected by the magnitude of reward.* The literature shows that in many situations the greater the magnitude of the reward, the higher the level of instrumental responding.

The Importance of Contiguity You help a friend change a tire on his or her car; you're thanked for your assistance. The effect of the social reward is to increase your likelihood of future helping behavior. However, if your friend waits several minutes before thanking you, the impact of the reward is reduced. This observation points to the importance of contiguity on instrumental conditioning: Reward can lead to the acquisition of an instrumental response if it immediately follows the behavior, whereas instrumental learning is impaired if reward is delayed. Furthermore, the longer the delay between the response and reward, the less conditioning that occurs. Many studies have documented the effect of delay

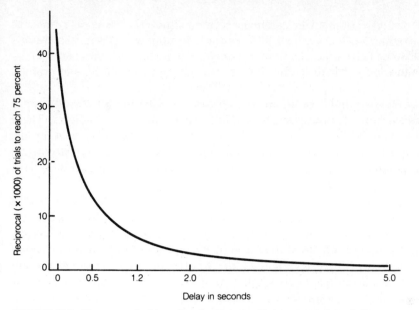

FIGURE 5-7   The amount of learning decreases with increased delay between the instrumental response and reward. The measure of level of learning is the reciprocal × 1000 of the number of trials to reach 75 percent correct choices; thus, the higher the value, the greater the level of learning. From Grice, G. R. (1948). The relation of secondary reinforcement to delayed reward in visual discrimination learning. *Journal of Experimental Psychology, 38,* 1–16. Copyright 1948 by the American Psychological Association. Reprinted by permission.

on the acquisition of an instrumental behavior; several of them are discussed next.

The Effect of Delay   In a classic study, Grice (1948) investigated the role of reward delay on the rat's learning to go into a black chamber instead of a white one. Grice varied the delay between the correct response and reward. In his study, the delay interval was either 0, 0.5, 1.2, 2, 5, or 10 seconds. As seen in Figure 5-7, there is a very steep delay gradient: Little conditioning occurred with delay intervals as short as 1.2 seconds.

However, not all experiments (see Logan, 1952; Perin, 1943; Skinner, 1938) have reported a delay gradient comparable to Grice's data. For example, Perin (1943) found moderate levels of conditioning of bar-press responses even with a 10-second delay, while with a delay of 30 seconds or more, rats were unable to learn to bar press to obtain reinforcement.

Why do the delay gradients differ in Grice's and Perin's experiments? The presence or absence of secondary reward cues is important. The presence of a secondary reward during the interval can strengthen the instrumental behavior and lessen the influence of delay. In contrast, when cues associated with reward are not present during the interval, even a very short delay produces little conditioning. In support of this view, animals in Grice's study spent the delay interval in an environment not associated with reward. In contrast, the rats in Perin's experiment remained in the conditioning environment (the operant chamber) associated with reinforcement during the interval between responding and primary reward.

Delay of Reward and Conditioning in Humans. The importance of reward delay has also been demonstrated by studies using children as subjects. These studies (see Hall, 1976) consistently show that the longer the delay between the instrumental behavior and reward, the poorer the conditioning of the instrumental response. Table 5-1 presents a sample of these delay of reward studies; let's examine one of them more closely.

Terrell and Ware (1961) gave kindergarten and first-grade children two easy problems to solve. The children received immediate reward for responding correctly to one of the problems; a 7-second delay of reward followed the correct solution of the other problem. Terrell and Ware reported that to learn the problems, the children required approximately 7 trials with immediate reward compared with an average of 17 trials when reward was delayed. These observations indicate that a delay between the correct response and the reward interferes with the acquisition of that response.

The Impact of Reward Magnitude

Acquisition of an Instrumental Response. Suppose parents decide to reward their children for learning vocabulary words. The rate of acquisition of the vocabulary words depends upon the magnitude of the reward provided; the larger the reward magnitude, the faster the acquisition of vocabulary words. Many studies (see Hall, 1976) show that the magnitude of reward affects the rate of acquisition of an instrumental response; let's look at several of these studies.

Crespi's 1942 study demonstrates the influence of reward magnitude on the acquisition of an instrumental running response in an alley. Upon reaching the goal box, Crespi's rats received either 1, 4, 16, 64, or 256 units of food. Crespi observed that the greater the reward magnitude, the faster the animals ran down the alley.

Researchers also have shown that reinforcer magnitude affects the acquisition of a bar-press response in an operant chamber. For example, Guttman (1953) varied the amount of reinforcement rats received for bar pressing; animals were given either a 4, 8, 16, or 32 percent sucrose solution following the operant response. Guttman discovered that the greater the reinforcer magnitude was, the faster the animals learned to bar press to obtain reinforcement (refer to Figure 5-8).

Performance of an Instrumental Response Some time ago, my youngest son informed me that $5 was no longer enough money for mowing the yard; he now wanted $10 to do the job. His behavior indicates the critical influence that the magnitude of reward has on the performance of an instrumental behavior. The likelihood and intensity of an instrumental response depends upon the mag-

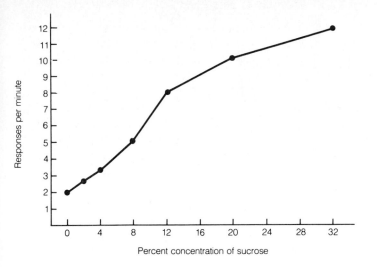

FIGURE 5-8   A rat's rate of responding, or the number of bar-press responses per minute, increases with higher concentrations of sucrose in the water, or the magnitude of reward. Adapted from Guttman, N. (1954). Equal reinforcing values for sucrose and glucose solutions compared with sweetness values. *Journal of Comparative and Physiological Psychology, 47,* 358–361. Copyright 1954 by the American Psychological Association. Reprinted by permission.

nitude of reward provided following the occurrence of a particular response. In many instances, the magnitude of reward must be of a sufficient level in order for the behavior to occur; thus, my son's mowing response would occur only if the payment was sufficiently high. At other times, the instrumental behavior may occur but the intensity of the response depends on the reward magnitude; under these circumstances, the greater the reward magnitude, the higher the level of performance of the instrumental response. The literature (see Pubols, 1960) consistently shows that reward magnitude affects instrumental task performance. This section examines several studies documenting this influence.

Crespi's 1942 study detailed earlier also evaluated the level of instrumental performance as a function of reward magnitude. Crespi discovered that the greater the magnitude was, the faster the rats ran down the alley to obtain reward, an observation which indicates that the magnitude of reward influences the level of instrumental behavior. Other studies also show that reward magnitude determines the level of instrumental performance in the runway situation (see Armus, 1959; Hill & Wallace, 1967; Mellgren, 1972; Reynolds & Pavlik, 1960) and in the operant chamber (see Butter & Thomas, 1958; Conrad & Sidman, 1956; Guttman, Sutterer, & Brush, 1975).

TABLE 5-1
SOME STUDIES INVESTIGATING DELAY OF REWARD WITH NORMAL AND RETARDED CHILDREN

Subjects	Task	Delay intervals	Response measure	Results	Investigators
Preschool children	2-stimulus, 1-choice apparatus, with reward delivered immediately to 1 stimulus and after 7 seconds to the other	0 and 7 seconds	Response speed and preference for one of the two stimuli	Subjects preferred to respond to immediate rewarded stimulus; no difference in response speed.	Lipsitt and Castaneda (1958)
Fourth-grade children	Simultaneous and successive discrimination tasks	0, 3, or 6 seconds	Number correct	No delay-of-reinforcement gradient obtained, although 6-second group performed most poorly.	Erickson and Lipsitt (1960)
Fourth-grade children	2-stimulus (easy) and 3-stimulus (difficult) successive discrimination problems	0, 10, or 30 seconds	Number correct	Increasing delay had progressively deleterious effect on difficult discrimination; no difference among groups with easy task.	Hockman and Lipsitt (1961)
Kindergarten and first-grade children	(1) Discrimination learning with subjects required to learn a size and form problem concurrently (2) 3-stimulus size and form problem learned concurrently	In both (1) and (2), one problem learned with 0-second delay, other problem with 7-second delay.	Number correct	Both (1) and (2) revealed delay resulted in poorer learning.	Terrell and Ware (1961)

Subjects	Task	Delay	Measure	Results	Reference
Moderately and severely retarded children; also normal first graders	2-choice discrimination problem	0, 1.5, 6, or 12 seconds	Errors and trials to criterion	12-second delay significantly increased errors and trials to criterion for all groups. No difference among other delay intervals.	Hetherington, Ross, and Pick (1964)
Mental retardates	Discrimination of geometric forms, e.g., square, subjects required to solve 10 problems (1 problem per day)	0 or 5 seconds	Errors	Delay increased difficulty of problem. Effect appeared to be limited to initial trials on each problem.	Schoelkopf and Orlando (1965)
Mental retardates	2-choice discrimination problem; chosen stimulus was visible or not visible during delay	0, 12, or 18 seconds	Errors and trials to criterion	Zero-second delay significantly superior to 12- or 18-second groups for both conditions.	Ross, Hetherington, and Wray (1965)
Normal and moderately retarded children	Simple discrimination	0 or 12 seconds	Errors and trials to criterion	12-second delay increased errors for retardates; no difference between 0- and 12-second delay for normals.	Hetherington and Ross (1967)
Mental retardates	2-choice discrimination problem	0 or 15 seconds	Number of correct responses	Zero-second delay significantly superior to 15 seconds.	Keeley and Sprague (1969)

Source: Hall, J. F. (1976). *Classical conditioning and instrumental learning: A contemporary approach.* Philadelphia: Lippincott.

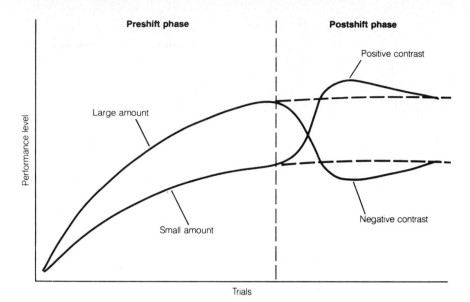

FIGURE 5-9   A higher level of performance occurs with a large reward magnitude during preshift phase. Not only does the level of responding following a shift from high to low reward magnitude decline, but it is also lower than that which would be exhibited if the level of reward had always been low (a depression or negative contrast effect). In contrast, a shift from low to high reward magnitude not only leads to a higher level of responding but also produces a level of responding greater than that which would occur if the higher level had always been used (an elation or positive contrast effect). The contrast effects last for only a few trials, and responding returns to the level appropriate for that reward magnitude.

You may have the impression that the magnitude of reward influences the level of conditioning. However, evidence indicates that the differences in performance reflect motivational rather than learning differences. According to this view, the greater the reward magnitude, the greater the motivation to obtain the reward. How can this approach be validated? In order to assess the relative contribution of learning and motivation, the reward value must be shifted to a higher (or lower) level. If the reward magnitude shift causes a gradual alteration in behavior, the change in responding is thought to reflect a learning influence since learning changes occur slowly; if the alteration in behavior following the shift is rapid, motivational processes are assumed to cause the behavior change.

Many studies (see Crespi, 1942; Zeaman, 1949) report a rapid change in behavior when reward magnitude is shifted, which indicates that motivational differences are responsible for the performance differences associated with differences in reward magnitude (refer to Figure 5-9). For example, Crespi (1942) shifted some animals from a high reward magnitude (256 units) to a moderate reward level (16 units) on trial 20; other animals were shifted from a low (1 pellet) to a moderate reward magnitude. The animals showed a rapid change in behavior on the trial following the shift in reward magnitude: The high-to-moderate-shift animals exhibited a significantly lowered response time on trial 21, whereas the low-to-moderate-shift subjects ran significantly faster on trial 21 than on the preceding trial. Other experiments have documented this rapid change in behavior after a shift in the magnitude of reward; see Zeaman (1949) for another example of this effect.

Importance of Past Experience   Suppose your boss's marginal profits cause your salary to be decreased. Under these conditions, your behavior will be less efficient as the result of the lowered magnitude of reward. How much will your output decline? Research (Crespi, 1942) indicates that you will exhibit less output now than if your salary had always been low (see Figure 5-9). The process in which a shift from a high to a low reward magnitude produces a level of instrumental behavior below that which would be exhibited if the level of reward had always been low is called the *depression effect*.

Perhaps your boss's profits increase and you receive a raise. Under these conditions, your behavior will become more efficient as a result of the higher magnitude of reward. In contrast to the depression effect, a shift from low to high reward magnitude produces a level of instrumental behavior greater than that which would occur if the higher level had always been used. The heightened performance produced by a shift from low to high reward and occurring above that exhibited with a constant high level of reward is called an *elation effect*.

Zeaman (1949) suggested replacing the terms *elation* and *depression* with *positive* and *negative contrast* effects to indicate that the specific context in which a stimulus is experienced can produce exaggerated or reduced effects of this stimulus. Thus, experience with low reward heightens the influence of a high reward (positive contrast effect); that is, a large reward is more effective than it normally would be because of previous experience with a small reward. In contrast, experience exaggerates the impact of a low reward magnitude (negative contrast effect); that is, a small reward is less effective than it would normally be because of experience with a large reward.

Investigations (see Flaherty, 1982) since Crespi's original study have consistently produced a negative contrast effect; yet, research conducted during the 1960s seemed to indicate that the positive contrast effect could not be induced (see Black, 1968). However, Bower (1981) suggested that a ceiling effect was responsible for the inability to produce a positive contrast effect; that is, high reward magnitude alone was causing maximum responding, and therefore the shift from low to high could not raise performance above that of the level exhibited by animals always experiencing the high reward magnitude. Studies (see Mellgren, 1972; Shanab, Sanders, & Premack, 1969) conducted in the late 1960s and early 1970s demonstrated that a positive contrast effect can be produced if animals are initially responding at a level below the upper limit.

We should note that the contrast effects last for only short periods of time. Thus, animals shifted from high to low (or low to high) reward respond at a lower (or higher) level than animals always experiencing the low (or high) reward magnitude for only a few trials.

Why do the contrast effects occur? The emotion of frustration seems to play an important role in the negative contrast effect. According to Flaherty (1985), an animal establishes an expected level of reward during initial acquisition training. The presentation of a lower than expected level of reward in the second phase causes frustration, which interferes with instrumental activity and thereby produces a response level lower than would have been found had the low reward magnitude been the expected reward. Support for this view is provided by the observation that drugs that reduce anxiety in humans eliminate the negative contrast effect; this result has been found with the tranquilizer Librium (Becker & Flaherty, 1983), with alcohol (Becker & Flaherty, 1982), and with barbiturates (Flaherty & Driscoll, 1980; Ridgers & Gray, 1973). Flaherty suggests that the emotional response of elation produced by receiving a reward greater than the expected magnitude may explain the positive contrast effect; however, evidence validating this view is not available.

Influence of Reward Magnitude in Humans We learned in Chapter 2 that many psychologists assume that reward magnitude (or incentive value) influences the acquisition and performance of an instrumental behavior. Although most of the research on reward magnitude has used animals as subjects, some research with people has indicated that reward value affects the performance of an instrumental response. However, differences in reward magnitude are not always reflected in behavioral differences.

Research with young children (see Hall, 1976) has shown that the magnitude of reward does affect the development of an instrumental response. For example, Siegel and Andrews (1962) found that 4- and 5-year-old children responded correctly more often on a task when provided a large reward (for example, a small prize) rather than a small reward (a button). Studies also have shown that reward magnitude influences instrumental behavior in adults. For example, Atkinson's research (see Atkinson, 1958) found that the amount of money paid for successful performance influences the level of achievement behavior.

The Nature of Reinforcement

Skinner (1938) defined a reinforcer as an event whose occurrence will increase the frequency of behavior that produces it. While Skinner was not concerned about when an event would be reinforcing, other psychologists have been interested in specifying the conditions that determine whether or not an event is reinforcing. Premack's probability-differential theory addresses this issue; we start our discussion of the nature of reinforcement with his view.

Premack's Probability-Differential Theory We typically assume that reinforcers are things like food or water. However, activities can also be reinforcers. For example, allowing children to watch television or go to the movies can be a reinforcement for studying. Although food and going to the movies appear to be very different types of reinforcers, Premack's (1959, 1965) *probability-differential theory* indicates that all reinforcers share a common attribute. According to Premack, a reinforcer is any activity whose probability of occurring is greater than that of the reinforced behavior. Therefore, a movie can be a reinforcer for studying if the likelihood of going to the movie is greater than the probability of studying. In Premack's view, it is the eating response to food, not food per se, that is the reinforcer for a rat. Since eating is a more probable behavior than bar pressing, eating can reinforce bar pressing.

Premack's (1959) study using children as subjects illustrates the reinforcing character of high-probability activities. Premack placed a pinball machine next to a candy dispenser. In the first phase of the study, he observed the children's relative rate of responding to each activity. Some children played pinball more frequently than they ate candy and were labeled "manipulators"; other children ate candy more often than they played pinball and were labeled "eaters." During the second phase of the study, mainpulators had to eat in order to play the pinball machine, while eaters were required to play the pinball machine in order to get candy. Premack reported that the contingency increased the number of times the "eaters" played the pinball machine and the amount of pieces of candy eaten by the "manipulators."

Application: The Use of Activity Reinforcers   The use of activities as reinforcers to establish desired modes of behavior has been widespread and quite successful (see Allison, 1989). We will examine several studies that are representative of the application of Premack's probability-differential theory to establish desired behaviors. These studies demonstrate that techniques that alter the behavior-reinforcement contingencies of an individual can be used to establish desired, and eliminate undesired, behaviors.

Nursery school–aged children have short attention spans and have a tendency to become unruly. Homme, de Baca, Devine, Steinhorst, and Rickert (1963) provide an early application of Premack's probability-differential theory to encourage desired behavior in young children. High-probability behaviors, such as running around the room and pushing chairs, were used as reinforcers for low-probability behaviors, such as, sitting quietly and looking at the blackboard. These researchers reported that the procedure produced relatively quiet and attentive children in just a few days.

In more recent work, Konarski and his associates (see Konarski, 1985; Konarski, Johnson, Crowell, & Whitman, 1980) found that activities as reinforcers could be used to increase academic performance in educable mentally retarded students. The academic behaviors involved were reading, coloring, cursive writing, and arithmetic. These researchers found that each of the behaviors could be increased by restricting access to another activity. For example, if reading activity were a low-frequency behavior, its occurrence was increased if it were necessary for coloring, a higher-frequency behavior.

The application of Premack's ideas has not been limited to educational settings; the business environment has proven to be an ideal location to modify behavior using activities as reinforcers. For example, Luthans, Paul, and Baker (1981) reported that total sales increased among department store salespersons when a contingency was established between low-probability sales activity and high-probability time-off-with-pay activity. In other words, the salespersons increased their sales performance when that activity allowed them time off with pay. O'Hara, Johnson, and Beehr (1985) noted a similar increase in sales with this contingency in telephone solicitors.

Psychologists using activities as reinforcers have made an important discovery. Not only can the use of an activity as a reinforcer increase performance of the target behavior, but it can also decrease the level of the activity used as the reinforcer (see Allison, 1989). And if the activity used as a reinforcer is undesirable, this represents an effective method to suppress an inappropriate behavior. To illustrate this application, suppose a child occasionally screams. Even though screaming may not occur frequently, it can be annoying. A parent could decrease screaming by allowing a child to scream contingent upon the occurrence of the target behavior (for example, reading). This contingency would act to increase a desired activity such as reading and decrease an undesired behavior such as screaming.

Premack's probability-differential theory assumes that an activity will be reinforcing if its probability of occurrence is greater than that of the activity being reinforced. Timberlake and Allison's response deprivation theory presents a different view of conditions under which an activity can be a reinforcer.

Response Deprivation Theory   William Timberlake and James Allison proposed that response deprivation created by the establishment of a behavior-reinforcer contingency causes an activity to be a reinforcer (see Timberlake & Allison, 1974). According to Timberlake and Allison, animals respond at a specific level when given free access to objects important to their survival. For example, a rat given free access to food will consume approximately the same amount of food each day; the rat responds to food at the same level each day because this behavior is adaptive and enhances the rat's chances of survival. When an animal's access to an object is restricted and, therefore, its level of responding is lowered, the animal will be motivated to return to its previous level of responding. Thus, food deprivation will cause a rat to engage in behaviors that will gain access to food and thereby restore responding to the predeprivation level. Further, Timberlake and Allison assert that a certain activity becomes a reinforcer because the establishment of a behavior-reinforcer contingency restricts the opportunity to participate in that activity. When a contingency is established, the animal increases the level of operant behavior in order to return the performance of the restricted activity to its baseline level of responding.

Timberlake and Allison (1974) conducted a number of studies that support their *response deprivation theory*. Let's briefly examine one of these studies. A rat was deprived of access to a running wheel, and a contingency was established so that the rat was required to drink in order to gain access to the wheel. Even though the rat's baseline level of responding was higher for drinking than running, Timberlake and Allison found that the contingency between drinking and running led to an increase in the rat's level of drinking. Apparently, restricting access to an activity results in that activity's becoming a reinforcer. These results also indicate that the relative level of responding does not determine whether or not an activity acts as a reinforcer. Instead, restricting access to low-frequency activity, such as running, can increase the response level of another, high-frequency activity, such as drinking, if performing the first activity will provide access to the restricted one.

Behavioral Allocation   We have learned that a contingency restricts an animal's access to an activity. Consider the rat that must bar press to obtain food. It cannot eat freely but instead must bar press to have access to food. How many times will the rat bar press? Intuitively, one might say that the rat would bar press until it was no longer motivated to eat. Unfortunately, in many circumstances, the contingency would require more responses than the animal is willing to emit to satisfy its desire for the food. Under these conditions, the rat will not bar press enough to reach its predeprivation baseline level of food consumption. A number of psychologists (see Allison, 1983, 1989; Rachlin & Burkhard, 1978; Staddon, 1988) have provided some insight into the question of how many times a rat will bar press to obtain reward.

Suppose an animal could freely engage in two activities. It might not respond equally, but instead its level of responding would be higher for one behavior than for the other. As an example, the animal might show 50 A responses and 150 B responses. Allison referred to the free operant level of two responses as the *paired basepoint* or *blisspoint*. The blisspoint would be the unrestricted level of performance of both behaviors.

When a contingency is established, free access to one behavior is restricted and the animal must emit a second behavior to have access to the first. Returning to our example, the contingency could be that one response A leads to one response B. This contingency means that the animal cannot attain blisspoint; that is, it cannot emit response B three times as much as A.

What does an animal do when it cannot attain blisspoint? According to Allison (1989), the animal will respond in a manner that allows it to be as close to the paired basepoint as possible. Figure 5-10 shows how this process works. As can be seen in this figure, blisspoint is three B responses to one A response, but the contingency specifies one B to one A. Does the animal emit 50, 100, 150, or 200 A responses? The closest point on the contingency line is point 1. At this point, the animal would emit 100 A responses to receive 100 B responses (reinforcer). This level of A responding would bring the animal closest to blisspoint.

The concept of blisspoint suggests that an animal does not randomly emit contingent responses. Instead, the animal allocates a certain number of responses so that it can be closest to blisspoint. The concept of blisspoint comes from economic theory and assumes that a person acts to minimize cost and maximize gain. If we think of a contingent behavior as a cost and reinforcing activity as a

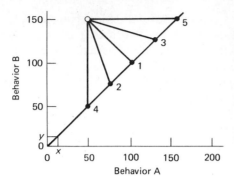

FIGURE 5-10
This graph shows the blisspoint (open circle) for behaviors A and B. The contingency states that one behavior A is necessary for access to one behavior B. The equilibrium point, or minimum distance to blisspoint, on the contingency line is point 1. Responding at other points takes animal farther away from blisspoint. From Allison, J. (1989). The nature of reinforcement. In S. B. Klein & R. R. Mowrer (Eds.), *Contemporary learning theories: Instrumental conditioning theory and the impact of biological constraints on learning.* Hillsdale, N.J.: Erlbaum.

gain, the *behavioral allocation view* assumes that the animal is emitting the minimum number of contingent responses in order to obtain the maximum level of reinforcing activities. This approach assumes that the economic principles that apply to purchasing products tell us about the level of responding in an operant conditioning setting.

The Matching Law   There are many circumstances in which a simple behavior-reinforcement contingency is not operative. Instead, the animal or person must choose from two or more contingencies. To illustrate this type of situation, suppose that an operant chamber has two keys instead of one, and the subject (in this case, a pigeon) receives reinforcement on a VI 1-minute schedule on one key and a VI 3-minute schedule on the other key. How would the subject respond on this task? Richard Herrnstein's *matching law* (see Herrnstein, 1961; Herrnstein & Vaughn, 1980) describes how the subject would act in this two-choice situation.

According to Herrnstein's matching law, when a subject has free access to different schedules of reinforcement, the subject allocates its responding in proportion to the level of reinforcement available on each schedule. In terms of our previous example, a pigeon can obtain three times as much reward on a VI 1-minute schedule as on a VI 3-minute schedule. The matching law predicts that the subject will respond three times as much on the key with the VI 1-minute schedule as on the key with the VI 3-minute schedule.

The matching law can be stated mathematically to provide for a precise prediction of the subject's behavior in a choice situation. The mathematical formula for the matching law is

$$\frac{X}{X + Y} = \frac{R(X)}{R(X) + R(Y)}$$

In the equation, X represents the number of responses on key X, Y is the number of responses on key Y, $R(X)$ represents the number of reinforcements received

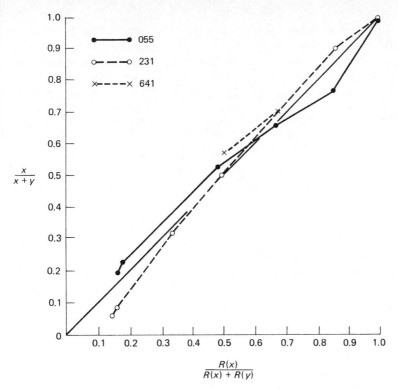

FIGURE 5-11   The proportion of key pecks on X and Y is proportional to the reinforcements available on keys X and Y. From Herrnstein, R. J. (1961). Relative and absolute strength of response as a function of frequency of reinforcement. *Journal of the Experimental Analysis of Behavior, 4,* 267–272. Copyright 1961 by the Society for the Experimental Analysis of Behavior, Inc.

on key X, and $R(Y)$ is the number of reinforcements on key Y. In terms of our example, the pigeon can receive three times as many rewards on key X as on key Y. The matching law shows that we can expect the pigeon to key peck three times as much on key X as on key Y.

Does the matching law accurately predict the subject's behavior in a choice situation? Herrnstein tested the theory by varying the proportion of reinforcements that could be obtained on each key and then determining the pigeon's proportion of key pecks on each key. The data from this study is shown in Figure 5-11. Herrnstein's results show exceptional matching; that is, the subject's responses on each key is a function of the reinforcements available on each key.

The matching law is a simple economic principle describing an animal's behavior in many choice situations. The student of economics soon discovers that simple principles are not always valid, and more complex processes are needed to accurately describe economic activity. The same complexity holds true for behavioral economics. While the matching law have been shown to describe behavior in a variety of situations, it is not always valid. More complex behavior economic principles have been developed to explain the complex situations. For example, the matching law is not valid when fixed ratio schedules are used. Such complex behavioral economic principles are beyond the scope of this text. The interested reader should see Allison (1989) for a discussion of these principles.

Section Review

A contingency not only specifies the response that will lead to reinforcement but also the manner in which the behavior must occur. In fixed-ratio schedules, a fixed number of responses is necessary to produce reinforcement, while with the variable-ratio schedule, an average number of responses leads to reinforcement. In contrast, the first response occurring after a specified interval of time produces reinforcement on an interval schedule of reinforcement; the interval remains constant with a fixed-interval schedule but varies from reinforcement to reinforcement on a variable-interval schedule. Compound schedules are a combination of two or more schedules of reinforcement.

A number of variables can affect the acquisition of an instrumental response. Contiguity between the appropriate response and reward influences conditioning: The instrumental response will be acquired rapidly if reward immediately follows the instrumental response. The magnitude of reward also affects instrumental conditioning. Performance of the instrumental response is higher with a large reward. This performance difference between large and small rewards is due to the greater motivational impact of a large reward. A shift in the magnitude of reward from large to small leads to a rapid decrease in responding, whereas a shift from small to large causes a significant increase in responding. The negative contrast (or depression) effect is a lower level of performance when the reward magnitude is shifted from high to low than when the reward magnitude always is low; the positive contrast (or elation) effect is a higher level of performance when the reward magnitude is shifted from low to high than when the reward magnitude always is high.

Premack's probability-differential theory indicates that activities, such as watching television or going to a dance, can serve as reinforcers. According to Premack, high-probability activities reinforce lower-probability activities. Timberlake and Allison's response deprivation hypothesis states that an activity will serve as a reinforcer when a response contingency limits access to that activity; such a contingency causes an increase in the operant response in order to restore access to the restricted activity to its baseline level. The paired basepoint or blisspoint is the free operant level of two responses. The behavioral allocation view assumes that an animal emits the number of contingent responses needed to come as close to blisspoint as possible. The matching law states that when two or more operant responses can be used to obtain reinforcement, the rate of responding is in direct proportion to the level of reinforcement available through each response.

EXTINCTION OF AN OPERANT OR INSTRUMENTAL RESPONSE

An operant or instrumental response, acquired when reinforcement follows the occurrence of behavior, can be extinguished when the reinforcer no longer follows the response. Continued failure of the operant or instrumental behavior to produce reinforcement causes the strength of the response to diminish until eventually the operant or instrumental action is no longer performed.

Consider the following examples to illustrate the *extinction* of an operant or instrumental response: (1) A hungry rat has been given food reinforcement for bar pressing, which has resulted in the development of an operant bar-press response. During extinction, food reinforcement is no longer presented, and the rate of bar pressing declines until the rat stops pressing the bar. (2) A child shopping with his mother sees a favorite candy bar and discovers that a temper tantrum persuades his mother to buy the candy. The contingency between the temper tantrum and the candy teaches the child to have a tantrum whenever he wants a candy bar. The child's mother, tired of being manipulated, decides to no longer submit to her child's unruly behavior. The mother no longer reinforces the child's tantrums with candy, and the incidence of tantrums declines slowly until the child learns to enter a store and behave when candy is refused. (3) A man eats in a specific restaurant nightly; it is not the quality of the food drawing him there but the attractive waitress. Arriving at the restaurant one night, he finds that the waitress has quit. Although the man continues to eat at the restaurant infrequently, he eventually stops. Many studies have shown that when reinforcement is no longer provided, the operant or instrumental behavior ceases to be performed; let's now examine several experiments demonstrating the extinction of an operant or instrumental response when reinforcement is discontinued.

Extinction Procedure

In 1938, Skinner observed that the failure to reinforce a previously acquired bar-press response in rats caused the extinction of that response. When reinforcement is first discontinued, the rate of responding is high (see Figure 5-12). Continued failure of the response to produce reinforcement causes the rate of responding to decline until the rat stops bar pressing. Responding is erratic during extinction; there are periods of high response rates and times when no responding occurs. Other psychologists (see Perin, 1942; Williams, 1938) have reported that animals cease bar pressing when reinforcement is no longer provided following an operant bar-press response. Furthermore, researchers have found that extinction of a previously rewarded instrumental response occurs when reward is no longer presented in a runway apparatus (see Bacon, 1962; Hill & Spear, 1963; Weinstock, 1958).

Extinction of a previously reinforced behavior has been also documented in humans. For example, Lewis and Duncan (1956, 1957, 1958) reinforced college students for pulling the lever of a slot machine. When reinforcement (a disk exchangeable for five cents) was discontinued, the students eventually stopped

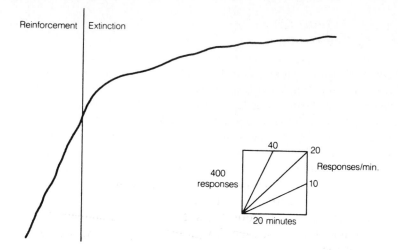

FIGURE 5-12   Cumulative response record during the extinction of a bar-press response. The animal quickly stops responding when reinforcement is discontinued.

pulling the lever. Lewis (1952) noted a similar extinction pattern in 6- and 7-year-old children who were no longer reinforced with toys for pressing a button.

The Nature of Extinction

Development of Inhibition   In Chapter 2, we learned that Hull suggested that nonreward occurring during extinction inhibits a previously rewarded instrumental habit. Initially, a temporary reactive inhibition (I_R) suppresses all responding due to fatigue occurring when behavior does not produce reinforcement. When fatigue dissipates, the instrumental behavior reappears. This increase in responding shortly after extinction is called *spontaneous recovery* (see Chapter 3). If the behavior continues to be unrewarded, a permanent conditioned inhibition ($_SI_R$) develops specifically to the nonrewarded behavior. According to Hull, the conditioned inhibition of a response occurs because the environmental events present during performance of the nonrewarded behavior become associated with the inhibitory nonreward state. When these cues are experienced again, the inhibitory state is aroused and the instrumental behavior suppressed. The continued nonreward also leads to a loss of spontaneous recovery.

Consider the following example to illustrate Hull's view of extinction. A rat runs down an alley but is not rewarded; nonreward elicits an inhibition response, which, in turn, becomes associated with the alley through the instrumental conditioning process. When the rat is again placed in the alley, inhibition is elicited as a conditioned response, and the rat's running response is suppressed. Inhibition is not the only impact of nonreward on responding; the influence of the aversive quality of nonreward is examined next.

Aversive Quality of Nonreward   Abram Amsel (1958) suggested that nonreward elicits an aversive internal frustration state. Stimuli associated with nonreward become able to elicit frustration as a conditioned response and escape from this aversive situation is reinforcing. Adelman and Maatsch (1956) provided evidence of the aversiveness of frustration and the reinforcing quality of escaping from a frustrating situation. They found that animals jumped out of a box previously associated with reward and up onto a ledge within 5 seconds if they were not rewarded. In contrast, animals that had been rewarded with food for jumping onto the ledge took 20 seconds to jump. Further, while the rewarded animals stopped jumping after about 60 extinction trials, the frustrated animals did not quit responding even after 100 trials, even though their only reward was escape from a frustrating situation.

Other researchers (see Brooks, 1980; Daly, 1974) have shown that the cues associated with nonreward develop aversive qualities. Let's briefly examine Daly's study to demonstrate the aversive quality of cues associated with nonreward. Daly presented a cue (either a distinctive box or a light) during nonreinforced trials in the first phase of her study; during the second part of the experiment, the rats learned a response—jumping a hurdle—that enabled them to turn off the light or to escape from the box. Apparently, the cues (distinctive box or light) had acquired aversive qualities during nonrewarded trials; the presence of these cues subsequently motivated the escape response. Termination of these cues reinforced the acquisition of the hurdle jump response.

Activation of Instrumental Behavior   One additional point about the influence of nonreward on instrumental behavior deserves our attention. Nonreward sometimes increases rather than decreases the intensity of instrumental behavior. Instrumental appetitive responding will be motivated by nonreward when frustration cues have been conditioned to elicit appetitive instead of avoidance behavior. An animal's behavior on a single alternation task illustrates that nonreward can become conditioned to motivate an appetitive instrumental response (see Burns, 1976; Capaldi, 1971; Flaherty & Davenport, 1972). In the single alternation situation, reward and nonreward trials are alternated. Studies using the single alternation task report that the intensity of responding increases following a nonrewarded trial but declines after a rewarded trial.

Why does response latency decrease after nonreward but increase after reward in the single alternation task? E. J. Capaldi's sequential theory (see Capaldi, 1966, 1967, 1971) explains this conditioning process. According to Capaldi, at the beginning of each trial, a subject remembers whether reward or nonreward occurred on the last trial; Capaldi labels the memory of reward as S^R and the memory of nonreward, S^N. When reward follows a nonrewarded trial, the memory of the nonreward (S^N) becomes associated with the instrumental response. The conditioning of the memory of nonreward (S^N) to elicit the instrumental response leads to an increase in responding following nonreward; the increased intensity of the instrumental appetitive response after nonrewarded trials supports this view. Furthermore, since nonreward always follows a rewarded trial, the memory of reward (S^R) is associated with nonreward, which results in the conditioning of an avoidance response to (S^R). Thus, the memory of reward elicits instrumental avoidance behavior; the decreased intensity of the instrumental appetitive response after rewarded trials provides support for Capaldi's approach.

Resistance to Extinction

Three factors appear to significantly contribute to the resistance to extinction of an instrumental response. First, *the reward magnitude experienced during acquisition influences the degree of resistance to extinction of an instrumental response.* The effect of the reward magnitude on the extinction of an instrumental behavior depends upon the level of acquisition training: When the level of training is minimal, higher reward magnitudes in acquisition produce greater resistance to extinction. In contrast, extended acquisition training results in an inverse relationship between the reward magnitude and the resistance to extinction; that is, the higher the reward magnitude used in acquisition, the less resistance to extinction. Second, *resistance to extinction is affected by the delay of reward used in acquisition training.* Research on the influence of the delay of reward indicates that if reward is sometimes delayed during acquisition, resistance to extinction is enhanced. However, the resistance to extinction is not affected if reward is always delayed. Third, *the consistency of reinforcement in acquisition influences the resistance to extinction of an operant response.* During extinction, an operant response that has not been reinforced every time it occurred continues for a longer period than does a response that has always been reinforced.

The Influence of Reward Magnitude D'Amato (1970) suggested that the influence of the reward magnitude experienced in acquisition on the resistance to extinction depends upon the amount of acquisition training. As seen in Figure 5-13, when the level of acquisition training is low, a large reward produces a greater resistance to extinction than does a small reward. However, the opposite effect is observed with extended acquisition: A small reward magnitude in acquisition produces more resistance to extinction of the instrumental behavior than does the use of a large reward magnitude.

The literature provides support for D'Amato's theory. Hill and Spear (1963), giving their subjects only a few acquisition trials in the runway and providing either a small or large reward in the goal box, found that the large reward was associated with more resistance to extinction than was the small reward. Armus (1959) and Hulse (1958) provided a large number of acquisition trials in the runway and presented either a small or a large reward magnitude in the goal box. Both studies observed that resistance to extinction was greater for the animals given the small than the large reward during acquisition. Furthermore, several

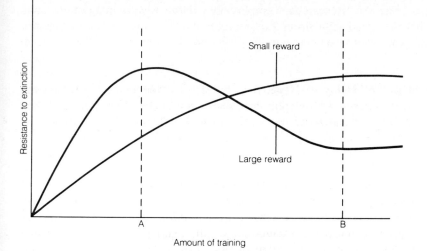

FIGURE 5-13   Hypothesized resistance to extinction of an instrumental response as a function of level of acquisition training and magnitude of reinforcement. From D'Amato, M. R. (1970). *Experimental psychology: Methodology, psychophysics, and learning.* New York: McGraw-Hill.

studies (see Ison & Cook, 1964; Senkowski, 1978; Traupmanni, 1972) varied both the acquisition reward magnitude and the number of acquisition trials; the results of the studies support the relationship depicted in Figure 5-13.

Why does the influence of reward magnitude on the resistance to extinction depend on the level of acquisition training? According to D'Amato (1970), when a small reward magnitude is used in acquisition, the r_G-s_G mechanism develops very slowly (see Chapter 2 for a discussion of this acquired motive concept). During extinction, there will not be substantial differences in the level of the r_G-s_G and, therefore, the frustration produced during extinction will be small. (This assertion is based on the view that frustration is not produced until reward is anticipated and that the amount of frustration produced is dependent upon the strength of the anticipatory goal response.) Since frustration is minimal, resistance to extinction should depend only on the amount of acquisition training. The results of studies using a small reward magnitude support this prediction; the greater the level of acquisition training with a small reward magnitude, the more resistant the instrumental behavior to extinction.

In contrast, the anticipatory goal mechanism (r_G-s_G) is conditioned rapidly when a large reward is used in acquisition. Frustration will not be elicited if extinction occurs following low levels of training; however, resistance to extinction will increase as r_G-s_G is conditioned. Once the r_G-s_G association is strong enough to produce frustration, increases in r_G-s_G should lead to higher levels of frustration during extinction. These increases in frustration, produced as a result of extended training with a large reward, lead to a more rapid extinction of the instrumental response. Researchers employing a large reward magnitude have observed that increased acquisition training first leads to an increase in resistance to extinction, followed by a decline in the difficulty of eliminating an instrumental response.

The Influence of Delay of Reward The effect of delay of reward on the resistance to extinction depends upon the consistency of the reward delay. When a constant delay is used in acquisition, resistance to extinction is not affected by acquisition delay. In contrast, inconsistent delay of reward in acquisition increases resistance to extinction. Terminal acquisition differences are produced with different delay intervals and these terminal differences must be equated; Anderson (1963) suggested guidelines for controlling for asymptotic performance.

Consider Tombaugh's 1966 study to illustrate the influence of consistent delay of reward in acquisition on the resistance to extinction. Tombaugh's rats were given 70 acquisition trials in a runway apparatus, with reward in the goal box delayed for periods of 0, 5, 10, or 20 seconds. During the 60 extinction trials, the rats were confined to the goal box for a period of delay equivalent to that experienced during acquisition. Controlling for terminal acquisition performance levels, Tombaugh found no differences in the resistance of extinction as a function of the delay of reward used in acquisition.

By comparing varied and constant delay of reward in acquisition, it is clear that the inconsistent delay of reinforcement does influence resistance to extinction. A number of researchers (see Logan, 1960; Schoonard & Lawrence, 1962; Shanab & Birnbaum, 1974) reported a greater resistance to extinction when reward was sometimes delayed compared to when reward was never delayed. However, varied delay increases persistence effectively in extinction only if the delay is substantial (20 to 30 seconds).

The Importance of Consistency of Reinforcement Earlier in the chapter we described an example of a mother extinguishing her child's temper tantrums in a grocery store. Suppose that after several nonreinforced trips to the store, and a reduction in the duration and intensity of the temper tantrums, the mother, on the next trip to the store, has a headache when the child starts to cry. The headache seems to intensify the unpleasantness of the tantrum, thus, she decides to buy her child candy in order to stop the crying. If the mother had headaches infrequently but reinforces a tantrum whenever she does have a headache, she is now intermittently rather than continuously reinforcing her child's temper tantrums. As we learned earlier, this intermittent reinforcement causes the intensity of the temper tantrum to return to its original strength. We also learned that the intensity of the child's behavior will soon exceed that of the level produced when the response was continuously reinforced. Despite how she feels, in all likelihood, the mother will eventually become so annoyed that she decides that she will no longer tolerate her child's temper tantrums; unfortunately, extinguishing this behavior will be extremely difficult because she has intermittently reinforced the child's temper tantrums.

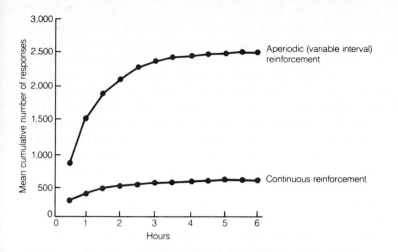

FIGURE 5-14 The mean cumulative bar-press responding during extinction is higher in rats receiving intermittent reinforcement than in those receiving continuous reinforcement. From Jenkins, W. O., McFann, H., & Clayton, F. L. (1950). A methodological study of extinction following aperiodic and continuous reinforcement. *Journal of Comparative and Physiological Psychology, 43,* 155–167. Copyright 1950 by the American Psychological Association. Reprinted by permission.

Partial Reinforcement Effect   The previous example illustrates the influence of consistency of reinforcement on the extinction of an instrumental behavior: Extinction is slower following partial rather than continuous reinforcement. The greater resistance to extinction which occurs with intermittent rather than continuous reinforcement is referred to as the *partial reinforcement effect*. (PRE). Humphreys (1939) and Skinner (1938) were the first to describe this greater resistance to extinction with partial than with continuous reinforcement. Many subsequent studies have demonstrated a partial reinforcement effect; this effect is one of the most reliable phenomena in psychology. Several studies are presented next to document the effect of consistency of reinforcement in acquisition on resistance to extinction.

Jenkins, McFann, and Clayton (1950) trained rats to bar press for food reinforcement. Half of the rats were reinforced on a VI schedule; the others, on a continuous schedule. As can be seen in Figure 5-14, rats receiving intermittent reinforcement emitted five times as many responses during extinction as did rats given continuous reinforcement.

Much research on the partial reinforcement effect has used the runway apparatus; the results of these studies have consistently demonstrated the PRE effect. Consider Weinstock's 1958 study to illustrate this effect in the runway. Weinstock's rats received 108 acquisition trials with reward occurring on either 16.7, percent, 33.5 percent, 50.0 percent, 66.7 percent, 83.3 percent, or 100 percent of the trials; each rat was then given 60 extinction trials. Weinstock found an inverse relationship between resistance to extinction and the percentage of rewarded trials. These results indicate that as the likelihood of an instrumental response producing reward in acquisition decreases, the resistance to extinction increases. Many other experiments have demonstrated that intermittent reward during acquisition increases resistance to extinction in the runway; see Nation and Boyajian (1981) for a review of this literature.

The partial reinforcement effect has also been demonstrated with in adults (see Lewis & Duncan, 1958) and children (see Lewis, 1952). To illustrate the impact of partial reinforcement on humans, let's examine the Lewis and Duncan (1958) study. College students were given reinforcement (a disk exchangeable for five cents) for pulling the arm of a slot machine. The percentage of reinforced lever pulling responses varied: Subjects received reinforcement after 33 percent, 67 percent, or 100 percent of the responses. Lewis and Duncan allowed subjects to play the slot machine as long as they liked during extinction, reporting that the lower the percentage of responses reinforced during acquisition, the greater the resistance to extinction.

The percentage of reinforced trials cannot be too low (see Lewis, 1960) or learning will be minimal and extinction rapid. Studies using a very small or very large percentage of reinforced trials generally produce a U-shaped relationship between the percentage of reinforced responses and resistance to extinction; that is, a low or high percentage of reinforcement produces a more rapid extinction than does reinforcement of an operant response on some but not all of its occurrences.

The Nature of the Partial Reinforcement Effect   Many explanations of the partial reinforcement effect have been proposed since Humphrey's and Skinner's initial observations: E. J. Capaldi's sequential theory (see Capaldi, 1966, 1967, 1971) appears to best describe the process responsible for the increased resistance to extinction following intermittent compared with continuous reinforcement. Capaldi provides a complex explanation of the partial reinforcement effect. A brief summary is offered here; the interested reader should see Capaldi (1971) for a more detailed description of his theory.

Recall that if reward follows a nonrewarded trial, the animal will then associate the memory of the nonrewarded experience (S^N) with the instrumental response. According to Capaldi, the conditioning of the S^N-R (memory of nonreward–instrumental behavior) association is responsible for the increased resistance to extinction with partial reward.

During extinction, the only memory present after the first nonrewarded experience is S^N. Animals receiving continuous reward do not experience S^N during acquisition; therefore, S^N is not associated with the instrumental response. The presence of S^N in continuously rewarded animals during extinction changes the stimulus context from that present during acquisition. The change in the stimulus context during extinction produces a reduction in response strength due to *generalization decrement,* a reduced intensity of a response when the stimulus present is dissimilar to the stimulus conditioned to the response (see Chapter 7 for a discussion of generalization). The loss of response strength due to generalization decrement combined with the inhibition developed during extinction produce a rapid extinction of the instrumental response in animals receiving continuous reward in acquisition. However, a different process occurs in animals receiving partial reward in acquisition: S^N is associated with the instrumental response during acquisition, and therefore no generalization decrement occurs during extinction. The absence of the generalization decrement causes the strength of the instrumental response at the beginning of extinction to remain at the level conditioned during acquisition. Thus, the inhibition developed during extinction only slowly suppresses the instrumental response; as a result, extinction is slower with partial than with continuous reward.

Capaldi and his associates (see Capaldi, Hart, & Stanley, 1963; Capaldi & Spivey, 1964) conducted several studies to demonstrate the importance of S^N experienced during a reinforced trial on the resistance to extinction. In these studies, during the interval between the nonrewarded and rewarded trials, reward was given in an environment other than the runway. The effect of this intertrial reward procedure is the replacement of the memory of nonreward (S^N) with a memory of reward (S^R) and thus a reduced resistance to extinction. Rats given intertrial reward showed a faster extinction of the instrumental response than control animals receiving only partial reward.

Capaldi suggests that two sequential factors influence the level of resistance to extinction produced by partial reward. First, *the greater the number of NR transitions occurring during acquisition, the greater the resistance to extinction.* In Capaldi's view, *NR transitions* (or sequence of nonrewarded and rewarded trials) act to condition the memory of S^N to the instrumental response; therefore, the greater the number of conditioning trials (NR transitions), the stronger the association of S^N to the instrumental response. To support his theory, Capaldi (1964) gave his rats either 3, 10, or 20 NR transitions during the acquisition of a running response. He found that the resistance to extinction increased as the number of NR transitions experienced in acquisition increased.

Second, *the greater the number of consecutive nonrewarded trials occurring prior to reward, the slower the extinction of the instrumental response.* According to Capaldi, the memory of nonreward (S^N) intensifies with consecutive nonrewarded trials. The presentation of reward causes a stronger S^N to be associated with the instrumental response when more than one nonreward trial precedes reward than when only a single nonrewarded experience occurs prior to reward. Furthermore, the larger the number of nonrewarded trials, or *N-length,* the stronger the S^N conditioned to the instrumental response.

The literature shows that the longer the N-length, the greater the resistance to extinction. Consider Capaldi's (1964) experiment to illustrate the influence of N-length. Two groups of rats in Capaldi's study received an identical sequence of rewarded and nonrewarded during trails (RNNRRNNR) during each acquisition session. The groups also received two intertrial rewards during training. The intertrial reward for one group occurred between nonreward trials (RN_rNRRN_rNR); this procedure caused the N-length to be reduced from 2 to 1. The subjects in the other group received the intertrial rewards after reward trials (R_rNNRR_rNNR);

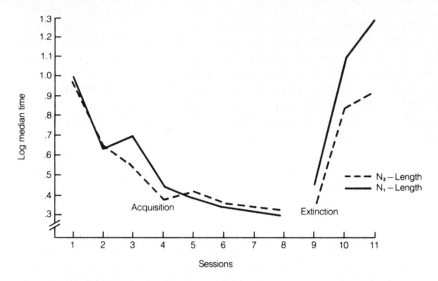

FIGURE 5-15 Mean log response latency to reach the goal box during acquisition and extinction in rats having one or two nonrewarded trials prior to reward during acquisition. The resistance to extinction is greater in animals experiencing two rather than one nonreward prior to reward in acquisition. From Capaldi, E. J. (1964). Effect of N-length, number of different N-lengths, and number of reinforcements on resistance to extinction. *Journal of Experimental Psychology, 68,* 230–239. Copyright 1964 by the American Psychological Association. Reprinted by permission.

this technique enabled the N-length to remain at 2. Although the two groups did not differ in the acquisition of the running response, the subjects in the group with an N-length of 2 were more resistant to extinction than were animals in the group with an N-length of 1 (see Figure 5-15). These results indicate that the greater the N-length experienced in acquisition, the slower the extinction of the instrumental response.

What is the significance of the partial reinforcement effect? According to Flaherty (1985), observations of animals in their natural environments indicate that animals' attempts to attain a desired goal are sometimes successful, while at other times the animals fail to reach the goal. Flaherty asserts that the PRE is adaptive because it motivates animals not to give up too soon and thus lose an opportunity to be successful. Yet, animals receiving partial reward do not continue responding indefinitely without reward, an observation that indicates that animals do not persist forever, and, therefore, experience continued frustration.

Section Review

The strength of the instrumental response increases during acquisition; the frequency and intensity of the instrumental behavior decline during extinction. Extinction of an instrumental response occurs when that behavior no longer produces reward. Nonreward of the instrumental response leads to an inhibition of that response, as well as to an elicitation of avoidance behavior. The avoidance behavior initially is an escape response from the frustration induced by nonreward. Association of environmental cues with nonreward motivates avoidance of nonreward and, therefore, decreases the strength of the instrumental response. However, nonreward sometimes increases the intensity of instrumental behavior. Capaldi argued that this intensification occurs when the memory of nonreward has been conditioned to elicit the instrumental response.

A number of variables can affect the extinction of an instrumental response. A large reward magnitude produces greater resistance to extinction than does a small reward magnitude when the amount of acquisition training is low, but the opposite is true with extended acquisition training. Also, resistance to extinction is greater when reward delay is varied rather than constant. Furthermore, partial rather than continuous reward leads to a slower extinction of the instrumental behavior. Capaldi's research indicates that the conditioning of the memory of nonreward in the partial reward condition, but not in the continuous reward condition, is responsible for the greater resistance to extinction with partial reward.

In this chapter we have learned that the way we act is affected by the presentation of reward and nonreward. The importance of reward and nonreward on instrumental or operant behavior has impressed many psychologists, who have designed conditioning procedures to control human behavior. These psychologists have used reward to institute more effective patterns of behavior and nonreward to eliminate inappropriate behavior patterns. We end our discussion of appetitive conditioning by examining its use in controlling human behavior.

APPLICATION: CONTINGENCY MANAGEMENT

In 1953, B. F. Skinner suggested that poorly arranged reinforcer contingencies are sometimes responsible for people's behavior problems. In many instances, effective operant responding does not occur because reinforcement is unavailable. At other times, reinforcing people's behavior problems sustains their occurrence. Skinner believed that rearranging reinforcement contingencies could eliminate behavior pathology and increase the occurrence of more effective ways of responding. Many psychologists (see Ullman & Krasner, 1965) accepted Skinner's view, and the restructuring of reinforcement contingencies emerged as an effective way of altering human behavior. The use of reinforcement and nonreinforcement to control people's behavior was initially labeled *behavior modification*. However, behavior modification refers to all types of behavioral treatments; thus, behavior therapists (refer to Rimm & Masters, 1979) now use the term *contingency management* to indicate that contingent reinforcement and nonreinforcement are being used to increase the frequency of appropriate behaviors and to eliminate or reduce inappropriate responses. We begin by examining the procedures necessary for effective use of reinforcement and nonreinforcement to alter operant behavior. Evidence of the effectiveness of contingency management is described later in this section.

There are three main stages in the effective implementation of a contingency management program (see Rimm & Masters, 1979, for a more detailed discussion of these procedures). The initial stage of therapy assesses the frequency of appropriate and inappropriate behaviors and determines the situations in which these operant behaviors occur. In addition, the reinforcement maintaining the inappropriate responding, as well as potential reinforcers for the appropriate behavior, is determined in the assessment phase. The second phase of therapy, the contingency contracting stage of treatment, specifies the relationship between responding and reinforcement. Also, the method of administering the reinforcement contingent upon appropriate behaviors is determined. During the next stage of contingency management, the treatment is implemented. The changes in responding during and following treatment are evaluated in the last phase of contingency management. This procedure ensures that (1) behavioral changes are produced by the therapy program and (2) these changes continue after the termination of formal treatment. As we discover shortly, contingency management is an effective way to alter behavior; the failure of the treatment to change responding often means that the program was not developed and/or implemented correctly, and changes in the treatment are necessary to ensure behavioral change.

Assessment Phase

The therapist must define the behavior problem and determine the situations in which it does or does not occur. Discussions with the client, others who are familiar with the patient, or both, are the initial source of information concerning the behavior problem. However, the therapist cannot rely solely on this subjective reporting, which merely provides the therapist with an impression of the problem. Direct observations are necessary to establish the precise baseline level of the target behaviors. The observations may be made by the staff of an institution, other people around the client, or the client. Regardless of who observes the target behavior, accurate observations are essential and training is needed to ensure reliable data recording.

Consider the following example to illustrate the observational training process. Parents complain to a behavior therapist that their child frequently has temper tantrums, which they have tried but failed to eliminate. The therapist instructs the parents to fill in a chart (see Table 5-2) indicating both the number and duration of tantrums occurring each day for a week as well as their responses to each tantrum. The parents' observation provides a relatively accurate recording of the frequency and intensity of the problem behavior.

The parents' observations also indicate the reinforcement of the problem behavior. As can be seen from Table 5-2, parental response to the tantrum increased the frequency of the behavior; ignoring the behavior decreased the frequency of temper tantrums. It is essential in the assessment phase to record the events following the target behavior; this information signifies the reinforcer of the problem behavior.

TABLE 5-2
INSTANCES OF TANTRUM BEHAVIOR AND PARENTAL REACTION TO TANTRUMS
DURING 7-DAY BASELINE ASSESSMENT PERIOD

Day	Tantrums	Duration (minutes)	Response
1	1	4	Comforted child when he slipped and banged head during crying
2	1	5	Told child to be quiet but finally gave cookie to quiet him down
	1	6	Ignored until couldn't stand it; gave cookie
3	1	5	Ignored
	2	6	Ignored
	3	8	Ignored until child took cookie himself; spanked child
4	1	4	Ignored; child stopped spontaneously
5	1	4	Company present; gave child cookie to quiet him
	2	5	Ignored; finally gave in
6	1	8	Ignored; went into bathroom, had cigarette, read magazine until child quieted himself
	2	4	Ignored; just as I was about to give in, child stopped
7	1	3	Ignored; child stopped, began to play

Source: Rimm, D. C., & Masters, J. C. (1979). *Behavior therapy: Techniques and empirical findings* (2d ed.). New York: Academic.

The assessment must indicate when and where the target behavior occurs. For example, the child may be having tantrums at home every day after school but not at school. This information about the target behavior shows the extent of the behavior problem as well as the stimulus conditions that precipate the response.

Based on information obtained in the assessment phase, the reinforcer to be used during therapy is determined. In some cases, the behavioral recording indicates what can be used as a reinforcer for appropriate behavior; in other instances, the therapist must discover what can be employed. Behavior therapists (see Rimm & Masters, 1979) have developed a number of reinforcer assessment techniques. For example, the Mediation-Reinforcer Incomplete Blank (MRB), a modified incomplete-sentence test developed by Tharp and Wetzel (1969), reveals the client's view of a reinforcer. A client's response to the question "I will do almost anything to get _____" shows what the client considers to be a material reinforcer.

Contingency Contracting Phase

In this phase, the desired instrumental response is specified, and the precise relationship between that response and reinforcement is indicated. This indication involves deciding the schedule of reinforcement necessary to establish the desired response. In addition, if a shaping procedure is needed, the contract will detail the changes in the contingency to occur at various stages of treatment. Furthermore, an inappropriate operant response often has elicited reinforcement in the past; the contingency will indicate that this inappropriate response will no longer be reinforced.

Who will administer the reinforcer? In the traditional application of contingency management, people other than the client (for example, a nurse in a mental hospital, a teacher in a school setting, or a parent in the home) have provided reinforcement contingent upon the occurrence of the appropriate operant behavior. During the contracting stage, the individuals administering reinforcement are trained to identify and reinforce appropriate behavior.

Enlisting people around the client to provide reinforcement is ideally suited to many types of situations. However, there are circumstances in which this technique is not feasible. This is especially true of adults seeking to change their behavior by using outpatient therapy; the use of the self-reinforcement procedure has often proven effective in these situations. Although psychologists (see Skinner, 1953) were initially skeptical of the efficacy of self-reinforcement in behavioral management, Bandura and Perloff (1967) demonstrated the self-reinforcement technique to be as effective in changing behavior as the typical reinforcement procedure. In their study, 7- to 10-year-old children received reinforcement for exerting effort on a wheel-turning task. Some children were given a supply of tokens at the beginning of the experiment, which they used to provide their own reinforcement (the tokens could be exchanged for prizes) for attaining a high level of performance; other children attaining a high level of performance received tokens from the experimenter. Bandura and Perloff reported that both the self-imposed reinforcement groups and the externally imposed reinforcement groups showed an equivalent level of performance, responding at a higher level than children given reinforcement prior to the task or no reinforcement. Self-reinforcement procedures have effectively modifed a number of undesired behaviors: impulsive overspending (Paulsen, Rimm, Woodburn, & Rimm, 1977), depression (Fuchs & Rehm, 1977; Rehm, 1977), inadequate study habits (Beneke & Harris, 1972; Greiner & Karoly, 1976) and overeating (Harris, 1969; Stuart, 1971).

Contingency management programs in which other persons provide reward have yielded impressive results for changing a wide variety of behaviors in many different situations. A brief discussion of their effectiveness completes our examination of contingency management.

Implementation of a Contingency Management Program

Skinner's idea that reinforcement could be systematically employed to modify behavior was empirically tested in the early 1960s by Ayllon and Azrin at Anna State Hospital in Illinois (see Ayllon & Azrin, 1965, 1968). Ayllon and Azrin established a contingency management program for institutionalized adult female

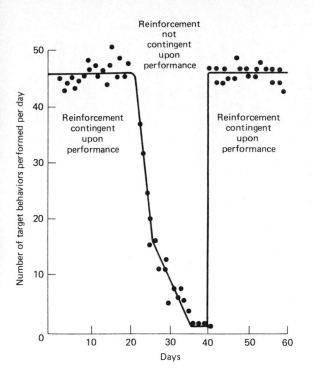

FIGURE 5-16
Illustration shows that presentation of reinforcement contingent upon target behaviors increases the frequency of appropriate responding. The target behaviors' frequency declined when reinforcement was discontinued but increased when contingent reinforcement was restored. From Ayllon, T., & Azrin, N. H. (1965). The measurement and reinforcement of behavior of psychotics. *Journal of the Experimental Analysis of Behavior, 8,* 357–383. Copyright 1965 by the Society for the Experimental Analysis of Behavior, Inc.

psychotic clients. These clients received tokens, which could later be exchanged for desired primary reinforcers, when they engaged in operant responses that would be needed for effective adjustment outside of the hospital. Two classes of operant behaviors were reinforced: (1) self-care activities, such as grooming and bathing, and (2) job activities, such as washing dishes and serving food. Allyon and Azrin reported that the frequency of appropriate responding significantly increased as the result of the contingency management program (see Figure 5-16). (Their approach is often called a token economy program because of the use of tokens as secondary reinforcers.)

Ayllon and Azrin's treatment shows that psychiatric patients can develop behaviors necessary for successful adjustment through the reinforcement of those behaviors. In fact, many studies (see Fairweather, Sanders, Maynard, & Cressler, 1969; Paul & Lentz, 1977; Schaefer & Martin, 1969) have found that psychotic patients receiving a contingency management treatment exhibit a significantly better adjustment to daily living than do patients given standard hospital treatment. The efficacy of operant conditioning to alter the behavior of hospitalized psychotic clients appears to be a well-established finding.

Contingency management programs have been used to alter behavior in a wide variety of settings. A sample of these programs is given in Table 5-3. Contingency management appears to be an effective treatment for a number of behavior

TABLE 5-3
SAMPLE OF BEHAVIORS INFLUENCED BY A CONTINGENCY MANAGEMENT PROGRAM

Target	Behavior/competency	Population	Outcome	Source of report
Social	Social and emotional behaviors	Handicapped children	Increased	Cooke & Apolloni (1976)
	Prosocial verbal behavior	Delinquent adolescent	Increased	Emshoff, Redd, & Davidson, (1976)
	Social interaction	Chronic psychotic adults	Increased	Fichter, Wallace, Liberman, & Davis (1976)
	Social interaction	Retarded adolescents	Increased	L. Williams, Martin, McDonald, Hardy, & Lambert (1975)
	Sharing, praising	Children	Increased	Rogers-Warren & Baer (1976)
	Social speech	Retarded children	Increased	Mithaug & Wolfe (1976)
	Social greeting	Retarded children	Increased	Stokes, Baer, & Jackson (1974)
	Social skills	Predelinquent adolescents	Increased	D. M. Maloney, Harper, Braukmann, Fixsen, Phillips, & Wolf (1976)
	Extreme withdrawal	Children	Improved	Allen, Hart, Buell, Harris, & Wolf (1964); Brawley, Harris, Allen, Fleming, & Peterson (1969)
	Extreme passivity	Children	Improved	Johnston, Kelley, Harris, & Wolf (1966)
	Sharing	Children	Increased	Warren, Rogers-Warren, & Baer (1976)
	Social disruption	Children	Decreased	MacPherson, Candee, & Hohman (1974)
Self-control	Hyperactivity/attention span	Retarded children	Decreased/ increased	Alabiso (1975)
	Hyperactivity	Children	Decreased	Wulbert & Dries (1977)
	Obesity	Children	Decreased	Epstein, Parker, McCoy, & McGee (1976)
	Classroom disruption	Children	Decreased	Todd, Scott, Bostow, & Alexander (1976)
	Family interaction	Mother and adolescent	Improved responsibility	Blechman, Olson, Schornagle, Halsdorf, & Turner (1976)
	Enuresis	Adolescent	Eliminated	Popler (1976)
	Rumination	Infant	Eliminated	Linscheid & Cunningham (1977)

Category	Behavior	Population	Outcome	Reference
	Classroom disruption	Children	Decreased	Robertson, DeReus, & Drabman (1976)
	Classroom disruption	Children	Decreased	Ayllon, Garber, & Pisor (1975)
	Classroom task attention	Children	Increased	Hay, Hay, & Nelson (1977b)
	Classroom task attention	Children	Increased	Marholin & Steinman (1977)
	Homework	Children	Improved	Harris & Sherman (1974)
	School attendance	Predelinquent	Improved	Alexander, Corbett, & Smigel (1976)
	Curfew obedience	Adolescents	Improved	Alexander, Corbett, & Smigel (1976)
	Writer's block	Adult	Eliminated	Passman (1976)
	Stuttering	Adults	Eliminated	Ingham & Andrews (1973)
Cognitive-emotional	Complex language	Autistic child	Acquired	Stevens-Long & Rasmussen (1974)
	Creativity	Children	Increased	Henson (1975)
	Intelligence score	Handicapped children	Increased	Smeets & Striefel (1975)
	Intelligence/vocabulary	Normal children	Increased	Clingman & Fowler (1976)
	Creativity	Normal children	Increased	Glover & Gary (1976)
	School performance	Adolescent	Improved	Schumaker, Hovell, & Sherman (1977)
	Reading/comprehension	Autistic child	Improved	Rosenbaum & Breiling (1976)
	Arithmetic competence	Children	Improved	Hundert (1976)
	Autisticlike behavior	Child	Eliminated	Moore & Bailey (1973)
	Anxiety and depression	Adult	Eliminated	Vasta (1975)
	Phobia	Adults	Eliminated	Marshall, Boutilier, & Minnes (1974)
	Conversion reaction	Adult	Eliminated	Kallman, Hersen, & O'Toole (1975)
	Autism	Children	Improved	Lovaas (1968); Wetzel, Baker, Rooney, & Martin (1966)
	Mutism	Adults	Improved	Sherman (1965); Straughan (1968)
	School phobia	Children	Eliminated	G. R. Patterson (1965)
	Psychogenic seizures			Gardner (1967)
	Pain	Adult	Eliminated	Cautela (1971)
	Stuttering	Adults	Reduced	Ingham & Andrews (1973)

Source: Rimm. D. C., & Masters, J. C. (1979). *Behavior therapy: Techniques and empirical findings* (2d ed.). New York: Academic.

pathologies other than the lack of living skills. Depression is one behavior problem that has been modified by contingent reinforcement (see Burgess, 1968; Lieberman & Raskin, 1971). Contingency management also has been employed in the treatment of anxiety (for example, Marshall, Boutilier, & Minnes, 1974; Reisinger, 1972; Rimm & Mahoney, 1969; Vasta, 1975) and pain (see Cautela, 1977; Kallman, Herzen, & O'Toole, 1975; Sand & Biglan, 1974). In these studies, reinforcement occurred when the clients showed decreases in anxiety, depression, or pain and increases in responses incompatible with the behavior problem.

Token economy systems have been established at a number of residential treatment centers for delinquent and predelinquent children and adolescents. The aim of these contingency management programs is to establish appropriate social and lawful behavior as well as academic competencies. These programs (see Bailey, Wolf, & Phillips, 1970; Emshoff, Redd, & Davidson, 1976; Kirigin, Braukman, Atwater, & Wolf, 1982) have shown that contingent reinforcement can decrease the incidence of inappropriate social behavior and increase the occurrence of desired social and academic responses.

A contingency management program can also be employed to increase effective responding in retarded children and adults. For example, contingent reinforcement has been used with retarded children to teach toilet training (see Azrin, Sneed, & Fox, 1973; Giles & Wolf, 1966; Siegel, 1977), personal grooming (Horner & Keilitz, 1975), and mealtime behavior (Plummer, Baer, & LeBlanc, 1977). Furthermore, contingency management can suppress several behaviors characteristic of some retarded children; for example, the incidence of self-injurious behavior (see Griffin, Locke, & Landers, 1975; Solnick, Rincover, & Peterson, 1977), aggression and disruptive behavior (Plummer et al., 1977), and self-stimulation (Wells, Forehand, Hickey, & Green, 1977) will decrease when reinforcement is made contingent upon the suppression of these behaviors.

The academic performance of normal children and adults is responsive to contingency management treatment. For example, Lovitt, Guppy, and Blattner (1969) found that contingent free time and permission to listen to the radio increased the accuracy of spelling in fourth-grade children. Other studies have found that academic competency in children can be increased with a contingency management procedure; refer to Harris and Sherman (1973), McLaughlin and Malaby (1972), or Rapport and Bostow (1976) for examples. Also, contingent reinforcement has been shown to increase the studying behavior of college students; however, this procedure appears to be effective only with students of below-average ability (Bristol & Sloane, 1974) or students with low or medium grade averages (Du Nann & Weber, 1976). It is likely that the other students already are exhibiting effective studying behavior, therefore, reinforcement is not likely to increase their responding. Thus, contingent reinforcement will increase academic performance for only those students not already responding effectively.

Not only is contingency management successful in changing the behavior of individuals, but it is also effective with large groups of people. For example, Hayes and Cone (1977) found that direct payments to efficient energy users produced large reductions in energy consumption, and Seaver and Patterson (1976) discovered that informational feedback and a contingent decal for efficient energy use resulted in a significant decrease in home fuel consumption. Also, McCalden and Davis (1972) discovered that reserving a special lane of the Oakland–San Francisco Bay Bridge for cars with several passengers increased car pooling and improved traffic flow. Finally, Geller and Hahn (1984) found that seat-belt use increased at a large industrial plant when the opportunity to obtain reinforcement was made contingent upon the use of selt-belts.

SUMMARY

1 Reinforcers have a powerful influence on human behavior. According to Skinner, a reinforcer is an event whose occurrence increases the frequency of behavior that produces it. A contingency is a specified relationship between behavior and reinforcement. An animal or a person learns to emit the appropriate behavior in order to obtain reinforcement. Instrumental conditioning refers to situations in which there are constraints on the opportunity to gain reward; operant conditioning involves no constraints and the animal or person can freely respond to obtain reinforcement.

2 Primary reinforcers possess innate reinforcing properties, whereas secondary reinforcers develop the capacity to reinforce operant or instrumental behavior. The reinforcing property of a secondary reinforcer is determined by the amount of primary reinforcement associated with the secondary reinforcer, the number of pairings of primary and secondary reinforcers, and the delay between primary and secondary reinforcement. A positive reinforcer is an event like food or money whose occurrence has reinforcing properties; in contrast, a negative reinforcer is the termination of an aversive event.

3 When the baseline response rate is zero, the operant response will not increase in frequency despite a contingency between reinforcement and the operant response. Furthermore, learning is slow if the rate of responding is low. The shaping procedure can be used to ensure rapid conditioning. Shaping involves reinforcing a high operant rate response, then changing the contingency so that closer and closer approximations to the final behavior are necessary to produce reinforcement.

4 The contingency also specifies the manner in which the behavior must occur. In fixed-ratio schedules, a fixed number of responses are necessary to produce reinforcement; in a variable-ratio schedule, an average number of responses leads to reinforcement, but the number of responses necessary varies over the course of training. In contrast, the first response occurring after a specified interval of time produces reinforcement on an interval schedule of reinforcement; the interval remains constant throughout a fixed-interval schedule but varies over the course of training on a variable-interval schedule. Compound schedules are a combination of two or more schedules of reinforcement.

5 A number of variables can affect the acquisition of an instrumental response. Contiguity between the appropriate response and reward influences conditioning: The instrumental response will be acquired rapidly if reward immediately follows the instrumental response. The magnitude of reward also affects instrumental conditioning. Performance of the instrumental response is greater with a large reward than with a small reward. This performance difference between large and small rewards is due to the greater motivational impact of a large reward. A shift from large to small reward magnitude leads to a rapid decrease in responding, whereas a shift from small to large reward magnitude causes a significant increase in responding. The negative contrast (or depression) effect is a lower level of performance when the reward magnitude is shifted from

high to low than when the reward magnitude always is low; the positive contrast (or elation) effect is a higher level of performance when the reward magnitude is shifted from low to high than when the reward magnitude always is high.

6 Premack's probability-differential theory indicates that activities, such as watching television or going to a dance, can serve as reinforcers. According to Premack, high-probability activities reinforce lower-probability activities. Timberlake and Allison's response deprivation hypothesis states that an activity will serve as a reinforcer when a response contingency limits access to that activity; such a contingency causes an increase in responding needed to restore access to the restricted activity to its baseline level. The blisspoint is the free operant level of two responses. The behavioral allocation view assumes that an animal emits the number of contingent responses in order to come as close to blisspoint as possible. The matching law states that when two or more operant responses can be used to obtain reinforcement, the rate of responding is in direct proportion to the level of reinforcement available through each response.

7 Extinction of an instrumental response occurs when that behavior no longer produces reward. Nonreward of the instrumental response leads to an inhibition of that response as well as an elicitation of avoidance behavior. The avoidance behavior initially is an escape response from the frustration induced by nonreward. Association of environmental cues with nonreward motivates avoidance of nonreward and thereby leads to a decrease in the strength of the instrumental response. However, nonreward sometimes increases the intensity of instrumental behavior. Capaldi argued that this intensification occurs when the memory of nonreward has been conditioned to elicit the appetitive response.

8 A number of variables can affect the extinction of an instrumental response. A large reward magnitude produces greater resistance to extinction than does a small reward magnitude when the amount of acquisition training is low, but the opposite is true with extended acquisition training. Also, resistance to extinction is higher when reward delay is varied rather than constant. Furthermore, partial rather than continuous reward leads to a slower extinction of the instrumental behavior. Capaldi's research indicates that the conditioning of the memory of nonreward in the partial reward condition, but not in the continuous reward condition, is responsible for the greater resistance to extinction with partial than with continuous reward.

9 Contingent reinforcement has been used in many real-world situations to increase appropriate behaviors and decrease inappropriate responses. The application of the operant conditioning process to alter human behavior is called contingency management. There are three phases of contingency management: assessment, contracting, and implementation. In the assessment phase, the level of appropriate and inappropriate behavior is determined, along with the situations in which these behaviors occur and the potential reinforcers of the appropriate operant response. The precise relationship between the operant response and reinforcement is decided during the contracting phase. Implementation of the contingency contract involves providing reinforcement contingent upon the appropriate response or absence of the inappropriate behavior, or both. Contingency management has been used to modify many different behaviors, including inadequate living skills, phobias, depression, poor study habits, and antisocial responses.

6

PRINCIPLES AND APPLICATIONS OF AVERSIVE CONDITIONING

THE PAIN OF FAILURE

Charles dreads next week. He has a major project due at work and he is not anywhere near being finished. His boss had given him the assignment three weeks ago. It was a difficult task that required a lot of effort. But Charles has not been able to focus his attention on the project. Instead, much of his time has been spent worrying about being fired.

Charles joined the accounting firm three months ago after graduating from college. He was very excited about working after 4 years of school. He had enjoyed the first few weeks at work, everything was new and people willingly answered all of his questions. Charles was pleased with his job until last month. His anxiety began when he made a major mistake on a report. The error was caught by a senior officer at the firm, who was furious with him. Charles received a very strong criticism from his boss, which had a very adverse effect on Charles. He did not sleep well that night and was very anxious the next day at work.

Over the next few days, Charles tried to stay away from his boss but could not avoid him. His boss looked angry even a week after the reprimand. By the end of each day, Charles was so nervous that he began frequenting a bar on his way home. Several beers eased his pain. Charles was anxious again by the time he got home, so he had several more beers before dinner and a few more while watching television. He did not enjoy drinking, but it at least allowed him to sleep.

When his boss gave him the new project, Charles knew he was in trouble. He was told that the project was extremely important and that he had better not make any mistakes. This threat made him extremely nervous, and he got really drunk that night. As the due date approached, his nervousness increased, as did his drinking.

Charles is sure he is going to get fired. His world is falling apart and he does not know what to do to prevent its collapse.

Charles's fear represents a reaction to his reprimand from his boss (see Chapter 3 for a discussion of the conditioning of fear). Charles responded to the situation by drinking. The alcohol dulled his nervousness, and his increased drinking had become a habitual way to cope with fear. People who find themselves in unpleasant circumstances may drink to reduce their distress. Others may respond in more constructive ways to terminate unpleasant feelings. This chapter details how people learn to respond to adversity.

THE ADVERSITY AROUND US

Throughout life, people encounter many unpleasant events. No one is immune to adversity; each of us experiences an unpleasant circumstance from time to time. Unless we learn how to cope with adversity, our lives will be quite miserable. Aversive conditioning refers to the process of learning how to cope with adversity; we will discuss aversive conditioning in this chapter.

Some events can be escaped but not avoided. We cannot anticipate these circumstances but must be prepared to respond in order to terminate them. For example, while walking to the store, you are attacked by a thief who wants your money. You might be able to end the mugging by counterattacking. You will escape if your aggressive response is effective; however, if it is not, your counterattack probably will lead to even greater adversity.

Other events can be avoided. In order to prevent adversity, you must learn when the adversive event will occur and how you can act to prevent it. For example, many elderly people know that they may be mugged if they go out at night; therefore, not leaving their homes after dark allows them to avoid being mugged. This chapter describes the learning processes governing the escape or avoidance of adversity.

A parent punishes his or her child after receiving a teacher's note indicating poor behavior. The punishment is intended to inhibit future misbehavior in the classroom. If the punishment is effective, the child will no longer misbehave in school. The factors that determine whether or not punishment suppresses inappropriate behavior will be detailed later in the chapter.

You might think that a parent punishing a child for misbehaving has no relationship to an elderly person remaining inside at night to avoid being mugged. Yet, punishment and avoidance conditioning typically detail two aspects of the same process: The child can avoid being punished by not misbehaving in school, and the elderly person can avoid being mugged by not going out at night. Thus, for punishment to be effective, it must motivate the inhibition of the inappropriate response. However, there are some circumstances in which a person, or an animal, learns to prevent punishment—but with a response other than stopping the inappropriate behavior. For example, a child may be able to avoid punishment by crying, rather than by not misbehaving. Although we will describe punishment and avoidance behavior separately in this chapter, it is important to realize that if punishment is to be successful, inhibition of the inappropriate response must be the only response that will prevent punishment.

Some events cannot be escaped or avoided. For example, a child who is abused by a parent cannot escape or prevent the abuse. In Chapter 8, we will discover that helplessness develops as a result of learning that adversive events can neither be escaped nor avoided. We begin this chapter with an examination of escape conditioning, followed by a discussion of avoidance learning and punishment.

ESCAPE CONDITIONING

Many people close their eyes during a scary scene in a horror movie, opening them when they believe the unpleasant scene has ended. This behavior is one example of an *escape response,* an instrumental behavior motivated by adversity (for example, the scary scene) and rewarded by the termination of that adversity.

Many studies (see Brush, 1970; Campbell & Church, 1969) show that people and animals will try to escape adversity; let's examine two of these experiments. Miller's classic 1948 study (see Chapter 3) showed that rats could learn to escape painful electric shock. Miller placed rats in the white compartment of a shuttle box and exposed them to electric shock. The rats could escape the shock by turning a wheel and running into the black compartment; Miller reported that the rats rapidly learned to use this escape route. In a similar study using human subjects, Hiroto (1974) exposed college students to an unpleasant noise, which they could terminate by moving their finger from one side of a shuttle box to the other. Hiroto found that his subjects quickly learned how to escape the noise.

Escape from Adversity

Three factors play an important role in determining whether a person or animal learns to escape from adversity and how efficient the escape response is. First, *the intensity of adversity affects escape conditioning.* Research indicates that the greater the intensity of adversity, the faster the conditioning of the escape response as well as the higher the asymptotic level of responding. Second, *the amount of negative reward influences the acquisition of an escape response.* An evaluation of the effect of reward magnitude shows that the greater the decrease in the severity of adversity, the faster the acquisition of the escape response as well as the higher the final level of escape responding. Third, *the delay of reward affects the development of an escape response.* Research demonstrates that the longer the delay in the termination of adversity, the slower the acquisition of the escape response and the lower the asymptotic response level.

Intensity of Adversity   While walking to class, you see a student stumble and fall. Will you stop to help? A number of variables affect helping behavior. One critical factor is the seriousness of the emergency. According to Jane Piliavin and her associates (see Piliavin, Dovidio, Gaertner, & Clark, 1981), the more unpleasant the situation, the higher the cost of helping, and, therefore, the greater the motive to escape from the emergency. Thus, the more serious the injury is, the less likely you are to help.

Many studies have supported this cost analysis of helping. For example, Piliavin, Piliavin, and Roden (1975) simulated an emergency on subway cars in New York City. A confederate acting as a victim would moan and then faint. The experimenters increased the discomfort of some bystanders by having the victim expose an ugly birthmark just before fainting. The victim did not expose the unpleasant birthmark to other bystanders. Piliavin et al.'s results indicate that the bystanders who saw the ugly birthmark helped the victim less often than those who did not. As the cost of helping increases—in this case, the cost included enduring the sight of an ugly birthmark—the likelihood of helping behavior decreases.

Our discussion indicates that the greater the seriousness of an emergency, the greater the motivation to escape the situation. The escape response when anticipating failure on a task provides another illustration of the influence of the intensity of adversity. The more unpleasant the task—in this case, the greater the expectation of failure—the higher the motivation to escape and, therefore, the less persistence exhibited by subjects (see Atkinson, 1964; Feather, 1967).

Research with animals has documented the effect of the intensity of adversity on escape behavior. Most studies have used electric shock as the unpleasant event. For example, Trapold and Fowler (1960) trained rats to escape electric shock in the start box of an alley by running to an uncharged goal box. The rats received either 120, 160, 240, 300, or 400 volts of electric shock in the start box. Trapold and Fowler reported that the greater the shock intensity, the shorter the latency to escape from the start box (see Figure 6-1). Other research showed that escape latency is influenced by the intensity of loud noise (see Bolles & Seelbach, 1964; Masterson, 1969) and light (see Kaplan, Jackson, & Sparer, 1965).

Absence of Reward   Many people experience unsatisfying social relationships but remain in those relationships. Why do these people fail to escape? One likely reason is that past escape reactions from other unpleasant relationships did not lead to positive ones, so these individuals have not learned to use an escape response as a way of getting out of unpleasant situations. Many studies have shown that the intensity of escape behavior is affected by the amount of negative reward (or the degree of decrease in adversity). In these experiments, the greater the negative reward, the higher the asymptotic level of escape performance. Let's now examine one of these studies.

Campbell and Kraeling (1953) exposed rats to a 400-volt electric shock in the start box of an alley. Upon reaching the goal box, the shock was reduced to 0, 100, 200, or 300 volts. Campbell and Kraeling reported that the greater the

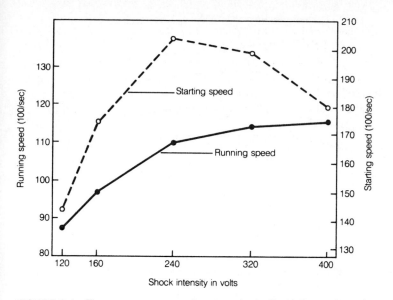

FIGURE 6-1   The mean escape performance for both starting and running speed increases over last eight trials of training with higher shock intensity. Adapted from Trapold, M. A., & Fowler, H. (1960). Instrumental escape performance as a function of the intensity of noxious stimulation. *Journal of Experimental Psychology, 60,* 323–326. Copyright 1960 by the American Psychological Association. Reprinted by permission.

reduction in shock intensity was, the faster the rats escaped from the 400-volt electric shock. Other researchers (see Bower, Fowler, & Trapold, 1959) have reported that the level of escape behavior is directly related to the level of shock reduction produced by the escape response. The positive influence of negative reward magnitude on the asymptotic level of escape performance has also been found with cold water as the adversive stimulus (see Woods, Davidson, & Peters, 1964).

Impact of Delayed Reward   Research has indicated that escape behavior is also influenced by the delay of reward. The longer that reward is delayed after an escape response, the slower the acquisition of the escape behavior, as well as the lower the final level of excape performance.

Fowler and Trapold's (1962) study illustrates the impact of reward delay on escape conditioning. In their study, the termination of electric shock was delayed 0, 1, 2, 4, 8, or 16 seconds after the rats entered the goal box of the alley. Fowler and Trapold reported that the time it took the rats to reach the goal box was a direct function of reward delay: The longer the delay, the slower the acquisition of an escape response (see Figure 6-2). Furthermore, the maximum escape speed was determined by reward delay; the longer the delay, the lower the final level of escape performance. Other studies using animals (see Milby, 1971; Tarpy &

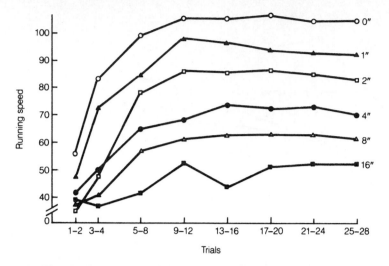

FIGURE 6-2   The mean running speed during escape training increases with a longer delay in shock termination. Adapted from Fowler, H., & Trapold, M. A. (1962). Escape performance as a function of delay of reinforcement. *Journal of Experimental Psychology, 63,* 464–467. Copyright 1962 by the American Psychological Association. Reprinted by permission.

Koster, 1970) and humans (see Penney, 1967) have found that delay of negative reward influences escape conditioning.

However, some experiments reported that a delay as short as 3 seconds results in no escape conditioning. According to Tarpy and Sawabini (1974), differences in delay gradients reflect the presence or absence of cues associated with negative reinforcement (termination of aversive event). The experiments showing very short delay gradients have used the operant chamber, with bar pressing as the escape response to terminate shock. Since no cues are typically associated with shock termination in the bar-press situation, no secondary reinforcement cues can enhance performance when reinforcement is delayed. If cues are presented following a bar-press response, these stimuli will be associated with shock termination, and some escape conditioning will occur despite a short delay of reinforcement. Recall from Chapter 5 that a similar influence of cues associated with reinforcements occurs when positive reinforcement is delayed. Thus, one significant influence of secondary reinforcers is to counter the effect of a delay of the primary reinforcer and, therefore, promote the conditioning of an escape response.

Elimination of an Escape Response

A rat shocked in the start box of an alley learns to escape by running into the goal box. A researcher can train the rat to no longer escape from the start box. Elimination of an escape response can be accomplished by no longer presenting

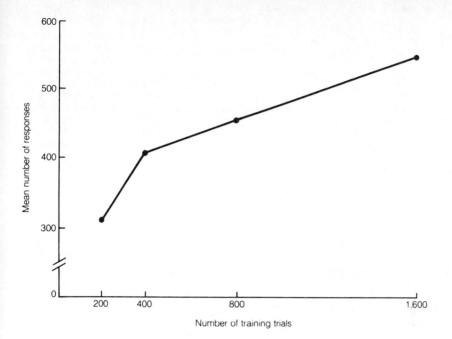

FIGURE 6-3   The mean number of escape responses during extinction increases with the greater number of acquisition trials. From Fazzaro, J., & D'Amato, M. R. (1969). Resistance to extinction after varying amounts of nondiscriminative or cue-correlated escape training. *Journal of Comparative and Physiological Psychology, 68,* 373–376. Copyright 1969 by the American Psychological Association. Reprinted by permission.

the adversive event or by no longer terminating the adversity following the escape response.

Removal of Negative Reward   An escape response is eliminated when the adversity continues despite the performance of the escape response. However, an animal or a person will continue to respond for some time; the adversity continues to motivate the escape response until the subject has learned that the escape response no longer terminates the adversity.

The strength of the escape response affects the resistance to extinction: The greater the acquisition training, the slower the extinction of the escape behavior. To illustrate the influence of the acquisition level on resistance to extinction, Fazzaro and D'Amato (1969) trained rats to bar press to terminate electric shock. Rats received 200, 400, 800, or 1600 training trials prior to extinction. Fazzaro and D'Amato found that the number of bar-press responses emitted during extinction increased with greater numbers of acquisition trials (see Figure 6-3).

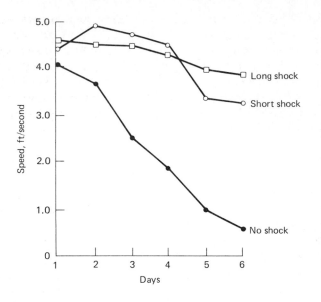

FIGURE 6-4
The mean escape latency during extinction for animals receiving either no shock in the alley, shock in the entire 6-foot alley (long-shock condition), or shock only in the last 2 feet of alley before goal box (short-shock condition). The resistance to extinction is higher in the long- and short-shock conditions than in the no-shock condition. From Brown, J. S., Martin, R. C., & Morrow, M. W. (1964). Self-punitive behavior in the rat: Facilitative effects of punishment on resistance to extinction. *Journal of Comparative and Physiological Psychology, 57,* 127–133. Copyright 1964 by the American Psychological Association. Reprinted by permission.

Absence of Adversity   Elimination of an escape response also occurs when the adversity is no longer experienced; yet, an animal or a person exhibits escape responses for awhile even though the adversive event no longer occurs. Why do escape responses occur when the adversity is not present?

D'Amato (1970) suggested an explanation for why escape responses occur after the adversity has been discontinued. According to D'Amato, the cues that were present when the adversive event occurred become able to elicit the r_p-s_p (anticipatory pain response mechanism; see Chapter 2). These conditioned stimuli produce the r_p-s_p and therefore motivate the escape response even though the adversity is no longer being presented. Escape responses will continue until the anticipatory pain response is extinguished.

Vicious-Circle Behavior   Judson Brown and his associates (see Brown, Martin, & Morrow, 1964) observed that punishment does not always eliminate escape behavior. In the Brown, Martin, and Morrow (1964) study, three groups of rats initially were placed in a 10-foot alley, which was electrified except for the goal box. All of these animals learned to run to the goal box to escape the shock. Animals in the no-shock condition had shock eliminated in the second phase of study. As seen in Figure 6-4, the speed of their escape response declined quickly when shock was stopped. The animals in the long-shock group continued to receive shock in the alley but not in the start box; the rats in the short-shock group received shock only in the final 2-foot segment before the goal box. Brown et al. observed that escape responding continued despite punishment of the escape response in both the long-shock and short-shock groups (refer to Figure 6-4). They referred to these animals' actions as self-punitive or *vicious-circle behavior*.

Vicious-circle behavior also has been observed in human subjects (see Renner & Tinsley, 1976; Tinsley & Renner, 1975). Renner and Tinsley trained human subjects to key press to escape shock in reaction to a warning light. These subjects stopped responding when the shock was discontinued. Other subjects had their first key press on each trial produce shock. These subjects failed to stop key pressing.

Why do animals show vicious-circle behavior? Brown and colleagues (1964) suggested that fear motivates running and that the conditioning of fear to the start box maintained the escape response. In contrast, Renner and Tinsley (see Renner & Tinsley, 1976; Tinsley & Renner, 1975) argued that vicious-circle behavior occurs because the animals or people failed to recognize that punishment would not occur if they did not respond. Renner and Tinsley observed that human subjects in a vicious-circle condition stop responding when told that key pressing would not result in shock. This observation indicates that subjects' behavior is affected by perception of behavior-outcome contingencies. We will discuss the importance of contingency learning in Chapter 8.

Section Review

Animals and people can learn to escape from adversity. Three variables affect the rate of acquisition of a behavior that terminates adversity: (1) the intensity of adversity—the greater the intensity of the adversity, faster the acquisition of an escape response; (2) the amount of reward—the greater the decrease in the severity of adversity following the escape behavior, the more rapid the learning of the escape response; and (3) the delay of reward—the longer the delay in the termination of adversity, the slower the acquisition of the escape response.

An escape response can also be extinguished. An animal or a person may stop responding if the adversity is no longer presented; however, fear conditioned during escape learning may prevent extinction of the escape response. Extinction typically occurs if the escape response is punished. The exception is vicious-circle behavior, in which the termination of adversity follows punishment of the escape response. In vicious-circle behavior, the escape response continues despite the fact that the failure to escape is not punished.

Our discussion indicates that we can learn how to escape from adverse situations. However, it is more desirable to avoid rather than escape adversity. In the next section we will examine the development of responses that allow us to prevent adversity.

THE AVOIDANCE OF ADVERSITY

A teenager is invited to a party by a boy whom she does not like. Not wanting to hurt his feelings, she says that she would like to go but cannot because she must study for a test. This teenager is exhibiting an avoidance response: Her "little white lie" enabled her to prevent an unpleasant evening without harming the boy.

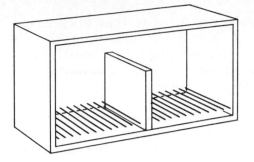

FIGURE 6-5
Illustration shows shuttle box used to study avoidance learning. When the conditioned stimulus is presented, animal must jump to other compartment to avoid electric shock.

Types of Avoidance Behavior

There are two classes of avoidance behavior: active and passive avoidance responses. Under some circumstances, an overt response, or an *active avoidance response,* is necessary to avoid the adverse situation. The teenager exhibited an active avoidance response: She formulated an excuse in order to prevent adversity. In other circumstances, not responding, or a *passive avoidance response,* will prevent adversity. Suppose you receive a note from your dentist indicating that it is time for your six-month checkup. Since you do not like going to the dentist, you ignore the note. This is an example of passive avoidance behavior: You avoid the dentist by not responding to the note.

Active Avoidance Learning O. H. Mowrer's classic research (see Mowrer, 1938, 1939) showed that rats could learn to exhibit an overt response to avoid electric shock. In these studies, a cue (for example, a buzzer) was paired with painful electric shock in one chamber of a shuttle box (see Figure 6-5). The rats could avoid shock by jumping across a barrier between the two compartments when the cue (CS) was presented but before the shock onset (UCS). The animals in Mowrer's studies learned to exhibit the active avoidance hurdle jump response when exposed to the CS and, therefore, avoided the electric shock. Many other psychologists since Mowrer's initial studies have observed that rats can learn to cross a barrier to avoid electric shock in the shuttle box apparatus (see Bower, Starr, & Lazarovitz, 1965; Kamin, 1956; Moyer & Korn, 1966; Theios, Lynch, & Lowe, 1966). The shuttle box apparatus also has been used to train other animal species to avoid adversity. This research indicates that to avoid shock, dogs (see Moscovitch & LoLordo, 1968; Solomon & Wynne, 1953), cats (Lockhart & Steinbrecher, 1965; Steinbrecher & Lockhart, 1966), mice (Winston, Lindzey, & Connor, 1967), and rabbits (Flakus & Steinbrecher, 1964) can learn to jump over the hurdle in a shuttle box.

The hurdle-jumping response in the shuttle box is one of many behaviors that animals can learn in order to avoid adverse events. Miller (1941, 1948) discovered that rats could learn to turn a wheel to avoid electric shock. Other psychologists have reported that rats can learn to press a bar in an operant chamber (Biederman,

D'Amato, & Keller, 1964; Hurwitz, 1964) or even rear up on their hind legs (Bolles & Tuttle, 1967) to prevent shock.

People learn many different responses to avoid adversity. A person opening an umbrella in order to stay dry, a child doing homework to avoid failing, or an adult paying the mortgage to avoid foreclosure are three examples of humans responding to avoid unpleasant events.

Many, perhaps most, of our avoidance responses are acquired during child-hood. Research with children shows that they are very adept in learning to avoid adversity. Several studies (Penney & Kirwin, 1965; Robinson & Robinson, 1961) using loud tones as the unpleasant event reported that preschool-aged children learned to press a lever to prevent hearing the noise.

Passive Avoidance Learning   Psychologists have also shown that animals can learn to avoid adversity passively. In one setting, an animal placed on top of a ledge above a grid floor receives an electric shock upon stepping down. Re-searchers (Chorover & Schiller, 1965; Hines & Paolino, 1970; McGaugh & Land-field, 1970) reported that rats refuse to leave the platform after a single training trial. Other studies demonstrated that animals readily learn to avoid shock by not entering an environment where they had been shocked the previous day (Baron, 1965; Kamin, 1959), or by failing to bar press after having been shocked for bar pressing (Camp, Raymond, & Church, 1967; Seligman & Campbell, 1965; Storms, Boroczi, & Broen, 1962).

The Nature of Avoidance Learning

We have discovered that animals and people can readily learn to avoid unpleasant events. What process enables animals or people to prevent adversity? The avoid-ance learning research of the 1930s created problems for the Hullian drive theory (see Chapter 2). The observation that animals can act to avoid unpleasant events suggests a cognitive process; that is, they are behaving in order to prevent ad-versity. Yet, the Hullian drive theory argued that mechanistic rather than cognitive processes govern behavior. O. H. Mowrer (1939, 1947, 1956) developed a drive-based view of avoidance behavior, an approach regarded as an accurate expla-nation of avoidance behavior until problems with this theory became apparent during the 1960s.

Two-Factor Theory of Avoidance Learning   Mowrer proposed a *two-factor theory of avoidance learning* which did not assume that avoidance behavior is motivated to prevent future adversity, a cognitive process. According to Mowrer, although it appears that animals or people are avoiding painful events, they are actually escaping a feared stimulus. Thus, their behavior is an escape response from a feared object, not an avoidance response to future adversity. Consider Miller's classic study (1948) to illustrate Mowrer's view of avoidance behavior.

In Miller's study, rats were shocked in a white chamber and learned to avoid shock by running from the white chamber through a doorway into a nonshocked black chamber. According to Mowrer, the rats were simply escaping the feared white compartment and were not behaving to avoid being shocked. In his view, the fear reduction which resulted from termination of the feared stimulus (white compartment) rewarded the rats' behavior. Mowrer believed that the motivation is to escape fear, not to avoid an adverse event, and that the instrumental response is rewarded by fear reduction, not by the avoidance of adversity.

Initial research evaluating Mowrer's theory was positive. Several studies (for example, Brown & Jacobs, 1949; Miller, 1948) reported that once fear of a distinctive cue was established, an animal learned a new response to escape from the feared stimulus. Psychologists (see Miller, 1951) believed that they had discovered how avoidance behavior is learned. However, some problems with Mowrer's view surfaced during the 1950s and 1960s.

Criticisms of Two-Factor Theory Several problems exist with Mowrer's two-factor theory of avoidance learning. First, although exposure to the conditioned stimulus should eliminate avoidance behavior, avoidance behavior is often extremely resistant to extinction. For example, Solomon and Wynne (1954) reported that dogs, even after receiving over 200 extinction trials, continued to perform a previously established avoidance response. The apparent failure of extinction represents a problem for the two-factor theory: If fear is acquired through classical conditioning and is responsible for motivating the avoidance behavior, then the presentation of the CS during extinction should cause a reduction in fear and a cessation of avoidance behavior.

Levis and Boyd (1979) offered one answer to this problem: It is not the number of extinction trials but rather the duration of exposure to the CS that determines the reduction of fear and thus the elimination of an avoidance response. Levis and Boyd found that the persistence of avoidance behavior is dependent on the duration of exposure to the feared stimulus: the longer the exposure, the weaker the avoidance response. Additionally, Levis (1989) suggests that a rapid avoidance response prevents the extinction of cues close to the time of the UCS. Suppose the adversive event (UCS) does not occur until 10 seconds after the CS begins. If the animal avoids after 2 seconds, the short latency cues will extinguish but not the longer latency ones. When the avoidance response slows, the long latency cues will elicit fear, which will act to recondition fear to the short latency cues. In support of this view, Levis found that extinction of the avoidance response is much slower if there are separate cues associated with short and long latency than if a single cue is present during the entire CS-UCS interval.

A second problem for the two-factor theory concerns the apparent absence of fear in a well-established avoidance response. For example, Kamin, Brimer, and Black (1963) observed that a CS for a well-learned avoidance behavior did not suppress an operant response for food reinforcement. The failure to reduce responding is thought to reflect an absence of fear, because one indication of fear is the suppression of appetitive behavior. However, it is possible that the absence of suppression does not indicate that an animal shows no fear in response to the CS, but rather that an animal's motivation for food is stronger than the fear induced by the CS. Further, strong fear is not necessary to motivate a habitual avoidance response—an observation consistent with Hull's idea that the tendency to respond is a joint function of drive and habit strength.

The Sidman avoidance procedure represents a third problem for two-factor theory. In the *Sidman avoidance task,* an animal receives periodic adversity unless it responds to prevent the adverse event. The avoidance response acts to delay the occurrence of the next adverse event for a specific period of time. The interval between adverse events is the S-S interval, while the time that the adversity is delayed is the R-S interval. If an animal responds consistently prior to the end of the R-S interval, it will not experience adversity. There is no external warning stimulus in the Sidman avoidance procedure. The lack of an external warning stimulus should prevent avoidance learning since there is no external conditioned stimulus to arouse fear prior to the avoidance behavior nor any external conditioned stimulus terminating after the avoidance response and producing fear reduction. Yet, researchers (see Anger, 1963; Sidman, 1953; Weisman & Litner, 1971) have observed that animals can learn to avoid adversity with the Sidman avoidance procedure.

Kamin's experiment (1956) demonstrating the importance of the avoidance of adversity during conditioning is perhaps the most damaging evidence against Mowrer's theory. Kamin compared avoidance learning in four groups of rats: (1) rats whose response both terminated the CS and prevented the UCS (normal condition), (2) animals shocked at a predetermined time but whose behavior terminated the CS (terminate-CS group), (3) rats that avoided the UCS while the CS remained for a short time after the response (avoid-UCS group), and (4) rats in a control group given CS and UCS but not allowed to escape or avoid the shock (classical conditioning group). Although the two-factor theory would predict that the avoid-UCS group would not learn because their fear remained after their response, these subjects showed greater avoidance responding than did control animals. Also, the avoid-UCS subjects responded as often as the rats whose behavior terminated the CS but did not prevent shock (terminate-CS group). Figure 6-6 presents the results of Kamin's study, which indicate that two factors— termination of the CS and avoidance of the UCS—play an important role in avoidance learning.

D'Amato's View of Avoidance Learning   Michael D'Amato (1970) developed an acquired motive view to explain why prevention of the adversive event is important for avoidance behavior (see Chapter 2). According to D'Amato, an adverse event such as a shock elicits an unconditioned pain response (R_P), and the stimulus consequences of the painful event (S_P) motivate escape behavior. As the result of conditioning, the environmental cues present during shock can eventually produce an anticipatory pain response (r_p), with its stimulus aftereffects (s_p) also motivating escape behavior.

D'Amato's r_p-s_p mechanism motivates escape from the conditioned stimulus. The termination of an adverse event (the UCS; for example, shock) produces an unconditioned relief response (R_R). The stimulus consequences (S_R) of the

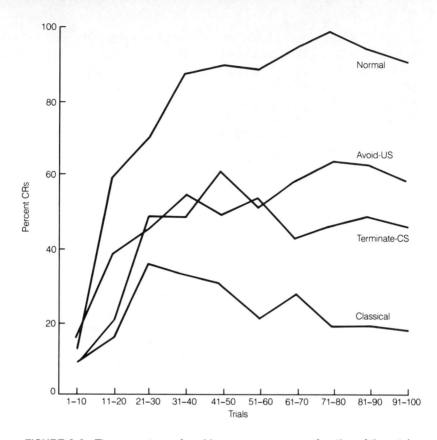

FIGURE 6-6 The percentage of avoidance responses as a function of the rats' ability to terminate the CS, avoid the UCS, or both. The level of avoidance behavior is greatest when the rats could both terminate the CS and avoid the UCS. From Kamin, L. J. (1956). The effects of termination of the CS and the avoidance of the UCS on avoidance learning. *Journal of Comparative and Physiological Psychology, 49,* 420–424. Copyright 1956 by the American Psychological Association. Reprinted by permission.

relief response are rewarding. According to D'Amato, the stimuli associated with the termination of adversity develop the ability to elicit an anticipatory relief response (r_R). The stimulus aftereffects (s_R) of this anticipatory response are also rewarding. Furthermore, the sight of the cues associated with anticipatory relief motivates approach behavior in a manner comparable to Spence's description of the approach response to anticipatory goal-related cues (see Chapter 2). This idea suggests a second motivational basis of avoidance behavior. The animal or human is not only escaping from an adverse situation but also approaching a rewarding one. According to D'Amato, the avoidance of adversity is important because if the animal does not avoid, the r_R-s_R mechanism will not develop and, therefore, the avoidance response will not be rewarded.

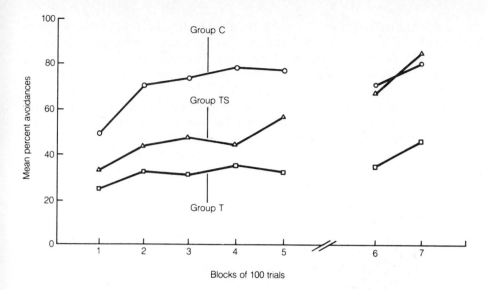

FIGURE 6-7   The percentage of avoidance responses during 700 trials for standard delayed-conditioning group (group C), trace-conditioning group (group T), and group receiving a cue for 5 seconds after each avoidance response (group TS). The feedback stimulus overcame the poor performance observed with trace-conditioning procedure. The break in curves indicates that a 24-hour interval elapsed between the fifth and sixth blocks of trials. From D'Amato, M. R., Fazzaro, J., & Etkin, M. (1968). Anticipatory responding and avoidance discrimination as factors in avoidance conditioning. *Journal of Experimental Psychology, 77,* 41–47. Copyright 1968 by the American Psychological Association. Reprinted by permission.

A number of studies support D'Amato's view of avoidance learning. D'Amato, Fazzaro, and Etkin (1968) suggested that an avoidance response is not learned when a trace conditioning procedure is used (in this technique, the CS terminates prior to the UCS presentation) because there is no distinctive cue associated with the absence of the UCS. If a cue were present when adversity ended, an avoidance response would be learned. In order to demonstrate this idea, D'Amato and colleagues presented a second cue (in addition to the CS) when their subjects exhibited an avoidance response. Although learning was slow—only reaching the level observed with the delayed conditioning procedure (the CS and UCS terminated at the same time) after 500 trials—these subjects performed at a higher level than observed when the second cue is present (see Figure 6-7). According to D'Amato, once the second cue was associated with the termination of shock, the r_R-s_R mechanism was acquired, which then acted to reward avoidance behavior.

The importance of a discriminative cue signaling the absence of adversity can be used to explain avoidance learning with the Sidman avoidance procedure. Recall that there is no external warning stimulus with the Sidman avoidance task. According to Levis (1989), the periodic adverse events experienced early in learning condition high levels of fear to the training environment. This fear produces high levels of activity, which motivate the avoidance response. Response-produced cues predict the absence of adversity. The relief experienced following the avoidance response reinforces the avoidance behavior and results in effective learning.

D'Amato's view asserts that we are motivated to approach situations associated with relief, as well as to escape those events paired with adversity. Furthermore, the relief experienced following avoidance behavior rewards that response. M. Ray Denny's research (see Denny, 1971) demonstrates the motivational and rewarding character of relief. Let's examine Denny's evidence validating both aspects of D'Amato's view.

Denny and Weisman (1964) demonstrated that animals anticipating pain will approach events that are associated with relief. They trained rats to escape or to avoid shock in a striped shock compartment of a T-maze by turning either right into a black compartment or left into a white chamber. One of the chambers was associated with a 100-second delay before the next trial, but the rat spent only 20 seconds between trials in the other compartment. The authors found that the rats learned to go to the compartment associated with the longer intertrial interval. These results suggest that when the rats anticipated adversity, they were motivated to seek an environment associated with the greatest relief.

Denny asserts that the amount of relief depends upon the length of time between adversive events: the longer the nonshock interval (or intertrial interval, ITI), the greater the conditioned relief. In Denny's view, the greater the relief, the faster the acquisition of an avoidance habit. To test this idea, Denny and Weisman varied the time between trials from 10 to 225 seconds and observed that acquisition of an avoidance response was directly related to intertrial interval: Animals allowed a longer interval between trials learned the avoidance response more readily than did those given a shorter time between trials. These results show that the longer the period of relief after an adverse event, the more readily the rats learned to avoid adversity.

A Cognitive View   Several psychologists (see Bandura, 1986; Bolles, 1978; Seligman & Johnston, 1973) theorized that expectancies play an important role in avoidance behavior. According to the cognitive approach, two types of expectancies—stimulus outcome and behavior outcome—affect avoidance behavior (see Chapter 2 for a review of expectancy theory). Stimulus outcome expectancies indicate when and where adverse events will occur. Also, stimulus outcome expectancies tell us which events are associated with the absence of adversity. The behavior outcome expectancies indicate when responding will prevent adversity. Consider Charles's avoidance behavior detailed in the chapter-opening vignette. Charles expects that poor performance will lead to verbal criticism (stimulus outcome expectancy) and that drinking alcohol will decrease his distress (behavior outcome expectancy). The role of expectancies in avoidance learning will be explored in Chapter 8.

A Combined Drive and Cognitive View Bolles (1978) pointed to one weakness in the cognitive approach. What process transforms an expectation into overt behavior? Some psychologists have suggested that cognitive processes determine how we interpret our emotions but that once we are aroused, drive processes automatically motivate behavior. The combined influence of cognitive and drive processes has been suggested for a number of behaviors, including achievement behavior (see Atkinson, 1958, 1964), aggression (see Berkowitz, 1980), interpersonal attraction (see Berscheid & Walster, 1978), and sexual behavior (see Klein, 1982).

How Readily Is Avoidance Behavior Learned?

Two variables appear to have an important influence on avoidance learning. First, *the severity of adversity influences avoidance behavior.* The influence of severity depends on the type of avoidance task. In simple tasks, the more severe the adversity, the faster the acquisition and the higher the asymptotic level of avoidance behavior. In contrast, the effect of severity is the opposite with difficult avoidance tasks: the greater the severity of the adversive event the slower the acquisition and the lower the final level of performance of an avoidance response. Second, *the length of the interval between presentation of the feared object and adversity influences avoidance behavior.* Research shows that as the CS-UCS interval increases, so does the time needed for the acquisition of avoidance response.

Severity of Adversity You might suspect that the greater the adversity of an event, the more likely it is that the situation will be avoided. This relationship is true in most avoidance situations; that is, the greater the adversity of an event, the more readily the avoidance response will be learned and the higher the final level of avoidance performance will be. However, the opposite relationship is true in a two-way active avoidance task. In this type of avoidance task, the greater the severity of adversity is, the slower the avoidance response will be acquired and the lower the final level of avoidance performance will be. We will first examine evidence indicating the influence of the severity of adversity on avoidance learning, then discuss why severity influences two-way avoidance behavior differently than it does other avoidance responses.

Passive Avoidance Behavior Investigators (see Camp, Raymond, & Church, 1967; Church, Raymond, & Beauchamp, 1967; Seligman & Campbell, 1965; Storms et al., 1962) have evaluated the effect of shock severity on the acquisition of a passive avoidance response. In these studies, rats were initially trained to bar press for food. After learning to bar press, the animals were shocked following a bar-press response; each rat could avoid being shocked by emitting a bar-press response. The severity of shock varied: Subjects received low-, moderate-, or high-severity electric shock. The results showed that the higher the shock severity, the faster the acquisition of the passive avoidance response and the higher the final performance level of the passive avoidance behavior.

One-Way Active Avoidance Behavior Shock severity also has an important influence on the acquisition and performance of a one-way active avoidance response. In this situation, the animal is shocked in one chamber of a shuttle box and can avoid shock by running to the other chamber. The shocked chamber is painted one color (for example, white) and the goal box another (for example, black). Many studies (see McAllister, McAllister, & Douglass 1971; Moyer & Korn, 1966; Theios et al., 1966) have discovered that increasing the severity of the shock leads to faster acquisition of the one-way active avoidance response, as well as a higher level of asymptotic avoidance performance. Let's examine the Moyer and Korn (1966) study to document the role of shock intensity on a one-way active avoidance response.

Moyer and Korn placed their rats on one side of a shuttle box, shocking them if they had not run to the other compartment within 5 seconds. Each rat remained in the "safe" chamber for 15 seconds and was then placed in the "dangerous" chamber to begin another trial. Animals received 0.5, 1.5, 2.5, or 3.5 mA (milliampere) of shock during acquisition training. Each subject was given 50 acquisition trials on a single day. Moyer and Korn reported that the more severe the shock was, the faster the animals learned to avoid the shock (see Figure 6-8). Furthermore, the higher the intensity of shock, the more rapidly the animals ran from the dangerous to the safe compartment of the shuttle box.

Two-Way Active Avoidance Behavior In a two-way active avoidance situation, the animal is placed in one chamber (side A) of the shuttle box and exposed to a specific stimulus (for example, a light) prior to the presentation of shock. In order to avoid the shock, the animal must run to the chamber (side B) before the electric shock is presented. After this trial, the animal remains in side B for a short time (for example, 60 seconds). At the end of this intertrial interval (ITI), the stimulus is again presented, and the animal must run from side B to side A in order to avoid being shocked; thus, the animal in this situation avoids the adverse event only by returning to the place where it had been shocked. Learning a two-way active avoidance response requires an animal to ignore situational cues (the place where shock was presented) and attend to a specific cue (for example, the light). The two-way active avoidance training continues until the animal responds consistently to the specific cue (CS) and avoids the aversive electric shock.

We learned earlier that increases in the adversity of an event facilitate the acquisition of a passive avoidance response and a one-way active avoidance behavior. In contrast, the literature (see McAllister et al., 1971, Moyer & Korn, 1964; Theois et al., 1966) clearly shows that a severe event impairs rather than enhances the acquisition and the asymptotic performance level of a two-way active avoidance response. Let's examine one study to illustrate the influence of severity on two-way active avoidance learning.

Moyer and Korn (1964) gave their rats two-way active avoidance response training in periods of 30 trials a day for 4 days. In their study, a tone was presented in one chamber and the rats had 5 seconds to run to the other chamber in order to avoid being shocked. Rats failing to respond within the 5-second

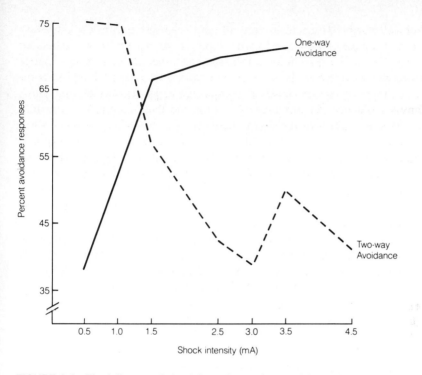

FIGURE 6-8 The influence of shock intensity on the acquisition of a two-way
and a one-way active avoidance response. Increases in shock intensity
facilitate one-way avoidance learning but impair two-way avoidance acquisition.
From Flaherty, C. F., Hamilton, L. W., Gandelman, R. J., & Spear, N. E. (1977).
Learning and memory. Chicago: Rand McNally.

interval received a 0.5, 1.0, 1.5, or 2.5 mA shock. Moyer and Korn found that
as shock intensity increased, the percentage of avoidance responses made during
acquisition declined (refer to Figure 6-8). These results show that high levels of
electric shock impair an animal's ability to avoid being shocked in a two-way
active avoidance task.

Why do increases in shock severity impair two-way active avoidance learning,
yet facilitate other forms of avoidance learning? Theois and colleagues (1966)
suggested that in a two-way active avoidance task, the animal experiences conflict
between running away from the feared stimulus and running into an environment
where adversity occurred on the previous trial. According to Theois et al., the
more severe the adversity, the greater the animal's reluctance to enter the environment associated with adversity and, therefore, the poorer the acquisition of an
avoidance response. Many studies (see Tarpy & Mayer, 1978) support this view;
let's examine one of them.

Freedman, Hennessy, and Groner (1974) compared the efficiency of avoidance
behavior occurring when animals were running from a compartment associated

with a high level of adversity into a compartment associated with less adversity to avoidance performance that occurred when both compartments were associated with equal shock adversity. Freedman and associates assumed that the reluctance to avoid shock would decrease if animals had to run to a less adversive compartment rather than an equally adverse compartment. In support of this view, they found that avoidance performance was enhanced if an animal had run into a chamber associated with a lower shock intensity.

Delay Interval between CS and UCS We learned in Chapter 3 that the level of fear conditioning depends upon the CS-UCS interval; the longer the interval, the weaker the conditioning of the fear response. The interval between the CS and the UCS also affects the acquisition of an avoidance response. The literature (see Hall, 1979) shows that the longer the CS-UCS interval, the slower the acquisition of the avoidance behavior. It seems reasonable to assume that the influence of the CS-UCS interval on fear conditioning is also responsible for its affect on avoidance learning; as the level of fear diminishes with longer CS-UCS intervals, motivation to escape the feared stimulus weakens and, therefore, the opportunity to learn to avoid lessens. Let's next consider one study that examined the influence of the CS-UCS interval on avoidance behavior.

Kamin (1954) trained dogs to avoid shock by jumping over a barrier in a two-way active avoidance situation. The CS, a 2-second buzzer, preceded the shock UCS. The interval between the CS-UCS varied: Subjects received a 5-, 10-, 20-, or 40-second CS-UCS interval. Kamin reported that the shorter the interval between the CS and the UCS, the quicker the acquisition of the avoidance response.

Application: Response Prevention or Flooding

Some psychologists, beginning with John Watson, have hypothesized that phobias are learned avoidance behaviors. On the basis of this assumption, techniques that are effective in eliminating avoidance behavior in animals also should be effective in eliminating phobic behavior. The problem with trying to extinguish phobic behavior is that because fear motivates avoidance of the phobic stimulus, the subject will not experience the CS long enough to be associated with the absence of the UCS. Two treatments of phobic behavior, flooding and systematic desensitization, have been used to overcome this problem. We learned in Chapter 4 that systematic desensitization works by conditioning a relaxation response that is antagonistic to fear of the phobic object. Flooding forces the person to experience the feared stimulus and associate the CS with the absence of UCS, thereby eliminating the avoidance behavior.

Flooding differs from the typical extinction procedure in that the feared stimulus cannot be escaped. Otherwise, the two procedures are identical: The animal or human is exposed to the conditioned fear stimulus without an aversive consequence. Research investigating response prevention, or *flooding,* has demonstrated it to be an effective technique for eliminating avoidance behavior in animals (see Baum, 1970). Baum found that the effectiveness of flooding increased with longer exposure to the fear stimulus. In addition, Coulter, Riccio, and Page (1969) found that flooding suppressed an avoidance response faster than a typical extinction procedure did.

Clinical Effectiveness   Malleson (1959) first reported the successful use of flooding to treat avoidance behavior in humans. Since Malleson's experiment, numerous studies have demonstrated the effectiveness of flooding to eliminate a wide variety of behavior disorders, including phobias (for example, Yule, Sacks, & Hersov, 1974), anxiety and neurosis (see Girodo, 1974), and obsessive-compulsive behavior (for example, Hackman & McLean, 1975).

Flooding seems to be especially effective in treating obsessive-compulsive behavior. The following case history, reported by Meyer, Robertson, and Tatlow in 1975, provides an example of the technique and its successful implementation. An adult female client had become extremely disturbed about anything associated with death—even the newspaper obituary column elicited anxiety. When anxious, she compulsively washed herself and changed her clothes. Treatment began by identifying anxiety-inducing stimuli. The most aversive stimulus was dead bodies. Thus, the therapist and the patient handled a corpse at a local hospital mortuary. The patient encountered other aversive stimuli—for example, a picture of a dead man. In order to prevent her ritualistic compulsive behavior, the therapist remained with her following her exposures to the feared stimuli. The authors reported that on the second treatment day the patient was completely able to suppress the rituals. Eight months after the therapy, the woman had no inclination to exhibit ritualistic behavior and demonstrated only a low level of anxiety to death-related stimuli.

The Nature of the Flooding Process   Investigations of flooding indicate that extinction of a fear response is not completely responsible for the effectiveness of this procedure (see Mineka, 1979, for a review of this literature). Mineka and Gino (1979) showed that animals receiving enough flooding (20 trials) to extinguish a well-learned avoidance response did not show reduced fear of the conditioned stimulus.

Mineka and Gino (1979) reported that additional flooding can eliminate the fear of the CS. Also, Monti and Smith (1976) observed that response prevention produced faster extinction of the CS-induced fear than did the typical self-exposure extinction procedure. Although flooding can eventually extinguish a fear response, the suppression of avoidance responding occurs independently of fear extinction. These results indicate that the extinction of the avoidance contingency can occur without extinction of the Pavlovian conditioned fear association and that avoidance learning reflects more than a response motivated by fear and reinforced by fear reduction.

The mechanism responsible for the effectiveness of flooding remains undetermined. Baum (1970) suggested that the conditioning of the relaxation response during flooding causes the elimination of avoidance responding. A study by Hawk and Riccio (1977) supports this view. Their research demonstrated that the introduction of a stimulus associated with the absence of shock facilitated the flooding-induced suppression of avoidance behavior; this cue produced relaxation and therefore enhanced conditioning of the relaxation response to the feared environment. Hussain's (1971) observation that the use of relaxing drugs increased the effectiveness of flooding also supports Baum's view. However, our earlier discussion indicated that with a moderate level of flooding treatment, fear persisted even though the avoidance behavior did not occur. It may be that relaxation is responsible for the eventual elimination of fear but does not cause the suppression of avoidance behavior. An understanding of the mechanisms responsible for the success of flooding may lie in the cognitive approaches to avoidance behavior; these cognitive views are discussed in Chapter 8.

Section Review

Some unpleasant circumstances can be prevented, and in these cases a specific overt behavior can be used to avoid adversity; in other instances, the suppression of responding will prevent the adverse event. Psychologists have speculated about the nature of avoidance learning. Mowrer suggested that fear is conditioned during the first phase of learning. In the second stage, fear motivates responding to any behavior that successfully terminates the fear. This effective behavior will be rewarded and elicited upon future presentations of the feared stimulus. According to Mowrer, adversity will be prevented only if the escape response to the feared stimulus also will result in the avoidance of painful events.

D'Amato proposed that avoidance behavior is motivated not only by the anticipation of pain but also by the anticipation of relief. D'Amato theorized that the anticipatory relief response cannot be acquired if the avoidance response does not prevent adversity. In contrast, Bolles suggested a cognitive view of avoidance behavior: Expectations that an adverse event will occur in the absence of avoidance behavior and that the avoidance response will prevent adversity are acquired during avoidance learning. One contemporary view of avoidance learning suggests that both drives and cognitions play an important role in avoidance behavior.

Two variables affect the rate of acquisition of an avoidance response. First, the severity of the event influences the acquisition of the avoidance response. In some tasks (passive avoidance learning and one-way active avoidance learning), increases in adversity lead to faster avoidance learning; in other tasks (two-way active avoidance learning), an increase in the intensity of the adversive event produces slower acquisition. Second, the rate of avoidance acquisition is influenced by the CS-UCS interval: the longer the interval between the CS and the UCS, the slower the acquisition of the avoidance response.

Flooding represents a viable treatment of human phobias and obsessive-compulsive behavior. In flooding, or response prevention, the person is prevented from exhibiting the avoidance response. The success of flooding depends upon providing sufficient exposure to the feared stimulus to extinguish the avoidance response.

PUNISHMENT

A parent takes away a child's television privileges for hitting a younger sibling. A teacher sends a disruptive student to the principal to be suspended for three days from school. A soldier absent without leave is ordered to the stockade by the military police. An employee who is late for work is reprimanded by the boss. Each of these situations is an example of punishment. *Punishment* is defined as the use of an adverse event contingent upon the occurrence of an inappropriate behavior. The intent of punishment is to suppress an undesired behavior; if punishment is effective, the frequency and intensity, or both, of the punished behavior will decline. For example, the parent who takes away a child's television privileges for hitting a younger sibling is using punishment to decrease the occurrence of the child's aggressive behavior. The loss of television is an effective punishment, if, after being punished, the youngster hits the sibling less frequently.

Types of Punishers

We have defined punishment as the response-contingent presentation of an adverse event. There are two types of punishment: positive punishment and negative punishment. *Positive punishment* refers to the use of a physically or psychologically painful event as the punishment. A spanking is one example of a positive punisher; verbal criticism is another. In *negative punishment,* reinforcement is lost or unavailable as the consequence of the occurrence of an inappropriate behavior. The term *omission training* is often used instead of negative punishment. In omission training, reinforcement is provided when the undesired response does not occur. However, the occurrence of the inappropriate behavior leads to a failure to obtain or a loss of reinforcement.

There are two categories of negative punishment. One of these is *response cost,* in which an undesired response results in either the withdrawal of or failure to obtain reinforcement. In laboratory settings, a response cost contingency means that an undesired response will cause an animal or a person to lose or not obtain either a primary reinforcer (for example, candy or food) or a secondary reinforcer (for example, chips, tokens, or points). Real-world examples of response cost punishment include the withdrawal or failure to obtain material reinforcers (money) or social reinforcers (approval). Losing television privileges for hitting a sibling is one example of response cost; being fined by an employer for being late for work is another.

The other kind of negative punishment is called *time-out* (or time-out from reinforcement). Time-out from reinforcement is a period of time during which reinforcement is unavailable. A child being sent to his or her room after misbehaving is one example of time-out; another is the soldier going to the stockade for being AWOL.

Is punishment effective? The extensive use of it in our society suggests that we believe punishment to represent an effective technique to suppress inappropriate behavior. However, psychology's view of the effectiveness of punishment has changed dramatically during the past 100 years. In the next section, we will examine how psychologists have viewed the effectiveness of punishment as a method of suppressing behavior.

The Effectiveness of Punishment

In Chapter 2, we learned that Thorndike (1898) proposed that stimulus-response associations are strengthened when followed by a satisfying state of affairs (or reward). Although he initially believed that unpleasant events weakened the S-R bond, Thorndike (1932) later suggested that annoying events or punishments do not weaken S-R associations. Thorndike's studies caused him to revise his view of punishment. In a typical experiment, human subjects were read a long list of words and were told that a number from 1 to 10 was associated with each word. The subjects were instructed to guess the number for each word. Some of the subjects' responses were rewarded with the feedback "Yes, that's right"; other responses were punished with the response "No, that's wrong." Most of the items were followed by no feedback. Whereas reward increased the rate of the subjects' correctness, the repetition of responses followed by punishment did not decline. On the basis of this research, Thorndike concluded that S-R bonds could be strengthened by reward but not weakened by punishment.

Estes (1944) and Skinner (1953) assumed that punishment could only *temporarily* suppress behavior. The classic Skinner study (1938) supports their view. In his experiment, two rats were trained to bar press for food reinforcement. The rats' bar-press responding was then extinguished by discontinuing reinforcement. One rat was also punished for bar pressing by having his paw slapped when it touched the bar during the first few responses of extinction. The other rat did not receive punishment. Skinner observed that the initial effect of punishment was a lower response rate (see Figure 6-9). However, the suppressive effect of punishment was short-lived; the rate of bar pressing was equivalent in the punished and the nonpunished rat within 30 minutes after punishment. Skinner also noted that the punished rat continued to respond at a high rate even after the nonpunished rat had slowed down. When both rats had finally stopped responding, both had made the same number of responses. Skinner's observations show that punishment may temporarily suppress responding but does not eliminate it.

Estes (1944) conducted a more extensive investigation of the effects of punishment. Instead of a slap on the paw, Estes used electric shock as the punisher. Estes also observed that the suppressive effects of punishment were only temporary. These results and similar observations led Estes (1944) and Skinner (1953) to conclude that punishment is an ineffective technique for eliminating an undesired behavior. They suggested that extinction instead of punishment should be used to permanently suppress an inappropriate response. Their conclusions certainly conflict with our society's belief that punishment is an effective method of suppressing inappropriate behavior.

Research evaluating the influence of punishment on behavior during the 1950s and 1960s shows that under some conditions, punishment does permanently sup-

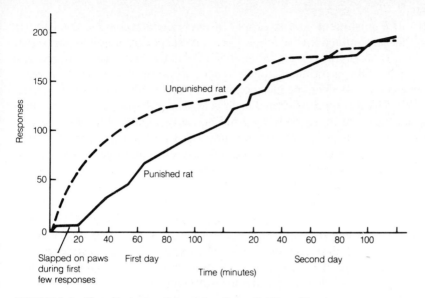

FIGURE 6-9   The effect of punishment on the extinction of bar-press response. Punishment produced a temporary reduction in bar pressing, but by the end of the second day, there were no longer any effects of punishment. Adapted from Skinner, B. F. (1938). *The behavior of organisms: An experimental analysis.* New York: Appleton-Century-Crofts.

press inappropriate behavior (see Campbell & Church, 1969). However, in other circumstances, punishment either has no effect on behavior or will only temporarily suppress behavior.

A number of variables determine whether or not punishment will suppress behavior, as well as how long the punished behavior will be inhibited. We will next discuss the conditions necessary for effective punishment and the circumstances in which punishment does not suppress inappropriate behavior.

When Is Punishment Effective?

Three factors have an important influence on the effectiveness of punishment. First, *the severity of the punishment affects the degree of behavioral suppression produced by punishment.* The literature shows that the more severe the punishment, the greater the suppression of the punished behavior. Second, *the level of suppression is influenced by the consistency of the administration of punishment.* Research documents that the greater the consistency with which punishment follows an inappropriate behavior, the greater the suppression of that behavior. Third, *the delay of punishment affects the influence of punishment on behavior.* The level of behavioral suppression is reduced as the interval between the behavior and punishment increases.

Severity of Punishment   Most people in our society recognize the dangers of driving under the influence of alcohol. Local newspapers routinely report traffic fatalities caused by drunk drivers. Over 650,000 individuals were injured and 46,000 killed in 1986 in traffic accidents related to drunk drivers (U.S. Department of Justice, 1988). Yet, people continue to drive while intoxicated. And thousands of drunk drivers are ticketed each year. These drivers, though punished when apprehended, are most likely to drink and drive again. About 48 percent of people charged with drunk driving are repeaters (U.S. Department of Justice, 1988). Why are the punishments given to drunk drivers so ineffective? One reason may be that the punishment is too mild to suppress drunk driving effectively. In most cases, the first offense is punished by mandatory participation in an alcohol treatment program rather than a jail sentence. Even repeat offenders rarely spend more than one year in prison.

Research investigating the influence of the severity of adversity on the effectiveness of punishment has consistently shown that mild punishment produces little if any suppression of the punished response. And if any suppression does occur, it will be short-lived. The effectiveness of punishment also has been found to increase as the severity increases (see Campbell & Church, 1969). Thus, a moderately severe punishment produces more suppression of an inappropriate behavior than does a mild punishment, while a strong punishment is more likely to produce complete suppression of the punished behavior. Also, the more severe the punishment is, the longer the punished behavior is inhibited. In fact, a severe punishment may lead to a permanent suppression of the punished response. Several studies showing that the effectiveness of punishment is dependent upon the severity of punishment are examined next.

Numerous studies using animal subjects have reported that the greater the intensity of punishment, the more complete the suppression of the punished behavior (see Church, 1969). Camp and colleagues' 1967 study provides an excellent example of the influence of the intensity of punishment on the degree of suppression of an operant behavior. In their study, 48 rats initially were given eight sessions of training to bar press for food reinforcement on a VI 1-minute schedule. Following initial training, the rats were divided into six groups and given 0, 0.1, 0.2, 0.3, 0.5, or 2.0 mA shock punishment lasting for 2.0 seconds. An animal was punished if its response rate had not changed within the minute since it had last received punishment. As can be seen in Figure 6-10, the higher the intensity of shock, the greater the suppression of the operant response. Apparently, the more severe the punisher is, the more effective the shock will be in suppressing the punished response. The effect of shock intensity on the suppression of an operant response has been shown in a number of animal species, including monkeys (Appel, 1963; Hake, Azrin, & Oxford, 1967), pigeons (Azrin & Holz, 1966), and rats (Karsh, 1962; Storms et al., 1962).

Research conducted with human subjects has demonstrated that the severity of punishment affects its effectiveness. There have been a number of studies (Aronfreed & Leff, 1963; Cheyne, Goyeche, & Walters, 1969; Parke & Walters, 1967) evaluating the effect of the intensity of punishment on the suppression of

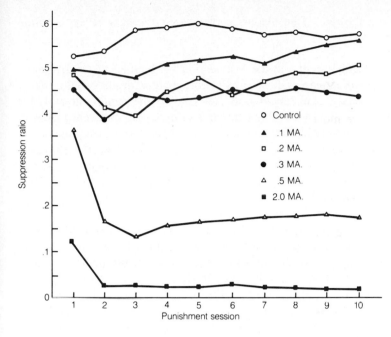

FIGURE 6-10 The mean suppression ratio increases with higher intensities of electric shock during punishment training. To obtain a suppression ratio, the number of responses to the CS and the number of responses to an equal amount of time without the CS are recorded. The suppression ratio is the number of responses to the CS divided by the total number of responses; the lower the suppression ratio, the greater the conditioning of fear to the CS. Adapted from Camp, D. S., Raymond, G. A., & Church, R. M. (1962). Temporal relationship between response and punishment. *Journal of Experimental Psychology, 74,* 114–123. Copyright 1967 by the American Psychological Association. Reprinted by permission.

playing with a forbidden toy. In these studies, children were punished with a loud noise for selecting one of a pair of toys. The noises ranged from 52 to 96 dB (decibels), with 60 dB being the loudness of normal conversation. After punishment, each child was isolated with toys that were either identical or similar to the toys presented at the beginning of the experiment. The studies recorded the latency that each child touched the ''wrong'' toy as well as the length of time the child played with this toy. The results of these experiments show that the more intense the punishment, the greater the suppression of the child's playing with the toy associated with punishment.

The severity of punishment also affects the level of response suppression in adults. Powell and Azrin (1968) punished their subjects for smoking cigarettes by using a specially designed cigarette case which delivers an electric shock when opened. Powell and Azrin reported that the smoking rate decreased as the intensity of shock increased. Similarly, Davidson (1972) found that as the punishment intensity increased, the rate of an alcoholic patient's pressing a lever to obtain alcohol declined.

Consistency of Punishment In the last section we learned that punishment must be severe to eliminate an undesired behavior, such as drunk driving. However, the use of a severe punishment may not lead to the suppression of this behavior. The literature shows that punishment also must be consistently administered if it is to successfully eliminate inappropriate behavior. Thus, punishment should be given every time a person drives while intoxicated. Unfortunately, the odds of a drunk driver being caught are 1 in 2000 (*Newsweek,* Sept. 13, 1982). Rigorous observation is essential to detect drunk drivers; however, this high level of recording is not always feasible, and therefore drunk driving probably will continue despite the institution of more severe penalties.

Numerous studies (see Walters & Grusec, 1977) have demonstrated the importance of administering punishment consistently. In one of these studies, Azrin, Holz, and Hake (1963) trained rats to bar press for food reinforcement on a 3-minute variable interval schedule. A 240-volt punishment was delivered following responding on fixed-ratio punishment schedules ranging from FR-1 to FR-1000. As can be seen in Figure 6-11, the level of suppression decreases as the punishment schedule increases. These results indicate that the less consistently the punishment is administered following bar pressing, the less effective the punishment is in suppressing bar-press responding.

Research (see Walters & Grusec, 1977) also points out that consistency influences the effectiveness of punishment in humans. For example, Parke and Deur (1972) reinforced 6- to 9-year-old boys with marbles for hitting a life-size Bobo doll. Then, without informing the subjects, Parke and Deur began punishing half of them with a loud buzzer every time they hit the doll; the other half were punished only 50 percent of the time they hit the doll and were reinforced the rest of the time. Parke and Deur found that the boys who received consistent punishment stopped hitting the doll sooner than those boys who were punished only intermittently. In another experiment, Leff (1969) demonstrated that continuous punishment, compared with intermittent punishment, more effectively caused children to stop choosing an attractive toy and to select an unattractive toy instead.

Several correlational studies have evaluated the relationship between delinquency and the consistency of parental punishment. This research (Glueck & Glueck, 1950; McCord, McCord, & Zola, 1959) reported that delinquent boys were more likely to have received inconsistent parental discipline than were nondelinquent boys. Apparently, parents who want to suppress their children's socially inappropriate behavior must be consistent in punishing that behavior.

Delay of Punishment We have learned that in order for punishment to suppress drunk driving effectively, it must be severe and consistently administered. In this section, we will discover that punishment also must be immediate. The literature shows that the longer the delay is between the inappropriate response

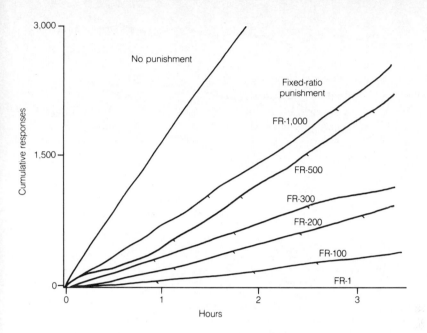

FIGURE 6-11   This graph shows that the rate of bar-press responding for food reinforcement delivered on a 3-minute variable-interval schedule increases with higher fixed-ratio schedules of punishment. Short oblique lines indicate when punishment was delivered. From Azrin, N. H., Holz, W. C., & Hake, D. F. (1963). Fixed-ratio punishment. *Journal for the Experimental Analysis of Behavior, 6,* 141–148. Copyright 1963 by the Society for the Experimental Analysis of Behavior, Inc.

and punishment, the less effective the punishment will be in suppressing the punished behavior. In our society, there is usually a long delay between the time a person is apprehended for drunk driving and the time he or she receives a fine or jail sentence. Because research on delay of punishment shows this method to be ineffective, a shorter interval between the time that the offense occurs and the time of sentencing should be implemented in order to maximize the effect of punishing drunk driving.

The literature using animal subjects (see Church, 1969) consistently demonstrates that immediate punishment is more effective than delayed punishment. The Camp et al. (1967) study provides an excellent example of this observation. After being trained to bar press for food reinforcement, rats received a 0.25 mA 1-second shock punishment either immediately or 30 seconds after a bar-press response. Camp et al. reported significantly greater suppression of the bar-press response when shock occurred immediately after responding than when shock occurred after 30 seconds (see Figure 6-12).

Banks and Vogel-Sprott (1965) investigated the influence of delay of punishment (electric shock) on the level of suppression of their human subjects' reaction

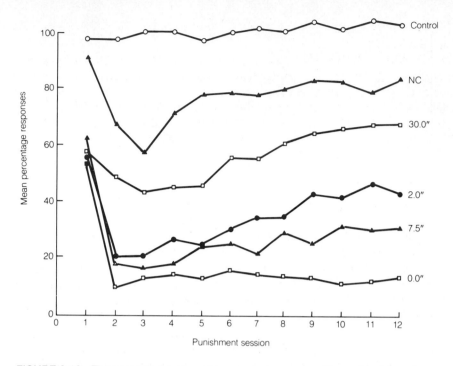

FIGURE 6-12   The mean percentage of responses increases with greater delay of punishment (in seconds). Control group did not receive electric shock, and NC group was given noncontingent shock. Adapted from Camp, D. S., Raymond, G. A., & Church, R. M. (1967). Temporal relationship between response and punishment. *Journal of Experimental Psychology, 74,* 114–123. Copyright by the American Psychological Association. Reprinted by permission.

to a tone in a digit-symbol task. These authors reported that although an immediate punishment inhibited responding, delayed punishment (for 30, 60, or 120 seconds) did not affect responding. A similar lack of effectiveness of delayed punishment was found in college students by Trenholme and Baron (1975) and in children by Walters (1964).

Section Review

Punishment is the presentation of an adverse event contingent on the occurrence of an undesired response. There are two classes of punishment: Positive punishment represents the presentation of a painful event after the occurrence of an undesired response, and negative punishment is the loss of reinforcement (response cost) or the inability to obtain reinforcement for a specified period of time (time-out) contingent on the occurrence of an inappropriate behavior. Although Estes and Skinner assumed that punishment only temporarily suppresses the punished response, in some circumstances behavior can be permanently suppressed by punishment.

The effectiveness of punishment is influenced by (1) severity of punishment—the more severe the event, the greater the behavioral suppression, (2) consistency of presentation of punishment—the more consistent the punishment, the more effective the suppression of the behavior, and (3) delay of punishment—the shorter the delay between punishment and occurrence of the undesired behavior, the more effective the suppression of the punished response.

The Nature of Punishment

Guthrie's Competing Response View   Edwin Guthrie (1934; see Chapter 2) suggested that an adverse event can elicit a number of unconditioned responses (for example, flinching, jumping, and freezing). These unconditioned responses will then be conditioned to the environmental cues present during the adversive event. According to Guthrie, the punished behavior will be suppressed if the response elicited by the event and conditioned to cues surrounding the adversity are incompatible with the punished response. Therefore, punishment suppresses bar pressing in Guthrie's view because a response preventing the rat from bar pressing has been conditioned to the operant chamber.

Fowler and Miller's (1963) classic study supports Guthrie's view of punishment. In this study, rats were initially trained to run down an alley for food reward. One group of rats was then shocked when their forepaws touched the metal rods, which were in front of the goal box. Electric shock applied to the forepaw elicits a flinching reaction, a response that is incompatible with forward running and, therefore, should result in rapid suppression of the running response. A second group of rats was shocked on the hindpaws; this elicits a lurching response, a behavior that is compatible with the running response, and therefore, should increase the speed of rats' response toward reward. A third group of rats was not shocked. Fowler and Miller reported that running was suppressed by forepaw shock but was facilitated by hindpaw shock. Apparently, the response elicited by punishment does influence the effectiveness of punishment.

Our discussion suggests that in order for punishment to be effective, it must elicit a behavior incompatible with the punished response. However, other research indicates that response competition alone is insufficient for punishment to be effective. Quite a few studies (Azrin, 1956; Boe & Church 1967; Camp et al., 1967; Schuster & Rachlin, 1968) show that the suppression of a response is significantly greater when an adverse event is contingent upon the occurrence of the response than when adversity occurs independently of behavior. Guthrie's view suggests that contingent and noncontingent adversity have an equivalent effect on behavior: Conditioning of a competing response should occur regardless of whether the presentation of the event was dependent on or independent of the occurrence of a response. The observation that contingency does influence the level of response suppression indicates that response competition alone cannot explain the nature of punishment. Mowrer's two-factor theory suggests why response contingency affects the influence of punishment on response suppression.

Mowrer's Two-Factor Theory   Mowrer's view of the process responsible for the effect of punishment on behavior is similar to his theory of avoidance learning described earlier in the chapter. According to Mowrer, the suppressive influence of punishment occurs in two stages. Fear, classically conditioned to the environmental cues present during punishment, is elicited when an animal or a person experiences the environmental cues preceding punishment; this fear acts to motivate escape from the feared stimulus. Any behavior, either an overt response or a failure to respond, that terminates the feared stimulus will be acquired. The rewarding consequences of escaping cause the animal or person to exhibit the escape response rather than the punished response. Thus, the suppressive effect of punishment reflects the elicitation of an escape behavior rather than the punished behavior.

Mowrer's view of avoidance learning and his view of punishment describe two aspects of the same process: Fear motivates an avoidance behavior, which enables an animal or a person to prevent punishment. Also, the occurrence of the avoidance behavior causes an animal or a person not to exhibit the punished response.

However, learning theorists (see Estes, 1969) have pointed to a weakness in Mowrer's view of punishment. It is often difficult to identify the overt behavior motivated by fear that prevents an animal from exhibiting the punished response. Estes's motivational view of punishment indicates why an overt response may not be essential. Let's briefly look at this view.

Estes's Motivational View of Punishment   According to Estes, when a behavior is rewarded, the motivational system present prior to reinforcement and the response become associated. When the motivational system is activated again, the response is elicited. For example, if a hungry rat is reinforced for bar pressing, the bar-pressing response and hunger become associated. The presence of hunger in the future will act to elicit bar pressing. Similarly, when a child is disruptive in school and obtains approval from classmates for these actions, the disruptive responding and the approval of peers become associated. When the child wants approval again, he or she will be disruptive. Suppose the rat is punished for bar pressing or the child for being disruptive. The effective use of punishment causes the rat to stop bar pressing or the child to no longer be disruptive.

Let's see how Estes's view of punishment explains the suppression of rats' bar pressing and children's disruptive classroom behavior. According to Estes's approach, punishment does not directly suppress rats' bar pressing or children's disruptive behavior; instead, punishment inhibits the rat's hunger or the child's need for approval. Therefore, because the punished rat or child is no longer motivated, the punished responses of bar pressing or disruptive behavior will no longer be elicited.

Wall, Walters, and England (1972) provide support for Estes's view. They trained water-deprived rats to lever press for water and to "dry lick" for air;

these behaviors were displayed on alternate days. The rate of both responses increased until it reached a stable level after 62 days of training. Each behavior was then punished. According to Walters and Grusec (1977), the internal stimuli associated with dry licking are more closely tied to the thirst motivational system than are the internal stimuli associated with lever pressing. Therefore, if punishment acts to decrease the thirsty rats' motivation for water, it should have a greater effect on dry licking than on lever pressing. Wall et al.'s results support this view: Punishing thirsty rats suppresses dry licking more effectively than lever pressing. However, punishing hungry rats does not produce more suppression of dry licking than lever pressing for food. According to Walters and Grusec, dry licking is not more closely associated with the hunger system than is lever pressing; therefore, reducing animals' motivation for food will not suppress dry licking any more than it will suppress lever pressing.

The Negative Consequences of Punishment

There are a number of negative consequences of punishment. In this section, we will examine these undesired effects.

Pain-Induced Aggression   When animals or people are punished, they experience pain. This pain response may elicit the emotion of anger, which, in turn, arouses aggressive behavior. This discussion begins by looking at evidence that supports the idea that pain can produce aggression, followed by studies that show why punishment can lead to aggression.

Azrin, Hutchinson, and Sallery (1964) observed that when primates are shocked, they attack other monkeys, rats, or mice. In addition, monkeys being shocked will attack a toy tiger (Plotnick, Mir, & Delgado, 1971) or a ball (Azrin, 1964). Shock-induced aggressive attack has also been reported in cats (Ulrich, Wolff, & Azrin, 1964).

During the past 20 years, Leon Berkowitz and his associates (see Berkowitz, 1962, 1969, 1971, 1978) have conducted research which supports the theory that anger induced by exposure to painful events can lead to aggression in humans. In one of these studies (Berkowitz & LePage, 1967), subjects were asked to list, within a period of 5 minutes, ideas that could be used by a publicity agent to increase sales of a product. A confederate then rated some subjects' performance as poor by giving these subjects seven electric shocks; this confederate shocked other subjects only once, to indicate a positive evaluation. According to Berkowitz and LePage, the seven-shock evaluation angered subjects, but the one-shock evaluation did not. Next, all the subjects evaluated the confederate's performance by giving the confederate from one to seven shocks. Subjects who received seven shocks retaliated by giving the confederate significantly more shocks than the other subjects did. These results indicate that painful events can motivate aggressive behavior.

We have seen that anger can result in aggressive behavior. However, this aggressive reaction is not motivated by the expectation of avoiding punishment; rather, it reflects an impulsive act energized by the emotional arousal characteristic of anger. Furthermore, the expression of aggressive behavior in angry animals or people appears to be highly reinforcing. Many studies show that annoyed animals will learn a behavior that provides them with the opportunity to be aggressive. For example, Azrin, Hutchinson, and McLaughlin (1965) discovered that squirrel monkeys bit inanimate objects (for example, a ball) after being shocked. However, if no object was present, they learned to pull a chain which provided them with a ball to bite.

Bramel, Taub, and Blum (1968) reported that irritated people report "feeling good" after being aggressive. During the early 1960s, Hokanson and his colleagues (see Hokanson & Burgess, 1962a, 1962b; Hokanson, Burgess, & Cohen, 1963; Hokanson & Shelter, 1961) found that angry people who were either verbally or physically aggressive toward the source of their anger showed a rapid decline in the level of systolic blood pressure. In contrast, the decline in systolic blood pressure was much slower in angry subjects who were not given the opportunity to be aggressive. Evidently, aggressive behavior reduces arousal.

Punishment does not always elicit aggressive behavior. Hokanson (1970) reported that people's previous experiences influence their reaction to painful events. If individuals have been reinforced for nonaggressive reactions to adversity, punished for aggressive responses to painful events, or both, the likelihood that punishment will elicit aggression is diminished. Furthermore, the level of anger produced by pain differs among individuals (see Klein, 1982). Some people react intensely to a level of adversity that only elicits mild anger in others. Since the probability that painful events will motivate aggression depends upon the level of anger induced by the adverse circumstance, individuals who respond strongly to adversity are much more likely to become aggressive than are people who are not very angered.

The Modeling of Aggression   A child who has been spanked for misbehaving may suppress the inappropriate behavior, may become aggressive, or may effectively learn to imitate the parent's aggressive behavior in an attempt to control other people's actions. The behavior that we learn not by receiving explicit reinforcement but by observing another person's actions is called *modeling* (see Bandura, 1971).

The classic experiment by Bandura, Ross, and Ross (1963) illustrates the influence of a model on aggressive behavior. In this study, children saw a preschool model act aggressively toward a life-size plastic doll called a Bobo doll. The model sat on this doll, punched it, hit it with a mallet, kicked it, and tossed it up and down (see Figure 6-13). Other children in the study did not watch a model behave in this manner. After the initial phase of the study, all children were allowed to play with attractive toys, then were frustrated by being required to leave these attractive toys for less attractive ones, including a Bobo doll. Bandura and colleagues recorded the level of imitative aggression (attacking the Bobo doll) and nonimitative aggression (behavior not performed by the model). They found that while all the children exhibited nonimitative forms of aggression when they were frustrated, only the children who had watched the model showed the

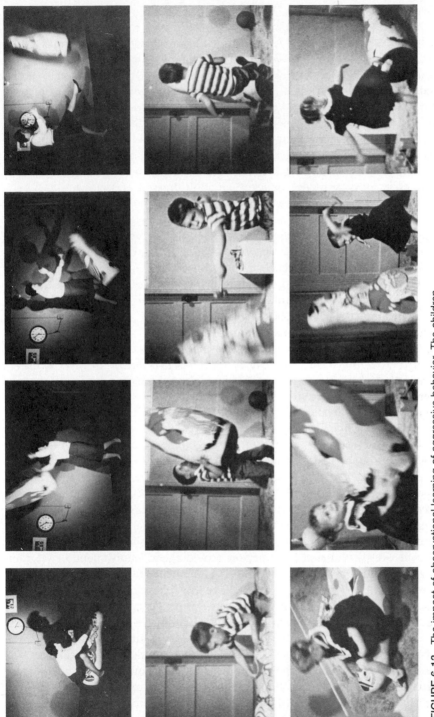

FIGURE 6-13 The impact of observational learning of aggressive behavior. The children first watched the adult attack the Bobo doll (top panel). When later frustrated, the children imitated the model's aggressive response toward the Bobo doll (middle and bottom panels). These children also would exhibit this form of aggressive behavior toward other children or adults. (Courtesy of Albert Bandura, Stanford University.)

imitative patterns of aggression. We apparently can learn how to perform a particular behavior merely by watching others exhibit it.

Other studies (see Grusec, 1972; Hanratty, Liebert, Morris, & Fernandez, 1969; Steuer, Applefield, & Smith, 1971) have also reported that children will imitate a model's aggressive behavior. For example, Steuer and colleagues (1971) discovered that children who had viewed cartoons depicting aggressive behavior became more aggressive toward other children, compared with children who did not see the cartoons. The imitated aggression included hitting, pushing, kicking, squeezing, choking, and throwing objects at the other children. Furthermore, Hanratty et al. (1969) reported that as the result of a modeling experience, children will even act aggressively toward an adult. In their study, young boys, after watching an aggressive model, attacked an adult dressed as a clown.

Do children who are physically punished, in turn, model this aggressive behavior? Two types of evidence support the view that they do. First, *experimental research shows that children punished during a study use the same method of punishment when attempting to control the actions of other children.* In one study, Mischel and Grusec (1966) verbally punished preschool-aged children for certain actions during a game; the children, in turn, employed verbal abuse toward other children playing the game. Similarly, Gelfand et al. (1974) found that children who had been penalized for incorrect responses during a game used this form of punishment when teaching another child to play.

Second, *correlational studies report a strong relationship between the use of punishment by parents and the level of aggressive behavior in their children.* Bandura and Walters (1959) reported that highly aggressive boys had parents who severely punished them for inappropriate behavior in the home. Furthermore, many studies (see Spinetta & Rigler, 1972) have found that parents who abuse their children were likely to have been abused as children by their parents. This observation suggests that children will imitate the abusive behavior of their parents and, in turn, may abuse their own children.

The Aversive Quality of a Punisher   We learned in Chapter 3 that environmental events present during adversity will become classically conditioned to elicit fear. In addition, we saw earlier in this chapter that fear motivates escape behavior. On the basis of these two observations, we should expect that since punishment is a painful event, the person providing the punishment, or the punisher, will become a conditioned stimulus capable of eliciting fear, which in turn should motivate the individual to escape from the punisher.

Azrin and colleagues' (1965) study provides evidence that escape behavior occurs as the result of the use of punishment. These psychologists first trained pigeons to key peck for food reinforcement on a fixed-ratio schedule, then punished each key peck response with electric shock. A distinctive stimulus was present during the punishment period, and the pigeons could peck at another key to terminate the cue signaling punishment. The escape response also produced another stimulus which indicated that the original reinforcement-punishment key could be pecked safely. After the pigeons pecked the original key and received reinforcement, the safe cue was terminated and the dangerous stimulus reintroduced. Azrin et al., reported that although the pigeons emitted few escape responses if the punishment was mild, the frequency of the escape response increased as the intensity of punishment increased until the pigeons spent the entire punishment period escaping from the cues associated with punishment.

The study by Redd, Morris, and Martin (1975) illustrates the adversive quality of a punisher in humans. In their study, 5-year-old children performed a task in the presence of an adult who made either positive comments (for example, "You're doing well") or negative comments (for example, "Stop throwing the tokens around" or "Don't play with the chair"). Redd and colleagues reported that although the punitive person was more effective in keeping the children working on their task, the children preferred working with the complimentary person.

However, little evidence of clients escaping a punitive behavior therapist has been reported (see Walters & Grusec, 1977). For example, Risley (1968) discovered that punishing autistic children's undesirable behavior with electric shock did not alter the children's eye contact with the therapist, who also reinforced the children's desirable responses. Other studies (see Lovaas & Simmons, 1969) have also reported absence of fear of and escape behavior from a therapist who had punished them. Walters and Grusec (1977) suggested that the use of reinforcement as well as punishment by the therapist prevented the therapist and the therapy situation from becoming adversive and thereby from motivating escape behavior.

Additional Negative Effects of Punishment   There are two additional negative effects of punishment. First, *the suppressive effects of punishment may generalize to similar behaviors*. The inhibition of these responses may be undesirable. For example, if a parent punishes a child for fighting with other children in the neighborhood, the punishment may generalize, causing the child to stop playing with these children. However, the effects of punishment do not always generalize to similar behavior. Chapter 7 discusses the circumstances under which punishment does or does not generalize to other responses. Second, *the contingency between punishment and the undesired behavior may not be recognized; the adversive events may be perceived as being independent of behavior*. In Chapter 8, we will discover that experiencing noncontingent aversive events leads to helplessness and depression. Punishment is most likely to be perceived as being noncontingent when a delay occurs between the undesirable behavior and punishment. The interval between a response and punishment makes it difficult for an animal or a person to recognize that the behavior is responsible for the punishment. People must be informed of the relationship between their actions and punishment so that helplessness does not result from noncontingent events.

Application: The Use of Punishment

The use of punishment to control human behavior is widespread in our society. The literature shows that most parents use punishment to govern the actions of their children. For example, Sears, Maccoby, and Levin (1957) reported that 99 percent of the parents of 379 kindergarten children used spanking as a form of punishment. In a more recent review, Erlanger (1974) reported that between 84 and 97 percent of all parents use physical punishment as a means of disciplining their children.

Teachers also employ negative events to modify students' disruptive actions. White's analysis (1975) of teacher-pupil interactions reported that while teachers showed approval of good academic performance, appropriate social behavior was also expected. Any disruptive behavior by a student produced strong disapproval from teachers. Also, Madsen, Madsen, Saudargas, Hammond, and Edgar (1970) found that 77 percent of elementary school teachers' interactions with their students were negative.

Other individuals in our culture employ punishment to control behavior. Police officers ticket traffic violators, the IRS jails tax evaders, the army court-martials AWOL soldiers, and employers fire employees who are often late for work. The following section examines several punishment procedures reported by psychologists to be successful in modifying undesired human activity.

Positive Punishment   We learned earlier in this chapter that positive punishment is the presentation of a painful event contingent upon the occurrence of an undesired behavior. We also discovered that punishment will be effective when it is severe, occurs immediately after the undesired response, and is consistently presented. But how effective is positive punishment in altering behavior problems in humans? The literature (see Rimm & Masters, 1979) shows that punishment can be quite successful in suppressing human behavior. Let's next examine evidence showing that punishment can be effectively used to modify human activity.

Lang and Melamed (1969) described the use of punishment to suppress the persistent vomiting of a 12-pound, 9-month-old child (see Figure 6-14). The child vomited most of his food within 10 minutes after eating, despite the use of various treatments (for example, dietary changes, use of antinauseants, and small feedings). Lang and Melamed detected the beginning of vomiting with an electromyogram (EMG), which measures muscle activity. When the EMG indicated that vomiting had begun, the child received an electric shock to the leg; the shock stopped when the child ceased vomiting. After the child had received six punishment sessions (one per day), vomiting no longer occurred after eating. Six months following treatment, the child showed no further vomiting and was of normal weight. Cunningham and Linscheid (1976) and Toister et al. (1975) also have found punishment to represent an effective way to suppress life-threatening vomiting in very young children. Furthermore, Galbraith, Byrick, and Rutledge (1970) successfully used punishment to curtail the vomiting of a 13-year-old retarded boy, and Kohlenberg (1970) reported that punishment suppressed the vomiting of a 21-year-old retarded adult.

We have learned that positive punishment can suppress the life-threatening vomiting of a young child. Many other behaviors have been successfully modified through the use of response-contingent punishment. Behaviors reported to have been suppressed by punishment include obsessive ideation (Kenny, Solyom, &

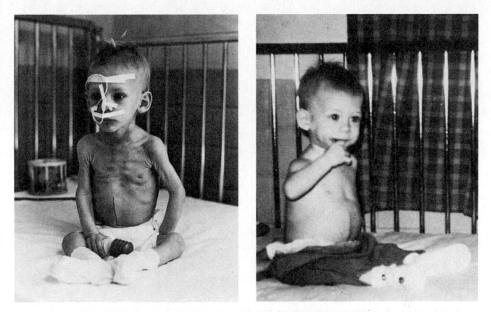

FIGURE 6-14 The photo on the left shows a 12-pound, 9-month-old child whose persistent vomiting left him seriously ill. The use of punishment suppressed vomiting within six sessions (one per day) and, as can be seen in the photo on the right, enabled the child to return to normal health. (Courtesy of Peter Lang.)

Solyom, 1973; Kushner & Sandler, 1966; McGuire & Vallance, 1964; Wolpe, 1958), hallucinations (Alford & Turner, 1976; Bucher & Fabricatore, 1970; McGuigan, 1966), self-mutilating behavior and tantrum activity of autistic and retarded children (Lovaas, Koegel, Simmons, & Long, 1973; Prochaska, Smith, Marzilli, Colby, & Donovan, 1974; Tanner & Zeiler, 1975), and chronic cough (Creer, Chai, & Hoffman, 1977).

Our discussion indicates that positive punishment has been used effectively to suppress a wide variety of undesired behavior. One problem sometimes encountered with punishment therapy is the patient's difficulty generalizing suppression from the therapy situation to the real world. The Risley (1968) study described next provides evidence that generalization of the suppression of a punished behavior can be produced. Risley used electric-shock punishment to treat the continual climbing behavior of a 6-year-old hyperactive girl. Although Risley's treatment suppressed the climbing during the therapy situation, there was no change in the frequency of this behavior at the girl's home. Risley then visited the home and showed the mother how to use the electric-shock device. When the mother punished her daughter's climbing, the frequency of this behavior declined from 29 to 2 instances a day within 4 days and disappeared completely within a few weeks. You might feel that this procedure is barbaric. However, the mother had attempted to control the climbing by spanking the child, and believed the spanking to be more unpleasant and ''brutalizing'' for both herself and her daughter than the shock, not to mention less effective. As Rimm and Masters (1979) point out, ''Many therapists feel that a minimal number of mild shocks is more humane than the continual but ineffective spanking or shaming of a child.''

Response Cost   A colleague recently told me of a problem with his daughter who was having trouble seeing the blackboard at school. When he suggested that she move to the front row of the classes, she informed him that she was already sitting there. She was examined by an optometrist, who discovered her eyesight to be extremely poor; she was to wear glasses all the time. Despite choosing a pair of glasses that she liked, she indicated an extreme dislike for wearing them. After waiting a reasonable adjustment period and discovering that encouragement and praise were ineffective in persuading his daughter to wear the glasses, the father informed her that she would lose 50 cents of her weekly allowance every time he saw her without them. Although she was not pleased with this arrangement, she did not lose any of her allowance and no longer expresses unhappiness about wearing her glasses.

My colleague was able to modify his daughter's behavior by using a response-cost procedure. As we learned earlier in the chapter, response cost refers to a penalty or fine that is contingent upon the occurrence of an undesired behavior. Thus, my colleague's daughter was to be fined when she did not wear her glasses. Psychologists (see Kalish, 1981) have consistently observed that response cost represents an effective technique for suppressing inappropriate behavior. Let's now examine one study that has examined the use of response cost to alter behavior.

Peterson and Peterson's (1968) study illustrates the effectiveness of response cost in suppressing self-injurious behavior. The subject was a 6-year-old boy who had been severely mutilating himself; the experimenters reinforced him with a small amount of food when no self-injurious behavior occurred during a 3-to-5-second period. However, if the boy exhibited self-injurious behavior, the reinforcer did not occur. Peterson and Peterson reported that they completely eliminated the boy's self-injurious behavior with their response-cost procedure.

A wide range of other undesired behaviors have been successfully eliminated by using a response-cost procedure. In an extensive investigation of the application of response cost, Kazdin (1972) discovered that response cost has been used to inhibit smoking, overeating, stuttering, psychotic speech, aggressiveness, and tardiness. In addition, response cost eliminated perseverative speech (Reichle, Brubakken, & Tetrault, 1976), anxious and depressive behavior (Reisinger, 1972), and hyperactive behavior (Wolf, Hanley, King, Lachowicz, & Giles, 1970).

Time-out from Reinforcement   Time-out from reinforcement refers to a program in which the occurrence of an inappropriate behavior results in a person's losing access to reinforcement for a specified period of time. In time-out, the individual can be removed either from a reinforcing environment or from the reinforcement itself. Examples of the use of time-out include a child who hits a sibling while watching television and is sent to his or her room for a half hour and an overweight person who is forbidden to dine out for a week for not sticking to his diet.

It is important that if a time-out area is employed, it must not be reinforcing. Thus, sending disruptive children to their rooms as a time-out may not stop the disruptive behavior if the room contains attractive toys and the child finds being there pleasurable. In fact, the frequency of disruptive behavior may actually increase if the time-out area is reinforcing. Solnick, Rincover, and Peterson's (1977) study illustrates the importance of ensuring that time-out is not reinforcing. They included a time-out contingent upon tantrum behavior in the treatment of a 6-year-old autistic child. Exposure to a sterile time-out environment was contingent upon the occurrence of self-stimulating behavior, and presentation of this environment increased rather than decreased the occurrence of tantrum behavior. When the investigators made physical restraint contingent upon tantrum behavior, the frequency of tantrums rapidly declined.

A wide variety of behaviors have been suppressed using time-out from reinforcement. For example, Drabman and Spitalnik (1973) reported that time-out suppressed disruptive behavior of male adolescents in a psychiatric hospital. Initial recordings showed that the adolescents exhibited very high rates of several disruptive behaviors including physical aggression, verbal abuse, and disregard of rules. The researchers instituted a time-out procedure during which the boys were placed in a small room for 10 minutes if they had been physically aggressive or had left their seat without permission. The verbal abuse was not a target of intervention and, therefore, its occurrence did not result in time-out. Drabman and Spitalnik found that the level of physical aggression and disregard of rules decreased significantly after the time-out procedure had been established. In contrast, the unpunished verbal abuse did not decline because its occurrence did not result in time-out. These observations demonstrate that time-out from reinforcement produces a specific reduction of behaviors contingent upon its presentation but does not affect unpunished activity.

Barton, Guess, Garcia, and Baer (1970) observed that the disruptive mealtime behavior of retarded children could be suppressed by the use of a time-out reinforcement procedure, and MacPherson et al. (1974) found that time-out could inhibit disruptive lunchroom activity in elementary school children. Other behaviors which have been suppressed by time-out include thumb-sucking (Baer, 1962), tantrum behavior in autistic children (Wolf, Risley, & Mees, 1964) and normal children (Wahler, Winkel, Peterson, & Morrison, 1965; Williams, 1959), self-stimulation in autistic children (Koegel, Firestone, Kramme, & Dunlap, 1974), and perseverative speech (Reichle et al., 1976).

The Ethical Use of Punishment When is the use of punishment permissible? The Eighth Amendment to the Constitution of the United States stipulates: ''Excessive bail shall not be required, nor excessive fines imposed, nor cruel and unusual punishments inflicted.'' What constitutes cruel and unusual punishment? When can a teacher use punishment to discipline a disruptive student, or a psychologist use punishment in therapy? The federal courts have indicated that some use of aversive remedial treatment is permissible. However, the treatment may be considered a violation of the Eighth Amendment if it "violates minimal standards of decency, is wholly disproportionate to the alleged offense, or goes beyond what is necessary" (see Schwitzgebel & Schwitzgebel, 1980).

There have been many unjustified uses of punishment in our society. For example, in *Wright* v. *McMann* (1972), the court found that punishing an inmate in a "psychiatric observation cell" by forcing him to sleep nude on a concrete floor in cold temperatures without soap, towels, or toilet paper constitutes cruel and unusual punishment. Similarly, the courts ruled that it is cruel and unusual punishment to administer apormorphine (to induce vomiting) to nonconsenting mental patients (*Knecht* v. *Gillman,* 1973) or to forcefully administer an intramuscular injection of a tranquilizer to a juvenile inmate for a rules infraction (*Nelson* v. *Heyne,* 1974).

Do these abuses mean that aversive-punishment procedures may never be employed? Punishment can be used to eliminate undesired behavior; however, the rights of the individual must be safeguarded. Recognition of the importance of protecting the individual was clearly evident in the American Psychological Association's *Ethical Principles of Psychologists* (1971). The preamble of this document states that "psychologists respect the dignity and worth of the individual and strive for the preservation and protection of fundamental human rights. They are committed to increasing knowledge of human behavior and of people's understanding of themselves and others and to the utilization of such knowledge for the promotion of human welfare. While pursuing these objectives, they make every effort to protect the welfare of those who seek their skills."

The welfare of the individual has been safeguarded in a number of ways (see Schwitzgebel & Schwitzgebel, 1980). For example, the doctrine of "the least restrictive alternative" indicates that less severe methods of punishment be tried before severe treatments are used. For example, Ohio law (1977) allows that "aversive stimuli" be used for seriously disruptive behavior only after other forms of therapy have been attempted. Further, an institutional review board or human rights committee should evaluate whether the use of punishment is justified. According to Stapleton (1975), justification should be based on "the guiding principle that the procedure should entail a relatively small amount of pain and discomfort relative to a large amount of pain and discomfort if left untreated."

Concern for the individual should not be limited to institutional use of punishment. The ethical concerns outlined by the American Psychological Association should apply to all instances in which punishment is used. Certainly, abuse by parents, family, and peers may be as great or greater than that by psychologists in the treatment of behavioral disorders. A child has as much right to be protected from cruel and unusual punishment by a parent as does a patient from abuse by a therapist. Adherence to ethical standards of administering punishment can allow an effective yet humane method of altering inappropriate behavior.

SUMMARY

1 Animals and people can learn to escape from adversity. Three variables affect the rate of acquisition of a behavior that terminates adversity: (1) the intensity of the adverse event—the greater the intensity of adversity the faster the acquisition of an escape response; (2) the amount of reward—the greater the decrease in adversity following the escape behavior, the more rapid the learning of the escape response; and (3) the delay of reward—the smaller the delay of reward following the escape behavior, the faster the acquisition of the escape response.

2 An escape response also can be extinguished. An animal or a person may stop responding if adversity is no longer presented; however, fear conditioned during escape learning may prevent extinction of the escape response. Extinction typically occurs when the escape response is punished. The exception is vicious-circle behavior, in which the termination of adversity follows punishment of the escape response. In vicious-circle behavior, the escape response continues even though the failure to escape is not punished.

3 Some unpleasant circumstances can be prevented. With active avoidance learning, an animal or a person must exhibit a specific overt behavior to avoid adversity; in passive avoidance situations, the absence of a response will prevent the adverse event.

4 Psychologists have proposed various theories about the nature of avoidance learning. Mowrer suggested that fear is conditioned during the first phase of avoidance learning. In the second stage, fear motivates responding. Any behavior that successfully terminates the fear will be reinforced and elicited upon future presentations of the feared stimulus.

5 D'Amato proposed that avoidance behavior is motivated not only by the anticipation of pain but also by the anticipation of relief. The anticipatory relief response cannot be acquired if the avoidance response does not prevent adversity. In contrast, Bolles suggested a cognitive view of avoidance behavior: expectations that (1) an adversive event will occur in the absence of avoidance behavior and that (2) the avoidance response will prevent adversity are acquired during avoidance learning. One contemporary view of avoidance learning suggests that both drives and cognitions play an important role in avoidance behavior.

6 Two variables affect the rate of acquisition of an avoidance response. First, the severity of the adversity influences the acquisition of the avoidance response. In some tasks (passive avoidance learning and one-way active avoidance learning), increases in adversity lead to faster avoidance learning; in other tasks (two-way active avoidance learning), increases in the intensity of adversity produce slower acquisition. Second, the rate of avoidance acquisition is influenced by the CS-UCS interval: the shorter the interval between the CS and the UCS, the faster the acquisition of the avoidance response.

7 Flooding represents a viable treatment of human avoidance behavior. In flooding or response prevention treatment, the person is prevented from exhibiting the avoidance response. The success of flooding depends upon providing sufficient exposure to the feared object to completely extinguish the avoidance response.

8 Punishment is the presentation of an adverse event contingent upon the occurrence of an undesired response. There are two classes of punishment: Positive punishment involves the presentation of a painful event after the occurrence of an undesired response, and negative punishment or omission training is the loss of reinforcement (response cost) or inability to obtain reinforcement for a specified period of time (time-

out) contingent upon the occurrence of an inappropriate behavior. Although Estes and Skinner assumed that punishment only temporarily suppresses the punished response, in some circumstances behavior can be permanently suppressed by punishment.

9 The effectiveness of punishment is influenced by (1) the severity of punishment—the more severe the adversity, the greater the behavioral suppression, (2) the consistency of presentation of punishment—the more consistent the punishment, the more effective the suppression of the behavior, and (3) the delay of punishment—the shorter the delay between punishment and occurrence of the undesired behavior, the more effective the suppression of the punished response.

10 Guthrie proposed that punishment elicits a specific behavior; if the response elicited by punishment is antagonistic to the punished behavior, punishment will suppress the undesired behavior, but punishment may increase the behavior if it elicits a compatible response. Mowrer assumed that fear is conditioned by the use of punishment and that it is this fear that motivates escape behavior. The escape behavior prevents the punished response from occurring. Estes's motivational view suggests that punishment reduces the motivation level; the absence of motivation suppresses the undesired response.

11 Punishment has a number of potential negative effects. First, punishment can elicit aggressive behavior. Second, the punished individual may model the use of punishment as a means of behavioral control. Third, the environment in which punishment occurs may become adversive, thereby motivating escape behavior. Fourth, the effects of punishment may generalize to other nonpunished behavior. Finally, the contingency between behavior and punishment may not be recognized and the failure to detect this contingency may result in feelings of helplessness.

12 Adversive events have been successfully used to alter undesired human behavior. However, safeguards must be established to protect individuals from cruel and unusual punishment. Adherence to ethical standards of conduct will allow the use of punishment as a method of influencing behavior while ensuring that those punished will experience less discomfort than if the treatment had not been employed.

7

STIMULUS CONTROL OF BEHAVIOR

A CASE OF MISTAKEN IDENTITY

While walking to the grocery store, James was approached by a tall man who suddenly jumped directly in front of him and drew a large knife. The stranger grabbed James's arm and demanded his money. Frightened, James surrendered the $25 with which he had planned to buy food. After grabbing the money, the thief bolted down the street, disappearing into an alley. James began yelling, "I've been robbed! I've been robbed!" But the criminal had fled, and the several people who had witnessed the robbery had dispersed.

A merchant hearing James's screams did call the police, who arrived within 5 minutes. The police first questioned James, asking him to describe the robber. The merchant, upon questioning, denied witnessing the crime and attested only to hearing James's screams.

Several weeks passed before the police contacted James, informing him that they had a suspect meeting James's description and having a record of attacks similar to the one on James. The police asked James to come to the police station to try to identify his assailant from a lineup. The lineup was a cinch; James immediately recognized his attacker. On the basis of his criminal record and James's identification, the suspect was charged with assault and robbery.

However, the person identified by James was not his assailant. Two weeks after the lineup, another man was apprehended while attempting to rob a woman on her way home from work. During his interrogation, the man confessed not only to this crime but also to robbing James.

Since James had had a close view of his assailant, why had he identified the wrong man? To answer, we must consider the five individuals in the lineup.

215

Although five men were in the lineup, only two were as tall as James's assailant. Of these two men, one was thin, the other, fat. The choice seemed obvious to James, and he picked the man he believed had robbed him. James's behavior illustrates discrimination learning: He had learned several important attributes of his assailant, and he used this knowledge to discriminate his assailant from the other men in the lineup. However, his discrimination was not perfect; although James's assailant and the man he identified in the lineup shared two attributes— they were both very thin and tall—their facial characteristics differed significantly. Unfortunately, James ignored facial attributes; instead, he responded only to the size characteristics of the men.

Chapter 7 discusses the impact of the stimulus environment on behavior. An animal or a person can respond in the same way to similar stimuli. The process of responding in the same manner to similar stimuli is called *generalization*. In the chapter-opening vignette, James responded in the same manner to both the assailant and the man in the lineup. Animals and people can also learn to respond in different ways to different stimuli; the process of responding to some stimuli but not others is called *discrimination*. James discriminated between the assailant and four of the five men in the police lineup.

Conditioned stimuli do not merely elicit conditioned responses. A conditioned stimulus sometimes prepares, or sets the occasion for, an animal to respond to a conditioned stimulus. For example, seeing an ad for food could prepare you to become hungry at dinnertime. Also, a conditioned stimulus can produce the motivational basis for instrumental or operant behavior. Dinnertime, now possessing the ability to elicit hunger, motivates a trip to the dining room.

We begin our discussion of stimulus control of behavior by examining the generalization of responding to stimuli similar to the conditioning stimulus. Other aspects of stimulus control will be addressed later in the chapter.

THE GENERALIZATION PROCESS

In December 1988, a Pan American airplane exploded over Scotland en route to New York. An Arab terrorist organization claimed credit for the explosion. Extensive media coverage of this and similar acts of violence has created the belief in many Americans that most Arab Moslems are terrorists. Generalization is responsible for the strong negative-conditioned emotional response toward this group.

Generalization frequently occurs in the real world. Sometimes, generalization is undesirable, as in the case of the dislike of many Americans for Arab Moslems. Racial, ethnic, and religious prejudice are examples of undesirable generalization that occurs when someone who has had an unpleasant experience with one member of a racial, ethnic, or religious group generalizes this dislike to other members of that group.

However, generalization is often adaptive. For example, parents read a book to their children, the children enjoy it, and a positive emotional experience is conditioned to the book. These children then generalize their positive emotional response to other books; thus, they read more and learn more about their environment. The children's generalization also enables them to like books that they have never read. To use another example, preschool children may enjoy playing with the other neighborhood children; this enjoyment reflects a conditioned response acquired through past experience. When these children attend school, they generalize their conditioned social responses to new children and are motivated to play with them. This generalization enables children to socialize with new children; otherwise, children would have to learn to like new acquaintances before they would want to play with them. Thus, generalization allows people to respond positively to strangers. Imagine how difficult life would be if you had to have a positive experience with someone before you would talk to him or her. Clearly, generalization makes our lives much easier.

Generalization causes us to respond to stimuli similar to the stimulus present during training. However, different amounts of generalization occur. In some instances, we respond the same to all stimuli resembling the stimulus associated with conditioning. For example, people who become ill after eating in a specific restaurant may generalize their negative emotional experiences and avoid eating out again. In other situations, less generalization is observed as the similarity to the conditioned stimulus lessens. Suppose a person has been bitten by a large dog. This individual may not show intense fear of all dogs, be moderately frightened of medium-sized dogs, and only slightly fearful of small dogs. In this case, the bigger the difference in size of the two dogs, the less generalization of fear that occurs. Or the person might be afraid only of large dogs; if so, only stimuli very similar to the conditioning stimulus (the large dog) will elicit fear.

To study level of generalization, psychologists have constructed generalization gradients. A *generalization gradient* is a visual representation of the strength of the response produced by stimuli of varying degrees of similarity to the stimulus associated with training; these gradients show the level of generalization that occurs to stimuli similar to the one present during conditioning. A steep generalization gradient indicates that people or animals respond very little to stimuli that are not very similar to the training stimulus, and a flat generalization gradient shows that responding occurs even to stimuli quite unlike the conditioning stimulus. Let's look at the research on generalization gradients.

Generalization Gradients

Most generalization studies have investigated generalization of excitatory conditioning. Recall from Chapter 3 that in excitatory conditioning, a specific stimulus is presented prior to the unconditioned stimulus. Following acquisition, the stimulus (S+) paired with the unconditioned stimulus and several test stimuli varying from very similar to very dissimilar to the S+ are presented. The amount of responding to the test stimulus in comparison to the amount of responding to the training stimulus indicates the level of generalization of excitatory conditioning. A graph of the response to each stimulus provides a visual display of the level of excitatory generalization.

Some research has studied the generalization of inhibitory conditioning. Remember that inhibitory conditioning develops when one colored stimulus is presented with either reward or punishment and another stimulus with the absence of the event (see Chapter 3). Conditioning of inhibition to the second colored stimulus (inhibitory stimulus; S−) will cause it to suppress responding to the first colored stimulus (excitatory stimulus; S+). After training, the second colored stimulus (S−) and several test stimuli varying in color from very similar to very dissimilar to the inhibitory colored stimulus are presented before the colored stimulus, which was paired with either reward or punishment (S+). The amount of suppression of responding produced by the inhibitory stimulus compared with that produced by the test stimuli indicates the amount of generalization of inhibition. A graph of the level of suppression produced by each stimulus can provide a visual display of the level of inhibitory generalization.

Excitatory Generalization Gradients   Much of the research on generalization gradients has been conducted using pigeons as subjects. Pigeons have excellent color vision, and their generalization to stimuli similar to the color used in training can be easily established. Guttman and Kalish's (1956) classic experiment trained hungry pigeons to peck a small illuminated disk to obtain food reinforcement. Four groups of pigeons were shown one of four colors or wavelengths of light (530, 550, 580, and 600 nanometers, or nm) ranging from yellowish green to red as training stimuli. During training, the key was illuminated for 60-second periods, and these periods alternated with 10-second periods of no illumination. The pigeons were reinforced on a VI 1-minute schedule of reinforcement when the key was illuminated; reinforcement was unavailable when the key was not illuminated. After acquisition training, Guttman and Kalish tested for generalization of responding to similar-colored stimuli. The generalization test consisted of presenting the color illuminated during training and 10 other stimuli (5 were higher on the wavelength color spectrum and 5 were lower). Each stimulus was presented randomly 12 times for a period of 30 seconds. Guttman and Kalish's results showed that the pigeons made the maximum number of responses to the training stimuli (see Figure 7-1). Guttman and Kalish noted that the level of responding declined as the difference between training and test stimuli increased. Note that Guttman and Kalish reported symmetrical generalization gradients. Furthermore, the general shape of each gradient was similar for all four subject groups, regardless of the training stimulus. Other experiments with pigeons have reported generalization gradients similar to that observed by Guttman and Kalish; see Blough and Blough (1977) for a review of the generalization gradient literature.

Researchers using species other than pigeons have reported generalization gradients similar to those found by Guttman and Kalish in pigeons. Moore (1972) provides an illustration of this generalization gradient form in rabbits. Moore initially conditioned an eye-blink response to a 1200-Hz tone. Following conditioning, the S+ and other stimuli varying from 400 Hz to 2000 Hz were presented to the rabbits. Moore reported that the highest percentage of responding was to

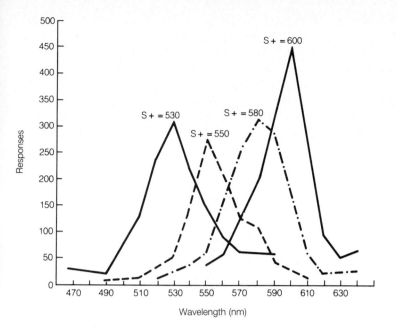

FIGURE 7-1 Generalization gradients obtained using four different wavelengths in separate groups of pigeons trained to key peck for food reinforcement. The results of this study showed that the amount of generalization decreased as the difference between the conditioning and the test stimuli increased. Adapted from Guttman, N., & Kalish, H. I. (1956). Discriminability and stimulus generalization. *Journal of Experimental Psychology, 51,* 79–88. Copyright 1956 by the American Psychological Association. Reprinted by permission.

the 1200-Hz tone (S +) and that the rabbits' responding declined as the similarity of the test and training stimulus decreased. Razran (1949) describes the results of 54 different experiments in Pavlov's laboratory examining the generalization of salivary conditioning in dogs. The results of these experiments show a convex upward generalization gradient.

Generalization gradients like those reported by Guttman and Kalish have been observed using a wide variety of stimuli and responses in humans (refer to Bass & Hull, 1934; Hoveland, 1937; Razran, 1949). For example, Hoveland (1937), pairing a tone (S +) with electric shock and then investigating the generalization of the galvanic skin response to other stimuli, reported that less generalization occurred as the test and conditioning tone became more dissimilar (refer to Figure 7-2). Bass and Hull (1934), using a tactile stimulus (stimulation of the shoulder) as the S + and electric shock as the UCS, presented the S + and other tactile stimuli after conditioning of the electrodermal response. The form of the generalization gradient for tactile stimuli observed by Bass and Hull was similar to that found by Hoveland for auditory stimuli. Razran (1949) examined generalization of a salivary response conditioned to words such as *style* and *urn* after

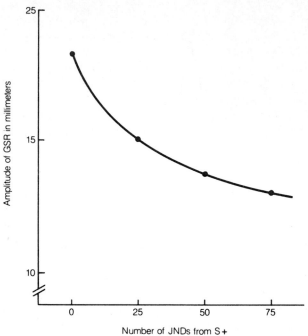

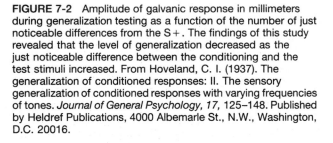

FIGURE 7-2 Amplitude of galvanic response in millimeters during generalization testing as a function of the number of just noticeable differences from the S+. The findings of this study revealed that the level of generalization decreased as the just noticeable difference between the conditioning and the test stimuli increased. From Hoveland, C. I. (1937). The generalization of conditioned responses: II. The sensory generalization of conditioned responses with varying frequencies of tones. *Journal of General Psychology, 17,* 125–148. Published by Heldref Publications, 4000 Albemarle St., N.W., Washington, D.C. 20016.

pairing the training words with stimuli such as *pretzels* and *candy*. Razran noted that synonyms and homophones of the training stimuli also elicited a salivary response, and the amount of generalization increased with greater semantic similarity.

Perhaps you think that the level of generalization shown in Figure 7-1 is characteristic of all situations. In many circumstances animals or persons will respond to stimuli similar to the conditioning stimulus, but in other situations animals or people may generalize to stimuli only remotely similar to the conditioning stimulus. Consider the following example: Some people who do not interact easily with others find that being around people elicits anxiety, and, although they may be lonely, they avoid contact. These socially anxious people probably experienced some unpleasantness with another person (or persons)— perhaps the other person rebuked an attempted social invitation or said something offensive. As a result of a painful social experience, a conditioned disliking to the other person occurred. Although everyone has had an unpleasant social experience, most people limit their disliking to the person associated with the pain or perhaps to similar individuals. Socially anxious individuals generalize their dislike to all people, and this generalization makes all interacting difficult.

Many studies have reported flat generalization gradients; that is, an animal or a person responds to stimuli that are quite dissimilar to the conditioning stimulus. The Jenkins and Harrison (1960) study is one example: Jenkins and Harrison trained two groups of pigeons to key peck for food reinforcement. A 1000-Hz tone was present during the entire conditioning phase in the control group. In contrast, animals in the experimental group received some training periods during which reinforcement was contingent on key pressing; reinforcement was unavailable despite key pecking during other training periods. The 1000-Hz tone was present during the training period when reinforcement was available; no tone was present when the reinforcement was not available. Thus, control-group animals had the 1000-Hz tone on for the entire period, while for the experimental group animals the tone was only on when reinforcement was available. Generalization testing followed conditioning for both groups of pigeons. Seven tones (300, 450, 670, 1000, 1500, 2250, and 3500 Hz) were presented during generalization testing. Jenkins and Harrison's results, presented in Figure 7-3, show that experimental animals exhibited a generalization gradient similar to that reported by Guttman and Kalish, and control animals responded to the stimulus present during conditioning and the other seven tones equally.

Inhibitory Generalization Gradients   In all likelihood, you are apprehensive when you start dating a person. If this is your initial date with this person, you did not acquire your fear directly; your fear could be caused by one of several factors (that is, excitatory generalizations from a negative experience with another person). Suppose your fears are unfounded and you have an enjoyable time. As the result of your experience, you will associate your date with the absence of adversity, the occurrence of a reinforcing experience, or both. This conditioning will diminish your apprehension about dating this person again. Fortunately, the inhibition of fear not only reduces your apprehensiveness about dating this particular person but also generalizes to dating other new people. Thus, the generalization of inhibition allows you to be less fearful of dating others.

Weisman and Palmer's (1969) study illustrates the generalization of inhibition. In their study, pigeons learned to peck at a green disk (S +) to receive reinforcement on a VI 1-minute schedule. When a white vertical line (S −) was presented, the pigeons were not reinforced for bar pressing. After conditioning, the pigeons received a conditioned-inhibition generalization test. In this phase of the study, the white vertical line (S −) plus six other lines, which departed from the vertical line by −90, −60, −30, +30, +60, and +90 degrees, were presented to the subjects. As can be seen in Figure 7-4, the presentation of the vertical line (S −) inhibited pecking. Furthermore, the amount of inhibition that generalized to other

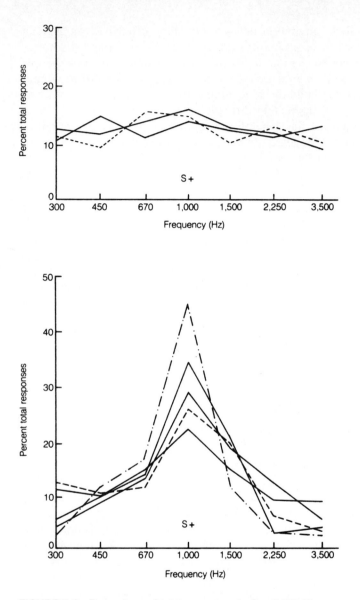

FIGURE 7-3 Percentage of total responses to S+ (1000-Hz tone) and other stimuli (ranging in loudness from 300 to 3500 Hz) during generalization testing for control-group subjects receiving only the S+ in acquisition (top graph) and for experimental group animals given both S+ and S− in acquisition (bottom graph). A steep generalization gradient was found in experimental subjects, while a flat gradient was obtained in control subjects. From Jenkins, H. M., & Harrison, R. H. (1960). Effect of discrimination training on auditory generalization. *Journal of Experimental Psychology, 59,* 246–253. Copyright 1960 by the American Psychological Association. Reprinted by permission.

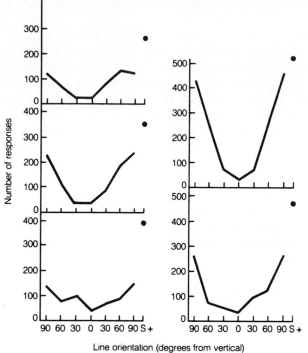

Line orientation (degrees from vertical)

FIGURE 7-4 Graphs show inhibitory generalization gradient for five subjects receiving vertical line as S−. The number of responses to the test stimuli and S+ are given. The results of this study showed that the level of inhibition generalizing to the test stimuli increased as the difference between the training and the test stimuli decreased. From Weisman, R. G., & Palmer, J. A. (1969). Factors influencing inhibitory stimulus control: Discrimination training and prior nondifferential reinforcement. *Journal of Experimental Analysis of Behavior, 12,* 229–237. Copyright 1969 by the Society for the Experimental Analysis of Behavior, Inc.

lines differed depending on the degree of similarity to the S−; the more dissimilar the line to the S−, or the extent to which the orientation of the line deviated from vertical, the less inhibited the responding.

The inhibitory generalization gradient shown in Figure 7-4 is similar in form to the excitatory generalization gradient observed by Guttman and Kalish (refer to Figure 7-1). In both examples of generalization, maximal excitation was conditioned to the S+ or maximal inhibition was conditioned to the S−, and the degree of generalization gradually declined with decreasing similarity to the S+ or S−. As is true of excitatory generalization gradients, in certain circumstances inhibition generalizes to stimuli quite dissimilar to the training stimulus. Even dissimilar stimuli can sometimes produce responding equivalent to that elicited by the conditioning stimulus.

Generalization of inhibition to stimuli quite dissimilar to the training stimulus can be seen in a study by Hoffman (1969). In his study, pigeons first learned to key peck for food reinforcement. Following this initial training phase, the birds were exposed to 24 conditioning sessions. During each session, a 2-minute, 88-dB noise preceding electric shock was presented three times, and a 2-minute, 88-dB, 1000-Hz tone not followed by electric shock was presented three times. Hoffman's procedure established the 88-dB noise (S+) as a feared stimulus, and the presentation of the 88-dB noise suppressed key pecking. In contrast, little suppression was noted when the tone (S−) was presented. Furthermore, the presence of the tone inhibited fear to the noise. Generalization of inhibition testing consisted of presenting the noise (S+) and several test tones. The tones varied in pitch from 300 to 3400 Hz. Hoffman reported that each tone equally inhibited the suppressive ability of the noise. Almost complete generalization of inhibition was noted; that is, tones with very dissimilar pitches produced about as much inhibition as did the S− (1000-Hz) tone.

The Nature of the Generalization Process

Why do we generalize our response to stimuli similar to the stimulus associated with conditioning at certain times but show no generalization to similar stimuli at other times? Many theories have been proposed to explain stimulus generalization (refer to Prokasy & Hall, 1963, for a review of these theories). The Lashley-Wade view of stimulus generalization is presented here, as it seems to best explain why generalization occurs on some occasions but not others.

Lashley and Wade (1946) suggested that animals and people respond to stimuli that differ from the training stimulus because they are unable to distinguish between the generalization test stimulus and the conditioning stimulus. Thus, they conclude that the failure to discriminate between the training and test stimuli is responsible for stimulus generalization. Furthermore, Lashley and Wade proposed that if animals or people could differentiate between the conditioning stimulus and other stimuli, they would not show a generalized response to the other stimuli. Therefore, according to Lashley and Wade, generalization represents the failure to discriminate; discrimination precludes generalization, and a failure to discriminate leads to generalization.

Several lines of evidence support the Lashley-Wade view of stimulus generalization. First, *generalization to stimuli even dissimilar to the training stimulus is found when nondifferential reinforcement training is used.* In this task, the conditioning stimulus is present during the entire training session when a nondifferential reinforcement is employed. Thus, the only stimulus the subject experiences during nondifferential reinforcement training is the excitatory stimulus (S+). The Lashley-Wade view assumes that without experience with stimuli other than the S+, the subject will generalize to all similar stimuli. The Jenkins and Harrison study (1960) provides an excellent example of the flat stimulus generalization gradient. In their study, control-group animals received nondifferential training where the 100-Hz tone was present during the entire conditioning session. Following training, each subject was exposed to seven tones ranging from 300 to 3500 Hz and to a nontone presentation. As can be seen in the top panel of Figure 7-3, the pigeons responded equally to all tones.

The second line of evidence is that *discrimination training results in generalization only to stimuli very similar to the conditioning stimulus*. As discussed earlier, during discrimination training, the excitatory stimulus (S +) is present when reinforcement is available and the inhibitory stimulus (S −) when reinforcement is unavailable. According to the Lashley-Wade view, an animal learns to differentiate between the S + and other stimuli as the result of discrimination training. This knowledge indicates that responses are almost always limited to the S +, and few or no responses are made to other stimuli; that is, little or no stimulus generalization occurs when an animal recognizes the specific stimulus associated with reinforcement.

A number of studies show that discrimination training leads to steep generalization gradients. We described a few of these experiments earlier in the chapter. The Jenkins and Harrison (1960) study evaluated the influence of discrimination training on stimulus generalization gradients. A brief review of their experiment will document the effect of discrimination training on the level of stimulus generalization. Jenkins and Harrison gave pigeons discrimination training in which pecking at the key with the S + (a 100-Hz tone) present resulted in reinforcement but key pecking with the S − (no tone presented) did not lead to reinforcement. After training, stimulus generalization testing consisted of seven tones ranging from 300 to 3500 Hz. The bottom panel of Figure 7-3 illustrates that this discrimination training produced a steep generalization gradient.

The third line of evidence, according to Lashley and Wade, is that *generalization occurs when an animal cannot differentiate between the training stimulus and generalization test stimuli*. An extension of this view suggests that little generalization should occur and that a discrimination should readily be formed when an animal can easily differentiate between S + and S −. The literature (see Kalish, 1969) indicates that the more able an animal is to differentiate between the S + and S −, the easier it learns a discrimination. Furthermore, a steeper generalization gradient is observed when an animal can easily distinguish between the S + and S − than when this discrimination is difficult.

Haber and Kalish's (1963) study illustrates the influence of discriminability on the ease of establishing a discrimination. Haber and Kalish initially showed that pigeons have more difficulty differentiating between a 550- and a 540-nm light than between a 540- and a 530-nm light. This observation was established by pairing either a 550-nm light or a 540-nm light with reinforcement; greater generalization developed to the 540-nm light with the 550-nm light as the S + than to the 530-nm light with the 540-nm light as the S +. Two other groups of pigeons learned to discriminate between these two pairs of stimuli; some pigeons had the 550-nm light as the S + and the 540-nm light as the S −; the other pigeons were trained with the 540-nm light as the S + and the 530-nm light as the S −. Haber and Kalish reported that animals more easily learned to discriminate between the 540-nm light and the 530-nm light than between the 550-nm light and the 540-nm light.

The final evidence supporting the Lashley-Wade theory is that *perceptual experience influences the amount of stimulus generalization*. The Lashley-Wade view assumes that animals learn to distinguish similarities and differences in environmental events. This perceptual learning is essential for an animal to discriminate between different stimuli yet generalize to similar stimuli. Without this perceptual experience, different environmental events would appear similar, thereby making discrimination very difficult. For example, a person with little or no experience with varied colors would find distinguishing between green and red difficult; this difficulty could result in failing to learn to observe traffic lights. Several studies have evaluated the influence of various levels of perceptual experience on the level of stimulus generalization (see Houston, 1986). These results show that as the perceptual experience increases, the generalization gradient becomes steeper. This perceptual experience allows animals or people to differentiate between similar stimuli and not to generalize their response from the S+ to other stimuli.

Peterson's (1962) classic study illustrates the effect of perceptual experience on the amount of stimulus generalization. Peterson raised two groups of ducks under different conditions. The experimental-group ducks were raised in cages illuminated by a 589-nm light and thereby experienced only a single color. In contrast, control-group animals were raised in normal light and, therefore, were exposed to a wide range of colors. During the initial phase of this study, Peterson trained the ducks to peck at a key illuminated by the 589-nm light. After training, both groups received generalization testing using stimuli varying from a 490-nm to 650-nm light. The top graph of Figure 7-5 illustrates that ducklings raised in a monochromatic environment showed a flat generalization gradient. These results indicate that ducklings without perceptual experience with various colors generalized their response to all colors. In contrast, the ducklings raised in normal light displayed the greatest response to the S+ (the 589-nm light) (see bottom graph of Figure 7-5). As the result of perceptual experience with various colors, animals apparently learn to differentiate between colors and, therefore, are less likely to generalize to similar colors. A similar influence of restricted perceptual experience on stimulus generalization was also observed in rats by Walk and Walters (1973), in ducks by Tracy (1970), in monkeys by Ganz and Riesen (1962), and in congenitally blind humans by Ganz (1968).

Section Review

Generalization is a process in which animals or people respond in the same way to similar stimuli; discrimination is a process in which animals or people learn to respond in different ways to different stimuli. Generalization enables us to respond to unfamiliar stimuli without having to discover directly their significance, and discrimination allows us to know when to respond and when not to

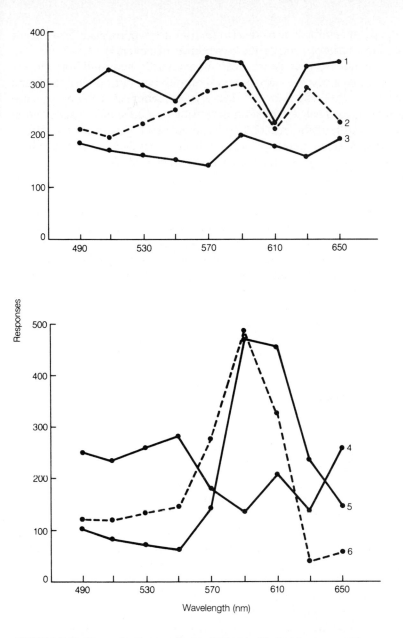

FIGURE 7-5 Generalization gradients obtained with ducklings reared in monochromatic light (top graph) and in white light (bottom graph). The results of the study showed that ducklings raised in monochromatic light exhibited flat generalization gradients, whereas those reared in white light demonstrated steep generalization gradients. From Peterson, N. (1962). Effect of monochromatic rearing on the control of responding by wavelength. *Science, 136,* 774–775. Copyright 1962 by the American Association for the Advancement of Science. Reprinted by permission.

respond. However, generalization or discrimination at inappropriate times leads to failure to obtain reinforcement, or the experience of adversity.

There are two major types of generalization: excitatory and inhibitory. In excitatory generalization, a cue is associated with reinforcement or punishment, and stimuli similar to the S+ will elicit the response. In contrast, in inhibitory generalization, a cue is associated with reinforcement or punishment, and stimuli similar to the S− will inhibit responding. The level of generalization differs between situations. A steep generalization gradient is obtained when an animal or a person only responds to stimuli very similar to the S+ or the S−. A flat generalization gradient occurs when the animal or person exhibits the same amount of excitation or inhibition to any stimuli resembling S+ or S−.

The Lashley-Wade view of generalization emphasizes the role of discriminability of the S+ and S− in the level of generalization. According to the Lashley-Wade view, animals and people generalize to stimuli quite dissimilar to the conditioning stimulus when they fail to distinguish between the S+ and other stimuli. In contrast, learning to differentiate between the S+ and other stimuli results in little or no generalization.

Under some circumstances, generalization is undesired. In these situations, reinforcement is available only when a specific stimulus is present, and generalized responses are ineffective in producing reinforcement. Reinforcement available only under certain conditions creates a situation in which an animal or a person must learn when responding is effective and when it is not; we turn our attention next to discrimination learning.

DISCRIMINATION LEARNING

We know that during some occasions reinforcement is available and will occur contingent upon an appropriate response and that during other occasions reinforcement is unavailable and will not occur despite continued responding. To respond when reinforcement is available and not when reinforcement is unavailable, we must learn to discriminate; that is, we must not only discover the conditions indicating reinforcement availability and respond when those conditions exist; we must also recognize the circumstances indicating the unavailability of reinforcement and not respond during these times. We are faced with thousands of discrimination learning tasks during our lives. For example, suppose you want to see a particular movie at your local theater. In many movie theaters you cannot just walk in; you must first get in the right line. If the line for the movie that you want to see is indicated by a blue line or specified number (S^Ds), then reinforcement (the movie) is available only if you get into the right line. However, you will not be able to see the movie if you get into the wrong line (S^{Δ}). The S^D is a stimulus signaling that the reinforcer is available, while the S^{Δ} is a stimulus which indicates that the reinforcer is unavailable.

We must learn to discriminate the conditions that indicate reinforcement availability (S^D) from the conditions that do not (S^{Δ}) to interact effectively with our environment. The failure to discriminate will cause us not to respond when reinforcement is available, to respond when reinforcement is unavailable, or both. Thus, you will miss the movie that you wanted to see if you get into the wrong line at the movie theater. In most cases, the failure to discriminate will cause you to be inconvenienced. For example, you lose time and effort going to the library if it's closed. Embarrassment may occur during some circumstances if you do not discriminate. If you go to the movies with friends, you will feel foolish if you have them get into the wrong line. In some cases, behavior pathology can result from discriminative failure. To illustrate this process, consider a sociopath who fails to discriminate between the acceptability of violence on television and the unacceptability of violent behavior in day-to-day life.

Discrimination learning involves discovering not only when reinforcement is available or unavailable but also when aversive events may or may not occur. For example, some conditions forecast rain, and some predict no rain. Since you get wet if you go out in the rain (typically an aversive event), you need to carry an umbrella when it rains to avoid becoming wet. If you fail to learn the conditions indicating impending rain, you will often become wet. Similarly, you need not carry an umbrella on a clear, sunny day. Nothing appears quite as foolish as someone carrying an umbrella when the sun is shining. However, it is difficult to learn when to carry an umbrella and when not to, because no stimuli always signal rain (the adversive event) or always indicate no rain (the absence of the adversive event). We will discuss the influence of predictiveness on discrimination learning later.

In many circumstances the occurrence or nonoccurrence of adversive events is easily predicted. A course outline for this class indicates that an exam will take place on specific days, but that the lack of an announcement means that you will have no exam. If you recognize the significance of the schedule, you will study before a scheduled exam, but you will not study if no exam is scheduled. The failure to discriminate may cause you to study even though you have no exam or fail to prepare for a scheduled exam. Another example of discrimination in adversive situations is seen in children who misbehave for a substitute teacher but behave appropriately with their regular teacher. Their behavior is based on the recognition that their regular teacher sometimes punishes them but that a substitute is not likely to do so.

You might have noticed that the abbreviations changed from $S+$ and $S-$ in the generalization discussion to S^D and S^Δ in the discussion of discrimination learning. This change reflects the conventional terms used in each area of research; it does not indicate that we are talking about different stimuli but instead that we are referring to different properties of the same stimulus. Consider the following example to illustrate that a stimulus can function as both a discriminative stimulus and a conditioned stimulus. On a hot summer day going to the beach can be quite reinforcing. The hot summer day is a discriminative stimulus which indicates that reinforcement is available; it is also a conditioned stimulus producing an anticipatory goal response and motivating the instrumental activity of going to the beach. We will describe the influence of conditioned stimuli on instrumental or operant behavior later in the chapter; we next discuss the conditions leading to discrimination learning as well as a failure to discriminate.

Discrimination Paradigms

Two-Choice Discrimination Tasks   In a two-choice discrimination learning situation, the S^D (the stimulus signaling reinforcement or punishment availability) and the S^Δ (the stimulus signaling reinforcement or punishment unavailability) are on the same stimulus dimension (for example, the S^D is a red light and the S^Δ a green light). Responding to the S^D produces reinforcement or punishment, and choosing the S^Δ leads to neither reinforcement nor punishment. Consider the following example: Suppose one of a child's parents is generous and the other parent is conservative. Asking one parent for money to go to the video arcade will be successful; a request to the other will result in failure. The first parent is an S^D since his or her presence indicates that reinforcement is available. Because reinforcement is unavailable when the other parent is asked, the presence of this parent is an S^Δ.

Research evaluating two-choice discrimination learning shows that animals or people begin by responding equally to the S^D and S^Δ. With continued training, response to the S^D increases and the response rate to S^Δ declines. At the end of training, an animal or a person is responding at a high rate to the S^D and responding very little or not at all to the S^Δ.

Reynolds (1961a) initially trained his pigeons to peck for food reinforcement on a multiple VI 3-minute, VI 3-minute schedule. (A multiple schedule is a compound schedule that consists of two or more independent schedules presented successively; each schedule is associated with a distinctive stimulus.) In the Reynolds study, a red light and a green light were associated with the separate components of the multiple schedule. As can be seen in Figure 7-6, Reynolds's pigeons exhibited equal response to the red and green lights during the prediscrimination phase of the study. In the discrimination stage, the schedule was changed to a multiple VI 3-minute extinction schedule. In this schedule, the red light continued to be correlated with reinforcement and the green light with the extinction (or nonreinforcement) component of the multiple schedule. During the discrimination phase of the study, Reynolds noted that the response rate to the red light (S^D) increased and response to the green light (S^Δ) declined (refer to Figure 7-6). To show that the change in response during the discrimination phase was due to differential reinforcement, Reynolds shifted the schedule back to a multiple VI 3, VI 3 schedule in the third phase of the study. Reynolds found that response to the red light declined and response to the green light increased during the third (nondiscrimination) phase until an equivalent response rate was made to both stimuli. This finding indicates that responding during the discrimination phase was controlled by the differential reinforcement procedure.

Two important observations should be made about the results of the Reynolds study. First, the animals stopped responding to the green light (S^Δ) associated

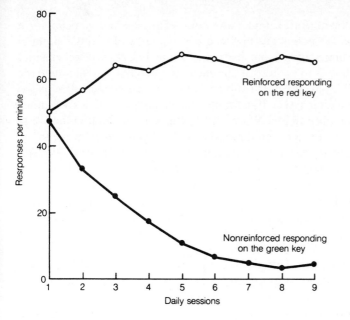

FIGURE 7-6   Mean number of responses per minute during discrimination learning. The pigeons' responses to the reinforced key increased as their responses to the nonreinforced key declined. From *A primer of operant conditioning* by G. S. Reynolds. Copyright 1968 by Scott, Foresman and Company. Reprinted by permission.

with the absence of reinforcement. Second, the pigeons increased their response rate to the red light (S^D) during the discrimination phase of the study. The increased responding to S^D and decreased responding to S^Δ is called *behavioral contrast*. The increased responding occurs to S^D despite the fact that the schedule associated with reinforcement has not changed. Behavioral contrast has been consistently observed by Reynolds (1961a, 1961b, 1961c) and other psychologists (see Lombardi & Flaherty, 1978; Rovee-Collier & Capatides, 1979; Woodruff, 1979).

The behavioral contrast phenomenon points to one problem with discrimination learning: It can have negative consequences. To recognize this problem, consider the following situation. The teacher of a disruptive child decides to extinguish the disruptive behavior by no longer reinforcing (perhaps by discontinuing attention) the child's disruptive activities. But the child's parents may continue to attend to the disruptive behavior. In this case, the child will be disruptive at home (S^D) but not at school (S^Δ). In fact, the parents will probably experience an increase in disruptive behavior at home due to behavioral contrast; that is, as the rate of disruptive behavior during school declines, the child will become more disruptive at home. Parents can deal with this situation only by discontinuing reinforcement (for example, attention) of the disruptive behavior in the home. This observation points out that one consequence of extinguishing an undesired behavior in one setting is an increase in that behavior in other situations. The desired method is to extinguish an undesired behavior in all situations.

Studies (see Hall, 1982) using human subjects indicate that people are sensitive to two-choice discrimination tasks. Illustrating the acquisition of a two-choice discrimination in people, Terrell and Ware (1961) trained kindergarten and first-grade children to discriminate between three-dimensional geometric forms. In one discrimination, the children needed to distinguish between large and small cubed boxes; in the other discrimination, between a sphere and pyramid. A light indicated a correct response. Terrell and Ware reported that the children quickly learned to discriminate between the geometric forms. These observations indicate that positive reinforcement is a critical ingredient for discrimination learning, even with humans.

Conditional Discrimination Tasks   According to D'Amato (1970), in a *conditional discrimination task,* the reinforcement contingency associated with a particular stimulus depends on the status of a second stimulus. In other words, a specific stimulus does not always signal either the availability or nonavailability of reinforcement in a conditional discrimination task. Instead, in some circumstances a particular cue indicates that reinforcement will be presented contingent upon the occurrence of an appropriate response, whereas under other conditions, the cue does not signal reinforcement availability.

Consider the following example to illustrate a conditional discrimination. Suppose a child wants a dollar to spend at the store. The child may ask his or her parents but knows that under most conditions the request will be denied. In contrast, when a relative is with the parents, the child's request is granted. This child will eventually learn to ask for money only when a relative is nearby. In this example, the parents' and relative's presence is an S^D signaling the availability of reinforcement. Thus, the child's request to the parents for money will be effective when a relative is present but ineffective when no relative is visiting (S^Δ). There are many instances of conditional discrimination situations in the real world. For example, a store is open at certain hours and closed at others, or a spouse is friendly sometimes but hostile at other times.

It is more difficult to learn that a particular cue signals reinforcement availability sometimes but not at other times than to learn that a specific stimulus always is associated with either reward availability or nonavailability. However, we must discover when a cue signals reinforcement availability and when it does not if we are to interact effectively with our environment. Psychologists (see D'Amato, 1970) have observed that both lower animals and people can learn a conditional discrimination; we will look at one of these studies next.

Nissen (1951) discovered that chimpanzees can learn a conditional discrimination. In Nissen's study, large and small squares were the discriminative stimuli; the brightness of the squares was the conditional stimulus. When the squares were white, the large square was the S^D and the small square was the S^Δ; when the squares were black, the small square was the S^D and the large square was the S^Δ. Nissen reported that chimpanzees learned to respond effectively; that is, they responded to the large square when it was white but not black and to the small square when it was black but not white.

We have learned that animals can learn to respond to S^D and not to S^Δ. The importance of having stimuli signal the unavailability as well as the availability of reinforcement is reviewed in the next section.

An Insoluble Discrimination Problem

Pavlov (1928) initially trained one group of dogs to discriminate between a circle and an ellipse by associating the circle with food, while the ellipse was not followed by food. After discrimination training, the ellipse was made progressively more like the circle. Pavlov observed that as the two stimuli became very similar, the dogs were no longer able to discriminate and responded to both stimuli. However, salivating to both stimuli was not the only change that Pavlov noted in the dogs' behavior. He observed that the dogs showed extreme agitation; they whined, howled, and tried to escape from the restraining harness. Further, Pavlov noted that these behaviors also occurred outside the experimental situation. According to Pavlov, the dogs experienced strong conflict, attempting to continue to respond to one stimulus but not to the other. This conflict caused the dogs to develop a behavioral disturbance which Pavlov called an *experimental neurosis*. This disorder causes the dogs to be unable to respond appropriately to the circle and ellipse, even when they were returned to original discrimination task.

Experimental neurosis has been consistently observed when animals are placed in an insoluble discrimination task (see Gantt, 1971, for a review of the literature). For example, Brown (1942) trained rats to discriminate between two lights of different brightness. Brown rewarded approach to the bright light and avoidance of the dim light. If the rats did not respond correctly, they received an electric shock. After the rats learned to discriminate, Brown changed the brightness of the two stimuli so that they were more similar. As the discrimination became more difficult, Brown noted that the rats became extremely agitated. The rats trembled, defecated, and urinated, and some even experienced convulsions.

In the previous examples, neurosis was produced when the two stimuli were made very similar and thus impossible to discriminate. Extreme behavioral disturbances (Maier, 1949; Maier, Glazer, & Klee, 1940; Maier & Klee, 1945) may also occur when an animal can perceive the differences between two stimuli but reward is randomly associated with the two stimuli. Maier and his associates studied the insoluble discrimination problem using a Lashley jumping stand, which forces the rat to jump (by shocking them for not jumping) across a space and through one of two doors. One door is usually black, the other white. In the soluble discrimination situation, one door is the S^D and the other is the S^Δ. If the rat responds to the S^D door it can safely pass through; if the rat responds to the other door, it runs into a closed door and falls into a net. The rats find it aversive to fall into the net and are highly motivated to learn how to avoid this adversity. To prevent the rat from learning to respond to one particular door, the safe and the dangerous doors are switched after each trial. The rats quickly learned to respond to the S^D in the soluble problem; however, although there was no solution to the insoluble problem, the rats responded in a specific manner. Some rats always jumped right or left, others to the black door, and the rest to the white door. In addition to developing a "fixated" way of responding, the rats lost muscle tone and became unresponsive. Also, they continued to exhibit the "fixated" response even when the problem was made soluble.

Predictiveness plays an important role in discrimination learning. Apparently, animals have a strong need for predictiveness, and severe behavioral disturbances results when animals experience insoluble discrimination problems. These animals can still receive reward half of the time, but the conflict produced by uncertain circumstances is disruptive even though no physical pain such as shock is experienced. Do these studies of experimental neurosis have relevance to humans? There are some studies (see Kazdin, 1978) that have demonstrated experimental neurosis in children using a Pavlovian discrimination training procedure. Additionally, certain analogous real-world situations involve insoluble discrimination problems. For example, parents who do not provide consistent reward and punishment create a home environment in which the child cannot discriminate when reward or punishment will occur. Considerable evidence indicates that inconsistent parental discipline leads to behavior problems in children; this information suggests that experiencing insoluble discrimination problems leads to self-doubt, conflict, uncertainty, and behavior pathology (see Baumrind, 1983, for a review of the literature on how parents' child-rearing styles affect their children's emotional development). Every attempt should be made to provide children (and adults) with an environmental structure in which they can predict when reward or punishment will and will not occur.

The Development of a Discrimination

We have seen that animals and people can learn when to respond to receive reinforcement or avoid punishment and when responding will be ineffective. The acquisition of a discrimination occurs in three stages: First, *animals or people must be able to differentiate (or distinguish) between the S^D and the S^Δ*. Second, *they must attend to the relevant dimension*. Third, *the discriminative stimuli must gain control over their behavior*. Two important points concerning the development of a discrimination need to be mentioned before we examine each stage. If an animal or person does not exhibit the behavior characteristic of each stage, the discrimination will not be learned. Thus, an animal or a person may be able to differentiate between the discriminative stimuli while attending to the relevant dimension and still not learn to discriminate because the discriminative stimuli did not gain control over the animal's or person's responding. Remember that these stages refer to the sequence of events involved in the development of a discrimination; since discrimination learning is a continuous process, when one stage ends and the next begins is impossible to discern.

Stimulus Differentiation   Recall from the chapter-opening vignette that a man wrongly accused a particular tall, thin man of attacking him. One likely cause of the victim's failure to discriminate was his inability to differentiate between tall, thin men. It also is possible that the victim was not attending to differential facial characteristics and did not discriminate. Selective attention and discrimination learning are discussed in the next section of this chapter.

There are obvious instances during which discrimination based on differences between stimuli in a particular dimension is impossible due to an inability to differentiate between discriminative stimuli. For example, some color-blind people cannot discriminate between red and green, and therefore cannot learn when to stop and go for red and green traffic lights. Because these color-blind people can use traffic light location cues, they can learn to discriminate between the red and green lights.

Does differentiation failure stem entirely from inherited deficiencies in an animal's or a person's perceptual system? Perceptual-system failure can be inherited; color blindness is merely one example of an inherited trait that can lead to discrimination failure. However, the ability to distinguish between discriminative stimuli also depends on perceptual experience, and the failure to discriminate can result from the absence of essential perceptual experience.

Eleanor Gibson's perceptual learning theory (1969) explains why perceptual experience is essential for discrimination learning. According to Gibson, animals and people have an inherent motivation to discover salient characteristics of their environment. These salient characteristics include the stimuli that remain the same despite changes in the surrounding environment. Perceptual constancies represent the outcome of this discovery. For example, we can recognize that a person's size remains constant despite changes in retinal image size caused by increased distance. While the retinal image of a 6-foot person becomes smaller as the person moves away from us, we can still recognize the size of this person standing 30 feet away from us. The recognition that size remains constant despite increased distance is one example of what Gibson calls *perceptual learning,* or an increase in an animal's or a person's sensitivity to the environment. According to Gibson, perceptual learning occurs as the result of experience but does not involve reinforcement; instead, it is motivated by an inherent need to discover important characteristics of the environment, which will enable survival. Perceptual learning involves not only learning existing constancies but also recognizing differences in the environment; it is the discovery of differences between stimuli that enables an animal or a person to discriminate between stimuli.

Many articles have evaluated the influence of perceptual experience on discrimination training (see Hall, 1982). In these studies, rats were raised in environments containing the stimuli that would serve as the S^D and S^Δ when the animals became adults. In the classic study by Gibson, Walk, and Tighe (1959), rats were raised in cages containing metal cutouts of circles and triangles. Remaining in these cages until 90 days of age, the rats were then trained to discriminate between a black triangle and black circle. The authors reported that rats given early perceptual experience learned to discriminate more readily than did those without this early experience. Apparently, the animals receiving early perceptual experience had already learned to differentiate between stimuli of a particular dimension and were able to use this knowledge to discriminate between stimuli of that dimension. Other studies by Gibson and her associates (Gibson et al., 1959; Walk, Gibson, Pick, & Tighe, 1959) have reported a similar facilitation of discrimination learning as the result of prior perceptual exposure.

Several recent studies (Channell & Hall, 1981; Hall, 1979) indicate that the facilitative influence of prior perceptual experience occurs only when the initial perceptual experience and later discrimination training take place in different environments. If the perceptual preexposure and subsequent discrimination training occur in the same environment, initial perceptual experience actually impairs subsequent discrimination learning. According to Mackintosh (1983), learned irrelevance is responsible for the impairment of discrimination learning when initial perceptual experience and subsequent discrimination occur in the same environment. As we learned in Chapter 4, learned irrelevance represents the knowledge that a particular stimulus has no significance. When different environments are used for perceptual preexposure and discrimination training, learned irrelevance is attenuated, and the animal's knowledge about the stimuli can act to enhance subsequent discrimination training.

Selective Attention   Recall the opening vignette of the chapter. The victim may have been able to recognize his assailant's physical characteristics that differentiated him from other people, but he did not attend to them. Instead, the victim attended only to the size of his assailant and was therefore unable to discriminate his assailant from other people.

The phenomenon of attending to one aspect of a situation while ignoring other dimensions is called *selective attention*. Selective attention has adaptive significance. If we attend to too much environmental information, we will be unable to detect important events effectively; thus, limiting the amount of information processed allows us to process information more efficiently. For example, suppose you are reading a textbook. If you attend to all the stimuli in the environment, you would be unable to study; the distraction of other events would prevent you from concentrating sufficiently to interpret the information presented in the text. Thus, you attend only to the text, not to other events in the environment.

While selective attention enables you to study effectively, it can prevent discrimination learning. If you do not attend to the relevant dimension, you cannot learn the discriminative stimuli and therefore will not interact effectively with the environment; that is, sometimes you will fail to respond to the S^D, responding to the S^Δ instead.

Suppose you sell automobiles. Some customers will buy a car; others are just looking. Which customers do you approach? If you learn whom to approach and whom not to approach, you will earn more money. Perhaps age is the relevant dimension. If so, attending to dress and not to age will cause you to approach some people who will not buy and fail to approach others who will. Obviously, to maximize your success, you must attend to the *dimension* associated with reward.

The Filter Theory of Selective Attention Why are people sensitive to some environmental information but unaware of other events? Broadbent (1958) has proposed a *selective filter* explanation of selective attention. Broadbent suggested that animals and people have a limited information-processing capacity. To process information effectively, some information reaching an animal's or a person's sensory receptors is not processed: It is rejected because a selective filter allows some information to be processed and rejects other information. The selective filter works by permitting information on only one "channel" to be transmitted beyond the sensory receptors and processed by the central nervous system while preventing other information from being transmitted by the sensory receptors.

Broadbent proposed that the selective filter blocks information on unattended channels from being processed. However, evidence (Treisman, 1960) indicates that the selective filter attenuates the intensity of unattended messages rather than blocks the processing of information on unattended channels. The attenuation rather than blocking has considerable adaptive significance. Because the intensity of unattended information is reduced, most of this information is not processed. However, important information coming over the unattended channel could not be detected if it was blocked. People can detect important information by increasing their sensitivity to it.

Consider the following example: You are reading; visual information from your book is the attended information. You are not attending to auditory information. Your selective filter attenuates the noise around you, and you are unaware of the noise. We have all undoubtedly experienced not hearing someone talking to us while we're reading. However, what if the fire alarm sounds or a baby cries? If our selective filter did not allow any auditory information to pass, we would hear neither sound. Although the intensity of the message is reduced, our sensitivity to important auditory stimuli allows us to hear the fire alarm or the baby's cry.

Selective-Listening Experiments Selective-listening studies have documented the selectivity of discernment. In these studies, a subject is exposed to two messages simultaneously. The task for the subject is to attend to only one message, an objective accomplished by having the subject repeat the words presented in one of the messages (see Figure 7-7). This technique is called *shadowing,* and subjects who practice can effectively shadow the desired message. Research on selective listening has shown that usually a subject is unaware of information presented in the nonshadowed message. Let's look briefly at evidence of the selectivity of a person's attention.

Moray's (1959) study shows that subjects can be unaware of information presented on a nonshadowed channel. In a selective-listening study, Moray presented

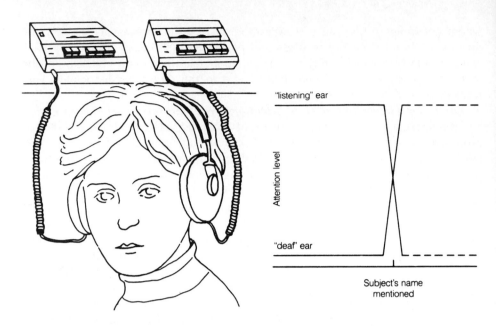

FIGURE 7-7 Selective-listening study. Each subject is presented two different messages, one message over each earphone. The subject is instructed "to listen" to one message by repeating the words presented to one ear. This procedure, called shadowing, typically causes subjects to be unaware of words presented to the unattended or deaf ear. Note that when an important item (for example, the subject's name) is presented to the "deaf" ear, the subject hears it. From *Psychology* (2d ed.) by G. R. Lefrancois. Copyright 1983 by Wadsworth, Inc. Reprinted by permission of the publisher.

a list of words 35 times over the nonshadowed channel. Subjects were then presented a larger list of words and were asked to identify words from it which they had heard over the nonshadowed channel. Moray reported that subjects had no recognition of the words presented over the nonshadowed channel. To evaluate the possibility that subjects had heard the words but could not remember them, Treisman and Geffen (1967) asked subjects to tap when certain target words were presented. Although the subjects identified the target words presented over the shadowed channel 86.5 percent of the time, the target words presented over the nonshadowed channel were detected only 8.1 percent of the time. These results indicate that failure to report information presented over the nonshadowed channel is a perceptual process, not a memory process. Cherry's (1953) investigation provides dramatic evidence that subjects can be unaware of information coming over the nonshadowed channel. Cherry presented two different messages in a selective-listening study; halfway through the study, the message over the nonshadowed channel switched from English to German, and the subjects did not notice the change.

You might think that the selective-listening studies indicate that subjects are always unaware of information presented over a nonshadowed channel. However,

under some conditions subjects do report information presented on a nonshadowed channel. For example, Moray (1959) reported that subjects can often detect
their own name presented over a nonshadowed channel. This research shows that
the sensory systems do not block all information of an unattended message but
instead only process important material. Thus, a person can detect important
information (that is, a name) in a nonshadowed message.

Recall Cherry's subjects who did not detect a shift from English to German.
Interestingly, Cherry (1953) reported that starting with a male's voice in both
messages followed by switching the nonshadowed message to that of a female's
voice causes subjects to notice a change. Subjects detected a difference in the
nonshadowed message when it was changed from a recorded human voice to that
of a 400-Hz pure tone. Also, Lawson (1966) reported that subjects could detect
target tones, but not words, of the nonshadowed message as well as those presented over the shadowed channel. This research demonstrates that some information is processed prior to the selective-attention stage; however, this processing
is based on the physical characteristics of an event but not on the content of a
message.

Controlled versus Automatic Processing of Information   Recent research
(Howard, 1983) argues against a filter explanation of selective attention because
people can process more than one piece of information at a time. For example,
many people can converse with a passenger while driving an automobile without
having an accident.

How can two different pieces of information be processed simultaneously?
Shiffrin and Schneider (1977) suggest that there are two types of information
processing: controlled processing and automatic processing. *Controlled processs-
ing* requires attention, and usually only one piece of information can be attended
to at one time. In our example, to understand the conversation, the driver must
attend to it; thus, understanding a conversation requires controlled processing. In
contrast, *automatic processing* requires little or no attention and occurs when a
person is participating in a highly practiced activity, such as driving.

Let's look at one study by Schneider and Shiffrin (1977) to illustrate the difference between automatic and controlled processing. In this study, subjects were
visually presented a target letter or number to identify. For some subjects, the
target was a letter mixed with other letters in a visual array, a treatment referred
to as the same-category condition. For other subjects, the target was a number,
and the other items in the visual array were letters (different-category condition).
The experimenters also varied the number of other items in the visual array, called
the frame size, from one to four. On some trials the target item was present; on
others, it was not. The subject's task was to indicate whether the target item was
present. Figure 7-8 presents a diagram of the two treatment conditions in Schneider and Shiffrin's study.

Schneider and Shiffrin observed that with or without the target present, subjects
in the same-category condition required more time to identify the target accurately
than did subjects in the different-category condition. According to Schneider and
Shiffrin, subjects began the study with a great deal of practice detecting numbers
among letters and therefore could readily detect the presence of the target number

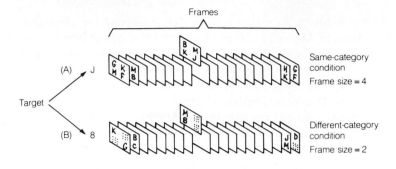

FIGURE 7-8   Trials from each of the two treatment conditions in the Schneider and Schiffrin experiment: (a) The same category condition, in which the target and distractors are letters and (b) the different-category condition, in which the target is a number and letters, the distractors. Adopted from Schneider, W., & Shiffrin, R. M. (1977). Controlled and automatic human information processing: I. Detection, search, and attention. *Psychological Review, 84,* 1–66. Copyright 1977 by the American Psychological Association. Reprinted by permission.

in the different-category condition. In contrast, subjects trying to identify a target letter from other letters in the same-category condition needed to inspect each item to determine the target's presence or absence accurately. These observations indicate that automatic processing was sufficient for effective performance in the different-category condition but that controlled processing was necessary in the same-category condition.

Our discussion indicates that to learn a discrimination we must differentiate between the S^D and S^Δ, then process the information in the relevant dimension. However, even if we can differentiate between the discriminative stimuli and are processing data in the relevant dimension, we still might respond to the S^Δ. To learn a discrimination, the S^D must also gain control over our behavior; that is, an animal or a person must respond to the S^D but not to other stimuli.

Stimulus Selection   The literature (D'Amato, 1970) points out that stimuli in some modalities gain control over responding, whereas stimuli in other modalities are not used because an animal or a person cannot detect when to respond and when not to respond. An animal or a person may not respond to stimuli in a particular modality even though (1) these stimuli are correlated with reinforcement, (2) the stimuli can be differentiated, and (3) the animal or person is attending to the stimuli.

D'Amato and Fazzaro's (1966) study demonstrates the stimulus selection process. The researchers trained two capuchin monkeys to discriminate using a compound S^D (a vertical white line superimposed on a red background) and a compound S^Δ (a horizontal white line superimposed on a green background). These compound stimuli were simultaneously presented on 20 of the 40 trials that the monkeys received each day. The color components were presented on only 10 trials; the horizontal-vertical bar components were presented on the remaining 10 trials. On the 20 trials providing one component, the monkeys could respond on the basis of the single compound, or they could press a white illuminated key and see the compound stimuli. Thus, by pressing the white key, called a *cue-producing response,* the monkeys were indicating that they needed the other dimension stimuli to respond effectively. D'Amato and Fazzaro reported that although the monkeys exhibited few cue-producing responses when the color component was given, they almost always emitted the cue-producing response when the bar component was presented. These results indicate that the color dimension controlled the monkeys' behavior and that the bar component had little control over behavior. You might think that primates cannot learn a horizontal-vertical discrimination. However, monkeys can learn to discriminate between horizontal and vertical lines if no other cues are associated with reinforcement. But when color is also associated with reinforcement, the horizontal-vertical cues just do not influence the responding of primates.

Other psychologists have reported that when more than one stimulus dimension is associated with reinforcement, one cue will gain control while the other cue (or cues) will not influence an animal's responding. For example, Reynolds (1961b) trained pigeons to discriminate between a triangle on a red background (S^D) and a circle on a green background (S^Δ). He reported that the pigeons responded to one of the cues but not to the other. The stimulus dimension that gained control differed: For some pigeons, the color dimension gained control; for others, the form controlled behavior (see Figure 7-9).

Stimulus selection also has been demonstrated in studies with human subjects. Trabasso and Bower (1968) trained college students in a concept-identification task (see Chapter 9). In their experiment, two dimensions (shape and location of a dot) were the relevant cues, and three other dimensions were irrelevant. Following the students' training, Trabasso and Bower tested for the learning which occurred to the shape and dot-location dimension. They found that most subjects solved the concept based entirely on one dimension; that is, they could identify the correct stimulus when one dimension was present but responded only at a chance in the presence of the other dimension. These observations indicate that in the concept-identification task, one dimension gained control of behavior and the other dimension did not.

There is one treatment that can enable other stimulus elements to gain control over responding. Research (D'Amato, 1970) indicates that overtraining can increase the number of stimulus elements controlling behavior. D'Amato (1970) trained capuchin monkeys on a compound discrimination task. In the training phase of the study, a vertical line and a circle served as the S^D; a horizontal line and a plus, as the S^Δ. Control subjects were trained to a criterion of 90 percent correct responses; experimental subjects received 800 trials beyond the 90 percent criterion. After training, the monkeys were tested on each stimulus element. D'Amato reported that the experimental subjects responded appropriately to both cues, although only one stimulus element affected the control subjects' behavior.

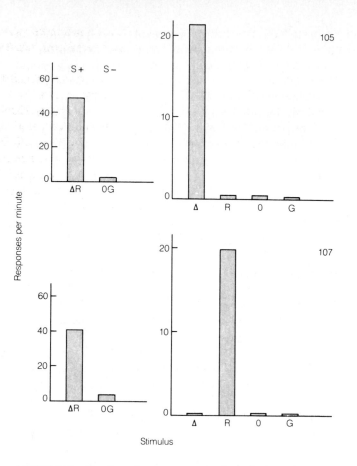

FIGURE 7-9 Number of responses per minute for two pigeons when both components of the compound were presented (left graphs) and when each component of the compound was presented separately (right graphs). The results of this study demonstrate that one stimulus dimension gains control of the pigeon's key pecking: The triangle controlled responding in pigeon 105; the red color controlled responding in pigeon 107. From Reynolds, G. S. (1961). Attention in the pigeon. *Journal of the Experimental Analysis of Behavior, 4,* 203–208. Copyright 1961 by the Society for the Experimental Analysis of Behavior.

This observation points out that overtraining can increase the number of stimuli that control responding.

Overtraining also can increase the number of stimuli gaining control in humans. James and Greeno (1967) trained college students on a paired–associate learning task using a compound consisting of a three-letter word and a nonsense syllable as the stimulus elements and digits from 1 to 8 as the responses. Control subjects who did not receive overtraining responded to the word but not to the

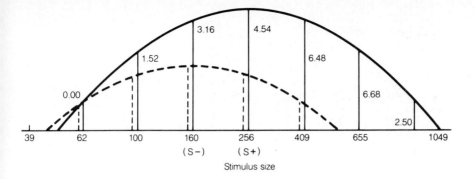

FIGURE 7-10 Graph presents Spence's theoretical view of the interaction of excitatory and inhibitory generalization gradients on discriminated behavior. During acquisition, reward is available when 256 stimulus size is present but not when 160 stimulus size is present. Excitatory potential (solid lines) generalizes to similar stimuli, as does inhibitory potential (broken lines). The resultant reaction tendency, indicated by the value above each stimulus size, is obtained by subtracting the inhibitory from the excitatory potential. From Spence, K. W. (1937). The differential response in animals to stimuli varying within a single dimension. *Psychological Review, 44,* 430–444. Copyright 1937 by the American Psychological Association. Reprinted by permission.

nonsense syllable, whereas 20 trials of overtraining in experimental subjects resulted in the nonsense syllables also gaining control of responding.

Overtraining does not always cause other stimulus elements to gain control over responding. For example, Houston (1967) used nonsense syllables and colors as the stimulus compound in a paired–associate learning task and did not find that overtraining increased the amount of responding controlled by the nonsense syllables. Discussing Houston's study, D'Amato (1970) suggested that color may be such a dominant or salient cue that the nonsalient nonsense syllable can gain little or no control of behavior.

The Nature of Discrimination Learning

Hull-Spence Theory   Clark Hull (1943) and Kenneth Spence (1936) provided us with an explanation of discrimination learning. Although not a completely accurate view of the nature of discrimination learning, their theory does describe some essential aspects of the discrimination-learning process.

Development of Conditioned Excitation and Inhibition   According to the Hull-Spence view, discrimination learning develops in three stages. First, conditioned excitation develops to the S^D as the result of reinforcement. Second, nonreinforcement in the presence of the S^Δ results in the development of conditioned inhibition to the S^Δ. As we learned earlier in the chapter, conditioned inhibition suppresses responding to the S^D. Finally, the excitation and inhibition generalize to other stimuli (see Figure 7-10); the combined influence of excitation and inhibition determines the level of responding to each stimuli. As can be seen in

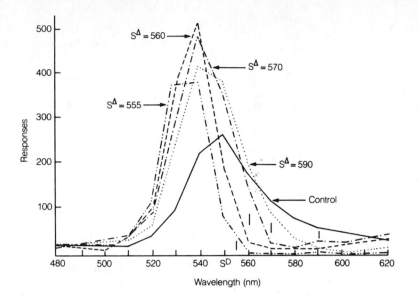

FIGURE 7-11 Mean number of responses on a generalization test (using wavelengths varying from 480 to 620 nm) for four experimental groups receiving prior discrimination training with 550 nm as the S^D and either 555, 560, 570, or 590 nm as the S^Δ; the control group did not receive discrimination training. Experimental subjects showed steeper generalization gradients and greater responding to stimuli similar to S^D than did control subjects. Also, the peak shift was seen in experimental but not in control subjects. From Hanson, H. (1959). Effects of discrimination training on stimulus generalization. *Journal of Experimental Psychology, 58*, 321–324. Copyright 1959 by the American Psychological Association. Reprinted by permission.

Figure 7-10, the Hull-Spence model predicts that a steeper generalization gradient is found with discrimination training than with nondiscrimination training. Also, the model assumes that maximum responding is not to the S^D but rather to a stimulus other than the S^D and in the stimulus direction opposite to that of the S^Δ. The reason for this prediction is that although the S^D (256 in the figure) has the greatest excitatory strength, it also has accrued inhibitory strength. Although another stimulus (409 in the figure) may have less excitatory strength than the S^D, it also has accrued little inhibitory strength. Thus, the resultant "effective" strength of the S^D will be less than that of the other stimulus.

The Peak Shift Phenomenon   Hanson (1959) tested the assumptions of the Hull-Spence model of discrimination learning. In Hanson's study, pigeons received either discrimination training using a 550-nm light as the S^D and a 555-, 560-, 570-, or 590-nm as the S^Δ or nondiscrimination training with a 550-nm light present during the entire training session. Following training, both groups of pigeons were given a generalization test using stimuli ranging from 480 to 620 nm. Hanson reported three important differences between discrimination and nondiscrimination generalization gradients (see Figure 7-11). First, a steeper generalization gradient was found with discrimination than with nondiscrimination training, a prediction in accord with the Hull-Spence model. Second, the greatest responding for discrimination-training subjects was not to the S^D but to the 540-nm stimulus. This observation, referred to as the *peak shift,* also agrees with the Hull-Spence view of discrimination training. In contrast, pigeons receiving nondiscrimination training responded maximally to the 550-nm stimulus. Third, the overall level of responding was higher with discrimination training than with nondiscrimination training, an observation not predicted by the Hull-Spence model.

The Aversive Character of S^Δ   Terrace (1964) suggested that behavioral contrast is responsible for the heightened responding with discrimination training. Terrace assumes that exposure to the S^Δ is an adversive event and that the "emotional effects of nonreinforced responding" or frustration produced during S^Δ periods increases the intensity of responding to other stimuli. Recall from Chapter 5 that nonreinforcement or stimuli associated with nonreinforcement are adversive, and exposure to either of these stimuli can increase the intensity of responding for reinforcement. Terrace's view that behavioral contrast is responsible for the heightened responding with discrimination training is consistent with the literature presented in Chapter 5.

Several other types of research support Terrace's approach. A number of drugs (for example, chlorpromazine, imipramine) appear to reduce the aversive effects of nonreinforcing events. Evidence of this effect is the elimination of frustration-induced behavior (for example, aggressive behavior) with their use. Another influence of these drugs is the disruption of performance on a discrimination task (Bloomfield, 1972; Terrace, 1963). Animals receiving chlorpromazine (an antipsychotic drug) or imipramine (an antidepressant drug) exhibit a high level of response to the S^Δ. It is thought that the reduced adversiveness of the S^Δ caused by the drugs is responsible for the lack of inhibition of response to the S^Δ. These drugs not only caused increased responding to the S^Δ but also eliminated both behavioral contrast and the peak shift. Thus, the heightened response to the S^D and the maximum responding to a stimulus other than the S^D, both of which are characteristic of discrimination learning, are not seen when either chlorpromazine or imipramine is administered. These observations suggest that (1) S^Δ must be an adversive event to inhibit responding and (2) the adversiveness of S^Δ causes both behavioral contrast and the peak shift.

The Hull-Spence model of discrimination learning suggests that conditioned excitation and inhibition lead to a steep excitatory generalization gradient and the peak shift. Hanson's (1959) research supports the Hull-Spence model. However, his study and Terrace's research indicate that nonreinforcement leads not only to the development of conditioned inhibition but also to the establishment of adversive properties to the S^Δ. This adversive character of the S^Δ contributes to the heightened responding to the S^D (behavioral contrast) and maximum responding to a stimulus other than the S^D (peak shift).

You should not conclude that discrimination learning merely reflects the development of excitatory tendencies to the S^D and inhibitory (and adversive) tendencies to the S^Δ. Although excitation and inhibition do play an important role in discrimination learning, other processes (for example, attention) also affect the establishment of a discrimination.

The Transposition Effect Although the peak shift phenomenon appears to support the Hull-Spence view, the noted Gestalt psychologist Wolfgang Kohler (1939) provides an alternative view of discrimination learning, which can also explain the peak shift. According to Kohler, stimuli are not evaluated in absolute terms but instead in relation to other stimuli. For example, a 75-dB tone may seem loud in a quiet room but soft in a noisy room. Thus, when we say that a noise is loud or soft, the perceived loudness depends on the context in which the noise is heard.

Kohler's view is important when applied to discrimination learning. For example, suppose that a rat learns to discriminate between an 80-dB S^D and a 60-dB S^Δ. Has the rat learned to respond to the 80-dB tone and not to the 60-dB tone? In Kohler's view, the animal has merely learned to respond to the louder of the two tones. How would the rat react to a 90-dB tone? Since the rat learned to respond to the louder tone, Kohler's theory predicts that the rat would react more intensely to the 90-dB tone than to the 80-dB tone. Kohler evaluated his view by training chickens and chimpanzees to respond to the brighter of the two stimuli (the S^D). When he tested his subjects with the S^D and a still brighter light stimulus, the animals chose the brighter of the two lights. Kohler called the phenomenon *transposition,* drawn from the analogy that the relation among notes comprising musical compositions does not change when the melodies are transposed to a different key.

Which view of discrimination learning is accurate: the Hull-Spence absolute view or the Kohler relational view? According to Schwartz (1989), there is evidence supporting both views. Studies that give animals choice between two stimuli support the relational or transposition view; that is, the animals respond to the relative rather than the absolute qualities of the stimuli. One study providing support for the relational view was conducted by Lawrence and DeRivera (1954). Lawrence and DeRivera initially exposed rats to cards that were divided in half. During training, the bottom half of the card was always an intermediate shade of gray, and the top half was one of three lighter or one of three darker shades of gray. A darker top half meant that the rats needed to turn left to obtain reward; a lighter top half signaled a right turn for reward. Figure 7-12 presents a diagram of this procedure. During testing, the intermediate shade of gray was no longer presented; instead, two of the six shades of gray presented during training were shown (one on the top, the other on the bottom). Although a number of combinations of these six shades were used, only one combination is described to illustrate how this study supports a relational view. On some test trials, two of the darker shades were used, with the lighter of the two on top (refer to Figure 7-12). If the animals had learned based on absolute values, they would turn left, since the dark shade had always been on the top in training. However, if the animals had learned based on the relation between stimuli, they would turn right during testing, since the darker stimulus was still on the bottom. Lawrence and

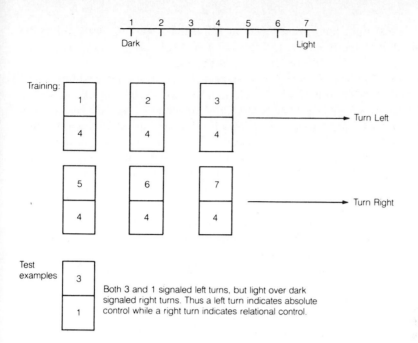

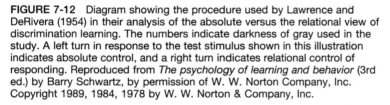

FIGURE 7-12 Diagram showing the procedure used by Lawrence and DeRivera (1954) in their analysis of the absolute versus the relational view of discrimination learning. The numbers indicate darkness of gray used in the study. A left turn in response to the test stimulus shown in this illustration indicates absolute control, and a right turn indicates relational control of responding. Reproduced from *The psychology of learning and behavior* (3rd ed.) by Barry Schwartz, by permission of W. W. Norton Company, Inc. Copyright 1989, 1984, 1978 by W. W. Norton & Company, Inc.

DeRivera reported that on the overwhelming majority of such test trials, the animals' responses were based on the relation between stimuli rather than on the absolute value of the stimuli. Thus, in our example, most of the animals turned right because the darker shade of gray was on the bottom half of the card.

Although some studies support a relational view of discrimination, other experiments support the Hull-Spence absolute stimulus view. Hanson's study (1959) provides support for the Hull-Spence theory. Hanson trained pigeons to peck at a 550-nm (S^D) lighted key to receive reinforcement; pecking at a 590-nm (S^Δ) light yielded no reinforcement. On generalization tests, the pigeons were presented a range of lighted keys varying from 480 to 620 nm. According to the Hull-Spence view, at a point on the stimulus continuum below the S^D the inhibitory generalization gradient does not affect excitatory responding. At this point on the gradient, responding to the S^D should be greater than the responding occurring at the lower wavelength test stimuli. In contrast, the relational view suggests that a lower wavelength of light will always produce responding greater than the S^D does. Hanson's results showed that while greater responding did occur to the 540-nm test light than to the 550-nm S^D, less responding occurred to the 530-nm light than to the S^D (refer to Figure 7-12). Thus, on generalization tests, greater responding occurs only to stimuli close to the S^D.

You might wonder why some results support the Hull-Spence absolute value view and others suggest that Kohler's relational approach is true. As Schwartz (1989) points out, the relational view is supported on a choice test; that is, subjects must choose to respond to one or two stimuli. In contrast, on a generalization test where a subject responds to only one stimulus, results support the Hull-Spence approach. In Schwartz's view, it is not unreasonable for both approaches to be valid; animals could learn about both the relation between stimuli and the absolute characteristics of the stimuli. In choice situations, the relation between stimuli is important, and the animal responds to the relational aspects of what it has learned. In contrast, when only a single stimulus is presented, the absolute character of a stimulus will determine its level of behavioral control.

Sutherland and Mackintosh's Attentional View   Sutherland and Mackintosh (1971) suggested that discrimination learning occurs in two stages. During the first stage, an animal's or a person's attention to the relevant dimension is strengthened. The second phase involves the association of a particular response to the relevant stimulus.

The Recognition of the Relevant Dimension   Recall that an animal or person viewing a compound stimulus attends to one dimension. According to Sutherland and Mackintosh, each stimulus dimension can activate an *analyzer*. The analyzer detects the presence of the salient or relevant aspect of a stimulus. The arousal of a particular analyzer causes an animal or a person to attend to that dimension. Thus, the presentation of a compound stimulus arouses the analyzer of the relevant dimension but not the analyzers of the other stimulus dimensions. Consider the following example to illustrate Sutherland and Mackintosh's view. A person viewing a 5-inch red horizontal bar projected onto a gray background could attend to several dimensions—for example, the color, brightness, length, or orientation of the bar. However, this person notices only the color of the bar. In Sutherland and Mackintosh's view, the reason for this phenomenon is that the analyzer for the color dimension is aroused, but the analyzers for the other dimensions are not.

What determines which analyzer will be aroused? Initially, the level of arousal of a particular analyzer is related to the intensity of the stimulus dimension; the greater the strength of a particular stimulus dimension, the more likely that dimension will activate the analyzer sufficiently to arouse attention. With certain types of experiences, the ability of analyzers to attract attention changes. According to Sutherland and Mackintosh, the predictive value of a particular stimulus dimension influences the amount of attention produced by the analyzer of a particular stimulus dimension. The analyzer will arouse more attention if the stimulus dimension predicts important events. However, an analyzer will arouse less attention if the stimulus dimension for that analyzer does not predict future events.

In the second phase of discrimination learning, the output from the analyzer is attached to a particular response. The connection between the analyzer output and the response is strengthened as the result of reinforcement. Thus, in Sutherland and Mackintosh's view, reinforcement increases both the attention to a particular dimension and the ability of a particular stimulus to elicit the response.

Predictive Value of Discriminative Stimuli   Research indicates that predictiveness has an important influence on discrimination learning. Recall from Chapter 3 that the predictive value of the CS determines whether it becomes able to elicit a CR. Similarly, the ability of the S^D to predict reinforcement is important; the predictiveness of the S^D determines whether it will gain control over responding. If the S^D is predictive of reinforcement, it will control responding. However, the S^D will not control responding if it does not reliably predict the occurrence of reinforcement.

Wagner and colleagues (1968) investigated the influence of predictiveness of the S^D on its control of operant responding. Two groups of rats were trained to bar press for reinforcement. Subjects in the first group were reinforced on 50 percent of the trials in which the light and the first tone compound stimulus were presented, and they were reinforced on 50 percent of the trials in which the light and the second tone compound stimulus were presented (see Figure 7-13). The rats in the second group received the light with the first tone stimulus paired with reinforcement 100 percent of the time; the light with the second tone stimulus was presented 0 percent of the time. These investigators were interested in the degree of control gained by the light cue. For subjects in the first group, the light and both tones were equally predictive of reinforcement. In contrast, the first tone was much more predictive of reinforcement than the light cue for subjects in the second group: For these subjects, tone 1 was present 100 percent of the trials on which reinforcement was available, but the light was paired with reinforcement on only 50 percent of the trials. Although the light was paired with reinforcement availability on 50 percent of the trials in both groups, the light was a better predictor in the first group than in the second: No cue in the first group predicted reinforcement more reliably than did the light, whereas the first tone predicted reinforcement better than the light in the second group. Wagner et al. reported that the light better controlled responding for subjects in the first group than in the second group. These results indicate that it is the relative predictiveness of an S^D, not the percentage of trials in which the S^D is associated with reinforcement, that determines its ability to control responding.

Continuity versus Noncontinuity   The Hull-Spence view asserts that excitation and inhibition gradually increase during the acquisition of a discrimination. This position is referred to as a *continuity theory* of discrimination learning because it assumes that the development of a discrimination is continuous and is due to the gradual acquisition of excitation to the S^D and inhibition to the S^Δ. Krechevsky (1932) and Lashley (1929) presented a view of discrimination learning that was quite different from the Hull-Spence approach. According to Krechevsky and Lashley, the learning of a discrimination is not a gradual, con-

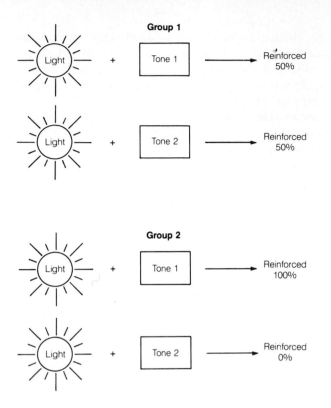

FIGURE 7-13 Two treatment conditions in the Wagner, Logan, Haberlandt, and Price (1968) study. For subjects in group 1, the light was equally predictive of reinforcement as either tone, but it was a worse predictor than tone 1 and a better predictor than tone 2 for subjects in group 2. From *The principles of learning and behavior* by M. Domjan and B. Burkhard. Copyright 1986 by Wadsworth, Inc. Reprinted by permission of the Brooks/Cole Publishing Company, Monterey, Calif., 93940.

tinuous process. Instead, they believed that an animal or a person acquires a discrimination by establishing a "hypothesis" about which stimulus is associated with reinforcement. While testing this hypothesis, the subject attends to the stimulus relevant to its hypothesis and learns nothing about other stimuli. The view espoused by Krechevsky and Lashley is referred to as a *noncontinuity theory* of discrimination learning because it assumes that once a subject focuses its attention on the relevant stimuli, the discrimination is rapidly acquired.

A considerable amount of research has been conducted in attempts to evaluate the continuity versus noncontinuity view. Some studies support the continuity approach of Hull and Spence, and other research has agreed with the noncontinuity approach of Krechevsky and Lashley. It is not surprising that there is research to validate both points of view, since discrimination learning reflects the acquisition of excitatory and inhibitory strength and the development of attention to predictive events in the environment. It seems reasonable that continuity theory explains how the emotional components of a discrimination are learned and that noncontinuity theory describes the attentional aspects of discrimination learning.

Section Review

Reinforcement is available in some circumstances and unavailable in others. In discrimination learning, an animal or a person discovers the stimuli (S^D) signaling the availability of reinforcement and the events (S^Δ) indicating the unavailability of reinforcement. Learning the discrimination results in responding when the S^D, but not the S^Δ, is present. Animals and people must also learn to discriminate between when punishment will occur and when it will not.

Experimental neurosis occurs when animals are exposed to insoluble discrimination problems; these insoluble problems involve either changing the S^D and the S^Δ so that they are no longer discriminable or presenting reinforcement or punishment inconsistently so that they are not controllable. The behavioral disturbances produced by insoluble discrimination tasks were extreme agitation or unresponsiveness.

Discrimination learning occurs in three stages. In the first stage, animals or people must be able to differentiate between the S^D and the S^Δ. In the second phase, they must attend to the relevant dimension. In the last phase, the discriminative stimuli must gain control over responding. The discrimination is not learned (1) if the animal or person cannot differentiate between the discriminative stimuli, (2) if the animal or person is not attending to the relevant dimension, or (3) if the discriminative stimulus does not gain control over responding.

According to the Hull-Spence view, conditioned excitation develops to the S^D as the result of reward; this conditioned excitation allows the S^D to produce the instrumental response. After conditioned excitation is established, nonreward in the presence of the S^Δ results in the development of conditioned inhibition to the S^Δ; this decreases responding to the S^Δ.

Kohler's relational or transposition view assumes that animals or people learn the relative relationship between the S^D and the S^Δ. Rather than just responding to a particular stimulus, they learn, for example, to choose the larger or smaller stimulus, or the louder or softer stimulus.

Sutherland and Mackintosh suggest that during discrimination learning, an animal's or a person's attention to relevant dimensions is strengthened. The ability of a stimulus analyzer to attract attention enables the animal or person to respond appropriately to the discriminative stimuli. After a subject person is attending to the relevant dimension, the association between the instrumental response and the relevant stimulus is strengthened.

The continuity view of discrimination learning assumes that excitation and inhibition gradually increase during the acquisition of a discrimination; this approach appears to describe the development of the emotional components of discrimination learning. In contrast, the noncontinuity approach asserts that there is an abrupt recognition of the salient features of a discrimination; this approach seems to describe the attentional aspects of discrimination learning.

THE IMPACT OF CONDITIONED STIMULI

Conditioned stimuli do not merely elicit or inhibit conditioned responses. There are two other properties of a conditioned stimulus besides excitation or inhibition of a conditioned response. First, conditioned stimuli sometimes prepare, or "set the occasion," for an animal to respond to another conditioned stimulus. Second, conditioned stimuli produce the motivation necessary for instrumental or operant behavior. We will examine next these two additional functions of conditioned stimuli.

The Occasion-Setting Function of a Conditioned Stimulus

A conditioned stimulus can have an excitatory property other than elicitation of the conditioned response. In some circumstances, a conditioned stimulus also can create the conditions necessary for another stimulus to have excitatory properties. In the absence of the conditioned stimulus, the other stimulus has no effect on behavior.

Holland (1983) has referred to the ability of one stimulus to enhance responding to another stimulus as *occasion-setting,* because one stimulus "sets the occasion" for another stimulus to elicit the conditioned response. Rescorla (1985) suggested that the occasion-setting stimulus facilitates responding to conditioned stimulus.

When will a conditioned stimulus be able to facilitate responding to another stimulus? Holland (1983) and Rescorla (1985) conducted a number of studies investigating the occasion-setting ability of a stimulus. In a typical experiment, pigeons experience stimulus A (for example, a localized lighted key on the wall of the operant chamber) without the unconditioned stimulus on some trials. On other trials, stimulus A follows a diffuse stimulus B (for example, an 1800-Hz tone) and both stimuli are paired with the unconditioned stimulus of food. (In this research, the conditioned response is the key peck to the lighted key; that is, the pigeons' conditioned response to the lighted key is the same as their unconditioned pecking response to food. The significance of this conditioned key-peck response will be explored further in Chapter 13.) Both investigators found that the presentation of stimulus A (light) alone elicited no responding. In contrast, the presentation of stimulus B or occasion-setting stimulus (1800-Hz tone) prior to stimulus A (lighted key) resulted in stimulus A's eliciting the conditioned key-peck response. In other words, the pigeons will not peck at the lighted key when it was presented alone, but the lighted key will elicited a conditioned key-peck response when it followed the tone.

You might think that the response to stimulus A (lighted key) in the presence of stimulus B (tone) is merely due to excitatory conditioning to stimulus B. However, both Holland (1983) and Rescorla (1985) argue that conditioned excitation and facilitation are separate properties of a conditioned stimulus. Conditioned excitation refers to a stimulus eliciting a conditioned response, and facilitation represents the occasion-setting function of a stimulus.

Several lines of evidence demonstrate the separate facilitation and excitation properties of a conditioned stimulus. Excitatory conditioning to stimulus B or the occasion-setter is not sufficient for that stimulus to facilitate responding to stimulus A (see Rescorla, 1985). Also, the establishment of stimulus B as a facilitator of responding to stimulus A does not result in the ability of stimulus B to elicit a conditioned response (see Holland, 1983). These observations provide strong support for the view that facilitation and excitation represent separate learning processes.

Two additional points deserve mentioning. First, the facilitation of responding by stimulus B develops only when stimulus B precedes stimulus A during compound conditioning. With the simultaneous pairing of stimuli A and B, stimulus B acts as a conditioned excitor but has no facilitatory properties. Recall our discussion of the development of within-compound associations in Chapter 4. We learned that the simultaneous pairing of two stimuli enhanced the formation of within-compound associations. Evidently, the development of a facilitatory capacity to a stimulus occurs only under conditions not favorable to the acquisition of within-compound associations. Second, the facilitating influence of stimulus B may transfer to conditioned stimuli other than stimulus A. Rescorla (1985) observed a general facilitating effect of an occasion-setting stimulus on conditioned responding. However, Holland (1986) reported that an occasion-setter had a general effect only when the excitatory stimulus used on the test was ambiguous. At this time, the extent of the facilitatory influence of an occasion-setting stimulus has not resolved.

What process enables a conditioned stimulus to facilitate responding to other stimuli? Rescorla (1986) argued that the facilitating effect of a stimulus is mediated by lowering the threshold of reaction to conditioned stimuli. He suggests that this facilitation effect is opposite that of conditioned inhibition, which raises the threshold reaction. Support for this conclusion can be found in the observation that stimulus B facilitates responding to excitatory conditioned stimuli but not to neutral stimuli (see Rescorla, 1985). Apparently, the facilitating effect of a stimulus is limited to stimuli possessing excitatory associative strength.

We have learned that conditioned stimuli can facilitate responding to other stimuli. Conditioned stimuli can also affect the level of operant responding or instrumental activity. In the next section, this additional influence of conditioned stimuli will be discussed.

Conditioned Stimuli and Operant/Instrumental Behavior

Consider the following two situations: (1) You are in a movie theater when a fire alarm sounds. The alarm causes you to stop watching the movie and rush from the theater. (2) You are studying for an exam to be taken tomorrow when you realize it's time for your favorite television show. You stop studying to watch the show. Both examples contain a particular element (the fire alarm and the scheduled time) that suppressed one behavior and evoked another. The fire alarm motivated you to terminate watching the movie and escape from the theater. In contrast, the scheduled time acted to inhibit your studying and motivated you to watch television.

The Influence of Central Motivational States Rescorla and Solomon's (1967) theory offers an explanation for the behavior exhibited in the previous two examples. According to Rescorla and Solomon, two central motivational states govern behavior. Arousal of an appetitive state motivates approach behavior; activation of an adversive state arouses avoidance behavior. Two types of conditioned stimuli stimulate the appetitive state and inhibit the adversive state. Why do you stop studying to watch your favorite television show? Since you associate the scheduled time of your favorite television show with past reward, that specific time can excite the central appetitive state and suppress the adversive state as a conditioned response. Spence (1956) called this response the *anticipatory goal response* (r_G; see Chapter 2); Mowrer (1960) called it *hope*.

The other conditioned stimulus that activates the central appetitive state and inhibits the adversive state is associated with the absence of an adversive event. For example, if you bolted from the theater when the fire alarm sounded, you would probably reenter when the alarm stopped (if, of course, you have been reassured of safety) and resume watching the movie. Rescorla and Solomon (1967) would assert that through conditioning, the termination of a stimulus (the fire alarm) associated with the absence of an adversive event (fire) stimulated the central appetitive state and suppressed the adversive state. D'Amato (1970) labeled this response an *anticipatory relief response* (r_R; Chapter 2); Mowrer (1960) labeled it *relief*. Thus, hope and relief motivate appetitive behavior and suppress avoidance behavior by influencing the functioning of the central motivational states.

Two types of conditioned stimuli also stimulate the central adversive state and inhibit the appetitive state. Because the fire alarm had been associated with fire, the alarm inhibited the appetitive state and therefore suppressed the watching of the movie. In addition, the alarm activated the adversive state, which in turn motivated escape behavior. Mowrer referred to this response as *fear;* D'Amato called it an *anticipatory pain response* (r_p; see Chapter 2). When a stimulus is associated with the absence of reward, the conditioned response produced by this stimulus can excite the central adversive state and inhibit the appetitive state. Amsel (1958) labeled this an *anticipatory frustration response* (r_F; see Chapter 2); Mowrer referred to it as *disappointment*. Thus, both *fear* and *frustration* stimulate avoidance behavior and suppress appetitive behavior by influencing the function of the central motivational states.

Why does a conditioned stimulus excite one state yet inhibit the other state? Suppose that the scheduled television show in our example aroused only the appetitive state and did not inhibit the adversive state. If this were the case, we would be unable to respond because our approach and avoidance tendencies

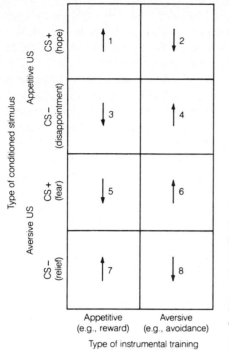

FIGURE 7-14
Matrix illustration of the interaction between conditioned stimuli and operant/instrumental behavior. Arrows indicate whether the conditioned stimulus facilitates (↑) or suppresses (↓) behavior. The terms in parentheses show the conditioned emotional response elicited by a particular conditioned stimulus. Adapted from Rescorla, R. A., & Solomon, R. L. (1967). Two-process theory: Relationships between Pavlovian conditioning and instrumental learning. *Psychological Review, 74,* 151–182. Copyright 1967 by the American Psychological Association. Reprinted by permission.

would have equal motive strength. Judson Brown's (1948) classic research on approach-avoidance conflict shows that equivalent approach and avoidance motive strengths produce vacillation; that is, the animal or person can neither approach reward nor avoid adversity. Therefore, the scheduled television show must inhibit the adversive state as well as excite the appetitive state to induce you to stop studying and turn on your favorite show.

Interaction Studies   Many studies support the theory that conditioned stimuli influence operant or instrumental behavior through their effect on the two central motivational states. To validate this theory, a study must classically condition a response to a specific stimulus, establish an operant or instrumental behavior, then evaluate how the conditioned stimulus affects the operant or instrumental activity. Figure 7-14 presents a diagram of the behavioral predictions of the Rescorla-Solomon theory. The figure indicates the predicated direction of behavioral change produced by each type of conditioned stimulus. For example, hope and relief should increase appetitive behavior (cells 1 and 3) and decrease aversive behavior (cells 2 and 8). Trapold and Winokur's (1967) study shows the influence of a conditioned stimulus paired with food on an operant appetitive bar-pressing behavior. The authors found, as predicted in cell 1, that the CS previously paired with food increased bar-pressing behavior. In contrast, Trapold and Winokur observed that another stimulus paired with the absence of food decreased the operant appetitive bar-press response. These results agree with the cell 3 prediction. Bolles and colleagues (1970) made a similar observation: Hope increased rats' appetitive instrumental alley running, whereas disappointment decreased it.

A study by Grossen, Kostensek, and Bolles (1969) illustrates how hope (cell 2) and disappointment (cell 4) influence aversive behavior. In the first phase of the study, rats were trained to postpone shock by running from one compartment of a shuttle box to a second chamber and then back to the original compartment. Following the establishment of the avoidance response, one group of rats was exposed to tone-food pairings and another group to tones with no food. Results indicated that the tone suppressed avoidance behavior for the rats that received tone-food pairings but increased response for the rats given tones with no food. Apparently, the emotional response of hope inhibits an aversive instrumental behavior; disappointment, in comparison, increases avoidance behavior.

The emotional responses (fear and relief) acquired in adversive situations also influence operant or instrumental behavior. A study by Annau and Kamin (1961) demonstrated how fear affects an appetitive bar-press response. The authors observed that a stimulus previously paired with shock suppressed rats' bar-press behavior for food. These results support the prediction of cell 5: The adversive state, when activated by a feared stimulus, suppresses operant appetitive behavior. In addition to suppressing appetitive behavior, fear enhances avoidance behavior (cell 6). The influence of fear on avoidance behavior is exemplified in a study by Martin and Riess (1969). Following the pairing of a light with shock, the conditioned fear stimulus increased the level of a previously learned operant bar-press avoidance response. Rescorla and LoLordo (1965) demonstrated that a stimulus associated with the absence of shock suppressed an avoidance response. These results support the prediction of cell 8: Stimuli associated with relief suppress avoidance behavior by activating the central appetitive state. Finally, Hammond (1966) showed that a stimulus paired with the absence of shock enhanced appetitive responding for food (see cell 7).

Our discussion indicates that emotional responses acquired through classical conditioning influence operant or instrumental behavior. It should not be surprising that an appetitive emotional response (hope or disappointment) affects appetitive behavior or that an adversive emotional response (fear or relief) influences aversive behavior. What is surprising is the influence of appetitive conditioned responses on aversive behavior and aversive conditioned responses on appetitive behavior. Why should your relief, which occurred when the fire alarm terminated, stimulate your return to the theater and the movie? Or why should your anticipation of a pleasant television show reduce your aversive studying behavior? In asserting the existence of two central motivational states, Rescorla and Solomon's theory provides an answer to these questions. The aversive state is activated by stimuli associated with pain and frustration; the appetitive state stimulated by cues associated with reward and relief. An aversive conditioned response motivates avoidance behavior and suppresses approach behavior. However, an appetitive conditioned response initiates approach behavior and inhibits avoidance behavior. Considerable evidence indicates that there are two neural systems involved in the functions of the two central motivational states; that is, one system motivates us to approach reward, and the other system motivates us to avoid adversity. Furthermore, the appetitive system is activated by reward or stimuli associated with reward; the aversive system is aroused by adversity or stimuli associated with adversity. Chapter 13 offers a description of where these two motivational states are located in the central nervous system, as well as evidence that these two particular neural systems represent the two central motivational states in Rescorla and Solomon's theory.

SUMMARY

1 Generalization is a process in which animals or people respond in the same way to similar stimuli; discrimination is a process in which animals or people learn to respond in different ways to different stimuli. Generalization enables us to respond to unfamiliar stimuli without having to discover directly their significance, and discrimination allows us to know when to respond and when not to respond. However, generalization or discrimination at inappropriate times leads to failure to obtain reinforcement, or the experience of adversity.

2 There are two major types of generalization: excitatory and inhibitory. In excitatory generalization, a cue is associated with reward or punishment, and stimuli similar to the S + will elicit the response. In contrast, in inhibitory generalization, a cue is associated with reward or punishment and stimuli similar to the S − will inhibit responding. The level of generalization can differ. A steep generalization gradient is obtained when an animal or a person responds only to stimuli very similar to the S + or the S −. A flat generalization gradient occurs when the animal or person exhibits the same amount of excitation or inhibition to any stimuli resembling S + or S −.

3 The Lashley-Wade view assumes that animals and people generalize to stimuli quite dissimilar to the conditioning stimulus when they fail to distinguish between the S + and other stimuli. In their view, learning to differentiate between the S + and other stimuli results in little or no generalization.

4 Reinforcement is available in some circumstances and unavailable in others. In discrimination learning, an animal or a person discovers the stimuli (S^D) signaling that reinforcement is available and the events (S^Δ) indicating that reinforcement is unavailable. Learning the discrimination results in responding when the S^D, but not the S^Δ, is present. Animals and people must also learn to discriminate between when punishment will occur and when it will not.

5 Animals and people have an inherent need to know when reinforcement or punishment is available. Experimental neurosis occurs when animals are exposed to insoluble discrimination problems; these insoluble problems involve either changing the S^D and the S^Δ so that they are no longer discriminable or presenting reinforcement or punishment inconsistently so that they are not controllable. The behavioral disturbances produced by insoluble discrimination tasks were extreme agitation or unresponsiveness.

6 Discrimination learning occurs in three stages. In the first stage, animals or people must be able to differentiate between the S^D and the S^Δ. In the second phase, they must attend to the relevant dimension. In the last phase, the discriminative stimuli must gain control over responding. The discrimination is not learned (1) if an animal or person cannot differentiate between he discriminative stimuli, (2) if the animal or

person is not attending to the relevant dimension, or (3) if the discriminative stimulus does not gain control over responding.

7 Several processes contribute to learning to discriminate. According to the Hull-Spence view, conditioned excitation develops to the S^D as the result of reward; this conditioned excitation allows the S^D to produce the instrumental response. After conditioned excitation is established, nonreward in the presence of the S^Δ results in the development of conditioned inhibition to the S^Δ; this decreases responding to the S^Δ. Terrace suggested that the association of the S^Δ with nonreinforcement results not only in the development of conditioned inhibition but also in the establishment of aversive properties to the S^Δ.

8 Kohler's relational or transposition view assumes that animals or people learn the relative relationship between the S^D and the S^Δ. Rather than just responding to a particular stimulus, they learn, for example, to choose the larger or smaller stimulus, or the louder or softer stimulus.

9 Attentional processes also play an important role in discrimination learning. Sutherland and Mackintosh suggest that during discrimination learning, an animal's or a person's attention to relevant dimensions is strengthened. The ability of a stimulus analyzer to attract attention enables the animal or person to respond appropriately to the discriminative stimuli. After an animal or a person is attending to the relevant dimension, the association between the instrumental response and the relevant stimulus is strengthened.

10 The continuity view of discrimination learning assumes that excitation and inhibition gradually increase during the acquisition of a discrimination; this approach appears to describe the development of the emotional components of discrimination learning. In contrast, the noncontinuity approach asserts that there is an abrupt recognition of the salient features of a discrimination; this approach seems to describe the attentional aspects of discrimination learning.

11 Conditioned stimuli not only elicit conditioned responses but also can influence responding to other conditioned stimuli. When a conditioned stimulus signals the occurrence of another conditioned stimulus and the unconditioned stimuli, the presence of the first conditioned stimulus enhances responding to the second conditioned stimulus. A stimulus develops occasion-setting properties when the second stimulus (CS) and the UCS follows the occasion-setting stimulus and the second stimulus (CS) occurs when both the UCS and the occasion-setting stimulus are not present. Rescorla suggests that a stimulus facilitates, or "sets the occasion" for, responding to another stimulus by lowering the threshold of elicitation of the conditioned response to the other stimulus. Further, Rescorla's work points to separate excitatory and facilitating functions of a conditioned stimulus.

12 The level of instrumental or operant activity can be enhanced or reduced by conditioned stimuli. The stimuli paired with reward or with the absence of adversity motivate appetitive behavior and suppress avoidance responding. These stimuli influence behavior due to their activation of a central appetitive motivational state or inhibition of a central adverse motivational state as a conditioned response. Other stimuli that are present with adversity or with the absence of reward motivate avoidance behavior and suppress appetitive behavior. These stimuli's ability to affect behavior is caused by their arousal of the central adverse motivational state and their inhibition of the central appetitive motivational state.

8

COGNITIVE CONTROL
OF BEHAVIOR

THE INSURMOUNTABLE BARRIER

Math has always been an obstacle for Martha. Her distaste for arithmetic was
evident even in elementary school. She dreaded working with numbers, and her
lowest grade was always in math. Martha's high marks in her other classes
came without much effort, but she always had to struggle to earn an acceptable
grade in her math courses. In college, she avoided the high-level math courses
and chose only the ones that other students had said were easy. She did well in
these courses because they resembled her high school math classes.

During her junior year in college, Martha decided to major in political
science. Two Bs in college math were the only marks to mar her superior grade
record. To earn her political science degree, Martha should have completed a
statistics course during her junior year, but she did not. The hour was not right
that fall semester, and she did not like the professor who taught during the
spring. Determined, Martha enrolled in the statistics course this past fall—only
to drop out three weeks later. She could not comprehend the material and
had failed the first exam.

Martha knows that she cannot finish in political science without the statistics
class, and only one semester remains until she is scheduled to graduate.
However, she does not believe that she can pass the course. She had discussed
her problem with her parents and friends, and they, in turn, regularly offered
encouragement. Unfortunately, their good wishes could not make her problem
go away.

Yesterday, Martha learned from a friend that he had a similar problem with
chemistry and that a psychologist at the University Counseling Center helped
him overcome his "chemistry phobia." This friend suggested to Martha that the
center might help her, too. Martha had never considered her math aversion a

psychological problem and was reluctant to accept any need for clinical treatment. She knew that she must decide before next week's registration whether to seek help at the center.

If Martha does go for help, she may learn several things: Her fear of the course was caused by her belief that past failures were due to a lack of ability in math. On the basis of this belief, Martha expects to fail in the future. Also, Martha believes that she cannot even attend the class regularly; this belief developed because of her recent inability to remain in the course. Later in the chapter we suggest a cognitive explanation of Martha's math phobia, as well as a treatment which has successfully modified the expectations that maintain the phobic behavior of people like Martha.

The term *cognition* refers to an animal's or a person's knowledge of the environment. Psychologists investigating cognitive processes have focused on two distinctively different areas of inquiry. Many psychologists have evaluated an animal's or a person's understanding of the structure of the psychological environment (that is, when events occur and what has to be done to obtain reward or avoid punishment) and how this understanding, which is referred to as an *expectancy,* acts to control responding. The role of cognitions in governing behavior will be discussed in this chapter. Other psychologists have evaluated the processes that enable an animal or a person to have knowledge of the environment. This research has investigated learning processes such as concept formation, problem solving, decision making, language acquisition, and memory. These processes provide the mental structure for thinking and will be discussed in later chapters.

TOLMAN'S PURPOSIVE BEHAVIORISM

Recall the discussion of cognitive approaches to learning, which were described in Chapter 2. Although Edward Tolman proposed a cognitive view of learning during the 1930s and 1940s, this approach was unacceptable to most psychologists. Hull's mechanistic approach was the accepted view of learning during that period. The cognitive view gained some acceptance during the 1950s as other psychologists expanded Tolman's original cognitive approach, but only in the past decade have psychologists recognized the important contribution of cognitions in the learning process. Our discussion begins with Tolman's work. Later in the chapter, we look at the ideas and research of these contemporary cognitive psychologists.

Learning Principles

Edward Tolman's (1932, 1959) view of learning contrasts with the mechanistic view described in Chapter 2. Tolman did not envision that behavior reflects an automatic response to an environmental event; rather, he thought that our behavior has both direction and purpose. According to Tolman, our behavior is goal-oriented because we are motivated either to approach a particular reward or to avoid a specific adverse event. In addition, we are capable of understanding the structure of our environment. There are (1) paths leading to our goals and (2) tools that we can employ to obtain these goals. Through experience, we gain an expectation of how to use these paths and tools to reach goals. Although Tolman used the terms *purpose* and *expectation* to describe the process that motivates our behavior, he did not mean that we are aware of either the purpose or the direction of our behavior. He theorized that we act *as if* we expect a particular action to lead to a specific goal.

According to Tolman, not only is our behavior goal-oriented, but also we expect specific outcomes to follow specific behaviors. For example, we expect that going to a favorite restaurant will result in a great meal. If we do not obtain our goal, we will continue to search for the reward and will not be satisfied with a less-valued goal object. If our favorite restaurant is closed, we will not accept any restaurant and instead choose only a suitable alternative. Also, certain events in the environment convey information about where our goals are located. According to Tolman, we are able to reach our goals only after we have learned the signs leading to reward or punishment in our environment. Thus, we know where our favorite restaurant is located and use this information to guide us to that restaurant.

Tolman suggests that we do not have to be reinforced to learn. However, our expectations will not be translated into behavior unless we are motivated. Tolman proposed that motivation has two functions: (1) It produces a state of internal tension that creates a demand for the goal object, and (2) it determines the environmental features to which we will attend. For example, if we are not hungry, we are less likely to learn where food is located than if we are starving. However, tension does not possess the mechanistic quality that it did in Hull's theory. According to Tolman, our expectations control the direction of our drives. Therefore, when we are motivated, we do not respond in a fixed, automatic, or stereotyped way to reduce our drive; rather, our behavior will remain flexible enough to enable us to reach our goal.

Much research has been conducted to evaluate the validity of Hull's mechanistic approach. In comparison, the research effort to validate Tolman's cognitive view has been meager, although Tolman and his students conducted several key studies providing support for his approach. The next sections examine these studies and describe what they tell us about learning.

Place-Learning Studies

Tolman asserted that people expect reward in a certain place and that they follow the paths leading to that place. In contrast, Hull proposed that environmental cues elicit specific motor responses that have led to reward in the past. How do we know which view is valid? Under normal conditions, we cannot determine whether our expectations or habits will lead us to reward. Tolman designed his place-learning studies to provide us with an answer.

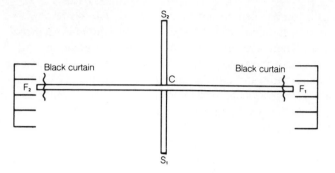

FIGURE 8-1 Schematic diagram of typical apparatus for a place-learning study. Rats can start at either S_1 or S_2 and receive reward in either F_1 or F_2. From Tolman, E. C., Ritchie, B. F., & Kalish, D. (1946). Studies of spatial learning: II. Place learning versus response learning. *Journal of Experimental Psychology, 36,* 221–229. Copyright 1946 by the American Psychological Association. Reprinted by permission.

T-Maze Experiments Tolman, Ritchie, and Kalish (1946) designed a study to distinguish behavior based on movement habits from behavior based on spatial expectations. Figure 8-1 depicts the apparatus in which they placed the rats for half of the trials in place S_1; on the other trials, the rats began in place S_2. For the place-learning condition, reward was always in the same location (for example, F_1), but the turning response necessary to produce reward differed for each trial, depending on whether the rat started at S_1 or S_2. In contrast, although the response-learning-condition rats received reward in both places, only one response—either right or left— produced reward. Tolman and colleagues found that all the place-condition animals learned within 8 trials and continued to behave without errors for the next 10 trials. None of the rats in the response condition learned this rapidly; even after responding correctly, they continued to make errors. Tolman et al.'s results illustrate that superior learning occurs when we can obtain reward in a certain place rather than by using a specific habit.

A second study by Tolman et al. (1946) demonstrates that a rat will go to a place associated with reward even though an entirely new motor response is required to reach the place containing the reward. During the first phase of the study, the researchers always put their rats in location S_1 and placed reward in F_1. For these rats, both a habit (right turn) and an expectation of where food is located (F_1) produce reward. During the second phase of the study, the researchers placed the rats at location S_2. In this stage, the rats reached the goal only by turning left toward F_1; the habitual right response led to an empty goal box. Tolman et al. reported that the subjects turned left and went to F_1, the place associated with reward. These results suggest that expectancies, not habits, controlled behavior in this study.

Numerous studies have compared place versus response learning. However, the results of some of the studies indicate that response learning is superior to place learning. Fortunately, there are several likely explanations for these different results. One cause of the conflicting results is the presence of cues to guide behavior (Blodgett & McCutchan, 1947, 1948). For example, place learning is superior to response learning when extra maze cues are present to allow spatial orientation to guide the rats to the correct location. Without extra maze cues, the animals are forced to rely on motor responses to produce reward.

The degree of experience with the task is another reason for the different results. I have sometimes experienced the following situation while driving home. Instead of turning from my typical path to run a planned errand, I continue past the turn and arrive home. Why did I drive my usual route home rather than turn off on the route necessary to do my errand? One likely answer is that I have driven home so often that the response has become the habitual route home. Kendler and Gasser's (1948) study indicates that well-learned behavior is typically governed by mechanistic processes rather than by cognitive ones. They found that with fewer than 20 trials, animals responded to place cues, whereas with greater training, the rats exhibited the appropriate motor response.

Alternate-Path Studies   Examine the map in Figure 8-2. Pretend that these paths represents routes to school. Which path would you choose? In all likelihood, you would use path A, the shortest path. However, what would you do if path A were blocked at point Y? If you were behaving according to your spatial knowledge, you would choose path C. Even though path C is longer than B, your

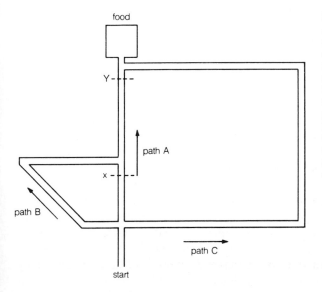

food

Y –

path A

x –

path B

path C

start

FIGURE 8-2
Apparatus used in Tolman and Honzik's alternate-path experiment. Obstacle Y blocks not only the shortest path A but also the middle-length path B. With paths A and B blocked, the only available route to the goal is the longest route, path C. From Tolman, E. C., & Honzik, C. H. (1930). "Insight" in rats. *University of California Publications in Psychology, 4,* 215–232.

cognitive map would produce the expectation that B also is blocked and thus would motivate the choice of C. In contrast, a drive interpretation predicts that you would choose B since it represents the second dominant habit. Path C is your choice if you behave like the rats did in Tolman and Honzik's (1930a, 1930b) study. In the study, animals were familiar with the maze but usually chose path A to reach the goal. However, most rats chose path C when path A was blocked at point Y. These results point out that knowledge of our environment, rather than "blind habit," often influences our behavior.

Other psychologists attempted to replicate the results of Tolman and Honzik's study (see Caldwell & Jones, 1954). However, animals in these studies have not always chosen path C. For example, Keller and Hull (1936) discovered that changing the width of the alleys caused the rats to respond according to habit and choose the blocked path. Unfortunately, there has been no definitive evaluation of why the blocked path is sometimes chosen. We can conclude from our prior discussion that the salience of cues leading to the goal and the degree of experience with the paths probably determine the processes controlling behavior. Thus, if we attend to paths leading to reward and the paths have not been employed frequently, our expectations rather than habits will determine our action.

Is Reward Necessary for Learning?

Recall our discussion of the law of effect in Chapter 2. According to Thorndike, S-R associations are established when the response leads to a satisfying state of affairs. Hull (1943) expanded Thorndike's early view and asserted that habit strength increases when a particular response decreases the drive state. Tolman (1932) thought that reward is not necessary for learning to occur and that the simultaneous experiencing of two events is sufficient. Chapter 2 discussed the development of the incentive motivation process initially detailed by Hull in 1952 and then later described by Spence in 1956. The research of Tolman and his students strongly influenced the nature of the incentive motivation concept.

Latent-Learning Studies Tolman felt that knowledge of the spatial characteristics of a specific environment can be acquired merely by exploring the environment. Reward is not necessary for the development of a cognitive map; reward influences behavior only when we must use that information to obtain reward. Tolman distinguished between learning and performance by asserting that reward motivates behavior but does not affect learning.

Tolman and Honzik's (1930a) classic study directly assessed the importance of reward on learning and performance. Tolman and Honzik assigned their subjects to one of three conditions: (1) Hungry rats in the R group always received reward (food) in the goal box of a 22-unit maze, (2) rats in the NR group were hungry but never received reward in the goal box, and (3) hungry rats in the NR-R group were not given reward on the first 10 days of conditioning; they received reward for the last 10 days. Tolman and Honzik found that rats that received reward on each trial (R group) showed a steady decrease in the number

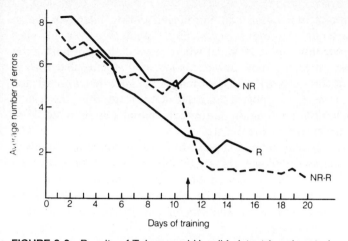

Days of training

FIGURE 8-3 Results of Tolman and Honzik's latent-learning study. Animals in the NR group received no reward during the experiment; those in the R group received reward throughout the study; those in the NR-R group received reward from day 11 to day 20. The results of this study showed that shifting reward on day 11 led to a rapid decline in the number of errors made by subjects in group NR-R to the level seen in animals receiving reward from the first trial (group R). From Tolman, E. C., & Honzik, C. H. (1930). Degrees of hunger; reward and nonreward; and maze learning in rats. *University of California Publications in Psychology, 4,* 241–256.

of errors during training, whereas those not given reward (NR group) showed little improvement in their performance (see Figure 8-3). Does this failure of the unrewarded rats to perform indicate a failure to learn? Or have the nonrewarded rats developed a spatial or *cognitive map* which they are not motivated to use? The behavior of those rats that did not receive reward until the 11th trial answers this question. Because the development of a habit was envisioned by Hull (1943) as a slow process, rats in the NR-R group should have shown a slow decline in errors when reward began. However, if learning has already occurred by the 11th trial but all that these rats needed was to be motivated, they should have performed well on the 12th trial. The results indicate that on day 12 and all subsequent days, animals in the R group (which were always rewarded) performed no differently than did those in the NR-R group (which were only rewarded beginning on trial 11). Apparently, NR-R subjects were learning during the initial trials even though they did not receive any reward.

While Tolman and Honzik's results suggest that learning can occur without reward, not all studies have found latent learning. MacCorquodale and Meehl (1954) reported that 30 of 48 studies were able to replicate the latent-learning effect. Although latent learning appears to be a real phenomenon, under some conditions it is likely and in other circumstances it is not. MacCorquodale and Meehl observed that in studies where reward was present for nondeprived animals during the initial trials and motivation was introduced during later experience with the same reward, latent learning was typically found. However, in other studies, latent learning was not typically found where rewards present during the initial trials were irrelevant to the motivation existing at that time and reward only became relevant during later trials. These results suggest that a motivated animal will ignore the presence of a potent but irrelevant reward; thus, the results agree with Tolman's belief that motivation narrows an animal's attention to those cues which are salient to its motivational state.

Johnson's (1952) study provides direct support for this interpretation. Johnson varied the level of deprivation during initial exploration in a T-maze and found that as deprivation increased, the likelihood of observing latent learning decreased. Apparently, we learn about the general aspects of our environment unless our motivation restricts our attention to some specific part of the environment.

The Drive Response The most consistent observation of latent learning occurs in animals not deprived when initially exposed to reward. The r_G-s_G mechanism described in Chapter 2 was developed to explain the results of these latent-learning studies. The anticipatory goal response (r_G-s_G) is established during initial exposure with reward but is not apparent until the motivating influence of deprivation is added. However, some latent-learning studies—the original Tolman and Honzik study is one example—employ no obvious reward. Yet, the nonrewarded animals in those studies, such as Tolman and Honzik's, do show a slight improvement in their performance; according to drive-view advocates (see Kimble, 1961), this result indicated that reward was present in these animals. These advocates suggested that handling or removing the animals from the strange maze to the familiar home cage represented sufficient reward to sometimes establish the r_G-s_G during initial nonreward. Although the strength of the r_G-s_G was not intense enough to motivate behavior, additional arousal produced by the introduction of reward resulted in rapid improvement in performance.

Section Review

Cognitive psychology began in the 1930s and 1940s with Edward Tolman's ideas. Although Tolman's cognitive approach did not receive much initial acceptance, his views represent the foundation for current cognitive theories. Tolman proposed that our behavior is goal-oriented; we are motivated to reach specific goals and continue to search until we obtain them. Rather than representing behavior as an inflexible habit, Tolman assumed that our behavior remains flexible enough to allow us to reach our goals. Our expectations determine the specific behavior we use to obtain reward or avoid punishment. According to Tolman, we expect that behaving in a particular fashion will enable us to obtain reward or avoid adversity. In addition to understanding the means needed to reach goals, Tolman felt that environmental events guide us to our goals. Tolman theorized that although we may know both how to obtain our goals and where these goals are located, we will not behave unless we are motivated.

Tolman's research changed the drive theory. For instance, the anticipatory goal mechanism developed in response to Tolman's incentive motivation and latent-learning studies. However, the drive-dominated psychology of the 1950s and 1960s all but forgot his cognitive approach. In contrast, the importance of Tolman's view is quite evident in the thinking of current psychologists studying the influence of cognition on learning.

THE CONCEPT OF AN EXPECTANCY

A Mental Representation of Events

What is an *expectancy?* Several psychologists have suggested that an expectancy is a mental representation of event contingencies (see Dickinson, 1989; Hulse, Fowler, & Honig, 1978; Roitblat, Bever, & Terrace, 1984). According to this view, an internal or mental representation of an experience is established when an animal or a person experiences an event. This representation contains information about the relations among previously experienced events and about relations between behavior and the consequences of this behavior.

Types of Mental Representations

Anthony Dickinson (1989) suggested that there are two main classes of declarative knowledge or factual information contained in an expectancy. First, contiguity between two events establishes an expectancy that contains an associative-link representation of two events. The establishment of an *associative-link expectancy* allows one event to excite or inhibit the representation of the other event. For example, suppose that a person experiences a great steak in a particular restaurant. In Dickinson's view, the person's expectancy would contain knowledge of the restaurant and the steak. Seeing the restaurant would cause the person to expect a great steak. According to Dickinson, associative-link representations mediate the impact of Pavlovian conditioning experiences. An excitatory-link representation of the CS and the UCS allows the CS to activate the representation of the UCS and thereby elicit the conditioned response. In terms of our example, seeing the restaurant would excite the representation of the great steak and thereby elicit hunger. In contrast, inhibitory-link representations allow a conditioned stimulus to inhibit a conditioned response.

The second type of declarative knowledge contained in an expectancy involves an understanding of the consequences of a specific action. This knowledge is represented in propositional form as a belief that action A causes reinforcer B. For example, the person in the above example would undoubtedly learn to go back to the restaurant serving the great steak. According to Dickinson's view, this individual's expectancy would contain the knowledge that going to that restaurant yields a great steak. Dickinson suggests that the representation of behavior and outcomes controls operant activity. The intent of an animal's behavior is to obtain desired reinforcement, and activation of the relevant *behavior-belief representation* enables an animal to obtain reinforcement.

In Dickinson's view, the existence of two classes of mental representations explains some important differences between Pavlovian and operant conditioning. As we discovered in Chapter 4, Pavlovian conditioning involves the acquisition of CS-UCS associations and the substitution of the CR for the UCR. Dickinson suggests that CS-UCS associative-link expectancies operate mechanistically; this mechanistic expectancy process causes the CS to involuntarily elicit the CR. In contrast, operant or instrumental conditioning involves the acquisition of behavior-outcome beliefs. According to Dickinson, intentionality is a property of belief expectancies. Operant or instrumental behavior is emitted based on inferences about the consequences of specific actions.

Dickinson suggests that expectancies contain knowledge of environmental circumstance. How can the idea that expectancies contain representations of stimuli, actions, and reinforcers be validated? According to Dickinson, research must show that a representation of the training stimuli and reinforcer is stored during Pavlovian conditioning. Experimentation also must demonstrate that, during operant or instrumental conditioning, knowledge contained in the expectancy stands in declarative relation to the conditioning contingency; that is, the knowledge in the expectancy represents a belief about the impact of a behavior on the environment. Dickinson presents a number of studies supporting an expectancy view; we examine several of them next.

Pavlovian Conditioning Associative-Link Expectancies. Suppose that some thirsty rats were trained to bar press for a sodium solution and other thirsty rats were reinforced with a potassium solution. After this initial training, both groups of rats were sodium deprived as their operant response was extinguished. How would these two groups of rats act during extinction if the drive state was switched from water deprivation to sodium deprivation? Dickinson and Nicholas (1983) conducted such a study. They found that the rats initially reinforced for bar pressing with sodium showed a higher response rate during extinction than did animals initially reinforced with potassium. Dickinson and Nicholas also reported that there were no extinction differences between animals if the animals were extinguished either when satiated or thirsty (see Figure 8-4). These results show that rats reinforced with sodium responded at a higher level during extinction than did rats reinforced with potassium, but only when the motivational state was more relevant to sodium than potassium.

What process was responsible for the *irrelevant incentive effect,* or the higher rate of responding in thirsty animals reinforced during training with sodium rather than potassium during extinction in the sodium drive state? According to Dickinson, an excitatory-link association developed during training between the contextual cues and the irrelevant incentive (sodium or potassium). When the animals were later deprived of sodium, activation of this excitatory-link association led to a general enhancement of responding, but only when the expectancy contained knowledge that the incentive was relevant. In other words, arousing the associative-link expectancy in sodium-deprived animals increased responding for sodium because the incentive was relevant to the drive, whereas the responding

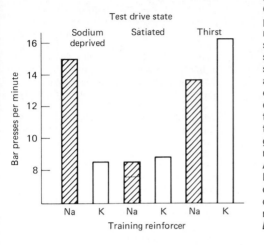

FIGURE 8-4
Graph illustrating the mean rate of bar pressing during extinction for animals reinforced for bar pressing with either sodium or potassium and tested while sodium deprived, water deprived, or saturated for water. The results show that animals receiving sodium during training exhibited a higher response rate when deprivation was shifted from water to sodium than did animals given potassium during training; this finding indicates that animals gain declarative knowledge of the specific reinforcer experienced during training. Adapted from Dickinson, A., & Nicholas, D. J. (1983). Irrelevant incentive learning during instrumental conditioning: The role of drive-reinforcer and response-reinforcer relationships. *Quarterly Journal of Experimental Psychology, 35B,* 249–263.

was low in the animals reinforced with potassium because their incentive experienced during training was irrelevant to the drive state experienced during extinction. Because both groups received equivalent training and the response rate during extinction under the thirst state (where the drive state was the same for both groups) also was equal for both groups, Dickinson concluded that declarative knowledge was gained about the incentive experienced during initial training. Further, knowledge of the incentive was contained in an excitatory-link association; activation of this excitatory-link association under relevant drive conditions enhanced responding.

Dickinson suggested the existence of two types of mental representations: an excitatory-link association and a behavior-reinforcer belief. Perhaps the greater responding by the sodium- rather than potassium-reinforced animals under sodium-deprivation conditions in the Dickinson and Nicholas study was due to a behavior-reinforcer belief rather than an excitatory-link association; that is, animals developed an expectancy that responding produced sodium or potassium rather than an association that sodium or potassium was experienced in a particular environment.

Dickinson and Dawson (1987) determined if the irrelevant incentive effect was due to the development of a Pavlovian excitatory-link association or an operant behavior-reinforcer belief. The irrelevant incentive effect caused the increased responding in animals reinforced with sodium during training when the deprivation state was shifted from thirst to sodium deprivation. In the Dickinson and Dawson study, all animals received four experiences during initial training in the hunger state. Two experiences involved Pavlovian conditioning: Cue A was paired with a sucrose solution and cue B was paired with food. These animals also were given two operant conditioning experiences: They were reinforced with sucrose with cue C present and were reinforced with food with cue D present.

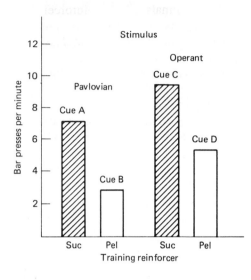

FIGURE 8-5
Graph illustrating the mean rate of bar pressing during extinction under water deprivation in the presence of a Pavlovian conditioned stimulus paired with sucrose solution or food pellets during training or in the presence of an operant discriminative stimulus signaling either sucrose or food availability during training. The results show that the level of responding during extinction under water deprivation was equal to both a Pavlovian conditioned stimulus associated with sucrose and a discriminative stimulus for sucrose availability; this finding indicates that Pavlovian conditioning involves the development of associative-link representations of stimulus and reinforcer. Adapted from Dickinson, A., & Dawson, G. R. (1987). Pavlovian processes in the motivation control of instrumental performance. *Quarterly Journal of Experimental Psychology, 39B,* 201–213.

The drive state was then switched from hunger to thirst during extinction and responding to all four stimuli determined. Dickinson and Dawson found that responding during extinction was greater to cues A and C than to cues B and D (see Figure 8-5). This result means that responding was higher to stimuli paired with sucrose than food. Since these animals were now thirsty, only an expectancy containing knowledge of sucrose would be relevant to the thirst state. The researchers also found equal responding to cues A and C. This finding indicates that responding was controlled by a Pavlovian excitatory-link representation, since cue A was paired with sucrose in a Pavlovian conditioning paradigm but was not associated with any operant contingency.

Operant Conditioning Behavior-Reinforcer Beliefs. According to Dickinson, animals also develop behavior-reinforcer beliefs; that is, an expectancy can contain declarative knowledge that emitting a specific behavior will result in the occurrence of a specific behavior. How can we validate the existence of a behavior-reinforcer belief? Dickinson uses the *reinforcer devaluation effect* to demonstrate such an expectancy.

Suppose animals are first trained to bar press for sucrose reinforcement, then the value of the sucrose reinforcer is devalued by pairing sucrose with illness. How would an animal respond following reinforcer devaluation? Adams and Dickinson (1981) investigated the effects of reinforcer devaluation. They presented sucrose and food to two groups of animals. One group received sucrose for bar pressing and was given food independently of responding; the other group had to bar press for food but received sucrose noncontingently. Adams and Dickinson observed that bar pressing during extinction was significantly lower for animals receiving behavior-contingent sucrose devaluation than behavior-noncontingent sucrose devaluation. In other words, the animals whose reinforcer (sucrose) was devalued responded much less during extinction than did animals whose reinforcer (food) was not devalued. This observation indicates that animals developed a belief that a specific behavior yields a specific reinforcer and this expectancy will control responding unless the reinforcer is no longer valued.

The Importance of Habits   Some learning theorists (Levis, 1976; Rescorla & Wagner, 1972) reject the idea that subjective representations of event contingencies are formed. Instead, they argue that stimulus-response associations rather than expectancies are formed as the result of experience and that concrete environmental events rather than subjective representations motivate behavior.

Dickinson (1989) does not reject the idea that habits exist; instead, he argues that habits as well as expectancies can control responding. In Dickinson's view, continued training leads habits rather expectancies to govern behavior. Two lines of evidence demonstrate that habits can control behavior. First, Adams (1982) trained two groups of rats to bar press for sucrose reinforcement on an FR 1 schedule. One group received 100 reinforcements (50/day); the other group was given 500 reinforcements (50/day). A third group of animals had to bar press 500 times to receive 100 reinforcements (FR 5 schedule; 50 reinforcements/day). After training, the sucrose was devalued for half of the animals in each group. Adams found that devaluation reduced responding in the groups receiving 100 reinforcements but had no effect on animals given 500 reinforcements. According to Dickinson, operant behavior initially is under the control of behavior-reinforcer beliefs. With more training, S-R habits develop and behavior can be controlled by habits rather than expectancies. The behavior of the animals receiving 500 reinforcements supports this view; that is, these animals continued to respond despite the fact that their actions produced a devalued reinforcer. Second, Colwill and Rescorla (1985) observed that reinforcer devaluation does not lead to a total absence of responding; that is, animals respond despite reinforcer devaluation. This observation further supports the suggestion that habits develop even when responding is being controlled by expectancies. When the influence of expectancies is eliminated by reinforcer devaluation, responding continues to some degree due to the control of S-R habits. We saw a similar dual learning when we discussed place learning earlier in the chapter. Dickinson refers to the control of responding by habit rather than by expectancy as *behavioral autonomy*.

Section Review

An expectancy is a mental representation of event contingencies. Dickinson suggested that mental representations or expectancies contain declarative knowledge gained through experience which guides an animal's behavior. According to Dickinson, there are two classes of declarative knowledge contained in expectancies. First, an expectancy contains associative-link representations of two events. This associative link allows one event to excite or inhibit the representation of the other event. In Dickinson's view, associative-link representations mediate the impact of Pavlovian conditioning experiences. An excitatory link between the CS and the UCS allows the CS to activate this UCS representation and thereby elicit the conditioned response. In contrast, inhibitory-link representations allow a conditioned stimulus to inhibit a conditioned response.

The second type of declarative knowledge contained in an expectancy involves an understanding of the consequences of a specific action. This knowledge is represented in propositional form as a belief that action A causes reinforcer B. According to Dickinson, the representation of behavior and outcomes controls operant activity. An animal develops a belief that a specific behavior produces a particular reinforcer. The intent of an animal's behavior is to obtain reinforcement, and the relevent mental representation enables an animal to obtain reinforcement.

According to Dickinson, operant behavior initially is under the control of behavior-reinforcer beliefs. With more training, S-R habits develop and behavior can be controlled by habits rather than by expectancies. Dickinson refers to the control of responding by habit rather than by expectancy as behavioral autonomy.

Our discussion suggests that animals develop expectancies during their exploration of the environment. Some expectancies involve stimuli and reinforcers; other expectancies involve behavior and reinforcers. We learned in Chapter 4 that a stimulus is not always predictive of reinforcement; that is, sometimes a CS occurs without a UCS and at other times, the UCS occurs without the CS. Similarly, a specific behavior may not always produce reinforcement.

What happens when an animal or a person discovers that events are unrelated? In Chapter 7, we learned that experimental neurosis occurs when animals or people experience unpredictable events. This neurosis is characterized by extreme agitation and apprehension. In the next section, we will discover that the acquisition of a belief that events are unrelated can lead to the behavior pathology of depression. We will discuss helplessness at length: It represents an area where an extensive amount of research has shown that cognitions developed through experience affect behavior.

A COGNITIVE VIEW OF DEPRESSION

Martin Seligman (1975) described depression as the "common cold of psychopathology." No one is immune to the sense of despair indicative of depression; each of us has become depressed following a disappointment or failure. For most, this unhappiness quickly wanes and normal activity resumes. For others, the feelings of sadness characteristic of depression last for a long time and impair the ability to interact effectively with the environment.

Why do people become depressed? According to Seligman, depression is learned and occurs when individuals assume that their failures are due to uncontrollable events and that they expect to continue to fail as long as these events are beyond their control: Depression develops because these persons believe that they are helpless to control their own destiny. Seligman's learned helplessness theory outlines the basis for his view of depression.

Learned Helplessness Theory

Imagine that none of the medical schools to which you applied admitted you. Because your dream since childhood has been to be a physician, you certainly would feel distressed for a while. If you are like most who are at first rejected, you might decide to enroll in some additional courses, study harder, and apply again. Or you could search for an alternative future occupation. However, these rejections might cause you to become severely depressed. According to Seligman, if this last alternative is your fate, you probably believe that you are very capable of succeeding in medical school but think that continued rejection is inevitable. You based your expectation of future rejection from medical school on your assumption that no matter how well you perform in school, you will be rejected. The belief that there is nothing you can do to be accepted leads you to become depressed. Depression, according to Seligman, is produced when individuals learn that events are independent of their behavior. Seligman labeled the expectation that events are uncontrollable *learned helplessness.*

Original Animal Research   Seligman developed his learned helplessness theory of depression from his animal studies (see Maier & Seligman, 1976, for a review of this literature). The original studies (Overmier & Seligman, 1967; Seligman & Maier, 1967) used dogs as subjects. Some of these dogs were strapped in hammocks and then exposed to a series of 64 intense inescapable shocks. Other dogs in a second group received a series of 64 escapable shocks; their shock terminated when they pressed a panel with their heads. The amount of shock received by dogs in both the inescapable and the escapable condition was equal: The shock ended for the dogs that received inescapable shock when the dogs in the escapable treatment successfully terminated their shock. A third group of dogs did not receive any shock during the initial stage of these studies. The experimenters placed each of the dogs in the three groups into a shuttle box 24 hours after the first stage. In the shuttle box, each dog received 10 trials of signaled escape-avoidance training (see Chapter 6). Once the CS was presented, each dog had 10 seconds to jump over the hurdle to avoid shock. At the end of the 10-second interval, the shock was presented and the dogs could terminate (escape) the shock by jumping the hurdle. The shock remained on for 50 seconds or until the dog escaped. The experimenters reported that two-thirds of the animals which 24 hours earlier had received inescapable shocks did not learn either to escape or to avoid the intense electrical shock in the shuttle box (refer to Figure 8-6). The dogs appeared helpless: They sat in the box and endured the intense shock for the entire 50-second interval. A few of the helpless dogs occasionally jumped the hurdle and either escaped or avoided shock. However, these dogs again acted helpless on the next trial; apparently, they did not benefit from

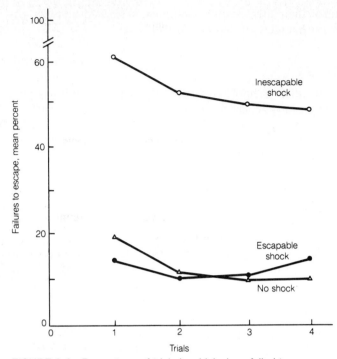

FIGURE 8-6   Percentage of trials in which dogs failed to escape shock in the shuttle box after receiving escapable shock, inescapable shock, or no shock in a harness. The mean percent failures to escape were significantly greater for animals exposed to inescapable shock than either escapable or no shock. From Seligman, M. E. P., & Maier, S. F. (1967). Failure to escape traumatic shock. *Journal of Experimental Psychology, 74,* 1–9. Copyright 1967 by the American Psychological Association. Reprinted by permission.

their successful experiences. In contrast, the dogs that had been given either escapable shock or no shock in the earlier phase quickly escaped shock during their initial trials in the shuttle box, and in their later trials they learned to respond to the signal and thereby avoid shock.

A wide range of animal species is susceptible to negative impact of uncontrollable experiences. Psychologists have observed the helplessness phenomenon in cats (Seward & Humphrey, 1967; Thomas & DeWald, 1977), fish (Frumkin & Brookshire, 1969; Padilla, 1973), rats (Jackson, Alexander, & Maier, 1980; Seligman, Rosellini, & Kozak, 1975), and humans (Fosco & Geer, 1971; Hiroto, 1974; Hiroto & Seligman, 1975; Klein & Seligman, 1976; Miller & Seligman, 1975; Roth & Kubal, 1975). Although the human studies have demonstrated an influence of uncontrollable experiences, the effects are small when compared to those found in lower animals. These results are not surprising; the aversive stimuli used are considerably less unpleasant in the human than in the nonhuman studies.

Exposing individuals to a treatment sufficiently intense to induce helplessness is unethical. Thus, human experiments in this area are primarily intended to demonstrate a similar directional influence of uncontrollable experiences in humans and lower animals.

Helplessness in Human Subjects   Hiroto's (1974) experiment with human subjects provides a good duplication of the original helplessness studies with dogs. Hiroto also employed the three-group design of the dog experiments. Let's briefly examine Hiroto's study to illustrate the influence of uncontrollable experiences on human subjects. College students who volunteered to participate were assigned to one of three treatment groups. Some could terminate an unpleasant noise by pushing a button four times. Although subjects in the uncontrollable group were told that their correct response would end the noise, there was actually no response with which they could terminate the noise. Parallel to the animal studies, the noise ended (uncontrollable-condition subjects) when a comparable (controllable-condition) subject in the escapable treatment successfully terminated the noise. A third group of subjects did not receive either of these noise treatments during the first stage of the study. Following the initial part of the study, Hiroto trained all subjects to avoid or escape noise in a finger shuttle box. The noise ended when subjects moved their finger from one side of the shuttle box to the other. Hiroto reported that subjects in the uncontrollable-noise condition failed to learn either to escape or to avoid the noise in the shuttle box and listened passively until the noise terminated at the end of a trial. In contrast, the group that received the controllable noise, as well as the group that was not given any initial trials, quickly learned to escape and then to avoid noise in the shuttle box. Apparently, uncontrollable experiences produce a similar negative effect on learning in both humans and lower animals.

Characteristics of Helplessness   Seligman (1975) proposed that exposure to uncontrollable events produces helplessness because of the development of an expectation that these events are independent of behavior. Once animals or humans acquire the belief that they cannot influence the occurrence of aversive events, helplessness ensues. Thus, the behavioral symptoms characteristic of helplessness are caused, according to Seligman, by the expectation of a lack of control. In Seligman's view, there are three major behavior components of helplessness: (1) *motivational deficits,* (2) *cognitive deficits,* and (3) *emotional disturbance.*

Motivational Impairments   After the establishment of helplessness, animals or humans are unable to initiate voluntary behavior. The passivity of dogs or humans following uncontrollable events is thought to reflect an inability to initiate instrumental behavior. Many different behaviors appear susceptible to the influence of uncontrollable events. For example, Braud, Wepman, and Russo (1969) observed that mice exposed to uncontrollable shock later were significantly slower to escape from a water maze than were mice receiving controllable shock. Rosellini and Seligman (1975) found that rats that had previously received inescapable shock did not escape from a frustrating experience; these rats sat passively in a situation formerly associated with reward. In contrast, rats that had received either escapable shock or no shock readily learned to escape from the frustrating situation.

Hiroto and Seligman's (1975) study readily exhibits the nonspecific character of helplessness. Human subjects received uncontrollable experiences in either a cognitive task (insoluble problems) or an instrumental task (inescapable noise). Hiroto and Seligman evaluated the effect of these uncontrollable events by using either a cognitive task (unscrambling anagrams) or an instrumental task (finger shuttle box). Results indicated that poorer performance followed uncontrollable rather than controllable events; this effect was found regardless of the nature of the uncontrollable events or the type of test situation. In addition, Hiroto and Seligman found that the uncontrollable experience and test situation did not need to be similar. For example, subjects who received uncontrollable experience in a cognitive task (insoluble problems) performed an instrumental task (anagram problems) more poorly than did subjects exposed to solvable problems.

Intellectual Impairments Cognitive deficits also characterize helplessness. The creation of the expectation that an animal has no control over environmental events renders this animal incapable of benefiting from future experiences. When animals or humans do not expect their lack of control to change, successful experiences fail to influence subsequent behavior. Overmier and Seligman (1967) and Seligman and Maier (1967) reported that their helpless dogs occasionally jumped over the hurdle and either escaped or avoided the electric shock. Despite this successful experience, these dogs did not change their behavior on subsequent trials; instead, they remained on the shock side of the shuttle box on the next trial. However, dogs in the escapable or no-shock condition learned from success: After a successful avoidance response, they were more likely to respond correctly on the next trial. In addition, normal dogs changed their ineffective behavior; helpless dogs continued not to respond even though they had received punishment on each trial.

The Miller and Seligman (1975) study shows (1) a similar failure to change behavior in human subjects who were previously exposed to uncontrollable events and (2) that the reason for this failure is that the individual expects future events to be uncontrollable. The first phase of this study exposed college students to a series of escapable, inescapable, or no-noise treatments. The experimenters then required all subjects to sort 15 cards into 10 categories within 15 seconds and told them that the rapidity of sorting depended on their skill. In reality, the experimenters controlled the subjects' success or failure on the sorting task; all subjects succeeded on 50 percent of the trials and failed on 50 percent of them. The experimenters determined success or failure by controlling the length of each trial so that the subjects experienced a predetermined sequence of successes and failures. They asked all subjects at the end of each trial to rate (on a scale of 0 to 10) their expectation of their success on the next trial. Miller and Seligman discovered that subjects who received the inescapable noise treatment showed little expectancy change after either success or failure; these subjects did not believe that their behavior influenced future events. In contrast, the subjects who were given either the escapable or no-noise treatments displayed large expectancy changes after each trial; a successful trial increased their expectation of future success and a failure on a trial decreased it. Apparently, our expectations of future events depend on our belief that we control present and past experiences. And it is the perceived ability to control events that is important, since none of Miller and Seligman's subjects in reality controlled the likelihood of success and failure.

Emotional Trauma   The expectation that events are uncontrollable, according to Seligman (1975), produces emotional disturbance. Animals exposed to uncontrollable events are obviously experiencing a traumatic emotional state. For example, the dogs in the original helplessness studies sat in a corner of the shuttle box and whined until the shock ended. Human helplessness studies show a similar emotional response. For example, Roth and Kubal (1975) administered questionnaires to their human subjects following uncontrollable experiences and reported increases in feelings of helplessness, incompetence, frustration, and depression. In addition, Gatchel and Proctor (1976) found that helplessness training lowered electrodermal activity; this lowered activity is thought to be correlated with lowered motivational level (Malmo, 1965) and occurs with clinical depression (McCarron, 1973).

Similarities of Helplessness and Depression   The importance of the learned helplessness phenomenon lies in its proposed relation to the clinical disorder of depression. Although a direct causal test cannot be ethically conducted, the correlational evidence supports Seligman's statement that the expectation of an inability to control events produces human depression. These comparisons show that depressed people display the cognitive characteristics of learned helplessness.

Animals and humans exposed to uncontrollable events exhibit motivational deficits. For example, college students who had previously received uncontrollable noise failed to learn to escape noise in the finger shuttle box (Hiroto, 1974). Klein and Seligman's (1976) depressed subjects similarly failed to escape noise in the shuttle box. Their studies contained four groups of subjects: One group was classified as depressed according to the Beck Depression Inventory, and the other three groups contained nondepressed subjects. Klein and Seligman exposed one group of nondepressed subjects to uncontrollable noise—a procedure that produces helplessness. The second nondepressed group received escapable noise; the third nondepressed group and the depressed group received no noise treatment. The study's results indicated that the nondepressed subjects who were exposed to inescapable noise (the helpless group) and the depressed subjects escaped more slowly than did nondepressed subjects who received either the escapable noise or no-noise treatment (see Figure 8-7). Evidently, these nondepressed individuals, as a result of uncontrollable laboratory experiences, behaved as did the clinically depressed persons. We should assume not that this treatment produced clinical depression but rather that both groups did not expect to be able to control laboratory noise. Depressives have a generalized expectation of no control; their failure to escape in the study merely reflects this generalized expectancy.

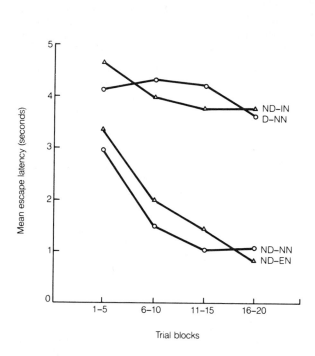

FIGURE 8-7
Escape latency to terminate noise for depressed subjects (on Beck Depression Inventory) who were not previously exposed to noise (group D-NN), for nondepressed subjects who were not previously exposed to noise (group ND-NN), for nondepressed subjects who were previously exposed to inescapable noise (group ND-IN), and for nondepressed subjects who were previously exposed to escapable noise (group ND-EN). The escape latency was greater for nondepressed subjects exposed to inescapable noise and depressed subjects not exposed to noise than for nondepressed subjects exposed to escapable noise or nondepressed subjects exposed to no noise. From Klein, D. C., & Seligman, M. E. P. (1976). Reversal of performance deficits and perceptual deficits in learned helplessness and depression. *Journal of Abnormal Psychology, 85,* 11–26. Copyright 1976 by the American Psychological Association. Reprinted by permission.

Our prior discussion indicates that subjects exposed to uncontrollable events do not benefit from their experiences: These subjects do not change their expectations of future success after experiencing either success or failure. Depressives show a similar failure to change their expectations after a successful experience (see Miller & Seligman, 1973). Miller and Seligman classified college students as either depressed or nondepressed and then exposed them to one of two tasks. The first task, involving a test of skill, required the subjects to move a platform upward in an appropriate manner to prevent a steel ball from falling. The second task, a game of chance, requested the subjects to guess which one of two slides would be presented on a given trial. Since the presentation of slides was random, success on this task was simply due to chance. All subjects estimated after each trial whether they expected to be successful on the next trial.

Miller and Seligman reported that success in the skill task increased nondepressed subjects' expectation of future success, but depressed individuals showed significantly less expectancy change after having performed a successful skill task (see Figure 8-8). Thus, the depressed subjects behaved as did individuals exposed to uncontrollable events: Neither changed their expectation of success very much

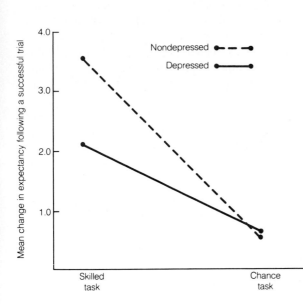

FIGURE 8-8
Average change in the expectation of future success in depressed and nondepressed subjects after success on either a skilled task or a chance task. The results showed that the change in the expectation of future success after success in a skilled task was much less for depressed than for nondepressed subjects. An equivalent expectation of future success following failure was found in depressed and nondepressed subjects. From Miller, W. R., & Seligman, M. E. P. (1973). Depression and the perception of reinforcement. *Journal of Abnormal Psychology, 82,* 62–73. Copyright 1973 by the American Psychological Association. Reprinted by permission.

after success. Why don't depressed and helpless subjects increase their expectation of success as much as nondepressed subjects do after a successful experience? The answer lies in the chance task behavior of both depressed and nondepressed subjects. After a successful trial on the chance task, neither depressed nor nondepressed subjects increased their expectation of future success. There was no reason to increase it, since all the subjects in this task knew that their success was due to chance and was therefore beyond their control. Depressed and helpless subjects, in Seligman's view, assumed that chance must be credited for any of their successful skill experiences, since they believed these events were uncontrollable.

Criticism of Learned Helplessness Approach   Seligman's original learned helplessness model generated interest in the role of cognitive processes involved in depression. However, his theory encountered difficulties; it was too simplistic and did not precisely reflect the process that produces depression. We next look at these problems with the original helplessness theory.

Recall from the prior description of Seligman's original theory that human subjects, following exposure to uncontrollable events, did not change their future expectations in a skill task even after having success on a previous task. These results suggest that the helpless subjects believed that their success was due to chance. During the experiment, helpless subjects behaved as if skill tasks were chance tasks; however, when questioned after the experiment, helplessness subjects described the situation as a skill test. The original helplessness model cannot explain why helpless subjects responded as if they had no control over events when they were aware that other people were able to control these same events.

A second problem with the original helplessness model is that some other studies have not observed performance deficits following uncontrollable experiences. In fact, several (Roth & Kubal, 1975; Tennen & Eller, 1977) have demonstrated improved subject performance after exposure to insoluble problems; their human subjects exposed to insoluble problems actually scored higher on subsequent tasks than did those who were exposed to solvable problems. This facilitation of subject performance after uncontrollable tasks is inconsistent with Seligman's original model of helplessness, which maintains that uncontrollable experiences should create expectations that impair—not improve—later behavior.

Rizley's study (1978) illustrates a final problem with Seligman's original helplessness theory. Rizley presented depressed and nondepressed subjects with a series of 50 numbers (either 0 to 1) and then instructed the subjects to guess the next number. Although there was no pattern to the numbers, Rizley told his subjects that there were number-order trends and tendencies and that their score would be above chance if they were aware of them. The subjects were told after the presentation of 50 numbers whether they succeeded (passed the test) by scoring 26 or more or had failed by scoring 25 or less. (Since there were only two choices, a score of 25 meant chance-level performance.) The subjects then indicated the reason for their score from a list of several possibilities—luck, task difficulty, effort, or ability. Rizley's results demonstrated that depressed people attributed their success to the external factors of luck and task ease and their failure to internal factors of lack of effort and ability. In contrast, nondepressed people thought that internal factors accounted for their success, and that external factors caused their failure. Thus, depressives attribute their failure to internal processes, but they also feel helpless because they can do nothing to prevent future failures. Seligman's learned helplessness theory could not explain Rizley's observations. Fortunately, Seligman's attributional model of helplessness provides an answer to the problems inherent in the original learned helplessness theory.

An Attributional Model

Seligman and his associates (Abramson, Garber, & Seligman, 1980; Abramson, Seligman, & Teasdale, 1978) proposed that the attributions that people make for their failures determine whether they become depressed. An attribution is a perceived cause of an event. Causal attributions of failure can be made on three dimensions: personal-universal (internal-external), global-specific, and stable-unstable. A personal attribution is the belief that internal characteristics caused the outcome; an external attribution represents the view that environmental forces determine success (reward) or failure (adversity). A stable attribution is the belief that the perceived cause of past success or failure will determine future outcomes; an unstable attribution represents the belief that new factors may determine success or failure in the future. A specific attribution reflects the view that the cause

TABLE 8-1
THE ATTRIBUTIONAL MODEL OF DEPRESSION: A WOMAN REJECTED

Dimension	Internal		External	
	Stable	Unstable	Stable	Unstable
Global	I'm unattractive to men.	My conversation sometimes bores men.	Men are overly competitive with intelligent women.	Men get into a rejecting mood.
Specific	I'm unattractive to him.	My conversation bores him.	He's overly competitive with women.	He was in a rejecting mood.

Note: The attribution of uncontrollability to internal causes produced personal helplessness, whereas an external causal attribution results in universal helplessness.
Source: Abramson, L. Y., Seligman, M. E. P., & Teasdale, J. D. (1978). Learned helplessness in humans: Critique and reformulation. *Journal of Abnormal Psychology, 87,* 49–74. Copyright 1978 by the American Psychological Association. Reprinted by permission.

of an outcome relates only to a specific task; a global attribution is the belief that the cause of the outcome in this task will determine outcomes in very diverse situations. The combination of these three dimensions produces eight possible attributional outcomes (see Table 8-1). The specific attribution will determine (1) if depression occurs, (2) if depression generalizes to other situations, and (3) if the depression is temporary or permanent. In the examples presented in Table 8-1, if the woman attributes her rejection to an internal, stable, global factor ("I'm unattractive to all men") she will become depressed. In contrast, the woman will not become depressed if she attributes rejection to an external, unstable, specific factor ("He was in a rejecting mood"). This attributional model, while certainly complex, provides us with an explanation for people's varied responses to uncontrollable experiences.

Personal versus Universal Helplessness　Consider the following examples: (1) The economy is depressed, and the automobile industry's failure to sell enough cars forces several plants to close. An automobile worker loses her job and becomes depressed. (2) A 16-year-old who wants to play for the high school basketball team has diligently practiced summer and fall; he was not selected for the team and became depressed. In both examples, depression occurred, according to Seligman, because of each individual's perceived inability to control future events: The automobile worker could not get a job and the student could not be on the team. However, the helplessness of the automobile worker and student is quite different.

The attributional model maintains two kinds of helplessness: personal and universal. The student's failure to be picked for the team is an example of *personal helplessness:* This student's inability caused failure, but other, more competent students were selected for the team. *Universal helplessness* occurs when the environment is structured so that no one can control future events: The automobile worker could not control the economy; therefore, the lack of control is attributed to external forces.

Abramson (1977) ascertained from her experiments that both personal and universal helplessness produced the cognitions (expectation of future inability to control events) and motivational deficits (lack of ability to initiate voluntary behavior) which are both characteristic of depression. In addition, Abramson and Sackeim (1977) examined the attributions of depressed people and found that those who were personally depressed made internal attributions for failure, whereas those who were universally depressed made external attributions.

The nature of the helplessness determines whether loss of esteem appears. People who attribute their failure to external forces—universal helplessness—experience no loss of self-esteem, since they do not consider themselves responsible for their failure. However, the attribution of failure to internal factors—personal helplessness—produces loss of self-esteem; the incompetency of these individuals causes their failure. In support of this view, Abramson (1977) found that lowered self-esteem occurs only with personal helplessness.

Global versus Specific Causal Attributions   People who are exposed to uncontrollable events may not become depressed; their failure could be attributed to a *specific* situation, and the helplessness would not occur in other circumstances. Or people could feel that their helplessness is *global,* will happen at other times, and become depressed. For instance, the automobile worker believes that a job does not exist in any other company and stops searching. In contrast, the student attributing the failure to make the team to the coach could change schools and try again next year. Thus, the attribution of lack of control to global rather than to specific factors will produce helplessness, which will generalize to new situations, but helplessness will be limited to a single situation if the attribution is specific.

Roth and Kubal's (1975) experiment supports the idea that global-specific attributions are important when determining whether people are helpless in new situations. First-year college students volunteered to participate in the Roth and Kubal study in two separate, very different experiments on the same day and in the same building. The first experiment was designed to fail all students. Subjects in one group (important condition) of this first experiment were told that the failed task was a "good predictor of college grades"; those in the other group (unimportant condition) were informed that they were participating in "an experiment in learning." Following the first experiment, all subjects proceeded to the second study. Because both groups experienced failure on the first experiment, the original helplessness model would predict that both groups would not perform well in the second study. However, the subjects who were told that the first experiment was a learning one did significantly better on the second experiment than did subjects who thought that the first experiment was a predictor of future success. According to the attributional model, the subjects in the important condition attributed their failure to a more global factor (absence of ability to succeed in college) than did subjects in the unimportant condition, who attributed their failure to a single task. As a result, the helplessness generalized to the new situation for subjects in the important condition but not for the subjects in the unimportant treatment condition.

Stable versus Unstable Causal Attributions   Seligman proposed that a person's attribution of helplessness to a stable or unstable factor also influences the effect of uncontrollable experience on behavior. Ability is considered a stable factor; effort, an unstable one. If someone attributes failure in an uncontrollable experience to lack of effort, the attribution will increase this person's subsequent effort. However, attribution of failure to the stable factor of lack of ability will lead to helplessness, since people can change their effort but not their ability. As an example of this approach, consider what would happen if the high school student, rather than having attributed failure to lack of control, felt that not enough effort was exerted. Under this condition, failure might increase rather than decrease behavior. Thus, the facilitation which follows uncontrollable experiences in some studies probably results from the subjects' belief that increased effort leads to success. However, continued failure will eventually cause an expectation of no control over failure. A test of this view is found in Roth and Kubal's (1975) study. Roth and Kubal gave their subjects one or two learned helplessness training tasks and found that those who had one task showed more motivation than control subjects but those who had two tasks exhibited helplessness.

The idea that stability or instability of the perceived cause influences helplessness also explains why depression is temporary under some situations and permanent under others. For example, with our automobile worker, the attribution to the external factor of the poor economy caused depression which will stay if the economy remains down. However, the depression will be temporary if the economy recovers (which is typical) and the worker gets a job. (If the economy improves but the worker fails to find employment, the worker may then attribute that failure to uncontrollable personal stable factors and continue to be depressed.)

Severity of Depression   Helplessness apparently can follow several different types of uncontrollable experiences. However, severe depression typically appears when individuals attribute their failure to internal, global, and stable factors (see Peterson & Seligman, 1984). Their depression is intense because they perceive themselves as incompetent (internal attribution) in many situations (global attribution), and they believe that their incompetence is unlikely to change (stable attribution). In support of this notion, Hammen and Krantz (1976) found that depressed women attributed interpersonal failure (for example, being alone on a Friday night) to internal, global, and stable factors. In contrast, nondepressed women blamed their failure on external, specific, and unstable factors. Other researchers (see Rizley, 1978; Robins, 1988; Sweeney, Anderson, & Bailey, 1986) observed a similar difference in causal attribution of failure between depressed and nondepressed people.

Depressives' Attributional Style   Seligman's attributional model assumes that attributional style or a tendency to perceive the same factors cause all events influences the likelihood that a person will become depressed. To validate the attributional model, differences in attributional style between depressed and nondepressed people must be shown to be present prior to the onset of depression. Recent evidence provides more direct support of the attributional model. Metalsky and associates (1982) found that knowledge of a person's attributional style enabled prediction of susceptibility to depression following failure. In their study the attributional style of college students was measured at the beginning of a semester. They discovered that those students who attributed past failures to internal, global, and stable factors were more likely to become depressed after earning a poor grade (in the student's view) on a midsemester exam than were students who had attributed their poor grade to external, specific, and unstable factors. Apparently, a person's attributional style influences the likelihood of becoming depressed when he or she fails.

The Importance of Optimism   Ellen Langer (1983) suggests that "perceived control is basic to human functioning." According to Langer, individuals strive to acquire feelings of competency and being able to master life's circumstances. Optimists feel that they are able to control external events; pessimists believe that they have no control. An optimistic view leads to greater successes than does a pessimistic view. For example, Seligman and Schulman (1986) reported that new insurance salespersons who were optimists sold more policies and were 50 percent less likely to quit within one year than salespersons who habitually explain failures as being uncontrollable ("I always fail" or "This is impossible"). Also, Maddux and Stanley (1986) observed that students who felt competent were less anxious and depressed and more academically successful than other students.

Albert Bandura (1986) proposes that a perceived self-efficacy or competency allows a person to persist despite failure. Our discussion suggests that feelings of competency enable people to cope better with life events. We will discover shortly that self-efficacy also positively influences a person's interaction with phobic objects.

Other Perspectives of Learned Helplessness

Although our discussion indicates that cognitions influence the development of depressive behavior, it is important to recognize that other factors are involved in depression. Several lines of research suggest that a few factors either alone or in combination can produce depression.

Disturbances in the functioning of the brain's amine chemical transmitter system (the catecholamines and indoleamines) are involved in depression. Numerous studies (see Depue & Evans, 1976) have shown that a deficiency in norepinephrine or dopamine correlates with depression, and an elevation of either reverses depression. Biochemical deficits can be caused by biological deficiencies or can be the result of experience. Jay Weiss and his associates (Weiss, Stone, & Harrell,

1970) have shown that exposing rats to uncontrollable events produced the biochemical and behavioral characteristics of depression.

However, the biochemical changes are transient; that is, they are found 24 hours but not 48 hours after exposure to uncontrollable events. These changes in biochemical state are related to the occurrence of helplessness: Weiss et al. observed helplessness 24 hours but not 48 hours after uncontrollable experiences. Furthermore, a number of studies (Sherman, Sacquitne, & Petty, 1982; Weiss, Glazer, & Pohorecky, 1976) reported that antidepressant drugs eliminated the learned helplessness effect in rats.

Although these results indicate that biochemical changes are related to depression, physiological recovery does not automatically mean that feelings of helplessness will decline. Helplessness may remain after an animal's or a person's physiological recovery. In support of this view, Overmier and Seligman (1967) found that dogs, after receiving two experiences with uncontrollable events, were helpless even a month after the second experience. In contrast, a single uncontrollable experience produced only a transient helplessness. We will look again at the biochemical basis of depression in Chapter 13.

Frustration also appears to be involved in producing depression. Amsel's (1972) behavioral persistence model suggests that nonreward initially elicits frustration, anxiety, and hostility. These behaviors act to impair goal-oriented behavior. Continued nonreward results in the conditioning of disruptive behavior; these behaviors persist with repeated nonreward and become an animal's or a person's repetitive response to frustrative nonreward.

Levis (1976) proposed that behavioral persistence is responsible for the development of learned helplessness. According to Levis, animals or people exposed to uncontrollable events experience a great deal of nonreward; this experience results in the development of persistent, disruptive, frustration-induced behaviors. When shifted to a controllable situation, the habitual disruptive activities prevent an animal or a person from experiencing reward; this in turn results in nonreward continuing to be experienced. This nonreward experience acts to increase the level of arousal, thereby increasing the level of conditioning of the persistent, frustration-induced, disruptive activities. These persistent disruptive behaviors produce behavioral deficits characteristic of learned helplessness. A number of studies have reported that animals exposed to uncontrollable events develop fixed or stereotyped response patterns. This observation has been found in both rats (MacKinnon, 1968; Maier et al., 1940; Rashotte & Amsel, 1968; Ross, 1964) and people (Deur & Parke, 1968; Linden, 1974; Vogel-Sprott & Thurstone, 1968).

A COGNITIVE VIEW OF PHOBIC BEHAVIOR

All of us have fears. In most cases, these fears are realistic and enable us to avoid adversity. For example, people are afraid to cross a street when cars are approaching; their fear motivates them to avoid walking in front of a car, thereby preventing them from being killed. However, some people's fears are unrealistic. These individuals have a *phobia,* a fear that was once appropriate (because an adversive event did occur) but is no longer realistic. This fear motivates avoidance behavior, which prevents learning that the phobia is unrealistic. In many situations, the original adversive event may not be readily apparent. An individual may have forgotten the unpleasant event, or the phobic response may have developed through high-order conditioning or vicarious conditioning. The phobic response also may result from stimulus generalization; for example, a child attacked by a peer generalizes this fear to all children. We next examine research indicating that cognitive processes affect the development of phobias.

A Phobic's Expectancies

Recall our description of Martha's math phobia from the chapter-opening vignette. In 1977, Albert Bandura presented a cognitive theory of phobic behavior according to which two classes of expectancies—outcome and efficacy—maintain Martha's phobia. Outcome expectancies reflect the perceived consequences of either a behavior or an event. Martha expects a statistics class to be very aversive—a *stimulus-outcome expectancy*—and she believes that she cannot pass the course—a *response-outcome expectancy*. Also, Martha knows that she can prevent the adversive experience by not enrolling in the statistics course; this response-outcome expectancy motivates her phobic behavior.

Martha's phobia presents her with a dilemma typical of phobic situations. Although her phobic behavior enables her to avoid the course, her phobic actions have definite negative consequences. She realizes that she must pass this course to graduate, but her phobic behavior prevents her from obtaining her desired goal. Thus, she continues to avoid the course even though she cannot graduate without it.

Bandura's theory suggests that a second type of expectancy is involved in motivating Martha's phobic behavior. According to Bandura's approach, Martha feels incapable of enduring the adversive experience. Bandura labeled this belief that one can or cannot execute a particular action an *efficacy expectancy*. In Bandura's view, Martha's lack of self-efficacy has caused her either to fail to register for the course or to withdraw from the courses shortly after it begins.

The Importance of Our Experiences

What factors account for Martha's outcome and efficacy expectations? Martha's outcome expectancy that she will fail the statistics course could have developed through direct personal experiences, through observations of the experiences of other people, or through information provided by others. Since Martha has not failed this course or any other course, her outcome expectancies cannot reflect any direct personal experience. Probably Martha has observed others whom she perceived as similar to herself fail. In addition, she probably has received information from other people that the course is difficult and therefore feels that she will fail it.

Bandura (1977) suggested that we use four types of information to establish an efficacy expectancy: (1) *Personal accomplishments indicate our degree of self-efficacy.* Successful experiences generally increase our mastery expectancy, and failure usually decreases our sense of self-efficacy. Bandura, Jeffrey, and Gajdos (1975) discovered that the influence of success or failure on efficacy expectancies depends on task difficulty, the amount of effort expended, and the pattern and rate of success. We are more apt to feel competent if we usually succeed at a difficult task that requires considerable effort than if we succeed without trying. (2) *Our sense of self-efficacy is developed by observing the successes or failures of other people whom we perceive as similar to ourselves.* Seeing others successfully cope with perceived adverse events enhances our belief that we also can be effective, and observing others fail decreases our belief that we can cope with adversity. Several factors determine the effectiveness of a vicarious modeling experience. The success of the other person's behavior, or the model's behavior, must be clear; we cannot develop a sense of self-efficacy if the outcome of this other person's behavior is ambiguous (Kazdin, 1974a). Also, we acquire a stronger mastery expectation when we see several people rather than a single person cope with an adversive situation (see Bandura & Menlove, 1968; Kazdin, 1974b). Finally, Meichenbaum (1972) discovered that we develop greater self-efficacy when we see other people initially struggle with adversity and become effective slowly rather than the first time we see them succeed. (3) *We can be persuaded that we are capable of coping or are unable to deal with adversity.* For example, Martha's family or her peers could attempt to convince her that she could pass the statistics course if she would try. To test the idea that verbal persuasion could alter expectancies, Lick and Bootzin (1975) suggested to their patients that they could successfully interact with a feared object. Unfortunately, they found little evidence of behavioral change with their use of verbal persuasion. Bandura (1977) proposed that the influence of verbal persuasion is short-lived unless personal experiences confirmed the altered expectancy change. (4) *Emotional arousal influences our sense of competence; we feel less able to cope with an aversive event when we are agitated or tense.* Although Bandura feels that emotional arousal plays a part in motivating phobic behavior, his view certainly differs from the drive approach outlined in Chapter 6. Bandura does not believe that fear directly causes avoidance behavior; instead, he suggests that fear and defensive action are correlated but do not reflect a causal relationship. We are more likely to display avoidance behavior when we are afraid—but only because fear makes us feel less effective. However, because emotional arousal is only one source of information used when developing a sense of self-efficacy, other information may enable us to feel competent even though we are afraid. Under these conditions, we will interact with feared objects while we are still afraid because we perceive ourselves able to cope with adversity. Our emotional arousal extinguishes after we have interacted with an aversive event.

Bandura and Adams's (1977) study demonstrates how efficacy expectations play a role in phobic behavior. Snake-phobic clients received the systematic desensitization therapy described in Chapter 4. Bandura and Adams discovered that

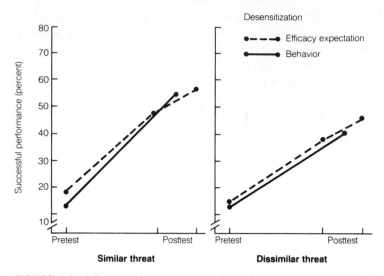

FIGURE 8-9 Influence of desensitization therapy on the subject's level of self-efficacy and ability to approach a snake. The success of therapy on the posttest was evaluated using both the same snake used in therapy ("similar threat") and a different snake ("dissimilar threat"). The results of this study showed that desensitization therapy increased a person's perceived self-efficacy and interaction with either the same or a different snake. From Bandura, A., & Adams, N. E. (1977) Analysis of self-efficacy theory of behavioral change. *Cognitive Therapy and Research, 1,* 287–310.

when patients no longer became emotionally disturbed by an imagined aversive scene, differences still existed in their ability to approach a snake. In contrast, the clients' self-efficacy expectation corresponded closely to their ability to interact with the snake: The greater the patients' perceived efficacy was, the more able they were to inhibit phobic behavior and approach the snake (refer to Figure 8-9). Thus, these clients believed that they could hold the snake, and this belief allowed them to overcome their phobia. This relation between self-efficacy and an absence of phobic behavior held true even after therapy when a new snake, different from the one used before the pretherapy and during desensitization training, was employed. These results demonstrate that if we believe ourselves competent, we will generalize our self-efficacy expectations to new situations.

Application: Modeling Treatments of Phobia

Our discussion points to the critical role of outcome and efficacy expectations in motivating phobic behavior. These expectations develop both through our experiences and through our observations of the experiences of other people. During the past 20 years, behavior therapists have employed models to interact with feared objects to treat phobic clients. The aim of this modeling treatment is to alter clients' phobic behavior by vicariously modifying their expectations.

Graduated Modeling   In graduated-modeling therapy, clients see the model move closer and closer until the feared object is encountered. A study by Bandura, Grusec, and Menlove (1967) shows the effectiveness of modeling in treating phobic behavior. These psychologists allowed children who feared dogs to watch a peer model interact with a dog. The children received eight 10-minute therapy sessions during a 3-day period. At first, the children saw the model pat the dog while it was in a pen. During later observations, the children watched the model walk the dog around the room. In the final sessions, the model climbed into the pen and played with the dog. Other children did not see the model but saw only the dog, which occupied the pen for the first therapy session and was leashed in the last sessions. Bandura and associates assessed the effectiveness of modeling by determining if the phobic children could approach and play with either the dog seen in therapy sessions or a new dog. The results indicated that modeling reduced the children's phobic behavior and increased their interaction with the dog seen in the study or a new dog.

According to Bandura's approach, the success of modeling therapy must be attributed to the vicarious modifications of a client's expectations. Support for this view is evident in a study by Bandura, Adams, and Beyer (1977). They exposed adult snake phobics to models interacting with a snake and assessed the influence of this modeling treatment on the subjects' approach response to the snake and their efficacy expectation, that is, their expectation of being able to interact fearlessly with the snake. Bandura and colleagues found that this modeling treatment's degree of success corresponded to the increase in the phobic's self-efficacy expectation; the more the model's action altered the client's efficacy expectation, the greater the client's approach to the snake. In other words, the individuals who felt most capable of handling the snake were the most likely to do so.

Participant Modeling   In 1969, Bandura and associates introduced a change in the modeling therapy that significantly enhanced its effectiveness. They suggested that the model (or therapist) encourage the patient to interact with the feared object. In participant modeling, the model slowly moves nearer and nearer to a phobic object. After each modeled behavior, the model (or therapist) asks the client to imitate that action. During the imitation, the model (or therapist) either stands close to or is in direct physical contact with the client. After the model (or therapist) has helped the client interact with the feared object, the treatment's success is evaluated by having the client encounter the feared object alone.

Bandura et al. (1969) compared the efficacy of participant modeling with that of symbolic modeling and systematic desensitization in curing snake phobias. The symbolic-modeling clients saw a 35-minute film of children, adolescents, and adults with a snake. The desensitization treatment, identical to the procedure described in Chapter 4, employed a 35-item hierarchy. Control subjects who did not receive formal therapy were assessed for their level of fear. Desensitization therapy continued until the patients could imagine the most feared item in the film without displaying any emotional response; participant-modeling therapy continued until patients could interact with their most feared item when the therapist was with them. The symbolic-modeling clients received as much modeling exposure as did clients in the participant-modeling treatment. Bandura and associates found that while participant-modeling clients needed only 2 hours to reach the criterion, desensitization clients required 4.5 hours of therapy to imagine their most feared hierarchy item. In addition, 92 percent of the participant-modeling clients could interact alone with a snake, compared to 33 percent of the symbolic-modeling clients, 25 percent of the systematic desensitization clients, and 0 percent of the control subjects. Thus, symbolic-modeling and desensitization therapies are effective when compared with no treatment; both are much less effective than participant modeling. Other studies have also documented participant modeling's effectiveness in treating phobic behavior. For example, participant modeling has successfully treated phobia of heights (Ritter, 1969) and phobia of water-related activities (Hunziker, 1972).

What factors contribute to the rapid elimination of phobic behavior when participant modeling is used? Modeling provides a vicarious change in a client's expectancies, and two processes probably account for the therapy's enhanced effectiveness when participation is also included: (1) A model (or therapist) provides clients with a sense of security. Many psychologists have realized that other people's presence can reduce the emotionality produced by adversive events (refer to Klein, 1982, for a discussion of the influence of other people on emotionality). Because Bandura's approach assumes that the emotionality level influences our efficacy expectations, the reduced arousal induced by a model's presence will increase a client's perceived efficacy, thereby enhancing the interaction with a feared object. (2) A model's (or therapist's) encouragement places social pressure on a client to encounter a feared object (see Klein, 1982, for a review of the social influence process). This personal experience enables clients to discover that they can interact with phobic objects without aversive consequences.

We suggested that participation alters a client's efficacy expectations by increasing modeling therapy's effectiveness. The Bandura et al. (1977) study supports this view. The researchers discovered that the efficacy expectations of being able to fearlessly encounter a snake were higher with participant modeling than with modeling alone (refer to Figure 8-10). Furthermore, the higher the level of self-efficacy produced by participant modeling, the more able each client was to approach the snake. Many clinical psychologists (see Franks & Wilson, 1974) suggest that participant modeling represents one of the most powerful ways of altering phobic behavior. Clearly, its effectiveness lies in its ability to modify the phobics' cognitions.

An Alternative View

Not all psychologists have adopted Bandura's view of the role of anxiety in motivating avoidance behavior. Some psychologists (see Eysenck, 1978; Wolpe, 1978) have continued to advocate a drive-based view of avoidance behavior (see

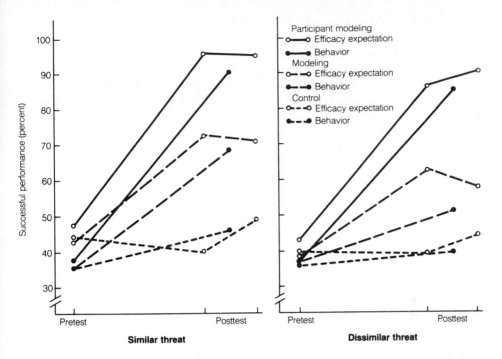

FIGURE 8-10 Influence of participant modeling, modeling, and control treatment on both the subjects' level of self-efficacy and their ability to approach a snake. (Subjects' self-efficacy and avoidance behavior were measured before (pretest) and after (posttest) the treatments.) Treatment effects were evaluated on the posttest with the same snake used in therapy ("similar threat") and a new snake ("dissimilar threat"). Increases in self-efficacy and interactions with the phobic object were greatest when people received participant modeling compared to modeling or control treatment. From Bandura, A., Adams, N. E., & Beyer, J. (1977). Cognitive processes mediating behavioral change. *Journal of Personality and Social Psychology, 35,* 125–129. Copyright 1977 by the American Psychological Association. Reprinted by permission.

Chapter 6). According to these psychologists, cognitions are elicited by anxiety but do not affect the occurrence of avoidance responding. Eysenck considers efficacy expectations to be merely "epiphenomenological" by-products of anxiety. Other psychologists (Borkovec, 1976, 1978; Lang, 1978) suggest that there are three types of anxiety: cognitive, physiological, and behavioral. Cognitive anxiety involves the effect of anxiety on self-efficacy, physiological anxiety affects the physiological state, and behavioral anxiety directly influences behavior. The influence of anxiety on behavior can be mediated by a cognition or a physiological state, or anxiety can directly motivate behavior. According to Lang, the relative contribution of each type of anxiety differs depending on the individual's learning history and type of situation. Sometimes cognitions will mediate the effect of anxiety on behavior; under other conditions, anxiety will directly affect behavior.

Our discussion suggests that both cognitive and noncognitive processes motivate avoidance behavior. A study by Feltz (1982) supports this view. Feltz examined the variables controlling whether female college students would execute a difficult back dive. Feltz discovered that self-efficacy predicted whether the subjects executed or avoided the task on the first trial; however, the influence of self-efficacy diminished on subsequent trials, indicating an influence other than cognitive anxiety. Feltz discovered that physiological arousal also influenced whether the subjects avoided the back dive; that is, physiological measures of anxiety (that is, heart rate) predicted behavior on trials 1 and 3. Furthermore, Feltz's research demonstrates that anxiety can directly affect behavior. On trial 2, the subjects' self-reported anxiety level was the only predictor of whether they completed the back dive or avoided it. Interestingly, self-efficacy and heart rate did correlate with self-reported anxiety prior to the first dive; however, self-reported anxiety did not correlate with either efficacy or heart rate on subsequent dives. On the basis of her research, Feltz suggested that anxiety can either directly or indirectly affect behavior by altering cognitive or physiological processes. Her study also supports the idea that both cognitive and noncognitive processes motivate avoidance behavior.

SUMMARY

1 During the past two decades, many psychologists have recognized the important role of cognitions in determining how we act. In contrast to the mechanistic view that we automatically respond to environmental events, a cognitive approach assumes that we have an active role in determining our responses to environmental circumstances.

2 Cognitive psychology began in the 1930s and 1940s with Edward Tolman's ideas. Although Tolman's cognitive approach did not receive much initial acceptance, his views represent the foundation for current cognitive theories. Tolman proposed that our behavior is goal-oriented; we are motivated to reach specific goals and continue to search until we obtain them. Rather than representing behavior as an inflexible habit, Tolman assumed that our behavior remains flexible enough to allow us to reach our goals. Our expectations determine the specific behavior we use to obtain reward or avoid punishment. According to Tolman, we expect that behaving in a particular fashion will enable us to obtain reward or avoid adversity. In addition to understanding the means needed to reach goals, Tolman felt that environmental events guide us to our goals. Tolman theorized that although we may know both how to obtain our goals and where these goals are located, we will not behave unless we are motivated.

3 Tolman's view altered the drive theory's character (for instance, the anticipatory goal mechanism developed in response to Tolman's incentive motivation and latent-learning studies), but the drive-dominated psychology of the 1950s and 1960s all but forgot his cognitive approach. In contrast, the importance of Tolman's view is quite evident in the thinking of current psychologists investigating the influence of cognition on learning.

4 An expectancy is a mental representation of event contingencies. Dickinson suggested that mental representations or expectancies contain declarative knowledge. This declarative knowledge is gained through experience and guides an animal's behavior. According to Dickinson, there are two main classes of declarative knowledge contained in expectancies. First, an expectancy contains associative representations of two events. This associative-link expectancy allows one event to excite or inhibit the representation

of the other event. In Dickinson's view, associative representations mediate the impact of Pavlovian conditioning experiences. An excitatory link between the CS and the UCS allows the CS to activate this UCS representation and thereby elicit the conditioned response. In contrast, inhibitory-link representations allow a conditioned stimulus to inhibit a conditioned response.

5 The second type of declarative knowledge contained in an expectancy involves an understanding of the consequences of a specific action. This knowledge is represented in propositional form as a belief that action A causes reinforcer B. According to Dickinson, the mental representation of behavior and outcomes controls operant activity. An animal develops a belief that a specific behavior produces a particular reinforcer. The intent of an animal's behavior is to obtain reinforcement, and the relevant mental representation enables an animal to obtain a desired reinforcer.

6 According to Dickinson, operant behavior initially is under the control of behavior-reinforcer beliefs. With more training, S-R habits develop and behavior can be controlled by habits rather than expectancies. Dickinson refers to the control of responding by habit rather than by expectancy as behavioral autonomy.

7 In some circumstances, animals or people perceive no relationship between behavior and outcomes. The literature implicates the occurrence of this perception in the behavior pathology of depression. There appear to be two types of helplessness or depression: personal helplessness, which occurs when people consider themselves incapable of obtaining reward or avoiding punishment, and universal helplessness, which occurs when people consider the attainment of reward or the avoidance of punishment to be impossible. The duration of depression is determined by whether people make a stable attribution, which leads to long-lasting depression, or an unstable causal attribution, which results in short-lived depression.

8 The extent of depression depends on whether a person makes a global or specific attribution; when a person makes a specific attribution, helplessness is restricted to a particular circumstance, but a global attribution leads to depression in many situations. Severe depression occurs when people believe that (1) their inabilities rather than external forces cause events to be uncontrollable, (2) their inability to control events will happen in many different situations, and (3) their inability to obtain reward and avoid failure will not change with time.

9 Cognitions also have a powerful impact on phobias. Phobic behavior occurs when individuals expect that (1) an aversive event will occur, (2) an avoidance behavior is the only way to respond to prevent the aversive event, and (3) they cannot interact with the phobic object. Participant modeling represents an effective treatment of phobias, because it alters the cognitions that motivate the phobic's avoidance behavior.

9

COGNITIVE LEARNING PROCESSES

A DAY AT THE BEACH

It was a lovely summer day. The temperature was about 85° and the humidity was quite moderate. It would be hard to find a better day to go to the beach. Despite the fact that it was the middle of the summer, Jill had not been to the beach this year. She had always enjoyed the beach, but with a full-time job, she had not found the time to go. Her two best friends, Gail and Sue, had asked her to go with them on numerous occasions, but she always seemed to have commitments at work that prevented her from accepting their invitations.

When Gail called on Monday, Jill thought that she would be able to go to the beach on Saturday. She had just completed a major project and certainly could handle the minor jobs that were on her desk during the week. On Tuesday, Jill's boss informed her that a report was needed a week earlier than planned and would have to be on her desk by Monday morning. Jill was devastated. She really wanted to go to the beach, but she did not feel that she could get the report done on time if she went. Gail probably would not ask her again if she backed out this time, but the report had to be done. What could she do?

Perhaps she could go to her boss, tell her about her commitment to Gail, and ask for an extension on the project. She had always handed in her work on time; maybe the boss would be agreeable. However, Jill decided not to ask for more time; it would look bad, and her boss probably would not agree, anyway. Another option would be to stay up late for the remainder of the week to get the project done. Jill did not function well on little sleep and dismissed this option. Could anyone else help her? Her coworker, Richard, was familiar with the project. Although he was definitely busy, maybe he would help her. He would understand her social dilemma. She could make it up to him by helping him with his work at some other time. This seemed like a reasonable solution. She would talk with him after lunch.

In this vignette, Jill has a problem. She must find a way to go to the beach on Saturday while still completing her project at work on time. In the story, Jill recognized the problem, identified her goal, and generated a number of possible solutions. After considering the possibilities and the likelihood of success of each, she decided on the solution that she perceived as most likely to be successful.

Each of us is faced with many problems to solve in our lives. In some instances, we adopt a systematic strategy to solve the problem, while in other cases, we use the first solution that comes to mind. In this chapter we examine how problems are solved and consider reasons why we might or might not be able to solve a particular problem.

This chapter introduces four major cognitive processes by which complex tasks are mastered. First, we explore how concepts are formed. A *concept* is a symbol that represents a class or group of objects or events with common characteristics. Second, we discuss problem solving. A *problem* exists when obstacles prevent attainment of a desired goal. To reach the goal, the problem must be solved. Third, we explore how decisions are made. People often have to choose between alternative actions. A *decision* involves selecting the action that is most likely to be successful in solving a problem. Finally, we examine the structure of language and how we learn to use it. *Language* is a means of communicating our thoughts and feelings. We begin our discussion by looking at the context in which cognitive processes operate.

THINKING

Suppose another student asks you for your notes from the last class. You might not say yes or no right away but instead tell the student that you will think about the request. What is meant when you say that you will think about the request? Thought involves some internal processes directed at coping with the environment; in this case, thinking involves the operation of internal processes directed at deciding whether or not you will give the other student your notes.

The purpose of thinking is to make sense out of our perceptions of the physical and social environment. A diverse group of cognitive processes are involved in thinking. One of these cognitive processes is decision making. Problem solving is another thought process. When we use thinking to solve problems, we are able to explore various solutions mentally without having to go through all of the physical activities that might be used to solve the problem. We also can use thought processes to understand written or spoken language, and to create language to communicate our thoughts to others.

What is the content of our thoughts? Thoughts can consist of mental images of our experiences. For example, thinking about your next vacation can involve images of sailing on a lake or walking in a forest. Thoughts can also contain words. Thinking about your next vacation may contain statements about the beauty of a lake or the tranquility of a forest. Words are instances of concepts; in our example, the words *lake* and *forest* represent objects possessing certain characteristics. We next look at the nature of concepts and how concepts are learned. Our discussion will provide insight about the content of our thoughts.

CONCEPT LEARNING

What is an airplane? *Webster's International Dictionary* defines it as a "fixed-wing aircraft, heavier than air, which is driven by a screw propeller or by a high velocity rearward jet and supported by the dynamic reactions of the air against its wings." The word *airplane* is a concept. A *concept* is a symbol that represents a class or group of objects or events with common properties. Thus, the concept "airplane" refers to all objects that (1) have fixed wings, (2) are heavier than air, (3) are driven by a screw propeller or high-velocity rearward jet, and (4) are supported by the dynamic reactions of the air against the wings. Airplanes come in various sizes and shapes, but as long as they have the four properties listed above, they are easily identified as airplanes. We are all familiar with many concepts. *Chair, book,* and *hat* are three such concepts: They stand for groups of objects with common properties.

Concepts significantly enhance the thinking process. Instead of separately labeling and categorizing each new object or event we encounter, we simply incorporate them into existing concepts. For example, suppose a child sees a large German shepherd. Even though this child may have been exposed only to smaller dogs like poodles and cocker spaniels, he or she will easily identify the barking animal with four legs and a tail as a dog. Thus, concepts enable us to group objects or events that share common properties and to respond in a similar manner to each example of the concept.

The Structure of a Concept

Attributes and Rules Concepts have two main properties: attributes and rules. An *attribute* is any feature of an object or event that varies from one instance to another. For example, height, weight, and coloring differ from person to person and therefore are attributes of each individual.

An attribute can have a fixed value; for example, the attribute of gender can be only either male or female. In other cases, attributes have continuous values; for instance, the shade of a certain color can vary from light to dark.

Certain properties or attributes are relevant to particular objects or events. For example, the attribute of four legs is relevant for cats, but the attribute of

TABLE 9-1
RULES FOR DEFINING ATTRIBUTES IN A CONCEPT

Rule	Symbolic description	Verbal description
Affirmation	L	Any large object
Negation	$\bar{L}$	Any object not large
Conjunction	L ∩ C	Any object both large and a circle
Disjunction	L ∪ C	Any object either large or a circle or both

Source: Haygood, R. C., & Bourne, L. E., Jr. (1965). Attribute and rule learning aspects of conceptual behavior. *Psychological Review, 72,* 175–195. Copyright 1965 by the American Psychological Association, Reprinted by permission.

wings is not. To understand a concept, one must learn what attributes are relevant to it.

For each concept, a rule defines which objects or events are examples of that particular concept. In terms of the concept "airplane" discussed earlier, the defining rule indicates that to be an airplane, an object must have fixed wings, be heavier than air, be driven by a screw propeller or high-velocity rearward jet, and be supported by the dynamic reactions of the air against its wings.

Types of Rules A number of different rules may be used to define the attributes of a concept (see Table 9-1). In some instances, the rules are simple; in other cases, they are more complex. When the rule is simple, an object or event must possess only one attribute to be an example of that particular concept. Suppose an object is green. This object belongs to the concept of green whether it is a green car, a green shirt, or a green pea.

The concept "green" is defined by the affirmative rule. The *affirmative rule* specifies that a particular attribute defines a concept. In Figure 9-1, the affirmative rule indicates that "large" is the concept. A *negative rule* states that any object or event having a certain attribute is not a member of the concept. Figure 9-1 shows that any object that is not large is not an example of the concept. Another example of a concept defined by a negative rule is blindness: Anyone who can see is not blind.

The rules defining other concepts may be more complex. For example, a *conjunctive rule* defines a concept based on the simultaneous presence of two or more attributes; all the specified attributes must be present for an object or event to be an example of the concept (see Figure 9-1). To illustrate the conjunctive rule, consider the question, "What is poison ivy?" Poison ivy is a *vine* that has *three-leaf clusters,* each leaf is *pointed* and *tooth-edged,* and each vine is *red* at the base of the branch of leaves. To be an example of the concept "poison ivy,"

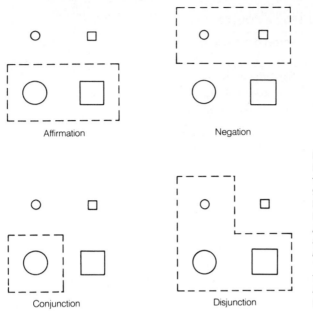

FIGURE 9-1
Positive instances for each of the four rules presented in Table 9-1 are enclosed by dashed lines. Adapted from Haygood, R. C., & Bourne, L. E., Jr. (1965). Attribute and rule learning aspects of conceptual behavior. *Psychological Review, 72,* 175–195. Copyright 1965 by the American Psychological Association. Reprinted by permission.

a plant must have all five attributes listed above. The Virginia creeper vine is like the poison ivy but has five-leaf clusters; seedlings of the box elder also look like poison ivy but have straight instead of vinelike stems. Many of us have mistaken other plants for poison ivy because we have not accurately learned the concept of poison ivy.

The disjunctive rule specifies that concepts can be defined by the presence of one of two, or both, common attributes; that is, an example of the concept can possess either of the two common attributes, or it can possess both of them. In Figure 9-1, the *disjunctive rule* is "circle" or "large" or both. A large circle is an example of the concept, as are both a large square and a small circle. As another example of a concept defined by a disjunctive rule, consider the question, "What is schizophrenia?" Schizophrenia is characterized by persistent hallucinations and/or delusions. Thus, a person who has either or both of the attributes may suffer from schizophrenia. We have examined four simple rules which specify the attributes of a concept. There are other complex rules that define concepts; interested readers are referred to Kintsch (1977) for a detailed discussion of the rules governing concept identification.

Our discussion suggests that for a specific object or event to be an example of a concept, it must have all the attributes characteristic of that concept. Yet, this is not always true. Consider the concept "bird." We know that birds can fly, are relatively the same size, have feathers, build nests, and head for warmer climates during the winter. However, not all birds have all these attributes; a

TABLE 9-2
RANKING OF FURNITURE AND VEGETABLES BY HOW WELL THEY EXEMPLIFY
THEIR CATEGORY

Furniture		Vegetables	
Exemplar	Goodness-of-example rank	Exemplar	Goodness-of-example rank
Chair	1.5	Peas	1
Sofa	1.5	Carrots	2
Couch	3.5	Green beans	3
Table	3.5	String beans	4
Easy chair	5	Spinach	5
Dresser	6.5	Broccoli	6
Rocking chair	6.5	Asparagus	7
Coffee table	8	Corn	8
Rocker	9	Cauliflower	9
Love seat	10	Brussels sprouts	10
Chest of drawers	11	Squash	11
Desk	12	Lettuce	12
Bed	13	Celery	13
Bureau	14	Cucumber	14
End table	15.5	Beets	15

Source: Rosch, E. (1975). Cognitive representations of semantic categories. *Journal of Experimental Psychology: General, 104,* 92–253. Copyright 1975 by the American Psychological Association. Reprinted by permission.

chicken, for example, has only one or two of these characteristics, while a robin has them all. Yet, we classify both the chicken and the robin as birds. Is a robin more of a bird because it has more of the attributes?

The Prototype of a Concept   Rosch (1973, 1975, 1978) demonstrated that all examples of a concept do not necessarily have all the attributes characteristic of that concept. Consider the concept "furniture." How exemplary of this concept is a desk, a table, or a chair? Rosch found that subjects could rank the degree to which a particular item fit a certain concept. As can be seen in Table 9-2, different pieces of furniture vary in the extent to which they are examples of the concept of furniture. "Chair" and "sofa" exemplify the concept to the greatest degree; "bureau" and "end table" to the least.

Why are some objects or events better examples of a concept than are others? Rosch (1975) assumes that the degree to which a member of a concept exemplifies the concept depends on the degree of *family resemblance:* The more attributes a specific object or event shares with other members of a concept, the more the object or event exemplifies the concept. Thus, compared with bureau and end table, sofa and chair are better examples of the concept "furniture" because they share more attributes with other members of the concept. Rosch and Mervis

(1978) found that the 5 most typical members of the concept "furniture" had 13 attributes in common, whereas the 5 least typical members had only 2 attributes in common.

When you think of the concept "vegetable," you are most likely to imagine a pea. Why? According to Rosch (1978), the *prototype* of a concept is the object that has the greatest number of attributes in common with other members of the concept and is therefore the most typical member of a category. As can be seen in Table 9-2, the pea is the prototype of the concept "vegetable." Members of the concept that have many attributes in common with the prototype are considered typical of the concept; thus, carrots and green beans are typical of "vegetable" because they have many of the same attributes as the pea. In contrast, celery, cucumbers, and beets are atypical of the concept because they share only a few attributes with the pea.

The degree to which an object or event exemplifies a concept is important. Rosch (1978) asked subjects to indicate whether a particular object or event was a member of a specific concept. For example, subjects were asked if robins and penguins are birds. Rosch reported that subjects took less time to respond affirmatively when the object or event was a good example of the concept (robin) than when it was a poor example (penguin). Thus, the more an object or event differs from the prototype, the more difficult it is to identify it as an example of the concept.

Boundaries of the Concept Two objects or events may share certain attributes but not be examples of the same concept. For example, although robins and bats both have wings, the robin is a bird and the bat is a mammal. Certain rules define the boundaries of a concept. These rules indicate whether differences between the prototype of a concept and another object or event indicate either that the other object or event is less typical of the concept or that it is an example of another concept. Thus, even though robins and bats both have wings, the other differences between them mean that the bat and the robin are not members of the same concept.

Sometimes boundaries between concepts are not clearly defined (Zazdeh, Fu, Tanak, & Shimura, 1975). For example, what is the difference between a river and a stream? When the boundary of a concept is vague, it is difficult to know whether an object or event is a member of that concept. Rosch (1978) reported that subjects easily answered that a stone is not a bird, but they had difficulty indicating that a bat is not a bird. In fact, many subjects thought that a bat was a kind of bird. This study suggests that we do not always know the boundaries defining certain concepts.

Studying Concept Learning

Psychologists have conducted numerous experiments examining concept learning. An early study by Smoke (1933) is representative. Smoke presented subjects with a large number of figures that differed in terms of the shape, size, number, and

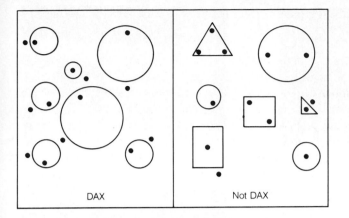

FIGURE 9-2 Samples of DAX and non-DAX figures. The DAX concept was defined as a circle with one dot inside and one dot outside its boundary. All objects possessing these attributes were examples of the DAX concept. From Smoke, K. L. (1932). An objective study of concept formation. *Psychological Monographs, 42,* whole no. 191. Copyright 1932 by the American Psychological Association. Reprinted by permission.

location of their dots. The subjects' task was to learn the concept of DAX, which consisted of a circle with one dot inside and another dot outside (refer to Figure 9-2). The DAX concept uses the conjunctive rule; a figure that (1) is not a circle, (2) has more than two dots, or (3) has two dots inside or outside the circle is not an example of the DAX concept. Subjects saw each figure, indicated whether they thought it was an example of the concept, and received feedback about the correctness of their response. Smoke reported that subjects readily learned the concept of DAX.

Concept Learning in Animals

Concept learning involves identification of the properties that characterize a concept as well as those that do not. Can animals learn concepts? The research of Richard Herrnstein and associates (Herrnstein, 1979; Herrnstein & de Villiers, 1980; Herrnstein, Loveland, & Cable, 1976) clearly shows that animals can learn a concept.

Herrnstein and colleagues (1976) presented a series of 80 slides to a group of pigeons. Half of the slides were S^D, and pecking at these slides resulted in a food reinforcement. The other 40 slides were S^Δ, and the pigeons did not receive a reinforcer for pecking at them. The S^D slides were examples of natural objects; for example, the S^D slides for some pigeons were pictures of water, for some pigeons the pictures were of trees, and for some pigeons the pictures were of a specific woman. The S^Δ slides did not show examples of the appropriate objects.

FIGURE 9-3 Examples of stimuli used in the Herrnstein, Loveland, and Cable (1976) study. Figures A, C, and E are S^{D}s. Figures B, D, and F are S$^\Delta$s. The concept "water" is present in Figure A but not in Figure B. The concept "trees" is present in Figure C but not in Figure D. The particular person present in Figure E is not in Figure F. (Photographs provided by Richard Herrnstein.)

Figure 9-3 shows positive (S^D) and negative (S$^\Delta$) instances of each concept. During each daily session, each of the 80 slides was briefly exposed to the pigeons. Herrnstein et al. found that the pigeons quickly learned to respond to the S^D and not to the S$^\Delta$.

Did these pigeons really learn a concept? Did they discover which stimuli contained examples of the concept and which did not? Or did they merely learn to respond to some particular stimuli but not to others? Herrnstein and de Villiers (1980) evaluated whether the pigeons had actually learned a concept in two ways. First, they presented the same 80 slides to the pigeons, but this time not just the S^D slides contained examples of the concept; that is, the slides were randomly assigned to S^D and S^Δ. If the pigeons were just learning to respond to some stimuli but not to others, then the random assignment of slides should not affect how fast the pigeons learned the discrimination. Although the pigeons did learn the discrimination when the slides were randomly presented as S^D and S^Δ, Herrnstein and de Villiers reported that learning was much slower when no concept defined S^D and S^Δ. Herrnstein and de Villiers also used a positive-transfer test to show that the pigeons did learn a concept. After the pigeons had learned the discrimination in which S^D contained an example of the concept and S^Δ did not, they were shown two new slides of S^D and S^Δ. According to Herrnstein and de Villiers, if the pigeons had learned to respond only to certain stimuli, then learning to discriminate new slides of S^D and S^Δ should proceed at the same rate as original learning. However, if the pigeons had learned the concept, positive transfer should occur, and the pigeons should readily learn how to respond to the new slides. Herrnstein and de Villiers observed considerable positive transfer to the new slides. The pigeons responded differentially to the new examples of S^D and S^Δ; their response was almost as effective as it had been to the original slides.

Our discussion indicates that pigeons can learn which stimuli are examples of a concept and which are not. Evidently animals as well as people can organize their environment according to those events which are examples of concepts and those which are not. However, the stimuli used in the preceding studies were natural concepts; that is, the stimuli represented concrete aspects of the natural environment. Can animals also learn abstract concepts such as "same" or "different"? D'Amato and associates (D'Amato & Salmon, 1984; D'Amato, Salmon, & Colombo, 1985) used a procedure called *matching to sample* to investigate whether primates can learn abstract concepts. The matching-to-sample procedure involves first presenting a stimulus item (for example, a square) and then presenting two stimuli (for example, a square and a dot). The subjects are reinforced if they choose the appropriate stimulus on the second presentation. To evaluate whether monkeys can learn the abstract concepts of "same" and "different," sample and test stimuli were presented. If the monkey is learning the abstract concept, the level of performance should improve with each trial. Further, if the monkey has learned to choose on the basis of sameness (or differentness), presentation of a new test stimulus should not affect performance. D'Amato and associates reported that the monkeys' level of performance improved with each trial and that monkeys did perform well when presented with new stimuli. These studies suggest that primates (and humans) can learn abstract concepts, but whether pigeons can also acquire abstract concepts such as "same" and "different" is unclear (see Lea, 1984, for a review of this literature).

Theories of Concept Learning

There are two main theories of concept learning. One view assumes that concept learning is an associative process; the other, that concept learning is a cognitive process.

Associative Theory   Clark Hull (1920) envisioned concept learning as a form of discrimination learning (see Chapter 7). In his view, concepts have both relevant and irrelevant attributes. On each trial of a concept-learning study, a subject determines whether the object or event shown is characteristic of the concept. A subject responding correctly is reinforced by feedback (told that the response was correct). As a result of reinforcement, response strength to the attributes characteristic of the concept is increased.

Consider the Smoke (1933) study described earlier. The subjects were reinforced when they recognized DAX figures (figures of a circle with one dot on the inside of the circle and another dot on the outside). As the result of reinforcement, the stimulus (figure) and response (DAX) were associated. In contrast, subjects that identified as DAX figures those that were not examples of the concept were not reinforced. The result of nonreinforcement was a diminished response to nonexamples of the concept of DAX.

Hull's (1920) classic study provides evidence for an associative view of concept learning. In this study, adult subjects learned 6 lists of 12 paired associates. The stimuli were Chinese characters containing 12 different features. The stimuli changed from task to task, but the features did not. (Six of the features are shown in Figure 9-4.) Nonsense syllables paired with each feature were the responses. The same feature-syllable pairs were used in all of the lists. Hull found that the subjects learned each successive list more rapidly than the preceding one. According to Hull, the subjects were able to learn later lists more quickly because they had learned the common feature of each stimulus in the category. Hull believed that subjects were not consciously aware of the association but instead had become trained to respond to a specific stimulus event.

Hull proposed that associative processes control concept learning. This view was advocated by most psychologists until the late 1950s, when further research revealed that cognitions also are involved in concept learning.

Cognitive Process in Concept Learning

Testing Hypotheses   How does a person learn a concept? According to Bruner, Goodnow, and Austin (1956), a concept is learned by testing hypotheses about the correct solution. If the first hypothesis formed is correct, the individual has learned the concept. However, if the hypothesis is incorrect, another hypothesis will be generated and tested. Hypothesis testing will continue until a correct solution is discovered.

Consider the DAX concept. Suppose on the first trial (see Figure 9-5) a figure of a circle and a dot was shown, and one subject's first guess or hypothesis was that this figure was an example of the concept DAX. Since DAX is a figure with

Feature	List 1	List 2	List 3	List 4	List 5	List 6

FIGURE 9-4 The stimuli used in Hull's concept learning study. Notice that the features shown on the left are contained in each list presented on the right. From Hull, C. L. (1920). Quantitative aspects of the evolution of concepts: An experimental study. *Psychological Monographs, 28,* whole no. 123. Copyright 1920 by the American Psychological Association. Reprinted by permission.

a circle and two dots, the subject who responded ''DAX'' to the first figure was wrong. Thus, the initial hypothesis was incorrect and the subject needed to generate a new one. On trial 2, the subject hypothesized that DAX was a dot to the left of the circle. The subject learned that this hypothesis also was wrong and on trial 3 guessed that two dots represent the concept. Again the subject learned that this guess was wrong. The subject's next hypothesis was that the concept was two dots and a circle. Although trial 4 suggests that this is a possibility, trial 5 proves it to be incorrect. The subject then hypothesized that the concept of DAX is one dot inside a circle and one dot outside. The subject tested this hypothesis on trials 6, 7, and 8 and finally concluded that it was correct. Our example suggests that, in addition to forming hypotheses to learn concepts, individuals adopt a win-stay, lose-shift strategy; that is, they will stick with a hypothesis as long as it works and will generate a new one when evidence indicates that the old hypothesis is not valid. What evidence demonstrates that hypotheses are tested in concept learning? Levine's (1966) classic study provides support for a hypothesis-testing view of concept learning.

Levine (1966) developed a blank-trials procedure to evaluate the theory that people learn concepts by testing hypotheses. On each trial, subjects were shown

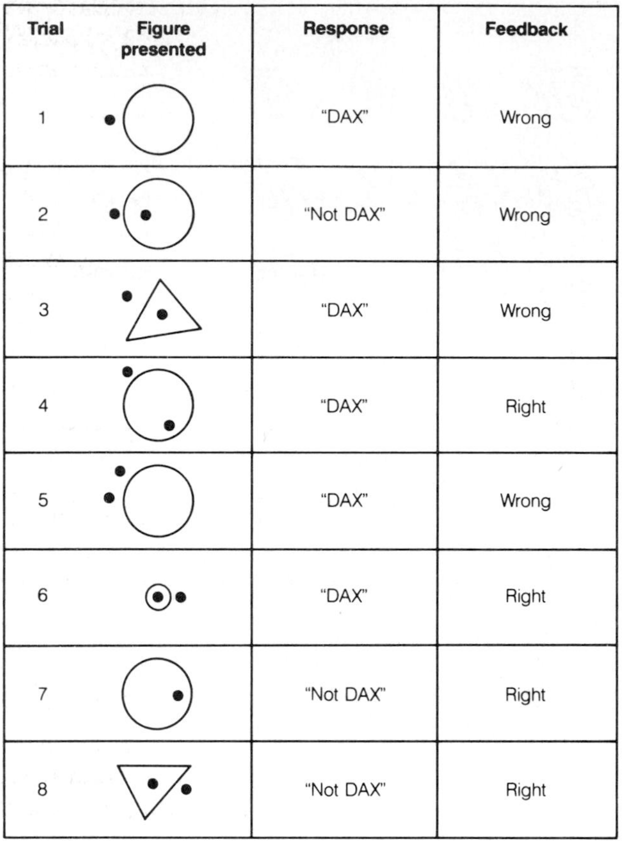

Trial	Figure presented	Response	Feedback
1		"DAX"	Wrong
2		"Not DAX"	Wrong
3		"DAX"	Wrong
4		"DAX"	Right
5		"DAX"	Wrong
6		"DAX"	Right
7		"Not DAX"	Right
8		"Not DAX"	Right

FIGURE 9-5   A hypothetical series of eight trials of the DAX problem. Successive rows show, trial by trial, the stimulus presented, the response given, and the feedback provided by the experimenter. From Kimble, G. A., Garmezy, N., & Zigler, E. (1984). *Psychology* (6th ed.). New York: Wiley.

two letters. The letters differed in terms of color (black or white), identity (*X* or *T*), size (large or small), and position (left or right). One attribute (for example, white) was chosen by Levine to be the concept; the subjects' task was to learn which attribute had been chosen. On each trial, the subjects chose one of the two stimuli and were told whether their response contained the correct attribute. After each study trial, subjects were given four blank trials. On each blank trial, two stimuli were presented, and the subjects again tried to choose the one that represented the concept. However, no feedback was given on these trials. The subjects' responses on the blank trials indicated whether they were testing a hypothesis about the correct attribute. If they were, a particular pattern of responses

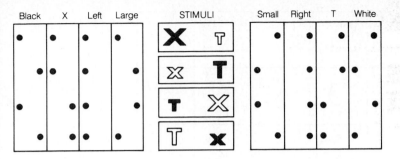

FIGURE 9-6   The stimuli used by Levine in his blank trials are presented in the middle of the figure. The eight possible hypotheses are to the left and right of the stimuli. The column below each hypothesis shows the pattern of choices that test the hypothesis. From Levine, M. (1966). Hypothesis behavior by humans during discrimination learning. *Journal of Experimental Psychology, 71,* 331–338. Copyright 1966 by the American Psychological Association. Reprinted by permission.

would be seen. Figure 9-6 presents eight patterns of responses. Suppose a subject hypothesized that black was the correct attribute. This subject's responses should match those depicted in the first column of Figure 9-6. In contrast, the responses of a subject who thought that large was correct should match those in the fourth column, while a random pattern of responses would be seen if subjects had not been testing hypotheses to learn the concept.

Levine found that subjects engaged in hypothesis testing on over 95 percent of the trials. Furthermore, he found that subjects adopted a win-stay, lose-shift strategy. When a hypothesis was confirmed on a feedback trial, subjects retained this hypothesis throughout the blank trials and continued to use it until they received feedback that the attribute was incorrect. When a hypothesis was found to be incorrect on a study trial, a new hypothesis was generated and used on the four subsequent blank trials and then on study trials until disconfirmed.

Two additional aspects of Levine's research are important to note. First, subjects typically do not use a specific hypothesis more than once while learning a concept. Once a hypothesis has proven to be incorrect, that hypothesis will not be evaluated again during the study. Apparently, people can remember past hypotheses that have been proven invalid and test different hypotheses until they find the correct one. Second, Levine showed that subjects can test more than one hypothesis at a time. Consider the subjects' response on the first study trial. Suppose a subject chose a large black *X* on the left, thinking that either black or *X* was the correct concept. The subject was told that the response was incorrect. This information indicates that neither black nor *X* is the correct attribute. Levine's results showed that subjects learned that both attributes were incorrect and, remembering that information, did not guess either black or *X* on blank trials.

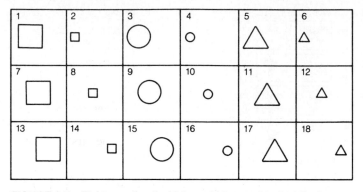

FIGURE 9-7 Eighteen stimuli which could be used to test the large circle strategy. From *An introduction to cognitive psychology* by Danny R. Moates and Gary M. Schumacher. Copyright 1980 by Wadsworth, Inc. Reprinted by permission of the publisher.

Do people randomly generate hypotheses, or do they use a specific strategy to learn a concept? A number of psychologists have reported that most people use particular strategies to learn concepts.

Strategies of Concept Learning   A strategy, or a systematic procedure, can be used to learn a concept. Bruner and associates (1956) conducted an extensive investigation of the strategies used to learn the attributes characteristic of a concept, the prototype of a concept, or the rule defining a concept. They identified a number of major strategies; we will discuss two strategies to illustrate that people do not randomly generate hypotheses to learn a concept.

One type of strategy used to learn a concept is *conservative focusing,* which entails focusing on the first positive instance of a concept and then choosing on each subsequent trial a stimulus that differs in only one attribute from the focal stimulus. The subject continues to select stimuli differing in only one attribute from the focal stimulus until the concept is learned. Conservative focusing is a very efficient strategy of learning a concept; it requires only one more trial than the number of dimensions.

Consider the following example: A subject is shown stimuli differing in three dimensions: shape, size, and position (refer to Figure 9-7). The correct concept is that of a large circle. On the first trial, the subject is shown card 3, a large circle on the left side of the card. The subject learns that this is a positive instance of the concept. Using this card as the focus, the subject chooses card 1, a large square also on the left. When told that the card is negative, the subject knows that shape is relevant and that circle must be a part of the concept. To see if position is relevant, the subject chooses card 9; this stimulus differs from card 3 only in that the large circle is on the right. When told that this card is a positive instance of concept, the subject knows that position is not a relevant dimension.

On the final trial, the subject selects card 4, which is the same as the focal stimulus except that the circle is small instead of large. The subject discovers that this card is not an example of the concept and now knows that size is relevant. Having systematically tested the three dimensions, the subject can identify the concept as a large circle.

Simultaneous scanning occurs when several different hypotheses are tested on a single trial. Although this is a very efficient strategy, it involves remembering a lot of information and often leads to errors. Using the large-circle concept, the following example illustrates this strategy. After learning on the first trial that card 3 (large circle on the left) was a positive instance of the concept, subjects could hypothesize that position is relevant and that shape is irrelevant. This hypothesis could be tested by choosing card 5 (large triangle on left). When told that this arrangement is not an example of the concept, the subject could deduce that shape (circle) is an attribute of the concept but that position is not.

Do not assume that associative learning and hypothesis testing are mutually exclusive means of learning a concept. A concept can be learned using either method, but it is learned best when both means are employed. For example, Reber, Kassin, Lewis, and Cantor (1980) found that subjects acquired a concept most rapidly when they learned both the rules defining the concept and the specific instances of the concept.

Section Review

A concept is a symbol that represents a class or group of objects or events that have common characteristics. Concepts enhance the thinking process by incorporating new objects and events into existing categories. A number of different rules define the characteristics, or attributes, of a particular concept. The affirmative rule states that the presence of a particular attribute defines the concept. The negative rule states that a member of the concept cannot possess a specific attribute. The presence of two or more attributes defines a concept by the conjunctive rule. The disjunctive rule states that the presence of one of two or both attributes defines the concept.

In some cases, not all members of a concept will have all the attributes characteristic of the concept. The prototype best exemplifies the concept because it possesses more attributes than the other members of the concept. Boundaries specify the point at which a particular object or event is not a member of a specific concept.

Concepts are learned by associating the concept name with specific instances of the concept. A concept can also be learned by testing hypotheses about the attributes of the concept or about the rules defining the concept. Various strategies can be used to systematically test hypotheses and thereby learn the concept. Several strategies have been identified. Conservative focusing entails focusing on the first positive instance of a concept and systematically determining which aspect of that positive instance defines the concept, whereas simultaneous scanning tests several hypotheses at the same time.

PROBLEM SOLVING

The Missionaries-and-Cannibals Problem

On one side of a river there are three missionaries and three cannibals. They have a boat on their side that is capable of carrying two people at a time across the river. The goal is to transport all six people across to the other side of the river. At no point can the cannibals on either side of the river outnumber the missionaries on that side of the river (or the cannibals would eat the outnumbered missionaries). This constraint only holds when there is at least one missionary on the side of the river where there are more cannibals. That is, it is all right to have one, two or three cannibals on the same side of the river with zero missionaries, because they would have no missionaries to eat. (Wickelgren, 1974, page 86).

Can you solve this problem? (Remember that someone will have to row the boat back after each trip across.) Spend several minutes trying to find a solution.

Were you able to transport the missionaries and cannibals without losing any missionaries? If you are like most people, you had some difficulty solving this problem. Figure 9-8 provides the series of trips necessary to move all the cannibals and missionaries to the other side of the river. Each box indicates where the missionaries, cannibals, and boat are after each trip. The arrows show which people take the boat ride on each trip. The trips following the even numbers are to return the boat to the original side.

Why is this problem difficult to solve? The difficulty lies on trip 6. On this trip, it is necessary to have both a cannibal and a missionary return across the river; otherwise, the cannibals will outnumber the missionaries on one side or the other. People usually pause for a long time at this point and are very likely to make an error. Why? The reason is that this choice (and the solution to the problem) appears to lead away from the solution to the problem; that is, this choice takes some of the missionaries and cannibals to the original side of the river. Like this problem, solutions to many real-life problems are not necessarily a straight line toward the goal. We now examine how problems are solved and suggest some methods that you might use to enhance your ability to solve the problems that you encounter.

The Nature of the Problem

What is a problem? A *problem* is a situation in which a person is motivated to reach a goal but attainment of the goal is blocked by some obstacle or obstacles. The person's task is to find a solution to the problem, that is, to discover a way to overcome the obstacles.

Edward Thorndike (1898) proposed that animals and people solve problems by trial and error (see Chapter 2). For example, Thorndike did not believe that the cats in his famous puzzle box study were able to figure out how to open the latch to escape from the box. Instead, the cats performed a large number of responses, and those that enabled the goal to be reached were rewarded. Wolfgang Kohler (1925) suggested a quite different view of problem solving. Ac-

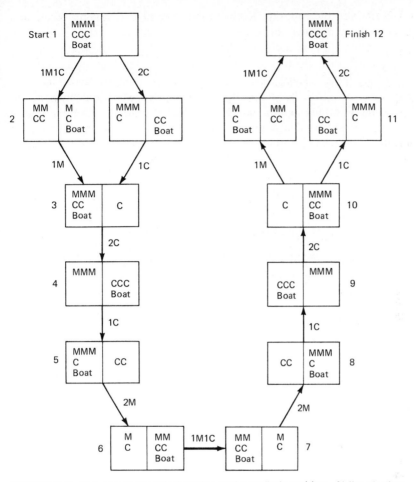

FIGURE 9-8 Solution to the missionaries-and-cannibals problem. At the starting point, the three missionaries and cannibals are on the left side of the river. On each boat ride, two people can be transported. The problem is that at no point can the cannibals outnumber missionaries on either side. The odd-numbered trips are across the river and the even numbers are return trips. The key to the solution of this problem is on trip 6; only by returning both a cannibal and a missionary to the original side of the river can the problem be solved.

cording to Kohler, an animal internally or mentally explores the problem before exhibiting a specific response. The exploration involves considering and rejecting possible solutions and finally developing insight as to the correct solution to the problem.

Consider Kohler's classic primate studies. Kohler presented several chimpanzees with the problem of reaching a piece of fruit that was suspended over their heads in their play area. The problem was structured so that the chimps could not reach the fruit even by jumping. Kohler randomly placed several boxes and sticks throughout the play area. According to Kohler, the chimpanzees initially attempted to reach the fruit by jumping. When that failed, they stopped jumping and paced back and forth. Kohler observed that the chimps abruptly stopped pacing and, looking quite resolute, used the boxes and sticks to reach the fruit. One chimp obtained the fruit by gathering several boxes, stacking them on top of each other, and climbing up the boxes to reach the fruit. Another chimp climbed on one box and used a stick to knock down the fruit. A third chimp collected two hollow sticks and made one long stick by inserting the end of one stick into the other.

Several critical observations led Kohler to suggest that insight was responsible for the chimpanzees' solutions to the problem: First, the chimps solved the problem with few or no mistakes. Second, once they had solved the problem, the chimps were able to solve other similar problems quickly.

Chimpanzees are not the only animals to insightfully solve problems. Epstein (1981) observed a similar phenomenon in pigeons. In his study, Epstein initially trained pigeons to peck at a model banana to obtain food reinforcement. The pigeons were also taught to move a box across the floor of a compartment by pecking at the box. Finally, the pigeons were placed in the compartment with the movable box at one end and the model banana suspended out of reach at the other end. The pigeons' feathers had been clipped so they could not fly to reach the banana. Epstein reported that the pigeons initially looked back and forth from the box to the banana. Finally, they stopped looking, moved the box under the banana, and climbed onto the box to peck at the banana. What cognitive processes enabled Kohler's chimpanzees and Epstein's pigeons to solve the problem? Let's look at possible answers to this question.

There are four steps to solving a problem: (1) define the problem, (2) devise a strategy to solve the problem, (3) execute the strategy, and (4) evaluate the effectiveness of the strategy.

Defining the Problem

Developing a definition of the problem entails identifying both the starting point, or *initial state,* of the problem and the end point, or *goal state,* of the problem. Consider the following example to illustrate this aspect of problem solving. How can you get from your car to the store without getting wet in the rain when you have no umbrella? The initial state of this problem is that you are in your car when it is raining. The goal state of this problem is getting to the store without becoming wet.

A representation of the problem involves two additional processes: First, the operations that solve the problem need to be identified. For example, suppose you want to receive a grade of A in this course. Some operations that would help you gain the knowledge needed to get an A include reading this text, attending class, and taking notes. Second, restrictions limit what can be done to solve a problem. In our example of how to receive an A, some restrictions are that cheating on tests and changing computer cards are not acceptable solutions to the problem.

Well-Defined versus Ill-Defined Problems   Some problems are well defined: Both the initial state and the goal state of the problem are clear. Our example of arriving at the store without becoming wet is well defined; that is, the starting points and goal states are obvious. However, some problems are ill defined: They have no clear starting point or end point. Consider the problem of an instructor who wants to teach a good class. How does the instructor determine whether a class is good? Since there are no definite standards to measure the success of a course, how can the instructor know that the goal state has been reached? In this example, the end point is unclear. In other cases, the starting point is unclear. For example, a person may recognize that a car must be in good working order to run smoothly, but the individual may not be able to check the condition of the car and therefore cannot identify the starting point of the problem.

Solving Ill-Defined Problems   Reitman (1965) suggested that identifying the starting point and end point is the key to bringing an ill-defined problem closer to a well-defined one and that this objective can be accomplished by generating additional structures (subproblems). Consider the following example: Suppose you are asked to write a term paper for a biology class. How can you best accomplish this goal? The starting point is a large body of literature that you need to analyze. The end point is a finished term paper that has a beginning, a middle, and an end, is sufficient in length and depth, and is an accurate discussion of the topic. To begin the definition of the problem, you must first choose a specific topic, such as genetics. The problem can be defined further by identifying several subtopics of genetics, and these subtopics can then be broken down into even more specific groups. In Reitman's view, the subtopics establish a series of subproblems which can then be solved one at a time. Commenting on Reitman's approach, Simon (1973) suggested that creating a set of manageable subproblems provides the structure for converting an ill-defined problem into a well-defined one. Wessels (1982) asserted that creating a hierarchy of clearly stated subproblems makes an ill-defined problem easier to solve. Several studies have found that the use of subproblems facilitated the solving of such ill-defined problems as designing a shop (Hayes, 1978), writing a fugue (Reitman, 1965), and building a warship (Simon, 1973).

A Strategy for Solving Problems

After the problem has been defined, the next step is to develop a plan of attack. There are two major strategies—algorithms and heuristics—that can be used to solve problems; next we briefly describe the use of algorithms and heuristics in problem solving.

Algorithms   An *algorithm* is a precise set of rules used to solve a particular type of problem. To illustrate, consider the algorithm for subtracting: One number is deducted from another to obtain the correct answer. If the algorithm is applied correctly, the solution will be accurate; in this case, following the rules of subtraction produces a correct calculation.

In some cases, a simple algorithm is all that is needed to solve the problem. The application of the subtraction algorithm, for instance, quickly leads to a correct answer. However, in many cases the set of rules that will solve the problem is not easily identified. In these situations, many alternatives must be tried before the correct solution is found. This process of trial and error often uses an enormous amount of time to solve a problem, as illustrated by Samuel's (1963) analysis of the application of this strategy to the game of checkers. Using an algorithm to develop a plan to win a checkers game would involve (1) identifying all possible opening moves, (2) predicting an opponent's response to each of these moves, and (3) anticipating all further responses of both players until all possible outcomes of the game had been analyzed. Samuel calculated that discovering a series of moves that would guarantee a win would involve considering 10^{40} moves and take 10^{21} centuries to complete. Obviously, using an algorithm to play checkers is not very practical.

Heuristics   A *heuristic* is a "best guess" or "rule of thumb" solution to a problem. The use of a heuristic is an alternative to the exhaustive search that the algorithm strategy usually entails. Heuristics increase the likelihood but do not guarantee that the problem will be solved. Suppose you are playing chess. Using an algorithm to discover a winning solution is not practical. You could decide to use a heuristic strategy such as maximizing the protection of the queen. However, you may not always be able to protect your queen and win (for example, when the only way to win is to sacrifice your queen), but usually heuristics will help you find a winning approach.

Consider the following real-world example of a problem solved both by an algorithm and by a heuristic. You need a special tool to fix your car, but you do not have the tool nor do you know which hardware store carries that tool. One way to solve your problem is to call every hardware store in the telephone book—using an algorithm to solve the problem. However, you might find this strategy time consuming, especially if there are hundreds of hardware stores in the telephone book. An alternative would be to call the hardware stores that have large ads in the phone book, since these stores would be more likely to stock the desired tool. Solving the problem this way uses a heuristic strategy.

Heuristics can be used to solve various problems (see Nisbett & Ross, 1980, for a review of this literature). Yet, heuristics represent cognitive shortcuts to solving problems, and the use of heuristics can lead to inaccurate solutions. Later in the chapter we will discuss the possible effects of a failure to use all available information to solve problems.

Execution of the Strategy

Once a strategy has been chosen, the next step is to decide how to execute it. In many instances, the execution of the strategy is straightforward. Simple, well-defined problems can be executed in a short time. For example, suppose you need a hammer to repair a chair. This problem can be quickly solved by going to the hardware store and buying a hammer. However, if you need a more sophisticated tool, you may have problems fixing the chair. The chosen strategy usually requires more time and effort to execute when the problem is ill defined. Some of this difficulty may stem back to the first stage in the problem-solving process, identifying the problem. Failing to make a precise identification of (1) the initial and goal states of an ill-defined problem, (2) the operations that can solve the problem, or (3) the restrictions to the solution can result in complications in executing the strategy and solving the problem.

The Problem Solved

The final stage of problem solving is determining the accuracy of the solution. Although we may not always know if we have solved a problem correctly, feedback often indicates whether our solution was effective. This information about the accuracy of the solution is important for two reasons. First, when we know we have chosen the right solution, we can then overcome the obstacles and reach our goals. If our solution is not accurate, this feedback lets us know that we need to find another way to solve the problem. At this point, we will start at the beginning of the problem-solving process. Second, the success or failure of our attempt to solve a problem can influence future problem solving by prompting us to continue to use effective approaches and to abandon ineffective ones. However, in some cases, present problem solving can negatively affect future decisions by causing us to retain previously effective problem-solving approaches that are no longer effective and to overlook approaches that may have been ineffective in one situation but might be effective in another. We look at these effects of experience next.

The Consequences of Past Experience

Functional Fixedness   After shopping at a local mall, you walk back to your car and notice that your license plate is loose. You know that it will probably fall off if you don't tighten the screws holding the plate to the frame, but how do you tighten the screws without a screwdriver? Although you might think of using a coin as a screwdriver, many other people would fail to recognize that a coin can be used in ways other than to buy things. Solving a problem often requires that we use a familiar object in a novel way. However, it is often hard to recognize these solutions. *Functional fixedness* refers to the difficulty involved in recognizing novel uses for an object. In the above example, because of functional fixedness, many people would not think to use a coin as a screwdriver.

Prior experience using an object to solve one problem makes it difficult to recognize that the same object can be used in a different manner to solve another problem.

The idea of functional fixedness was first discussed by Maier in 1931, and many studies have since demonstrated this phenomenon (see Weisberg, DiCamillo, & Phillips, 1979, for a review of this literature). To study functional fixedness, Birch and Rabinowitz (1951) gave their subjects in the experimental groups two problems to solve. For the first problem, subjects were asked to complete an electrical circuit. Some of the subjects received a switch to use; others had a relay. Control subjects did not receive this initial problem. All subjects were then shown two strings hanging from the ceiling and told to tie the ends of the strings together. The problem was that the two strings were too far apart to hold one and reach the other. To solve this problem, subjects were given access to two heavy objects, a switch and a relay. The subjects should have then tied a heavy object to the end of one string, swung that string like a pendulum, grabbed the end of the other string, caught the first string when it swung back to them, and then tied the two strings together. Birch and Rabinowitz reported that subjects who had used the relay to complete the circuit in the first problem chose the switch as the weight in the pendulum problem. In contrast, subjects who had used the switch to solve the first problem chose the relay as the weight in the second problem. Control subjects used the relay and switch equally often. These results indicate that once the experimental-group subjects had established a function for an object (relay or switch) during the first problem, they did not think of using that object in a different manner to solve the second problem. Because control subjects had no prior experience with either object, the function of the objects had not been fixed, and either one could have been used to solve the pendulum problem.

Functional fixedness reflects an inability to perceive objects as having more than one function. This rigidity can impair problem solving; however, there are ways to overcome functional fixedness. One way is to learn that objects can function in many ways. To illustrate this concept, Flavell, Cooper, and Loiselle (1958) asked subjects to use objects such as a switch and pliers in various ways before exposing them to the pendulum problem. Flavell and associates reported that using one of these objects in several different ways prompted subjects to use that object again as a weight in the pendulum problem. However, if a subject had used the object in only one way, the subject did not use that object to solve the pendulum problem.

Set Functional fixedness is not the only source of negative transfer in problem solving. People also have a tendency to attack new problems in the same way that they have solved earlier problems. The tendency to continue to use an established problem-solving method for future tasks is referred to as a *set*. It is important to note that a set is a source of negative transfer only if a new approach to solving a problem is needed. In fact, if the habitual approach will effectively

TABLE 9-3
LUCHINS'S WATER-MEASUREMENT PROBLEMS

Problem	Given jars of the following sizes			Obtain the amount
	A	B	C	
1.	29	3		20
2. E1	21	127	3	100
3. E2	14	163	25	99
4. E3	18	43	10	5
5. E4	9	42	6	21
6. E5	20	59	4	31
7. C1	23	49	3	20
8. C2	15	39	3	18
9.	28	76	3	25
10. C3	18	48	4	22
11. C4	14	36	8	6

Note: E = Experimental group; C = Control group.
Source: Luchins, A. S. (1942). Mechanization in problem solving. *Psychological Monographs,* 54, Whole 24B. Copyright 1942 by the American Psychological Association. Reprinted by permission.

solve the new problem, the set will actually be a source of positive transfer; that is, new problem solving will be enhanced as a result of the set.

Luchins's (1942) classic study showed the impact of set on problem solving. Subjects were given a series of problems that involved measuring out a given amount of water by using a water tap and three jars of different sizes. Table 9-3 presents the sizes of the jars and the amount of water needed to solve the 11 problems. All subjects received problem 1, which could be solved by filling jar A and pouring three times the water into jar B. Subjects in the experimental group received problems 2 through 11; control-group subjects were given only problems 7 through 11. Most of the subjects in the experimental group learned that a single approach, $B - A - 2C$, could solve problems 2 through 6. Although problems 7 through 11 could also be solved using this approach, a simpler strategy, $A + C$ or $A - C$, could be used to solve these problems. Control subjects used the shorter solution for problems 7 through 11; in contrast, experimental subjects continued to use the longer method. This study demonstrated that the experimental-group subjects established a set, or habitual method of problem solving, as they solved problems 2 through 6, and they continued to use this approach for the remaining problems. Why did subjects in the experimental group continue to use the less efficient strategy? The reason for the use of the prior strategy is that it still was successful in solving the problem. Unfortunately, according to Luchins, a set also "blinded people to fresh ways of exploring problems," especially when other solutions are more efficient.

Application: Becoming a Better Problem Solver

Can you improve your ability to solve problems? The answer to this question is yes. Let's examine some methods experts use to solve problems and some approaches you can use to enhance your ability to solve problems.

The Nature of Expertise   People differ in terms of their ability to solve problems: Some are extremely good at solving problems; others are not. Why this is true has been examined by research comparing chess masters with novice players (see Chase & Simon, 1973, for a review of this literature). This research has shown that, because of repeated practice, the chess master has learned thousands of different patterns, perhaps as many as 50,000 in some cases, and can therefore predict the effectiveness of all possible moves before choosing a particular one. In contrast, the novice player, before every move, must generate from scratch several possible responses to the opponent's last move and then try to anticipate the consequences of each possible reaction before deciding which move to choose. Thus, an expert has more knowledge than the novice. But expertise involves more than greater knowledge; an expert also possesses more abstractions and uses more general concepts than does the novice who is more concrete and employs specific bits of information. In terms of chess, experts have a general understanding of the utility of each piece and how each piece can be moved to the greatest advantage, whereas the novice has memorized some moves that in the past have been successful.

The Improvement of Problem Solving Ability   Some psychologists (Wicklegren, 1974) have asserted that problem solving in any area can be improved. Wicklegren suggests several points for improving the ability to solve problems. First, it is important to be aware of the *problem space*. The problem space is the start and end points of the problem as well as all the possible solutions to the problem. The expert chess player's knowledge of various chess positions, possible moves from each of these positions, and consequences of each move constitutes an awareness of the problem space. Second, awareness of the *various strategies for solving the problem* and knowledge of *when a particular strategy should be used* are also necessary. As discussed earlier, a number of strategies usually can be used to solve a particular problem, and the effectiveness of a certain strategy depends on the various aspects of that problem. Knowledge of different heuristic strategies (for example, defending the queen) and of when each strategy should be employed contribute to the expert chess player's success. Third, the *most effective solution* must be selected. The problem solver must consider many possible solutions and then choose the one that provides the greatest likelihood of success. Finally, problem solvers must *avoid fixating on a particular strategy or a specific solution*. Changes in the nature of a problem may cause a chosen strategy to become ineffective; a problem solver must be prepared to recognize these changes and to try a new strategy to overcome them. Although knowledge of how to improve problem solving is important, only practice can significantly improve the ability to solve problems. One way to get this practice is to use Wickelgren's book, which provides examples of many problems and describes how these problems can be solved.

Section Review

A problem exists when attainment of a desired goal is blocked by an obstacle or obstacles. Thorndike argued that problems are solved by trial and error. In contrast, Kohler argued that a problem is first explored internally. Possible solutions are then tested, and finally insight into the correct solution is gained. Insight then enables the problem to be solved.

Research indicates that there are four steps to solving a problem. Defining the problem—identifying both the starting point, or initial state, and the end point, or goal state, of the problem—is the first step. In some cases, the problem is well defined, with clear starting and end points; however, some problems are ill defined. The key to solving an ill-defined problem is generating subproblems. The initial step in problem solving also involves identifying the operations that can be used to solve the problem as well as restrictions that will not help to solve the problem.

The second step in problem solving is developing a strategy. There are two types of strategies: algorithms, which are precise rules, and heuristics, which are best-guess strategies. Executing the strategy is the third step, and solving the problem is the final step.

Difficulties are common in solving a problem. These difficulties are sometimes caused by the influence of past experiences. In the case of functional fixedness, inability to recognize new uses for familiar objects impairs problem solving. Solving problems may also be impaired by a set, which motivates a person to approach new problems in the same ways that earlier problems had been solved, even though the old strategies are no longer effective.

There are situations in which more than one solution can be used to solve a problem. In these circumstances, the person must decide which solution to use to solve the problem. In the next section, we discuss how decisions are made.

DECISION MAKING

We have to make many choices in our lives. Daily decisions include selection of clothes to wear, foods to eat, and television shows to watch. More long-lasting choices involve selection of a college, a major, or a job. Many decisions can be easily made; yet, other choices may be quite difficult. For example, many students have no difficulty selecting a major, but for other students, the choice is an extremely difficult one. It is not unusual for college students to change majors several times; for these students, the selection of a major is a difficult process.

How does a student select a major? Some students will systematically evaluate the advantages and disadvantages of each major before making a decision; other students might select a major because the area is interesting, or because a parent or friend majored in that field in college. This observation suggests that people use different strategies to make decisions: Some decisions are made by a systematic evaluation of the alternatives, whereas other decisions involve the use of less formal analysis. We next examine these two types of approaches to decision making.

Decision-Making Strategies

As a high school senior, you were faced with the decision about which college to attend. One way to make this difficult decision was to list all of the pluses and minuses about each school and then select the college that had the most positive attributes and the least negative ones. Using this approach, you were likely to select the college that was best for you; this approach to decision making is a rational one.

Why is a selection based on a comparison of positive and negative attributes rational? The answer lies in the use of deductive reasoning. You began the decision process with certain general assumptions or premises; that is, there were positive and negative attributes of all schools and you were best suited for the college with the most pluses and least minuses. Your decision was based on your assumptions; thus, you selected the school with the most positive attributes and least negative ones. It should be mentioned that deductive reasoning is not always accurate. If the assumptions used to make a decision are flawed, the use of deductive reasoning will lead to a flawed decision.

There are two major classes of rational approaches to decision making (see Hammond & Arkes, 1986). *Compensatory models* propose that decision making is based on a systematic evaluation of the advantages and disadvantages of all possible alternatives. In contrast, *noncompensatory models* suggest that decisions are made comparing only certain aspects of each alternative. We will look briefly at both models next.

Compensatory Models   Recall the example of your deciding which university to attend. Suppose you identified four possible universities. Each can be evaluated on a number of dimensions: the size of the university, its location, the quality of its dormitories, and its cost, to name a few. You could rate each school on each dimension.

One compensatory model to decide which college to attend is the additive model. Using the *additive model,* you could add up the ratings for each school. As seen in Table 9-4, university A receives the highest ranking. If you made the selection based on the additive model, you would select university A to attend.

Noncompensatory Models   A decision can be made without comparing all of the features of each choice. Instead, specific features of each possibility can be compared to select a specific alternative. Noncompensatory models of decision making use a critical attribute or attributes in the decision process, rather than

TABLE 9-4
HYPOTHETICAL APPLICATION OF THE ADDITIVE
MODEL OF DECISION MAKING

Attributes	University			
	A	B	C	D
Size	+3	+1	+1	−2
Location	+1	−1	+2	+1
Quality of Dorms	−1	+1	−2	−2
Cost	+2	+1	+1	+4
	+5	+2	+2	+1

Note: Decisions based on additive model add up ratings on each quality or attribute, and the alternative with highest rating is chosen. In this example, university A would be chosen since it has the highest rating.

comparing all identifiable features. For example, you can select a college based on a comparison of one attribute rather than all possible attributes.

An example of a noncompensatory model is the *maximax strategy*. Using this strategy, the alternative with the highest rating on the most important attribute is selected. Suppose you rate each university on the four attributes but feel that cost is the most important factor. Using the maximax strategy, you would select the school that had the highest ranking on the cost factor. In our example seen in Table 9-4, university D is rated favorably in terms of cost. Using the maximax strategy, you would select this university.

When do people use compensatory or noncompensatory strategies to make decisions? One important factor is the complexity of the decision. Payne (1976) found that subjects used a compensatory strategy if the decision was easy, whereas the use of a compensatory strategy declined and a noncompensatory strategy increased as the decision became more difficult. To investigate the impact of complexity on decision making, Payne gave subjects information about apartments and asked them to select one of them. Subjects received either 4, 8, or 12 types of information about each apartment and had to select from 2, 6, or 12 different apartments. Specific information about each apartment was typed on individual cards (see Figure 9-9). The cards were placed face down, and the subjects were instructed to turn over the cards one at a time. The subjects were asked to think aloud as they choose specific cards. The experimenter determined the subjects' decision-making strategies by examining the order that the cards were turned over as well as subjects' statements during the course of the study. Payne discovered that when the decision involved few attributes and few apartments, the subjects used compensatory strategies in decision making. However, he reported that the more attributes and/or apartments that had to be considered in making the decision, the more subjects used noncompensatory rather than compensatory strategies. The switch to noncompensatory strategies occurred because too much information needed to be analyzed to use a compensatory strategy.

Apartment A

Noise level	Cleanliness	Distance	Rent
Low	Fair	20 minutes	$110

Apartment B

Noise level	Cleanliness	Distance	$170
High	Good	30 minutes	Rent

FIGURE 9-9
The subjects in Payne's study received information about different apartments. In the condition shown in this illustration, four types of information about two apartments were presented on cards to subjects. The cards were face down, and the subjects could turn the cards over one at a time to reveal pertinent information. Adapted from Payne, J. W. (1976). Task complexity and contingent processing in decision making: An information search and protocol analysis. *Organizational Behavior and Performance, 16,* 366–387. Reprinted by permission.

Pitfalls of Decision Making

The use of a rational strategy usually leads to good choices. However, there are conditions in which decision making is flawed, and poor choices are made.

Entrapment   There is a saying that a person should not "throw good money after bad." Another related saying is that there are times when "one should cut his or her losses." What do these sayings mean? Suppose a person goes to Atlantic City and loses a significant sum of money. Should the person continue or stop gambling? The above sayings suggest that the logical choice would be to stop playing and not risk losing additional money. Yet, many people do not stop despite losing a lot of money. The media reports of people selling their jewelry, cars, or even airline tickets to continue gambling points to the illogical choice of continued gambling.

Why do people continue to gamble when the logical choice is to stop? The process of *entrapment* is a likely reason for this decision-making error. When people feel committed to a choice, that commitment entraps them in sticking with that choice even though the continued commitment is harmful. Thus, the person feels committed to gambling to win money, and this choice causes the person to be entrapped. This entrapment causes the gambler to "throw good money after bad," because the likelihood of winning at Atlantic City is not very good. Many studies have shown that entrapment leads to judgment errors (see Brockner & Rubin, 1985); we will look at one of these studies next.

Schoorman (1988) gained access to the performance rating that managers in a large organization gave to their clerical workers. In some instances, the managers had been involved in the hiring of the clerical workers, whereas in other cases, the managers had either recommended not hiring the clerical worker or had no involvement in the hiring. Schoorman found that the performance ratings of the clerical workers was highest when the manager had recommended the hiring and lowest when the manager opposed hiring (see Figure 9-10). These observations indicate that the manager's previous decisions concerning hiring had biased his or her later evaluation.

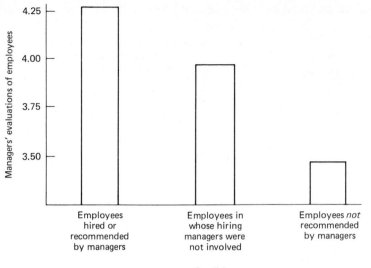

FIGURE 9-10   The entrapment process leads people to be committed to past decisions. The impact of entrapment can be seen in managers' evaluations of employee performance. Managers rated more favorably those employees whom they hired or recommended to be employed and less favorably those employees whom they did not recommend to be hired and those in whose hiring they had not been involved. Adapted from Schoorman, F. D. (1988). Escalation bias in performance appraisals: An unintended consequence of supervisor participation in hiring decisions. *Journal of Applied Psychology, 73,* 58–62. Copyright 1988 by the American Psychological Association. Reprinted by permission.

Overestimation   People believe themselves to be much better decisions makers than they are in reality (see Arkes, Dawes, & Christensen, 1986). This *overestimation effect* causes people to ignore objective data and rely on their own judgments. For example, Arvey and Campion (1982) reported that the best employment decisions are made when managers use statistical formulas. Yet, they found that many managers ignore formulaic approaches to decision making and instead rely on their judgment formed on the basis of a brief interview.

Why do people overestimate their ability to make decisions? Dawes (1976) suggests that the use of the availability heuristic causes the overestimation error. According to Dawes, people are more likely to remember their successes than failures. This memory bias causes people to overestimate their ability to make decisions.

The overestimation flaw in decision making can be overcome. Arkes, Christensen, Lai, and Blummer (1987) had subjects make two sets of judgments. They also were asked to indicate their confidence in the correctness of their responses. Some subjects were given feedback after the first set of judgments indicating that their responses were poorer than they had estimated; other subjects were not given feedback on their judgments. The researchers discovered that the confidence of the subjects on the second set of judgments was significantly lower for those subjects receiving feedback than no feedback. These observations indicate that a person's overconfidence can be reduced by direct evidence of the inaccuracy of his or her previous decision.

Section Review

We are often faced with choices. Some decisions are made in a systematic, logical fashion by considering the utility value of each alternative as well as the probability that specific outcomes will follow each choice. Compensatory models of decision making involve a systematic comparison of all of the desirable and undesirable attributes of each alternative. In contrast, noncompensatory models make decisions based on a comparison of specific attributes of each alternative.

There can be serious pitfalls to decision making. The entrapment bias leads a person to stick with a decision even though it is not proving to be effective. People often rely on incomplete information because the overestimation effect causes them to believe that their judgments are more effective than they really are. Direct evidence of errors can cause a person to take a more realistic view of his or her decision-making ability.

LANGUAGE

The Nature of Language

Language serves three very important functions in our lives. First, *language allows us to communicate with other people*. Just imagine how difficult life would be if we could not express our ideas to our family and friends. We could not, for example, complain to our friends about how much schoolwork we have to do this weekend or call home to ask for money. Second, *language facilitates the thinking process*. The first three sections of this chapter discussed concept learning, problem solving, and decision making. Although these three processes, like most cognitions, can occur without language, language facilitates them by providing a system of interrelated symbols and rules. Third, *language allows us to recall information beyond the limits of our memory stores*.

A subdiscipline of psychology has been developed to study language: psycholinguistics. At its most elemental level, psycholinguistics describes the nature of speech sounds, called *phonemes,* and how phonemes combine to form words. A higher level of analysis, called *grammar,* discusses the rules by which words combine to form phrases and sentences. The highest level of study deals with semantics. Semantics is the study of the meaning of language. Psycholinguists have studied how language is learned as well as whether primates can also communicate with language.

The Structure of Language

Phonemes   A phoneme is the simplest functional speech sound. For example, consider the words *pin* and *bin*. These two words have different meanings and can be distinguished only because their initial sounds, /p/ and /b/, are different phonemes. Note that these distinguishing sounds can occur anywhere in the word. The word pairs *but, bet* and *top, ton* illustrate that the different phonemes occurring at various places in words enable us to distinguish the meanings of different words.

Any language has a limited number of different sounds or phonemes. English is comprised of 45 basic sounds, but some languages have a few as 15 basic sounds or as many as 85 (Mills, 1980). Also, phonemes differ from one language to the next. For example, English contains the /l/-/r/ distinction (as in the words *late* and *rate*), but no such sound difference exists in Japanese. In fact, Miyawaki and associates (1975) reported that the Japanese do not hear the difference between the two sounds and when learning to speak English have difficulty mastering the phoneme distinction between /l/ and /r/. This research indicates that we only distinguish the phonemes that exist in the languages with which we are familiar. No wonder we have such difficulty learning a new language!

How do we learn to recognize phonemes? Eimas and Corbit (1973) discovered that phonemes have distinctive psychological meaning; that is, each sound has its own categorical boundaries and can be distinguished from other sounds. Consider the two syllables *ba* and *pa*. Using a speech synthesizer, Eimas and Corbit slowly changed the sound from the phoneme /b/ to the phoneme /p/, thus changing the syllable *ba* to the syllable *pa*. Although the synthesizer changed the speech sound gradually, the subjects did not respond to the subtle changes. Instead, they reported hearing an abrupt change in the syllable. Apparently, physical boundaries delineate different phonemes.

Interestingly, Eimas, Siqueland, Jusczyk, and Vigorito (1971) showed that even 1-month-old babies make similar categorical distinctions between phonemes. Infants from Spanish-speaking homes who had never been exposed to English react the same way as do infants from English-speaking homes (see Lasky, Syrdal-Lasky, & Klein, 1975). These observations suggest an innate ability to detect specific phonemes. However, experience determines which sounds gain significance and become part of our everyday vocabulary. The finding that different languages use different phonemes indicates that cultural experience governs which phonemes adults will be able to recognize. Additional support for this view is provided by studies in which subjects are trained to make phoneme distinctions they normally do not make. For example, Streeter and Landauer (1976) reported that Spanish children could be taught to distinguish between *ba* and *pa,* a discrimination that is not part of the Spanish language.

Morphemes   A morpheme is the smallest meaningful unit of language. Whereas phonemes are single sounds that enable us to distinguish the different meanings of different words, morphemes are the simplest combinations of phonemes that can be formed and still have meaning. Some morphemes are single phonemes, such as the words *a* and *I*. Other morphemes are comprised of two or more phonemes—the words *fun, joy,* and *car,* for example. A morpheme does not have to be a word; prefixes (for example, *un-* and *re-*) and suffixes (*-er* and *-able*) also are morphemes. Similarly, inflections that make a noun plural (*leaf* to *leaves*) or indicate that a verb is present or past (*catch, caught*) also are morphemes. Consider the words *pill* and *pillow.* Adding *-ow* to the word *pill* creates a word with a different meaning. The word *pill* is a *free morpheme,* because it can stand alone; *-ow* is a *bound morpheme* because it must be bound to a free morpheme to have meaning.

Sentences Words can be combined into a *phrase,* a group of two or more related words that expresses a single thought, and phrases can be connected to form a sentence. A *sentence* consists of two or more phrases and conveys assertion, question, command, wish, or exclamation. For example, the sentence *The couple bought the house* consists of two major phrases: the noun phrase *the couple* and the verb phrase *bought the house.*

How is a sentence constructed? Phrases cannot be randomly combined to form a sentence. Rules govern the formation of sentences; they determine how phonemes are grouped to form words and how words are combined to express various ideas. The rules that govern language are called *syntax.*

Syntax: The Rules of Language

Syntax is the system of rules for combining the various units of speech. An infinite number of morphemes, phrases, and sentences can be formed by these rules. Thus, human language is generative: Syntax enables us to create an infinite number of meaningful expressions. Every language has its own syntax and, therefore, its own unique way of communicating ideas.

Phonology Languages do not use every possible phoneme combination. For example, the two phonemes /p/ and /z/ cannot be combined to begin a word in the English language. Each language restricts the way in which phonemes can be combined to produce meaningful morphemes. *Phonology* refers to the rules that dictate how phonemes can be combined into morphemes.

Grammar Grammar rules establish the ways that words can be combined into meaningful phrases, clauses, and sentences. Words must be arranged to indicate mutual relations; they cannot be grouped haphazardly. Consider the following example cited by the noted psycholinguist Noam Chomsky (1957): *Colorless green ideas sleep furiously* is a meaningful, although somewhat ridiculous, sentence, whereas the same five words arranged as *Furiously sleep ideas green colorless* is not even a sentence. When words are organized according to the rules of grammar, the resulting sentence conveys some kind of meaning. However, words strung together randomly will not express a coherent thought or idea.

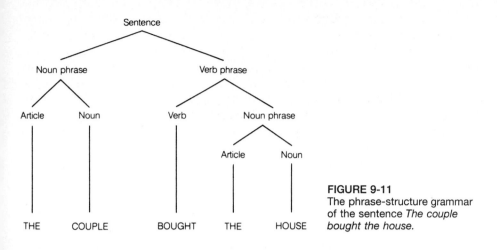

FIGURE 9-11
The phrase-structure grammar of the sentence *The couple bought the house.*

Linguists have studied the structure of the sentence in terms of phrases. This analysis of the constituents of a sentence is called *phrase-structure grammar*. The analysis begins by dividing a sentence into a noun phrase and a verb phrase. Figure 9-11 presents a diagram of the phrase-structure grammar for the sentence *The couple bought the house.* As the diagram illustrates, the noun and verb phrase can then be divided further. This detailed linguistic analysis identifies all the constituent structures of the sentence. The phrase-structure analysis of a simple sentence can be easy; obviously, complex sentences can be difficult to diagram. I still remember my seventh-grade English class and the considerable frustration I experienced trying to construct "grammar trees." Perhaps you have similar memories.

The rules of grammar are elaborate and not always followed. However, because they are generally accepted, using these rules of grammar allows us to communicate effectively with each other.

Semantics: The Meaning of Language Consider the following two sentences: *The boy hit the ball. The ball was hit by the boy.* Shown in Figure 9-12, the grammar trees for these two sentences are quite different, but these two sentences convey the same meaning. According to Houston (1986), the fact that different sentences may have the same meaning points to one important problem of the phrase-structure grammar approach to language. Also, according to Houston, there is a second difficulty with this approach: One sentence may have two different meanings. For example, the sentence *They are growing trees* can mean either that a group of people are in the business of growing trees, or that certain trees are in the process of growing. Figure 9-13 presents the phrase-structure analyses of this ambiguous sentence.

Analyzing the grammar of a sentence is not the same as analyzing the meaning. Noam Chomsky (1965) recognized this difference. In Chomsky's view, the ar-

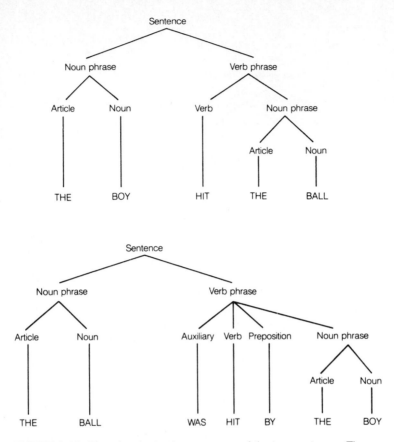

FIGURE 9-12   The phrase-structure grammar of the two sentences *The boy hit the ball* and *The ball was hit by the boy.*

rangement of the words in a sentence represents the *surface structure.* The meaning or idea conveyed by the sentence is the *deep structure.* Only by determining the deep structure can the meaning of a sentence be understood.

How do we figure out the meaning of a sentence? A number of psycholinguists have described this process (Forster, 1979; Wanner & Maratsos, 1978). The first step in the comprehension of a sentence is to divide it into *clauses.* For example, the sentence *The pitcher threw the ball, and the batter hit it* expresses two complete thoughts or propositions; these two thoughts are clauses. Evidence of the application of clause analysis is provided by a study of Fodor, Bever, and Garrett (1974) in which subjects heard a clicking sound either in the middle of the first clause or between the two clauses. Regardless of when the click was actually presented, subjects reported hearing a click between the two clauses. This study indicates that a clause is a cognitive unit that resists disruption. Thus, the click

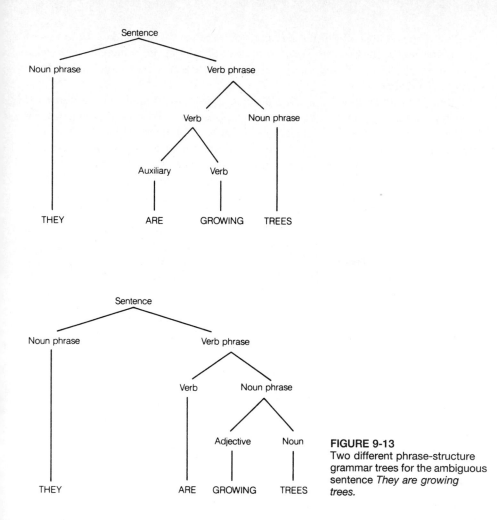

FIGURE 9-13
Two different phrase-structure
grammar trees for the ambiguous
sentence *They are growing
trees.*

presented in the middle of the first clause "migrated" to the end of the clause, and a click presented at either point in the sentence represented a "mental comma" between the two clauses.

After a sentence has been divided into clauses, its meaning can then be determined. Let's use the sentence *The cat chased the mouse* to illustrate this process. To understand the sentence, the reader must determine who is the "doer" and who is the "done to." One approach is to use the "first-noun-phrase-did-it" strategy (Bever, 1970). Using this strategy, the sentence is assumed to be in the active voice, and the first noun clause is tentatively identified as the doer and the second noun clause as the done to. This strategy can convey the meaning of the above sentence, and of most sentences, since the active voice is used much more frequently than the passive voice. However, it will communicate an incorrect meaning if the sentence is in the passive voice. Several clues indicate the use of the passive voice, for example, the words *was* and *by* in the sentence *The mouse was chased by the cat*. These cue words indicate that the first-noun-phrase-did-it strategy is invalid.

Slobin (1966) suggested that an elaborate grammatical analysis is often used to determine deep structure of passive-voice sentences. To provide evidence for this view, Slobin asked his subjects to listen to a sentence, look at a picture, then decide whether the sentence described the picture. Slobin reported that subjects took longer to react to passive-voice sentences than to active-voice sentences. The differences in the elaborateness of grammatical analysis was responsible for the longer reaction times for passive-voice sentences than active-voice ones.

Note that shortcuts sometimes can be used to determine meaning (Slobin, 1966). For example, consider the sentence *The flowers are watered by the girl*. Even though the sentence is in the passive voice, logically, the meaning can be quickly determined. It is plausible that girls water flowers; flowers do not water girls. However, this shortcut will not work for sentences with reversible meanings, for example, *The cat is chased by the dog*.

Not only do we receive and interpret language, we also generate it. According to Chomsky (1965), ideas can be expressed in a number of ways; that is, deep structures can be transmitted through various surface structures. Chomsky suggested that transformational rules enable the same deep structure to generate many different surface structures. Each language has its own acceptable rules of transformational grammar. Individuals in particular cultures must learn these rules so that their use of language will comply with accepted grammatical principles and thus be understood by other members of that culture.

Acquisition of Language

There are two major views of how the ability to use language is acquired. A learning view, first proposed by B. F. Skinner in 1957, assumed that language is acquired through the operant conditioning process (see Chapter 5). According to this approach, children learn to use language because their parents and other people in their environment reinforce it. The psycholinguistic theory, initially described by Noam Chomsky in 1965, proposed that language acquisition is innate. In this view, humans are born with certain mechanisms that enable them to learn to communicate with only a minimal amount of linguistic experience.

A Reinforcement View Suppose that a mother hears her young child say "mama." In all likelihood, the mother will be pleased, and she will give the child a hug and kiss. This affection reinforces the child's behavior and thus increases the frequency of the child's use of language.

Skinner (1957) argued that all responses, including language, are acquired according to the laws of operant conditioning (see Chapter 5). In Skinner's view, shaping is used to encourage children to learn to communicate with words. Initially, approximations of a desired verbal response are reinforced, but eventually adults expect a closer resemblance to the final behavior before providing reinforcement. Consider Anne, a baby learning to talk. When Anne first makes any sound resembling a real word, such as the *m* sound for *mama,* Anne's parents are delighted and reinforce her with praise and affection. However, as Anne continues to make nonsense sounds, her parents gradually stop responding to them. To again receive reinforcement, Anne must learn to say something closer to the actual word *mama.*

Words are not the only language units that can be acquired through the use of reinforcement. Skinner argued that phrases and sentences can also be learned by the process of shaping; initially, nongrammatical phrases and sentences may be reinforced, but eventually only correct language use will be reinforced.

Psycholinguists have been extremely critical of Skinner's reinforcement view of language acquisition (see Lenneberg, 1969, for a discussion of these criticisms). There are three major aspects of this criticism. The first problem is that Skinner's view assumes that parents will reinforce correct use of language and ignore or penalize incorrect use, but observations (McNeill, 1966) show that parents use reinforcements and punishments to influence only the content, not the grammatical correctness, of their children's language. Thus, a parent will allow a grammatically incorrect sentence to be used as long as the content is accurate. Brown, Cazden, and Bellugi's (1969) description of the language of two children, Eve and Adam, provides an excellent illustration of the influence of parental approval and disapproval on a child's use of language.

> Gross errors of word choice were sometimes corrected, as when Eve said, "What the guy idea." Once in a while an error of pronunciation was noticed and corrected. More commonly, however, the grounds on which an utterance was approved or disapproved . . . were not strictly linguistic at all. When Eve expressed the opinion that her mother was a girl by saying, "She a girl," mother answered, "That's right." The child's utterance was ungrammatical but the mother did not respond to that fact; instead she responded to the truth . . . of the proposition the child intended to express. . . . Adam's "Walt Disney comes on Tuesday" was disapproved because Walt Disney came on some other day. It seems then to be truth value rather than syntactic well-formedness that chiefly governs explicit verbal reinforcement by parents—which renders mildly paradoxical the fact that the usual product of such [training] is an adult whose speech is highly grammatical but not notably truthful. (pp. 70–71)

A second problem that psycholinguists have cited with the reinforcement view concerns the creative aspect of language. Children (as well as adults) frequently use an original combination of words to convey an idea. The fact that people can generate new but grammatically accurate language is difficult to explain in terms of operant conditioning principles; how can children (or adults) use a combination of words that they have never said nor heard and that therefore has never been reinforced? Consider Miller's (1965) statement to illustrate this criticism of the reinforcement theory:

> By a rough, but conservative calculation there are 10^{20} sentences 20 words long, and if a child were to learn only these it would take him something on the order of 1000 times the estimated age of the earth just to learn them. . . . Any attempt to account for

language acquisition that does not have a generative character will encounter this difficulty. . . .

Since the variety of admissible word combinations is so great, no child could learn all of them. Instead of learning specific combinations of words, he learns rules for generating admissible combinations. (pp. 176, 178)

The final and perhaps strongest criticism comes from Lenneberg's research showing that despite widely varying social conditions, most children acquire language in a relatively constant pattern. It seems reasonable to expect that children living in different cultures would show various patterns of language acquisition. Yet, Lenneberg found that nonsense sounds are always followed by one-word speech, which develops into the use of two-word sentences, followed by telegraphic speech, and then the use of complex sentences. The observation that even children raised by deaf parents show the same pattern of language development suggests that social reinforcement is not a critical determinant of language acquisition.

Carlson (1984) argued that criticisms of the reinforcement theory overlooked an important point. According to Carlson, language can be reinforced in ways other than direct intervention, and that, in fact, it is the effect of language, not the actual words, that is reinforced. For example, suppose that 2-year-old Billy says "milk" and is then given a glass of milk by his father. Although his father did not consider the glass of milk a reinforcer for his son's saying "milk," to Billy, the glass of milk served as a reinforcement for the verbal behavior that was instrumental in attaining it. The success of this verbal behavior will prompt Billy to use it again whenever he wants a glass of milk. Further, the effects of this reinforcement will be generative, causing Billy to realize that he can use words to get other things he wants, such as books and toys. Verbal behavior can also be used to obtain social reinforcers such as praise or sympathy, and receiving this kind of reinforcement will increase a child's use of language in social situations.

Increasing verbal behavior is one role of reinforcement in language acquisition. Reinforcement also affects the learning of grammar rules. According to Carlson, simple speech is sufficient to express simple ideas, while more complex language is needed for complex expressions. The future tense is one example of complex language; this tense is especially hard for children to learn because the idea expressed in a future-tense sentence is not immediately experienced and therefore not immediately reinforced. For example, the statement *We're going to the circus now* is much easier for a child to understand than the sentence *We're going to the circus next week*.

A Psycholinguistic Approach   Noam Chomsky (1965, 1968, 1975) was very impressed with how easily young children learned their native language. He described the universal sequence of language development from nonsense sounds to the generation of complex sentences and, on the basis of these observations, suggested that children are born with a language-generating mechanism called the *language acquisition device* (LAD). The LAD "knows" the universal aspects of language. This knowledge allows children to readily grasp the syntax relevant to their native language. In Chomsky's view, however, this biological prepared-ness does not result in automatic language acquisition; a child must be exposed to language to learn it. Usually, though, parents eager for their child to start talking provide more than adequate stimulation.

Chomsky's view that children are inherently prepared to learn language re-ceived a considerable amount of support from psycholinguists during the 1960s and 1970s (Dodd & White, 1980). For example, Eric Lenneberg (1967, 1969) argued that language acquisition is an innate species-specific characteristic and that its expression depends only on physical maturation and minimal exposure to language. According to Lenneberg, language is acquired in a fixed order and at a particular rate. Even when maturation is abnormally slow, as in the case of children with Down's syndrome, language is still learned in the same sequence but at a slower rate.

In recent years, however, a number of psychologists (see Bruner, 1978; Glea-son & Weintraub, 1978; Newport, 1977; Snow, 1979) have suggested that the LAD theory expressed by Chomsky and Lenneberg may not completely explain how language is acquired. These psychologists believe that the social aspects of language, rather than simply exposure to language, govern language acquisition. Language is a method of communicating our desires to others; children are mo-tivated to use language by various forms of reinforcement. This view does not imply that children are not prepared to learn to use language but suggests that this preparedness alone is insufficient to explain language acquisition. The idea that the ability to use language is the result of a combination of biological pre-paredness and reinforced experience is consistent with the material presented in Chapter 13.

Consider Moskowitz's (1978) observations to illustrate the importance of the social function of language. Moskowitz studied the language acquisition of a boy with normal hearing whose deaf parents communicated through American Sign Language. The parents had their son watch television every day in hopes that it would teach him English. Unfortunately, their idea failed; at the age of 3 their son was fluent in sign language, but he neither understood nor spoke English. This case indicates that children must interact verbally with others to learn language.

Application: Teaching Chimpanzees Language

Monkeys use sounds to communicate with each other. A primate can express a variety of different emotional states in a manner that other primates understand and to which they respond. Observations of vervet monkeys in Kenya (see Sey-farth, Cheney, & Marler, 1980) reveal both the sophistication of primates' vo-calizations and the reactions of other primates to these vocalizations. For example, the vervet monkeys made distinctive alarm calls when they spotted predators. The sight of a leopard caused them to emit a series of short, tonal calls. The sight of an eagle elicited a low-pitched grunt. The reaction to a snake consisted of a series of high-pitched "chutters." Each of these calls elicited a different response from vervet monkeys nearby: They ran for cover when hearing the eagle-alarm call; they looked down when hearing the snake-alarm call. These observations indicate that primates can communicate through vocalizations; however, these vocalizations are not language. Can primates learn to use language to communicate?

Early investigations suggested that primates could not learn language. Winthrop Kellogg and Luella Kellogg (1933) raised the baby chimpanzee Gua in their home with their infant son Donald. Despite many attempts to teach Gua to speak, the chimp never uttered any English words, although she did learn to obey certain commands. Cathy Hayes and Keith Hayes (1951) were somewhat more successful in teaching the chimpanzee Vicki to speak. Vicki learned to say three words— *papa, mama,* and *cup.* Yet, these words were acquired only after a long period of training, which included manipulating the chimp's lips.

Compared with the Kelloggs and the Hayes, Beatrice Gardner and Allen Gardner (1971) were much more successful in teaching language to their chimp Washoe. The Gardners believed that intellectual impairment was not responsible for earlier failures to teach chimpanzees language; instead, these failures were caused by the chimpanzees' physical inability to produce the complex vocalizations necessary for speech. So instead of trying to teach Washoe to speak English, they taught her American Sign Language. Washoe lived in a trailer in the Gardners' backyard and during all her waking hours had the companionship of one or two people who talked to her only in sign language. After 4 years of training, Washoe had learned over 200 signs and was able to combine them into sentences, such as *Please tickle more* or *Give me sweet drink.*

Did Washoe learn to use language to communicate? The Gardners think so. Washoe's "language" certainly has many of the characteristics of human language. First, it makes sense. For example, Washoe used the sign for *cat* to point out a cat and the sign for *dog* to identify a dog. Second, Washoe's verbalizations were in sentence form. Third, sentences created by Washoe were structured according to the rules of grammar; the sentence *Please tickle more* illustrates Washoe's mastery of syntax. Finally, Washoe responded to questions. For example, if the Gardners asked in sign language the question, "Who pretty?," Washoe answered, "Washoe."

The Gardners are not the only psychologists who have taught primates to use language. For example, Penny Patterson (1978) taught Koko, a gorilla, over 600 signs. Koko's use of language was spontaneous, and she could even generate new language. In fact, she scored only slightly below average on an intelligence test designed for humans her age.

Techniques other than sign language have been used to teach primates to communicate. Duane Rumbaugh and colleagues (Rumbaugh & Gill, 1976; Savage-Rumbaugh, Rumbaugh, & Boysen, 1980) taught chimpanzees language with the aid of a computer. To obtain what they wanted, the chimpanzees had to press the keys that corresponded to specific words. For example, their chimpanzee Lana learned to send the following message, "Please machine make movie period."

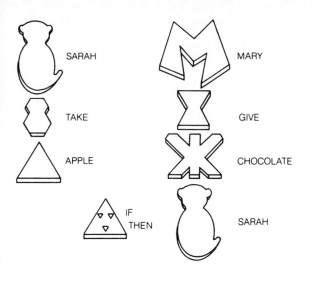

SARAH

TAKE

APPLE

MARY

GIVE

CHOCOLATE

IF
THEN

SARAH

FIGURE 9-14
A few of Sarah's "words," which
she arranged to form complex
sentences. From Premack, A. J.,
& Premack, D. (1972). Teaching
language to an ape. *Scientific
American, 227*, 92–99.

Two other chimpanzees, Austin and Sherman, even learned to communicate with each other through the computer. For example, Rumbaugh and his colleagues sometimes gave either Austin or Sherman food; the "unfed" chimpanzee had to ask the "fed" chimpanzee for food. Austin and Sherman learned to ask each other for food and for many other things. David Premack (1976) taught his chimpanzee Sarah to "read" and "write" by arranging plastic tokens into "sentences." Each plastic token represented an object, action, or attribute (see Figure 9-14). Sarah was able to construct and understand a number of different sentences. For example, she learned the agent-action-object word order and created new sentences such as *Debby cut banana.*

Despite the fact that primates appear to use language to communicate, many psychologists do not believe that primates are capable of learning language. Herbert Terrace (1979), for example, teaching American Sign Language to a chimpanzee named Nim Chimpsky, noted some important differences between Nim's vocalizations and human language. An intense, directed effort was required to teach Nim even very simple signs, whereas children do not need to be taught language; they learn to talk simply by being in an environment where language is used. Also, Terrace found no evidence that Nim could create unique, grammatically correct sentences. According to Terrace, the chimpanzee did not learn the creative aspect of language; that is, she did not know how to use rules to create an infinite number of new experiences and complex sentences. Instead, Terrace argued that the chimpanzee's multiword sentences merely imitated the order used by the trainer. Reviewing the transcripts of communications of Washoe and several other chimpanzees, Terrace concluded that these animals were unable to generate syntactically correct novel combinations of signs. Terrace also noted that few of Nim's statements were spontaneous; most of them were in response to a human's statement. This lack of spontaneous speech is quite different from human speech.

Although a number of psychologists (Marx, 1980; Thompson & Church, 1980) have supported Terrace's view, others (Bindra, 1981; Gardner & Gardner, 1980; Pate & Rumbaugh, 1983; Patterson, 1981; Savage-Rumbaugh, 1986) have disagreed with him. For example, Beatrice Gardner (1981) argued that Nim was raised quite differently from Washoe and that this difference was responsible for Terrace's observations. The debate about primate ability to learn language continues, and future research will attempt to determine whether primates do in fact use language to communicate.

SUMMARY

1 A concept is a symbol that represents a class or group of objects or events that have common characteristics. Concepts enhance the thinking process by incorporating new objects and events into existing categories. A number of different rules define the characteristics, or attributes, of a particular concept. The affirmative rule states that the presence of a particular attribute defines the concept. The negative rule states that a member of the concept cannot possess a specific attribute. The presence of two or more attributes defines a concept by the conjunctive rule. The disjunctive rule states that the presence of one of two or both attributes defines the concept.

2 In some cases, not all members of a concept will have all the attributes characteristic of the concept. The prototype best exemplifies the concept because it possesses more attributes than the other members of the concept. Boundaries specify the point at which a particular object or event is not a member of a specific concept.

3 Concepts can be learned by associating the concept name with specific instances of the concept. A concept can also be learned by testing hypotheses. Various strategies can be used to systematically test hypotheses and thereby learn the concept. Conservative focusing entails focusing on the first positive instance of a concept and systematically determining which aspect of that positive instance defines the concept, whereas simultaneous scanning tests several hypotheses at the same time.

4 A problem exists when attainment of a desired goal is blocked by an obstacle or obstacles. Thorndike argued that problems are solved by trial and error. In contrast, Kohler argued that a problem is first explored internally. Possible solutions are then tested, and finally insight into the correct solution is gained. Insight then enables the problem to be solved.

5 Research indicates that there are four steps to solving a problem. Defining the problem—identifying both the starting point, or initial state, and the end point, or goal state, of the problem—is the first step. In some cases, the problem is well defined and has clear starting and end points; however, some problems are ill defined. The key to solving an ill-defined problem is generating subproblems. The initial step in problem solving also involves identifying the operations that can be used to solve the problem as well as restrictions that will not help to solve the problem.

6 The second step in problem solving is developing a strategy. There are two types of strategies: algorithms, which are precise rules, and heuristics, which are best-guess strategies. Executing the strategy is the third step, and solving the problem is the final step.

7 Difficulties are common in solving a problem; these difficulties are sometimes caused by the influence of past experiences. In the case of functional fixedness, the inability

to recognize new uses for familiar objects impairs problem solving. Development of a set causes people to attack new problems in the same ways that earlier problems had been solved, even though the old strategies are no longer effective.

8 We are often faced with choices. Some decisions are made in a systematic, logical fashion by considering the utility value of each alternative as well as the probability that specific outcomes will follow each choice. Compensatory models of decision making involve a systematic comparison of all of the desirable and undesirable attributes of each alternative. In contrast, noncompensatory models make decisions based on a comparison of specific attributes of each alternative.

9 There can be serious pitfalls to decision making. The entrapment bias leads a person to stick with a decision even though the decision may have been a poor one. People often rely on incomplete information because the overestimation effect causes them to believe that their judgments are more effective than they really are. Knowledge of poor decisions can cause a person to take a more realistic view of his or her decision-making ability.

10 Language serves three important functions: It allows us to communicate with others, it facilitates the thinking process, and it enables us to recall information beyond the limits of our memory stores. Psycholinguists have studied the nature of language. The phoneme is the simplest speech sound. Although we have an innate ability to detect many different phonemes, our culture determines how many different sounds we learn to use.

11 Phonemes are combined to form a morpheme, the smallest meaningful unit of language. Morphemes are words (free morphemes) as well as prefixes and suffixes (bound morphemes). Words can be combined into a phrase, which expresses a single thought, and phrases can be grouped to form a sentence, which conveys an assertion, question, command, wish, or exclamation.

12 Syntax is the system of rules governing the ways in which various units of speech can be combined. Phonology refers to the rules specifying how phonemes can be combined into words, whereas the rules of grammar establish how words are combined into meaningful phrases and sentences. Grammar refers to the surface structure of a sentence; the meaning conveyed by the sentence is called the deep structure.

13 The study of the meaning of language, called semantics, has shown that the same sentence can have different meanings and different sentences can have the same meaning. According to Chomsky, transformational rules of grammar allow a specific deep structure to generate varied surface-structure sentences.

14 Two major theories of language acquisition have been proposed. Skinner argued that children acquire language because of reinforcement of appropriate language use. In contrast, Chomsky argued that humans have an innate ability to learn language and that language can be used to communicate after only a minimal amount of linguistic experience. A contemporary view suggests that both preparedness and the use of conditioning influence language; humans may be prepared to learn language, but they must also discover that language can be used to obtain nonsocial and social reinforcers.

15 Primates have been taught sign language and can use signs in sentences. Some psycholinguists believe that these primates communicate with language and therefore argue that language is not limited to humans. However, other psycholinguists believe that primates are not actually using language but are merely imitating behavior which has been reinforced by their trainers. Whether primates can use language remains a topic for future discovery.

10

THE STORAGE OF OUR EXPERIENCES

A FLEETING EXPERIENCE

While working at a construction site last year, Donald was hit in the head by a piece of wood. Although the accident left Donald unconscious for only a few minutes, it completely altered his life. Donald can still recall events that occurred prior to the injury, but once new thoughts leave his consciousness, they are lost.

Two experiences occurred today that are typical of Donald's memory problem. Donald and his wife were shopping when a man whom Donald had no recollection of ever meeting approached them with a friendly greeting, "Hello, Helen and Don." The man commented that it was a beautiful day to go shopping. He was looking for a sweater for his daughter's birthday but so far had had no luck finding the right one. Helen mentioned that the clothing store at the other end of the mall had nice sweaters, and the man said that he would try that store. After the man had walked away, Helen identified the "stranger" as a neighbor, Bill Jones, who had moved into a house down the block several months ago. Don became frustrated when Helen told him that he frequently talked with this neighbor. Helen, too, was frustrated; she often wished that Don would remember what she told him. She knew Don would ask her again about Bill Jones the next time they met.

When they arrived home, Don received a telegram from his aunt, informing him of his uncle's death. Don, immediately struck with an intense grief, cried for almost an hour over the loss of his favorite uncle. Yet, after being distracted by a phone call, Donald no longer remembered his uncle's death. Helen told him again, and he experienced the intense grief once more.

Donald suffers from a disorder called *anterograde amnesia*. His memory problems are the direct result of his accident, which caused an injury to an area of the brain called the dorsomedial thalamus. The dorsomedial thalamus is an area of the brain involved in the storage of recent experiences in a permanent, or relatively permanent, way. As the result of brain damage, Donald cannot store experiences that have occurred since the accident. To recall an event, three processes must take place. First, the experience must be stored as a memory. Second, the stored memory must be encoded or organized into a meaningful form. Third, the memory must be retrieved. This chapter describes the storage of experiences into memories; Chapter 11 explores the encoding of experiences, and Chapter 12 looks at retrieval of memory. Forgetting as a result of retrieval failure will be discussed in Chapter 12. Memory losses that result from storage failure are examined in this chapter. Also in this chapter we describe the physiological basis of memory storage.

A THREE-STAGE VIEW OF MEMORY STORAGE

Richard Atkinson and Richard Shiffrin (1971) suggested that there are three stages in the storage of information: sensory register, short-term store, and long-term store. As can be seen in Figure 10-1, external input (or external events) is initially stored in the *sensory register* for a very brief time, usually one-half to one second. The information contained in the sensory register is an initial impression of the

FIGURE 10-1   A diagram illustrating the Atkinson-Shiffrin three-stage model of memory storage. Initially, experiences are stored in the sensory register. The interpretation and organization of experiences are accomplished by the second stage of memory storage, or the short-term store. The final stage, or long-term store, represents the site of permanent (or almost permanent) memory storage. Adapted from Atkinson, R. C., & Shiffrin, R. M. (1968). Human memory: A proposed system and its control processes. In K. W. Spence & J. T. Spence (Eds.), *The psychology of learning and motivation* (Vol. 2). New York: Academic.

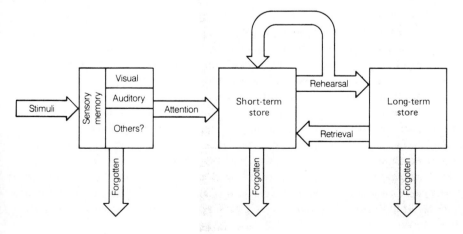

external environment; experiences stored in the sensory register are exact duplications of external stimuli. However, not all information in the external environment is stored in the sensory register. Information decays rapidly after leaving the sensory register and will be lost unless processed into the short-term store.

The *short-term store* is a temporary storage facility for our experiences. Memories can remain in the short-term store for 5, 10, 15 seconds, or even longer. The length of time that information remains in short-term store depends on two processes. First, experiences can be rehearsed or repeated. *Rehearsal* holds information in the short-term store. Without rehearsal, information can be lost from the short-term store before it is stored in a meaningful way. Rehearsal also serves to organize information in the short-term store. This organization makes an experience more meaningful, enhancing the likelihood that the memory will later be recalled. The longer that information in the short-term store is rehearsed, the more likely it is that the information will be remembered later. Second, only a limited amount of information can be retained in the short-term store. When new information enters the short-term store, old information will be "bumped out" unless the short-term store has enough room for both the old and the new information. Rehearsal of information in the short-term store can prevent new information from entering the short-term store; thus, rehearsal prevents information from being "bumped" from the short-term store, thereby increasing its chances of being remembered later.

Most information contained in the short-term store is transferred into the *long-term store,* the site of permanent memory storage. Although Atkinson and Shiffrin suggest that information can be lost from the long-term store because of slow decay, the issue of whether information is lost from the long-term store has not been settled. Most research indicates that all information in the long-term store remains there permanently; some research suggests that decay causes some memories to be lost.

Storage of a memory in the long-term store does not guarantee the ability to recall that particular memory. Two processes may hinder recall of information from the long-term store. First, the presence of other memories in the long-term store may prevent recollection of a particular experience; this failure to recall a specific memory because of the presence of other memories in long-term store is called *interference.* Second, according to Underwood (1983), failure to recall a memory from the long-term store may result from the absence of a specific stimulus that can retrieve the memory. People can use salient aspects of an event, called *memory attributes,* to remember the event. For example, a friend's visit may remind you of a past experience with this friend. Or, returning to a place you have not been for several years may cause you to remember something you did there years earlier. Your friend's presence or the place you revisited is the memory attribute enabling you to retrieve the earlier experiences. The absence of these environmental events can result in the failure to recall a memory from the long-term store. The identification of the salient aspects of an event for use as memory attributes occurs during the short-term storage phase of memory storage. The failure to identify a salient aspect of an experience for use as a memory attribute can prevent later recall of the experience.

The organization of experience can occur even after a memory is transferred to long-term store. The retrieval of a memory from the long-term store results in the return of the memory to the short-term store; returning the memory to the short-term store enables a person to be consciously aware of a previous experience. While the memory remains in the short-term store, it can receive additional processing. This processing may facilitate recall of the experience later. Processing can also alter the memory, making the memory more logical or appealing. Thus, memories that have received additional processing may not accurately reflect the actual experience.

One additional point needs to be made regarding the Atkinson-Shiffrin three-stage model of memory storage. This view is one of several ways of conceptualizing the processing of information. For example, Craik and Lockhart (1972) levels of processing view assumes that memories differ in the extent to which they have been processed rather than existing in different storage systems. These views are not necessarily antagonistic. Instead, they may be describing different aspects of the storage of our experiences. We describe the Atkinson-Shiffrin three-stage model in this chapter; alternative approaches will be discussed in Chapter 11.

THE METAPHOR OF MEMORY PROCESSES

Our discussion suggests that new experiences are stored and later recalled. However, the memory storage and recall processes are not entirely analogous to the storage and retrieval systems with which we are familiar. For example, we can store data on a computer disk or write data on an index card, but the brain does not store memory in a concrete location.

The metaphor of memory storage and retrieval (see Roediger, 1980) allows us to appreciate the characteristics of how experiences are stored as memories and later recalled from storage. However, this language should not reify the storage and retrieval processes. For example, we suggest that the short-term store acts to organize information, but the short-term store is merely a hypothetical construct, not an actual object. Although experiences are organized, we are not consciously aware of this organization nor do we understand how it is accomplished. With this idea in mind, let's next examine each stage of memory storage in greater detail.

SENSORY REGISTER

How are memories stored? Is an exact duplicate of the initial experience stored, or is a partial replica of an event stored? Several lines of evidence suggest that an exact copy of an experience is stored in the sensory register. However, the copy lasts for only a very short time (no more than one-half to one second).

Research on the characteristics of the sensory store has investigated two sensory systems: the visual system and the auditory system. The visual copy contained in the sensory store is referred to as an *icon,* and the copy is stored in *iconic memory. Echoic memory* contains a replica of an auditory experience, and the *echo* is stored in the sensory store.

Iconic Memory

In Search of an Icon   The classic research of George Sperling (1960, 1963) examined the storage of visual information in the sensory register; Sperling's findings also demonstrated that (1) an icon is an exact copy of a visual experience and (2) an iconic memory lasts for only a very brief time following the event. Sperling presented to subjects an array of letters arranged in three horizontal rows of four letters each (see Figure 10-2). An apparatus called a tachistoscope was used to present the letters on a screen for 0.05 second. The screen was then blank for a specified retention interval of 0 to 1 second. Some of Sperling's subjects received a *partial report technique;* they were asked at the end of the interval to recall all the letters in one of the three rows. The subjects were not informed before the end of the retention interval which line they were to recall. A tone presented at the end of the retention interval indicated which line should be recalled: A high pitch indicated the first row; a medium tone, the second row; and a low tone, the third row. Presenting the tone very soon after the presentation of the array of letters enabled the subjects to remember most of the letters. However, if the retention interval was greater than 0.25 second, the subjects' performance declined significantly, and they could remember only about one letter per line (refer to Figure 10-3). That retention is high on an immediate but not on a delayed retention test indicates that even though subjects have access to all information contained in the sensory store, the visual copy fades quickly following entry into the sensory register.

FIGURE 10-2   Sperling's procedure for investigating the visual sensory memory. This illustration shows one trial using the partial report technique. In this procedure, subjects see 12 letters for 1/20 second. A tone is presented at the appropriate time to indicate which row of letters the subjects should attempt to recall. A high-pitched tone means the top row; a medium-pitched tone, the middle row; and a low-pitched tone, the bottom row.

Phase 1	Phase 2	Phase 3
Experimenter presents array for $\frac{1}{20}$ second.	Tone signals which row subject is to recall	Suspect tries to recall correct row

X	G	O	B
T	M	L	R
V	A	S	F

High tone means recall top row.
Medium tone means recall middle row
Low tone means recall bottom row.

For example
high tone signals
subject to recall
X   G   O   B

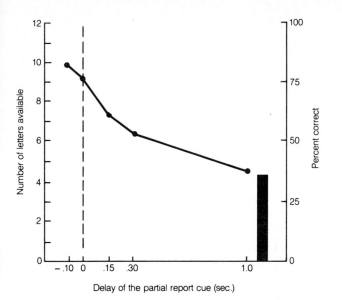

Delay of the partial report cue (sec.)

FIGURE 10-3   Performance level in Sperling's investigation of visual sensory memory. The solid line on the graph shows the number of letters recalled (left axis) and the percentage recalled (right axis) for subjects given the partial report technique as a function of the delay between signal and recall. The bar at the right presents the number and percentage correct for the whole report technique. As can be seen in the graph, a subject can report all of the letters immediately after the stimuli end; however, the recall of letters declines rapidly following stimuli presentation. From Sperling, G. (1960). The information available in brief visual presentations. *Psychological Monographs, 74,* whole no. 498. Copyright 1960 by the American Psychological Association. Reprinted by permission.

Sperling asked some of his subjects to recall as many of the 12 letters in the array as possible. When recall occurred immediately after stimulus presentation had ended, this procedure, referred to as a *whole report technique,* resulted in subjects' remembering only approximately 4.5 of the letters (see Figure 10-3). Sperling's observations with the partial report technique indicated that all 12 letters were encoded into the sensory store; why, then, could subjects receiving the whole report technique remember only about one-third of them? The answer is that since experiences stored in the sensory register decay rapidly, the image fades before the subjects can recall more than four or five of the letters.

Note that when the retention interval was longer than 0.25 second, subjects were able to recall approximately 4.5 of all the letters or 1.5 of the letters in a particular row. As we learned earlier in this chapter, only a limited amount of information can be transferred from the sensory register to short-term memory. The ability of Sperling's subjects to recall only 4.5 of all letters or 1.5 of the letters in a particular row after a 0.5- or 1-second delay suggests that only these

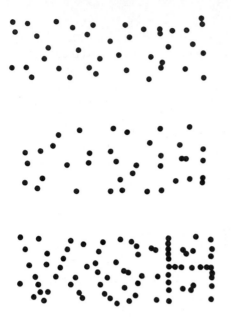

FIGURE 10-4
The stimuli used by Eriksen and Collins to study iconic memory. The top two stimuli were presented sequentially to subjects; if the two stimuli were not separated by more than 0.25 second, the subjects saw the nonsense syllable *VOH,* which is presented in the bottom panel. From Eriksen, C. W., & Collins, J. F. (1967). Some temporal characteristics of visual pattern perception. *Journal of Experimental Psychology, 74,* 476–484. Copyright 1967 by the American Psychological Association. Reprinted by permission.

letters were transferred from the sensory store to short-term memory and that decay caused the rest to be lost.

Our discussion indicates that a ''snapshot'' of a visual experience is encoded in the sensory information store. Sperling's results provide evidence that an exact visual image of an event is stored in the sensory register. Many other studies (refer to Wingfield & Byrnes, 1981) have also shown that the sensory register contains a ''mental'' picture of a visual experience and that for a brief period following the event, a person can recall any of the information stored in the sensory register. These studies have also demonstrated that the icon, or visual memory, decays rapidly from the sensory register; we next examine one of them.

Eriksen and Collins (1967) presented to subjects some stimuli separated by an interval varying from 0 to 1 second. As can be seen in Figure 10-4, each separate stimulus is meaningless; however, when the stimuli overlap, the letters *VOH* can be seen. According to Eriksen and Collins, if an exact copy of the one stimulus had been stored in the sensory register when the next stimulus was presented, the subjects would be able to detect the *VOH* letter pattern. Eriksen and Collins reported that their subjects accurately identified the letters when an interval of up to 0.25 second was inserted between the stimulus patterns, and they also found that the ability of the subjects to recognize the *VOH* letters declined to a level of no recognition when given a 1-second interval between successive stimulus presentations. Other studies have also observed that a combined image is experienced when separate stimulus events are presented close together; see Haber and Standing (1969) for another example.

The Duration of an Icon   Sperling's (1960) article suggests that visual images are stored in the sensory register for 0.25 second. However, depending on conditions, icons may persist for as much as a second or for less than 0.25 second. The intensity of the visual events appears to affect the duration of an icon. For example, Keele and Chase (1967) and Mackworth (1963) reported that iconic memory is longer when a bright rather than a dim display of letters is used. Similarly, if the preletter and postletter exposure displays are very bright, Averbach and Sperling (1961) observed that the icon may last less than 0.25 second, whereas the icon may persist for more than a second when the displays following a visual event are very dark. Apparently, an intense stimulus experience produces a long-duration iconic memory, and a strong second visual experience can reduce the duration of the visual image of the first stimulus.

The backward-masking literature (see Breitmeyer & Ganz, 1976) shows that a visual experience can be erased from the sensory register by presentation of a second stimulus. Thus, a second event may shorten the duration of the icon. The Averbach and Coriell study (1961) provides an excellent example of this backward-masking phenomenon. Averbach and Coriell showed their subjects an 8-by-2 array of letters for 0.05 second. The letters were followed by a white field for a duration ranging from 0 to 0.5 second. At the end of the retention interval, the subjects were instructed to recall a specific letter; the letter to be recalled was indicated by a marker. The marker was either a circle around the position the letter had occupied in the initial array or a bar over the position of the letter.

Averbach and Coriell reported that with the bar marker, retention was high immediately after the array of letters terminated, but declined to a recall of only 4 or 5 out of 16 letters when the retention interval was longer than 0.25 second (refer to Figure 10-5). However, the use of the circle marker substantially reduced recall of the letters for intermediate intervals (0.1 to 0.2 second). According to Breitmeyer and Ganz (1976), no masking occurs when the circle marker either (1) comes on immediately after the letters, integrating the marker into the visual image, or (2) comes on after 0.25 second, in which case the information has already been transferred to the short-term store. Only when the information is in the sensory register will the circle marker "mask" the letter by taking the letter's place in the visual image. In contrast, the bar is far enough away from the letter to act as a marker rather than a mask. Other masking studies (Averbach, 1963; Sperling, 1963) report that any patterned visual event (for example, a closely meshed grid) following the letters will erase the visual image of the letters from the sensory register.

The Nature of Iconic Memory   Our discussion indicates that for a brief time following a visual event, an exact copy of that experience is stored in the sensory register. Does visual information undergo any processing while in the sensory register? The evidence (see Howard, 1983) indicates that analysis of visual experiences occurs *after* the sensory register stage. Information from the sensory register can be recalled only in an unprocessed form. Subjects required to report

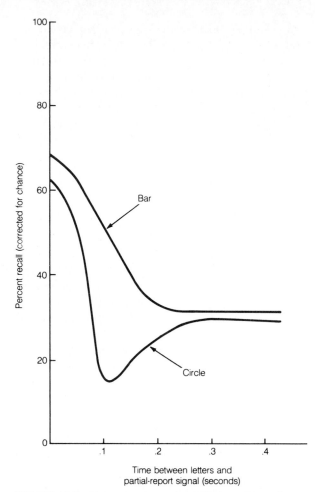

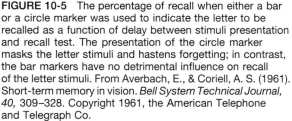

Time between letters and
partial-report signal (seconds)

FIGURE 10-5 The percentage of recall when either a bar or a circle marker was used to indicate the letter to be recalled as a function of delay between stimuli presentation and recall test. The presentation of the circle marker masks the letter stimuli and hastens forgetting; in contrast, the bar markers have no detrimental influence on recall of the letter stimuli. From Averbach, E., & Coriell, A. S. (1961). Short-term memory in vision. *Bell System Technical Journal, 40,* 309–328. Copyright 1961, the American Telephone and Telegraph Co.

organized visual experiences while the memory is stored in the sensory register are unable to do so. Thus, only unprocessed information is available to the subject while a memory is in the sensory register.

Coltheart, Lea, and Thompson (1974) modified Sperling's partial report technique to investigate the nature of iconic memory. They presented subjects on each trial with an array consisting of two rows of four letters each. Half the letters were red; the other half, black. Half the letters had a long *e* sound (*B, C, D, G, P,* and *T*); the other half, a short *e* sound (*F, L, M, S,* and *X*). Subjects were asked on each trial to report three kinds of information. On some trials, subjects were asked to report the top or bottom row of letters. On other trials, they were required to report all the black letters or all the red letters. Finally, on the remaining trials, subjects were instructed to report all the letters with the long sound or all the letters with the short sound.

The image that subjects were shown contained two types of information: the row and the color. To report these two types of information, subjects did not need to process any information; they simply needed to have the information in the sensory register. Coltheart and associates reported that subjects asked to report either one row of letters or all the letters of one color had high recall. The other type of information, the sound of the letter, was not contained in the visual image. Thus, the task of reporting the sound of the letters required the subjects to process information contained in the sensory register. The authors found that recall of the sounds was low. These observations demonstrate that information stored in the sensory register is not processed at this stage of memory storage.

Echoic Memory

In Search of an Echo The sensory register can also contain an exact duplication of an auditory experience. Neisser (1967) called the memory of an auditory experience in the sensory register *echoic memory,* or an ''echo'' of a recent event. Moray, Bates, and Barnett (1965) conducted an evaluation of echoic memory comparable to Sperling's study of iconic memory. Each subject sat alone in a room containing four high-fidelity loudspeakers placed far enough apart so that subjects could discriminate the sounds coming from each speaker. At various times during the study, a list of spoken letters was emitted from each loudspeaker. The list ranged from one to four letters, transmitted simultaneously from each loudspeaker. For example, at the same instant, loudspeaker 1 produced letter *e;* loudspeaker 2, letter *k;* loudspeaker 3, letter *g,* and loudspeaker 4, letter *t.*

For some trials, each subject was required to report as many letters as possible, a procedure analogous to Sperling's whole report technique. Moray et al. reported that subjects remembered only a small proportion of the letters presented from the four loudspeakers. On other trials, subjects were asked to recall the letters coming from only one of the four loudspeakers. This procedure, analogous to Sperling's partial report technique, resulted in subjects' recalling the letter on most of the trials.

Remember from the discussion of iconic memory the reason subjects did not recall all the visual information presented: An icon is only a brief, transient copy, and subjects forgot some information stored in the icon before they had a chance to transfer it to the short-term store. An echo is also stored for only a brief time, and some of the information decays before the subjects can recall it using the whole report technique.

Darwin, Turvey, and Crowder (1972) reported results that also show that an echo lasts a very short time. Their experiment was similar to the Moray et al. (1965) study, with two exceptions: First, subjects heard simultaneous lists of letters from three rather than four locations; second, after the termination of the list, the time delay before the subjects were required to recall the letters varied. Darwin and colleagues used four delay intervals: 0 second (immediately after the letters were presented) and 1, 2, or 4 seconds later. As seen in Figure 10-6, using the partial report technique, the level of recall declined as the interval between the auditory event and testing increased. Furthermore, using a 4-second retention interval, recall with the partial report technique was similar to recall with the whole report technique. These results point out that the copy of an auditory experience stored in echoic memory is only temporary. We learned in our discussion of iconic memory that the typical duration of an icon is approximately 0.25 second. Inspection of Figure 10-6 suggests that an echo lasts several seconds. Why does the representation of an auditory experience stored in sensory memory decay more slowly than the trace of a visual event?

The Duration of an Echo   Although you would anticipate that an echo would have the same duration as that of an icon, Wingfield and Byrnes (1981) suggest that the typical duration of an echo is 2 seconds. To examine why an auditory event is stored in the sensory register longer than a visual event, consider this example. Suppose you look at a chair. All the information needed to detect that the object is a chair is contained in the visual snapshot of the chair. Thus, salient physical characteristics of visual events can be detected by examining a single visual image of an event from a particular moment. However, suppose that someone says ''chair'' to you. Five separate sounds, or phonemes, are contained in the word *chair* (see Chapter 9 for a discussion of phonemes). To detect that the word is *chair,* you must combine the five sounds into one word. Although this combining of sounds into a word takes place in the short-term store, the detection of each of the phonemes occurs in the sensory register.

The duration of an echo must be longer than that of an icon, since the average duration of a spoken syllable is between 0.2 and 0.3 second. Thus, unless the memory of an auditory syllable lasts for longer than 0.3 second, the memory of the beginning of the syllable would be lost before the speaker is able to finish the syllable. Furthermore, the recognition of a particular phoneme is ''context dependent''; that is, the way an individual sound will be perceived depends on the nature of the sounds preceding or following it. Illustrating this process, Liberman, Delattre, and Cooper (1952) presented subjects with a very brief, 15-second burst of noise followed by one of several different vowel sounds. Subjects heard the burst of noise as a /p/ if it preceded the vowel /i/ but heard the sound of /k/ if the burst occurred prior to the vowel /a/. Thus, the echo of a sound must continue after the sound ends so that sound can be detected.

Backward masking has also been observed with auditory events. Elliot's (1967) study represents one example of backward masking using auditory stimuli. Presenting a very brief 10-millisecond tone followed at various intervals by a

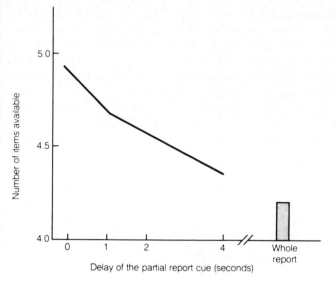

FIGURE 10-6 Performance level in Darwin, Turvey, and Crowder's study of the auditory sensory system. The graph presents the number of items available as a function of the delay between signal offset and recall test. The bar at the right shows performance with the whole report technique. The results of this study show rapid forgetting of auditory stimuli stored in the sensory register. From Darwin, C. T., Turvey, M. T., & Crowder, R. G. (1972). An auditory analogue of the Sperling partial report procedure: Evidence for brief auditory storage. *Cognitive Psychology, 3,* 255–267.

100-millisecond noise burst, Elliot found that if the noise burst occurred in any time less than 100 milliseconds after the tone, the subjects reported that they did not hear the tone. However, if the noise occurred 100 milliseconds (0.1 second) or more after the tone, the subjects did hear the tone. This observation suggests that the duration of an echo is 0.1 second, a result that is inconsistent with the earlier statement that the duration of the echo is 2 seconds. Yet, other studies (see Efron, 1970) have reported results similar to Elliot's.

Turvey (1978) suggested an explanation for the results of these backward-masking studies. Turvey found that with a simple stimulus, such as a tone, only a very short time is needed to detect the tone. Once detected, the information is transferred to the short-term store. However, with a more complex auditory event, such as the detection of phonemes, a longer echo is needed for detection. Thus, the backward-masking studies reflect the shorter duration of an echo required for detection of a simple auditory event. Yet, echoes can and typically do last much longer than 0.1 second for the detection of complex auditory information.

Crowder and Morton (1969) used a serial learning procedure to estimate the duration of echoic memory. (A serial learning procedure is used to demonstrate the serial position effect. In the typical serial learning study, subjects are presented a list of items to learn. Each subject's task is to learn the items in the exact order in which they are presented. Experiments in serial learning demonstrate consistently that subjects do not learn each item on the list at the same rate. Instead, they learn items at the beginning and at the end of the list more readily than items in the middle of the list. This difference in the rate of learning of serial lists is called the *serial position effect.* Many studies have reported the serial position effect; see Hall [1982] for a review of this literature.) Crowder and Morton presented to subjects several lists of random digits; each list contained seven digits presented at a rate of 100 milliseconds per digit. After finishing each list, a brief 400-millisecond delay was followed by subjects' recalling as many of the seven digits as possible. Although all the digits were presented visually, some subjects were told to look at the digits and remain silent until the time for recall. Other subjects were instructed to say the name of each digit aloud when it was presented. As can be seen in Figure 10-7, although the rate of recall did not differ for items early in the list using either the visual (silent) or auditory (aloud) presentations, the retention of the last few digits was greater with auditory than with visual presentation.

One explanation for this difference is that iconic and echoic memory have different durations. According to Crowder and Morton, with visual presentation, subjects have poor recall of the last items on the list because the visual trace of these digits has faded before the end of the 400-millisecond retention interval. In contrast, recall of the last digits is higher with the auditory presentation because the echo of the last few digits remains through the 400-millisecond delay. If it is assumed that several hundred milliseconds are required to present the last few items of the list and 400 milliseconds intervene between the last digit and recall, the duration of echoic memory is close to the 2-second estimate suggested by Darwin et al. (1972).

The Nature of Echoic Memory   Recall from earlier in the chapter that an icon is an unprocessed sensory impression of a visual experience. Similarly, an echo is an exact copy of an auditory experience, and the organization and interpretation of this auditory event occurs in the short-term memory stage. Support for this view of the nature of echoic memory is provided by the selective listening studies described in Chapter 7. Recall that subjects in these tasks are presented two different messages. The subject is required to repeat, or shadow, the information presented in one message. As we discovered, nonshadowed information is detected by the sensory system; that is, the auditory experience presented over the nonattended channel is stored in the sensory register. However, unless this information is significant, it is not transferred to the short-term store and, therefore, cannot be recalled.

What types of information presented through the nonattended channel are detected? We learned that subjects can detect physical changes; for example, subjects will notice a change in the pitch of the message, such as when the speaker is switched from a male to a female. However, subjects are unable to detect a difference in meaning over the unattended channel; for example, subjects will not

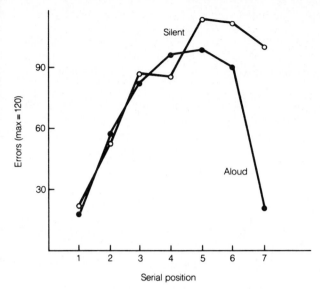

FIGURE 10-7   The number of errors as a function of the serial position of the letters for subjects who received either silent or aloud presentation of stimuli. The recall of the letters at the end of the list was significantly higher when the letters were read silently rather than aloud. From Crowder, R. G., & Morton, J. (1969). Precategorical acoustic storage (PAS). *Perception and Psychophysics, 5,* 365–373.

notice a change if the language of the unattended message is shifted from English to German (or vice versa). This indicates that a person can detect physical changes in auditory experiences stored in sensory register. However, subjects are unable to detect a difference in meaning over the unattended channel.

Section Review

The sensory register of memory formation is the first stage of the storage of an event. An exact copy of the external stimuli is stored in the sensory register. The visual copy contained in the sensory store is referred to as an icon and is stored in the iconic memory. Echoic memory contains an exact replica of an auditory experience, and an echo is stored in the sensory store.

Data are stored in the sensory register for only a very short time; icons usually last about 0.25 second, and echoes approximately 2 seconds. Echoes last longer than icons because, although a visual experience conveys all the information needed to detect the salient characteristics, recognition of an auditory event requires that individual sounds be retained in the sensory store until the whole event is detected. Information in the sensory register decays rapidly and is lost unless transferred to the short-term store.

SHORT-TERM STORE

Information stored in the sensory register is transferred to short-term store, where it is retained for a brief time before being permanently (or nearly permanently) stored in long-term store. The duration of a memory in the short-term store typically is 15 to 20 seconds.

Although experiences are transferred from short-term to long-term store, short-term memory is not merely a temporary holding facility for a memory between the sensory register and the long-term store. Instead, experiences in the short-term store are interpreted for their meaning and organized in logical ways.

Several psychologists (Feigenbaum, 1970; Greeno, 1974) have referred to short-term store as the "working memory," a phrase suggesting a dynamic memory process that is the central characteristic of the short-term store. The interpretation and organization of experiences involves not only the physical representation of an event from the sensory register but also the use of prior information stored in long-term memory. The use of information from long-term store allows people to analyze and organize new experiences as well as to reinterpret previous events.

We have identified two major characteristics of the short-term store: It has a brief storage span and its function is to organize and analyze information. The short-term store has three additional characteristics: its storage capacity is limited—only a small amount of information can be maintained there; memories contained in the short-term store are easily disrupted by new experiences; and the short-term store has a rehearsal function; that is, the short-term store can rehearse or replay memories of prior experiences. The impact of rehearsal is to enhance the recall of a prior event: The more an event is rehearsed in the short-term store, the more likely the information can be recalled later.

Why does rehearsal increase the likelihood of recall of an event? One likely explanation is that rehearsal allows an experience to remain in the short-term store and therefore increases the chances that the event will be transferred to the long-term store. Another explanation is that rehearsal allows for greater analysis and interpretation of experiences; the enhanced organization facilitates recall once the memory has been transferred to the long-term store. We next examine three characteristics of the short-term store—the span of the short-term memory, the limited storage capacity, and the susceptibility of the short-term store. The organization and rehearsal of memories will be discussed in the next chapter.

The Span of Short-Term Memory

Say the nonsense syllable *txz,* then start counting backward by threes, beginning with the number 632 and continuing with 629, 626, 623, 620, 617, 614, 611, 608, 605, 602, 599, 596, 593, 590, 587, 584, 581, 578, and 575. Do you remember the nonsense syllable? In all likelihood, you do not. The nonsense syllable was detected by the sensory receptors, and the memory of the nonsense syllable was registered in the sensory register and entered into the short-term store. Yet, the

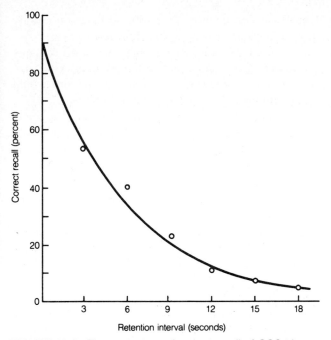

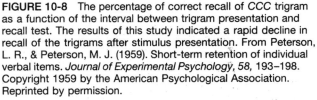

FIGURE 10-8 The percentage of correct recall of *CCC* trigram as a function of the interval between trigram presentation and recall test. The results of this study indicated a rapid decline in recall of the trigrams after stimulus presentation. From Peterson, L. R., & Peterson, M. J. (1959). Short-term retention of individual verbal items. *Journal of Experimental Psychology, 58,* 193–198. Copyright 1959 by the American Psychological Association. Reprinted by permission.

memory of the nonsense syllable was lost as the result of the backward-counting task. Because this task required only approximately 20 seconds to complete, it appears that the memory of the nonsense syllable is rapidly forgotten after leaving the short-term store.

The preceding example was modeled after the classic Peterson and Peterson (1959) study. In this study, subjects were presented a number of three-consonant trigrams, and after saying the three letters of each trigram, the subjects were given a number and required to start counting backward by threes. The numbers used were different following each trigram. The subjects were given a signal to designate when to stop counting backward and to recall the trigram; the signal was presented at different retention intervals varying from 3 to 18 seconds. Figure 10-8 presents the level of recall of a trigram as a function of the interval between presentation of a trigram and testing. As can be seen from the figure, recall of a nonsense syllable declines rapidly: The likelihood that a subject can remember the trigram is 80 percent with a 3-second interval, compared with only about an

18 percent rate of recall with an 18-second interval. Peterson and Peterson's study illustrates the brief retention of an item after leaving the short-term store.

The brief retention span of a short-term memory has adaptive significance— it allows us to quickly shift attention from one event to the next. As Gleitman (1987) points out, imagine how difficult a long-distance telephone operator would find remembering one telephone number while dialing another.

Limited Storage Capacity

Repeat the following list of nonsense trigrams:

SYX	GXL
TRZ	QNW
BGC	RDH
KDM	HCX
NFQ	FZJ
PHY	YPC
JBD	GBX
LCN	CQT
OTS	DZP

Now repeat as many of the nonsense syllables as you can remember. If your memory is like that of most college students, you will be able to remember four or five or even six or seven of the nonsense syllables. Your inability to recall all or most of the nonsense syllables reflects the limited storage capacity of the short-term store.

In 1956, George Miller published a classic paper entitled ''The Magical Number Seven, Plus or Minus Two: Some Limits on Our Capacity for Processing Information.'' Miller presented evidence that people can hold approximately five to nine items at a time in short-term store. An item may be a single letter or number; an item can also be a word or an idea. Miller referred to a meaningful item as a *chunk* of information. Information is ''chunked'' in the short-term store; for example, three letters are chunked into a word. *Chunking,* an organizational function of the short-term store, increases memory capacity from 7 separate letters to 21 letters existing as seven 3-letter words.

A number of studies suggest that the capacity of the short-term store is seven plus or minus two items of information. For example, Pollack (1952) and Garner (1953) reported that people can easily label two to four tones (or levels of loudness) but have difficulty when asked to make five or more judgments. Similarly, Kaufman and associates (1949) reported that subjects could accurately estimate the number of dots when six or fewer dots were presented on a screen for 0.2 second; however, subjects could only guess when more than six dots appeared in the pattern. Furthermore, Hayes (1952) and Pollack (1953) found that listeners recalled only six or seven items from a list of words, letters, or digits that had been read at a fast and constant rate. Based on this and other information, Miller (1956) concluded that a seven ± 2 item limit exists for the amount of information that can be contained in the short-term store.

However, Watkins (1974) demonstrated that the true capacity of the short-term store may be only three to four chunks. According to Watkins, although the capacity of the short-term store appears to be seven plus or minus two units or chunks, some recall actually reflects information stored in the long-term store; that is, Watkins argued that information presented early in an experience has already been permanently stored. Thus, the capacity of the short-term store is actually three to four chunks. Evidence to support this view will be presented in the next chapter.

Disrupting a Short-term Memory

Consider the following series of events to illustrate how easily a memory contained in the short-term store can be disrupted: After locating a number in the telephone book, you begin dialing; then your roommate says something to you, and you stop dialing to respond. After responding, you begin to dial the number again but cannot remember it.

Evidence of the disruption of short-term memory can be seen in the memory-span studies discussed earlier. Recall that Peterson and Peterson (1959) found that subjects asked to count backward after the presentation of a trigram were unable to recall the trigram just 18 seconds after it had been presented. Numbers had replaced the trigram in the short-term store, and subjects were unable to recall the trigram. Memories in the short-term store are easily disrupted because the storage capacity of this store is so limited. As the capacity is reached, new memories automatically replace older ones. And, unless stored in a meaningful way, the events will be lost forever. Thus, you forget a telephone number when someone distracts you because a telephone number contains seven units of information (seven numbers). The memory of the number is displaced by your roommate's words. You must look up the number again because it has not been stored in a retrievable way in the long-term store.

How can the easy disruption and limited storage capacity of the short-term store be overcome? The short-term store has a natural organizational ability that condenses the amount of information contained in a message, and thus allows the short-term store to retain more total information. Under most conditions, this organization allows the memory of an event to be stored in a meaningful way in the long-term store. Chapter 11 looks more closely at the organizational function of the short-term store.

Short-Term Memory in Animals

Do animals have a short-term store that is comparable to humans' short-term store? The evidence does suggest that animals have a short-term store with qualities comparable to those seen in humans. Researchers have used a number of techniques to study short-term memory in animals. One important method involves using a delayed matching-to-sample procedure. In this task, a subject is presented with a specific sample stimulus. After a retention interval, the subject receives several test stimuli one of which is the sample stimulus. The animal is reinforced for selecting the correct test stimuli. Figure 10-9 shows a representative delayed matching-to-sample task for a pigeon. The pigeon was initially shown a red sample stimulus for 5 seconds on the middle key. After a certain interval, the pigeon was presented two-choice test stimuli: a red key on the left and a green key on the right. Pecking at the red key produced reinforcement, but nonreinforcement followed pecking at the green key. A considerable number of studies with both pigeons (Grant, 1981; Roitblat, 1980) and monkeys (D'Amato, 1973) indicate that the longer the interval between termination of the sample and presentation of the test stimuli, the poorer the performance during testing.

Grant's (1976) study illustrates the rapid forgetting that occurs following the termination of the sample stimulus. Grant used pigeons as subjects and presented two test stimuli 0, 20, 40, or 60 seconds after the sample stimulus. As can be seen in Figure 10-10, the level of performance declined with longer retention intervals. These results indicate that a minute interval between the sample stimulus and test stimuli caused the pigeons to forget the sample stimulus.

FIGURE 10-9 A representative delayed matching-to-sample task in pigeons. The pigeon first sees the sample stimulus. After various intervals, the sample stimulus and another stimulus are presented. A response to the sample stimulus yields reinforcement; in contrast, a responding to the other stimulus results in no reinforcement. Reproduced from *The psychology of learning and behavior* (3d ed.) by Barry Schwartz, by permission of W. W. Norton & Company, Inc. Copyright 1989, 1984, 1978 by W. W. Norton & Company, Inc.

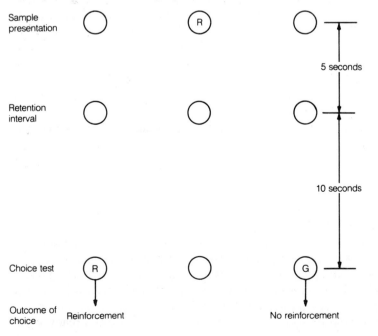

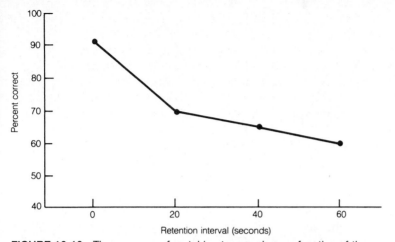

FIGURE 10-10 The accuracy of matching to sample as a function of the interval between the sample stimulus and the test stimuli. The results show that responding to the sample stimulus, or recall of the prior stimulus, declined rapidly after the sample stimulus ended. From Grant, D. S. (1976). Effect of sample presentation time on long-delay matching in the pigeon. *Learning and Motivation, 7,* 580–590.

What is the value of the short-term store in animals? One benefit is as an aid to an animal in searching for food. How can it locate food in its environment? In addition to knowing specific instrumental activities that will successfully obtain food, the animal must also know where food is located. As we discovered in Chapter 8, Tolman suggested that animals develop cognitive maps of the environment and use this spatial knowledge to guide them to reward. As an animal explores its environment, it will encounter places where reward is not located. To effectively interact with its environment, the animal must remember what places do not contain reward and avoid returning to those places. The animal must also remember where reward is located and then return to those places. The research of a number of psychologists (Gould, 1982; Menzel, 1978; O'Keefe & Nadel, 1978; Olton, 1979; Shettleworth & Krebs, 1982) indicates that animals can use their cognitive maps to remember where they previously have or have not found reward.

Olton and associates (Olton, 1978, 1979; Olton, Collison, & Werz, 1977; Olton & Samuelson, 1976) constructed an eight-arm radial maze (see Figure 10-11) to investigate whether an animal has a "spatial memory," or a cognitive map, which it can use to remember where it did or did not find food. Unlike the typical maze-learning study in which food is placed in only one arm of a maze, Olton placed food in each of the eight arms. The rat's task is to remember which arm it went to on the last trial and to not go to that arm again (because there is no longer any food, returning to that arm will result in no food on that trial). The animal must use its spatial memory to go to an arm to which it has not already gone.

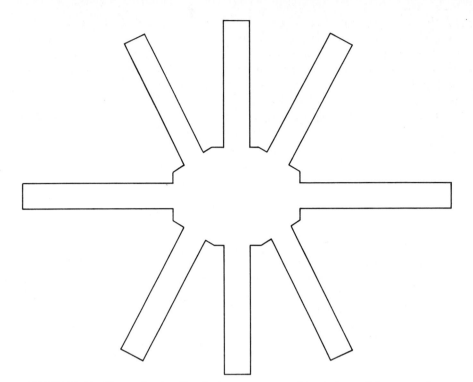

FIGURE 10-11 Figure showing the eight-arm maze used to study spatial memory. In studies of spatial memory with this maze, Olton and associates placed food in each arm of the maze and required rats to learn to visit each arm of the maze without returning to a previously visited arm to obtain food. From Olton, D. C., & Samuelson, R. J. (1976). Remembrance of places passed: Spatial memory in rats. *Journal of Experimental Psychology: Animal Behavior Processes, 2,* 96–116. Copyright 1976 by the American Psychological Association. Reprinted by permission.

Obviously, the task becomes more difficult when only one or two arms containing food are left. Once an animal has successfully gone to each arm, food will again be placed in each arm, and the entire process is repeated. Olton reported that animals readily learned how to obtain food on every trial. He found that usually by 20 trials, the rats rarely returned to an arm that they had already visited until food was returned to all the arms.

How does the rat learn to find food in the eight-arm maze? Olton observed that the rats do not learn to respond to the eight arms in a specific manner; instead, the pattern of response is seemingly random. Also, odor cues do not seem to guide the rat to reward; Olton reported that placing strong-smelling after-shave lotion in the maze after each trial to prevent the use of odor cues did not impair the rat's performance. Apparently, the rats used the cues contained in their spatial memory to guide their performance. Olton found that rotating the maze so that accurate information was no longer provided by spatial cues caused a deterioration of the rat's performance. These observations suggest that the rat learns to get food on each trial by developing a cognitive map of the maze and uses its spatial short-term memory to keep track of where it has and has not been since the beginning of the trial. The efficient use of spatial memory is not limited to rats; it has been observed in other species including birds (Shettleworth, 1983; Shettleworth & Krebs, 1982) and primates (Menzel, 1978).

Recall our discussion of the characteristics of the short-term store. We learned that the short-term store has a limited storage capacity and lasts for a brief period of time. The short-term store in animals appears to have a larger storage capacity than is seen in humans. Olton and colleagues (1977) found that rats do almost as well remembering where food was previously located in a 15-arm radial maze as in an 8-arm radial maze. This observation indicates that at least 15 units of information can be recalled by the rat's short-term memory. The duration of the short-term store also is longer in animals than humans. Beatty and Shavalia (1980) allowed rats to visit four arms of an eight-arm radial maze. The animals were then removed from the maze and returned to the maze from a few minutes to 24 hours later. Beatty and Shavalia reported that the rats would go to the four arms that they previously had not visited if they were returned to the maze within 4 hours. This result suggests that the duration of an animal's short-term store can last for up to 4 hours. Why is the short-term memory capacity greater and duration longer in animals than in humans? An answer to this question can be found in Chapter 12.

Section Review

The short-term store serves as a temporary storage facility, and people are consciously aware of information stored there. Information remains in the short-term store for approximately 15 to 20 seconds, and during this time memory is interpreted and organized to produce a more meaningful experience.

The short-term store has limited storage capacity, only three or four units of information can be retained at one time. One effect of the interpretation and organization of memories is to overcome this limited storage capacity. Memories contained in the short-term store are easily disrupted and replaced by new information. The short-term store can rehearse or replay prior experiences, and this rehearsal functions to retain information in the short-term store for a longer period. This increased rehearsal enhances interpretation and organization of the memory, improving the likelihood that the memory will later be available for recall.

LONG-TERM STORE

Memories are permanently (or relatively permanently) encoded in the long-term store. Let's now explore two aspects of the long-term storage of experiences. First, we examine evidence that there are several different types of long-term memories. Second, we discuss the physiological processes governing the long-

TABLE 10-1
CHARACTERISTICS OF EPISODIC AND SEMANTIC MEMORY

Diagnostic feature	Episodic	Semantic
Information		
Source	Sensation	Comprehension
Units	Events; episodes	Fact; ideas; concepts
Organization	Temporal	Conceptual
Reference	Self	Universe
Veridicality	Personal belief	Social agreement
Operations		
Registration	Experiential	Symbolic
Temporal coding	Present; direct	Absent; indirect
Affect	More important	Less important
Inferential capability	Limited	Rich
Context dependency	More pronounced	Less pronounced
Vulnerability	Great	Small
Access	Deliberate	Automatic
Retrieval queries	Time? Place?	What?
Retrieval consequences	Change system	System unchanged
Retrieval mechanisms	Synergy	Unfolding
Recollective experience	Remembered past	Actualized knowledge
Retrieval report	Remember	Know
Developmental sequence	Late	Early
Childhood amnesia	Affected	Unaffected

Source: Tulving, E. (1983). *Elements of episodic memory;* Clarendon Press/Oxford University Press.

term storage of an event, as well as the psychological and physiological circumstances that can result in the failure to store an experience. A memory may be permanently stored yet still not be recalled; the processes that result in the failure to recall a prior event are described in Chapter 12.

Episodic versus Semantic Memories

Endel Tulving (1972, 1983) suggested that there are two types of long-term memories: episodic and semantic. An *episodic memory* consists of information about temporally related events, whereas a *semantic memory* contains knowledge necessary for the use of language. Thus, an episodic memory may be of an event that you experienced at a particular time and place; a semantic memory includes information about words and other symbols, their meaning and referents, relations among the words and symbols, and the rules, formulas, or algorithms for the development of concepts or solutions to problems. Tulving emphasizes that the difference between episodic and semantic memory is greater than just the different types of information stored in each memory. Tulving argues that the episodic memory system is functionally distinct from the semantic memory system. Table 10-1 presents a list of the informational and operational differences between the episodic and semantic memory. The interested reader should refer to Tulving's 1983 book *Elements of Episodic Memory* for a detailed discussion of episodic and semantic memory.

Types of Information   The types of information stored in the episodic and semantic memory systems differ. Episodic memory contains recollections of a specific event that occurred in the past. In contrast, no single unit of information is stored in the semantic memory system. Instead, information contained in the semantic memory consists of facts, ideas, concepts, rules, propositions, schemata, and scripts that define a culture's knowledge of the world. Information contained in the episodic memory system is organized temporally; that is, one event precedes, occurs at the same time, or follows another event. In contrast, knowledge contained in the semantic memory system is organized conceptually. The source of episodic memory is sensory stimulation; comprehension of cultural knowledge is the source of semantic memory.

Separate Operations   The processes involved in the storage and retrieval of episodic and semantic memories also differ. According to Tulving, the episodic memory system registers immediate sensory experiences, whereas the semantic memory system records knowledge conveyed by language. The temporal order of events can be detected by the episodic memory system; problems of temporal order can be solved only by inference in the semantic memory system. Tulving reports that the episodic memory system has limited inferential capacity; that is, information stored in the episodic memory is based mainly on direct sensory impressions. In contrast, the semantic memory system has a rich inferential capacity and can discover the rules of a language merely from experience with that language.

Tulving has found that the recollection of memories from the episodic system is deliberate and often requires conscious effort, whereas recall of information contained in the semantic system is automatic and can therefore occur without conscious knowledge. Although we can be aware of knowledge contained in both memory systems, we interpret episodic memories as part of our personal past and semantic memories as part of the impersonal present. Thus, we use the term *remember* when referring to episodic memories and the term *know* to describe semantic memories. According to Tulving, when information is retrieved from episodic memory, it is often changed, but memories recalled from the semantic memory are not altered. Thus, the episodic memory system is much more vulnerable to distortion than are memories contained in the semantic system.

Two Functionally Different Memory Systems?   Tulving (1983) detailed the results of many experiments documenting the existence of separate episodic and semantic memory systems. Let's briefly examine one study supporting the distinction between episodic and semantic memory.

A study by Wood and associates (1980) provides compelling evidence in support of separate episodic and semantic memory systems. These researchers compared the regional cerebral blood flow of two groups of subjects; one group was involved in a semantic memory task, the other in an episodic memory task. The authors observed differences in regional cerebral blood flow of the two groups and suggested that their results indicate "an anatomical basis for the distinction between episodic and semantic memory."

A number of psychologists (Craik, 1979; Kintsch, 1980; Naus & Halasz, 1979) disagree with the idea that episodic and semantic memory systems represent two separate memory systems. Instead, they suggest that there is a single memory system and that the content of a memory in this system varies from highly context-specific episodes to abstract generalizations. Tulving (1983) asserts that the dissociation studies provide convincing evidence that there are in fact two separate memory systems. However, Tulving does recognize that the episodic and semantic memory systems are highly interdependent. Thus, an event takes on more meaning if semantic as well as episodic knowledge is involved in the storing of that experience. Yet, Tulving believes that these two memory systems can also operate independently. For example, a person can store information about a particular temporal event that is both novel and meaningless, a result which can occur only if the episodic memory system is independent of the semantic memory system.

Procedural versus Declarative Memories

I have not been on a bicycle in several years. Yet, I would certainly remember how to ride a bicycle. As a child, I had many experiences riding bicycles. The storage of these past experiences of riding bicycles would allow me to ride a bicycle today. My storage of memories of bicycle riding is an example of a procedural memory.

According to Squire (1986), *procedural memory* is skill memory. Procedural memories are not accessible to conscious awareness; instead, evidence of a procedural memory can be gained only through observations of performance. These memories represent knowledge of how to do things like tie shoelaces or play the piano which are stored as a result of instrumental conditioning experiences. Procedural memories also can represent emotional reactions to environmental events such as becoming hungry when arriving at the movie theater or fearful before driving over a high bridge. These emotional reactions are stored as a result of Pavlovian conditioning.

Procedural memories are acquired slowly through repeated experience. The extensive practice required to learn how to play the piano is one example of the importance of repeated experience for the storage of procedural memories. Evidence of the existence of a procedural memory lies in how well or poorly the animal or person responds. For example, the intensity of a person's fear when driving over a high bridge indicates the strength of the person's procedural memory. Similarly, the quality of piano playing documents the strength of this procedural memory.

Your favorite television show is on at 8:30 p.m. on Tuesday. Remembering the day and time that your favorite television show airs is an example of *declar-*

ative memory. Squire refers to declarative memory as factual memory. The time and day of the television show is a fact, and you stored this information as a declarative memory. Other examples of declarative memory include remembering the route to school or recognizing a familiar face.

We are consciously aware of declarative memories. According to Squire, a declarative memory can exist as a verbal thought or a nonverbal image. Thus, you are verbally aware of when your favorite television show can be seen, whereas knowledge of the route to school can exist as a nonverbal image. A declarative memory can be formed in a single experience; however, practice can enhance the ability to recall a declarative memory.

Recall our discussion of the interdependence of episodic and semantic memories. A similar interdependence exists for procedural and declarative memory. For example, tying a shoe can be a declarative memory; that is, you can have knowledge of how a shoe is tied, which is a declarative memory. Yet, tying one's shoe also exists as a procedural memory. Similarly, repeated practice can transform the conscious knowledge (or declarative memory) of the route to school into an unconscious habit (or procedural memory).

The Memory Consolidation Process

Donald Hebb (1949) proposed that the memory of an event is not immediately stored in a permanent form but instead is initially stored in a fragile form. According to Hebb, experiencing an event activates a neural circuit in the central nervous system. The activity in this neural circuit "reverberates," or lasts for a short time following the termination of the event. Hebb suggested that one function of the reverberatory activity is to act as a temporary store and retain a record of an event until it can be consolidated into a permanent representation of the event.

In Hebb's view, physiological changes in the central nervous system occur following an event and represent the permanent record of the event. Because these physiological changes occur slowly, the reverberating activity must be maintained until the storage process is completed. If reverberatory activity is disrupted, the consolidation process stops, and no further physiological changes take place.

The strength of a memory depends on the amount of time that the memory had to consolidate. Disruption of reverberating activity early in the consolidation process leads to a weak or nonexistent permanent memory of an event, and thus to an inability to recall the event. However, disruption late in the consolidation process usually has little impact: The permanent physiological changes have almost been completed, the permanent memory is strong, and recall of the event is probable.

Next we discuss evidence that reverberatory neural activity (1) follows an event, (2) is essential for the storage of a memory into permanent form, and (3) is followed by permanent physiological changes representing the permanent record of an event. We can only briefly examine the physiological basis of memory;

for a more detailed discussion of this topic, see Rosenzweig and Bennett (1976) or Thompson, Hicks, and Shvyrok (1980).

Do Reverberatory Circuits Exist? Considerable evidence supports Hebb's (1949) idea that following an event, activity reverberates in a neural circuit. This neural activity continues sequentially through the circuit, and the activity is sustained for a short time following the event. Attempting to document the existence of a reverberating circuit, Burns (1958) first isolated a section of cortical tissue by undercutting a section of the cortex so that the section was no longer neurally connected to other parts of the brain. Next, he electrically stimulated part of the neural tissue and observed bursts of activity. This electrical activity continued following termination of the stimulation. Depending on the intensity of the electrical stimulation, the continued neural activity lasted up to 30 minutes. Although reverberation seems to be the most reasonable explanation for the sustained neural activity following an event, Burns provided more direct evidence of reverberation. He reasoned that if all the neurons in the circuit were stimulated simultaneously, then the sustained activity would stop when all the neurons were in the refractory period. To test this hypothesis, Burns applied a single intense shock to the middle of the cortical tissue. He noted an initial activity in the entire neural tissue followed by a cessation of neural activity. Apparently, for the continued neural activity to continue after an event, it must reverberate only through a specific neural circuit.

Other studies (Verzeano, Laufer, Spear, & McDonald, 1970; Verzeano, & Negishi, 1960) also demonstrate reverberatory activity in neural tissue. In these studies, electrodes were implanted close together (30 to 200 micrometers apart) and arranged in a row to record electrical activity in adjacent neurons. Results show that brain stimulation produced a wave of neural activity which began with the stimulated neurons and continued sequentially in adjacent neurons. Furthermore, the activity occurred in recurrent waves of excitation from one neuron to another. These observations suggest that recirculating or reverberating activity is initiated by stimulation. Verzeano and associates also observed that the pattern of neural activity varied as a function of the stimulus presented, implying that different reverberatory circuits are activated by different events. It seems reasonable to assume that the activation of different neural circuits by various events accounts for the differentiation of memories.

Is Reverberatory Activity Essential for Memory Storage? Hebb's (1949) theory proposes not only that activity reverberates in a neural circuit after an event but also that consolidation requires this reverberation. If the encoding of an event in the long-term store requires reverberatory activity, disruption of activity in the neural circuit early in the consolidation of a memory should prevent encoding of the event as a memory. Duncan's (1949) study provided evidence supporting the critical role of reverberating activity in memory consolidation.

Duncan (1949) trained rats to avoid electric shock in the shuttle box. A light serving as the conditioned stimulus was presented 10 seconds prior to the shock.

Each animal received one trial per day for 18 days. After each training trial, the rats in eight experimental groups received an electroconvulsive shock (ECS). The time lapse between the end of the training trial and the ECS varied from 20 seconds to 14 hours. A control group of rats did not receive the ECS. Because electroconvulsive shock produces intense activity in many neurons, Duncan hypothesized that synchronized reverberating activity would be disrupted, and that this in turn would disrupt memory consolidation. Duncan further hypothesized that the shorter the interval between the training trial and the ECS, the less of the memory that would be stored and the lower the recall of the experience. As he predicted, Duncan reported that the longer the interval between training trial and ECS, the higher the level of memory recall as indicated by avoidance performance (see Figure 10-12). The reduced memory following ECS treatment is called *retrograde amnesia,* and it is assumed to result from the disruption of memory consolidation caused by the ECS-induced termination of reverberating activity. Note that Duncan's study showed that consolidation occurred slowly. Avoidance performance was impaired even when several hours passed between training and ECS.

Following Duncan's initial observations, a number of studies (Leukel, 1957; Ransmeier, 1953; Thompson & Dean, 1955) reported that ECS produced deficits in the retention of a response. The studies also showed that when ECS immediately follows an event, a retention test shows no recall of that event. Furthermore, the effects of ECS on retention were observed in a variety of tasks: Leukel (1957) and Ransmeier (1953) used a maze-learning situation, and Thompson and Dean (1955) employed a visual discrimination task. Retrograde amnesia with ECS has also been reported in human subjects (Cronholm & Molander, 1958; Flesher, 1941; Williams, 1950; Zubin & Barrera, 1941).

However, these early studies contain methodological problems. Subjects were exposed to a series of ECSs, and because electroconvulsive shocks are an adversive event, using multiple ECS presentations may lead to the association of the adversive properties of ECS to the environment in which ECS was presented. The adversive qualities of this environment may lead to longer latencies, and the longer latencies which have been attributed to poor recall may, in fact, have been caused by avoidance of the situation in which ECS was received. The temporal gradient showing greater performance as the interval between the learning trial and ECS increased, which has been attributed to more consolidation, may, in fact, have resulted from less aversive conditioning caused by the delay between the end of the training trial and ECS.

Support for the argument that the poor performance of subjects in these ECS studies resulted from aversive conditioning rather than interrupted consolidation is provided by Miller and Coons's study (1955), which shows that ECS does have aversive properties and that multiple ECSs can lead to increased avoidance latency. Miller and Coons first trained rats to run down an alley to obtain food and then shocked them while they ate. Electroconvulsive shocks were delivered at various intervals after the electrical shock was presented. If ECS does indeed disrupt consolidation of the shock experience, the rats should have forgotten being

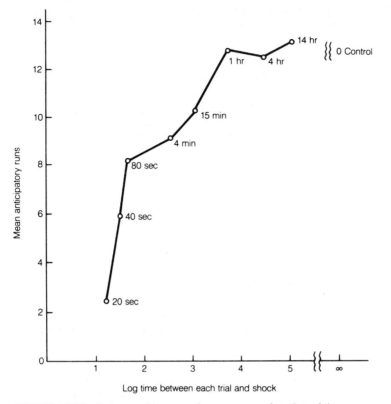

FIGURE 10-12   Active-avoidance performance as a function of the interval between avoidance training and presentation of ECS. Anticipatory runs are trials in which shock is avoided. The results of this study suggested that the amnesic influence of electroconvulsive shock declined with increased interval between training and electroconvulsive shock. From Duncan, C. P. (1949). The retroactive effect of electroshock on learning. *Journal of Comparative and Physiological Psychology, 42,* 32–44. Copyright 1949 by the American Psychological Association. Reprinted by permission.

shocked and should have run quickly to food. However, if ECS has aversive properties, avoidance latency would have increased. Miller and Coons reported that rats given ECS after being shocked showed greater avoidance latency than did rats that received shocks but not ECS. Furthermore, the longer the interval between the shock and the ECS, the shorter the latency to run for food. A similar development of anxiety as the result of ECS has been observed in humans (Gallinek, 1956).

Because multiple ECSs produce fear and lead to poorer active avoidance performance, studies employing ECS after the 1950s have used a single ECS. This procedure minimizes the aversive conditioning by the ECS. Experimenters have also employed passive avoidance tasks (see Chapter 6). In the passive avoidance

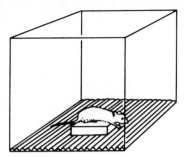

FIGURE 10-13
Step-down apparatus used for training passive
avoidance response. When animal steps off the
platform, it receives electrical footshock. Reluctance
to step off platform on test indicates the level of
conditioning of passive avoidance response.

task, the aversive qualities of ECS would lead to greater avoidance performance.
If ECS does affect memory, it could be detected; If ECS induces memory deficits,
then the use of ECS would result in decreased avoidance performance; but if
ECS causes aversive conditioning, then the result will be greater avoidance performance. Studies using single-trial passive avoidance tasks have reported that
ECS will induce memory deficits only when administered very shortly after passive avoidance training (Lewis, 1969); we next look at one of these studies.

Chorover and Schiller (1965) used a step-down apparatus to train rats to avoid
electric shock passively. This step-down apparatus consists of a chamber with a
grid floor and a small wooden platform in the middle of the chamber (see Figure
10-13). Rats stepping off the platform were shocked. After being shocked, rats
in the experimental groups received ECS. Chorover and Schiller varied the interval between the end of training and ECS from 3 to 30 seconds. Control-group
rats either did not receive ECS after being shocked or were given neither training
nor ECS. Chorover and Schiller reported that when tested the next day, control-
group rats that had not received ECS after training demonstrated that they remembered being shocked in the apparatus by refusing to step off the platform;
however, the control animals that had not received either shock or ECS the previous day readily stepped off the platform. The presentation of ECS after training
did disrupt passive avoidance performance; animals that had received ECS after
passive avoidance training stepped off the platform quickly on the retention test.

Chorover and Schiller also established the temporal gradient of retrograde amnesia; that is, they measured the amount of time required before the ECS no
longer affected the performance of a learned response. Unlike the results of Duncan (1949) and other studies using multiple training trials and ECS, Chorover
and Schiller found ECS to be ineffective when presented more than 30 seconds
after training (refer to Figure 10-14). These observations suggest that memory
consolidation occurs quickly, within a matter of seconds, and that the behavioral
deficits following ECS gradients observed in other studies were caused by
processes other than the failure to consolidate. Other experiments have also found
that ECS is effective for only a short time following training; see Quartermain,
Paolino, and Miller (1965) for another example.

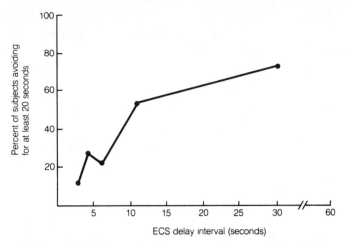

FIGURE 10-14 Percentage of subjects avoiding stepping off platform for at least 20 seconds as a function of training–electroconvulsive shock interval. This study's results indicated that the effective interval of amnesia from electroconvulsive shock was extremely short. From Chorover, S. L., & Schiller, P. H. (1965). Short-term retrograde amnesia in rats. *Journal of Comparative and Physiological Psychology, 59,* 73–78. Copyright 1965 by the American Psychological Association. Reprinted by permission.

Our discussion suggests that a memory consolidates quickly, and that consolidation is susceptible to disruption for only a few seconds after an event. A number of studies (Lewis, 1979; Miller & Springer, 1973) suggest that memories are consolidated in a fraction of a second. Furthermore, these articles argue that one function of the short-term store is to organize or elaborate on the stored memory; this organization or elaboration enhances the ability to later retrieve the memory. This theory suggests that ECS affects not the consolidation or storage of a memory but rather the retrieval of that memory.

Misanin, Miller, and Lewis (1968) provide evidence that ECS interferes with the retrieval of a memory. They trained their rats to avoid electric shock in a one-trial passive avoidance step-down situation. Twenty-four hours after training, some subjects received the light CS followed by an ECS. The authors reported that ECS produced retrograde amnesia 24 hours after original training. Because consolidation of the memory of passive avoidance training was completed within 24 hours, the retrograde amnesia could not have resulted from disruption of memory consolidation. Instead, Misanin et al. suggested that there are two kinds of memory systems: active and passive. The active memory system corresponds to the short-term store; the passive memory system, to the long-term store. In their view, retrograde amnesia can be produced only when a memory is active; that is, ECS can interfere with retrieval only when the memory of an event is being actively recalled. Why did ECS, presented 24 hours after training, produce retrograde amnesia? In Misanin et al.'s view, the CS reactivated the memory of original training, and the recall of the passive avoidance response enabled ECS to produce amnesia.

In Search of the Engram

What physical changes provide the basis for the permanent record of an event? Many scientists (see Agranoff, 1980; Dunn, 1980) have suggested that a change in nucleic acids (RNA and DNA) represents the storage site of memories. This view, called *nucleotide rearrangement theory,* assumes that a permanent change in RNA and DNA occurs as the result of learning. The modified RNA and DNA contains information about the experience. Other researchers (see Lynch, 1986; Rosenzweig, 1984) have proposed that consolidation represents changes in neural responsiveness. This view, referred to as *cellular modification theory,* suggests that learning permanently alters the functioning of specific neural systems. This change can reflect either enhanced functioning of existing neural circuits or the establishment of new neural connections. We briefly examine both the nucleotide rearrangement and cellular modification views next.

Nucleotide Rearrangement Theory   The nucleotide rearrangement theory suggests that learning represents a permanent change in RNA and DNA. For several reasons, scientists have found the nucleotide rearrangement theory attractive. First, considerable evidence implies that hereditary information is stored in the DNA molecule. Because innate information can be stored, it seems reasonable to assume that acquired information could also be stored in DNA. Second, an enormous amount of information is accumulated in a lifetime. DNA possesses sufficient complexity to store this vast amount of information. A considerable number of studies evaluating the nucleotide rearrangement theory have provided evidence that seems to support this view.

We next examine two approaches that have been employed to validate the nucleotide rearrangement view of memory storage. Some studies have measured biochemical changes associated with learning. Other experiments have attempted to inhibit changes in nucleotides.

Chemical Changes Associated with Learning   Many studies have evaluated whether learning produces quantitative or qualitative changes in RNA. (Since the life span of RNA is limited and its manufacture is controlled by DNA, changes in RNA are assumed to reflect DNA changes.) Some of these studies have measured RNA changes after learning. While not all these experiments have reported positive results, many have found RNA changes following learning (see Squire, 1987, for a review of this literature). For example, Hyden and Egyhazi (1964) found that rats forced to reach for food with their nonpreferred paw showed a significant increase in cortical RNA in the hemisphere contralateral to the nonpreferred paw, compared with control rats allowed to reach with their preferred paw. Qualitative changes in RNA were also observed by Hyden and

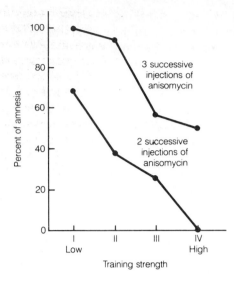

FIGURE 10-15
The percentage of mice showing amnesia as a function of level of training and the number of injections of anisomycin, a protein inhibitor. The amnesic effect of anisomycin was increased with a higher dose but reduced with additional training. From Flood, J. F., Bennett, E. L., Rosenzweig, M. R., & Orme, A. E. (1973). The influence of duration of protein synthesis inhibition on memory. *Physiology and Behavior, 10,* 555–562. Copyright 1973, Pergamon Press, Ltd.

Egyhazi. They found changes in the ratios of nucleotide bases, the building blocks of RNA and DNA, for experimental animals, but reported no changes in control subjects.

Other studies have attempted to discover a specific protein change following learning. (Since protein synthesis is controlled by RNA, altered protein synthesis is assumed to reflect nucleotide alteration.) George Ungar and associates (Ungar, Galvan, & Clark, 1968) identified a protein specific to fear. To identify this protein, rats were shocked when they entered a dimly lit chamber. Analysis of the brains of these animals revealed a protein not present in untrained animals. Ungar and associates named the protein *scotophobin* after the Greek word for "fear of the dark."

Inhibition of RNA Synthesis   Another way to access the nucleotide arrangement theory is to administer drugs that temporarily impair or prevent RNA synthesis. The effect of these drugs should be to block memory storage, as the result of the temporary reduction or elimination of RNA synthesis. Many studies have reported that inhibition of RNA synthesis results in memory impairment (see Quartermain, 1976, for a review of this literature); we next examine one important study in this area.

Flood and associates (1973) found anisomycin, a drug that inhibits protein synthesis, to be an effective amnesic at low doses; the lethal dose is 25 times the effective amnesic level. Furthermore, since low doses are safe, the drug can be given in repeated uses. Flood et al. reported that repeated injections produce amnesia, even after extended training. Figure 10-15 shows the results of their study in which mice were trained to avoid electric shock passively. The level of training was manipulated by varying shock intensity; the greater the intensity of shock, the higher the training strength. The mice received one, two, or three successive injections of anisomycin. The first injection was given 15 minutes before training; the subsequent injections were given at 2-hour intervals after training. As can be seen in Figure 10-15, the more injections, the greater the amnesia of prior avoidance training. Furthermore, at a high level of training three injections were needed to produce amnesia, indicating that with stronger training, protein synthesis must be inhibited longer to produce forgetting. Flood and associates (1975) observed a similar influence of training strength and length of inhibition on the level of amnesia of an active avoidance response.

Our discussion suggests that nucleic acids may be involved in the storage of information; however, this idea remains unproved, and many researchers are still skeptical. Some scientists (see Briggs & Kitto, 1962) argue that DNA structure cannot be changed by neural activity. Other psychologists (John, 1967; Rosenblatt, 1967; Ungar, 1976) assert that the nucleic acids represent a logical basis of memory storage. How might memories be stored in nucleic acid? In an elegant discussion, John (1967) details a mechanism by which experience can lead to a change in nucleotide action. We can only briefly describe John's theory, but interested readers are referred to John's *Mechanisms of Memory* for a complete discussion of his theory and evidence supporting it.

John's Theory of Memory Storage John (1967) suggests that every event produces a unique and distinctive spacial-temporal pattern of neural activity. The representation of this experience is then permanently stored in the central nervous system. According to John, the storage of a memory occurs in three phases. In the first phase, an experience is registered in the nervous system. This stage corresponds to the sensory register and is almost instantaneous.

John's second phase, containing two parts, corresponds to the short-term store. One part of this phase provides the temporary retention characteristic of the short-term store; the second aspect serves as the template for long-term information storage. In John's view, short-term recall results from prolonged cellular responsiveness. Considerable evidence supports John's theory that increased neural responsivity is responsible for short-term recall. For example, Haycock, van Buskirk, and McGaugh (1977) observed that recall is enhanced by injections of catecholamines, which increase neural reactivity when the drug is administered immediately following training. Similarly, Stein, Belluzzi, and Wise (1975) and Jensen and associates (1978) found that when injected shortly after learning, drugs that lower catecholamine levels and thereby decrease neuron responsivity impair short-term recall.

The short-term store also serves as the template for long-term information storage. John (1967) suggests that, instead of an experience permanently changing DNA, DNA action is modified as a result of an event. According to John, neural responsivity is governed by DNA action. The activity of small segments of DNA is in turn controlled by repressor genes; modification of repressor gene activity also modifies DNA action, thereby changing responsivity of a neuron or neurons.

How does an event modify repressor gene function? In John's view, a newly synthesized RNA molecule, produced in response to an event, alters repressor

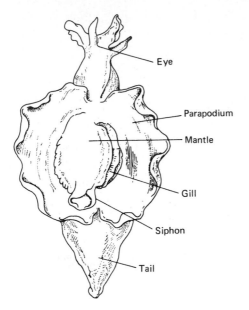

Eye

Parapodium

Mantle

Gill

Siphon

Tail

FIGURE 10-16
Aplysia californica. In this shell-less marine mollusk, touching either the siphon or the mantle elicits a defensive retraction of the three external organs—the gill, the mantle, and the siphon.

gene function. This new RNA molecule has a limited life span and serves as the holding mechanism only until the memory is permanently stored. John presents a number of studies supporting his view. For example, Barondes and Cohen (1966) found that actinomycin D_1, a compound that inhibits RNA synthesis, interferes with the acquisition (storage) of a response but not with its retention (retrieval).

Information, in John's view, is permanently stored in the last phase of memory processing. According to John, the modified DNA action produces new RNA and proteins. The new RNA and protein have two effects: (1) to reproduce the spacial-temporal neural activity associated with the event and (2) to maintain the altered DNA action through the continued influence on repressor gene function. John presents evidence to support this aspect of his theory. For example, he suggests that the drug puromycin interferes with long-term retention by inhibiting the use of newly formed RNA and protein.

Cellular Modification Theory Research also has demonstrated that structural changes in neurons occur as a result of experience. We next examine these neuronal modifications.

Learning in the **Aplysia Californica** Eric Kandel and associates (see Carew, Hawkins, & Kandel, 1983; Hawkins, Abrams, Carew, & Kandel, 1983; Kandel & Schwartz, 1982; Klein & Kandel, 1978) have investigated changes in neuron responsivity following learning in the sea hare *Aplysia californica* (see Figure 10-16). This simple shell-less marine mollusck exhibits a significant increase in neural responsivity as a result of certain experiences.

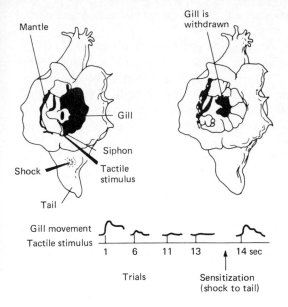

FIGURE 10-17
Illustration of the habituation and sensitization of the gill withdrawal response in *Aplysia californica*. Repeated exposure to a weak tactile stimulus leads to a reduced withdrawal reaction (habituation), while an intense electric shock increases the withdrawal reaction to a weak tactile stimulus (sensitization). From Kandel, E. R., & Schwartz, J. H. (1982). Molecular biology of learning: Modulation of transmitter release. *Science, 218,* 433–443. Copyright 1982 by the American Association for the Advancement of Science.

Kandel's early studies examined the habituation and sensitization (see Chapter 1) of a protective response in the *Aplysia*. The *Aplysia* has three external organs—the gill, the mantle, and the siphon—that retract when either the mantle or the siphon is touched. Kandel observed that when a weak tactile stimulus is used, repeated presentations of this stimulus yield less defensive reaction (see Figure 10-17). This habituation of the defensive reaction is site specific, and any change in the location of the touch will produce an increased defensive response. The use of an intense electric shock produces sensitization or an increased defensive reaction. Kandel found that even a mild stimulus would elicit a strong defensive reaction after the electric shock.

What physiological changes underlie increased neural responsivity? When a neuron is stimulated, sodium (Na +) and calcium (Ca +) ions rush into the channels or gates in the cell. The influx of sodium and calcium ions is followed by an expulsion of potassium (K +) ions from the cell. The influx of calcium ions is necessary for the release of neurotransmitter substances, while the outflow of potassium ions is necessary for the neuron to return to normal responsivity. However, following a sensitizing electric-shock experience, Kandel found that the potassium channels remain closed and, therefore, these ions cannot leave the cell. The failure of the potassium ions to leave the cell prolongs the neuron's reaction to stimulation.

The facilitation of neural functioning following a strong electric shock occurs at the presynaptic membrane. Kandel reported that this enhanced reactivity occurred in the neurons that activate the presynaptic membrane of sensory neurons.

This enhanced presynaptic facilitation results in a heightened reaction to external stimulation.

The defensive reaction in the *Aplysia* can be conditioned. Carew et al. (1983) paired a light touch applied to the mantle or siphon (CS) with a strong electric shock to the mollusk's tail (UCS). These investigators reported that the pairing of the light touch (CS) with electric shock (UCS) allowed the light touch to elicit the withdrawal response as the CR. Enhanced neural responsivity also was observed to the CS following the conditioning experience. This increased reaction was the result of reduced outflow of potassium in response to the CS. Thus, according to Carew et al. the effect of the CS was to enhance activation of those sensory neurons, which resulted in the continued release of neurotransmitter substances and enhanced elicitation of the withdrawal response.

How does the CS increase sensory responsivity and thereby elicit the CR? The research of Gary Lynch (see Lynch, 1986) provides an explanation of the neural basis of conditioning; we look at his work next.

Structural Changes and Experience Lynch found that experience enhances the level of calcium ions that can enter the nerve cell. This increased level activates a dormant enzyme called calpain. The effect of calpain is to break down the protein fodrin, which is a major component of neural dendrites, as well as being the coating around the dendrites (see Figure 10-18). The breakdown of the dendrite's coating exposes more of the dendrite to stimulation from other neurons; that is, as the coating breaks down, the neuron becomes more sensitive. With continued experience, the breakdown process continues, which results in even greater sensitivity of the neuron.

Lynch (1986) suggests that continued experience causes the dendrites to become a "skeleton." The lack of cellular coating allows the dendrites to change shape and spread out. These changes in dendrite structure lead to the establishment of new neural connections. In Lynch's view, the establishment of new neural connections, due to the breakdown of the dendrite coating, and the resulting arborization of the dendrite tree of the neuron represents the neural changes produced by learning.

These neural changes also are necessary for recall of prior learning. Lynch and Baudry (1984) trained rats to find food in an eight-arm radial maze. They then implanted a pump that could infuse a chemical called leupeptin into the lateral ventricle of the brain. This chemical prevents the breakdown of fodrin and thereby the establishment of new neural connections. These researchers found that the experimental animals recalled nothing of their past learning experience. The rats entered the arms of the radial maze randomly. Control animals that did not receive the drug showed good recall of the prior experiences. Evidently, learning cannot occur without structural changes taking place in the neuron. The absence of these neural changes prevents recall of prior experiences.

We have discovered that experiences produce structural changes in the nervous system. Rosenzweig (1984) has demonstrated that exposure to an enriched environment produces significant changes in the nervous system; we conclude our discussion of the cellular modification view with his work.

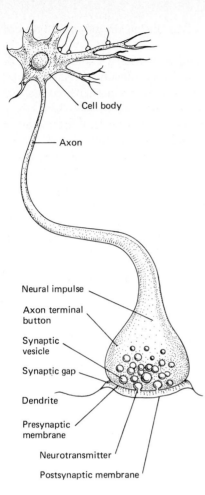

Cell body

Axon

Neural impulse

Axon terminal
button

Synaptic
vesicle

Synaptic gap

Dendrite

Presynaptic
membrane

Neurotransmitter

Postsynaptic membrane

FIGURE 10-18
Diagram illustrating the chemical communication of
information between neurons. When a neural impulse
reaches the axon's terminal button, chemical
transmitter substances stored in the synaptic
vesicles are released into the synaptic gap. The
neurotransmitter substances migrate from the
presynaptic membrane of transmitting neuron to the
postsynaptic membrane. The neurotransmitter
substances either depolarize (excite) or hyperpolarize
(inhibit) the postsynaptic membrane.

The Impact of an Enriched Environment   Rosenzweig and colleagues (see
Diamond, Linder, Johnson, Bennett, & Rosenzweig, 1975; Globus, Rosenzweig,
Bennett, & Diamond, 1973) have examined the neural changes that occur as a
result of an enrichment experience. These researchers took litters of rats and
exposed them to an enriched environment, which consisted of running wheels,
ladders, and objects to explore and manipulate. Several objects in the enriched
environment, were changed daily. Other litters of rats were raised in an impov-
erished environment, which consisted of a plain cage in a dimly lit, quiet room.
Analysis of the brains of animals raised in each environment showed that the rats
reared in the enriched environments had a thicker cortex, greater dendrite connections, and more area of contact at the synapses than did rats raised in impov-
erished environments. These observations provide additional support for the view

that structural changes in the nervous system occur during the physical basis of memory consolidation.

You might perceive that the nucleotide rearrangement theory and cellular modification approach present antagonistic views of memory consolidation. However, this interpretation is not valid. The ability to recall past experiences can be due to structural changes in the nervous system that are controlled by RNA and DNA. This fact would lead analysis of biological changes following learning to reveal both nucleotide rearrangements and structural neural modifications.

The storage of information can also be influenced by the action of several key central nervous system structures. Damage to these structures can lead to anterograde, or posttraumatic, amnesia. *Anterograde amnesia* is an inability to recall events that occur after some disturbance to the brain, such as a brain injury or certain degenerative brain diseases. The case described in the opening vignette of the chapter is one example of the inability to permanently store information as the result of an injury to the brain.

Anatomical Basis of Memory Formation

In 1889, the Russian neurologist Sergei Korsakoff described a serious and dramatic memory deficit. His patients failed to recall past events; if an event recurred, these individuals showed no evidence of having experienced the event. This disorder, called *Korsakoff's syndrome,* is typically seen in chronic alcoholics and occurs when certain brain structures malfunction.

Patients with Korsakoff's syndrome suffer from anterograde amnesia, or an inability to store certain experiences. A person with anterograde amnesia can remember an experience for only a short time. However, once the person shifts his or her attention, the ability to recall the event is lost. This observation indicates that with anterograde amnesia, information about an event cannot be transformed from short-term to long-term store. While a person suffering from anterograde amnesia cannot store information, the individual can remember events that occurred prior to the onset of amnesia. In fact, while the amnesic will forget an event several minutes after it happened, he or she can remember experiences that took place years earlier. This finding shows that anterograde amnesia does not reflect a retrieval failure.

Anterograde amnesia can occur for reasons other than Korsakoff's syndrome. This memory disorder can be produced by a head trauma; infections of the brain including syphilis; strokes and other permanent disorders of the blood flow to the brain; tumors of brain structures involved in memory storage; brain damage due to exposure to toxic substances; and some forms of dementia, such as Alzheimer's disease.

Research on anterograde amnesia has focused on two important issues, the first being the extent of the memory impairment in patients suffering from this disease. According to Squire (1986), evidence indicates that amnesic patients suffer from an inability to code information efficiently in the short-term store. This inefficient coding impairs the ability to store an event in a meaningful fashion, which in turn results in an inability to remember the event at a later date. Early research with these patients suggested an inability to store any information; however, more recent studies show that amnesic patients can remember certain types of information or events that do not require coding. For example, Sidman, Stoddard, and Mohr (1968) trained a patient with Korsakoff's syndrome to press a square containing the image of a circle, giving a penny as a reinforcement for each correct response. The patient quickly learned to press the circle, and could select a circle from a display containing one circle and seven ellipses of various shapes. Even after several minutes of working on other tasks, the patient could select the appropriate stimulus. These observations indicate that this particular patient could remember the correct response.

However, although the patient responded appropriately physically, he soon forgot the words for what he had learned. When asked during the first task what he was doing, he replied that he was choosing the circle. However, after several minutes, he could no longer verbally describe his actions. Apparently, the patient retained knowledge of the contingency between behavior and reinforcement but forgot exactly what he was doing. In a similar study with additional patients, El-Wakil (1975) observed that patients with Korsakoff's syndrome could remember previously acquired contingencies but could not recall the logic behind their actions. Recall our prior discussion of procedural and declarative memories earlier in the chapter. Our observations indicate that the memory deficit in Korsakoff's syndrome patients represents a loss of declarative but not procedural memories.

Psychologists have conducted research to identify nonfunctioning structures that cause anterograde amnesia. In 1954, Scoville demonstrated that bilateral removal of the medial temporal lobe in humans resulted in memory impairment identical to that seen in Korsakoff's syndrome patients. These operations, conducted on 30 psychotic patients in an attempt to reduce their behavioral problems, resulted in anterograde amnesia.

Patient H. M. is perhaps the most famous case of anterograde amnesia (see Corkin, Sullivan, Twitchell, & Grove, 1981; Milner, 1970; Scoville & Milner, 1957). In 1953, H. M. had his temporal lobes removed as a treatment for severe epilepsy. Although the operation successfully treated his epilepsy, H. M. now had severe anterograde amnesia. He could remember events prior to his surgery, could carry on a conversation about those events, and still write or perform mathematics. Unfortunately, H. M. could not recall anything that happened after his surgery. On each visit he would have to be reintroduced to his doctors. He would read a magazine article many times without recalling having previously read that article. Our earlier discussion indicated that Korsakoff's syndrome patients could store procedural but not declarative memories. A similar pattern is seen with H. M., who can perform a task that he had learned earlier but could not recall having learned that task.

Other studies (Penfield & Mathieson, 1974; Penfield & Milner, 1958) have implicated the hippocampus, a structure in the limbic system, as being responsible for the consolidation of memories. These experiments demonstrated that removing the temporal lobe alone does not lead to memory impairments, but removal of

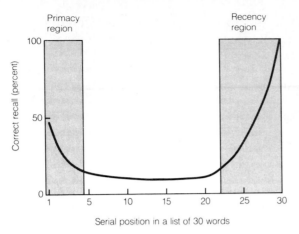

FIGURE 10-19
Graph shows the serial-position effect in terms of percentage of correct recall. The shaded areas indicate that recall is better for items at the beginning (primacy portion) and the end (recency portion) of the list than for items in the middle of the list. From Howard, D. V. (1983). *Cognitive psychology.* New York: Macmillan.

the hippocampus, which often is also removed with the temporal lobe, does result in severe anterograde amnesia.

Evidence collected by Horel and associates (see Horel & Misantone, 1974, 1976) also indicates that the destruction of the dorsomedial thalamic nucleus can lead to memory impairments characteristic of Korsakoff's syndrome. Horel (1978), examining published studies concerning memory loss in humans suffering from Korsakoff's syndrome, reported that the memory impairments seen with this disease correlate with damage to the dorsomedial thalamus. Furthermore, Horel and Misantone (1974, 1976) observed that destruction of the dorsomedial thalamus affected primates' ability to distinguish new from familiar objects. In contrast, dorsomedial thalamic lesions had no influence on the animals' retention of a visual discrimination. These results suggest that the memory deficits observed in patients with Korsakoff's syndrome can be reproduced in primates by destroying the dorsomedial thalamus.

We have seen that several structures are involved in the storage of our experiences. Structures mediating the retrieval of past experiences will be examined in Chapter 12.

SUPPORT OF MULTISTAGE VIEW OF MEMORY STORAGE

This chapter has been discussing the Atkinson-Shiffrin multistage memory model. Most psychologists support the idea that experiences can be retained in stores of differing permanence. Next we examine some additional evidence that validates the Atkinson-Shiffrin model.

Strong support for the theory of distinct memory stores is provided by research on the serial-position effect. Recall that people learn the items at the beginning and end of a list more readily than items in the middle of the list. The serial-position effect also is observed during recall (see Figure 10-19). One interpretation of the effect argues that the recency aspect of the serial-position effect—the better recall of the last items— results from continued rehearsal of these items during testing and, therefore, reflects the operation of the short-term store. In contrast, the primacy aspect of the serial-position effect—the higher recall of initial items—is thought to occur because subjects can spend more time processing the initial items and storing them in the long-term store. This interpretation suggests that two distinct memory-storage systems are involved in the serial-position effect—the short-term store causes the recency effect, and the long-term store accounts for the primacy effect.

Is this dual-storage theory of the serial-position effect valid? A considerable amount of research (refer to Howard, 1983) indicates that different variables influence the primacy and recency effects; these observations are consistent with the idea that different memory systems are responsible for the primacy and recency effects. For example, Murdock (1962) and Postman and Phillips (1965) presented some of their subjects with a list of 30 words and then asked them to count backward by threes for 2 minutes; other subjects were tested immediately. A multistage memory model predicts that this procedure should influence the recency but not the primacy effect, since counting backward affects short-term but not long-term memory. In support of this prediction, the researchers found that although the counting-backward technique did not influence recall of the items presented at the beginning of the list, recall was significantly poorer for end-of-the-list items when testing was delayed rather than immediate.

Murdock (1962) and Postman and Phillips (1965) also varied the rate at which the words were presented. It is assumed that the presentation rate should not influence short-term memory and, therefore, the recency effect. In contrast, a slower rate of presentation should allow for more long-term storage of information and thus increase the primacy effect and lead to greater recall of items early in the list. Consistent with this view, the authors reported that increasing the rate of presentation affected the primacy but not the recency effect.

SUMMARY

1 The Atkinson-Shiffrin three-stage model assumes that there are three stages involved in the storage of an experience. The first stage is the sensory register, which stores an exact copy of the external stimulus. The visual copy contained in the sensory store is referred to as an icon and is stored in the iconic memory. Echoic memory contains an exact replica of an auditory experience, and echo is stored in the sensory store.

2 Data are stored in the sensory register for only a very short time; icons usually last about 0.25 second, and echoes approximately 2 seconds. While a visual experience provides all the information needed to detect the salient characteristics, the recognition of an auditory event requires sounds to be retained in the sensory store until the whole event is detected. Information decays rapidly after leaving the sensory register and is lost unless transferred into the short-term store.

3 The short-term store serves as a temporary storage facility, and people are consciously aware of information stored there. Information remains in the short-term store for approximately 15 to 20 seconds, and during this time experiences are interpreted for meaning and then organized in logical ways. This interpretation and organization produces a more meaningful experience, which in turn increases the likelihood of recall occurring at a later time.

4 The short-term store also has limited storage capacity; only three or four units of information can be retained at one time. One effect of the interpretation and organization of experiences is to overcome this limited storage capacity. Memories contained in the short-term store are easily disrupted and replaced by new information. The short-term store can rehearse or replay prior experiences, and this rehearsal functions to retain information in the short-term store for a longer period. This increased rehearsal enhances interpretation and organization of the memory, improving the likelihood that the memory will later be available for recall.

5 Most information in the short-term store is transferred into the long-term store, the site of permanent memory. There are several classes of long-term memories. An episodic memory contains information about temporally dated events, and a semantic memory contains knowledge of words or other symbols or of the rules, formulas, or algorithms for developing concepts or solutions to problems. The episodic and semantic memory systems also are functionally distinct. An episodic memory is easy to store but difficult to retrieve; in contrast, a semantic memory is difficult to store but easy to retrieve. Procedural memories contain information about the performance of specific skills, and declarative memories contain knowledge about the environment. A procedural memory represents an unconscious automatic reaction to the environment; in contrast, a declarative memory is a conscious thought or image.

6 Activity reverberates in a neural circuit following the experience of an event. This reverberatory activity represents the interpretive and organizational function of the short-term store. Disruption of this neural activity prior to the elaboration of an experience can produce a memory that cannot be retrieved from the long-term store.

7 The nucleotide rearrangement theory suggests that learning represents a permanent modification in DNA and RNA. The RNA changes that occur following learning and the memory impairments that occur when protein synthesis is suppressed provide support for the nucleotide rearrangement theory.

8 According to John, modification of repressor gene action occurs following an experience; the change in repressor gene function alters the action of DNA. The modified DNA acts to change neural responsivity and also represents the site of permanent memory storage. Changes in RNA have been observed following an event; these findings provide support for John's theory of memory storage.

9 Specific changes in neural functioning have been suggested to underlie the structural basis of memory. Kandel discovered that sensitization of the withdrawal response in the sea mollusck *Aplysia Californica,* produced by exposure to a strong electric shock, increased neural responsiveness. This withdrawal response also can be classically conditioned, with exposure to the conditioned stimulus producing increased neural responsiveness.

10 As a result of experience, the fodrin coating of the dendrites breaks down, which leads to the establishment of new connections between neurons as the dendrites change shape and spread out to adjacent neurons. The enhanced area of contact between neurons and the formation of greater neuron connections that occurs when animals are exposed to enriched environments provide additional evidence of the structural changes in the nervous system which underlie the permanent storage of experiences.

11 Anterograde amnesia, a failure to remember recent experiences, occurs from a number of brain disorders including alcoholism (Korsakoff's syndrome), head trauma, brain infections such as syphilis, strokes, tumors, and some forms of dementia such as Alzheimer's disease. Patients suffering from anterograde amnesia can recall events taking place prior to the onset of the disorder, but events experienced after the amnesia begins will be forgotten as soon as the person is no longer attending to the event. The amnesic can remember how to perform previously learned habits (procedural memory) but cannot recall having experienced the event (declarative memory). Several brain structures, including the temporal lobes, hippocampus, and dorsomedial thalamus, function to code and store declarative memories.

12 The serial-position effect provides support for the multistage view of memory storage. People remember the items at the beginning and the end of the list more readily than the items in the middle of the list. The recency aspect the serial-position effect—the better recall of the last items—is thought to result from continued rehearsal of these items during testing and, therefore, reflect the operation of the short-term store. In contrast, the primacy aspect of the serial-position effect—the better recall of initial items—is thought to occur because subjects can spend more time processing the initial items and storing them in the long-term store. This interpretation suggests that two distinct memory-storage systems are involved in the serial-position effect—the short-term store causes the recency effect, and the long-term store accounts for the primacy effect.

11

THE ENCODING OF OUR EXPERIENCES

A MEMORABLE EXPERIENCE

Reading the morning newspaper, Rene was drawn to an ad for a workshop that taught techniques in memory improvement. "Techniques are available to enable you to remember better. Let us teach you these techniques in only one day." Rene has a terrible memory. She often forgets her errands and even forgets to attend meetings, both of which are detrimental to her career as a real estate agent. Although skeptical about the prospects for improvement in her memory, Rene decided to attend the workshop anyway.

Jim Brewer, the instructor of the workshop, is somewhat of a celebrity. Rene has seen him on several television shows where he demonstrated a remarkable memory, recalling all the names of people in the audience or pages of telephone numbers from the local directory. Rene thought that Jim Brewer's extraordinary memory capacity must have been inherited; however, if Rene could learn just a few techniques to improve her feeble memory, she certainly would be grateful.

The large number of people attending the workshop surprised Rene. Jim Brewer began the session by saying that everyone has the capacity for a good memory but that the ability to remember previous experiences must be developed. He explained that a number of techniques called *mnemonics* have been developed to improve memory and that the aim of the workshop would be to learn these techniques. Brewer continued by emphasizing that these mnemonic techniques are easily learned and can readily enhance the ability to remember. To illustrate this point, he asked members of the workshop to perform a mnemonic exercise to learn the name of the person sitting in front of them. Rene, surprised by the effectiveness of the technique, still remembers the name.

382

However, Brewer also emphasized that the techniques must be practiced to have a significant effect. The workshop lasted only one day, but Rene learned many techniques to help her remember things like names, appointments, and phone numbers. She even learned how to use her memory to improve her bridge game. Rene was very pleased with the workshop and vowed to practice the techniques she had learned.

Rene's memory improvement course allowed her to develop more effective ways of recalling past experiences. Yet, there is nothing mystical about mnemonics. Instead, mnemonics represent the effective utilization of naturally occurring organizational properties of the short-term store.

In the last chapter, we described the three stages involved in the storage of our experiences. In this chapter, we examine the encoding of information. We discuss the importance of the analysis of experiences in the storage and retrieval, as well as the specific changes that occur as memories are encoded.

THE ANALYSIS OF AN EXPERIENCE

Levels of Processing View

Fergus Craik and Robert Lockhart (1972) offer an alternative to the Atkinson-Shiffrin three-stage model of memory storage presented in the last chapter. They suggest that memories differ in the extent to which they have been processed. Their *levels of processing view* assumes that a memory can be processed at many different levels (see Table 11-1). An event can receive only shallow, superficial analysis, or it can be interpreted at a deeper level. Consider the various levels at which the word *car* can be processed. The initial processing involves analysis of the physical characteristics of the word, such as determining the lines and angles of those individual letters. A deeper level of processing involves identifying the three letters. A still deeper level of processing leads to identifying the word, and

TABLE 11-1
THE DEPTH OF PROCESSING VIEW OF THE MEMORY
OF A BEAUTIFUL AUTOMOBILE

Depth of Processing	Example of level of processing
Shallow processing (physical and perceptual aspects)	Detection of the lines, angles, and contour of an automobile
Intermediate processing (object is recognized and labeled)	The person recognizes that the object seen is an automobile
Deep processing (semantic meaning)	The attributes of a beautiful automobile (styling, color) are compared to automobile seen; this automobile is identified as being beautiful.

determining the meaning of the word represents a further level of memory processing.

The level of processing that an event receives has an effect on recall of the event, according to Craik and Lockhart's view. They propose that all experiences result in a permanent memory trace, but that the strength of the trace depends on the level of processing that memory has received. Craik and Lockhart propose that the more an event is processed, the more durable its memory trace will be and the greater the likelihood that it will be recalled.

The Importance of Elaboration

Craik and Tulving (1975) discuss how the analysis or elaboration of experiences influences the recall of those events. According to Craik and Tulving, the elaborateness of memory encoding refers to the extent to which events are related to or organized with other events. For example, suppose you learn a list containing the words *grief, love, forgotten,* and *spinster.* The words in the list could be encoded in an elaborate fashion by relating them to each other—such as by using them together in a sentence. A less elaborate encoding would be to analyze the meaning of the words without attempting to relate the words to each other.

According to Craik and Tulving, there also are differences in the extent to which an event is analyzed independent of its relation to other events. An experience can be interpreted phonetically in terms of its physical characteristics and semantically in terms of its meaning. Craik and Tulving suggest that although both the physical and semantic features of an event are analyzed, events differ in terms of the levels of phonetic and semantic elaboration. Some events may receive little semantic or physical elaboration, whereas other experiences undergo substantial physical or semantic elaboration.

Consider the following two examples to illustrate how semantic and phonetic elaboration may vary. In the first case, you are reading about the predatory behavior of lions. While reading, you concentrate on the meaning of the words rather than the physical attributes of the words. In the second case, you are attempting to evaluate the rhythm of a poem. In this case, you need to analyze the physical features of the words more than the semantic aspects.

We have discovered that experiences undergo varying degrees of elaboration prior to storage. Craik and Tulving (1975) performed an experiment to demonstrate that the level of elaboration determines the ability to recall previously experienced events. In this study, they presented to subjects several words and asked them whether each word made sense in various sentences. For example, one word was *watch,* and two sentences that different subjects received for the word *watch* were: *He dropped the* _____ and *The old man hobbled across the room and picked up the valuable* _____ *from the mahogany table.* According to Craik and Tulving, semantic analysis is required to determine whether the insertion of the word *watch* makes sense in each case, but subjects given the second sentence have to use greater elaboration than did subjects receiving the first sentence. An unannounced memory test showed that the level of recall was affected by the degree of elaboration: the greater the elaboration, the higher the level of retention of the word. Other studies have also shown that the level of recall of previously experienced events depends on the elaborateness of processing; see Cermack and Craik (1979) for a review of this literature.

The Importance of Distinctiveness

Why does memory elaboration enhance the recall of a prior experience? The formation of a distinctive memory is one reason that elaboration improves retention; that is, we are more likely to remember a distinctive event than a nondistinctive one (see Ellis, 1987, Hunt & Mitchell, 1982). The following example illustrates the significance of a distinctive memory.

Suppose you witness a person being hit by an automobile. The driver of the automobile does not stop to see if the person is injured, but instead drives away. The police question you about the accident. One likely question will be to describe the automobile involved in the accident. How well will you be able to remember the automobile? Perhaps you noticed that the automobile was a dark blue late model Ford Mustang with one hubcap missing. Your processing of the accident would have to have been quite extensive to provide such a detailed recollection of the automobile. This analysis would create a memory of an automobile that was quite distinctive; that is, there are not too many dark blue late model Ford Mustangs missing one hubcap. Your description will undoubtedly be very helpful to the police. However, suppose you only are able to remember that the automobile was dark blue. This memory would have received little elaboration. It also is not very distinctive, since there are probably many dark blue cars in your town. The police are not likely to gain much information from your recollection of the event.

How does distinctiveness enhance recall? First, interference between memories is less likely when the experiences can be differentiated. In terms of the preceding example, the memory that the automobile was a dark blue late model Ford Mustang with one hubcap missing will prevent confusion between the automobile involved in the accident and other automobiles. Second, a distinctive memory will contain a representation of stimuli that are unique to that memory. The presence of these unique stimuli will act to facilitate retrieval of the appropriate memory. For example, the recognition of the distinctive aspects of the automobile involved in the accident will allow you to identify that automobile. However, you are not likely to recall the automobile involved in the accident if the only information stored was the automobile was dark blue. In the next chapter, we will look closely at the impact of distinctiveness on memory retrieval and forgetting. We next examine the encoding processes that provide distinctive memories.

Section Review

The level of elaboration that an experience receives during processing influences the recall of that event; the more elaborately an event is encoded, the more likely the memory will be retrievable later. Elaboration affects retrieval presumably by enhancing the identification of the important aspects of an experience.

The distinctiveness of our experiences also is increased as a result of memory elaboration. This enhanced elaboration can identify memory attributes which later allow retrieval during testing as well as enable the memory to be distinguished from other experiences, thereby reducing interference as a source of forgetting.

THE ORGANIZATION OF OUR EXPERIENCES

We learned in the last chapter that the main function of the short-term store is to organize information arriving from the sensory register. The experience then is retained in the long-term store until recalled in the organized fashion. One type of organization accomplished by the short-term store is *chunking*. Chunking involves combining two or more units or *bits* of information into a single unit. For example, the six letters *s, i, g, n, a, l* can be chunked into the single word *signal*.

A second type of organization of experiences is *coding*. Coding is the transformation of information into a new form. For example, persons using Morse code change letters into dots and dashes to transmit a message. Similarly, subjects in an experiment can code nonsense syllables into words by adding letters. The coding of the nonsense syllable *ROG* into the word *frog* illustrates this kind of coding.

The formation of associations is a third organizational process carried out by the short-term store. An *association* indicates the detection of a relation between events. Some associations are based on temporal contiguity—the occurrence of events together in time. Other associations are based on the semantic similarity of events; for example, a person can associate a dog and a cat because both are animals. The temporal and semantic relations between events are identified while a memory is in the short-term store.

The organization of information by the short-term store provides some significant advantages. People can reduce the impact of the limited storage capacity of the short-term store by organizing incoming information from the sensory register. As a result of this organization, an event can become more significant or meaningful and thus more likely to be remembered. The recall of our experiences from the long-term store is greatly enhanced by these organizational processes. Evidence that information is organized by the short-term store and that this organization increases the recall of our experiences is examined next.

Chunking

Suppose you hear the three letters *B A T*. You are not likely to hear the three letters, but instead will hear the word *BAT*. The combining of the three letters into a single word reflects a process of the short-term store called chunking. Chunking is an automatic process reflective of the organizational functioning of the short-term store. It also significantly enhances our ability to recall past experiences. Let's next look at these two aspects of chunking.

The Short-term Store and Chunking   People automatically chunk information contained in the short-term store. For example, presenting six-digit numbers to subjects to memorize, Bower and Springston (1970) found that most people chunked the six digits into groups of three digits, each separated by a pause and distinct melodic pattern. Thus, the six-digit number 427316 became 427-316. The division of a seven-digit telephone number into two separate chunks is another use of chunking. Norman (1976) describes another example of the natural use of chunking by the short-term store: Children learn the 26 letters of the alphabet by using rhyming and melodic rhythm to create three chunks; each chunk contains two elements, and each element has two units of 1 to 4 letters. Norman diagrammed the chunking of the alphabet: [*(ab-cd) (ef-g)*] [*(hi-jk) (lmno-p)*] [*qrs-tuv) (w-xyz)*].

People not only chunk letters into words but also chunk words into sentences and sentences into a chunk or chunks of related ideas (Johnson, 1968). Johnson assumed that people learning sentences chunk the words into higher-order units (see Chapter 9 for a discussion of language learning). For example, a noun phrase represents a chunk of the sequence *the* + adjective + noun.

What evidence indicates that the words contained in a sentence are chunked into one or more units? Consider this sentence: *The tall boy saved the dying woman.* How likely will the word *boy* in the sentence be recalled? Johnson argued that the recall of one word within a unit (or chunk) is more related to the recall of other words within that unit than to the recall of words in another unit. Thus, the likelihood that a subject could recall the noun *boy* should be more influenced by the recall of the adjective *tall* than by the recall of the verb *saved.* This is true even though the noun *boy* is adjacent to both the adjective *tall* and the verb *saved.* Johnson's research shows that a subject is more likely to remember an adjacent word in the same unit than an adjacent word in a different chunk.

Does chunking increase the amount of information that can be retained in the short-term store? Simon (1974) evaluated the view that the short-term store can retain seven chunks of information, regardless of the absolute amount of information contained in each chunk. Using himself as a subject, Simon found that he could immediately recall seven 1-syllable words, about seven 2-syllable words, and about six 3-syllable words. However, Simon found that he could remember only four 2-word phrases (for example, *Milky Way, criminal lawyer*) and only about three longer phrases (for example, *All's fair in love and war.*) Although Simon's observations indicate that chunking can increase the absolute amount of information retained in the short-term store, they also indicate that the short-term store does not contain seven chunks. Recall that Watkins (1974) suggested that the true capacity of the short-term store is three to four chunks. Watkins reported that when only a small amount of information is contained in each chunk, the capacity of the short-term store appears to be five to nine chunks; however, some of the subjects' recall actually reflects information stored in the long-term store. Thus, the short-term and long-term stores contribute to the level of retention shown by a subject.

The Effect of Chunking on Recall   We have learned that more information can be retained in the short-term store as the result of chunking. There are two additional issues related to the impact of chunking. First, does chunking improve the short-term recall of our experiences? Second, are memories recalled from the long-term store in an organized fashion? We next address these two questions.

Murdock's (1961) classic study evaluated the role of chunking in the short-term recall of our experiences. Murdock presented his subjects a 3-consonant trigram, a 3-letter word, or three 3-letter words and then required them to count backward for 0, 3, 6, 9, 12, 15, or 18 seconds. As can be seen in Figure 11-1, the retention of the 3-consonant trigram was identical to that found by Peterson and Peterson (1959); recall of the trigram declined dramatically over the 18-second retention interval. However, Murdock's subjects after 18 seconds exhibited a high level of recall of the 1-word unit. Furthermore, on the 18-second recall test, the retention of the 3-word unit containing nine letters equaled that of the 3-letter trigram.

Chunking does not merely improve recall; instead, the information is recalled from the long-term store in a specific order. Suppose a subject is given the following list of items:

tea	cabbage	lion	coffee
milk	seal	potato	orange
cow	spinach	lemon	elephant
apple	pear	soda	carrot

This list contains four categories of items: beverages, animals, vegetables, and fruit. How would subjects recall the items on the list? Subjects receiving the above list will recall the items in each category together, even though the items were presented separately. The recall of material in terms of categories is called *clustering* (see Bousfield, 1953, for an early study on clustering or Tulving & Donaldson, 1972, for a review of this literature). The organization of material allows us to relate similar events and contributes to a structured and meaningful world. Organization is a very important aspect of the learning process; its significance should be apparent throughout the text.

Coding

We have discovered that information is combined into smaller units of information by the short-term store. The short-term store can also code information, that is, transform an event into a totally new form. There are three major codes or ways that the short-term store codes experiences. First, visual experiences can be coded into an auditory code, or an acoustic code. Second, information can be encoded as a word, or a verbal code. Third, words or ideas can become an image, or a visual code. While the transformation or coding of experiences is a natural property of the short-term store, most people do not use the coding properties of the short-term store effectively. Yet, people can learn to transform their experiences effectively; the use of these coding systems in mnemonic or memory en-

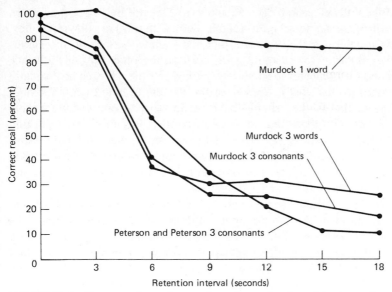

FIGURE 11-1   The percentage of correct recall as a function of the type of stimulus material and the length of the retention interval. The results of this study show that the recall of a 3-letter word is greater on an 18-second test than either three consonants or three words. Adapted from Melton, A. W. (1963). Implications of short-term memory for a general theory of memory. *Journal of Verbal Learning and Verbal Behavior, 2,* 1–21.

hancement techniques will be detailed later in this chapter. Although coding can enhance the storage of information, it will increase the recall of that information only if the memory can readily be decoded. This section also addresses the problem of decoding experiences.

Auditory Codes   Suppose you see the word *car* on a sign. In all likelihood, your short-term store will transform the visual image of the word *car* into the sound of the word. This observation suggests that we encode a visual experience as a sound or as an *auditory code*.

Conrad's (1964) study illustrates the acoustical coding of visual information. He presented visually a set of letters to his subjects and then asked them to recall all the letters. Analyzing the type of errors made by subjects on the recall test, Conrad found that errors were made based on the sound of the letters rather than on their physical appearance. For example, subjects were very likely to recall the letter *P* as the similar sounding *T,* but they were unlikely to recall the visually similar *F*. Many other studies have shown that acoustic confusions are much more common than visual confusions; see Wickelgren (1965) for another example.

People learn, through repeated experience, to use *acoustical coding* for visual experiences. Conrad (1971) presented 5- and 12-year-old children with a series of pictures and then placed each picture face down. The children were then given a duplicate set of pictures and asked to match them with the face-down pictures. On half the trials, names of the duplicate pictures sounded similar to the names of the face-down pictures (for example, *mat, bat*); on the other half of the trials, the names sounded different (for example, *fish, house*). If the children acoustically coded the original pictures (that is, they used the names) to help them remember the pictures they had seen, they should have made more errors with items that sounded similar than with those that sounded dissimilar. In fact, Conrad did find that 12-year-old subjects made more errors with the similar than with the dissimilar list; however, the 5-year-olds made the same number of errors on both types of lists. These observations suggest that older children use acoustical coding, but younger children simply remember visual patterns.

Why does the short-term store transform visual events into an auditory representation? Why do older but not younger children use acoustical coding? According to Howard (1983), the short-term store is a working memory; it not only retains specific information but also represents a space for thinking. Since language plays a central role in thinking (see Chapter 9), it seems logical both that visual events would be acoustically coded to aid the thinking process and that acoustical coding would be more important as children mature and learn to use language in their thinking.

Verbal Codes   Underwood (1983) suggests that relatively meaningless nonsense syllables can be recoded to create more meaningful verbal units. For example, the nonsense syllable *rac* can become the word *car*.

Another use of verbal coding of information involves natural language mediators. Consider the following example of the use of verbal coding. Suppose a person is asked to learn the two words *dog* and *car*. If the person injects the word *chase* between *dog* and *car,* the natural language mediator is *dog-chase-car*. According to Underwood (1983), the mediator produces a meaningful link between the stimulus and the response. Underwood reports that subjects attempting to learn verbal material use language mediators. For example, subjects learning a serial list of words often will add a word or two to the list to create a story.

Can use of natural language mediators enhance the recall of verbal information? Many studies (Spear, 1971) have reported that retrieval of verbal material is increased by the use of natural language mediators. In one of the studies, Montague, Adams, and Kiess (1966) gave to subjects a single presentation of a list of 25 pairs of nonsense syllables and then asked the subjects to report whether they used natural language mediators to learn each pair. The subjects returned to the laboratory 24 hours later to recall the pairs of nonsense syllables. Montague et al. observed greater recall of pairs learned with a mediator than without one.

Visual Codes   Look at, but do not name, the objects in Figure 11-2 for 30 seconds. Now, close your book and see how many of these objects you can name. If you have a good visual memory, you probably can recall most of the objects. In fact, most people would be able to recall more of the objects seen in a picture

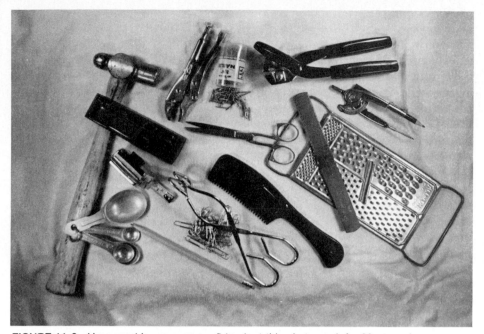

FIGURE 11-2   How good is your memory? Look at this photograph for 30 seconds but do not name the objects. Close the book and try to recall as many of the objects as you can (Courtesy of Fran Smith).

than objects presented verbally (see Paivio, 1986). This observation indicates that encoding objects as images can be more effective than storing them as words.

Words or ideas can be transformed into images. For example, the word *car* can be transformed into the image of a car. According to Underwood (1983), encoding the word as an image can enhance the recall of the word.

Research by Allan Paivio (1969, 1986) showed that the use of imagery enhances the recall of experiences. In one study, Paivio, Yuille, and Madigan (1968) asked people to rate on a scale of 1 to 7 a large number of nouns based on how easily they could form images of the words. In general, concrete nouns such as *blood* or *hyena* were rated high, and abstract nouns such as *democracy* or *truth* were rated low. Paivio reported that his subjects remembered high-imagery words much more readily than low-imagery words.

Why does the amount of imagery elicited by a word affect the amount of recall? According to Paivio, both high- and low-imagery words activate verbal codes. However, only high-imagery words also elicit visual codes. In Paivio's view, the fact that high-imagery words activate two codes, whereas low-imagery words activate only one code, accounts for the greater recall of high-imagery words.

People differ in their ability to store experiences as images. About 1 percent of adults have excellent visual memories (see Haber, 1969). These individuals are able to recall a sharp image of previous experiences. This visual memory or *eidetic image* lasts about 4 minutes and provides for excellent retention of prior events. An eidetic image, or photographic memory, is more common in children than adults. Recall our previous discussion of acoustic coding. We suggested that as children learn to use language to think, they begin to code their experiences acoustically. In all likelihood, the greater use of acoustic coding occurs at the expense of visual coding of experiences. We can learn to make greater use of visual codes; we will examine this topic in our discussion of mnemonics later in this chapter.

The Importance of Decoding   Recall our previous discussion of natural language mediators. We learned that a person could encode the two words *dog* and *car* as *dog-chase-car*. Although natural language mediators can enhance the retrieval of verbal material, this is not always true. Underwood (1983) observed that subjects attempting to recall a particular verbal unit often make errors. In Underwood's view, in order for a subject to accurately recall a response that had been coded by a natural language mediator, the subject's memory of the verbal unit must contain decoding information (or knowledge of words to be deleted). Errors occur because subjects lack a systematic decoding procedure. In our discussion of mnemonics, we will discover that some very effective mnemonic techniques use natural language mediators and contain specific decoding procedures.

As was true of the use of natural language mediators, order transformations can increase the recall of verbal units. A number of studies (Spear, 1971) have shown that this type of coding can enhance recall. However, this is true only if subjects have available to them during recall a simple rule for rearranging the verbal units into the original form.

Underwood and Keppel (1963) presented college students with a list of 10 trigrams to learn. Each trigram could be arranged into words by changing two letters. Some subjects were instructed to rearrange the trigrams into words during training; other subjects were not. Underwood and Keppel reported that rearranging the trigrams into words during training facilitated recall of the trigrams only if the subjects were free to recall the words in any order. If the subject had to recall the trigrams in the correct order, recall was actually poorer than for subjects who had not rearranged the trigrams.

The poor recall of subjects instructed to rearrange the trigrams and then remember them in the original order reflects the absence of simple coding and decoding instructions. To show the importance of coding and decoding rules, Underwood and Erlebacher (1965) provided some of the subjects with specific rules for arranging (coding) and rearranging (decoding) the 12 trigrams they were to learn. Some subjects could code and decode each trigram with the same rule. For example, each trigram in the list could be coded into a word and decoded back into the correct trigram with the 1-3-2 rule (switching second and third letters). Other subjects had two or four rules to use, and a final group had no rules. Underwood and Erlebacher found that order transformation during training improved recall for subjects who had only a single rule to learn compared with subjects who did not code the words during training. In contrast, when subjects needed two or four rules to code and decode the trigrams, recall was impaired. One of the advantages of the mnemonic techniques to be discussed shortly is that they provide a simple rule for coding experiences and then decoding experiences.

The Association of Events

If someone asks you to respond to the word *day,* in all likelihood you will think of the word *night.* Recall from Chapter 2 that your response indicates that you have learned an association between the words *day* and *night.* One organizational function of the short-term store is to record the association of events. Two basic associations, *episodic* and *semantic,* are formed by the short-term store. As we learned in the last chapter, episodic associations are based on temporal contiguity. For example, if another person verbally abuses you, you will associate this person with the verbal abuse. Semantic associations are based on a similarity between the meaning of events. For example, the association of *day* and *night* reflects that both represent times of day.

Associative Network Theories   Does the short-term store randomly associate concepts? Some associations appear to be made in a logical, organized fashion. Episodic associations are organized temporally. Consider our encoding of the 12 months of the year. We do not merely associate the 12 months of the year, but rather learn the months in temporal order. However, we do not associate the months in alphabetical order. While recall of the months in temporal order would be easy, you would have difficulty remembering the months in alphabetical order.

Semantic memories seem to be organized hierarchically. This hierarchical structure is from general to specific concepts. Examine the hierarchy of the concept *minerals* presented in Figure 11-3. As can be seen in the illustration, there are four levels in the hierarchy. The concept *minerals* contains two types: metals and stones. Similarly, there are three types of metals: rare, common, and alloys. A number of psychologists have discussed the organizational structure of semantic memories; we begin with Collins and Quillian's hierarchical approach.

A Hierarchical Approach   Collins and Quillian (1969) suggested that semantic memory consists of hierarchical networks of interconnected concepts. Each concept is represented by a node, and two nodes or concepts are connected by an associative link. At each node there are paths to information about that concept. Figure 11-4 presents one of these associative networks. The superordinate concept *animal* is connected to its subordinate network *bird,* which then is linked to its subordinate, *canary.* The illustration also shows that each node has associated concept information; for example, the node *canary* contains the information that the canary can sing and is yellow.

How did Collins and Quillian verify that semantic memory contains networks of interconnected associations? They reasoned that response time for accessing

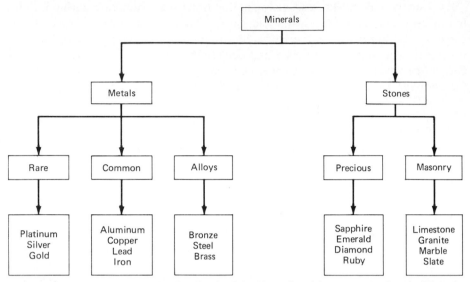

FIGURE 11-3   Illustration showing four levels of the hierarchy of the concept *minerals*. Minerals can be grouped into two types: metals and stones. In turn, metals can be classified as rare, common, and alloys; stones as precious or masonry. In the fourth level, platinum is an example of a rare metal, diamond of a precious stone.

information contained in a network would depend upon the number of links separating the information. According to Collins and Quillian, the greater the separation, the longer the reaction time. Consider the two questions: A canary can sing? or A canary has skin? The first question should be answered more readily since the information about singing is contained in the node *canary*. Yet, the information about skin is located in the animal node, which is separated from the node *canary* by two associative links. Verifying the statement that the canary has skin should take longer to answer than the question can a canary sing, because of the greater separation of information in the former statement.

Collins and Quillian investigated how the reaction time to verify statements is affected by the number of linkages separating the information. They observed that reaction time was positively related to the number of nodes separating information (see Figure 11-5). As seen in the figure, subjects could respond more rapidly to the statement that a canary can sing than to the statement that a canary has skin.

Our discussion suggests that concepts are stored in a hierarchy of interconnected concepts. While there is considerable evidence supporting this view, some researchers have found it be too simplistic. Studies (see Glass & Holyoak, 1986; Stern, 1985) have identified three main problems with the Collins and Quillian hierarchical approach. First, this theory assumes that concepts are stored in semantic memory in a logical hierarchy. Yet, research suggests that this may not always be true. Consider the two statements: ''The collie is an animal'' and ''The

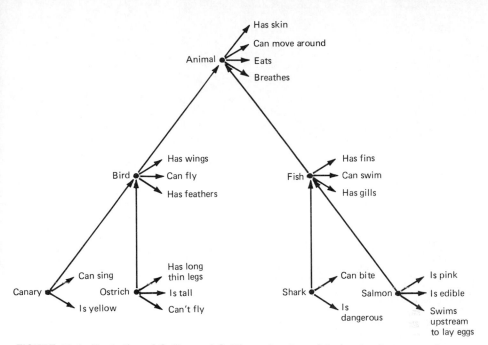

FIGURE 11-4   Illustration of Collins and Quillian network model of semantic memory for concept *animal.* The animal concept node contains four properties and is associated with the nodes of bird and fish, which also have associated properties. From Collins, A. M., & Quillian, M. R. (1969). Retrieval time from semantic memory. *Journal of Verbal Learning and Verbal Behavior,* 8, 240–247.

collie is a mammal.'' Quillian and Collins's view would suggest that reaction time would be longer for the first than for the second statement. The reason for this prediction is that the concept node *mammal* is closer to the node *collie* than is the concept node *animal* (the concept *animal* is superordinate to the concept *mammal*). Yet, Rips, Shoben, and Smith (1973) observed that subjects could verify the statement ''The collie is an animal'' more readily than ''The collie is a mammal.'' Evidently, the speed of reaction time is not always related to the number of levels of concepts separating information.

A second problem involves the idea that information is stored at only one node. For example, the information that animals breathe is only stored at the concept node *animal.* If this assumption is valid, it should take longer to verify the statement ''An ostrich can breathe'' than the statement ''An animal can breathe.'' Yet, Conrad (1972) reported no difference in reaction time for these types of sentences. This result suggests that information is stored at more than one node.

Finally, the Collins and Quillian view assumes that all subordinates of concept are equally representative of that concept. This approach assumes that a canary and an ostrich are equally representative of the concept *bird.* We discovered in

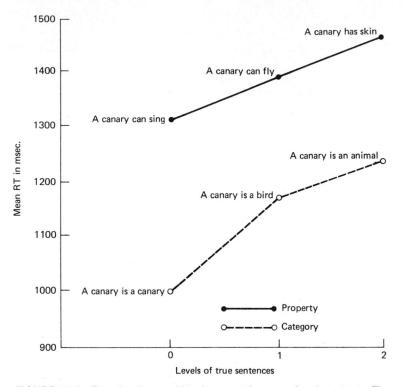

FIGURE 11-5 Reaction time and levels separating associated concepts. The results of this study showed that a person's reaction time to verify a statement was positively related to the number of nodes separating the information; that is, the greater the separation of nodes, the longer the period needed to verify the concept. From Collins, A. M., & Quillian, M. R. (1969). Retrieval time from semantic memory. *Journal of Verbal Learning and Verbal Behavior, 8,* 240–247.

Chapter 9 that all members of a particular concept are not equally representative of the concept; that is, members vary in how closely they resemble the prototype of the concept. In terms of the concept *bird,* a canary is more representative than an ostrich. This greater representativeness allows a person to verify the statement "A canary is a bird" more readily than the statement "An ostrich is a bird" (see Roth & Shoben, 1983).

Our discussion indicates that semantic memory is organized into a hierarchy of interconnected concepts. Several alternative associative models have been developed; we next look at the spreading activation theory developed by Collins and Loftus.

Spreading Activation Theory Collins and Loftus (1975) revised two main aspects of the Collins and Quillian model. First, they assumed that properties can be associated with more than one concept. For example, the property *red* can be associated with a number of concepts, for example, *fire engine, apple, roses,* and *sunset* (see Figure 11-6). Thus, you can have a red apple or a red fire engine. Second, a particular property can be more closely associated with some concepts than others. As seen in Figure 11-6, the property *red* is more closely associated with a fire engine than a sunset.

The spreading activation theory assumes that once a concept or property is activated, activation spreads to associated concepts or properties. For example, if you heard the word *red,* you would think of associated concepts, such as *fire engine* or *sunset.* According to Collins and Loftus (1975), the activation spreads and even more distant associations can be recalled. For example, the activation of the *fire engine* concept could activate the associated concept *vehicle.*

The different lengths of association between properties and concepts explain the differences in reaction time to verify various statements. The greater length of association between *red* and *sunset* than *red* and *fire engine* results in the ability to more rapidly verify the statement "Fire engines are red" than "Sunsets are red."

The spread of activation theory also can explain the *priming* phenomenon or the facilitation of recall of a specific information following exposure to closely related imformation. To show the effect of priming, Meyer and Schvanefeldt (1971) asked subjects to indicate as rapidly as possible when two items were both words (for example, *first-truck*) or were both not words (for example, *roast-brive*). Some of the word pairs were related (*bread-butter*) and other word pairs were not related (*rope-crystal*). Meyer and Schvaneveldt observed that the subjects were able to identify the pairs as both being words if the words were related than if they were not related. According to the spreading activation theory, the prime word activates related words, which leads to a rapid identification that both were words. The lack of priming slows the identification of the second string of letters as a word.

The spreading activation model assumes that semantic memory consists of associations between concepts and properties of concepts. A different theory of encoding was proposed by Smith, Shoben, and Rips, we next examine their feature comparison model.

Feature Comparison Model   Smith, Shoben, and Rips (1974) suggested that concepts in semantic memory are represented by specific properties or features. A few of these properties, called *defining features,* are necessary for definition of the concept. Consider the concept *robin* (see Table 11-2). The defining features of *robin* are (1) is living, (2) has feathers, and (3) has a red breast. The memory of a robin also contains other properties, or *characteristic features.* The characteristic features are (1) flies, (2) perches on trees, (3) is undomesticated, and (4) is smallish. These characteristic features are not essential to the definition of the concept *robin* and are present in other birds as well as the robin.

As seen in Table 11-2, the number of defining and characteristic features is greater in the narrower, subordinate concept *robin* than the broader superordinate concept *bird.* The reason for the differences in number of features is that it takes fewer features to define the broader concept *bird* than the narrower concept *robin.* Also, there are fewer common characteristic features of birds than robins.

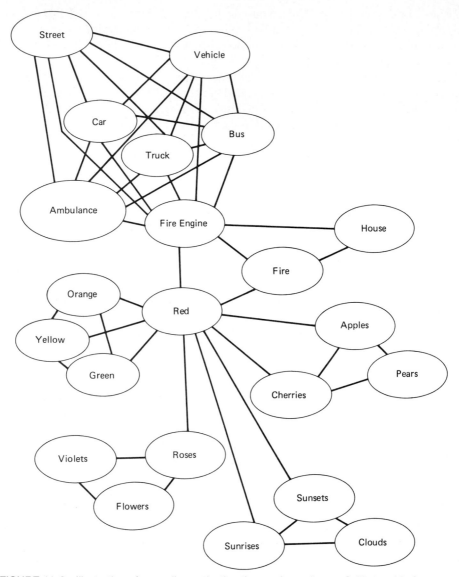

FIGURE 11-6 Illustration of spreading activation theory. According to Collins and Loftus, a property such as red can be associated with several concepts. Also, each concept can have associated properties. A particular property can be more closely associated with some concepts than others. From Collins, A. M., & Loftus, E. F. (1975). A spreading activating theory of semantic memory. *Psychological Review, 82,* 407–428. Copyright 1975 by the American Psychological Association. Reprinted by permission.

   Suppose a person is asked to verify the statement that a robin is a bird. How does the feature comparison model explain this process? The person will compare

TABLE 11-2
DEFINING AND CHARACTERISTIC FEATURES OF CONCEPTS
ROBIN AND *BIRD*

	Concept	
Features	Robin	Bird
Defining features	Is living Has feathers Has a red breast	Is living Has feathers
Characteristic features	Flies Perches in trees Is undomesticated Is smallish	Flies

Source Smith, E. E., Shoben, E. J., & Rips, L. J. (1974). Structure and process in semantic memory: A feature model for semantic decisions. *Psychological Review, 71,* 61–77. Copyright 1974 by the American Psychological Association. Reprinted by permission.

the defining and characteristic features of the subordinate concept (*robin*) with the superordinate concept (*bird*). Substantial overlap of features will lead the person to conclude that "a robin is a bird." A lack of overlap will allow the individual to recognize that a statement is false. The statement "A fish is a bird" is not true, since there is little overlap between the features of a fish and a bird.

The perfect overlap of features of robin and bird (see Table 11-2) allows a person to quickly verify the statement. People take longer to correctly verify statements when there is a moderate degree of overlap between concepts. Consider the statement "A chicken is a bird." A chicken is a bird but neither flies nor perches in trees. The fact that there is not a perfect match of features of chickens and birds forces the person to compare the defining features of the two concepts. This comparison, which indicates that a chicken is a bird, takes time and, therefore, results in a longer verification time than when all the features match.

We have learned that the feature comparison model asserts that each concept contains defining and characteristic features. A comparison of features indicates whether or not concepts are associated. However, there are important weaknesses of this view. For example, the feature comparison theory cannot explain how people disconfirm specific statements (see Glass & Holyoak, 1975). Suppose a person is asked to verify the statements "Some chairs are tables" and "Some rocks are tables." According to feature comparison theory, since the concept *rocks* and *tables* share fewer features than do *chairs* and *tables,* it should take less time to disconfirm the statement "Some rocks are tables" than "Some chairs are tables." Yet, Glass and Holyoak (1975) observed the opposite result: Subjects were able to disconfirm the statement "Some chairs are tables" faster than "Some rocks are tables." How can we explain these results? One way is with the parallel distributed processing model offered by Rumelhart and McClelland.

Parallel Distributed Processing Model Recall our discussion of Hebb's concept of reverberating circuits that we described in the last chapter. Each memory, according to Hebb, consists of separate neural connections. David Rumelhart, James McClelland and the PDP Research Group (1986) suggested that memory is not composed of separate circuits but rather of a series of interconnected associative networks. They propose that memory consists of a wide range of different connections that are simultaneously active. In their theory, thousands of connections are possible. A connection can be either excitatory or inhibitory. Experience can alter the strength of an excitatory or inhibitory connection.

The parallel distributed model assumes that ''knowledge'' is not located in any particular connection. Instead, knowledge is distributed throughout the entire system; that is, the total pattern of connection strengths represents the influence of a total experience. With each individual training experience, the strength of individual connections changes. With continued training, the connections' strength changes until the desired pattern is reached.

Suppose a person sees and smells a rose. How is this experience encoded? According to Rumelhart and McClelland (1986), the sight of the rose (visual input) arouses a certain pattern of neural units and the smell of the rose (olfaction input) activates a different pattern of neural units. Figure 11-7 presents a hypothetical pattern of a rose activating four neural visual units and four neural olfactory units.

As seen in the figure, the pattern of neural A units activated by the sight of rose is $+1$, -1, -1, and $+1$, and the pattern of neural B units activated by the smell of rose is -1, -1, $+1$, and $+1$. (A positive value indicates excitation of a neural unit, and a negative value indicates inhibition of a neural unit.) Rumelhart and McClelland propose that the neural A units elicited by the sight of rose become associated with the neural B units activated by the smell of rose.

Perhaps you see a rose in a vase on a table. This visual image is likely to cause you to recall the smell of a rose. Rumelhart and McClelland's parallel distributed processing model can explain how the sight of a rose caused you to remember the smell of the rose. According to Rumelhart and McClelland, each neural unit activated by the sight of rose is associated with each neural unit activated by the smell of rose. They suggest that stimulation of specific neural units by the sight of rose will arouse the pattern of neural units normally activated by the smell of rose. Stimulation of these olfactory neural units will produce the perception of the smell of a rose.

How does activating the visual units arouse the memory of a rose's smell? Using matrix algebra methods, Rumelhart and McClelland were able to construct a matrix of interconnected elements, or a pattern associator. This pattern associator matrix is formed during the associations of two events and enables the presentation of one event to elicit the recall of the other event. The pattern associator matrix shown in Figure 11.7 is established by association of the sight and smell of a rose and allows the sight of rose to activate the pattern of neural activity produced by the smell of rose. Similarly, the smell of rose can activate the pattern produced by sight of rose and cause us to remember the visual image of a rose.

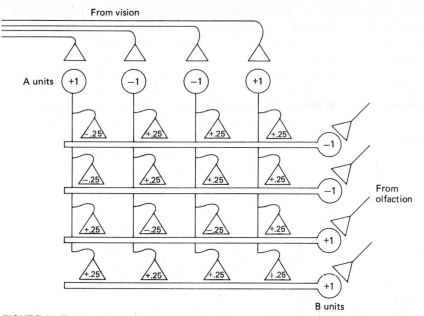

From vision

A units

From olfaction

B units

FIGURE 11-7   Hypothetical illustration of pattern associator matrix of visual and olfactory units activated by sight and smell of a rose. The sight of rose activates four A units in a +1, −1, −1, and +1 pattern, whereas the smell of rose activates four B units in a −1, −1, +1, +1 pattern. The interconnection of all visual A units with all olfactory B units allows the presence of the sight of rose to elicit the recall of a rose's smell. From McClelland, J. L., Rumelhart, D. E., & Hinton, G. E. (1986). The appeal of parallel distributed processing. In Rumelhart, D. E., McClelland, J. L., and the PDP Research Group (Eds). *Parallel distributed processing: Explorations in the microstructure of cognition*, Vol. 1. Cambridge, Mass.: MIT Press.

The main idea of the parallel distributed processing approach is that knowledge is derived from the connections rather than from the nodes. The extensive synaptic connections in the nervous system are consistent with a parallel rather than a serial processing model of memory. Karl Lashley's (1950) classic examination of the location of memory provides additional support for a parallel distributed processing view. Lashley trained rats in a simple discrimination and then destroyed small part of the animals' brains. The intent of this destruction was to locate the site of the animals' memory of the discrimination. Lashley discovered that the animals still showed retention of the discrimination despite the absence of the brain tissue. He continued the search for the engram by destroying other brain areas, but the animals remained able to recall their past learning. On the basis of his observations, Lashley (1950) stated:

It is not possible to demonstrate the isolated localization of a memory trace anywhere within the nervous system. Limited regions may be essential for learning or retention of a particular activity, but within such regions the parts are functionally equivalent. The engram is represented throughout the region.

Lashley's statement suggests that knowledge is distributed throughout an entire region of the nervous system. Interestingly, the parallel distributed processing model came to the same conclusion almost a half century later.

Section Review

The short-term store serves as a temporary storage facility. Information remains in the short-term store for approximately 15 to 20 seconds; during this time, experiences are interpreted for their meaning and then organized in logical ways. The interpretation and organization produce a more meaningful experience, which in turn increases the likelihood of recall occurring at a later time.

Chunking is an automatic process of the short-term store that combines units or bits of information. The amount of information contained in the short-term store is condensed by the chunking process. Information is chunked into smaller units of information at the time of storage, allowing a person to recall information from the long-term store in categories or clusters of chunked material.

Coding, another organizational process of the short-term store, transfers information into a new form. There are three types of memory codes. First, visual experiences can be coded into an auditory form or an acoustic code. Second, information can be coded as a word or verbal code. Third, words or ideas can become an image or visual code. Coding is a natural property of the short-term store, but it will only enhance recall when the memory can be decoded at the time of recall.

Another organizational function of the short-term store is the association of events. Associative network theories assume that associations are formed in a logical fashion. Our memories of personal events, or episodic memories, are associated temporally. Collins and Quillian suggest that semantic memory consists of interconnected concepts and properties associated to each concept node. According to Collins and Quillian, the response time to access information from semantic memory is determined by the number of linkages separating concept nodes.

Spreading activation theory assumes that a property can be associated with more than one concept, but any particular property will be more closely associated with some concepts. Once a concept or property is activated, activation spreads to associated concepts or properties. Differences in reaction time to verify statements are due to different lengths of various associations.

The feature comparison model suggests that concepts in semantic memory contain information about specific properties or features. Defining features are necessary to define the concept, whereas characteristic features are not essential to define the concept but are attributes of that concept. Questions concerning the content of semantic memory are answered by comparing defining and characteristic features of concepts.

The parallel distributed model assumes that knowledge is not contained in any particular location but instead is distributed throughout the entire system. According to this view, a memory consists of a series of interconnected associated networks with either excitatory or inhibitory properties. Experience acts to alter the combined influence of excitation and inhibition in the system.

THE REHEARSAL FUNCTION OF THE SHORT-TERM STORE

Suppose you are trying to learn the French word for *door*. To learn that the French word is *porte,* you must form an association between the words *door* and *porte*. In an attempt to learn the association, you repeat the two words to yourself several times. This process, called *rehearsal,* keeps the memories in the short-term store. Rehearsal has two main functions (see Eich, 1985). First, it keeps information in the short-term store so that it is not forgotten. Second, rehearsal can provide the opportunity to make information more meaningful.

There is an important difference between these two functions of rehearsal. We can merely repeat information contained in the short-term store. When we are simply repeating material that we have experienced, we are using *maintenance rehearsal*. This form of rehearsal will keep information in the short-term store and can lead to establishment of some associations. However, the likelihood of later recall of our experiences is greatly enhanced by the use of *elaborative rehearsal*. With elaborative rehearsal, information is altered to create a more meaningful memory. We may attempt to relate the experience to other information, form a mental image of the experience, or organize the experience in some new way.

Consider the following example to illustrate the difference between maintenance and elaborative rehearsal: You have an exam tomorrow and the material is quite complex. Attempts at trying to memorize the facts by repeating the information has not helped. You simply cannot recall the material for the exam and are quite worried. A friend suggests that instead of merely repeating the words, you relate this new information to concepts presented earlier in the class. The friend indicates several ways of relating current and previous concepts. You think about the relationships between the concepts and now you understand the material for the test.

We have suggested that you can repeat information contained in the short-term store (maintenance rehearsal) and can organize the material in the short-term store (elaborative rehearsal). In the remainder of this section, we examine evidence for these two aspects of the rehearsal process.

Sperling (1967) found that subjects rehearsing an item presented visually say the item to themselves, hear what they say, and then store the message in long-term storage. Sperling's observation implies that rehearsal is "subvocal," or "implicit," speech. Furthermore, a person may repeat the item several times during the rehearsal process until it is finally stored in long-term storage and a new memory is allowed to enter into the short-term store.

Several types of research suggest that rehearsal is subvocal, or implicit, speech. First, recall that visual information is stored acoustically. Second, the rate of rehearsal is the same as that of vocal, or overt, speech (Laudauer, 1962). Laudauer asked subjects either to rehearse a series of letters 10 times or to say the letters aloud. He found that subjects could either rehearse or say about three to six letters a second. Thus, subjects appear to rehearse letters at the same rate as they would say them.

Our discussion indicates that rehearsal represents a recycling of information several times during the short-term store. Does rehearsal increase the strength of a memory in the long-term store? Studies by Rundus (see Rundus, 1971; Rundus & Atkinson, 1970) suggest that rehearsal does enhance the recall of an event by increasing the strength of a memory stored in the long-term store. In one of Rundus's studies, subjects were given a list of words to recall; the words were presented at a rate of one word every 5 seconds. Subjects were instructed to study the list by repeating the words during the 5-second interval between the presentation of the words. After the entire list had been presented, the subjects were required to recall as many words as possible from the list. The level of recall of a particular word was compared to the number of times it had been rehearsed during the interval between the word presentations. Rundus observed that the more times a word is rehearsed, the higher the likelihood that a subject will be able to recall the word. In other words, the more a memory is rehearsed, the greater the chances that the memory will be recalled at a later time.

You may think that rehearsal always increases the level of recall. However, evidence (Craik & Watkins, 1973; Woodward, Bjork, & Jongeward, 1973) indicates that this is not so; in fact, unless rehearsal leads to the organization of an event, rehearsal will not improve recall. Craik and Watkins (1973) presented subjects with a list of 21 words and instructed them to repeat the last word that began with a given letter until the next word beginning with that letter was presented. For example, suppose the given letter was *G* and the list of words was *daughter, oil, rifle, garden, grain, table, football, anchor,* and *giraffe.* The subjects rehearsed *garden* until the word *grain* was presented; *grain* was rehearsed until *giraffe* was presented. Using this procedure, Craik and Watkins varied the amount of time words were rehearsed. Thus, in this list, *garden* was rehearsed for less time than *grain.* Each subject received 27 lists, and the number of words between critical words varied in each list. After completing the 27 lists, each subject was asked to recall as many words as possible from any of the lists. Craik and Watkins found that the amount of time a word was held in the short-term store had no impact on the level of recall, and thus the amount of rehearsal did not affect the recall of the critical word.

Why did rehearsal affect recall in the Rundus study but not in the Craik and Watkins study? The answer may lie in one of the differences between their studies: Subjects in the Craik and Watkins experiment rehearsed only a single word, whereas subjects in Rundus's study rehearsed several words. Thus, subjects could organize the information in the Rundus study, but no organization was possible in the Craik and Watkins study. This suggests that rehearsal will enhance recall only if the subject organized the information during rehearsal.

How might rehearsal enhance the organization of information? Consider the following list of words: *apple, peach, pear, orange.* These words are conceptually similar; each is a type of fruit. The word *fruit* is associated with each word in the list and is an example of an implicit associative response (IAR), because the word *fruit* will be elicited by each word in the list. Suppose these four words were presented within a larger list of 25 words. A subject would probably recall the four fruits together, even though they were not presented consecutively, and a subject able to recall the name of one of the fruits would be very likely to remember the others. Why would the fruits be remembered together? According to Underwood (1965) presentation of the second fruit elicits not only the IAR but also the first fruit. Thus, the IAR is the organizational basis that groups the names of the four fruits. This discussion suggests that rehearsal (remembering the first fruit as a result of the presentation of another fruit) can provide the opportunity to recall the IAR and other conceptually similar items in a list, thus tying all the items together.

Wood and Underwood's (1967) study evaluated the influence of an IAR on the recall of a list of words. They used a list of words such as *derby, coffee,* and *skunk,* words that are not ordinarily grouped together. However, adding the word *black* to the list creates an IAR for the other three words. Wood and Underwood, evaluating the influence of presenting an IAR with the list of other items conceptually related to the IAR, found that the IAR did enhance the recall of conceptually similar items. (It should be noted that the IAR must be included in the initial presentation of the list of words; the IAR has no influence if it is presented only on the recall task.) Wood and Underwood's results indicate that the IAR acts to increase the level of recall of items. Presumably, the IAR acts to increase recall by enhancing the organization of items during rehearsal.

THE RECONSTRUCTION OF THE PAST

How accurate is a person's recollection of an experience? Sir Fredrick Bartlett (1932) argued that a memory of an experience is often inaccurate. Sometimes details of an event are forgotten, creating an imperfect memory. To create a logical and realistic experience, people may add information to the memory during recall. Or an experience may not make sense to an individual, and some information will be deleted or new information added to establish a memory consistent with the individual's view of the world. The alteration of a memory to correspond to the individual's expectations is called *memory reconstruction.* This memory reconstruction process was first studied by Frederic Bartlett many years ago.

Memory Reconstruction Studies

Bartlett examined the alteration of a memory during recall. In one of his classic studies, he had subjects read the folktale "The War of the Ghosts." This story contains a number of details about the experiences and eventual death of a warrier who was engaged in combat with ghosts (see Figure 11-8). The students were tested for recall of the story immediately after reading it and then several hours or days later. Bartlett noted that the subjects' memory of the stories, when tested at both time intervals, often differed from the original story. He found that some

THE WAR OF THE GHOSTS

Original Story

One night two young men from Egulac went down to the river to hunt seals, and while they were there it became foggy and calm. Then they heard warcries, and they thought: "Maybe this is a war-party." He escaped to the shore, and hid behind a log. Now canoes came up, and they heard the noise of paddles, and saw one canoe coming up to them. There were five men in the canoe, and they said:

"What do you think? We wish to take you along. We are going up the river to make war on the people."

One of the young men said: "I have no arrows."

"Arrows are in the canoe," they said.

"I will not go along. I might be killed. My relatives do not know where I have gone. But you," he said, turning to the other, "may go with them."

So one of the young men went, but the other returned home.

And the warriors went on up the river to a town on the other side of Kalama. The people came down to the water, and they began to fight, and many were killed. But presently the young man heard one of the warriors say: "Quick, let us go home; that Indian has been hit." Now he thought: "Oh, they are ghosts." He did not feel sick, but they said he had been shot.

So the canoes went back to Egulac, and the young man went ashore to his house, and made a fire. And he told everybody and said: "Behold I accompanied the ghosts, and we went to fight. Many of our fellows were killed, and many of those who attacked us were killed. They said I was hit, and I did not feel sick."

He told it all, and then he became quiet. When the sun rose he fell down. Something black came out of his mouth. His face became contorted. The people jumped up and cried.

He was dead.

Remembered Story

Two men from Edulac went fishing. While thus occupied by the river they heard a noise in the distance.

"It sounds like a cry," said one, and presently there appeared some in canoes who invited them to join the party on their adventure. One of the young men refused to go, on the ground of family ties, but the other offered to go.

"But there are no arrows," he said.

"The arrows are in the boat," was the reply.

He thereupon took his place, while his friend returned home. The party paddled up the river to Kaloma, and began to land on the banks of the river. The enemy came rushing upon them, and some sharp fighting ensued. Presently someone was injured, and the cry was raised that the enemy were ghosts.

The party returned down the stream, and the young man arrived home feeling none the worse for his experience. The next morning at dawn he endeavored to recount his adventures. While he was talking, something black issued from his mouth. Suddenly he uttered a cry and fell down. His friends gathered around him.

But he was dead.

FIGURE 11-8 Bartlett had subjects read stories, such as "The War of the Ghosts." Subject recollections of these stories varied significantly from the original tales. An example of a remembered version is given here. From Bartlett, F. C. (1932). *Remembering: A study in experimental and social psychology.* Cambridge: Cambridge University Press.

aspects of the stories were deleted, some overemphasized; in other cases, new information was added. According to Bartlett, the content and structure of the folktale was quite different from actual events that the subjects had experienced. Because of their unfamiliarity with the story, the subjects reconstructed their

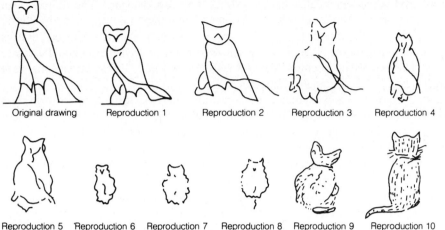

FIGURE 11-9   Subject 1 was shown original drawing and asked to reproduce it after half an hour. The reproduction of the original drawing was shown to subject 2, whose reproduction was presented to subject 3, and so on through subject 10. This figure presents the original drawing and the 10 reproductions. Note that the drawing changes with each successive reproduction. From Bartlett, F. C. (1932). *Remembering: A study in experimental and social psychology.* Cambridge: Cambridge University Press.

memory to be more consistent with their own cultural expectations. Bartlett reported that each subject retained some key facts and then used these key ideas to reconstruct the story. He found that the main features were retained, but since each subject was using personal knowledge to reconstruct the story, each subject's version differed. An example of a reconstructed story also is presented in Figure 11-8.

To demonstrate how extensively a memory can be altered by reconstruction, Bartlett presented a figure to a subject, then told the subject told to reproduce it for a second subject. In some cases, the transmission of information continued through 10 subjects. Bartlett noted that not only did the final drawing differ from the original, but the changes were quite extensive. Also, the figure changed from subject to subject. Figure 11-9 shows the change in each subject's recollection of the figure presented.

Bartlett argued that memories were reconstructed when the event was stored. Some research (see Kintsch, 1974) does show that experiences can be altered during storage, while other experimentation (see Hasher & Griffin, 1978) indicates that memories can be altered at the time of retrieval. We next examine the memory reconstruction of eyewitness testimony.

The Accuracy of Eyewitness Testimony

Elizabeth Loftus (1980) pointed out the significant relation between the memory reconstruction process and the accuracy of eyewitness testimony. According to

Loftus, trial witnesses recall what they think they saw or heard. The literature on memory reconstruction suggests that subjects' recollections may not always be accurate. In all likelihood, the incident witnesses are recalling occurred months or years earlier, and they may have forgotten some aspects of the event. To create a logical and realistic account, the witnesses will fill in information consistent with the aspects they actually remember.

Loftus (1980) contends that a memory also can be altered by information received from others. Because of this information, the memory of the past event is inaccurate, and memory is subsequently changed to conform to the information received from other people. Consider Loftus' (1975) study to illustrate this process. In her study, subjects first were shown a series of slides showing a red sports car headed for a collision. Two groups of subjects saw the same sequence of slides except for one difference: Some subjects saw the car approaching a stop sign; for the other group, the subjects saw a yield sign in the slide (see Figure 11-10). After seeing the slides, the subjects were asked a series of questions about the accident. One question was "Did you see the stop sign?" For half of these subjects, this question was consistent with the slides; that is, they actually saw the stop sign. Yet, for the other subjects, this question was inconsistent with their experiences, since they did not see a stop sign. The other half of the subjects were asked, "Did you see the yield sign?"

A week later, all subjects were asked to recall the accident. Testing involved showing subjects pairs of slides and then asking them to identify which slide they actually saw. Loftus reported that subjects who were asked the question consistent with actual experience correctly identified 75 percent of the time the actual slide (either stop sign or yield sign) that they had seen in the accident. However, subjects who were asked the inconsistent question identified the correct slide only 40 percent of the time.

Why did the inconsistent question cause many subjects to think that the other sign actually was in the scene? According to Loftus, the wording of the question implied that the other sign was present during the accident, and thus the subjects altered their memory of the accident to include the other sign. These results show that a memory can be altered by information received during recall.

The results of Loftus' study have special relevance to the reliability of eyewitness testimony. They demonstrate that a clever attorney may be able to change a witness's memory of a crime by asking leading questions, thereby altering the outcome of the trial. Other psychologists also have found that suggestion can alter the content of memory; see Dodd and Bradshaw (1980) for another example.

Changing a witness's memory can be accomplished by very subtle wording of a question. For example, Loftus and Zanni (1975) asked subjects one of two questions about a car accident. Some subjects were asked, "Did you see the broken headlight?" Other subjects were questioned, "Did you see a broken headlight?" Subjects who heard the word *the* were much more likely to say that they did see a broken headlight in the film. On the basis of the Loftus and Zanni study, as well as similar studies, it is no wonder that many psychologists and legal scholars question the accuracy of eyewitness testimony.

FIGURE 11-10
Didn't You See the Stop Sign? The top photo shows the actual scene of the car going
through the yield sign, while the bottom depicts the scene recalled when the experimenter
suggested that a stop sign was present. (Photos provided by Elizabeth Loftus.)

Is the original memory obliterated by the memory reconstruction process? The
evidence (see Zaragoza, McCloskey, & Jamis, 1987) suggests that the original
memory still exists, but the person is uncertain whether the original or the reconstructed memory is accurate. Recent research on eyewitness testimony (see
Schaller, Gerhard, & Loftus, 1986) indicates that an individual witnessing an
accident and then receiving misleading information cannot discriminate between
the real and suggested events. This inability to tell the real from the imaginary
leads to inaccurate eyewitness testimony.

Consider John Dean's recollections of the Watergate conversations to illustrate this inaccuracy. His testimony was a mixture of real and imagined events, and he was unable to distinguish what actually happened from what he thought took place. Dean received a lot of misleading information from the other participants in the Watergate affair; their information merged with his recollections to create the inconsistencies in his recollections.

Altering the Memories of Animals

Do animals reconstruct their memories? The research of William Gordon and associates (Gordon, 1983; Mowrer & Gordon, 1983; Wittrup & Gordon, 1982) indicates that information experienced during recall can change an animal's memory of a past event. Mowrer and Gordon's (1983) study provides an illustration of the reconstruction of memory process. In the study, rats were first trained to avoid shock in a shuttle box. Some rats received avoidance training and testing in the same context; other rats were trained and tested in different contexts. Mowrer and Gordon reported that retention of the avoidance response was impaired when the context was changed from training to testing. As we will discover in the next chapter, the absence of the environmental stimuli associated with training is responsible for forgetting observed in animals trained and tested in different environments. Mowrer and Gordon treated a third group of animals in yet another manner. These animals were trained in one context, were given a cueing treatment in a second context, and then were retested in the original training context. The cueing procedure involves exposure to a white translucent box that is identical to the white chamber of the avoidance apparatus. The researchers reported that animals in this third group performed poorly on the avoidance task when tested in the original context.

Why did exposure to the cueing treatment lead to poor recall in the training context? According to Mowrer and Gordon, the cueing treatment caused the animals to remember their previous avoidance training in the new context. This treatment altered the memory of avoidance learning by changing the memory to include the second rather than the first environment. Apparently, an animal's memory of past experiences can also be reconstructed by the presence of new information during recall. We will have more to say about the role of context in memory retrieval in the next chapter.

APPLICATION: MNEMONICS

My youngest son recently requested that I ask some questions for his science test. One question required him to list five items. As he recalled the list to me, it was evident that he had a system for remembering the list. He had memorized the first letter of each item and was using these letters to recall each item on the list. Although he was unaware of it, he was using a *mnemonic technique* to recall the list of items. People often unknowingly use mnemonic techniques to increase recall. For example, medical students trying to remember the bones in a person's hand often use a mnemonic device; they take the first letter of each bone, construct a word from the letters, and use the word to recall the bones on a test. Perhaps you have used a similar mnemonic technique to recall some information.

You may have noted that the two cases just described are examples of the coding process detailed earlier in the chapter. Your observation is accurate. There is nothing mystical about mnemonics. Mnemonic techniques merely use the short-term store efficiently. You have undoubtedly seen memory experts on television. Although they seem to possess an extraordinary memory, their ability to recall information stems from their use of mnemonic techniques. There are a number of these techniques, each having in common the ability to take unorganized material and store it in a meaningful way.

The remainder of this chapter discusses several mmemonic techniques. Students in my courses using these mnemonic techniques have found them to be effective ways of enhancing recall. Since this chapter gives only a brief discussion of mnemonics, interested readers should refer to *The Memory Book* by Lorayne and Lucas (1974) to master the use of mnemonics.

Method of Loci

Suppose you need to give a memorized speech in one of your classes. Trying to remember the words by rote memorization would be a time-consuming process and could cause you to make many mistakes. This method of loci is one mnemonic technique you might use to recall the speech. This method, developed by the Greeks to memorize speeches, first involves establishing an ordered series of known locations. For example, the person can take "a mental walk" through his or her home, such as entering the house through the living room, and so on. The individual would then separate the speech into several key thoughts. The key thoughts are then associated in the order corresponding to the walk through the house. Perhaps your speech will be on Pavlov's research on the classical conditioning process. The first key thought may be to remember that Pavlov used dogs to investigate conditioning. You need to associate this thought with your living room. To do this, you might form a mental image of Pavlov and a dog in your living room. When you give the speech, you need only to imagine going into the living room and seeing Pavlov and his dog there. This mental image will enable you to tell your class that Pavlov investigated the conditioning process using dogs. Perhaps you can see from our discussion that the method of loci represents a structured technique for using the associative and organizational capacities of the short-term store to remember a speech. The use of imagery increases the meaningfulness of the material and thus acts to enhance the recall of the speech.

The method of loci can be used to remember any list, either in a specific order or in a random one. For example, you need to buy six items at the grocery store (see Figure 11-11). You could write the items on a piece of paper or use the method of loci to remember them. Perhaps one item you need is sugar. You could

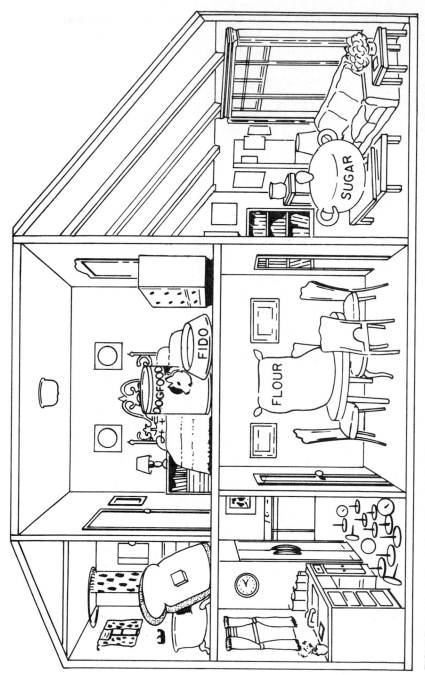

FIGURE 11-11 *A Mental Trip Through the House.* An illustration of how one could use the method of loci to remember a shopping list of six items: butter, bread, flour, thumbtacks, sugar, and dog food. This method involves associating the mental image of the item with a familiar place, such as a room in your house.

associate a container of sugar with your living room. Using this method to recall lists of items will show you that your memory can be improved and will document the power of the mmemonic techniques.

Peg Word System

Another popular mnemonic technique used to enhance recall of a list is the *peg word* system. An example of a popular peg word system is

One is a bun.
Two is a shoe.
Three is a tree.
Four is a door.
Five is a hive.
Six is sticks.
Seven is heaven.
Eight is a gate.
Nine is wine.
Ten is a hen.

Let's see how this peg word mnemonic system works. Suppose you wanted to learn the following list of words: *table, candle, firewood, glass, cigar, picture, book, ashtray, car,* and *lamp*. To use the peg word system to remember the list, first associate the word *table* with the first peg word, *bun*. To do this, perhaps imagine a bun sitting on a table. Next, associate the word *candle* with the second peg word, *shoe*. To do this, imagine a candle burning a hole in the shoe. Associate each word in the list with the appropriate peg word. The peg word system works like the method of loci: Both efficiently use the associative and organizational capacity of the short-term store. This system also is effective because a person can recall any item without having to start at the beginning of the list.

Lorayne and Lucas (1974) offer a different peg word system in *The Memory Book*. Although more difficult to learn, it provides more useful applications than the systems described above. For example, Lorayne and Lucas's peg word system can be used to remember a variety of things, including phone numbers, playing cards, weekly appointments, and anniversaries. The system begins by matching a letter to each of the numbers from 0 to 9. The pegs are

1 = *t* or *d*
2 = *n*
3 = *m*
4 = *r*
5 = *l*
6 = *sh, j, ch,* soft *g*
7 = *k, l, and c,* hard *g*
8 = *f, v, ph*
9 = *p* or *b*
0 = *z, s,* soft *c*

TABLE 11-3
ONE HUNDRED PEG WORDS

1.	tie	26.	notch	51.	lot	76.	cage
2.	Noah	27.	neck	52.	lion	77.	coke
3.	Ma	28.	knife	53.	loom	78.	cave
4.	rye	29.	knob	54.	lure	79.	cob
5.	law	30.	mouse	55.	lily	80.	fuzz
6.	shoe	31.	mat	56.	leech	81.	fit
7.	cow	32.	moon	57.	log	82.	phone
8.	ivy	33.	mummy	58.	lava	83.	foam
9.	bee	34.	mower	59.	lip	84.	fur
10.	toes	35.	mule	60.	cheese	85.	file
11.	tot	36.	match	61.	sheet	86.	fish
12.	tin	37.	mug	62.	chain	87.	fog
13.	tomb	38.	movie	63.	chum	88.	fife
14.	tire	39.	mop	64.	cherry	89.	fob
15.	towel	40.	rose	65.	jail	90.	bus
16.	dish	41.	rod	66.	choo choo	91.	bat
17.	tack	42.	rain	67.	chalk	92.	bone
18.	dove	43.	ram	68.	chef	93.	bum
19.	tub	44.	rower	69.	ship	94.	bear
20.	nose	45.	roll	70.	case	95.	bell
21.	net	46.	roach	71.	cot	96.	beach
22.	nun	47.	rock	72.	coin	97.	book
23.	name	48.	roof	73.	comb	98.	puff
24.	Nero	49.	rope	74.	car	99.	pipe
25.	nail	50.	lace	75.	coal	100.	disease

Source: Lorayne, H., & Lucas, J. (1974). *The Memory Book.* New York: Stein & Day.

There is a rationale for each of the pegs. For example, 4 is *r* because the word *four* ends in the letter *r*. The system so far is a code for transforming numbers to letters. To create the peg words, vowels and consonants not used for other pegs are added. For example, the peg for 5 is *law*. Peg words above 9 can be easily created; the peg word for 55 is *lily*. In fact, an infinite number of peg words can be created (refer to Table 11-3).

Let's look at one example of the use of this peg word system to remember a telephone number. Suppose your doctor's number is 940-8212. To learn this number, Lorayne and Lucas suggest that you associate *doctor* (perhaps by using a stethoscope) to *br*(a)*ss f*(ou)*nt*(ai)*n*. The italic letters refer to the letters that correspond to the numbers in the peg word system. To form this association, visualize a stethoscope around a brass fountain.

A word of caution: Much practice is needed to use this mnemonic system efficiently. You need to (1) learn the peg, (2) use the peg to code information, and (3) decode the peg word to recall information correctly. In our example, you need to know how to transform the peg words *brass fountain* into the correct phone number. The efficient use of this peg word system, like any skill, requires time and effort. Do not expect rapid results. However, if you work at it, you will in all likelihood be pleased with the outcome. One problem experienced by many people is difficulty remembering names. The last example of a mnemonic technique is a description of its use in recalling names.

Remembering Names

Why do many people have such a hard time remembering other people's names? To recall a name, an individual must associate the person with his or her name, store this association, then be able to retrieve the name. The main problem with remembering a person's name lies in the storage process: The association of a person's name with that individual is a difficult one to form. As is true with many recall problems, the association will eventually be formed with repeated repetition and, therefore, eventually will be recalled. Mnemonic techniques can enhance the association between a name and a person; the enhanced storage of this association enables a person to recall a name after a single experience.

Lorayne and Lucas (1974) provide many examples of the use of mnemonics to recall people's names. Let's examine several of them. Suppose you meet a person named Bill Gordon. Perhaps Bill Gordon has very bushy eyebrows. Lorayne and Lucas suggest that when you first meet him, you might visualize his eyebrows as being a *garden* with dollar *bills* growing there. The mental image formed when you first meet someone and then elicited when you see this person again will provide you with the information needed to recall the person's name.

What if you meet a woman named Ms. Pukcyva? How can you possibly use the mnemonic technique to recall her name? Perhaps she has a tall hairdo; you could see *shivering* hockey *pucks* flying out of her hair. After you have formed this association, the next time you meet Ms. Pukcyva you will remember her name.

This mnemonic technique can create a mental image that contains not only a person's name but also other bits of information about the individual. For example, suppose Mr. Gordon works for American Airlines. You can put this information into your mental image by seeing an United States flag (*American*) on an airplane (*Airlines*) flying. Note that practice is required before you will be able to rapidly form a mental image of a person's name and then remember the name. The more you practice, the more efficient you will become at remembering names.

Do mnemonic techniques work? The empirical evidence indicates that they are effective (see Norman, 1976, for a review of this literature). We will look at two studies demonstrating the effectiveness of mnemonics. Bugelski's (1968) study provides one example of the effectiveness of mnemonic techniques. Bugelski had an experimental group learn a list of words using the "one is a bun" peg word system and control subjects learn the list without the aid of the mnemonic technique. Bugelski then asked subjects to recall specific words; for example, he asked them, "What is the seventh word?" The study found that experimental subjects recalled significantly more words than did control subjects.

Crovitz (1971) demonstrated the effectiveness of the method of loci. He had subjects learn a list of 32 words either using the method of loci or not having any special instructions. Crovitz reported that experimental subjects who learned the list with the method of loci recalled 26 of the words, compared to 7 words for control subjects who did not have the benefit of this mnemonic technique.

SUMMARY

1. Craik and Lockhart suggest that an event can receive varying levels of processing or elaboration. The amount of elaboration that an experience receives during processing influences the recall of that event; the more elaborately an event is encoded, the more likely the memory will be retrieved later. Elaboration affects retrieval presumably by enhancing the identification of the important aspects of an experience. This enhanced identification can provide memory attributes that allow retrieval during testing as well as enable the memory to be distinguished from other experiences, thereby reducing interference as a source of forgetting.

2. The short-term store serves as a temporary storage facility. While in the short-term store, experiences are interpreted for their meaning and then organized in logical ways. The interpretation and organization produce a more meaningful experience, which in turn increases the likelihood of recall occurring at a later time.

3. Chunking is an automatic process of the short-term store that combines units or bits of information. The amount of information contained in the short-term store is condensed by the chunking process. By chunking information into smaller units at the time of storage, a person can recall information in categories or clusters of chunked material.

4. Coding, another organizational process of the short-term store, transforms information into a new type of code. There are three types of memory codes. First, visual experiences can be coded into an auditory form, or acoustic code. Second, information can be coded as a word, or verbal code. Third, words or ideas can become images, or visual codes. Coding is a natural property of the short-term store but will only enhance recall when the memory can be decoded at the time of recall.

5. Another organizational function of the short-term store is the association of events. Our memory of personal events, or episodic memories, are associated temporally. Collins and Quillian suggest that semantic memory consists of interconnected concepts and properties associated with each concept node. According to Collins and Quillian, the response time to access information from semantic memory is determined by the number of linkages separating concept nodes.

6. The spreading activation theory assumes that a property can be associated with more than one concept, but any particular property will be more closely associated with some concepts than with others. Once a concept or property is activated, activation spreads to associated concepts or properties. Differences in reaction time to verify statements are due to different lengths of various associations. According to spreading activation theory, the greater the length of the association, the longer the reaction time to access semantic memory.

7. The feature comparison model suggests that concepts in semantic memory contain information about specific properties or features. Defining features are needed to define the concept, whereas characteristic features are not essential to define the concept but

are attributes of that concept. Questions concerning the content of semantic memory are answered by comparing defining and characteristic features of concepts.

8 The parallel distributed model assumes that knowledge is not contained in any particular location but instead is distributed throughout the entire system. According to this view, a memory consists of a series of interconnected associated networks with either excitatory or inhibitory properties. Experience acts to alter the combined influence of excitation and inhibition in the system.

9 The short-term store can rehearse or replay prior experiences. This rehearsal can function to retain information in the short-term store for a longer period (maintenance rehearsal). This increased rehearsal also enhances the interpretation and organization of the memory (elaborative rehearsal), improving the likelihood that the memory will later be available for recall.

10 The memory of an experience is not always accurate. Sometimes details of an event are forgotten, creating an imperfect memory. To produce a logical and realistic memory of an event, information will be added to the memory during recall. If an experience does not make sense, some information may be deleted, new information may be added, or both, to establish a memory of an event that is consistent with the animal's or person's perception of the world.

11 Environmental input received during retrieval can also lead to a change in the memory of a past experience. The alteration of a memory after initial storage is called memory reconstruction. Research in the area of memory reconstruction has special significance because it relates to the accuracy of much or all eyewitness testimony. Misleading information can alter a person's recollections of an event that he or she witnessed. The original memory is not obliterated, but instead the person cannot discriminate between the real and suggested events.

12 Memory can be improved by the use of mnemonic techniques. There are a number of mnemonic techniques, and the effectiveness of each results from enhanced organization of information during the storage process. This increased organization leads to improved ability to remember information.

12

MEMORY RETRIEVAL
AND FORGETTING

A LOOK INTO THE PAST

Steve's grandfather died yesterday. His death surprised Steve. Although he was
90 when he died, his grandfather had been in relatively good health. He
suffered a massive coronary while riding in Steve's mother's car. He died
immediately, and Steve was glad that he did not suffer.

The plane ride home to his grandfather's funeral was long, and during the
trip, Steve had a lot of time to reminisce about childhood experiences with
his grandfather. His grandparents had lived in Brooklyn when he was young,
and Steve would stay with them for one week every summer. He remembered
those visits with his grandparents as being quite wonderful. His grandfather
would take him to see the Dodgers play at Ebbets Field at least twice during
each visit. He could still remember seeing Jackie Robinson, Roy Campanella,
and Duke Snider. Steve was sure that his passion for baseball began during
those trips.

Steve also went to Coney Island with his grandparents. He remembered
fondly the arcade where his grandfather would give him money to play the
games. Visits to Coney Island meant eating at Nathan's. He could still taste
Nathan's hotdogs, one of life's greatest treats. Remembering eating Nathan's
hotdogs also reminded him of becoming very ill after riding a roller coaster at
Coney Island. Not surprisingly, Steve no longer enjoys riding roller coasters.

He continued to reminisce about his childhood experiences with his
grandfather throughout the plane ride. Toward the end of the flight, Steve
realized that his grandfather always would be with him. His survival past death
was possible because of his grandson's ability to remember the past.

Remembering is a very important part of all of our lives. It allows us to recall a first love, or a vacation with our parents. Yet, we do not remember all of the events that happen to us. People often forget where they left their car in the parking lot of a large shopping mall, or where they last left their car keys. In this chapter, we discuss why sometimes we are able to recall events from the past, but at other times are unable to remember past experiences.

ATTRIBUTES OF MEMORY

Benton Underwood (1969, 1983) suggested that memory can be conceptualized as a collection of different types of information. Each type of information is called a *memory attribute*. For example, the memory of an event contains information regarding where the event occurred. This aspect is referred to as the *spatial* attribute of that memory. A memory also contains information about the temporal characteristics of an event; Underwood calls this the *temporal* attribute. According to Underwood, there are 10 major memory attributes: acoustic, orthographic, frequency, spatial, temporal, modality, context, affective, verbal associative, and transformational.

The Function of an Attribute

Before discussing each type of memory attribute, let's first look at the two basic functions of attributes as described by Underwood. First, *the establishment of a specific aspect of an experience as a memory attribute can act to decrease forgetting*. Interference, a major cause of forgetting, often occurs as a result of the failure to differentiate between memories. Information contained in a memory attribute provides a basis for distinguishing memories and thus can prevent forgetting. Second, *the presence of the stimulus contained in the memory attribute can act to retrieve a memory*. When we encounter or reexperience the stimulus that characterizes a salient aspect of a past event, the presence of that stimulus will cause us to recall the memory of the event. We will discuss the development of memory attributes and their role in the recall of past experiences in more detail later.

Although there are 10 major attributes of memory, information about each attribute may not be contained in every memory. Even though a stimulus may characterize a particular aspect of a past experience, if it is not a memory attribute of that experience, its presence will not lead to the recall of the event. For example, you have a traffic accident on a particular day. If the day of the accident is not an attribute of the memory, the anniversary of the accident will not remind you of this misfortune. The one or two most salient aspects of an experience will become memory attributes of the event, and retrieval will be based solely on the presence of the stimuli that represent these attributes.

Types of Attributes

Acoustic Attribute   Recall from Chapter 11 that experiences are acoustically coded by the short-term store. Underwood suggested that one attribute of a memory provides information about the acoustical properties of an event. Because speech communication would be impossible if people could not discriminate between verbal signals, acoustic properties of an event are clearly important.

Long and Allen's (1973) study illustrates the important influence of the acoustic attribute on the recall of an experience. Long and Allen presented to their subjects a list of 18 words organized in one of two ways: six groups of three rhyming words (for example, *Ted, red, head; Jack, black, back*) or six groups of three conceptually related words (for example, *Ted, Jack, Jean; red, black, green*). After the list was presented, the subjects were asked to recall as many words as they could. Remember that while the list is being presented, subjects organize the words into clusters. Long and Allen, interested in whether the subjects would cluster the words based on the acoustic attribute or the conceptual attribute, found that the words were clustered according to the way they sounded rather than their meaning. These observations indicate that the acoustic attribute had a dominant influence on the recall of the words.

Underwood (1969) suggested that the *acoustic attribute* does not always play the dominant role in memory. Sometimes acoustic features may not be the most salient aspect of the experience. In these circumstances, other types of information will become attributes and later be used to recall the experience.

Orthographic Attribute   Events differ in terms of structural characteristics. For example, different letters have different shapes. Words differ in length, in number of syllables, in number of repeated letters, and in terms of unusual or infrequently appearing sequences. Underwood referred to the feature characteristics of events as their *orthographic attribute.*

To differentiate items, for example, to distinguish an *A* from a *K,* a person must recognize feature characteristics of each item. Evidence indicates that people can detect these orthographic characteristics of an event. For example, Zechmeister (1969) reported that subjects rated words based on their orthographic distinctiveness.

Furthermore, people can use the orthographic attribute to recall a particular event. To illustrate the influence of orthographic attribute on the retrieval of a memory, Hintzman, Block, and Inskeep (1972) presented subjects with eight successive 18-word lists. Half of the words on each list were presented in uppercase block letters; the other half, in lowercase script letters. Hintzman and colleagues found that, on a free recall task (a task in which subjects can recall items in any order), subjects reported words in the script type in one group and words in the block type in another group. These results indicate that the orthographic attribute of type style was used to retrieve the words on the list. Other attributes also were used to recall the words, because all the subjects did not cluster the words based on type style. The use of the orthographic attribute to recall material has been

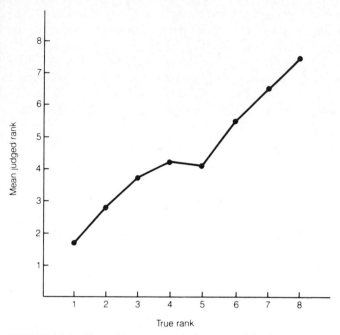

FIGURE 12-1   The subjects' mean judgments of the frequency with which words occur in printed discourse were highly related to the actual frequency of occurrence; the more often the words appeared, the higher the subjects' judgment of their occurrence in print. From *Attributes of memory* by B. J. Underwood. Copyright 1983 by Scott, Foresman and Company. Reprinted by permission.

reported by other researchers; for example, Kolers (1976) had subjects read some material upside down and found that subjects could recall items a year later based on whether they had been read upside down.

Frequency Attribute   According to Underwood, a counting mechanism that registers every experience provides a record of the number of times a specific event is experienced. In Underwood's view, the frequency of an event's occurrence, or the *frequency attribute,* can be used to recall the memory of that event.

Ekstrand, Wallace, and Underwood (1966) presented subjects with a list of eight 4-letter words and asked them to guess how frequently each of the words appeared in everyday print such as books and newspapers. The results showed that these estimates corresponded well with the actual frequency that the words did appear (Figure 12-1). Thus, people do store information about how frequently certain events occur.

Can this information about frequency be used to recall a specific memory? Ekstrand et al. (1966) also evaluated this aspect of memory attribute theory. Subjects in this study received a list of 75 words, 40 of which were presented only once; 20 were presented twice; 10, three times; and 5, four times. After the list had been presented, the subjects were shown pairs of the words from the list and asked to indicate which of the two words had occurred more frequently. If frequency is an attribute of memory, then the subjects should be able to recognize the word in the pair that had occurred more frequently. Ekstrand and colleagues reported that subjects did use the frequency information and identified the correct word. Note that identification was not perfect but that a greater difference in how frequently the two words appeared was correlated with greater accuracy of recall. For example, subjects were better able to identify the correct word if one word had been presented one time and the other word presented four times than if the words had been presented two and three times.

Spatial Attribute   Students will occasionally tell me that they can remember the number of the page where a particular study is described in a textbook. These people have stored information about the spatial location of a certain item. This knowledge represents the *spatial attribute* of a memory.

According to Underwood (1969, 1983), spatial information automatically becomes part of a person's memory of an event. A study by Weeks (1975) shows that the stimulus contained in the spatial attribute can prompt retrieval of a memory. In Weeks' study, subjects received five successive lists of trigrams presented through either a single speaker or two speakers placed 120 degrees apart. When all five lists were presented through the same speaker, interference caused the subjects to have difficulty remembering words from later lists. However, if the first four lists were presented through one speaker and the fifth through a second speaker, the subjects could readily remember the words presented in the last list. These results suggest that the spatial location of the speaker became an attribute for remembering the last list and was responsible for subjects' ability to recall the words on it.

Let's use one further example to show the influence of the spatial attribute. When trying to remember the details of a particular story, you recall the specific newspaper or magazine in which the story appeared. You can then use this spatial information to remember the story.

Temporal Attribute   When it is September 15th, I know that it's my birthday. Obviously, one attribute of my birthday is the date on which my birth occurred. The knowledge of my birth date is the *temporal attribute* of that event. Everyone knows the date of his or her birthday as well as the dates of other significant events. These observations indicate that time can be a very important part of a memory. Even so, research shows that only *significant* temporal information is used to recall an experience.

Underwood (1977) presented college students with a list of eight events; the events occurred approximately a year apart, and Underwood made certain that the subjects were familiar with the details of these events. The students were asked to rank the events in the order that they had taken place. Underwood reported that of 108 students, only 2 did so correctly. Apparently, the temporal attribute does not always contain sufficient information for retrieval; a person may know that an event occurred but may not know exactly when. For example, you may have received an excellent grade on a test on a particular date last year, but that date this year does not remind you of the test or grade. Only when the date becomes associated with the event will the temporal attribute contain the date of the occurrence and therefore lead to the retrieval of the memory of the event.

Modality Attribute   Underwood (1969, 1983) asserts that memories may also contain information regarding the sensory modality through which the event was experienced. Thus, one attribute of a memory is knowledge of whether the event was seen or heard or felt. What is the function of this *modality attribute* of a memory? In Underwood's view, the modality attribute serves the same purpose as any other attribute: It is used to differentiate among memories, and the presence of specific sensory information can prompt retrieval of a particular memory. Hintzman and colleagues' (1972) study provides support for this view.

Hintzman et al. (1972) presented several lists of words visually and other lists of words orally. Subjects were then asked to identify which words had been spoken and which had been shown. The authors reported that their subjects identified the words correctly 74 percent of the time, indicating that the memory of each word contained information regarding the sensory modality that had registered the word. Hintzman et al. also asked subjects to recall as many words as possible and found that subjects had clustered the words based on the method of presentation, indicating that they used the modality attribute to remember the words.

Underwood notes that although the input modality is an attribute of a memory, there is a high level of interchange among memories established through different modalities. To understand an experience often requires information received by other modalities. Underwood presents the following example to illustrate this cross-modality interchange: Suppose you use your index finger to write letters of the alphabet on the back of another person. Can this person tell which letters you have drawn? Evidence indicates the answer is yes. According to Underwood, the correct detection occurs because the tactile stimulation was translated into a memory system having access to visual information about the letters. This visual information is used to identify the letters that were experienced tactilely.

Context Attribute   The event's background can become an attribute of memory, and reexposure to that background context can prompt the retrieval of the memory of that event. For example, in the classic movie *Casablanca,* the song "As Time Goes By" reminded Humphrey Bogart of his love affair years earlier with Ingrid Bergman. The song was part of the context in which their love affair had taken place, and thus the song was a memory attribute of the affair. Hearing the song retrieved the memory of their romance and caused him to remember the

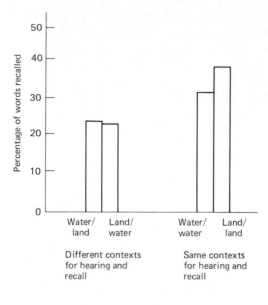

FIGURE 12-2
Illustration of the effect of a change in context on recall. Scuba divers remembered a list of words better in the same context as training than in a new context. Adapted from Gooden, D. R., & Baddeley, A. D. (1975). Context-dependent memory in two natural environments: On land and underwater. *British Journal of Psychology, 66,* 325–331.

events surrounding his affair. The experience of Humphrey Bogart's character is not unique. You have undoubtedly been reminded of a past event by reexperiencing some aspect of the context in which that event occurred.

Underwood's view suggests that context is a memory attribute. A considerable amount of research has been conducted to investigate the *context attribute*. Some of this research has involved human subjects (see Smith, Glenberg, & Bjork, 1978; Underwood, 1983); other studies have used animals as subjects (see Gordon, 1983; Spear, 1973, 1978). Both types of research show that context is an important memory attribute. We now briefly examine some of this research.

How can we know whether context has become a memory attribute? The way to demonstrate the influence of context on memory retrieval is to learn a response in one context and then see if a change in context produces a memory loss. Gooden and Baddeley (1975) conducted an interesting study showing the importance of context on memory. These investigators had scuba divers listen to a list of words. The divers were either 10 feet underwater or were sitting on the beach when they heard the words. The divers were tested either in the same context as they heard the words or in the second context. Gooden and Baddeley observed better recall when the scuba divers were tested in the same context than when they were tested in a different context (see Figure 12-2). In other words, the scuba divers who heard the words underwater (or on the beach) remembered the words better when tested underwater (or on the beach) than when on the beach (or underwater).

The influence of context in memory retrieval in animals was demonstrated by a study by Gordon, McCracken, Dess-Beech, and Mowrer (1981). Animals in this study were trained in a distinctive environment to actively respond to avoid

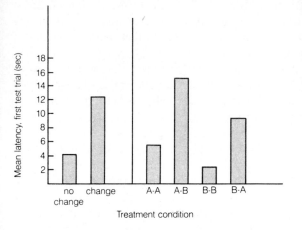

Mean latency, first test trial (sec)

Treatment condition

FIGURE 12-3

The mean latencies to cross to the black chamber on the retention test for groups A-A and B-B (trained and tested in the same environment) and groups A-B and B-A (trained in one environment and tested in another). The results showed that retention of past avoidance training was greater when rats were tested in the original rather than in the new context. From Gordon, W. C., McCraken, K. M., Dess-Beech, N., & Mowrer, R. R. (1981). Mechanisms for the cueing phenomenon: The addition of the cueing context to the training memory. *Learning and Motivation, 12,* 196–211.

shock in a shuttle box. Forty-eight hours later, the rats were placed either in the shuttle box in the original training room or in an identical shuttle box located in another room that differed from the training room in terms of size, lighting, odor, ambient noise level, and holding cage. Gordon and associates reported high retention when the rats were tested in the training context and significantly poorer performance when testing occurred in a novel context (refer to Figure 12-3).

Not all studies have shown that a change in context leads to forgetting (Underwood, 1983). Although context is one attribute of memory, a memory also contains information about other characteristics of an event. The significance and availability of other attributes influence whether a memory is recalled in another context. If the context is the most unique or significant aspect of a memory, retrieval will depend on the presence of the context; however, if other attributes are important and available, retrieval will occur even in a new context.

The reminder-treatment studies (Gordon, 1983) demonstrate that retrieval can occur in a new context when other attributes are able to produce recall. The reminder treatment involves presenting subjects during testing with a subset of the stimuli that were present in training. Although this reminder treatment is insufficient to produce learning, it can induce retrieval of a past experience, even in a novel context. The Gordon et al. (1981) study shows this influence of the reminder treatment. Recall that in this study, changing the context caused animals to forget their prior active avoidance responses. Another group of animals in the study received the reminder treatment 4 minutes before they were placed in the novel environment. The reminder treatment involved placing animals for 15 seconds in a cueing chamber—a white, translucent box identical to the white chamber of the avoidance apparatus where shock had occurred during training. Following the reminder treatment, animals were placed in a holding cage for 3.5 minutes and then transferred to the shuttle box in the novel context. Gordon et al. found that animals receiving the reminder treatment performed as well as the animals that had been in the training context. Exposure to the cueing chamber prevented the forgetting that normally occurs in a novel context. These observations indicate that the presence of stimuli contained in other memory attributes can reduce the impact of a change in context cues.

Smith (1979, 1982) discovered that a reminder treatment could be used with human subjects to reduce forgetting that occurs when context is changed from training to testing. In Smith's studies, one group of subjects was given a list of 32 words to learn in one context and then asked to recall the list in the same context; a second group was asked to recall the list in a new context. A third group of subjects was exposed to a context-recall technique prior to testing in a new context. The context-recall technique involved instructing subjects to think of the original training context and ignore the new context when trying to recall the list of words. Smith reported that subjects in the context-recall technique group remembered as many words in a new room as did subjects tested in their original learning room. In contrast, subjects who were tested in a new context but did not receive the reminder treatment showed poor recall of their prior training. These observations indicate that a reminder treatment can prevent forgetting that would normally be seen in both animals and humans as a result of a context change.

Affective Attribute   Underwood (1969, 1983) asserted that the emotional responses produced by various events can be attributes of memories. Some events are pleasant; others unpleasant. The memory of an event contains much information regarding the emotional character of that event. This *affective attribute* enables a person to distinguish among various memories as well as to retrieve the memory of a particular event.

Underwood theorized that the affective attribute could be viewed as an internal contextual attribute; that is, it contained information about the internal consequences of an event. Events not only produce internal changes, they also occur during a particular internal state. Suppose you are intoxicated at a party. The next day a friend asks you if you had an enjoyable time, but you do not remember. This situation is an example of *state-dependent learning* (Overton, 1964, 1971). In a state-dependent learning study, an experience encountered during one internal state will not be recalled when the internal state is changed. According to our memory attribute framework, internal state is an attribute of memory; that is, knowledge of the internal state is contained in our memory of an event. A change in internal state eliminates an attribute of memory, which can lead to a failure to recall the event. We next examine evidence that internal state is a memory attribute.

State-Dependent Learning   Donald Overton (1964) trained rats to obtain food in a T-maze. Half the animals were trained after receiving pentobarbital (a drug that depresses bodily functions); the remaining half were trained after receiving saline. The two groups of animals were subdivided again during testing: Half of each group was tested after receiving pentobarbital; the other half, after saline. As can be seen in Table 12-1, half the animals were tested when they were in

TABLE 12-1
RETENTION OF RESPONSE AS A FUNCTION OF
TRAINING AND TESTING CONDITIONS

	Testing	
Training	Drug	No drug
Drug	Good retention	Poor retention
No drug	Poor retention	Good retention

Note: The high level of retention occurred in the groups
experiencing the same conditions during both training and
testing.

the same internal state as they had been during training; the other half were tested during a state different from that experienced during training. Overton found a high recall of the instrumental response if rats had received pentobarbital or saline prior to both training and testing. In contrast, retention was impaired if animals had been given pentobarbital before training and saline prior to testing, or saline before training and pentobarbital prior to testing. Thus, forgetting of a previously learned response can occur when the internal state changes.

State-dependent learning has been reported for a variety of behaviors, including approach in the T-maze (Overton, 1964), escape and avoidance responding in the shuttle box (Holmgren, 1964), and bar pressing in an operant chamber (Kubena & Barry, 1969). State-dependent learning has been observed in rats, monkeys, cats, dogs, goldfish, and humans. The studies with humans have used alcohol (Goodwin, Powell, Bremer, Hoine, & Stein, 1969; Modill, 1967), amphetamine (Swanson & Kinsbourne, 1979), and marijuana (Eich, Weingartner, Stillman, & Gillin, 1975).

Events also can be experienced during a particular internal emotional state, and a change in this emotional state can lead to forgetting. Using hypnosis, Gordon Bower (1981) manipulated mood state (either happy or sad) before training and again prior to testing. Some subjects experienced the same mood prior to both training and testing, and other subjects experienced one mood state present before training and the other before testing. Bower found significantly better recall when the emotional state induced before testing matched the state present during training than when the training and testing states were not the same. Thus, a change in mood state, as well as drug state, can lead to forgetting.

The Kamin Effect   Changes in internal state can occur naturally; these changes also can lead to forgetting because of the absence of the internal attributes of a memory. In 1957, Kamin reported that rats were unable to perform a previously learned active avoidance response on an intermediate retention test (1 to 3 hours after original training), whereas avoidance performance was excellent both immediately and 24 hours after the initial adversive experience (see Figure 12-4). This U-shaped retention function, the *Kamin effect*, has been consistently replicated (Brush, 1971), and the poor performance on the intermediate retention

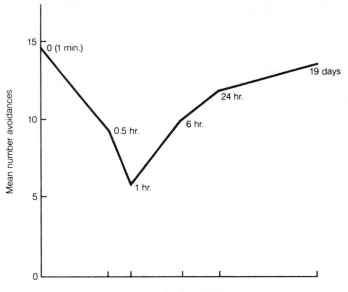

FIGURE 12-4   The mean number of active avoidance responses as a function of the time between training and testing. The animals in this study showed better performance of a previously learned avoidance response when tested either immediately or 24 hours after training than on an intermediate retention interval (1 hour). From Kamin, L. J. (1957). Retention of an incompletely learned avoidance response. *Journal of Comparative and Physiological Psychology, 50,* 457–460. Copyright 1957 by the American Psychological Association. Reprinted by permission.

interval has been attributed to retrieval failure. A number of studies (Baum, 1968; Bintz, 1970; Klein, 1972; Klein & Spear, 1969, 1970a, 1970b; Spear, Klein, & Riley, 1971) support a retrieval-failure explanation of the Kamin effect. When the memory of original training is available (both immediately and 24 hours after training), subjects show a high level of performance in the original training situation (Klein & Spear, 1969, 1970b). However, when the memory of prior avoidance responding is unavailable (on an intermediate retention test), subjects do not respond according to prior training in the original situation; that is, they act like untrained rats in a new situation.

Why are animals unable to recall the memory of a prior response on an intermediate retention test? The answer is that different internal states are experienced immediately or 24 hours after training and 1 to 3 hours after training. Because avoidance training is adversive, a number of physiological changes take place during the acquisition of the avoidance response. One physiological response that occurs during avoidance training is the release of adrenocorticotropic hormone (ACTH) from the pituitary gland. One effect of ACTH is the excitement of specific neural systems, and this excitement produces the motivational and emotional arousal characteristic of stressful experiences (Grossman, 1967). Approximately 1 hour after a stressful experience, a central inhibition of the ACTH release is caused by the presence of adrenocorticotropic hormones released by the adrenal cortex. This inhibition of ACTH release lasts several hours and results in a lowered responsivity to stressful experiences. Thus, performance of the avoidance response on the intermediate retention test is poor. The corticoid inhibition is no longer present on the 24-hour test, and, therefore, the internal responsivity and response performance have returned to the normal state.

Several studies support the theory that inhibition of ACTH is responsible for the poor performance on an intermediate retention test. First, Spear and colleagues (1971) found that avoidance learning acquired during the intermediate interval state was forgotten when animals were tested at the 24-hour interval. Second, Klein (1972) observed that direct injection of ACTH into the lateral anterior hypothalamus at the intermediate retention test resulted in a high level of performance of the learned response. These treatments are assumed to reinstate the internal state that had been present during training, and thus eliminate forgetting usually observed on an intermediate retention test.

Relative Contributions of Internal versus External Memory Attributes The internal state experienced during training is one attribute of memory. Although a change in internal state can lead to retrieval failure, in some circumstances forgetting does not occur despite a change in internal state. For example, although intoxicated people do forget some events, they can clearly remember others. The attribute model of memory suggests that the presence of other memory attributes can lead to retrieval, despite the change in internal state.

Eich and associates (1975) examined the state-dependent effects of marijuana. With the permission of appropriate government agencies, subjects smoked either a marijuana cigarette (drug condition) or a cigarette with the active ingredient THC removed (nondrug condition). Some subjects smoked the marijuana 20 minutes before learning a list of words and again before testing 4 hours after training. Other subjects were given the marijuana prior to training and the nondrug before testing; still other subjects received the nondrug before training and the marijuana before testing. A final group of subjects smoked the nondrug before both training and testing. Eich et al. evaluated the influence of marijuana by measuring heart rate (marijuana increases heart rate) and the subjective experience of being "high." They found that compared with the nondrug condition, marijuana produced a strong physiological and psychological effect.

The researchers tested half of the subjects using a free-recall task; the other half, using category names of the words given in training as retrieval cues. In the free-recall testing, state-dependent learning was observed: The subjects remembered more words when the same state was present during both training and testing than when the state differed during testing and training (see Table 12-2). The lower recall of words on the free-recall test was observed whether the subjects were in a drug state during training and a nondrug state during testing or a nondrug state during training and a drug state during testing. In contrast to the state-dependent effects with the free-recall test, subjects receiving the cued-recall

TABLE 12-2
TREATMENT CONDITIONS AND RESULTS OF A STATE-
DEPENDENT LEARNING STUDY

Condition		Average number of words recalled	
Study	Test	Free recall	Cued recall
Nondrug	Nondrug	11.5	24.0
Nondrug	Drug	9.9	23.7
Drug	Nondrug	6.7	22.6
Drug	Drug	10.5	22.3

Source: Eich, J. E., Weingartner, H., Stillman, R. C., & Gillin, J. C. (1975). State-dependent accessibility of retrieval cues in the retention of a categorized list. *Journal of Verbal Learning and Verbal Behavior, 14,* 408–417.

test did not demonstrate state-dependent effects. When the subjects received the category words at testing, they showed a high level of recall in all four treatment conditions.

Why did a change in internal state not lead to forgetting in the cued-recall testing procedure? Eich (1980) suggested that people typically rely on external cues. If these cues are unavailable, they will use subtle cues associated with their physiological or mental state to retrieve memories. The cued-recall procedure provided verbal associative cues that eliminated the need to use internal retrieval cues to recall the training.

Verbal Associative Attributes   According to Underwood (1983), when a person hears or sees a word, the word may produce a variety of verbal associates. For example, the word *cat* may elicit the associative response *animal.* The category word *animal* is a *verbal associative attribute* of the memory *cat,* and its presence may act to retrieve the word *cat* on a retrieval test. Verbal associative attributes are responsible for the enhanced recall that occurs as the result of associative learning. Underwood suggested that there are two types of verbal associative attributes: parallel associates and class associates.

Parallel Associative Attributes   Underwood (1983) proposed three major types of parallel associative attributes: antonyms, synonyms, and functional associates. Functional associative attributes are formed because of functional contiguity and include pairs such as *cup-saucer, table-chair,* and *key-lock.* The presence of a parallel associative attribute during testing can result in the retrieval of a memory that would not have been recalled if the associative attribute had not been present.

The influence of parallel associative attributes on retrieval was demonstrated by the study by Jenkins, Mink, and Russell (1958). The researchers constructed four lists of words, and each list consisted of 12 pairs of words. Thus, the four lists combined contained 48 pairs, all of which differed in terms of the strength of the individual associates. Some had high associative strength (for example, *man-woman*); others had low associative strength (for example, *comfort-chair*). Four different associative strengths were used—76, 43, 32, and 12; the strengths varied according to the number of subjects producing the same associative responses. Each list contained three pairs of each associative strength. As seen in Figure 12-5, the higher the associative strength of a pair, the higher the recall of the words, indicating that the presence of a parallel associate increased the recall of the associated word.

Class Associative Attribute   Underwood (1983) proposed that when a word elicits the category name that includes that word, the category name is a class associative attribute of the word. The presence of the category name can act to retrieve the word during testing. For example, the category name *animal* can act as a memory attribute of the word *cat*.

Recall the implicit associative response study conducted by Wood and Underwood (1967), which was described in Chapter 11. The presence of the word *black* on a list of words enhanced the retrieval of three apparently unrelated words: *derby, coffee,* and *skunk. Black* was a class associative attribute of each word; that is, it has conceptual similarity to each of the other three words. Thus, *black* was a memory attribute of each word: If subjects remembered the word *black,* they would also remember the three other words. The observation that the inclusion of the word *black* facilitated the recall of its class associative words but not the other words on the list supports Underwood's view.

Underwood points out that the class attribute must be elicited during conditioning and also during testing. If the class associative attribute is not present during both training and testing, retrieval will not be enhanced. For example, Wood and Underwood (1967) found that if the word *black* was present only during training or only during testing, the recall of its three class associative words was not better than if the word *black* had not been presented at all. Thus, class attributes can function to retrieve a memory if an association is formed between the class associative attribute and the word during training and if the class associative attribute is present during testing.

Transformational Attributes   The final class of memory attributes proposed by Underwood (1983) is the *transformational attribute*. Recall from Chapter 11 that information can be transformed by the short-term store. For example, the nonsense trigram *tfx* can be coded into the word *tax*. During testing, the word *tax* must be decoded into the nonsense syllable *tfx*. According to Underwood, a part of the memory of the nonsense syllable must consist of the information for decoding. This decoding information constitutes the transformational attribute. This section discusses three major types of transformational attributes: images, natural language mediators, and order transformations.

Images   Many words or ideas can be transformed into images. For example, the word *car* can be transformed into the image of a car. According to Underwood (1983), the image is a transformational attribute of the word or idea. Remembering the image will enable a person to recall the word or idea. Recall our discussion of mnemonic techniques in the last chapter. Mnemonic techniques make great

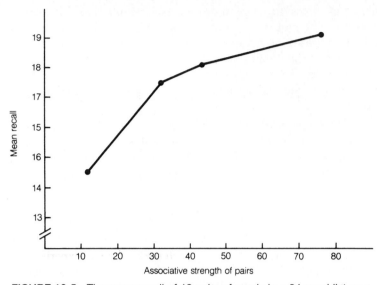

FIGURE 12-5   The mean recall of 12 pairs of words in a 24-word list as a function of the associative strength of word pairs. Subjects in this study recalled items better when the pairs of words were highly related than when they were unrelated. Adapted from Jenkins, J. J., Mink, W. P., & Russell, W. A. (1958). Associative clustering as a function of verbal association strength. *Psychological Reports, 4,* 127–136.

use of imagery in the storage of information, and they can enhance recall of past events.

Natural Language Mediators   Consider the following example: In a paired-associate learning task, a subject is learning the associate *dog-car.* if a subject injects the word *chase* between *dog* and *car,* the natural language mediator is *dog-chase-car.* According to Underwood (1983), the mediator produces a meaningful link between the two words. Underwood reports that subjects attempting to learn verbal material often use language mediators. For example, subjects learning a serial list of words often will add a word or two to the list to create a story. Underwood has found that the use of natural language mediators can enhance the recall of past verbal experiences, as long as the memory contains decoding information, or knowledge of words to be deleted.

Order Transformations   Underwood (1983) suggests that relatively meaningless nonsense syllables can be recoded to create more meaningful verbal units. For example, the nonsense syllable *rac* can become the word *car.* As was true of images and natural language mediators, order transformations can increase the recall of verbal units. However, this is true only if people have available to them during recall a rule for rearranging the verbal units into the original form. As we learned in the last chapter, one of the advantages of the mnemonic techniques is that they provide a simple rule for coding experiences and then decoding them during testing.

Section Review

According to Underwood, a memory is a collection of different types of information, called memory attributes. A memory attribute can decrease interference by providing a basis for distinguishing memories. When one aspect of an event is experienced, the attribute of that event prompts the recall of the entire memory.

There are 10 major memory attributes. The acoustic attribute stores information about the auditory properties of an event. The physical characteristics of an event are contained in the orthographic attribute. In the frequency attribute, a record of the number of times an event is experienced is stored. The time that an event occurred is recorded in the temporal attribute, and the place where it occurred is contained in the spatial attribute of the memory. The modality attribute provides information about the sensory modality through which the event was experienced. The background in which an event took place is stored in the context attribute.

The affective attribute of a memory provides information about the emotional condition surrounding an event. The affective attribute can be viewed as an internal contextual attribute: It registers internal changes in affect, changes which may be natural reactions to the event or may be drug-induced. The associates of verbal items are also attributes of a memory. There are two types of verbal associative attributes: parallel associative attributes (antonyms, synonyms, and functional associates of the verbal item) and class associative attributes (the category name of the verbal item). The transformational attribute contains information about how to decode items that were coded during learning. The three types of transformational attributes are images, natural language mediators, and order transformations.

FORGETTING

How Quickly We Forget

Left to itself, every mental content gradually loses its capacity for being retrieved. ... Facts crammed at examination time soon vanish. (Hermann Ebbinghaus, 1885)

The preceding quote characterizes Ebbinghaus's view of forgetting. His work contributed to our current attention to the forgetting of past events. Our discussion of forgetting begins with a description of his research.

Ebbinghaus conducted an extensive study of memory, using himself as the only subject, in the latter part of the 19th century. To study memory, Ebbinghaus invented the nonsense syllable—two consonants separated by a vowel (for example, *baf* and *xof*). He memorized relatively meaningless nonsense syllables, since he felt that these verbal units would be uncontaminated by his prior experience. He assumed that any difference in the recall of specific nonsense syllables

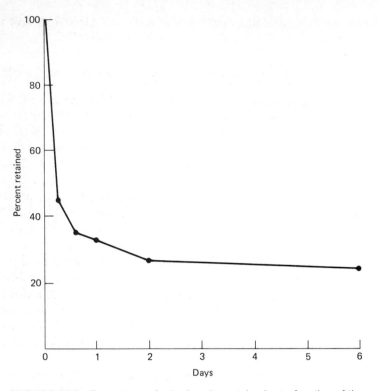

FIGURE 12-6   Percentage of prior learning retained as a function of the interval between training and testing. Ebbinghaus found that his recall of nonsense syllables declined rapidly as the interval between training and testing increased. Adapted from Ebbinghaus, H. (1885). *Memory: A contribution to experimental psychology.* H. A. Ruger & C. E. Bussenins (Trans.). New York: Dover.

would be due to forgetting and not to differential familiarity with the nonsense syllables.

After memorizing a list of 10 to 12 nonsense syllables, Ebbinghaus relearned the list. (In his study, savings in relearning the lists were used to indicate how much of the list was retained; the greater the savings, the higher the recall.) He memorized over 150 lists of nonsense syllables at various retention intervals. As can be seen in Figure 12-6, Ebbinghaus forgot almost half of a prior list after 24 hours, and 6 days later recalled only one-fourth of the prior learning. Ebbinghaus's results show a rapid forgetting following acquisition of a list of nonsense syllables.

Why did Ebbinghaus forget so much of his prior learning? Three theories have been proposed to explain the forgetting of previous experiences. First, some psychologists (McGeoch, 1932) have suggested that memories decay, a view which assumes that memory is lost through disuse; that is, memories that are not recalled will not survive. Second, interference among memories has been proposed as a cause of forgetting (McGeoch, 1932; Underwood, 1957). Interference refers to the inability to recall a specific event as the result of having experienced another event. The third theory is that the absence of a specific stimulus can lead to forgetting (Underwood, 1969, 1983). This view holds that a memory contains a collection of different types of information, and each type of information is an attribute of the memory. The retrieval of a memory depends on the presence of the stimulus contained in the memory attribute.

Decay of a Memory

It is generally assumed that specific physiological changes take place that relate to the event being experienced (see Chapter 10). The *engram,* or physical representation of an event, enables a person to recall the experience at a later time. A few psychologists (see McGeoch, 1932) have proposed that the engram fades with disuse; that is, the physiological changes that took place during learning and that represent the record of the experience will diminish unless the memory is retrieved from time to time. Retrieval may prevent decay or strengthen a decaying memory.

In a classic study, Jenkins and Dallenbach (1924) evaluated the decay view of forgetting by teaching subjects a list of nonsense syllables to a criterion of one trial without errors. The retention of the nonsense syllables was evaluated 1, 2, 4, or 8 hours later. Half the subjects spent their retention interval awake; the other half of the subjects slept during the interval. If the decay view is accurate and the time between learning and recall determines the level of forgetting, an equal amount of forgetting should be found regardless of whether the subjects were asleep or awake during the retention interval. As can be seen in Figure 12-7, more forgetting was seen in the subjects who were awake than in those asleep during the retention interval, suggesting that activities that occurred while the subjects were awake contributed to the amount of forgetting.

Note that subjects who slept during the interval forgot a considerable amount during that time. Is this forgetting a result of decay? According to Underwood (1957), the methods employed by Jenkins and Dallenbach (1924) were inadequate by contemporary standards. In addition, Jenkins and Dallenbach's subjects had been in other studies; this previous participation may have produced high levels of interference, which in turn may have caused the forgetting seen in the asleep condition.

Conducting a more controlled investigation of the effects of sleep on retention, Ekstrand (1967) used subjects who had not experienced prior paired-associate tasks. One group of subjects slept the 8-hour retention interval after learning a list of paired associates; the other group was awake during the retention interval. Ekstrand observed that subjects in the awake condition forgot 23 percent of the paired associates, whereas subjects in the sleep condition forgot only 11 percent. These observations suggest that interference, which resulted from prior experience with paired associates, caused much of the forgetting reported by Jenkins and

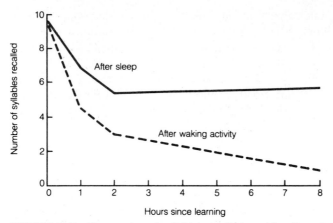

FIGURE 12-7 The number of syllables recalled as a function of time between training and testing in subjects who were either asleep or awake during the retention interval. The results of this study showed that recall was higher in subjects who slept during the retention interval than in subjects who spent the interval awake. From Jenkins, J. G., & Dallenbach, K. M. (1924). Oblivescence during sleep and waking. *American Journal of Psychology, 35,* 605–612.

Dallenbach in the asleep condition subjects. However, subjects in the asleep condition in the Ekstrand study did forget some material. Decay of memory may have been responsible for this forgetting. It is also feasible that extraexperimental sources of interference (interference from verbal material learned outside the laboratory) contributed to the forgetting seen in the asleep condition. We next examine some research supporting a decay view; extraexperimental sources of interference as a cause of forgetting will be discussed later in the chapter.

Rozin and Gleitman (cited in Gleitman, 1971) used fish as their subjects and trained them to avoid shock in a shuttle box. The fish spent either a 4-week or an 8-week retention interval in either the training temperature (25–26°C) or in a hot tank (33°C). Rozin and Gleitman reasoned that since fish are cold-blooded, heating the fish tank would accelerate their metabolic processes, thereby increasing the rate of decay of the memory of the avoidance training. Rozin and Gleitman reported that the fish kept in the hot tank forgot more during the retention interval than did the fish in the training tank.

Other investigators have attempted to slow down metabolic rate to decrease the decay of memory and thereby reduce the amount of forgetting. Rensch and Ducker (1966) observed that goldfish treated with chlorpromazine, a drug that suppresses nervous system activity, during the retention interval exhibited greater retention of a visual discrimination than did goldfish not given chlorpromazine. A similar decrease in forgetting was observed by Ducker and Rensch (1968) in goldfish kept in the dark during the retention interval and by Alloway (1969) in grain beetles kept in a cold environment after training.

TABLE 12-3
DESIGN OF A PROACTIVE INTERFERENCE STUDY

Group	Stage of experiment		
	I	II	III
Experimental	Learn first materials	Learn materials to be remembered	Test for recall
Control	Unrelated activity	Learn material to be remembered	Test for recall

Gleitman (1971) points to one problem in concluding that decay is a source of forgetting. Studies evaluating the decay view have inferred that treatments such as heat or sleep affect forgetting by altering the metabolic processes that govern erosion of the memory trace. Unfortunately, no study has proved that this relation exists; thus decay remains only a possible source of forgetting. In contrast, considerable evidence indicates that interference is a cause of forgetting.

Interference

There are two types of interference: proactive and retroactive. *Proactive interference* (PI) involves an inability to recall recent experiences because of the memory of earlier experiences. For example, a group of subjects learns one list of paired associates (A-B list) and then learns a second list of paired associates (A-C). (In a paired-associates learning task, subjects are presented a list of stimuli and responses. The list usually consists of 10 to 15 pairs, and subjects are required to learn the correct response to each stimulus.) When subjects are asked to recall the associates from the second list, they are unable to do so because the memory of the first list interferes. How do we know that these subjects would not have forgotten the response to the second list even if they had not learned the first list? To show that it is the memory of the first list that caused the forgetting of the second list, a control group of subjects learned only the second list (see Table 12-3 for a diagram of the treatments given to experimental and control subjects). Any poorer recall of the second list by the experimental subjects than by the control subjects is assumed to reflect proactive interference.

Retroactive interference (RI) occurs when people cannot remember distant events because the memory of more recent events intervenes. Retroactive interference can be observed with the following paradigm: Experimental subjects learn two lists of paired associates (A-B, A-C), then take a retention test that asks them to recall the responses from the first list. The retention of the first list of responses for experimental subjects is compared with the retention for a control group required to learn only the first list (refer to Table 12-4 for a diagram of the treatment given the experimental and control subjects). If the recall of the first list is poorer for experimental subjects than for control-group subjects, retroactive interference is assumed to be the cause of the difference.

TABLE 12-4
DESIGN OF A RETROACTIVE INTERFERENCE STUDY

	Stage of experiment		
Group	I	II	III
Experimental	Learn materials to be remembered	Learn new materials	Test for recall
Control	Learn materials to be remembered	Unrelated activity	Test for recall

Why does interference occur? Melton and Irwin offered a two-factor view of interference.

Melton and Irwin's Two-Factor Theory of Interference   According to Melton and Irwin (1940), competition between memories is a source of both proactive and retroactive interference. Consider the A-B, A-C paradigm, in which the same stimulus (A) has been associated with two responses (B and C). Because the task requires subjects to recall only one response, the task will elicit the response with the strongest association to the stimulus. Thus, a subject may forget response C because of competition from response B, which has a stronger association to stimulus A. However, if the stimulus response association A-C is stronger than that of A-B, the subject will be unable to recall the responses from task A-B.

Melton and Irwin proposed that although competition is the only cause of proactive interference, a second factor, unlearning, can also produce retroactive interference. According to Melton and Irwin, for subjects to learn the second list (A-C), they must unlearn or extinguish the first list (A-B). They do not view unlearning as an erasure of A-B associations. Instead, they suggest that A-B associations are suppressed so that subjects can learn the second task. Unlearning of the first task causes subjects to forget these responses when they take a retention test given immediately after second-list acquisition.

Melton and Irwin suggested that the suppression of first-list responses is only temporary and that the association will spontaneously recover during the interval after second-list learning. The recovery of the strength of first-task associations may lead to a recall of the first-list responses. As the memory of first-list responses becomes available, response competition becomes the sole determinant of which memory the subject will recall.

Evidence Supporting Melton and Irwin's View.   Several lines of evidence support the Melton and Irwin two-factor theory of interference. First we discuss research suggesting that competition influences the level of PI and RI, then describe evidence that implies that unlearning is a source of RI.

The competition theory suggests that the degree of first- and second-task associative learning should affect the level of PI and RI. If the level of first-task learning is greater than that of second-task learning, then associative strength to the first-task responses should be greater than to the second-task responses. According to the competition approach, the stronger first-task associations should lead to high levels of PI. A number of studies (Atwater, 1953; Postman & Riley, 1959; Underwood, 1945) have evaluated how the degree of original task learning relates to the amount of PI. These experiments show that as the level of first-list learning increases, PI also increases.

The competition view also assumes that increased degree of second-list, or interpolated, learning should cause greater levels of RI. The increased RI reflects the greater associative strength of the second-list responses that results from increased levels of interpolated list learning. The research (Lewis, Smith, & McAllister, 1952; Postman & Riley, 1959; Thune & Underwood, 1943) evaluating the role of the degree of interpolated list learning on RI has demonstrated that as interpolated lists are learned to greater degrees, the level of RI increases (see Hall, 1966, for a review of how the degree of original and interpolated list learning affects PI and RI).

Thus, the greater the degree of original (or interpolated) task learning, the higher the PI (or RI). A greater degree of learning increases the associative strength, and a stronger association enables the memory of a particular stimulus-response association to compete with the memory of another stimulus-response association, thereby increasing interference. These observations support Melton and Irwin's view that competition is a source of interference.

Melton and Irwin (1940) conducted a study to evaluate the second aspect of their theory that unlearning is a source of RI. They provided subjects with a list of 18 nonsense syllables to learn in serial order. After original training, subjects were given an interpolated 18-item list of nonsense syllables for 5, 10, 20, or 40 trials, followed by the relearning of the original list. Examining the total amount of RI, Melton and Irwin found that the greater the number of interpolated list trials, the higher the RI. Melton and Irwin also measured the interpolated list intrusions (or the recall of nonsense syllables from the second list) that occurred during the relearning of the original list. If competition is responsible for RI, interpolated list intrusions should be related to the level of RI; that is, as RI increases, so should the number of interpolated list intrusions. Melton and Irwin found no perfect relationship between the number of interpolated list intrusions and the total amount of retroactive interference. As can be seen in Figure 12-8, the amount of RI attributed to interpolated list intrusion (competition) increased to a maximum point, between 5 and 10 trials of interpolated list learning, and then declined. Note that even when interpolated list intrusions are greatest, they do not completely account for RI. Thus, Melton and Irwin assumed that a factor other than competition must be responsible for RI. They called this factor X, but they suggested that it represented unlearning as a source of RI. Similar results were obtained by Thune and Underwood (1943) with two lists of paired associates.

Although these observations indicate that a second factor contributes to the level of RI, they do not indicate that unlearning is necessarily that second cause.

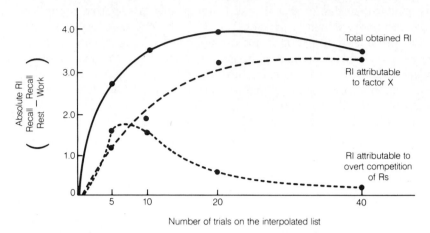

FIGURE 12-8   The amount of retroactive interference (RI) as a function of the degree of interpolated list training. The graph shows that the amount of retroactive interference attributed to competition first increased and then declined with increased interpolated list learning; in contrast, the residual retroactive interference is attributed to factor X. From Melton, A. W., & Irwin, J. M. (1940). The influence of degree of interpolated learning on retroactive inhibition and the overt transfer of specific responses. *American Journal of Psychology, 53,* 173–203.

However, a number of studies (see Hall, 1966) support Melton and Irwin's view that factor X is, indeed, unlearning.

Barnes and Underwood's (1959) experiment suggests that unlearning is a source of RI. Subjects learned two lists (A-B, A-C) of paired associates; the two lists had the same stimuli but different responses. After 1, 5, 10, or 20 trials of interpolated list learning, the subjects were asked to recall the two responses for each stimulus. If unlearning is a cause of RI, then subjects learning the second list would not be able to recall the responses of the first list. In contrast, if competition is the sole cause of RI, subjects given sufficient time should be able to recall both responses. Barnes and Underwood reported that the subjects' ability to report responses in the first list declined as they learned the responses of the second list (Figure 12-9). These observations indicate that first-list responses became increasingly unavailable as subjects learned the second list, an idea consistent with the view that unlearning is a source of RI.

Melton and Irwin (1940) conceptualized the unlearning of original task responses as analogous to the extinction of a conditioned response. Recall from Chapter 3 that conditioned responses will spontaneously recover several hours after extinction. If unlearning is a cause of RI, then the spontaneous recovery of the first-task response should result in reduced RI and increased PI. A number of studies (see Hall, 1966) have measured the changes in PI and RI following interpolated list learning. Experimentation demonstrates that immediately following the learning of the second task, subjects can remember only the second task.

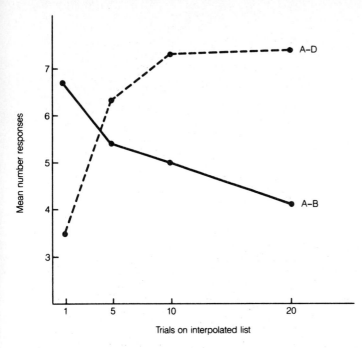

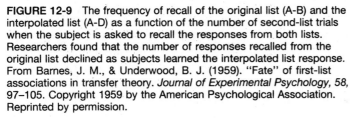

FIGURE 12-9   The frequency of recall of the original list (A-B) and the interpolated list (A-D) as a function of the number of second-list trials when the subject is asked to recall the responses from both lists. Researchers found that the number of responses recalled from the original list declined as subjects learned the interpolated list response. From Barnes, J. M., & Underwood, B. J. (1959). "Fate" of first-list associations in transfer theory. *Journal of Experimental Psychology, 58,* 97–105. Copyright 1959 by the American Psychological Association. Reprinted by permission.

Thus, RI is maximal, and no PI occurs when testing takes place immediately after acquisition of the second list. As the time lapse after learning of the second task increases, ability to remember the second list decreases while ability to recall the first list increases. Therefore, with an increased retention interval, the level of RI diminishes and PI increases. The changes in interference with time are assumed to reflect the spontaneous recovery of original-list responses.

We have learned that Melton and Irwin (1940) suggested that competition is the cause of PI and that competition and unlearning are causes of RI. In the past 50 years several changes in the interference theory of forgetting have been proposed. Our discussion of interference as a source of retrieval failure for long-term memories will conclude by examining these developments.

Extraexperimental Sources of Interference   Underwood and Postman (1960) addressed an important issue about forgetting. The issue concerns the forgetting that occurs after learning a single task. Recall our discussion of the classic

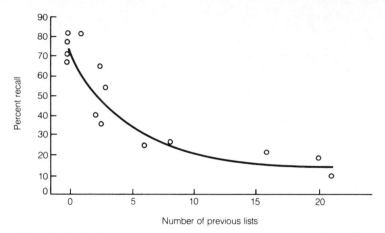

FIGURE 12-10   The amount of proactive interference as a function of the number of previously learned lists on the recall of a list of nonsense syllables on a 24-hour retention test. Underwood found that the retention of previous learning on a 24-hour test declined with increased previous learning. Adapted from Underwood, B. J. (1957). Interference and forgetting. *Psychological Review, 64,* 49–60. Copyright 1957 by the American Psychological Association. Reprinted by permission.

Ebbinghaus (1885) study, which showed rapid forgetting following acquisition of a list of nonsense syllables. Why did Ebbinghaus forget so much of the single list of nonsense syllables? Underwood (1951) examined 14 studies that reported the recall of a list of nonsense syllables on a 24-hour retention test and found considerable differences among the studies. Some articles reported minimal forgetting after 24 hours; others showed substantial forgetting. He reported that as the number of prior lists increased, so did the amount of forgetting (see Figure 12-10). These observations suggest that interference from prior lists caused forgetting 24 hours after original learning. Note that, in a number of studies, subjects had no experience in learning lists of nonsense syllables, but these studies still showed 15 to 25 percent forgetting after 24 hours.

Why did untrained subjects still forget some of their prior learning on a 24-hour retention test? According to Underwood and Postman, language habits acquired before entering the laboratory were responsible for the forgetting of a single list of nonsense syllables in untrained subjects. Underwood and Postman referred to the natural language habits that produce forgetting of laboratory material as *extraexperimental sources of interference*. Furthermore, two types of extraexperimental sources of interference have been identified. First, *letter sequences* used in the laboratory conflict with grammatically correct letter sequences. For example, if the nonsense syllable to be learned is *qtx,* the *qt* letter sequence conflicts with the previously learned *qu* letter sequence. To learn the *qt* sequence, the subject must unlearn the *qu* sequence; the spontaneous recovery of the *qu* letter sequence occurring after laboratory experience will cause the subject to forget the *qt* sequence. *Unit-sequence* interference is the second kind of extraexperimental source of interference. Suppose a subject must learn the paired associate *ice-dog* in the laboratory. This unit sequence conflicts with the previously learned sequence *ice-cold*. Again, the response *cold* must be unlearned as a subject learns the response *dog,* and the spontaneous recovery of the response *cold* will interfere with the recall of the response *dog*.

The Influence of Distributed Practice   Underwood and Postman (1960) assumed that language habits acquired outside the laboratory interfere with the recall of material learned in the laboratory, but the level of forgetting seen after a single task is only modest. Why do language habits not produce greater interference with laboratory material? The answer lies in the way in which language habits are typically learned in the real world. Although subjects usually learn material in the laboratory in a short time (under what psychologists call *massed practice*), language habits acquired in the real world are usually learned slowly (under *distributed practice*). According to Underwood and Postman, less interference occurs with distributed than with massed practice. A considerable amount of evidence (see Keppel, 1964; Underwood & Ekstrand, 1966) supports this view.

For example, in Underwood and Ekstrand's (1966) study, one group of subjects learned the initial list over a 4-day period (distributed practice); other subjects acquired the first list in a single session (massed practice). All subjects learned the second list under massed practice. Underwood and Ekstrand then evaluated the level of interference, finding greater interference with massed practice than with distributed practice. These observations show that materials acquired with distributed practice are less susceptible to the effects of interference. Our discussion has suggested why people do not forget massive amounts of linguistic activities. Because much of our verbal material is acquired under distributed practice, verbal memories are less likely to be a source of interference.

Why does distributed practice influence the level of forgetting? Underwood's list-differentiation view of interference provides one answer.

Underwood's List Differentiation View   Underwood (1969, 1983) suggested that interference is caused not by response competition, but instead by a failure of task differentiation. According to Underwood, subjects do remember responses from both tasks but are unable to remember with which task a particular response was associated. Thus, subjects asked to recall the response learned from the first task can remember the response from both tasks but will appear to have forgotten them because the subjects cannot remember which response came from the first list. A considerable amount of research indicates that the failure of *list differentiation,* rather than competition, is a source of forgetting. Let's briefly look at the evidence.

We learned earlier that interference is not displayed by subjects who learned one task in one environment and another task in a different environment. According to Underwood, learning in different environments enables subjects to differentiate between memories. Although responses from the two tasks are still in associative competition, interference will not occur because the subjects are able to differentiate between the two tasks. In Underwood's view, interference occurs when a subject cannot differentiate between memories.

According to Underwood, any treatment that increases the distinctiveness of memories will reduce the level of interference. We know that interference is reduced when the distribution of practice on the first list differs from that of the second list. Furthermore, Underwood and Freund (1968) observed less interference when original and interpolated list learning were separated by 3 days, even when the two lists were acquired with the same distribution of practice. Underwood argues that each of these treatments (different distributions of practice, different times, different environments) increased the distinctiveness of the memories, and this increased list differentiation was responsible for the reduced interference.

Postman's Generalized Competition View Barnes and Underwood (1959) noted that the level of proactive interference (PI) increases following interpolated list learning, whereas the amount of retroactive interference (RI) declines. These researchers argued that the changes in interference were caused by the spontaneous recovery of the original list responses. However, while some studies have observed spontaneous recovery, others have not (see Keppel, 1968; Postman, Stark, & Fraser, 1968). Based on this conflicting evidence, Postman, Stark, and Fraser (1968) held that "it is clear that long-term spontaneous recovery is not a dependable phenomenon."

These observations suggest that spontaneous recovery cannot be responsible for the predictable changes in interference that follow interpolated list learning. They also imply that unlearning is not responsible for the unavailability of original list responses during interpolated list acquisition. Postman and associates (Postman, 1967; Postman et al. 1968) suggest that *generalized competition* rather than unlearning is responsible for both an inability to recall first-list responses as the second list is acquired and the changes in interference after interpolated list learning.

According to Postman, generalized competition is a "set" or disposition to continue to respond in the manner learned most recently. A selector mechanism excludes from subjects' response repertoire all responses except those being learned. It is this selector mechanism, not unlearning, that prevents a subject from being able to remember original list responses. Postman suggests that following interpolated list acquisition, the "set" to respond dissipates or generalized competition declines; the reduced disposition to respond according to recency is responsible for the increased PI and decreased RI. Throughout the text we have seen that recency plays an important role in determining behavior. Postman's generalized competition proposes a mechanism which ensures that recency will have a significant impact on behavior.

What evidence indicates that generalized competition exists? Melton and Irwin (1940) argued that the relative strength of competing responses from each list determines the level of interference. Yet, it is the relative degree of learning of each list, not individual response strength, that indicates the amount of interference (see Runquist, 1957). The observation that the learning of the entire task, rather than the memory of individual responses, is a function of interference supports the view that a selector mechanism acts to limit responses to the most recent task for a short time following learning.

Forgetting and Short-term Memories

What causes the forgetting of information in the short-term store? Peterson and Peterson (1959) suggested that memories fade within a few seconds after leaving the short-term store. They suggested that the decay of a short-term memory is an automatic process, and that future recall of that memory will occur only if the memory has been transferred to the long-term store. Furthermore, these researchers argued that rehearsal postpones the onset of the decay of a short-term memory but that the memory begins to fade as soon as rehearsal stops.

Melton (1963), offering another interpretation of the rapid forgetting observed in the Peterson and Peterson (1959) study, claimed that interference was responsible for the rapid forgetting of the trigrams. In Melton's view, subjects recalling a specific trigram encounter two sources of interference. First, the backward-counting task is a source of retroactive interference; the memory of the numbers interfered with recall of the trigrams. Second, the memory of trigrams presented at the beginning of the study may have proactively interfered with the recall of trigrams presented later in the study. Because Peterson and Peterson reported only the average recall of all trigrams, Melton argued that the recall of the trigrams presented early in the study may have been greater than the reported average.

Gleitman (1987) offers an analogy which may help illustrate between the decay and interference theories. Suppose some packages are on a loading dock, ready to be stored in a warehouse. Packages can be lost if they either rot (decay) or are shoved off by other packages (interference). Which of the processes, decay or interference, causes the forgetting of short-term memories? The evidence (Wessels, 1982) indicates that in the Peterson and Peterson (1959) study, both decay and interference were responsible for an inability to recall a trigram presented 18 seconds earlier.

Keppel and Underwood (1962) provided evidence that proactive interference caused most of the retention loss observed by Peterson and Peterson. In the Keppel and Underwood study, three trigrams were presented on each of three trials. Two retention intervals (3 or 6 seconds) were used on each trial. Keppel and Underwood reported that on the first trial, subjects showed no decline in recall with the 3- to 6-second interval. In contrast, on the second trial, recall of the trigram was less with the 6-second interval, and an even greater loss of retention was seen on the third trial (refer to Figure 12-11). Thus, as subjects learned more trigrams, they became less able to remember them after

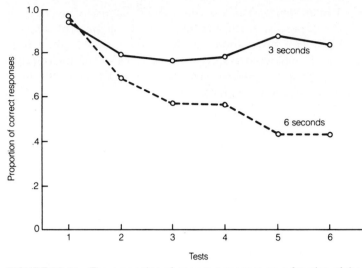

FIGURE 12-11   The proportion of correct responses as a function of the number of previous items and length of retention interval. The results of this study show that the amount of forgetting on the 6-second retention test increased with greater prior training. From Keppel, G., & Underwood, B. J. (1962). Proactive inhibition in short-term retention of single items. *Journal of Verbal Learning and Verbal Behavior, 1,* 153–161.

6 seconds. Keppel and Underwood argue that the memories of trigrams acquired on the early trials interfered with the recall of trigrams experienced on later trials.

Waugh and Norman (1965) evaluated the influence of retroactive interference on the recall of short-term memory. In this study, subjects received a list of digits (for example, 1, 7, 8, 3, 4, 2, 5, 6, 3, 4, 8, 2, 9, 7, *) followed by the presentation of a tone, which is indicated by the asterisk (*). The number that appeared before the tone is the *probe digit,* and subjects were asked to recall the digit that followed the probe digit the *first time* it was presented. Thus, in our example, the correct digit to recall is 8. Waugh and Norman varied the number of digits that intervened between the correct response and the probe digit. According to Waugh and Norman, the more digits that intervened, the greater the retroactive interference and the lower recall a subject should have of the correct digit. However, more time is required when the number of intervening units is increased, and because of this time lapse between the correct digit and recall, decay, not retroactive interference, would be responsible for the low recall. To control for the influence of time, Waugh and Norman used two rates of presentation: four digits per second (fast rate) and only one digit per second (slow rate). If interference is responsible for forgetting, then recall of a 12-item presentation, for example, should be the same, regardless of whether the items were presented 3 seconds apart or 12 seconds apart. However, if decay is responsible for forgetting, then recall should

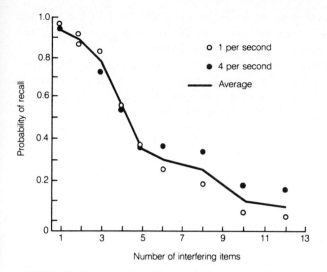

FIGURE 12-12   The probability of recall as a function of the rate of stimulus presentation and the number of intervening items. These results showed that the level of retroactive interference was affected by the number of intervening items; that is, the greater the number of intervening items, the poorer the recall. However, researchers found that rate of stimulus presentation did not influence recall. From Waugh, N. C., & Norman, D. A. (1965). Primary memory. *Psychological Review, 72,* 89–104. Copyright 1965 by the American Psychological Association. Reprinted by permission.

be affected by rate of presentation; that is, more forgetting should occur when it takes 12 seconds rather than 3 seconds to present the 12 digits. Figure 12-12 shows the results of Waugh and Norman's study. The number of intervening digits affected the level of recall; the percent correct declined from almost 100 percent with one intervening digit to less than 10 percent with 12 intervening digits. In contrast, the rate of presentation did not affect recall of the correct digit. These observations support the view that retroactive interference, not decay, affects the recall of memories from the short-term store.

Some evidence suggests that decay does occur but is simply not apparent because interference is a more powerful and common cause of forgetting. There are a number of studies (Baddeley, 1976; Baddeley & Scott, 1971; Shiffrin & Cook, 1978) that indicate that decay can be observed under certain conditions. For example, Shiffrin and Cook (1978) told their subjects that they were studying how well people forget information, not how well people can remember—a procedure Shiffrin and Cook believed would minimize rehearsal and enhance the detection of decay. Their subjects participated in a tone-detection task in which many times during a 40-second trial a tone was presented against a background of white noise. Also, in each 40-second trial, five consonants were presented for

2.5 seconds each. The subjects were instructed to repeat the five consonants, then put them out of their ''mind'' and continue with the tone-detection task. At the end of each trial, subjects were asked to recall the letters.

Shiffrin and Cook used two kinds of trials: on long-delay trials, the letters were presented early in the trial (32.5 seconds prior to the end of the trial); on short-delay trials, the letters were presented late in the trial (12.5 seconds before the end of the trial). According to Shiffrin and Cook, if decay is a cause of forgetting, more forgetting should be observed with a long-delay trial than with a short-delay trial. Shiffrin and Cook reported that subjects forgot 20 percent of the letters on the short-delay trials and 30 percent on the long-delay trials. This result is consistent with the decay theory.

Increased forgetting on long-delay trials may be caused by processes other than decay. Retroactive interference from events occurring during the retention interval may explain the greater degree of forgetting observed on long-delay trials; yet, the subjects' experiences during the interval were not similar to the letters and should thus have caused a minimal amount of interference. The recall differences may have been caused by proactive interference; however, Baddeley and Scott (1971), using a task similar to Shiffrin and Cook's, tested subjects after only one trial, a procedure designed to minimize the development of proactive interference. These experimeters also observed greater forgetting with a long-delay test than with a short-delay test. The results suggest that decay accounts for some forgetting of previously learned material.

Forgetting of Short-term Memories in Animals

Recall our discussion of matching-to-sample and short-term memory in animals in the last chapter. We learned that animals show a rapid forgetting of the sample following the termination of the sample stimulus. What causes the forgetting of the sample stimulus? Can the forgetting of a short-term memory be reduced?

Suppose the lights in the operant chamber are turned off after the sample is presented. Will this procedure affect the recall of the sample stimulus? A number of experiments (Grant & Roberts, 1976; Roberts & Grant, 1978) have turned off the lights in the experimental chamber during the interval between the end of the sample and the presentation of the test stimuli. These studies reported that this procedure enhanced retention of the sample. Why does this procedure lead to greater recall of the sample stimulus? According to Schwartz (1989), turning off the lights eliminates distracting stimuli. The absence of distracting stimuli allows the animal to rehearse the sample stimulus, and the rehearsal increases recall of the sample at testing.

The technique of turning off the lights in the experimental chamber during the retention interval may also enhance recall because of reduction in retroactive interference. We learned earlier that interference has a significant impact on short-term memory in humans. A number of articles (Grant, 1975; Grant & Roberts, 1973; Jarvik, Goldfarb, & Corley, 1969) have reported that interference also interferes with short-term memory in animals. In these studies, another stimulus is presented prior to the sample. The presence of the other stimulus produces a reduced recall of the sample. It is argued that proactive interference from the stimulus accounts for the lower retention of the sample.

ANATOMICAL BASIS OF MEMORY RETRIEVAL

In Chapter 10, we learned that several brain areas, the temporal lobe, the hippocampus, and the dorsomedial thalamus, are involved in memory processes. A number of studies (see Huppert & Piercy, 1979; Poon, 1980; Signoret & Lhermitte, 1976; Warrington & Weiskrantz, 1968, 1970; Weiskrantz & Warrington, 1975) have demonstrated that damage to the hippocampus also can lead to an inability to recall past events. We next examine evidence that hippocampal damage can lead to retrieval difficulty.

Warrington and Weiskrantz (Warrington & Weiskrantz, 1968, 1970; Weiskrantz & Warrington, 1975) conducted a number of studies comparing the memory of amnesics with the memory of individuals who were able to recall prior events. In one study (refer to Warrington & Weiskrantz, 1968), subjects were given a list of words to remember. The amnesics were unable to remember the words even after several repetitions; however, Warrington and Weiskrantz noted that as the amnesics had been given several lists, they began to give responses from earlier lists. In contrast, fewer prior-list intrusions were observed in nonamnesic subjects. These results indicate that the amnesics had stored the responses from earlier lists but were unable to retrieve the appropriate response. These observations further suggest that amnesics are more susceptible to interference than are nonamnesics and that interference was responsible for the higher level of retrieval failure in amnesics as compared to nonamnesic subjects.

Further evidence that amnesic patients suffer from problems in retrieval is provided by Warrington and Weiskrantz's 1970 study. The researchers used three testing procedures: recall, recognition, and fragmented words. With the recall procedure, subjects were asked to recall as many words as they could from a previously learned list. With the recognition procedure, subjects were asked to identify the words they had previously learned from an equal number of alternative words. With the fragmented words procedure, subjects were presented five-letter words in a partial form by omitting two or three of the letters. As can be seen in Figure 12-13, the percentage of correct responses for both amnesic and nonamnesic subjects was greater with the recognition than for the recall procedure. Further, the level of recall was equal for the amnesic and nonamnesic subjects with the fragmented words procedure. These results indicate that the amnesic subjects had stored the words but were unable to retrieve them on the recall test. According to Warrington and Weiskrantz, the recognition and fragmented word treatments provided the subjects with the cues necessary for retrieval and, therefore, enabled the amnesic to remember the words. Other studies by Weiskrantz and Warrington (1975) also showed that providing cues to amnesics at the time of testing significantly increased recall.

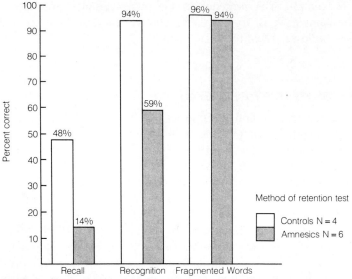

FIGURE 12-13 The percentage of correct responses for amnesic and control subjects on either a free-recall test, a recognition test, or a fragmented-word test. The level of recall in amnesics was equal to control subjects with the fragmented word test, but poorer than controls with either a free-recall or recognition test. From Warrington, E. L., & Weiskrantz, L. (1970). Amnesic syndrome: Consolidation or retrieval. *Nature, 228,* 628–630. Reprinted by permission from *Nature,* Vol. 228, pp. 628–630. Copyright 1970—Macmillan Journals Limited.

Our discussion suggests that retrieval failure caused the memory deficits of the amnesic subjects in Warrington and Weiskrantz's studies. Let's examine evidence that this retrieval failure results from hippocampal malfunctions; see Squire (1987) for a review of this literature.

Malamut, Saunders, and Mishkin (1984) evaluated the effect of damage to the hippocampus on the retention of a visual discrimination task in monkeys. They found that animals with hippocampal lesions required significantly more trials to relearn the task than did nonlesioned animals. In fact, hippocampal-lesioned animals required almost as many trials to relearn the task as they did during original training. Also, Zola-Morgan and Squire (1986) found that destruction of the hippocampus produced poor recall on a matching-to-sample task. Lesions did not affect learning but did disrupt recall of a response. These observations show that the hippocampus plays an important role in the retrieval of memories.

SUMMARY

1 According to Underwood, a memory is a collection of different types of information, called memory attributes. A memory attribute can decrease interference by providing a

basis for distinguishing memories. When one aspect of an event is reexperienced, the attribute of that event prompts the recall of the entire memory.

2 There are 10 major memory attributes. The acoustic attribute stores information about the auditory properties of an event. The physical characteristics of an event are contained in the orthographic attribute. In the frequency attribute, a record of the number of times an event is experienced is stored. The time that an event occurred is recorded in the temporal attribute, and the place where it occurred is contained in the spatial attribute of the memory. The modality attribute provides information about the sensory modality through which the event was experienced. The background in which an event took place is stored in the context attribute.

3 The affective attribute of a memory provides information about the emotional condition surrounding an event. The affective attribute can be viewed as an internal contextual attribute: It registers internal changes in affect, changes which may be natural reactions to the event or may be drug-induced. The associates of verbal items are also attributes of a memory. There are two types of verbal associative attributes: parallel associative attributes (antonyms, synonyms, and functional associates of the verbal item) and class associative attributes (the category name of the verbal item). The transformational attribute contains information about how to decode items that were coded during learning. The three types of transformational attributes are images, natural language mediators, and order transformations.

4 The failure to remember an experience can result from one of three processes. One is the absence of a stimulus associated with memory; another is decay. Memories decay when the physiological changes that took place during memory formation, and that represent the record of the event, diminish with time. Interference is the third cause of forgetting. Interference occurs when the memory of one experience prevents the retrieval of the memory of another event. There are two types of interference: Proactive interference is the inability to recall recent events because of the memory of a past experience; retroactive interference is the inability to remember distant events because of the memory of recent events.

5 Melton and Irwin's two-factor theory assumes that interference is caused by competition and unlearning. According to Melton and Irwin, competition among memories produces both proactive and retroactive interference, whereas unlearning, which is the temporary suppression of distant memories during current learning, causes only retroactive interference. As the effect of unlearning diminishes, competition alone determines which type of interference occurs.

6 A more contemporary view of forgetting proposes that list differentiation and generalized competition, rather than competition and unlearning, are responsible for interference. According to Underwood, the failure to distinguish memories is one cause of interference. Postman suggests that generalized competition, a ''set'' to continue to respond in the manner most recently learned, is another source of interference.

7 The hippocampus area of the central nervous system has been shown to govern the retrieval of memories. Hippocampal damage leads to amnesia because of an inability to retrieve stored memories.

13

BIOLOGICAL INFLUENCE ON LEARNING

A NAUSEATING EXPERIENCE

For weeks, Sean has looked forward to spending the spring semester break in Florida with his roommate John and John's parents. Never having visited Florida, Sean was certain that his anticipation would make the long 18-hour car ride tolerable. When they arrived, Sean felt genuinely welcome; John's parents had even planned many sightseeing tours for all of them during the week's stay. Sean was glad that he had come.

John had often mentioned that his mother was a gourmet cook. Sean was certainly relishing the thoughts of her meals, especially since his last enjoyable food had been his own mother's cooking. Sean was also quite tired of the many fast food restaurants at which they had stopped during their drive. When John's mother called them to dinner, Sean felt very hungry. However, the sight of lasagna on the dining table almost immediately turned Sean's hunger to nausea. As he sat down at the table, the smell of the lasagna intensified his nausea. Sean began to panic; he did not want to offend his hosts, but he hated lasagna. Although he had stopped John's mother after she had served only a small portion, Sean did not know if he could eat even one bite. When he put the lasagna to his mouth, he began to gag and the nausea became unbearable. He quickly asked to be excused, bolting to the bathroom, where he proceeded to vomit everything he had eaten that day. Embarrassed, Sean apologetically explained his aversion to lasagna. Although he liked most Italian food, he had become intensely ill several hours after eating lasagna, and now he cannot stand even the sight or smell of it. John's mother said that she understood: She herself had a similar aversion to seafood. She offered to make Sean a sandwich, and he readily accepted.

Why did Sean have such a strong reaction to lasagna? This chapter explores the learning process that caused Sean to develop his aversion to lasagna but not to other foods. We will discover that Sean's experience affected his instinctive feeding system, which caused him to develop a strong aversion to lasagna. A person's biological character and environmental circumstance also affect other types of learning; we examine in this chapter several instances where behavior is jointly determined by biological character and the environment.

GENERALITY OF THE LAWS OF LEARNING

Why do psychologists train rats or monkeys to press a bar for food or present a buzzer prior to food presentation for cats or dogs, since these situations bear little resemblance to those of the real world? (In natural settings, rats and monkeys do not have to bar press for food, just as cats and dogs do not hear a buzzer before they eat.) The answer to this question lies in the belief that there are some general laws of learning. These laws will be revealed by studying any behavior, even behaviors not exhibited in natural settings.

Psychologists investigating operant conditioning use the bar-press response because it is a behavior easily acquired in many different species. But the same rules governing the acquisition or extinction of an operant response could be demonstrated by using a maze or an alley to study the instrumental conditioning process. Furthermore, the unnaturalness of bar pressing is desirable because the animal comes into the conditioning situation without any past experience that may affect its behavior. The following statement by Skinner (1938) illustrates the belief that the study of any behavior shows that there are specific laws governing the operant conditioning process: "The general topography of operant behavior is not important, because most if not all specific operants are conditioned. I suggest that the dynamic properties of operant behavior may be studied with a single reflex" (pp. 45–46).

Although Skinner studied operant conditioning using the bar-press response, the observations reported in Chapter 5 show that the rules detailed by Skinner governing the acquisition and extinction of the bar-press response control the operant conditioning process with many different behaviors and in many species. Also, much research demonstrates that many varied reinforcers can be employed to increase the rate of bar pressing and that the rules described by Skinner have been found to operate in both laboratory and real-world settings. It is not surprising that psychologists felt confident in training rats and primates to bar press for food to reveal the general laws of operant conditioning.

Similarly, psychologists who present a buzzer prior to food assume that any rules uncovered governing the acquisition or extinction of a conditioned salivation response will represent general laws of classical conditioning. Further, the choice of a buzzer and food is arbitrary: Cats or dogs could be conditioned to salivate as readily to a wide variety of visual, auditory, or tactile stimuli. The following statement by Pavlov (1928) illustrates the view that all stimuli are capable of becoming conditioned stimuli: "Any natural phenomenon chosen at will may be converted into a conditioned stimulus . . . any visual stimulus, any desired sound, any odor, and the stimulation of any part of the skin'' (p. 86).

The specific UCS used also is arbitrary: Any event that can elicit an unconditioned response can become associated with the environmental events that precede it. Thus, Pavlov's buzzer could as easily have been conditioned to elicit fear through pairing it with shock as it was conditioned to elicit salivation through being presented prior to food. The equivalent associability of events is described in the following statement by Pavlov (1927): ''It is obvious that the reflex activity of any effector organ can be chosen for the purpose of investigation, since signaling stimuli can get linked up with any of the inborn reflexes'' (p. 17). Pavlov found that many different stimuli can become associated with the UCS of food. Other psychologists documented the conditioning of varied stimuli with a multitude of UCSs. Also, the literature points out that different CSs and UCSs can become associated in both laboratory and natural situations. The idea that any environmental stimulus can become associated with any unconditioned stimulus seemed a reasonable conclusion based on the research conducted on classical conditioning.

A BEHAVIOR SYSTEMS APPROACH

All organisms . . . possess the basic behavioral patterns that enable them to survive in their niches, but learning provides the fine tuning necessary for successful adaptation. (Garcia and Garcia y Robertson, 1985.)

The general laws of learning view described in the last section assumed that learning is the primary determinant of how an animal or human acts. According to this approach, learning functions to organize reflexes and random responses so that an animal or a person can effectively interact with the environment. In this view, the impact of learning is to allow the animal or person to adapt to the environment and thereby survive. However, the quote presented at the beginning of this section provides a different perspective on the impact of learning on behavior. Rather than assuming that learning organizes behavior, Garcia and Garcia y Robertson (1985) assume that the organization of behavior already exists in the animal. The function of learning is to enhance already existing organization rather than create a new organization. Many psychologists (see Garcia & Garcia y Robertson, 1985; Hogan, 1989; Johnston, 1981; Rozin & Schull, 1987; Timberlake, 1989) have suggested that learning modifies prexisting instinctive systems rather than constructing a new behavioral organization; we look at this idea next.

William Timberlake (see Timberlake, 1983, 1984; Timberlake & Lucas, 1989) offers an alternative to the general laws of learning concept. According to Timberlake, an animal possesses a set of instinctive behavior systems, such as feeding, mating, social bonding, care of young, and defense. These instinctive behavior systems are independent and serve a specific function or need within the animal. Figure 13-1 shows an example of the behavior system for feeding. As seen in the figure, there are several components of the animal's feeding response. Indi-

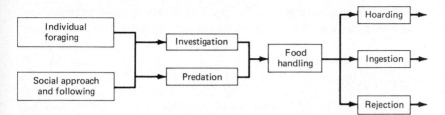

FIGURE 13-1   Illustration of the basic components of feeding system. Individual foraging and social approach and following place the animal in contact with food. Once food is contacted, investigation and/or predation leads to handling of food, which in turn results in the ingestion, rejection, or hoarding of food. From Timberlake, W. (1983). The functional organization of appetitive behavior: Behavior systems as learning. In M. D. Zeiler & P. Harzem (Eds.), *Advances in analysis of behavior: Vol. 3. Biological factors in learning.* Chichester, England: Wiley. Reprinted by permission of John Wiley & Sons, Ltd.

vidual foraging and social approach and following bring the animal into contact with food. Once in contact with food, the investigation and/or predation behaviors enable the animal to obtain food. The handling of obtained food can result in the ingestion, rejection, or hoarding of the food. This complex instinctive behavior system allows the animal to find and consume the nutrients that it needs to survive.

Timberlake's *behavior systems approach* suggests that learning evolved as a modifier of already existing behavior systems. According to Timberlake, the impact of learning is to change the integration, tuning, instigation, or linkages within a particular behavior system. For example, a new environmental stimulus could become able to release an instinctive feeding response as a result of a Pavlovian conditioning experience. Learning can also alter the intensity of a simple motor response due to its repetition or improve the efficiency of a complex behavior pattern as a result of the contingent delivery of a reinforcer.

According to Timberlake, one of the functional features of the behavior system approach is the variation in learning among species; that is, different species of animals learn at different rates. Also, there is considerable variation between different behaviors within a species in terms of the rate of learning. These differences exist in terms of response integration or stimulus responsiveness. What causes these variations among and within animal species? Timberlake suggests that the variations are due either to predispositions or constraints on what an animal can learn.

A *predisposition* represents instances where an animal learns more rapidly or in a different form than expected. Timberlake suggests that predispositions occur when environmental circumstance easily modifies the instinctive behavior system that the animal brings into the situation. Variations in learning also can reflect the impact of a *constraint* on learning. In Timberlake's view, a constraint on learning occurs when an animal learns less rapidly or less completely than expected. According to Timberlake, constraints on learning occur when environmental circumstance is not suited to the animal's instinctive behavior system. In the next sections we examine examples of predispositions and constraints on learning.

ANIMAL MISBEHAVIOR

Several summers ago my family visited Busch Gardens. We observed some unusual behavior in birds during our visit; they walked on a wire, pedaled a bicycle, pecked certain keys on a piano, and so on. The birds had been trained to exhibit these behaviors using the operant conditioning techniques detailed in Chapter 5. Keller Breland and Marian Breland (see Breland & Breland, 1961) initiated the use of operant procedures to teach exotic behaviors to animals. They conducted their research at Animal Behavior Enterprises, Hot Springs, Arkansas, to see if the techniques described by Skinner could be used in the real world.

The Brelands trained 38 species, including reindeer, cockatoos, raccoons, porpoises, and whales. In fact, they have trained over 6000 animals to emit a wide range of behaviors, including hens playing a five-note tune on a piano and performing a "tap dance," pigs turning on a radio and eating breakfast at a table, chicks running up an inclined platform and sliding off, a calf answering questions in a quiz show by lighting either a yes or no sign, and two turkeys playing hockey. Established by Breland and Breland and many other individuals, these exotic behaviors have been shown at many municipal zoos and museums of natural history, in department store displays, at fair and trade convention exhibits, at tourist attractions, and on television shows. These demonstrations have not only provided entertainment for millions of people but have also documented the power and generality of the operant conditioning procedures detailed by Skinner.

Although Breland and Breland (1961, 1966) were able to condition a wide variety of exotic behaviors using operant conditioning, they noted that the efficiency of some operant responses, although initially performed effectively, deteriorated with continued training despite repeated food reinforcements. According to Breland and Breland, elicitation by food of instinctive food-foraging and food-handling behaviors caused the decline in the effectiveness of an operant response reinforced by food. These instinctive behaviors, strengthened by food reinforcement, eventually dominate the operant behavior. Breland and Breland called the deterioration of an operant behavior with continued reinforcement *instinctive drift,* and the instinctive behavior that prevented the continued effectiveness of the operant response is an example of *animal misbehavior.*

Breland and Breland attempted to condition pigs to pick up a large wooden coin and deposit it in a piggy bank several feet away. Each pig was required to deposit four or five coins to receive one reinforcement. According to Breland and Breland, "pigs condition very rapidly, they have no trouble taking ratios, they have ravenous appetites (naturally), and in many ways are the most trainable animals we have worked with." However, each pig they conditioned exhibited an interesting pattern of behavior following conditioning (see Figure 13-2). At first, the pigs picked up a coin, carried it rapidly to the bank, deposited it, and readily returned for another coin. However, over a period of weeks, the pigs'

FIGURE 13-2
Breland and Breland attempted to train this pig to deposit the wooden disk into a piggy bank. Unfortunately, the pig's operant response deteriorated with repeated food reinforcements due to the elicitation of the instinctive foraging response of rooting. (Photo Courtesy of Animal Behavior Enterprises, Inc., Hot Springs, Arkansas. Used by permission of Marian Breland.)

operant behavior became slower and slower. Each pig still rapidly approached the coin, but rather than carry it until depositing it in the bank, the pigs "would repeatedly drop it, root it, drop it again, root it along the way, pick it up, toss it up in the air, drop it, root it some more, and so on."

Why did the pigs' operant behavior deteriorate after conditioning? According to Breland and Breland, the pigs merely exhibited instinctive behaviors associated with eating. The presentation of food during conditioning not only reinforces the operant response but also elicits instinctive food-related behaviors. The reinforcement of these instinctive food-gathering and food-handling behaviors strengthens these instinctive food-related behaviors, which results in the deterioration of the pigs' operant responses (depositing the coin in the bank). The more dominant the instinctive food-related behaviors become, the longer it takes for the operant response to occur. The slow deterioration of the operant depositing response provides support for Breland and Breland's instinctive drift view of animal misbehavior.

Breland and Breland have reported many other instances of animal misbehavior. For example, they found hamsters that stopped responding in a glass case, porpoises and whales that swallowed balls or inner tubes instead of responding to them to receive reinforcement, cats that refused to leave the area around the food dispenser, and rabbits that refused to approach their feeder. Breland and Breland also reported extreme difficulty in conditioning many bird species to vocalize to obtain food reinforcement. In each case of animal misbehavior, Breland and Breland suggested that the instinctive food-seeking behavior prevented the continued high level of performance of an operant response required to receive reinforcement. Apparently, the effectiveness of food reinforcement used to establish an operant behavior is limited.

Boakes and associates (1978) established a procedure for producing animal misbehavior in the laboratory. Boakes et al. trained rats to press a flap to obtain a ball bearing to be deposited in a chute to obtain food reinforcement. They reported that although all the rats initially released the ball bearing readily, the majority of the animals became reluctant to let go of the ball bearing after several training sessions. These rats repeatedly mouthed, pawed, and retrieved the ball bearing before finally depositing it in the chute.

Breland and Breland (1961, 1966) suggested that elicitation of instinctive food-related behaviors (food-seeking and ingestive behaviors) by reinforcement and the strengthening of these instinctive responses during operant conditioning is responsible for animal misbehavior. Boakes et al. (1978) proposed another explanation. In their view, animal misbehavior is produced by Pavlovian conditioning rather than by operant conditioning. The association of environmental events with food during conditioning causes these environmental events to elicit species-typical foraging and food-handling behaviors; the elicitation of these behaviors competes with the occurrence of efficient operant behavior. Consider the misbehavior of the pig detailed earlier. According to Breland and Breland, the pigs rooted the tokens because the reinforcement presented during operant conditioning produced rooting behavior and reinforcement strengthened the intensity of the instinctive food-related behavior; in contrast, Boakes et al. suggested that the association of the token with food caused the token to elicit the rooting behavior.

Timberlake, Wahl, and King (1982) conducted a series of studies to evaluate the validity of Breland and Breland's operant conditioning instinctive drift hypothesis and Boakes and associates' Pavlovian conditioning view of animal misbehavior. The results of the experiments conducted by Timberlake et al. show that both operant and Pavlovian conditioning contribute to producing animal misbehavior. In their *appetitive structure view,* misbehavior represents species-typical foraging and food-handling behaviors that are elicited by pairing food with the natural cues controlling food-gathering activities. Also, the instinctive food-gathering behaviors must be reinforced if the misbehavior is to dominate the operant behavior. Furthermore, animal misbehavior does not occur in most operant conditioning situations because (1) the cues present during conditioning do not resemble the natural cues eliciting instinctive foraging and food-handling behaviors and (2) these instinctive behaviors are not reinforced. Let's examine how Timberlake and associates validated their appetitive structure view of animal misbehavior.

Timberlake et al. used the ball bearing procedure developed by Boakes and associates to investigate animal misbehavior. Recall that rats in this situation repeatedly mouth, paw, and retrieve the ball bearing before releasing it down the chute to obtain food reinforcement. Timberlake and colleagues (experiment 1) assessed the contribution of Pavlovian conditioning to animal misbehavior by pairing the ball bearing with food in experimental subjects. Experimental-treatment animals received food after the ball bearing had rolled out of the chamber. Also, this study used two control conditions to evaluate the importance of ball bearing–food presentation: Animals in one control condition were given random pairings of the ball bearing and food (random group); subjects in the second control condition received only the ball bearing (CS-only group). The researchers reported that experimental-group animals exhibited a significant amount of misbehavior toward the ball bearing: They touched it, carried it about the cage, placed it in their mouth, and bit it while holding it in their forepaws. In contrast, infrequent misbehavior occurred in animals in the two control groups. These observations indicate that the ball bearing and food must be presented together for a high level of misbehavior to occur.

According to Timberlake and associates (1982), the pairings of the ball bearing with food are necessary but not sufficient for the development of misbehavior. They also assert that the misbehavior must be reinforced by food presentation for misbehavior to dominate operant responding. Timberlake et al.'s experiments 3 and 4 evaluated the importance of operant conditioning to the establishment of animal misbehavior. In experiment 3, contact with the ball bearing caused food to be omitted. The researchers assumed that if reinforcement of contact with the ball bearing is necessary for the dominance of animal misbehavior, the contingency that contact with the ball bearing would prevent reinforcement would lead to an absence of animal misbehavior. The results of experiment 3 show that if contact with the ball bearing prevents reinforcement, then the animals exhibit no contact with the ball bearing. The experimenters then reinforced contact with the ball bearing in experiment 4. If the animal did not touch the ball bearing, it received no food on that trial. Timberlake and associates reported that reinforcement of contact with the ball bearing produced a rapid increase in the level of animal misbehavior. Apparently, for misbehavior to develop, stimuli (for example, ball bearings) resembling the natural cues controlling food-gathering activities must be consistently paired with food (Pavlovian conditioning), and the presentation of food must reinforce the occurrence of species-typical foraging and food-handling behaviors elicited by the natural cues (operant conditioning).

Does misbehavior occur in humans? Research needs to be conducted to answer this question. However, a few years ago during the banquet of my youngest son's football team, a young girl seated across from me exhibited a pattern of eating behavior definitely resembling the misbehavior described by Breland and Breland. The girl spent several minutes playing with her eating utensils before putting a bite of food in her mouth. At the end of the 1½-hour banquet, she had not even half-finished her food. Her parents indicated that this was not atypical behavior for their daughter; it was not unusual for her to spend several hours eating, and she had, in fact, spent her entire last birthday party eating rather than playing with her friends. Furthermore, they said that her older brother also took a long time to eat but not nearly as long as his sister. Surely other children also show excessively long periods of eating behavior; undoubtedly, it may be the association of the utensils with food as well as the reinforcement of the misbehavior that contributes to their pattern of eating behavior.

Section Review

Psychologists have generally assumed that some laws govern the learning of all behaviors. This view has enabled psychologists in the laboratory to study behaviors not exhibited in natural settings. Further, these psychologists have proposed that learning functions to organize reflexes and random responses.

Timberlake's behavior systems approach suggests that animals possess highly organized instinctive behavior systems that serve a specific need or function in the animal. Learning evolves as a modifier of instinctive behavior systems and acts to change the integration, tuning, instigation, or linkages within a specific behavior system. Variations in learning are due either to predispositions, where an animal learns more rapidly or in a different form than expected, or constraints, where an animal learns less rapidly or completely than expected.

Breland and Breland trained many exotic behaviors in a wide variety of animal species; however, they found that some operant responses, although initially performed effectively, deteriorated with continued training despite repeated food reinforcements. The deterioration of the operant behavior is called instinctive drift, and the instinctive behavior that prevents continued effectiveness of the operant response is an example of animal misbehavior. Recent research indicates that animal misbehavior occurs when (1) the stimuli present during operant conditioning resemble the natural cues controlling food-gathering activities, (2) these stimuli are paired with food reinforcement, and (3) the instinctive food-gathering behaviors elicited by the stimuli present during conditioning are reinforced.

SCHEDULE-INDUCED BEHAVIOR

B. F. Skinner (1948) described an interesting pattern of behavior exhibited by pigeons reinforced for key pecking on a fixed-interval schedule. When food reinforcement was delivered to the pigeons on a fixed-interval, 15-second schedule, they developed a "ritualistic" stereotyped pattern of behavior during the interval. The pattern of behavior differed from bird to bird: Some walked in circles between food presentations; others scratched on the floor; still others moved their heads back and forth. Once a particular pattern of behavior emerged, the pigeons repeatedly exhibited it, with the frequency of the behavior increasing as the birds received more reinforcement. Skinner referred to the behavior of his pigeons on the interval schedule as an example of *superstitious behavior*.

Why do animals exhibit superstitious behavior? One reasonable explanation suggests that animals have associated superstitious behavior with reinforcement and that this association causes the animals to exhibit high levels of superstitious behavior. However, Staddon and Simmelhag's (1971) analysis of superstitious behavior indicates that it is not an example of the operant behavior detailed in Chapter 5. They identified two types of behavior produced when reinforcement (for example, food) is programmed to occur on a regular basis: (1) *Terminal behavior* occurs during the last few seconds of the interval between reinforcer presentations, and it is reinforcer oriented. Staddon and Simmelhag's pigeons pecking on or near the food hopper which delivered food is an example of terminal behavior. (2) *Interim behavior,* in contrast, is not reinforcer oriented. Although contiguity influences the development of terminal behavior, interim behavior does not occur contiguously with reinforcement. Terminal behavior falls between interim behavior and reinforcement but does not interfere with the exhibition of interim behavior.

According to Staddon and Simmelhag, terminal behavior occurs in stimulus situations that are highly predictive of the occurrence of reinforcement; that is, terminal behavior is typically emitted just prior to a reinforcement availability on a fixed-interval schedule. In contrast, interim behavior occurs during stimulus conditions that have a low probability of the occurrence of reinforcement; that is, interim behavior is observed most frequently in the period *following* reinforcement. Recall our discussion of the ethological approach in Chapter 1. Terminal behavior corresponds to appetitive behavior, interim behavior to consummatory behavior.

The strange superstitious behavior described initially by Skinner is only one example of interim behavior. Animals exhibit a wide variety of other behaviors (for example, drinking, running, grooming, nest building, aggression) when reinforcement occurs regularly. The elicitation of high levels of interim behavior by fixed-interval schedules of reinforcement is referred to as *adjunctive behavior*.

Schedule-Induced Polydipsia

The most extensively studied form of adjunctive behavior is the excessive intake of water (polydipsia) when animals are reinforced with food on a fixed-interval schedule. John Falk (1961) was the first investigator to observe *schedule-induced polydipsia*. Falk deprived rats of food until their body weight was approximately 70 to 80 percent of their initial body weight and then trained them to bar press for food reinforcement. When water was available in an operant chamber, Falk found that the rats consumed excessive amounts of water. Even though Falk's rats were not water deprived, they drank large amounts of water; in fact, under certain conditions animals provided food reinforcement on an interval schedule will consume as much as one-half their weight in water in a few hours. Note that this level of excessive drinking cannot be produced with water deprivation or heat stress or by providing a similar amount of food in one meal. Apparently, some important aspects of providing food on an interval schedule can elicit excessive drinking.

Is schedule-induced polydipsia an example of interim behavior? Recall Staddon and Simmelhag's (1971) definition—interim behavior occurs in stimulus situations that have a low probability of reinforcement occurrence. Schedule-induced drinking does fit their definition: Animals reinforced on an interval schedule typically drink in the period *following* food consumption. In contrast, drinking usually does not occur in the period preceding the availability of food reinforcement.

Schedule-induced polydipsia has been observed consistently in rats given food on an interval schedule (see Wetherington, 1982). A variety of different interval schedules of reinforcement have been found to produce polydipsia. For example, Falk (1966a) observed polydipsia in rats on a fixed-interval schedule, and Jacquet (1972) observed polydipsia on a variety of multiple schedules of reinforcement. Schedule-induced polydipsia has been found in species other than rats. For example, Shanab and Peterson (1969) reported this behavior in pigeons on an interval schedule of food reinforcement, and Schuster and Woods (1966) observed it in primates.

Level of Schedule-Induced Polydipsia Several factors contribute to the amount of polydipsia (see Wetherington, 1982). First, the intensity of food deprivation affects the level of polydipsia observed. Falk (1969) initially established polydipsia in animals of 70 to 80 percent normal body weight and then decreased the level of deprivation to 95 to 100 percent of their initial body weight. Falk discovered that the amount drunk declined as body weight increased. These results indicate that the level of polydipsia is influenced by motivation level: As the motivation level declines, the amount of polydipsia declines.

Second, Falk (1964, 1966a) reported that the palatability of the available fluid affects the amount of schedule-induced polydipsia. Falk observed that the level of intake declined when animals were given a sodium chloride solution instead of water. In a similar study, Gilbert (1974) discovered that rats drank less ethanol solution than water. Furthermore, as the concentration of ethanol was increased, the amount of polydipsia declined. Apparently, schedule-induced polydipsia can be reduced by the presence of an unattractive liquid.

Third, the level of polydipsia is affected by the length of time between reinforcements. A number of studies (Falk, 1966a, 1967; Flory, 1971) show that an inverted U-shaped relation exists between the time interval between reinforcements and the level of polydipsia: The amount of polydipsia increases as the interval length increases up to 180 seconds, then declines with increased interval length. Falk's (1966a) study illustrates this effect. He varied the fixed-interval (FI) length from 20 seconds to 300 seconds. As can be see in Figure 13-3, the level of polydipsia increased as the FI was increased to 180 seconds, then dropped sharply with a 300-second interval. Flory (1971) observed a gradual drop in the level of polydipsia from an FI of 240 seconds to an FI of 480 seconds.

Other Schedule-Induced Behaviors

Several other instinctive behaviors are observed in animals on interval schedules. A number of psychologists (King, 1974; Levitsky & Collier, 1968; Staddon & Ayres, 1975) have reported that interval schedules of reinforcement produce high levels of wheel running. These researchers found *schedule-induced wheel running* using both food and water reinforcement. Furthermore, Levitsky and Collier (1968) found that the highest rate of wheel running occurs in the time immediately following reinforcement, then decreases as the time for the next reinforcement nears. Moreover, Staddon and Ayres (1975) reported that as the interreinforcement interval increases, the intensity of wheel running initially increases and then declines.

Animals receiving reinforcement on an interval schedule will attack an appropriate target of aggressive behavior. For example, Azrin, Hutchinson, and Hake (1966), Cohen and Looney (1973), and Flory and Ellis (1973) reported that pi-

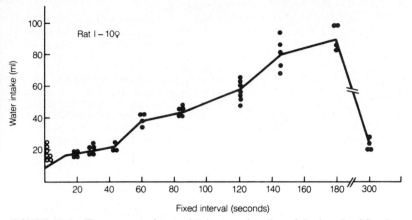

FIGURE 13-3   The amount of water intake as a function of the length of fixed-interval schedule of food reinforcement. As shown in the graph, the amount of water drunk first increased as the interreinforcement interval increased up to 180 seconds, then declined with a 300-second interval. Adapted from Falk, J. L. (1966). Schedule-induced polydipsia as a function of fixed-interval length. *Journal of the Experimental Analysis of Behavior, 9,* 37–39. Copyright 1966 by the Society for the Experimental Analysis of Behavior.

geons will attack another bird or a stuffed model of a bird that is present during key pecking for reinforcement on an interval schedule. Similar *schedule-induced aggression* has been observed in squirrel monkeys (Hutchinson, Azrin, & Hunt, 1968) and rats (Gentry & Schaeffer, 1969; Knutson & Kleinknecht, 1970), and on response-independent fixed-time schedules (Flory, 1969). Schedule-induced aggression has been found using a variety of interval schedules, including fixed-interval schedules (Richards & Rilling, 1972). Knutson and Kleinknecht (1970) reported that the greatest intensity of aggressive behavior occurred in the immediate postreinforcement period. Finally, an excessive level of aggressive behavior is produced on interval schedules of reinforcement. For example, Azrin et al. Observed that pigeons on an interval schedule of reinforcement often badly injure live target birds.

The Nature of Schedule-Induced Behavior

Riley and Wetherington (1989) proposed that schedule-induced behavior is an instinctive behavior elicited by periodic reinforcement. The elicited nature of schedule-induced behavior can be see in the fact that animals continue to drink a flavor that had been paired with illness. (Recall that an aversion to a flavor is established when the flavor is paired with illness.) The relative insensitivity of schedule-induced polydipsia to flavor-aversion learning provides the strongest evidence that adjunctive behavior is elicited by reinforcement. Riley, Lotter, and Kulkosky (1979) provide evidence of this insensitivity. They gave two groups

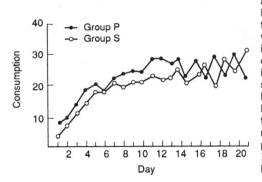

FIGURE 13-4
The mean consumption of water during first 12 days of polydipsia acquisition followed by saccharin and water presentations on alternating days. The animals in group P received a lithium chloride injection following saccharin consumption on day 14, while physiological saline followed saccharin in group S animals. The rapid extinction of the saccharin aversion suggests an insensitivity to an aversive flavor in a schedule-induced polydipsia situation. From Riley, A. L., Lotter, E. C., & Kulkoskey, P. J. (1979). The effects of conditioned taste aversions on the acquisition and maintenance of schedule-induced polydipsia. *Animal Learning and Behavior, 7,* 3–12. Reprinted by permission of Psychonomic Society, Inc.

of animals spaced food sessions with water available in 13 days. This procedure resulted in schedule-induced polydipsia or substantial water intake (see Figure 13-4). On day 14, animals in group P received an injection of lithium chloride after experiencing saccharin during the training session; this procedure paired saccharin consumption and illness and led to the establishment of an aversion to saccharin. Evidence of the aversion to saccharin in the group P animals was the significant reduction in saccharin intake on the first test day (day 16). The rats in group S received saline after the training session with saccharin. These animals did not have saccharin paired with illness and developed no aversion to saccharin.

A different result was obtained on the third test day. The saccharin intake in group P was equal to the saccharin intake in group S by the third test day (day 20; see Figure 13-4). The rapid extinction of a saccharin aversion in group P was much faster than is generally seen with flavor aversions (see Elkins, 1973). This rapid extinction suggests an insensitivity of schedule-induced polydipsia to an aversive flavor. It is possible, however, that only a weak aversion was established when saccharin was paired with illness in the schedule-induced polydipsia paradigm.

Hyson and colleagues (1981) evaluated the possibility that the rapid extinction of the saccharin aversion was due to a weak flavor aversion being established in a schedule-induced polydipsia situation. The researchers initially established a flavor aversion by pairing saccharin with illness in the animals' home cage. The animals were given either 1, 2, or 4 saccharin-illness pairings. After flavor-aversion conditioning, animals received either spaced or massed exposure to food in the training situation outside the home cage. The spaced feeding procedure (SIP treatment) produced excessive fluid consumption, whereas the massed feeding procedure (PD treatment) did not. The researchers found greater suppression of saccharin intake in the massed feeding procedure (PD treatment) than in the

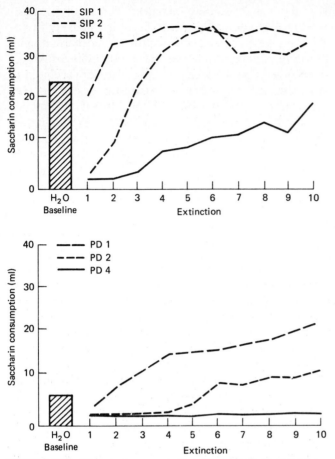

FIGURE 13-5   The mean consumption of saccharin for groups SIP-1, SIP-2, and SIP-4 (top graph) and for groups PD-1, PD-2, and PD-4 (bottom graph). The intake of saccharin was much higher for animals receiving periodic food reinforcements in the training environment (SIP groups) than for animals receiving food in a single meal (PD groups). Also, the greater the number of saccharin–lithium chloride pairings, the stronger the suppression of saccharin intake. From Hyson, R. L., Sickel, J. L., Kulkosky, P. J., & Riley, A. C. (1981). The insensitivity of schedule-induced polydipsia to conditioned taste aversions: Effect of amount consumed during conditioning. *Animal Learning and Behavior, 9,* 281–286. Reprinted by permission of Psychonomic Society, Inc.

spaced feeding procedure (SIP treatment) during the entire extinction period (see Figure 13-5). The suppression over the course of extinction trials in the massed feeding treatment indicates that a strong flavor aversion was established to the saccharin. Yet, animals in the spaced feeding treatment drank significantly more saccharin than did animals in the massed feeding treatment. This result provides strong support for the view that schedule-induced polydipsia is relatively insensitive to a flavor aversion. Further, the continued consumption of saccharin despite its aversion in the spaced feeding paradigm indicates that food elicits drinking.

Hyson et al. (1981) also observed that the level of suppression of saccharin in the spaced feeding procedure increased with greater saccharin-illness pairings (see Figure 13.5). Although continued pairings of saccharin and illness will produce consistently low levels of saccharin consumption (see Riley, Wetherington, Wachsman, Fishman, & Kautz, 1988), animals would sip the aversive saccharin flavor after food presentation before quickly stopping drinking. This cessation of drinking led to the observed suppression of saccharin intake. These results indicate that food elicits drinking, but intake will stop quickly if the flavor is aversive.

Does Schedule-Induced Behavior Occur in Humans?

In many situations in our society, reinforcement is programmed to occur on an interval schedule. Furthermore, excessive levels of instinctive appetitive behaviors do often occur in humans. Gilbert (1974) suggested that interval schedules could be responsible for the excessive drinking (or alcoholism) of many people. Gilbert's demonstration that excessive levels of ethanol were consumed by rats on an interval schedule supports his view. Note that animals do not normally drink any ethanol and that the use of an interval schedule of reinforcement is one of the few ways of producing drinking of alcohol in animals. A recent study by Granger, Porter, and Christoph (1983) with humans observed that water intake was increased when reinforcement (M&Ms) was presented on an interval schedule; the heightened water intake occurred after reinforcement presentation and, therefore, was a demonstration of adjunctive behavior in humans. Furthermore, several researchers (Cantor & Wilson, 1984; Cherek, 1982; Wallace, Singer, Wayner, & Cook, 1975) have observed excessive levels of activities such as eating, smoking, or nail biting in the interval following reinforcement in real-world settings.

Although there have been a number of demonstrations of schedule-induced behavior in humans, there are a number of important distinctions between research with animals and humans (see Sanger, 1986). Unlike the consistently powerful demonstration of schedule-induced behavior in animals, evidence indicates that schedule-induced behavior in humans is often weak and variable. Also, schedule-induced behavior develops slowly in animals but is seen on the first trial in humans. The reasons for differences between animals and humans await future investigation. Further, the relevance of the findings of schedule-induced behavior in human subjects to the real world is unclear. Schedule-induced behavior in humans decreases even with very short intervals (approximately 240 seconds) between reinforcements. As reinforcers typically occur farther apart in humans in the real world, it remains only speculative that spaced reinforcements lead to excessive consummatory behavior in humans.

FLAVOR-AVERSION LEARNING

I have a friend who refuses to walk down an aisle in a supermarket where tomato sauce is displayed; he says that even the sight of cans of tomatoes makes him ill. My oldest son once got sick after eating string beans, and now he refuses to touch them. I once was very nauseated several hours after eating at a local restaurant, and I have not returned since. Almost all of us have some food that we will not eat or a restaurant that we avoid. Often the reason for this behavior is that at some time we experienced illness after eating a particular food or in a particular place, and we associated the event with the illness through classical conditioning. Such an experience engenders a *conditioned aversion* to the taste of the food or the place itself. Subsequently, we avoid it.

Our discussion of flavor-aversion learning begins with the classic research of John Garcia and associates (see Garcia, Kimeldorf, & Hunt, 1957, Garcia, Kimeldorf, & Koelling, 1955). Although rats have a strong preference for saccharin, consuming large quantities even when nondeprived, Garcia and colleagues discovered that these animals will not subsequently drink saccharin if illness followed its consumption. In their studies, rats after consuming saccharin were made ill by agents such as *x-ray irradiation* or *lithium chloride;* they subsequently avoided the taste.

Long-Delay Learning

In Chapter 3 we learned that contiguity plays a critical role in the acquisition of a conditioned response: Little conditioning occurs if the CS precedes the UCS by several seconds or minutes. However, animals will develop aversions to taste cues even when the taste stimulus preceded illness by *several hours.* This observation indicates that unlike other conditioned responses, contiguity is not essential for the establishment of a flavor aversion. The association of a flavor with illness is often referred to as *long-delay learning;* the use of this term suggests a difference between flavor-aversion learning and other examples of classical conditioning.

The Selectivity of Conditioned Aversion Learning   We also discovered in Chapter 3 that stimuli differ in salience; that is, some stimuli are more likely to become associated with a particular UCS than other stimuli are. Garcia and Koelling's (1966) classic study shows that a taste is more salient when preceding illness than when preceding shock, whereas a light or tone is more salient when presented prior to shock than is illness. In Garcia and Koelling's study, rats were exposed to either a saccharin taste cue or a light and tone compound stimulus. Following exposure to one of these cues, animals received either an electric shock or irradiation-induced illness. Figure 13-6 presents the results of the study. The animals exhibited an aversion to saccharin when it was paired with illness but not when it was paired with shock. In addition, they developed a fear of the light and tone stimulus when it was paired with shock but not when it was paired with illness.

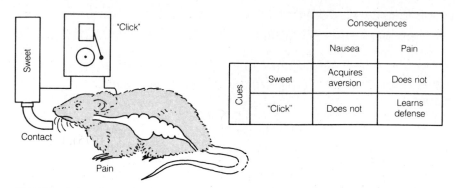

FIGURE 13-6 Effects of pairing a gustatory cue or an auditory cue with either external pain or internal illness. In this study, animals readily associated flavor with illness and click with electric shock, but did not associate food with electric shock and click with illness. Adapted from Garcia, J., Clark, J. C., & Hankins, W. G. (1973). Natural responses to scheduled rewards. In P. P. G. Bateson & P. H. Klopfer (Eds.), *Perspective in ethology* (vol. 1). New York: Plenum.

On the basis of the Garcia and Koelling study, Seligman (1970) proposed that rats have an evolutionary preparedness to associate tastes with illness. Further support for this view is the observation that an intense aversion to a flavor is acquired in adult rats after a single taste-illness pairing. Young animals also acquire a strong aversion after one pairing (see Galef & Sherry, 1973; Klein, Domato, Hallstead, Stephens, & Mikulka, 1975; Rudy & Cheatle, 1977). Apparently, taste cues are very salient in terms of their associability with illness.

Seligman also suggested that rats are contraprepared to become afraid of a light or tone paired with illness. However, other research (for example, Best, Best, & Mickley, 1973; Klein et al., 1985; Morrison & Collyer, 1974; Revusky & Parker, 1976) indicates that rats can associate an environmental cue with illness. Best and associates (1973) and Klein et al. (1985) found that rats avoided a distinctive black compartment previously paired with an illness-inducing apormorphine or lithium chloride injection. Morrison and Collyer (1974) reported that rats developed an aversion to a light cue preceded by illness, and Revusky and Parker (1976) observed that rats did not eat out of a container that had been paired with illness induced by lithium chloride. Although animals can acquire environmental aversions, more trial and careful training procedures are necessary to establish an environmental aversion than a flavor aversion (see Klein et al., 1985; Riccio & Haroutunian, 1977). Also, extinction is more rapid, and the delay interval during which an aversion can be acquired is shorter, with an environmental aversion than with a flavor aversion (Best, Best, & Henggeler, 1977).

Although rats form flavor aversions more readily than environmental aversions, other species do not show this pattern of stimulus salience. Unlike rats, birds acquire visual aversions more rapidly than taste aversions. For example, Wilcoxon, Dragoin, and Kral (1971) poisoned quail that had consumed sour blue water, reporting that an aversion was formed to the blue color but not to the sour taste. In the same vein, Capretta (1961) found greater salience of visual cues than taste cues in chickens.

Why are visual cues more salient than taste stimuli in birds? According to Garcia, Hankins, and Rusiniak (1974), this salience hierarchy is adaptive. Since birds' seeds are covered by a hard, flavorless shell, they must use visual cues to assess whether food is poisoned; thus, these visual cues enable birds to avoid consuming poisonous seeds. Although this view seems reasonable, it does not appear to be completely accurate. According to Braveman (1974, 1975), the feeding time characteristic of a particular species determines the relative salience of stimuli becoming associated with illness. Rats, which are nocturnal animals, locate their food at night and therefore rely less on visual information than on gustatory information to identify poisoned food. In contrast, birds search for their food during the day; thus, visual information plays an important role in controlling their food intake. Braveman evaluated this view by examining the salience hierarchy of guinea pigs, which, like birds, seek their food during the day. Braveman found visual cues to be more salient than taste stimuli for guinea pigs.

Flavor-Aversion Learning in Humans

Does a person's dislike for a particular food reflect the establishment of a flavor aversion? It seems reasonable that people's aversion to a specific food often develops after they eat it and become ill. Informally questioning the students in my learning class last year, I found that many of them indeed had an experience in which illness followed eating a certain food and that these students no longer could eat that food. If you have had a similar experience, perhaps you too can identify the cause of your aversion to some food. In a more formal investigation, Garb and Stunkard (1974) questioned 696 subjects about their food aversions, reporting that 38 percent of the subjects had at least one strong food aversion. Garb and Stunkard found that 89 percent of the people reporting a strong food aversion could identify a specific instance in which they became ill after eating the food, refusing to consume it thereafter. Even though most often the illness did not begin until several hours after consumption of the food, their subjects still avoided the food in the future. Also, Garb and Stunkard's survey indicated that the subjects were more likely to develop aversions between the ages of 6 and 12 than at any other time of life.

Experimentation has documented the establishment of food aversion in people (see Logue, 1985, for a review of this literature). In one study, Bernstein (1978) found that children in the early stages of cancer acquired an aversion to a distinctively flavored Mapletoff ice cream (maple and black walnut flavor) consumed before toxic chemotherapy in the gastrointestinal (GI) tract. Instead of eating Mapletoff ice cream, these children now preferred either to play with a toy or to eat another flavor ice cream. In contrast, both children who had previously received the toxic therapy to the GI tract without the Mapletoff ice cream and children who had been given the Mapletoff ice cream before toxic chemotherapy not involving the GI tract continued to eat the Mapletoff ice cream. Bernstein and Webster (1980) reported similar results in adults. Cancer patients receiving radiation therapy typically show a loss of appetite and weight (Morrison, 1976); the association of hospital food with illness could be reduced by presenting radiation therapy prior to meals, a procedure that would lead to greater eating and a better chance of recovery.

Nature of Flavor-Aversion Learning

Why do animals and people develop aversions to a specific food consumed prior to illness, despite a delay of several hours between consumption of the food and illness? Two very different explanations of long-delayed flavor-aversion learning have been proposed: (1) Kalat and Rozin's (1971) learned-safety theory and (2) Revusky's (1977) concurrent interference theory. Research evaluating both views suggests that each process contributes to flavor-aversion learning.

Learned-Safety View   Kalat and Rozin's (1971) learned-safety view suggests that a unique process is responsible for flavor-aversion learning. The contiguity process detailed in Chapter 3 has obvious adaptive significance for most classical conditioning situations. For example, a child touches a flame and experiences pain. The association of the flame with pain produces the conditioned response of fear; fear elicited on subsequent exposure to the flame motivates this child to avoid pain. However, since the consumption of poisoned food rarely produces immediate illness, the contiguity process characteristic of other classical conditioning situations will not enable an animal to associate food and illness. In Kalat and Rozin's view, a mechanism unique to learning a flavor aversion evolved to allow animals to avoid potentially lethal foods. Kalat and Rozin called this process used by animals to avoid poisoned food *learned safety.*

An animal exposed to a new food consumes only a small portion of it. This low intake of a novel food, *ingestional neophobia,* has adaptive significance: It prevents an animal from consuming a large quantity of a potentially poisonous food so that if the food is poisonous, the animal will become sick but not die. According to Kalat and Rozin, if an animal becomes sick within several hours after food consumption, it will associate the food with illness and develop an aversion to that food. However, if illness does not occur, the animal assumes that the food is not poisonous and that it can safely be consumed again. Learned safety overcomes an animal's reluctance to eat new foods, enabling it to eat foods that enhance its survival.

Kalat and Rozin (1973), providing support for their learned-safety view, gave animals one of three treatments: One group of rats received a novel flavor 4 hours before being poisoned (4-P treatment). A second group was poisoned half an hour after receiving the novel food (½-P treatment). A third group was given access to the novel flavor and was again exposed to it 3½ hours later; illness followed half an hour later (3½–½-P treatment). A contiguity view of classical conditioning predicts equal strength of the flavor aversion in the second and third groups,

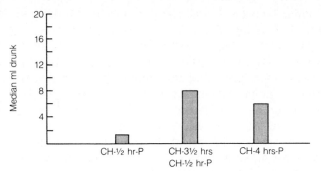

FIGURE 13-7 Mean casein hydrolysate consumption for ½-P, 3½–½-P, and 4-P treatment conditions. The results of this study showed that a significantly stronger aversion to casein hydrolysate developed in the ½-P treatment animals than in either the 3½–½-P or 4-P treatment animals. From Kalat, J. W., & Rozin, P. (1973). "Learned safety" as a mechanism in long-delay taste-aversion learning in rats. *Journal of Comparative and Physiological Psychology, 83,* 198–207. Copyright 1973 by the American Psychological Association. Reprinted by permission.

since a half-hour interval separated the flavor and illness in both groups, and a weaker aversion should be found in the first group because a 4-hour interval separated the flavor and illness. In contrast, the learned-safety view assumes a strong aversion in the second group and a weak aversion in the first and third groups, since the rats in both groups 1 and 3 had 4 hours after consumption of the novel flavor to learn it was safe. As can be seen in Figure 13-7, the results of Kalat and Rozin's study support a learned-safety view of flavor-aversion learning.

Concurrent-Interference View Revusky (1971) assumes that the associative processes influencing other forms of classical conditioning also affect flavor-aversion learning. In all cases, classical conditioning reflects the association a CS with a UCS. However, since animals often experience several stimuli prior to the UCS, which stimulus becomes associated with the UCS? According to Revusky, proximity is a critical factor in conditioning; the stimulus occurring closest to the UCS will become able to elicit the CR. In this view, a CS will be unable to elicit a CR if other stimuli occur between the CS and the UCS. The failure of conditioning to occur when a stimulus is experienced between the CS and the UCS probably will produce *concurrent interference*. However, after eating a food, an animal is unlikely to consume another food for several hours. Thus, long-delay learning occurs in flavor-aversion learning as a result of the absence of concurrent interference.

Revusky (1971) conducted a number of studies showing that the presence of other taste cues can interfere with the establishment of a flavor aversion. In a typical study, rats received initial exposure to saccharin (CS) followed by illness 75 minutes later. A second flavor was introduced 15 minutes after the CS and 1 hour before the UCS. For some subjects, tap water was the second solution; for others, it was vinegar. Revusky reported a weaker aversion to saccharin when vinegar rather than water was used as the second solution, indicating that the presentation of vinegar interfered with the establishment of the saccharin aversion. Furthermore, the amount of concurrent interference was related to the intensity of the vinegar: the stronger the vinegar, the weaker the aversion to saccharin. Revusky found maximum concurrent interference if the second flavor had previously been paired with illness and minimal concurrent interference if the second flavor had previously been experienced without illness.

Section Review

Animals receiving reinforcement on an interval schedule of reinforcement exhibit a wide variety of instinctive behaviors (for example, drinking, running, grooming, nest building, aggression). Although there is no contingency between these behaviors and reinforcement, excessive levels of these schedule-induced behaviors occur; the highest level, called adjunctive behavior, is observed in the time period following reinforcement. Schedule-induced behavior appears to reflect the elicitation of instinctive consummatory behavior by periodic reinforcements. The elicited quality of schedule-induced behavior causes a relative insensitivity of the schedule-induced polydipsia situation to flavor aversions. It also leads an animal to sip an aversive flavor after food reinforcement.

When an animal or a person experiences illness after eating a particular food, an association between the food and illness develops. Subsequently, this association causes the animal or person to avoid that food. A flavor aversion can be formed even when illness occurs several hours after experience with the food: The association of the flavor with delayed illness is often referred to as long-delayed learning. Salience affects the strength of flavor-aversion learning: Some stimuli are more likely to become associated with illness than others. Nocturnal animals, like rats, associate flavors more readily with illness than with environmental events. In contrast, visual stimuli are more salient than flavor cues in diurnal animals like birds or guinea pigs.

Two views have been offered to explain flavor-aversion learning: Kalat and Rozin's learned-safety view and Revusky's concurrent interference theory. When an animal eats a food and no illness results, it learns that the food can be safely consumed in the future; however, if the animal becomes ill after eating, an association between the food and illness is formed, and the animal will subsequently avoid that food. An aversion may not develop if other foods are experienced between the initial food and illness.

SIGN TRACKING

Konrad Lorenz (1969) suggested that the instinctive systems of lower animals and people are programmed to change in response to both successful and failed experiences. These experiences, referred to as *conditioning,* provide additional knowledge about the environment, which, in turn, enhances adaptability. According to Lorenz, conditioning can alter instinctive behavior, the stimuli that release instinctive behavior, or both. Only the *consummatory response* at the end of the behavior chain, according to Lorenz, is resistant to modification. Depending on the nature of the conditioning experience, this change can be either increased or decreased sensitivity. In addition, new behaviors or releasing stimuli can be developed through conditioning. All these modifications increase an animal's or a person's ability to adapt to the environment.

Howard Liddell's experiment (reported by Lorenz, 1969) illustrates Lorenz's view. Working in Pavlov's laboratory, Liddell observed that Pavlov's dogs, conditioned to salivate when a metronome was presented, ran to the machine when they were released from their harness. The dogs then wagged their tails, barked, and jumped on the machine. What caused this behavior? According to Lorenz, these dogs behaved as they would if begging another dog for food. Apparently as the result of conditioning, the machine developed the capacity to release in dogs the same instinctive actions as those that might have been produced by their seeking another dog with food.

Studying Sign Tracking

Psychologists have not always appreciated the importance of Liddell's and Lorenz's observations. Traditionally, Pavlovian conditioning has been viewed from a narrow perspective. Through Pavlovian conditioning, environmental events become able to elicit instinctive visceral and skeletal responses. Conditioned responses can motivate operant behavior, which enables an animal to obtain reinforcement or avoid punishment. However, the significance of conditioned stimuli to animals in natural settings has not been apparent until recently. During the late 1960s and 1970s, research conducted on *sign tracking* or *autoshaping* points to a valuable contribution of conditioned stimuli in the elicitation of instinctive behavior that enables animals to obtain reinforcement, a view consistent with the observations of Liddell and Lorenz (see Tomie, Brooks, & Zito, 1989, for a review of this literature).

Animals need to locate reinforcers (for example, food and water) in their natural environment. How do they find these reinforcers? Environmental events, or stimuli signaling the availability of reinforcement, are approached and contacted by animals seeking reinforcement. By tracking these environmental stimuli, an animal is able to obtain reinforcement. Consider a predator tracking its prey: Certain sights, movements, odors, and noises are characteristic of the prey. The predator can catch the prey only by approaching and then contacting these stimuli. Research indicates that experience increases a predatory animal's ability to aim its instinctive biting response toward the desired part of the prey (Eibl-Eibesfeldt, 1970) and to attack motionless prey (Eibl-Eibesfeldt, 1961; Fox, 1969). Operant conditioning is not responsible for the establishment of effective predatory behavior, since a young predator's attack response improves even when its predatory behavior is unsuccessful. Furthermore, although nonpredatory animals can learn to kill other animals for food, they do not exhibit the instinctive species-specific response characteristics of predatory behavior. Pavlovian conditioning undoubtedly contributes to the enhancement of the predatory attack by causing the animal to approach and contact the stimuli characteristic of the prey.

Brown and Jenkins (1968) conducted the first sign-tracking, or autoshaping, experiment. They placed pigeons in an operant chamber (see Figure 5-1); the environmental chamber contained a small circular key, which could be illuminated, and a food dispenser. Hungry pigeons were fed at 15-second intervals, and the key was illuminated for 8 seconds prior to each food presentation. The pigeons did not have to do anything to obtain food. Brown and Jenkins reported that the pigeons, instead of approaching the food dish when the food was presented, started to peck at the key. The pigeons did not have to peck at the key to obtain food, but the presentation of the illuminated key prior to food sufficiently established a key-pecking response.

Jenkins (1977) described several characteristics of the autoshaping process that point to an involvement of Pavlovian conditioning. First, pigeons' initial pecking at the illuminated key is not accidental: The pairing of the signal and food is necessary to produce pecking. Second, the predictiveness of the stimulus is a crucial element in the establishment of autoshaping. If the illuminated key does not reliably predict the occurrence of food, pigeons will not continue to peck at the key. Gamzu and Williams's (1971) study shows the influence of predictiveness on autoshaping. In the study, food was presented only when the key was illuminated for contingency subjects. Noncontingency subjects were given half their food when the key was illuminated and half when it was not. The results showed that when a noncontingency existed between the signal and food, autoshaping did not occur. Furthermore, Gamzu and Williams found that if the contingency was removed after the development of the key pecking, the pigeons stopped pecking at the key.

Perhaps you think that the pigeons' key pecking is an operant response reinforced by food rather than a conditioned response elicited by the illuminated key. If the key pecking is, indeed, an operant response, then its characteristics would not differ with the use of various reinforcers. However, if the illuminated key is producing an instinctive response identical to that previously elicited by reinforcement, then the animals' response will differ with various reinforcers. The research on autoshaping with reinforcers other than that of food reveals that the key-pecking response observed by Brown and Jenkins is a conditioned response rather than an operant behavior.

Jenkins and Moore (1973) used either food or water as the reinforcer in their autoshaping study. Observations of the pigeons' key-pecking responses demonstrated distinct differences between pigeons receiving the reinforcer of food and those receiving water. Pigeons autoshaped with food key pecked sharply and vigorously; their behavior resembled their responses toward food. Animals autoshaped with water exhibited a slower, more sustained contact with the key. Furthermore, these pigeons frequently made swallowing movements; their behavior toward the key resembled their response to water. Jenkins and Moore also

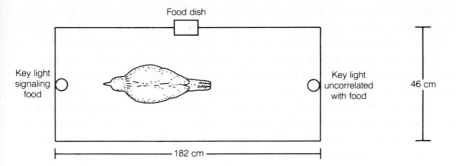

FIGURE 13-8   Illustration of top view of the apparatus used by Hearst and Jenkins to study sign tracking. Illumination of one key signaled food presentation, while illumination of the other key was uncorrelated with food. The pigeons pecked at the key signaling food presentation despite the fact that food presentation was not contingent upon key pecking. Further, pecking at the key correlated with food presentation often prevented the pigeon from obtaining food because of the short time between the illumination of the key and the termination of food availability. From *The principles of learning and behavior* by M. Domjan and B. Burkhard. Copyright 1986 by Wadsworth Inc. Reprinted by permission of Brooks/Cole Publishing Company, Monterey, Calif., 93940.

autoshaped pigeons using two keys: one with food reinforcement, the other with water reinforcement. They reported that these pigeons responded with intense short pecks to the key associated with food and with slow, sustained contact to the key paired with water.

In an interesting study of autoshaping, Rackham (1971) reported conditioned fetish behavior in pigeons. Rackham used four mated pairs of birds, housing the male and female of each pair in adjacent compartments of a large chamber with a sliding door separating the two birds. The stimulus, a light, was turned on daily just prior to the removal of the sliding door (moving the door allowed the male to initiate courtship with the female). Rackham initially observed that the pigeons' first reaction to the light was to approach it, nodding and bowing. The pigeons then began cooing, strutting, and pirouetting. Finally, midway through the study Rackham observed the pigeons emitting nest calls. The pigeons' response to the light stimulus was similar to that exhibited to the female. Also, the conditioned courtship response, like the autoshaped eating and drinking responses observed by Jenkins and Moore (1973), was directed toward the conditioned stimulus.

We have learned that animals approach and contact stimuli associated with reinforcement. Further, the autoshaping process enables animals to track distant reinforcers. The Hearst and Jenkins (1974) study illustrates the sign-tracking function of autoshaping. Hearst and Jenkins placed pigeons in a 6-foot alley with a food dish in the middle (see Figure 13-8); at each end of the alley a circular disk could be illuminated. One key was illuminated prior to food presentation; illumination of the other key was uncorrelated with food. Note that the pigeons had only 4 seconds to get food after the presentation; failure to walk to the food dish within 4 seconds resulted in no food on that trial.

Hearst and Jenkins reported that the pigeons, following several illuminated key-food pairings, ran to the end of the alley having the illuminated key associated with food, pecked at the key, then ran to the center of the alley for food. The pigeons did not respond to the key unassociated with food presentation. Because the alley was long, the pigeons did not always reach the food dish before removal of the food. However, they continued to respond to the illuminated key prior to going to the food, demonstrating the strong attraction of animals to stimuli associated with reinforcement: The pigeons in the Hearst and Jenkins study did not have to peck to obtain food; they simply had to sit in the middle of the alley and wait for it. The birds' responding to the light associated with food indicates the power of a classically conditioned signal of reinforcement.

Sign Tracking in Humans

Does the autoshaping process influence human behavior? Do we respond instinctively to signals for reinforcement? Consider our response to a refrigerator to answer these questions. Certainly your refrigerator is associated with food. Traditionally, going to it to obtain food is considered to be an operant response, that is, a response which a person learns to get food. However, this may not be the case. Your response to the refrigerator is similar to your response to food: You approach, contact, open the refrigerator, and check out the many foods in it. The automatic reflexive character of going to the refrigerator is consistent with the idea that it is an instinctive response conditioned to a signal rather than to an acquired operant response. People also show approach and contact behavior to signals associated with other reinforcers (for example, water and sex). Research is necessary to show conclusively an involvement of Pavlovian conditioned instinctive behavior in the attainment of reinforcement; the reflexive character of goal-seeking behavior in humans points to an influence of the autoshaping process in our responses to reach our goals.

IMPRINTING

Infant Love

You have undoubtedly seen ducklings swimming behind their mother in a lake. What process is responsible for the young birds' attachment to their mother? Konrad Lorenz (1952) investigated this social attachment process, calling it *imprinting*. Lorenz found that a newly hatched bird approaches, follows, and forms a social attachment to the first moving object it encounters. Although typically the first object that the young bird sees is its mother, birds have imprinted to many different and sometimes peculiar objects. In a classic demonstration of imprinting, newly hatched goslings imprinted on Konrad Lorenz and thereafter followed him everywhere. Birds have imprinted to colored boxes and other inanimate objects as well as to animals of different species. After imprinting, the young first prefers the imprinted objects to its real mother; this shows the strength of imprinting.

Although animals have imprinted to a wide variety of objects, certain characteristics of the object affect the likelihood of imprinting. For example, Klopfer
(1971) found that ducklings imprinted more readily to a moving object than to a
stationary object. Also, ducks are more likely to imprint to an object that (1)
makes "lifelike" rather than "gliding" movements (Fabricius, 1951), (2) vocal-
izes rather than remains silent (Collias & Collias, 1956), (3) emits short rhythmic
sounds rather than long, high-pitched sounds (Weidman, 1956), and (4) measures
about 10 centimeters in diameter (Schulman, Hale, & Graves, 1970).

Harry Harlow (1971) observed that primates readily became attached to a soft
terry cloth surrogate mother but developed no attachment to a wire mother. Harlow and Suomi (1970) found that infant monkeys preferred a terry cloth mother
over a rayon, vinyl, or sandpaper surrogate; liked clinging to a rocking mother
rather than to a stationary mother; and chose a warm (temperature) mother over
a cold one. Mary Ainsworth and associates (see Blehar, Lieberman, & Ainsworth,
1977), reporting a similar importance of a warm, responsive mother in the social
attachment of human infants, found a strong attachment to mothers who were
responsive and sensitive to their children's needs. In contrast, infants showed
little attachment to anxious or indifferent mothers.

Age plays an important role in the imprinting process. Not only does imprinting occur readily in certain sensitive periods, but it is also less likely to occur
following this sensitive period. Illustrating the importance of age in imprinting,
a study by Jaynes (1956) exposed newly hatched New Hampshire chicks to cardboard cubes at different times. Jaynes reported that five-sixths of the chicks imprinted within 1 to 6 hours after hatching. However, only five-sevenths of the
chicks met the criterion for imprinting when exposed to the cardboard cube 6 to
12 hours after hatching. The percentage declined to three-fifths at 24 to 30 hours,
two-fifths at 30 to 36 hours, and only one-fifth at 48 to 54 hours.

However, the sensitive period merely reflects a greater difficulty of forming
an attachment; when sufficient experience is given, imprinting will occur after
the sensitive period has lapsed. For example, Boyd and Fabricius (1965) reported
that ducklings not exposed to the imprinting object until 10 days after hatching
still formed an attachment. Brown (1975) trained ducklings ranging in age from
20 to 120 hours to follow an object to an equivalent degree. Brown found that
although the older the duck was, the longer the time required for the duckling to
follow the imprinting object, all the ducklings with sufficient training showed an
equal degree of attachment to the imprinted object.

The sensitive period for social attachment differs between species; in sheep
and goats, it is 2 to 3 hours after birth (see Klopfer, Adams, & Klopfer, 1964);
in primates, 3 to 6 months, and in humans, 6 to 12 months (Harlow, 1971).

Other Examples of Imprinting

A young animal's or person's attachment to "mother" is not the only form of
imprinting. We examine two other instances of imprinting—sexual and food preferences—in this section.

Sexual Preference Konrad Lorenz (1952) reported an interesting behavior in one of his male jackdaws. The bird attempted courtship feeding with him: It finely minced worms mixed with saliva and attempted to place the worms in Lorenz's mouth. When Lorenz did not open his mouth, he got an earful of worm pulp. Lorenz suggested that the male jackdaw had sexually imprinted to him. The sexual preference of many birds is established during a sensitive period (Eibl-Eibesfeldt, 1970; Lorenz, 1970). Also, the birds' sexual preference does not have to be for their own species; although in the absence of the preferred, imprinted species, sexual behavior will occur with their own species. Since sexual preference develops in immature birds when copulation is impossible, the establishment of the birds' sexual preference does not depend upon sexual reinforcement. Further, the imprinted bird's sexual preference is not modified even after sexual experience with another bird species. Perhaps this sexual imprinting is a cause of the development and persistence of human sexual preferences.

Food Preference According to Hess (1962, 1964), animals' experience with food during a sensitive period of development results in the establishment of a food preference. This preference can develop to a nonpreferred food and, once established, is permanent. Consider the following study by Hess (1973) to illustrate the imprinting of a food preference: Chicks innately prefer to peck at a white circle on a blue background rather than a white triangle on a green background. Hess gave different groups of chicks of various ages experience with the less-preferred stimulus. As can be seen in Figure 13-9, the chicks developed a strong preference for the green-triangle stimulus experienced during days 3 to 4 after the chicks had hatched. Preference did not change if the experience occurred on days 1 or 2 or days 7 or 9 after hatching. These observations indicate that the sensitive period for the establishment of food preference in chicks is 3 to 4 days following hatching. Hess suggests that this time period for the establishment of a food preference is critical because 3-day-old chicks (1) no longer use the yolk sac for nutrients and (2) can peck with maximum accuracy.

Humans differ considerably in their food preferences (Rozin, 1977). These preferences may, to some degree, reflect experience with a specific food during the sensitive period of development. People typically seem to prefer familiar foods, which suggests an imprinting influence in food preference. Food aversions in humans may also be sensitive to a developmental stage; Garb and Stunkard's (1974) observation that people are most apt to develop food aversions between the ages of 6 and 12 provides additional evidence that imprinting affects the establishment of food preferences and aversions.

Nature of Imprinting

What process accounts for animals' developing a social attachment (or food preference or sexual preference) during a specific developmental period? Two different views of imprinting have been offered: One suggests that associative learning is responsible for imprinting, and the other proposes that genetic

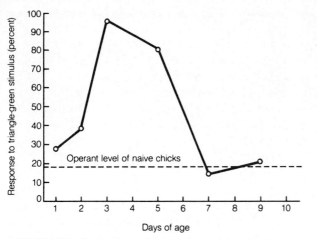

FIGURE 13-9 Percentage of responses to triangle-green stimulus as a function of age of initial exposure to stimulus. The imprinting to the triangle-green stimulus only developed during the sensitive period (3 to 5 days old), with imprinting not developing if exposure occurred either before or after the sensitive period. Adapted from Hess, E. H. (1964). Imprinting in birds. *Science, 113,* 1132–1139. Copyright 1964 by the American Association for the Advancement of Science.

programming produces imprinting. The evidence indicates that both instinctive and associative processes contribute to imprinting.

Associative Learning View Moltz (1960, 1963) proposed that classical and operant conditioning are responsible for social imprinting. Consider the imprinting of a chick to its mother to illustrate the associative learning view. When the chick is old enough to move around in its environment, large objects (for example, mother) in the environment attract the chick's attention, and it orients toward the objects. The chick at this developmental age has little fear of new objects in its environment; therefore, only a low level of arousal will be conditioned to these objects. When the chick's fear system does emerge, new environmental objects will elicit high levels of arousal. Because familiar objects produce only low levels of arousal, their presence elicits relief. This relief reduces the chick's fear and reinforces its approach response, which enables it to reach the familiar object. Thus, the chick develops an attachment to mother (or any other object) because her presence elicits relief and thereby reduces the young chick's fear. A considerable amount of literature indicates that the imprinted object does have fear-reducing properties. For example, Bateson (1969) and Hoffman (1968) noted that the imprinting object's presence reduced distress vocalizations in birds. Harry Harlow's (1971) classic research with primates clearly shows the fear-reducing properties of "mama."

FIGURE 13-10 Cloth and wire surrogate mothers. (Courtesy of Harlow Primate Laboratory, University of Wisconsin.)

Harlow (1971) observed that young primates up to 3 months old do not exhibit any fear of new events; after 3 months, a novel object elicits intense fear. Young primates experience a rapid reduction in fear when clinging to their mother. For example, 3-month-old primates are extremely frightened when introduced to a mechanical monster or plastic toy and will run to their mother; clinging to her apparently causes the young primates' fear to dissipate. Human children show a similar development of fear at approximately 6 months of age (Schaffer & Emerson, 1964). Before this time, they exhibit no fear of new objects. After children are 6 months old, an unfamiliar object elicits fear, and children react by running to mother and clinging to her, which causes fear to subside.

Is this fear reduction responsible for the young primate's or human's attachment to "mother"? Harlow developed two inanimate surrogate mothers to investigate the factors influencing the attachment to the mother (see Figure 13-10). Each mother had a bare body of welded wire; one mother retained only the wire body, and the other was covered with soft terry cloth. In typical studies, primates were raised with both a wire and a cloth-covered surrogate mother. While both the wire and cloth surrogate mothers were equally unresponsive, frightened young primates experienced fear reduction when clinging to the cloth mother but showed no loss of distress when with their wire mother. When aroused, the infants were extremely motivated to reach their cloth mother, even jumping over a high plexiglass barrier to get to it. In contrast, the frightened young primates showed no desire to approach the wire mother. Also, the young primate preferred to remain with the cloth mother in the presence of a dangerous object rather than to run away alone; however, if the wire mother was present, the frightened primate ran away. These observations indicate that the cloth mother contained the essential component necessary for infant bonding.

Blehar and associates (1977) reported a similar importance of security in human infants. They initially observed the maternal behavior of white middle-class Americans feeding their infants from birth to 54 weeks of age. They identified two categories of maternal care: One group of mothers showed responsivity and sensitivity to their children during feeding; the other mothers were indifferent to their infants' needs. During the second stage of their study, Blehar and associates examined the behavior of these infants at 1 year of age in a strange environment. In the unfamiliar place, the interested mothers' children occasionally sought their mothers' attention; when left alone in a strange situation, these children were highly motivated to remain with the mother when reunited. In addition, once these children felt secure in the new place, they explored and played with toys. The researchers called this type of mother-infant bond a *secure relationship*. The behavior of these secure children strikingly resembles the response of Harlow's rhesus monkeys to the cloth mother. In contrast to this secure relationship, children of indifferent mothers frequently cried and were apparently distressed. Their alarm was not reduced by the presence of the mother. Also, these researchers reported that these children avoided contact with their mothers, either because the mothers were uninterested or because the mothers actually rejected them. The researchers labeled this mother-infant interaction an *anxious relationship*. The failure of the mothers of these anxious children to induce security certainly parallels the infant primates' response to the wire surrogate mother.

Moltz's associative learning view suggests that initial conditioning of low arousal to the imprinting objects develops because the object is attention-provoking, orienting the animal toward the imprinting object. But we learned earlier that chicks imprint more readily to objects moving away than to objects moving toward them. One would assume that advancing objects would be more attention-provoking than retreating objects. Chicks' greater imprinting to objects moving away argues against an explanation of imprinting based only on simple associative learning. This observation points to another problem with an associative learning view. Some objects are more likely than others to become imprinting objects. For example, animals imprint more readily to objects having characteristics of adult members of their species. A simple associative explanation of imprinting would not assume that the characteristics of the imprinting objects are important: Any object attracting the animal's attention prior to the development of fear should become able to provide security and, therefore, a strong attachment should ensue. The importance of the specific attributes of the object in the formation of a social attachment argues against a purely associative explanation of imprinting.

Instinctive View of Imprinting   Konrad Lorenz (1935) suggested that imprinting is a genetically programmed form of learning. Imprinting is adaptive because it ensures that environmental events elicit instinctive reactions that enhance the animal's survival. Hess (1973) also proposed that inheritance governs the imprinting process. The following quotation by Hess eloquently describes his view of the role of instinct in the social attachment of the young mallard to its mother:

> We must consider that young ducks innately possess a schema of the natural imprinting object, so that the more a social object fits this schema, the stronger the imprinting that occurs to the object. This innate disposition with regard to the type of object learned indicates that social imprinting is not just simply an extremely powerful effect of the environment upon the behavior of an animal. Rather, there has been an evolutionary pressure for the young bird to learn the right thing—the natural parent—at the right time—the first day of life—the time of the sensitive period that has been genetically provided for. (p. 380)

Several observations indicate that imprinting differs from other forms of associative learning (Graham, 1981). The animal's response to the imprinting object is less susceptible to change than is an animal's reaction to events acquired through conventional associative learning. For example, conditioned stimuli that elicit saliva quickly extinguish when food is discontinued. Similarly, the absence of shock produces a rapid extinction of fear. In contrast, the elimination of reinforcement does not typically lead to a loss of reaction to an imprinting object. Hess (1962,1964) observed that once a 3- or 4-day-old chick developed a food preference to a less preferred object, this preference remained, despite the discontinuance of food reinforcement when the chick pecked at this object.

While punishment quickly alters an animal's response to conditioned stimuli associated with reinforcement, animals seem insensitive to punishment from an imprinting object. Kovach and Hess (1963) found that chicks approached the imprinting object despite its administration of electric shock. Harlow's (1971) classic research shows how powerful the social attachment of the infant primate is to its surrogate mother. Harlow constructed four very abusive "monster mothers." One rocked violently from time to time; a second projected an air blast in the infant's face. Primate infants clung to these mothers even while being abused. The other two monster mothers were even more abusive: one of them tossed the infant off her, and the other shot brass spikes as the infant approached. Although the infants were unable to cling to these mothers continuously, they resumed clinging as soon as possible when the abuse stopped. Harlow's observations indicated why abused children typically desire to return to their abusive parent (or parents). Apparently, a child's love for the parent makes possible the forgiveness of even the strongest abuse.

THE AVOIDANCE OF ADVERSITY

Species-Specific Defense Reactions

We discovered earlier in the chapter that animals possess instinctive responses enabling them to obtain reinforcement (that is, food, water, mate). Robert Bolles (1970, 1978) suggested that animals also have a *species-specific defense reaction* (SSDR), which allows them to avoid dangerous events. According to Bolles, animals have little opportunity to learn to avoid danger: They either possess instinctive means of keeping out of trouble or they perish. For example, a deer does not have time to learn to avoid its predator. Unless the deer possesses instinctive means of avoiding the predator, it probably will wind up as the predator's meal.

The instinctive responses that enable animals to avoid adversity differ. An animal's evolutionary history determines which behaviors will become SSDRs: Responses that enable animals to avoid adversity will remain in their genetic programming, whereas nonadaptive responses will not be passed on to future generations. According to Bolles, animals experiencing danger narrow their response repertoire to those behaviors which they expect will eliminate the danger. Since evolution has proved the species-specific defense reactions to be effective and other behaviors are likely to produce failure, behaviors other than the species-specific defense reactions probably would be nonadaptive. Thus, animals limit their reactions to SSDRs as they attempt to avoid danger.

Rats employ three different species-specific defense reactions: running, freezing, and fighting. Rats attempt to run from a distant danger; a close danger motivates freezing. When these two responses fail, rats use aggressive behavior to avoid adversity. Other animals employ different instinctive responses to avoid danger: the mouse, as Bolles suggests in a quote from Robert Burns's "To a Mouse", is "a wee timorous beastie" when experiencing danger because this is the only way this small and relatively defenseless animal can avoid danger. In contrast, the bird just flies away to avoid adversity.

A study by Bolles and Collier (1976) demonstrates that the cues that predict danger not only motivate defensive behavior but also determine which response rats will exhibit when they expect danger. Bolles and Collier's rats received shock in a square or a rectangular box. After they had shocked the rats, the rats either remained in the dangerous environment or were placed in the other box where no shocks were given. They found that defensive behavior occurred only when the rats remained in the previously shocked compartment. Also, Bolles and Collier found that a dangerous square compartment produced a freezing response, whereas a running behavior occurred in the rectangular box. Apparently, the particular SSDR produced depends on the nature of the dangerous environment.

Psychologists have found that animals easily learn to avoid an adversive event when they can use an SSDR. For example, rats readily learn to run to avoid being shocked. Similarly, pigeons easily learn to avoid shock by flying from perch to perch. In contrast, animals have difficulty learning to avoid an adversive event when they must emit a behavior other than an SSDR to avoid adversity. D'Amato and Schiff's (1964) study provides an example of this difficulty. Trying to train rats to bar press to avoid electric shock, D'Amato and Schiff reported that over half of their rats, even after having participated in more than 7000 trials over a 4-month period, failed to learn avoidance response.

Bolles (1969) provides additional evidence of the importance of instinct in avoidance learning. He reported that rats quickly learned to run in an activity wheel to avoid electric shock but found no evidence of learning when his rats

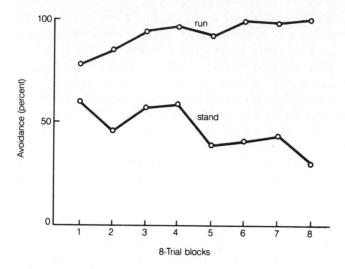

FIGURE 13-11   Percentage of avoidance responses during training in animals that could avoid shock by running or standing on their hind legs. The results of this study showed that the level of avoidance learning was significantly greater if the rats could run to avoid shock. From Bolles, R. C. (1969). Avoidance and escape learning. *Journal of Comparative and Physiological Psychology, 68,* 355–358. Copyright 1969 by the American Psychological Association. Reprinted by permission.

were required to stand on their hind legs to avoid shock (see Figure 13-11). Although Bolles's rats stood on their hind legs in an attempt to escape from the compartment where they were being shocked, these rats did not learn the same behavior to avoid shock. According to Bolles, the rats' natural response in a small compartment was to freeze, and this innate SSDR prevented their learning a non-species-specific defensive reaction as the avoidance behavior.

The Nature of Avoidance Learning

We saw earlier in the chapter that environmental events associated with reinforcement will acquire the ability to elicit instinctive food-gathering behaviors as a conditioned response. This conditioned response causes animals to approach and contact reinforcement, thereby enabling them to obtain reinforcement. This process is called sign tracking or autoshaping. Bolles (1978) suggested that *autoshaping* also is responsible for the development of avoidance learning. In Bolles's view, adversive events elicit instinctive species-specific defensive response. The environment present during adversity becomes able to produce these instinctive defensive reactions as a conditioned response. Whereas instinctive CRs to cues associated with reinforcement elicit approach and contact behavior that enables an animal to obtain reinforcement, stimuli associated with adversity produce instinctive defensive responses that allow the animal to avoid adverse events.

Bolles's approach assumes that Pavlovian conditioning rather than operant conditioning is responsible for avoidance learning. According to Bolles, the association of environmental stimuli with adversity rather than reinforcement is responsible for the development of avoidance behavior. Bolles and Riley's (1973) study shows that reinforcement is not responsible for the rapid acquisition of avoidance behavior. In their study, some animals could avoid being shocked by freezing. Bolles and Riley reported that after only a few minutes of training, their animals were freezing most of the time. Two additional groups were included in their study: One group punished for freezing could avoid shock by not freezing; the other group was shocked regardless of their behavior. Bolles and Riley observed that the rats punished for freezing still froze much of the time. Furthermore, rats punished for freezing froze as much as rats shocked regardless of their behavior. Bolles suggested that when an animal is in a small confined area and anticipates adversity, it freezes. The animals punished for freezing would still have frozen all the time, in Bolles's view, had frequent shocks not disrupted their freezing. Yet, as soon as the shock ended, the anticipation of future shock elicited the instinctive freezing response. Thus, with the exception of shock-induced disruption of freezing in animals punished for freezing, animals either reinforced or punished for freezing showed equivalent levels of freezing. Apparently, the contingency between responding and adversity did not affect the animals' behavior in Bolles and Riley's study.

Section Review

Animals need to locate reinforcers in their environment. Environmental events signaling the availability of reinforcement are approached and contacted by animals seeking reinforcement. The animal's response to these events enables it to obtain desired reinforcers. The ability of these events to elicit approach and contact behavior is acquired through classical conditioning. As the result of conditioning, the conditioned stimulus becomes able to elicit instinctive responses identical to those naturally elicited by reinforcement. The process of an animal learning to reach a desired reinforcer by using conditioned instinctive behaviors is called sign tracking or autoshaping.

Young animals through the imprinting process develop strong attachments to their mothers; this attachment has considerable adaptive significance during the young animals' years of dependency. Animals are more likely to imprint during a specified period of development called a sensitive period. Although animals can imprint to any object experienced during the sensitive period, they are more likely to imprint to objects having characteristics of their species. The animal's attachment to the imprinted object reflects both associative and instinctive processes. Sexual and food preferences are two other forms of imprinting.

Animals possess instinctive responses called species-specific defense reactions, which allow them to avoid dangerous events. These instinctive means of keeping out of trouble are programmed into animals' genetic structure, since they have little opportunity to learn to avoid danger in the real world. Bolles suggested that animals are prepared to learn the environmental events signaling danger. Once animals anticipate danger, they will readily learn to avoid it if a species-specific defense reaction is effective. However, if a non-species-specific defense reaction is required to avoid an adverse event, animals will learn with extreme difficulty or will not learn at all.

THE BIOLOGY OF REINFORCEMENT AND PUNISHMENT

Responses to reinforcement and punishment differ considerably. Some of us are intensely motivated to obtain reinforcement; others show a lack of interest in reinforcement. Similarly, punishment can readily modify some people's behavior; others seem totally oblivious to punishment. Although psychological factors clearly can affect our sensitivity to reinforcement and punishment, physiological research during the past 30 years demonstrates that several brain systems are significantly involved in our responses to both reinforcers and adversity. Effective functioning of these systems allows us to obtain socially acceptable reinforcers and avoid potential punishment. Malfunctions in these systems lead to pathological behavior.

Electrical Stimulation of the Brain

James Olds and Peter Milner's research (Olds & Milner, 1954) is a significant contribution to psychology. Olds and Milner found that stimulating some areas of the brain is reinforcing and that stimulating other areas is aversive. It is interesting that they made their classic observations accidentally when trying to determine the effects of activating the reticular formation. Their electrode placement mistakenly swung forward into the hypothalamus. When this area was aroused, their rats behaved as if stimulation was reinforcing. For example, the rats strongly preferred the place on the long table where they received the stimulation.

To evaluate their findings further, Olds and Milner made the electrical stimulation contingent on pressing a bar in an operant chamber (see Figure 13-12). They found that the rats pressed a bar to receive brain stimulation. The animals' behavior to obtain brain stimulation is called either *electrical stimulation of the brain* (ESB) or *intracranial self-stimulation* (ICSS). Many species, including pigeons (Goodman & Brown, 1966), rats (Olds & Milner, 1954), cats and dogs (Stark & Boyd, 1963), primates (Brady, 1961), and humans (Heath, 1955) have demonstrated that brain stimulation can be reinforcing.

Although Olds and Milner found that stimulating many brain areas provided reinforcement, activation of other brain areas was adversive. Animals receiving this adversive stimulation learned a new behavior to terminate or avoid it. For example, Delgado, Roberts, and Miller (1954) discovered that cats learned to turn

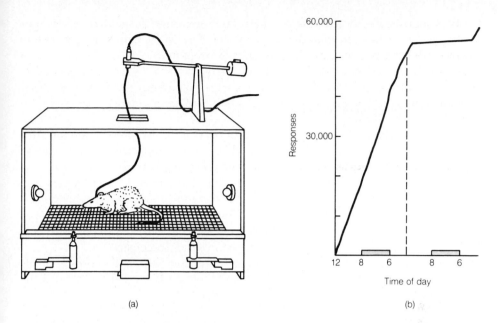

(a)   (b)

FIGURE 13-12   (a) Rat pressing a bar for electrical brain stimulation (ESB). (b) Sample cumulative record. Note extremely high rate of responding (over 2000 bar presses per hour) that occurred for more than 24 hours and was followed by a period of sleep. Adapted from Olds, J. (1958). Self-stimulation experiments and differentiated rewards. In H. H. Jasper, L. D. Proctor, R. S. Knighton, W. C. Noshav, & R. T. Costello (Eds.), *Reticular formation of the brain*. Boston: Little, Brown. Copyright 1958 by Little, Brown, and Company.

a paddlewheel to terminate brain stimulation, just as they would have done to escape an electrical shock to the feet.

Anatomical Location of Reinforcement and Punishment

Larry Stein and associates (Stein, 1969) presented evidence indicating that a group of nerve fibers, the *medial forebrain bundle* (MFB) located in the limbic system, is the brain's reinforcement center. Stimulation of the MFB motivates us to approach reinforcement. In addition, another limbic system fiber tract, the *periventricular tract* (PVT), represents the brain's punishment center. Activation of the PVT motivates us to avoid punishment.

Stein also described how the reinforcement (MFB) and punishment (PVT) systems exert control over operant behavior. Activity in the PVT inhibits our tendency to approach events. Stimulation of the MFB—by either internal activation or the presence of a reinforcing event—inhibits the amygdala. The amygdala excites the PVT through the medial thalamus and hypothalamus; inhibiting the amygdala lessens this excitation and thereby suppresses the effectiveness of the PVT punishment system. Stein's theory portrays animals and humans as normally cautious when encountering new events. The MFB reinforcement system inhibits our hesitancy and motivates approach behavior.

MFB Reinforcement System

Is This the Site of Reinforcement? Not only are most of the brain sites for reinforcement located in the MFB, but MFB stimulation causes more intense reinforcing effects than does stimulation of other brain areas (see Vaccarino, Schiff, & Glickman, 1989, for a review of this literature). Lesion studies also demonstrate the importance of the MFB in motivating reinforcer-seeking behavior. These experiments (Morgane, 1961; Teitelbaum & Epstein, 1962) showed that destruction of the MFB impairs reinforcer-seeking behavior. Apparently, the MFB must be intact if we are to be motivated by reinforcement.

MFB Influence Chapter 7 described Rescorla and Solomon's concept of the central appetitive motivational state. In this section we learn that the MFB is the site of the central appetitive motivational system.

The appetitive motivational state and stimulation of the MFB share four characteristics: (1) Activation of the central appetitive motivational state elicits appetitive behavior. Psychologists have discovered that MFB arousal also motivates approach behavior. (2) Stimulation of the MFB is highly reinforcing; animals will exert considerable effort to activate this system. We exert considerable effort to obtain stimuli (secondary reinforcers) that affect the central appetitive motivational state, indicating that arousal of this state also is reinforcing. (3) Reinforcement and stimuli associated with reinforcement activate the central appetitive motivational state, and evidence collected by numerous psychologists shows that reinforcement enhances MFB functioning. (4) Deprivation increases the intensity of the approach behavior activated by the central appetitive motivational state. A similar influence of drive is found in MFB effectiveness.

The MFB's reinforcing and motivational abilities should not be surprising, because conventional reinforcers (for example, money) also possess motivational properties. For example, the extreme measures taken by many children to obtain ice cream often motivate them to consume large servings of it. Evidence which indicates that MFB stimulation is both reinforcing and motivating follows in the next sections.

Reinforcing Power of Stimulation of the MFB Stimulation of the MFB is extremely reinforcing. Valenstein and Beer's (1964) study illustrating the impact of brain stimulation on rats found that for weeks, rats pressed a bar continuously up to 30 times per minute, stopping for only a short time to eat and groom. These rats responded until exhausted, fell asleep for several hours, and awoke to resume bar pressing.

Electrical stimulation of the brain (ESB) is more powerful than conventional reinforcers such as food, water, and sex. To illustrate that ESB has greater reinforcing value than other rewards, Routtenberg and Lindy (1965) constructed a situation in which pressing one lever caused brain stimulation and pressing another lever produced food. The experimental animals (rats) were placed in this situation for only one hour a day and had no other food source. All the rats spent the entire hour pressing for brain stimulation and eventually starved to death.

The pleasurable aspect of brain stimulation has also been demonstrated in humans. For example, Ervin, Mark, and Stevens (1969) reported that MFB stimulation not only eliminated pain in cancer patients but also produced a euphoric feeling (approximately equivalent to the effect of two martinis) lasting for several hours. Sem-Jacobson (1968) found brain stimulation to be pleasurable to patients suffering intense depression, fear, or physical pain; patients who felt well experienced only mild pleasure.

Motivational Influence of MFB Stimulation   The research of Elliot Valenstein and associates (Valenstein, Cox, & Kakolewski, 1969) demonstrated that activation of the reinforcement system also motivates behavior. The specific response motivated by brain stimulation depends on the prevailing environmental conditions. Thus, brain stimulation will motivate eating if food is available or drinking when water is present. Further, recent research (see Gratton & Wise, 1988) indicates that the same neurons in the MFB, which, when stimulated, elicit feeding, also will maintain electrical brain stimulation. This phenomenon is named *stimulus-bound behavior* to indicate that the stimulus environment determines which action is motivated by brain stimulation.

Electrical brain stimulation motivates behavior even when no internal deprivation exists. Why would brain stimulation cause an animal to eat food when not hungry or drink when not thirsty? Mendelson's (1966) study suggests that MFB activity makes environmental events more reinforcing and thereby motivates us to obtain these events. Mendelson placed his rats in a T-maze (see Chapter 5); movement to one side of the maze produced ESB; movement to the other side produced both ESB and food. What did Mendelson's rats do in this situation? The previous discussion pointed out that animals will learn a new behavior to obtain ESB. Thus, we might predict that Mendelson's rats would favor both sides equally since they are not hungry. However, Mendelson reported that his subjects learned to go to the side producing both ESB and food. Mendelson's rats first received the brain stimulation and then ate their food. Apparently, they experienced pleasurable brain stimulation, which made their eating more enjoyable.

Influence of Reinforcement   Many people report that sexual intercourse is more pleasurable after watching an erotic film (Klein, 1982). According to our view of MFB functioning, the movie activates the MFB reinforcement center, which then increases the reinforcing quality of sex. A number of studies have demonstrated that the presence of reinforcement or stimuli associated with reinforcement increases the reinforcing value of MFB activity.

Mendelson's (1967) study illustrates the influence of water on the reinforcement value of ESB. Mendelson compared how often his rats pressed a bar to obtain brain stimulation when water was available with how often they pressed it in the absence of water. His results showed that rats pressed significantly more often when water was present. Coons and Cruce (1968) found that the presence of food increased the effort expended to obtain brain stimulation, and Hoebel (1969) discovered that a peppermint odor or a few drops of sucrose in the mouth produced a heightened self-stimulation response. These results indicate that the presence of reinforcement makes brain stimulation more reinforcing.

Influence of Drive   Drinking ice water is very satisfying on a hot day, yet on a cold day ice water has little reinforcing quality. This example illustrates one characteristic of deprivation: Drive increases the value of reinforcers. In this example, the presence of thirst on a hot day enhances the reinforcement value of ice water. Increasing the activity of the brain's reinforcement system probably is one mechanism that accounts for this drive effect. Studies showing that drive increases the value of brain stimulation support that view.

Using rats, Brady (1961) showed that the rate of self-stimulation depends on the level of hunger; the longer his rats were deprived of food, the more intense was their rate of brain stimulation. Using water deprivation, Olds (1962) found that the value of brain stimulation is enhanced in rats deprived of water. The male sex hormone testosterone and the female sex hormone estrogen increase sexual motivation (Klein, 1982). Caggiula and Szechtman (1972) discovered that injecting rats with testosterone increased ESB; Prescott (1966) reported that rats' rate of brain stimulation increased when estrogen levels increased during the estrus cycle and decreased when estrogen levels declined.

PVT Punishment System   Chapter 7 detailed Rescorla and Solomon's central aversive motivational state, which is activated by adversive events and the anticipation of adversity. This stimulation results in terminating approach to reinforcement and avoiding adverse and potentially adverse events. Much research indicates that the periventricular tract (PVT) is the site of Rescorla and Solomon's punishment system. Let's examine some of this evidence.

Stimulation of the PVT produces three effects identical to those induced by aversive events such as electrical shock (see Olds, 1962). First, PVT stimulation elicits jumping, biting, and vocalizations, all behaviors which electrical shock and other painful agents can produce. Second, both PVT stimulation and conventional punishers suppress reinforcement-seeking behavior. Third, animals are motivated to terminate PVT stimulation as well as to acquire behaviors that prevent activation of the PVT. Shock and other adversive events also motivate escape and avoidance behaviors.

Destruction of the PVT produces animals insensitive to adversive events. For example, Margules and Stein (1969) noted that rats with PVT lesions showed large deficits in their ability to avoid electrical shock. Apparently, effective avoidance and escape from adversive events depend on the effective functioning of the PVT. In the next section we look at how malfunctions in the MFB and PVT can lead to behavior disturbances in humans.

Reinforcement and Punishment Systems in Behavior Pathology

Many prominent psychologists (Snyder, 1974; Stein & Wise, 1971, 1973; Valenstein, 1973) have suggested that behavioral disturbances can result from failure of the reinforcement and punishment systems to operate effectively. Two major categories of abnormal behavior—depression and phobias—have been linked to malfunctions in the reinforcement and punishment systems. Contemporary evidence implicates a reinforcement system that functions at low levels in depressives' failure to obtain satisfaction from reinforcement. Phobics' extreme fear is thought to be caused by intense arousal of the punishment system.

Chemistry of Reinforcement and Punishment

MFB Reinforcement System   Many studies support the idea that two catecholamine substances, *norepinephrine* and *dopamine,* are the neurotransmitter substances in the MFB reinforcement system (see Vaccarino et al., 1989). Several of these studies are briefly described.

Margules (1969) found that an injection of amphetamine, a drug that stimulates the release of both norepinephrine and dopamine, enhances the reinforcing value of ESB. Other experiments (Olds, 1975; Stein & Wise, 1973) have discovered that direct administration of the catecholamines into the MFB also increases the rate of brain stimulation.

Drugs that inhibit the MFB decrease the reinforcing effect of self-stimulation. Stein & Wise (1969) reported that administration of a-methyl-paratyrosine (AMPT), a drug that prevents the synthesis of both norepinephrine and dopamine, decreases the rate of brain stimulation. Also, administration of chlorpromazine, a drug that blocks both norepinephrine and dopamine neural transmission, attenuates the reinforcing value of ESB. Other experiments (see Gallistel, Boytim, Gomita, & Klebanoff, 1982; Liebman & Butcher, 1974; Stellar, Kelley, & Corbett, 1983) have also concluded that drugs that antagonize noradrenergic and dopaminergic neurons (those neurons for which norepinephrine and dopamine are the transmitter substances) either reduce or eliminate responding aimed at brain stimulation.

PVT Punishment System   The chemical transmitter substance *acetylcholine* has been implicated in the motivation of escape and avoidance behavior (Carlton, 1969; Stein, 1969). Injections of drugs that activate cholinergic neurons (those neurons for which acetylcholine is the transmitter substance) increase the influence of punishing agents. In contrast, drugs that block cholinergic activity reduce the effectiveness of punishment.

The experiments by Margules and Stein (1967) provide direct evidence of cholinergic transmission in the PVT punishment system. The researchers injected directly into the punishment area drugs that either increase cholinergic activity (for example, carbachol) or decrease it (for example, atropine). Before being injected, rats had been trained to bar press for a reinforcer (milk) and had experienced a tone paired with electrical shocks. Margules and Stein administered the injections while presenting this tone. They reported that drugs that aroused cholinergic neurons increased the effectiveness of the tone in suppressing bar pressing. In contrast, drugs that inhibit cholinergic neurons decreased the suppressive ability of the tone.

The Pharmacology of Behavioral Disturbance We have seen that adrenergic and dopaminergic neurons in the MFB are activated when we seek reinforcement. Moreover, cholinergic neurons in the PVT are aroused when we avoid adversity. Under ideal conditions, the effective functioning of these two systems enables us to obtain reinforcement and avoid punishment. Evidence suggests that malfunctions in either the reinforcement or the punishment system are involved in depression and phobic behavior.

Depression A central characteristic of depression is a lack of interest in reinforcement (Klein, 1982). Considerable evidence indicates that lowered responsivity of the catecholamine neurons in the MFB contributes to the development of depression in humans (see Chapter 8).

Studies evaluating amine levels have demonstrated a deficiency in depressed individuals (Depue & Evans, 1976). For example, Ashcroft, Crawford, and Eccleston (1966) measured the level of a serotonin metabolite (5-hydroxyindole acetic acid or 5HIAA) in the cerebrospinal fluid of depressed and nondepressed persons and found lower levels of 5HIAA in the depressives. Similarly, several other studies (for example, Maas, Dekirmenjian, & Fawcett, 1971) point to a low level of the cerebrospinal metabolite (3-methoxy-4-hydroxyphenylethylene glycol or MHPG) of norepinephrine in depressives.

Drugs that decrease brain amine levels induce depressive behavior. Lemieux, Davignon, and Genest (1956) reported that reserpine, a drug that reduces levels of serotonin and norepinephrine, produced depression. In contrast, drugs that elevate brain amine levels are able to decrease depressive symptoms. For example, the tricyclic compounds increase brain norepinephrine by interfering with its reuptake after the neuron fires. Davis, Klerman, and Schildkraut (1967) found tricyclic drugs effective in the treatment of many depressives.

Phobic Behavior Phobics are intensely motivated to avoid adversity. Although psychological processes undoubtedly contribute to phobic behavior, some evidence indicates that an overresponsive PVT punishment system contributes to a phobic's preoccupation with avoiding a specific adverse event.

Suppose you feel extremely anxious about your forthcoming examinations and do not know whether you can take them. Your doctor might prescribe a tranquilizer as treatment for this excessive fear. Two frequently prescribed tranquilizers used to treat anxiety are chlordiazepoxide (Librium) and diazepam (Valium). Other common antianxiety drugs are the barbiturates (for example, pentobarbital) and alcohol.

Animal research clearly demonstrates the capacity of the antianxiety drugs to reduce fear (see Gray, 1971). Conger (1951) trained rats to run down an alley to obtain food and then shocked them before they entered the goal box. This procedure established an approach-avoidance conflict (see Chapter 2). Conger discovered that an alcohol injection reduced the suppressive effects of the electrical shock: The animals that received alcohol ran into the goal box. In contrast, animals given a control injection of water would not approach the goal box. It is possible that the effect of alcohol was not to reduce fear but to increase hunger. Conger used Brown's concept of strength of approach-avoidance tendencies to test this assertion. He measured his rats' approach to reinforcement or avoidance of punishment. Testing either mildly drunk or sober rats, he found that alcohol reduced the adversiveness of punishment but had no effect on the attractiveness of reinforcement. These results demonstrate that alcohol directly antagonizes the suppressive effects of punishment.

The observation that the antianxiety drugs antagonize fear suggests that these drugs affect the PVT punishment system. Margules and Stein (1967) provided additional direct evidence by finding that the barbiturate oxazepam not only reduced the suppressive effects of conventional adversive events (for example, electric shock or bitter quinine) but also antagonized the punishing effects of brain stimulation.

SUMMARY

1 Psychologists generally have assumed that some laws govern the learning of all behaviors. This view has enabled psychologists in the laboratory to study behaviors not exhibited in natural settings. Further, these psychologists proposed that learning functions to organize reflexes and random responses.

2 Timberlake's behavior systems approach suggests that animals possess highly organized instinctive behavior systems which serve a specific need or function in the animal. Learning evolved as a modifier or instinctive behavior systems and acts to change the integration, tuning, instigation, or linkages within a specific behavior system. Variations in learning are due either to predispositions, where an animal learns more rapidly or in a different form than expected, or constraints, where an animal learns less rapidly or completely than expected.

3 Breland and Breland trained many exotic behaviors in a wide variety of animal species; however, they found that some operant responses, although initially performed effectively, deteriorated with continued training despite repeated food reinforcements. The deterioration of the operant behavior is called instinctive drift, and the instinctive feeding behavior that prevents continued effectiveness of the operant response is an example of animal misbehavior. Recent research indicates that animal misbehavior occurs when (1) the stimuli present during operant conditioning resemble the natural cues controlling food-gathering activities, (2) these stimuli are paired with food reinforcement, and (3) the instinctive food-gathering behaviors elicited by the stimuli present during conditioning are reinforced.

4 Animals receiving reinforcement on an interval schedule of reinforcement exhibit a wide variety of instinctive behaviors (for example, drinking, running, grooming, nest building, aggression). Although there is no contingency between these behaviors and reinforcement, excessive levels of these schedule-induced behaviors occur; the highest level, called adjunctive behavior, is observed in the time period following reinforce-

ment. Schedule-induced behavior appears to reflect the elicitation of instinctive consummatory behavior by periodic reinforcements. The elicited quality of schedule-induced behavior causes a relative insensitivity of the schedule-induce polydipsia situation to flavor aversions. It also leads an animal to sip an adversive flavor after food reinforcement.

5 When an animal or a person experiences illness after eating a particular food, an association between the food and illness develops. Subsequently, this association causes the animal or person to avoid that food. A flavor aversion can be formed even when illness occurs several hours after experience with the food: The association of the flavor with delayed illness is often referred to as long-delayed learning. Salience affects the strength of flavor-aversion learning: Some stimuli are more likely to become associated with illness than others. Nocturnal animals, like rats, associate flavors more readily with illness than with environmental events. In contrast, visual stimuli are more salient than flavor cues in diurnal animals like birds or guinea pigs.

6 Two views have been offered to explain flavor-aversion learning: Kalat and Rozin's learned-safety view and Revusky's concurrent interference theory. When an animal eats a food and no illness results, it learns that the food can be safely consumed in the future; however, if the animal becomes ill after eating, an association between the food and illness is formed, and the animal will subsequently avoid that food. An aversion may not develop if other foods are experienced between the initial food and illness.

7 Animals need to locate reinforcers in their environment. Environmental events signaling the availability of reinforcement are approached and contacted by animals seeking reinforcement. The animal's response to these events enables it to obtain desired reinforcers. The ability of these events to elicit approach and contact behavior is acquired through classical conditioning. As the result of conditioning, the conditioned stimulus becomes able to elicit instinctive responses identical to those naturally elicited by reinforcement. The process of an animal learning to reach a desired reinforcer with conditioned instinctive behaviors is called sign tracking or autoshaping.

8 Young animals through the imprinting process develop strong attachments to their mothers; this attachment has considerable adaptive significance during the young animals' years of dependency. Animals are more likely to imprint during a specified period of development called a sensitive period. Although animals can imprint to any object experienced during the sensitive period, they are more likely to imprint to objects having characteristics of their species. An animal's attachment to an imprinted object reflects both associative and instinctive processes. Sexual and food preferences are two other forms of imprinting.

9 Animals possess instinctive responses called species-specific defense reactions which allow them to avoid dangerous events. Bolles suggested that animals are prepared to learn the environmental events signaling danger. Once animals anticipate danger, they will readily learn to avoid it if a species-specific defense reaction is effective. However, if a non-species-specific defense reaction is required to avoid an adversive event, animals will learn with extreme difficulty or will not learn at all.

10 Specialized neural systems control our responses to reinforcers and punishers. Arousal of the medial forebrain bundle (MFB), the brain's reinforcement system, causes pleasure. Research indicates that the presence of reinforcement activates the MFB; arousal of the MFB motivates us to seek the reinforcement. Drive also increases MFB activity, thereby increasing the value of reinforcers. In contrast, activity in the peri-

ventricular tract (PVT), the brain's punishment center, is unpleasant. Punishers activate this system, motivating escape and avoidance behavior. Behavioral disturbances can result when reinforcement and punishment systems operate ineffectively. Contemporary evidence implicates a low-level functioning of the reinforcement system in depressives' failure to obtain satisfaction from reinforcement, and phobics' extreme fear is thought to be caused by intense arousal of the punishment system.

GLOSSARY

Acoustic attribute   The acoustic properties of an event serve as a retrieval cue for that experience.

Acquired drive   An environmental stimulus can elicit the internal drive state as a result of being paired with an unconditioned source of drive.

Action-specific energy   Internal force that motivates a specific action.

Active avoidance response   An overt response to feared stimulus that prevents adversive event.

Addiction   A habitual coping response to terminate an aversive opponent B state.

Additive model   A compensatory decision-making model where the alternative with the highest overall rating is selected.

Adjunctive behavior   The elicitation of interim behavior by interval schedules of reinforcement.

Affective Extension of SOP (or AESOP)   Wagner's view that a UCS elicits separate affective and sensory unconditioned response sequences.

Affective attribute   The mood state present during an event can serve as a memory attribute of that experience.

Affirmative rule   A concept defined by the rule that a particular attribute defines the concept.

Algorithm   A precise set of rules to solve a particular problem.

Analgesia   A reduced sensitivity to painful events.

Animal misbehavior   Operant behavior deteriorates rather than improves with continued reinforcement.

Anterograde amnesia   An inability to recall events that occur after some disturbance to the brain.

Anticipatory frustration response (r_F)   Stimuli associated with nonreward produce frustration state, which motivates escape from a nonrewarding environment.

Anticipatory goal response (r_G)   Stimuli associated with reward produce a conditioned arousal response, which motivates approach to reward.

Anticipatory pain response (r_P)   Stimuli associated with painful events produce fear response, which motivates escape from painful environment.

Anticipatory relief response (r_R)   Stimuli associated with termination of adversity motivate approach behavior.

Anxious relationship   The lack of a relationship to mother who was indifferent to her infant.

Appetitive behavior   Instinctive or learned response motivated by action-specific energy and attracted to a sign stimulus.

Appetitive structure view   Idea that animal misbehavior represents species-typical foraging and food-handling behaviors, which are elicited by pairing food with the natural cues controlling feeding.

Associative-link expectancy   A representation containing knowledge of the association of two events that occur together.

Associative network theory   The idea that associations are formed in a logical, organized fashion.

A state   The initial affective reaction to an environmental stimulus in opponent process theory.

Attribute   A feature of an object or event that varies from one instance to another.

Attributional style   A singular attribution made for all outcomes.

Auditory code   The transformation of a visual image into the sound of that word.

Automatic processing   A type of information processing that requires little attention in order to exhibit a highly practiced activity.

Autoshaping   A key-peck or bar-press response established by periodic reinforcements.

Backward blocking   The pairing of two stimuli (CS_1 and CS_2) with UCS followed by presentation of only one stimulus (CS_1) with UCS leads to reduced conditioned response to the other stimulus (CS_2).

Backward conditioning   With this paradigm, the UCS is presented and terminated prior to CS.

Behavioral allocation view   The idea that an animal emits the minimum number of contingent responses in order to obtain the maximum number of reinforcing activities.

Behavioral autonomy   The continued reinforcement of a specific behavior leads to the occurrence of the response despite devalued reinforcer.

Behavioral contrast   In a two-choice discrimination task, the increase in response to S^D that occurs at the same time as responding to S^Δ declines.

Behaviorism   A school of thought that emphasizes the role of experience in determining actions.

Behaviorist methodology   Skinner's view that environmental circumstances determine behavior.

Behavior modification   Behavioral treatments to alter inappropriate behavior.

Behavior-reinforcer expectancy   A representation in propositional form that action A causes the occurrence of reinforcer B.

Behavior systems approach   Timberlake's idea that learning evolved as a modifier of innate behavior systems and functions to change the integration, tuning, instigation, or linkages within a particular system.

Blocking   The conditioning to one stimulus (CS_1) prevents the acquisition of a CR to a second stimulus (CS_2) when both are paired with UCS.

B state   The opposite affective response that is elicited by the central reaction or A state in opponent process theory.

Cathexis   Tolman's idea that the ability of deprivation states to motivate behavior transfers to stimuli present during deprivation state.

Causal attribution   The perceived cause of a specific event.

Cellular modification theory   The view that learning permanently alters the functioning of specific neural systems.

Chunk   A meaningful unit of information.

Chunking   The combining of several units of information into a single unit.

Classical conditioning   The acquisition of conditioned response when the conditioned and unconditioned stimuli are paired.

Clause   A complete thought or proposition.

Clustering   The recall of information in specific categories.

Coding   The transformation of an experience into a totally new form.

Cognition   An understanding or knowledge of the structure of the psychological environment.

Comparator theory of conditioning   The ability of a particular stimulus to elicit a CR is dependent upon a comparison of the level of conditioning to that stimulus and other stimuli paired in compound with the UCS.

Compensatory models   Decision making based on a systematic evaluation of advantages and disadvantages of all possible alternatives.

Compound conditioning   The pairing of two or more stimuli with a UCS.

Compound schedule   A complex contingency where two or more schedules of reinforcement are combined.

Concept   A symbol that represents a class of objects or events with common characteristics.

Concurrent interference   The prevention of learning when a stimulus intervenes between the conditioned and unconditioned stimuli or when a behavior occurs between the operant response and reinforcement.

Conditional discrimination task   A task where the availability of reinforcement to a particular stimulus depends upon the presence of a second stimulus.

Conditioned aversion   An aversion to stimulus that precedes illness.

Conditioned emotional response   The long-lasting hypoactivity or freezing response to CS paired with painful event.

Conditioned hunger   Environmental stimuli associated with either food deprivation or food become able to elicit hunger response and motivate eating.

Conditioned inhibition   The permanent inhibition of a specific behavior as a result of the continued failure of that response to reduce drive state or a stimulus (CS−) develops ability to suppress responding to another stimulus (CS+) when CS+ is paired with UCS and CS− is presented without UCS.

Conditioned reflex   The acquisition of a new S-R association as a result of experience.

Conditioned response (CR)   A learned reaction to conditioned stimulus.

Conditioned stimulus (CS)   A stimulus that becomes able to elicit a learned response as a result of being paired with an unconditioned stimulus.

Conditioned withdrawal reaction   Environmental cues associated with withdrawal produce a conditioned craving and motivation to resume drug use.

Conditioning   The modification of instinctive systems as a result of experience.

Conjunctive rule   The simultaneous presence of two or more attributes defines concept.

Conservative focusing A concept-learning strategy of focusing on the first positive instance of a concept and then choosing on each subsequent trial a stimulus that differs in only one attribute from the focal stimulus.

Constraint Instances where learning occurs less rapidly or less completely than expected.

Context attribute The context in which an event occurred can be a retrieval cue.

Context blocking The idea that conditioning to the context can prevent acquisition of a CR to a stimulus paired with the UCS in that context.

Contingency management The use of contingent reinforcement and nonreinforcement to increase the frequency of appropriate behavior and eliminate inappropriate behaviors.

Contiguity The temporal pairing of CS and UCS.

Contiguity theory Guthrie's idea that if a response occurs when a particular stimulus is present, the stimulus and response will automatically become associated.

Contiguous The close temporal proximity of two events.

Contingency The specified relationship between a specific behavior and reinforcement.

Continuity theory of discrimination learning The idea that the development of a discrimination is a continuous and gradual acquisition of excitation to S^D and inhibition to S^Δ.

Contrapreparedness Some stimuli, despite repeated CS-UCS pairings, cannot become associated with a particular UCS.

Controlled processing A type of information processing requiring attention and only one piece of information can be attended to at one time.

Counterconditioning The elimination of a conditioned response when the conditioned stimulus is paired with an opponent or antagonistic unconditioned stimulus.

CS predictiveness Acquisition of a conditioned response is reduced when the UCS occurs without the CS and/or the CS occurs without the UCS.

CS preexposure effect The presentation of CS prior to conditioning impairs the acquisition of conditioned response when the CS is paired with UCS.

Cue-controlled relaxation A procedure of conditioning the relaxation response to a specific environmental event.

Cue deflation The extinction of response to one cue leads to increased reaction to the other conditioned stimulus.

Cue-producing response A response that allows an animal to have access to the stimulus dimension controlling behavior.

Decay of memory The idea that memory fades with disuse.

Decision The selection of an action that is most likely to be successful in solving a problem.

Declarative memory Factual memory or the memory of specific events.

Deep structure of sentences The meaning or idea conveyed by a sentence.

Delayed conditioning With this paradigm, the CS onset precedes the UCS, and CS termination occurs either with UCS onset or during UCS presentation.

Discrimination learning Responding in different ways to different stimuli.

Disinhibition The conditioned stimulus will elicit a conditioned response when a novel stimulus is presented during extinction.

Disjunctive rule The concept is defined by the rule that the concept can possess either or both of two attributes.

Displacement The activation of an instinctive response unrelated to presence of conflict in motives.

Distributed practice The spacing of learning experiences over time.

Drive An intense internal force that motivates behavior.

Echo The auditory record of an event contained in the sensory register.

Echoic memory The auditory memory of an event stored in the sensory register.

Efficacy expectancy A feeling that one can or cannot execute a particular behavior.

Elaborative rehearsal The organization of experiences while information is maintained in the short-term store.

Electrical stimulation of the brain (ESB) The high levels of operant behavior exhibited when responding leads to activation of reinforcement areas of brain.

Engram The physical representation of an experience.

Entrapment A decision-making pitfall where commitment to a solution leads to staying with that alternative even though that choice is harmful.

Episodic memory The memory of temporarily related events or the time and place of an experience.

Equivalence belief Secondary rewards (or subgoals) possess the same motivational properties as original goal object.

Escape conditioning A behavioral response to an aversive event which is reinforced by termination of adversity.

Evolution Changes in behavioral and physical characteristics that occur over generations when a species adapts to its new environment.

Excitation The ability of a conditioned stimulus to arouse conditioned response due to CS-UCS pairings.

Expectancy A mental representation of event contingencies.

Expectancy-value theory Rotter suggested that the likelihood of behavior is determined by the perceived probability of reward times the value of that reward.

Experimental neurosis The extreme emotional response when animals are exposed to an insoluable discrimination task.

External expectancy The belief that there is little connection between your behavior and reward.

External inhibition The presentation of novel stimulus during conditioning suppresses response to the conditioned stimulus.

Extinction of conditioned response The conditioned stimulus does not elicit conditioned response when the unconditioned stimulus no longer follows conditioned stimulus.

Extinction of instrumental or operant response The discontinuance of reinforcement leads to a suppression of responding.

Extraexperimental sources of interference The natural language habits represent a source of interference of laboratory material.

External attribution The belief that environmental factors were responsible for a specific outcome.

Family resemblance The more attributes that an object or event shares with other members of concept, the more the object or event exemplifies the concept.

Fear Conditioned response to stimuli associated with painful events that motivates avoidance of adversity.

Feature comparison model The view that statements are verified by comparing specific features or properties of related concepts.

Fixed action pattern (FAP) An instinctive response that is released by presence of effective sign stimulus.

Fixed-interval schedule   Contingency where reinforcement is available only after a specified period of time, and the first response emitted after the interval has elapsed is reinforced.

Fixed-ratio schedule   A contingency where a specific number of responses is needed to produce reinforcement.

Flavor-aversion learning   Avoidance of a flavor that precedes an illness experience.

Flooding (or response prevention) technique   A behavior therapy where phobia is eliminated by forced exposure to the fear stimulus without an adversive consequence.

Forgetting   The inability to recall a past experience.

Frequency attribute   The frequency of an event can be a retrieval cue.

Frustration state   Nonreward elicits the emotional state of frustration, which motivates escape behavior.

Functional fixedness   A difficulty recognizing novel uses for an object.

Functionalism   Early school of psychology that emphasized the instinctive origins and adaptive function of behavior.

Generalization   Responding in the same manner to similar stimuli.

Generalization decrement   The reduced intensity of a response when the stimulus conditions during testing are different than training.

Generalization gradient   A visual representation of the response strength produced by stimuli of varying degrees of similarity to the training stimulus.

Generalized competition   A temporary tendency or set to respond with most recent learning.

Global attribution   The assumption that a specific outcome will be repeated in many situations.

Goal-state of problem   The end point in the solution to a problem.

Graduated-modeling therapy   A behavioral technique of eliminating a phobia by observing a model move closer and closer to the feared object.

Grammar   The rules that define the ways that words can be combined into meaningful phrases, clauses, and sentences.

Habituation   A decrease in responsiveness to a specific stimulus as a result of repeated experience.

Habit hierarchy   The varying level of associative strengths between stimulus environment and behaviors associated with that environment.

Heuristic   A ''best guess'' solution to problem solving.

Higher-order conditioning   A stimulus (CS_2) can elicit CR even without being paired with UCS if CS_2 is paired with another conditioned stimulus (CS_1).

Hull-Spence theory of discrimination learning   The idea that conditioned excitation first develops to S^D followed by the conditioning of inhibition to S^Δ.

Hypoanalgesia   An increased sensitivity to a painful event.

Icon   The visual copy of an event contained in the sensory register.

Iconic memory   The visual memory of an event stored in the sensory register.

Ill-defined problem   A problem with no clear starting or goal state.

Imprinting   The development of a social attachment to stimuli experienced during a sensitive period of development.

Incentive motivation (K)   The level of motivation is affected by the magnitude of reward: the greater the reward magnitude, the higher the motivation to obtain that reward.

Ingestional neophobia   An instinctive avoidance of a novel food.

Inhibition Pavlov's idea that presentation of CS without UCS activates a central inhibitory state that suppresses the CR.

Inhibition of delay The inhibition of responding to CS until just prior to the UCS in a trace conditioning paradigm.

Initial state of problem The starting point in the solution to a problem.

Innate releasing mechanism (IRM) A hypothetical process by which a sign stimulus removes the block on the release of the fixed action pattern.

Instinctive drift Operant behavior deteriorates despite continued reinforcement due to the elicitation of instinctive behaviors.

Instrumental conditioning The environment constrains the opportunity for reward and a specific behavior can obtain reward.

Interference An inability to recall a specific memory due to the presence of other memories.

Interim behavior The responding that occurs following reinforcement.

Internal attribution The assumption that personal factors lead to a particular outcome.

Internal expectancy A belief that one's actions determines whether or not a goal is reached.

Interval schedule A contingency which specifies that reinforcement becomes available at a certain period of time after last reinforcement.

Irrelevant incentive effect The acquisition of an excitatory link expectancy that a particular stimulus is associated with a specific reinforcer under an irrelevant drive state.

Intracranial self-stimulation The high levels of operant behavior exhibited when responding leads to activation of the reinforcement areas of brain.

Kamin effect The poor retention of a prior aversive experience on intermediate retention test (1 to 4 hours after training) but good recall either immediately or 24 hours later.

Korsakoff's syndrome The inability to recall past events seen in alcoholics due to a failure to permanently store experiences.

Language A system of words and word meanings, and a set of rules for combining the words.

Language acquisition device (LAD) Chomsky's idea that an innate mechanism exists that allows children to grasp the syntax of their language with minimal experience.

Lashley-Wade view of generalization The idea that generalization occurs when animals are unable to distinguish between test stimulus and conditioning stimulus.

Latent-learning Knowledge of the environment is gained through experience but is not evident under current conditions.

Law of effect The process of a reward strengthening an S-R association.

Law of readiness Sufficient motivation must exist in order to develop an association or exhibit a previously established habit.

Learned helplessness Exposure to uncontrollable events leads to the belief that events are independent of behavior and results in emotional trauma as well as motivational and cognitive deficits.

Learned irrelevance The presentation of a stimulus without UCS leads to the recognition that the stimulus is irrelevant, stops attention to that stimulus, and impairs conditioning when the stimulus is paired with UCS.

Learned safety The recognition that a food can be safely consumed.

Learning A relatively permanent change in the ability to exhibit a specific behavior that occurs as a result of experience.

Levels of processing view The idea that an experience can receive different levels of processing and that the greater the processing, the better the recall.

List differentiation   An ability to distinguish between memories reduces the level of interference.

Locus of control   The generalized expectation that either internal or external factors control behavior.

Long-delay learning   The aversion that develops to a stimulus paired with illness despite a long interval between stimulus and illness.

Long-term store   The site of permanent memory storage.

Maintenance rehearsal   The mere repetition of information in the short-term store.

Massed practice   Material is learned in a short period of time.

Matching law   When an animal has free access to two different schedules of reinforcement, the portion of responding is proportional to the level of reinforcement available on each schedule.

Matching to sample   A procedure where subjects first are exposed to a stimulus and then later experience the initial stimulus and a second stimulus.

Maximax strategy   A noncompensatory decision-making model where the alternative with the highest rating on the most important attribute is selected.

Medial forebrain bundle (MFB)   The area of the limbic system that serves as the brain's reinforcement center.

Memory attribute   A salient aspect of an event whose presence can lead to retrieval of the past event.

Memory consolidation   The physical encoding of an event into a permanent record of the experience.

Memory elaboration   The analysis of an experience for its meaning.

Memory reconstruction   The alteration of a memory to provide a consistent view of the world.

Method of Loci   A mnemonic technique where items are stored in an ordered series of known locations and a specific item is recalled by visualizing that item in an appropriate location.

Mnemonics   A set of techniques to enhance the storage and retrieval of information.

Modality attribute   Information about sensory modality through which an event was experienced can serve as a memory attribute.

Modeling   The acquisition of behavior as a result of the observation of the experience of others.

Morpheme   The smallest meaningful amount of language.

Multistage memory storage view   Atkinson and Shiffrin's idea that an experience is stored sequentially in the sensory register, short-term store, and long-term store.

Negative contrast (or depression) effect   The lowering of performance below that exhibited with a low reward magnitude when the magnitude of reward is shifted from high to low.

Negative punishment   The occurrence of an inappropriate behavior leads either to loss or unavailability of reinforcement.

Negative reinforcer   The termination of an aversive event reinforces the behavior that terminated the adversity.

Negative rule   The concept is defined by the rule that any object or event having a certain attribute is not a member of the concept.

Neophobia   The reluctance of animals to consume novel flavors.

N-length   The number of nonreward trials that precedes reinforcement; the longer the N-length, the greater the resistance to extinction.

Noncompensatory models Decision making based on a comparison of only certain aspects of each alternative selection.

Noncontinuity theory of discrimination learning The idea that discrimination is learned rapidly once an animal discovers the relevant dimension and attends to relevant stimuli.

NR transition According to Capaldi, the sequence of nonreward and reward trials is responsible for the increased resistance to extinction produced by intermittent reinforcement.

Nucleotide rearrangement theory The view that a permanent change in RNA and DNA occurs as a result of learning.

Occasion setting The ability of one stimulus to enhance responding to another stimulus.

Operant chamber A simple structured environment where a specific response leads to reinforcement.

Operant conditioning Specific response produces reinforcement and the frequency of response determines the amount of reinforcement obtained.

Opponent process theory An event produces an initial instinctive affective response, which is followed by an opposite affective reaction.

Orthographic attribute The feature properties of an event serve as a memory attribute.

Outcome expectancy The perceived consequences of either a behavior or an event.

Overestimation effect The belief that a person is a better decision maker than he or she is in reality.

Overshadowing In a compound conditioning situation, the prevention of conditioning to one stimulus due to the presence of a more salient or intense stimulus.

Pain-induced aggression Punishment can elicit the emotion of anger and motivate aggressive behavior.

Paired basepoint (or blisspoint) The unrestricted level of performance of two behaviors.

Parallel distributed processing model The idea that memory is composed of a series of interconnected associative networks and that knowledge is distributed throughout the entire system.

Partial reinforcement effect (PRE) The greater resistance to extinction of an instrumental or operant response following intermittent rather than continuous reinforcement during acquisition.

Partial-report technique Sperling's procedure asking subjects to recall information presented in one of three rows shortly after event exposure.

Participant modeling therapy A behavioral treatment of phobias in which the patient is encouraged to interact with the feared object after observing the model exhibit nonphobic behavior.

Passive avoidance response The absence of responding leads to the prevention of adversity.

Peak shift phenomenon Maximum responding occurs to stimulus other than S^D and in the stimulus direction opposite that of the S^Δ.

Peg word system A mnemonic technique in which items are associated with the peg words appropriate to a particular system.

Perceptual learning An increased sensitivity to similarities and differences in the environment as a result of perceptual experience.

Periventricular tract (PVT) The area of the limbic system that represents the brain's punishment center.

Personal helplessness   A perceived incompetency leads to failure and feelings of helplessness.

Phobia   An unrealistic fear of a specific environmental event.

Phoneme   The simplest functional speech sound.

Phonology   The rules that dictate how phonemes can be combined in morphemes.

Phrase   A group of two or more related words that expresses a single thought.

Phrase-structure grammar   The analysis of the constituent elements of a sentence.

Positive contrast (or elation) effect   The greater level of performance to a high-reward magnitude when the magnitude of reward is shifted from low to high than is exhibited by animals only experiencing the high-reward magnitude.

Positive punishment   The use of a physical or psychological painful event as the punisher.

Positive reinforcer   An activity in which occurrence increases the frequency of the behavior that precedes the activity.

Postreinforcement pause   A cessation of behavior following reinforcement on a ratio schedule, which is followed by resumption of responding at the intensity characteristic of that ratio schedule.

Potentiation   The enhancement of an aversion to a nonsalient stimulus when a salient stimulus also is paired with UCS.

Predisposition   Instances where learning occurs more rapidly or in a different form than expected.

Preparedness   Seligman's idea that an evolutionary predisposition exists to associate a specific CS and UCS.

Primary reinforcer   The reinforcing properties of the activity are innate.

Proactive interference (PI)   The inability to recall recent experiences as a result of the memory of earlier experiences.

Probability-differential theory   Premack's idea that an activity will have reinforcing properties when its probability of occurrence is greater than that of the reinforced behavior.

Problem   An obstacle exists that prevents the attainment of a desired goal.

Procedural memory   Skill memory or the memory of a highly practiced behavior.

Prototype   The object that has the greatest number of attributes characteristic of concept and therefore is the most typical member of concept.

Punishment   A means of eliminating undesired behavior by the use of an adversive event contingent upon the occurrence of the inappropriate behavior.

Purposive behaviorism   Tolman's theory that behavior is goal-oriented and through experience knowledge of the environment's structure is gained which allows us to reach desired goals.

Ratio schedule   A contingency which specifies that a certain number of behaviors are necessary to produce reinforcement.

Reactive inhibition   In Hull's theory, the persistence of drive state due to unsuccessful behavior leads to temporary suppression of all behavior.

Reciprocal inhibition   Wolpe's term for the process in which only one emotional state can be experienced at a time.

Rehearsal   The repetition of an event that keeps the memory of an event in the short-term store.

Reinforcer   An event where occurrence increases the frequency of behavior and reinforcement.

Reinforcer devaluation effect   The association of reinforcer with adversive event reduces the behavioral control exerted by that reinforcer.

Rescorla-Wagner theory of conditioning   The view that a particular UCS can support only a specific level of conditioning and that when two or more stimuli are paired with UCS, each stimulus must compete for the associative strength available for conditioning.

Response cost   A negative punishment technique in which an undesired response results in either the withdrawal of or a failure to obtain reinforcement.

Response deprivation theory   Timberlake and Allison's idea that a contingency restricts access to an activity and causes that activity to become a reinforcer.

Retardation test   The reacquisition of an extinguished CR by pairing the CS with the UCS.

Retroactive interference (RI)   The inability to recall distant events because of the memory of more recent events.

Retrospective processing   The continual assessment of contingencies leads to a reevaluation of prior conditioning of a CS with UCS.

Retrograde amnesia   The inability to recall events that occurred prior to a traumatic event.

Reverberatory activity   The continued reactivation of a neural circuit for a time following an experience.

Reward   A satisfying state of affairs that can strengthen S-R (stimulus-response) associations.

Salience   The property of a specific stimulus to become readily associated with a particular UCS.

Scallop effect   A pattern of behavior characteristic of fixed interval schedule, where responding stops after reinforcement and then slowly increases as the time approaches when reinforcement will be available.

Schedule-induced aggression   The high levels of aggressive behavior exhibited following reinforcement on an interval schedule.

Schedule-induced polydipsia   The high levels of water consumed following food reinforcement on an interval schedule.

Schedule-induced wheel running   The high levels of wheel running following reinforcement on an interval schedule.

Schedule of reinforcement   A contingency that specifies how often or when we must act to receive reinforcement.

S^D   A stimulus that indicates the availability of reinforcement contingent upon the occurrence of an appropriate response.

S^Δ   A stimulus that indicates that reinforcement is unavailable and the operant response will be ineffective.

Secondary reinforcer   An activity that has developed its reinforcing properties through its association with primary reinforcers.

Secure relationship   The establishment a strong bond to the mother who was sensitive and responsive to her infant.

Selective attention   The process of responding to a specific stimulus dimension while ignoring other dimensions.

Selective filter theory   Broadbent's idea that some information reaching the sensory receptors are not processed.

Semantic memory   The memory of knowledge concerning the use of language, and the rules for the solution of problems or acquisition of concepts.

Semantics   The meaning of language.

Sensitization An increased reactivity to all environmental events following exposure to an intense stimulus.

Sensory preconditioning The initial pairing of two stimuli will enable one of the stimuli (CS_2) to elicit CR without being paired with UCS if the other stimulus (CS_1) is paired with UCS.

Sensory register The initial storage of memory for a very brief time as an exact duplicate of the event.

Sentence Two or more phrases that convey an assertion, question, command, wish, or exclamation.

Serial-position effect The faster learning and greater recall of items at the beginning and end than at the middle of the list.

Set The tendency to use an established method for solving problems.

Shadowing A technique requiring a subject to repeat information presented over a specific message.

Shaping or successive approximation procedure A technique of acquiring a desired behavior by first selecting a high operant behavior, then slowly changing the contingency until the desired behavior is learned.

Short-term store A temporary storage facility where information is modified to create a more meaningful experience.

Sign stimulus A distinctive environmental event that can activate the IRM and release stored energy.

Sign tracking The orientation toward stimuli that enables animals to approach and contact reinforcers.

Simultaneous conditioning The CS and UCS are presented together in this conditioning paradigm.

Simultaneous scanning A concept-learning strategy of testing several different hypotheses at a time.

Sometimes Opponent Process (SOP) theory Wagner's idea that the CS becomes able to elicit the secondary A2 component of the UCS as the CR, and the A_2 component is sometimes opposite the primary A1 component and sometimes the same as the A1 component.

Spatial attribute The spatial location of an item can serve as a memory attribute.

Spatial-temporal hierarchy A hierarchy where phobic scenes are related to distance (either physical or temporal) to the phobic object.

Species-specific defensive reaction (SSDR) An instinctive reaction that is elicited by signals of danger and allows the avoidance of adversity.

Specific attribution The belief that a particular outcome is limited to a specific situation.

Spontaneous recovery The return of a CR when an interval intervenes between extinction and testing without additional CS-UCS pairings, or the instrumental or operant response returns without additional reinforced experience.

Spreading activation theory The idea that once a concept or property of a concept is activated, activation spreads to associated concepts or properties.

Stable attribution The assumption that the factors which resulted in a particular outcome will not change.

State-dependent learning Events experienced in one state will not be recalled if tested in a different state.

Stimulus-bound behavior The prevailing environmental conditions determine which behavior is elicited by stimulation of the brain's reinforcement center.

Stimulus differentiation   The ability to distinguish between the discriminative stimuli.

Stimulus selection   The control of responding by one stimulus dimension.

Stimulus substitution model   Pavlov's view that the pairing of the CS and the UCS allows the CS to elicit the UCR as the CR.

Summation test   The presentation of an extinguished CS with another conditioned stimulus.

Superstitious behavior   "Ritualistic" stereotyped pattern of behavior exhibited during the interval between reinforcements.

Surface structure of a sentence   The arrangement of the words in a sentence.

Surprise   The occurrence of an unanticipated event, which is necessary for conditioning.

Sutherland-Mackintosh attentional view of discrimination learning   Attention to the relevant dimension is strengthened in the first stage and association of a particular response to the relevant stimulus occurs in the second stage of discrimination learning.

Syntax   The system of rules for combining the various units of speech.

Systematic desensitization   A graduated counterconditioning treatment for phobias in which the relaxation state is associated with the phobic object.

Temporal attribute   The time that an event occurred can be a retrieval cue for that experience.

Temporal conditioning   The presentation of the UCS at regular intervals leads to the time of the UCS becoming able to elicit the CR.

Terminal behavior   The operant behavior that occurs just prior to reinforcer presentations.

Thematic hierachy   A hierarchy in which phobic scenes are related to a basic theme.

Thought   The internal process directed at coping with the environment.

Time-out from reinforcement   A negative punishment technique in which an inappropriate behavior leads to a period of time during which reinforcement is unavailable.

Tolerance   The reduced reactivity to an event with repeated experience.

Trace conditioning   The CS is presented and terminated prior to UCS onset with this conditioning paradigm.

Transformational attribute   The transformed or altered event can serve as a memory attribute for that experience.

Transposition phenomenon   Kohler's idea that animals learn relationships between stimuli and that responding to different stimuli is based on the same relationship as original training stimuli.

Two-choice discrimination task   A task when the S^D and S^Δ are on the same stimulus dimension.

Two-factor theory of avoidance learning   Mowrer's view that fear is conditioned in the first stage through the classical conditioning process and in the second stage, an instrumental response is acquired which terminates the feared stimulus.

Two-factor theory of interference   Melton and Irwin's idea that competition between memory causes PI and RI and unlearning leads to RI.

UCS preexposure effect   The exposure to the UCS prior to conditioning impairs later conditioning when a CS is paired with that UCS.

Unconditioned reflex   An instinctual response to an environmental event.

Unconditioned response (UCR)   An innate reaction to the unconditioned stimulus.

Unconditioned stimulus (UCS)   An environmental event that can elicit an instinctive reaction without any experience.

Universal helplessness   A belief that environmental forces produced failure and results in helplessness.

Unstable attribution   The belief that in the future other factors may affect outcomes.

Variable-interval schedule   Contingency where there is an average interval of time between available reinforcements, but the interval varies from one reinforcement to the next contingency.

Variable-ratio schedule   A contingency where an average number of behaviors produces reinforcement, but the actual number of responses required to produce reinforcement varies over the course of training.

Verbal associative attribute   A word associate can act as a retrieval cue.

Verbal code   The transformation of a relatively meaningless nonsense syllable into a meaningful word.

Vicarious conditioning   The development of the CR to a stimulus after observing the CS being paired with the UCS.

Vicious-circle behavior   Escape response which continues despite punishment of escape response due to a failure to recognize that absence of escape behavior will not be punished.

Visual code   The transformation of a word into an image.

Well-defined problem   A problem with clear initial and goal states.

Whole report technique   Sperling's procedure asking subjects to recall all of the information shortly after event exposure.

Withdrawal   An increase in the intensity of the affective opponent B state following the termination of the event.

REFERENCES

Abramson, L. Y. (1977). Universal versus personal helplessness: An experimental test of the reformulated theory of learned helplessness and depression. Unpublished doctoral dissertation, University of Pennsylvania, Philadelphia.

Abramson, L. Y., Garber, J., & Seligman, M. E. P. (1980). Learned helplessness in humans: An attributional analysis. In J. Garber & M. E. P. Seligman (Eds.), *Human helplessness: Theory and applications* (pp. 3–34). New York: Academic.

Abramson, L. Y., & Sackeim, H. A. (1977). A paradox in depression: Uncontrollability and self-blame. *Psychological Bulletin, 84,* 838–851.

Abramson, L. Y., Seligman, M. E. P., & Teasdale, J. D. (1978). Learned helplessness in humans: Critique and reformulation. *Journal of Abnormal Psychology, 87,* 49–74.

Adams, C. D. (1982). Variations in the sensitivity of instrumental responding to reinforcer devaluation. *Quarterly Journal of Experimental Psychology, 34B,* 77–98.

Adams, C. D., & Dickinson, A. (1981). Instrumental responding following reinforcer devaluation. *Quarterly Journal of Experimental Psychology, 33B,* 109–122.

Adelman, H. M., & Maatsch, J. L. (1956). Learning and extinction based upon frustration, food reward and exploratory tendency. *Journal of Experimental Psychology, 52,* 311–315.

Ader, R., & Cohen, N. (1981). Conditioned immunopharmacologic responses. In R. Ader (Ed.), *Psychoneuroimmunology.* New York: Academic Press.

Ader, R., & Cohen, N. (1982). Behaviorally conditioned immuno suppression and murine systemic lupus erythematosus. *Science, 215,* 1534–1536.

Ader, R., & Cohen, N. (1985). CNS-immune system interactions: Conditioning phenomena. *Behavior and Brain Science, 8,* 379–394.

Agranoff, B. W. (1980). Biochemical events mediating the formation of short-term and long-term memory. In Y. Tsukada & B. W. Agranoff (Eds.), *Neurobiological basis of learning and memory.* New York: Wiley.

Alford, G. S., & Turner, S. M. (1976). Stimulus interference and conditioned inhibition of auditory hallucinations. *Journal of Behavior Therapy and Experimental Psychiatry, 7,* 155–160.

Allison, J. (1983). *Behavioral economics.* New York: Praeger.

Allison, J. (1989). The nature of reinforcement. In S. B. Klein & R. R. Mowrer (Eds.), *Contemporary learning theories: Instrumental conditional theory and the impact of biological constraints in learning* (pp. 13–39). Hillsdale, N.J.: Erlbaum.

Alloway, T. M. (1969). Effects of low temperature upon acquisition and retention in the grain beetle *(Tenebrio molitor). Journal of Comparative and Physiological Psychology, 69,* 1–8.

American Psychological Association (1982). *Ethical principles in the conduct of research with human participants.* Washington, DC: Author.

Amsel, A. (1950). The combination of primary appetitional need with primary and secondary emotionally derived needs. *Journal of Experimental Psychology, 40,* 1–14.

Amsel, A. (1958). The role of frustrative nonreward in noncontinuous reward situations. *Psychological Bulletin, 55,* 102–119.

Amsel, A. (1972). Behavior habituation, counterconditioning, and a general theory of persistence. In A. H. Black & W. F. Prokasy (Eds.), *Classical conditioning II: Current research and theory* (pp. 409–426). New York: Appleton-Century-Crofts.

Anderson, N. H. (1963) Comparison of different populations: Resistance to extinction and transfer. *Psychological Review, 70,* 162–179.

Anger, D. (1963). The role of temporal discriminations in the reinforcement of Sidman avoidance behavior. *Journal of Experimental Analysis of Behavior, 6,* 477–506.

Annau, Z., & Kamin, L. J. (1961). The conditioned emotional response as a function of intensity of the US. *Journal of Comparative and Physiological Psychology, 54,* 428–432.

Appel, J. B. (1963). Punishment and shock intensity. *Science, 14,* 528–529.

Arkes, H. R., Christensen, C., Lai, D., & Blummer, C. (1987). Two methods of reducing overconfidence. *Organizational Behavior and Human Decision Processes, 39,* 133–144.

Arkes, H. R., Dawes, R. M., & Christensen, C. (1986). Factors influencing the use of a decision rule in a probabilistic task. *Organizational Behavior and Human Decision Processes, 37,* 93–110.

Armus, H. L. (1959). Effect of magnitude of reinforcement on acquisition and extinction of a running response. *Journal of Experimental Psychology, 58,* 61–63.

Aronfreed, J., & Leff, R. (1963). The effects of intensity of punishment and complexity of discrimination upon the generalization of an internalized inhibition. Unpublished manuscript, University of Pennsylvania, Philadelphia.

Arvey, R. D., & Campion, J. E. (1982). The employment interview: A summary and review of recent research. *Personal Psychology, 35,* 281–322.

Ashcroft, G., Crawford, T., & Eccleston, E. (1966). Hydroxyindole compounds in the cerebrospinal fluid of patients with psychiatric or neurological disease. *Lancet, 2,* 1049–1052.

Atkinson, J. W. (1958). *Motives in fantasy, action and society.* Princeton, N.J.: Van Nostrand.

Atkinson, J. W. (1964). *An introduction to motivation.* Princeton, N.J.: Van Nostrand.

Atkinson, R. C., & Shiffrin, R. M. (1971). The control of short-term memory. *Scientific American, 225,* 82–90.

Atwater, S. K. (1953). Proactive inhibition and associative facilitation as affected by degree of prior learning. *Journal of Experimental Psychology, 46,* 400–404.

Averbach, E. (1963). The span of apprehension as a function of exposure duration. *Journal of Verbal Learning and Verbal Behavior, 2,* 60–64.

Averbach, E., & Coriell, A. S. (1961). Short-term memory in vision. *Bell System Technical Journal, 40,* 309–328.

Averbach, E., & Sperling, G. (1961). Short-term storage of information in vision. In C. Cherry (Ed.), *Fourth London Symposium on Information Theory.* London and Washington, D.C.: Butterworth.

Ayllon, T., & Azrin, N. H. (1965). The measurement and reinforcement of behavior of psychotics. *Journal of the Experimental Analysis of Behavior, 8,* 357–383.

Ayllon, T., & Azrin, N. H. (1968). *The token economy: A motivation system for therapy and rehabilitation.* New York: Appleton-Century-Crofts.

Azrin, N. H. (1956). Some effects of two intermittent schedules of immediate and non-immediate punishment. *Journal of Psychology, 42,* 3–21.

Azrin, N. H. (1964, September). Aggression. Paper presented at the meeting of the American Psychological Association, Los Angeles.

Azrin, N. H., Hake, D. F., Holz, W. C., & Hutchinson, R. R. (1965). Motivational aspects of escape from punishment. *Journal of the Experimental Analysis of Behavior, 8,* 31–44.

Azrin, N. H., & Holz, W. C. (1966). Punishment. In W. K. Honig (Ed.), *Operant behavior: Areas of research and application* (pp. 380–447). New York: Appleton-Century-Crofts.

Azrin, N. H., Holz, W. C., & Hake, D. F. (1963). Fixed-ratio punishment. *Journal of the Experimental Analysis of Behavior, 6,* 141–148.

Azrin, N. H., Hutchinson, R. R., & Hake, D. F. (1966). Extinction-induced aggression. *Journal of the Experimental Analysis of Behavior, 9,* 191–204.

Azrin, N. H., Hutchinson, R. R., & McLaughlin, R. (1965). The opportunity for aggression as an operant reinforcer during aversive stimulation. *Journal of the Experimental Analysis of Behavior, 8,* 171–180.

Azrin, N. H., Hutchinson, R. R., & Sallery, R. D. (1964). Pain aggression toward inanimate objects. *Journal of the Experimental Analysis of Behavior, 7,* 223–228.

Azrin, N. H., Sneed, T. J., & Foxx, R. M. (1973). A rapid method of eliminating bedwetting (enuresis) of the retarded. *Behavior Research and Therapy, 11,* 427–434.

Bacon, W. E. (1962). Partial-reinforcement extinction following different amounts of training. *Journal of Comparative and Physiological Psychology, 55,* 998–1003.

Baddeley, A. D.,(1976). *The psychology of memory.* New York: Basic Books.

Baddeley, A. D., & Scott, D. (1971). Short-term forgetting in the absence of proactive inhibition. *Quarterly Journal of Experimental Psychology, 23,* 275–283.

Baer, D. M. (1962). Laboratory control of thumbsucking by withdrawal and representation of reinforcement. *Journal of the Experimental Analysis of Behavior, 5,* 525–528.

Baerends, G. P., Brouwer, R., & Waterbolk, H. T. (1955). Ethological studies on *Lebistes reticulatus (Peters)*: I. An analysis of the male courtship pattern. *Behaviour, 8,* 249–334.

Bailey, J. S., Wolf, M. M., & Phillips, E. L. (1970). Home-based reinforcement and the modification of pre-delinquents' classroom behavior. *Journal of Applied Behavior Analysis, 3,* 223–233.

Baker, A. G. (1976). Learned irrelevance and learned helplessness: Rats learn that stimuli, reinforcers and responses are uncorrelated. *Journal of Experimental Psychology: Animal Behavior Processes, 2,* 130–141.

Baker, A. G., & Baker, P. A. (1985). Does inhibition differ from excitation: Proactive interference, contextual conditioning, and extinction. In R. R. Miller & N. S. Spear (Eds.), *Information processing in animals: Conditioned inhibition* (pp. 151–184). Hillsdale, N.J.: Erlbaum.

Baker, A. G., & Mackintosh, N. J. (1977). Excitatory and inhibitory conditioning following uncorrelated presentations of CS and US. *Animal Learning and Behavior, 5,* 315–319.

Baker, A. G., & Mackintosh, N. J. (1979). Pre-exposure to the CS alone, US alone, or CS and US uncorrelated: Latent inhibition, blocking by context, or learned irrelevance? *Learning and Motivation, 10,* 278–294.

Baker, A. G., & Mercier, P. (1989). Attention, retrospective processing and cognitive representations. In S. B. Klein & R. R. Mowrer (Eds.), *Contemporary learning theories: Pavlovian conditioning and the status of traditional learning theory* (pp. 85–101). Hillsdale, N.J.: Erlbaum.

Baker, A. G., & Mercier, P., Gabel, J., & Baker, P. A. (1981). Contextual conditioning and the US preexposure effect in conditioned fear. *Journal of Experimental Psychology: Animal Behavior Processes, 7,* 109–128.

Balsam, P. D. (1984). Relative time in trace conditioning. *Annals of the New York Academy of Sciences, 423,* 211–227.

Balsam, P. D., & Schwartz, A. L. (1981). Rapid contextual conditioning in autoshaping. *Journal of Experimental Psychology: Animal Behavior Processes, 7,* 382–393.

Bandura, A. (1971). *Social learning theory.* Morristown, N.J.: General Learning.

Bandura, A. (1977). Self-efficacy: Toward a unifying theory of behavior change. *Psychological Review, 84,* 191–215.

Bandura, A. (1986). *Social foundations of thought and action: A social cognition theory.* Englewood Cliffs, N.J.: Prentice-Hall.

Bandura, A., & Adams, N. E. (1977). Analysis of self-efficacy theory of behavioral change. *Journal of Personality and Social Psychology, 1,* 287–310.

Bandura, A., Adams, N. E., & Beyer, J. (1977). Cognitive processes mediating behavioral change. *Journal of Personality and Social Psychology, 35,* 125–129.

Bandura, A., Blanchard, E. B., & Ritter, B. (1969). The relative efficacy of desensitization and modeling approaches for inducing behavioral, affective, and attitudinal changes. *Journal of Personality and Social Psychology, 13,* 173–199.

Bandura, A., Grusec, J. E., & Menlove, F. L. (1967). Vicarious extinction of avoidance behavior. *Journal of Personality and Social Psychology, 5,* 16–23.

Bandura, A., Jeffrey, R. W., & Gajdos, F. (1975). Generalizing change through participant modeling with self-directed mastery. *Behavior Research and Therapy, 13,* 141–152.

Bandura, A., & Menlove, F. L. (1968). Factors determining vicarious extinction of avoidance behavior through symbolic modeling. *Journal of Personality and Social Psychology, 8,* 99–108.

Bandura, A., & Perloff, B. (1967). Relative efficacy of self-monitored and externally imposed reinforcement systems. *Journal of Personality and Social Psychology, 7,* 11–116.

Bandura, A., & Rosenthal, T. L. (1966). Vicarious classical conditioning as a function of arousal level. *Journal of Personality and Social Psychology, 3,* 54–62.

Bandura, A., Ross, D., & Ross, D. A. (1963). Imitation of film-mediated aggressive models. *Journal of Abnormal and Social Psychology, 66,* 3–11.

Bandura, A., & Walters, R. H. (1959). *Adolescent aggression.* New York: Ronald.

Banks, R. K., & Vogel-Sprott, M. (1965). Effect of delayed punishment on an immediately rewarded response in humans. *Journal of Experimental Psychology, 70,* 357–359.

Barnes, G. W. (1956). Conditioned stimulus intensity and temporal factors in spaced-trial classical conditioning. *Journal of Experimental Psychology, 51,* 192–198.

Barnes, J. M., & Underwood, B. J. (1959). "Fate" of first-list associations in transfer theory. *Journal of Experimental Psychology, 58,* 97–105.

Baron, A. (1965). Delayed punishment of a runway response. *Journal of Comparative and Physiological Psychology, 60,* 131–134.

Barondes, S. H., & Cohen, H. D. (1966). Puromycin effect on successive phases of memory storage. *Science, 151,* 594–595.

Bartlett, F. C. (1932). *Remembering: A study in experimental and social psychology.* London: Cambridge University Press.

Barton, E. S., Guess, D., Garcia, E., & Baer, D. M. (1970). Improvement of retardates' mealtime behaviors by time-out procedures using multiple baseline techniques. *Journal of Applied Behavior Analysis, 3,* 77–84.

Bass, M. J., & Hull, C. L. (1934). The irradiation of a tactile conditioned reflex in man. *Journal of Comparative Psychology, 17,* 47–65.

Bateson, P. P. G. (1969). Imprinting and the development of preferences. In A. Ambrose (Ed.), *Stimulation in early infancy* (pp. 109–132). New York: Academic.

Baum, M. (1968). Reversal learning of an avoidance response and the Kamin effect. *Journal of Comparative and Physiological Psychology, 66,* 495–497.

Baum, M. (1970). Extinction of avoidance responding through response prevention (flooding). *Psychological Bulletin, 74,* 276–284.

Baumind, D. (1983). Rejoiner to Lewis reinterpretation of parental firm control affects: Are authorative families rarely harmonious? *Psychological Bulletin, 94,* 132–142.

Beatty, W. W., & Shavalia, D. A. (1980). Rat spatial memory: Resistance to retroactive interference at long retention intervals. *Animal Learning and Behavior, 8,* 550–552.

Bechterev, V. M. (1913). *La psychologie objective.* Paris: Alcan.

Beck, A. T. (1963). Thinking and depression: I. Idiosyncratic content and cognitive distortions. *Archives of General Psychiatry, 9,* 324–333.

Becker, H. C., & Flaherty, C. F. (1982). Influence of ethanol on contrast in consummatory behavior. *Psychopharmacology, 77,* 253–258.

Becker, H. C., & Flaherty, C. F. (1983). Chlordiazepoxide and ethanol additively reduce gustatory negative contrast. *Psychopharmacology, 80,* 35–37.

Beneke, W. N., & Harris, M. B. (1972). Teaching self-control of study behavior. *Behaviour Research and Therapy, 10,* 35–41.

Berger, S. M. (1962). Conditioning through vicarious instigation. *Psychological Review, 69,* 450–466.

Berkowitz, L. (1962). *Aggression: A social psychological analysis.* New York: McGraw-Hill.

Berkowitz, L. (1969). *Roots of aggression.* New York: Atherton.

Berkowitz, L. (1971). The contagion of violence: An S-R mediational analysis of some effects of observed aggression. In M. Page (Ed.), *Nebraska Symposium on Motivation* (pp. 95–135). Lincoln: University of Nebraska Press.

Berkowitz, L. (1978). Do we have to believe we are angry with someone in order to display "angry" aggression toward that person? In L. Berkowitz (Ed.), *Cognitive theories in social psychology: Papers reprinted from the advances in Experimental Social Psychology* (pp. 455–463). New York: Academic.

Berkowitz, L. (1980). *A survey of social psychology* (2ed.). New York: Holt, Rinehart & Winston.

Berkowitz, L., & LePage, A. (1967). Weapons as aggression-eliciting stimuli. *Journal of Personality and Social Psychology, 7,* 202–207.

Berman, J., & Katzev, R. (1972). Factors involved in the rapid elimination of avoidance behavior. *Behaviour Research and Therapy, 10,* 247–256.

Bernard, L. L. (1924). *Instinct: A study in social psychology.* New York: Henry Holt.

Bernstein, I. L. (1978). Learned taste aversions in children receiving chemotherapy. *Science, 200,* 1302–1303.

Bernstein, I. L., & Webster, M. M. (1980). Learned taste aversions in humans. *Physiology and Behavior, 25,* 363–366.

Berscheid, E., & Walster, E. U. (1978). *Interpersonal attraction.* Reading, Mass.: Addison-Wesley.

Bersh, P. J. (1951). The influence of two variables upon the establishment of a secondary reinforcer for operant responses. *Journal of Experimental Psychology, 41,* 62–73.

Best, M. R., Batson, J. D., Meachum, C. L., Brown, E. R., and Ringer, M. (1979). Characteristics of taste-mediated environmental potential in rats. *Learning and Motivation, 16,* 190–209.

Best, M. R., & Domjan, M. (1979). Characteristics of the lithium-mediated proximal US-preexposure effect in flavor-aversion conditioning. *Animal Learning and Behavior, 7,* 433–440.

Best, M. R., & Gemberling, G. A. (1977). Role of short-term processes in the conditioned stimulus preexposure effect and the delay of reinforcement gradient in long-delay taste-aversion learning. *Journal of Experimental Psychology: Animal Behavior Processes, 3,* 253–263.

Best, P. J., Best, M. R., & Henggeler, S. (1977). The contribution of environmental non-ingestive cues in conditioning with aversive internal consequences. In L. M. Barker, M. R. Best, & M. Domjan (Eds.), *Learning mechanisms in food selection* (pp. 371–393). Waco, Tex.: Baylor University Press.

Best, P. J., Best, M. R., & Mickley, G. A. (1973). Conditioned aversion to distinct environmental stimuli resulting from gastrointestinal distress. *Journal of Comparative and Physiological Psychology, 85,* 250–257.

Bever, T. G. (1970). The cognitive basis for linguistic structures. In J. R. Hayes (Ed.), *Cognition and development of language.* New York: Wiley.

Biederman, G. B., D'Amato, M. R., & Keller, D. M. (1964). Facilitation of discriminated avoidance learning by dissociation of CS and manipulandum. *Psychonomic Science, 1,* 229–230.

Bindra, D. (1981). Ape language. *Science, 211,* 86.

Bintz, J. (1970). Time-dependent memory deficits of aversively motivated behavior. *Learning and Motivation, 1,* 405–406.

Birch, H. G., & Rabinowitz, H. S. (1951). The negative effect of previous experience on productive thinking. *Journal of Experimental Psychology, 41,* 121–125.

Black, R. W. (1968). Shifts in magnitude of reward and contrast effects in instrumental selective learning: A reinterpretation. *Psychological Review, 75,* 114–126.

Blanchard, R. J., & Blanchard, D. C. (1969). Crouching as an index of fear. *Journal of Comparative and Physiological Psychology, 67,* 370–375.

Blehar, M. C., Lieberman, A. F., & Ainsworth, M. D. S. (1977). Early face-to-face interaction and its relation to later infant-mother attachment. *Child Development, 48,* 182–194.

Blodgett, H. C., & McCutchan, K. (1947). Place versus response-learning in a simple T-maze. *Journal of Experimental Psychology, 37,* 412–422.

Blodgett, H. C., & McCutchan, K. (1948). The relative strength of place and response learning in the T-maze. *Journal of Comparative and Physiological Psychology, 41,* 17–24.

Bloomfield, T. M. (1972). Contrast and inhibition in discrimination learning by the pigeon: Analysis through drug effects. *Learning and Motivation, 3,* 162–178.

Blough, D., & Blough, P. (1977). Animal psychophysics. In W. K. Harris & J. E. R. Staddon (Eds.), *Handbook of operant behavior* (pp. 514–539). Englewood Cliffs, N.J.: Prentice-Hall.

Boakes, R. A., Poli, M., Lockwood, M. J., & Goodall, G. (1978). A study of misbehavior: Token reinforcement in the rat. *Journal of the Experimental Analysis of Behavior, 29,* 115–134.

Boe, E. E., & Church, R. M. (1967). Permanent effects of punishment during extinction. *Journal of Comparative and Physiological Psychology, 63,* 486–492.

Bolles, R. C. (1969). Avoidance and escape learning: Simultaneous acquisition of different responses. *Journal of Comparative and Physiological Psychology, 68,* 355–358.

Bolles, R. C. (1970). Species-specific defense reactions and avoidance learning. *Psychological Review, 77,* 32–48.

Bolles, R. C. (1972). Reinforcement, expectancy and learning. *Psychological Review, 79,* 394–409.

Bolles, R. C. (1975). *Theory of motivation* (2d ed.). New York: Harper & Row.

Bolles, R. C. (1978). The role of stimulus learning in defensive behavior. In S. H. Hulse, H. Fowler, & W. K. Honig (Eds.), *Cognitive processes in animal behavior* (pp. 89–108). Hillsdale, N.J.: Erlbaum.

Bolles, R. C. (1979). *Learning theory* (2d ed.). New York: Holt, Rinehart & Winston.

Bolles, R. C., & Collier, A. C. (1976). The effect of predictive cues on freezing in rats. *Animal Learning and Behavior, 4,* 6–8.

Bolles, R. C., Collier, A. C., Bouton, M. E., & Marlin, N. A. (1978). Some tracks for ameliorating the trace-conditioning deficit. *Bulletin of the Psychonomic Society, 11,* 403–406.

Bolles, R. C., Grossen, N. E., Hargrave, G. E., & Duncan, P. M. (1970). Effects of conditioned appetitive stimuli on the acquisition and extinction of a runway response. *Journal of Experimental Psychology, 85,* 138–140.

Bolles, R. C., & Riley, A. (1973). Freezing as an avoidance response: Another look at the operant-respondent distinction. *Learning and Motivation, 4,* 268–275.

Bolles, R. C., & Seelbach, S. (1964). Punishing and reinforcing effects of noise onset and termination for different responses. *Journal of Comparative and Physiological Psychology, 58,* 127–132.

Bolles, R. C., & Tuttle, A. V. (1967). A failure to reinforce instrumental behavior by terminating a stimulus that had been paired with shock. *Psychonomic Science, 9,* 255–256.

Booth, N. P. (1980). An opponent process theory of motivation for jogging. Cited in R. L. Solomon, The opponent-process theory of motivation. *American Psychologist, 35,* 691–712.

Borkovec, T. D. (1976). Physiological and cognitive processes in the regulation of fear. In G. E. Schwartz & D. Shapiro (Eds.), *Consciousness and self-regulation: Advances in research* (pp. 261–312). New York: Plenum.

Borkovec, T. D. (1978). Self-efficacy: Cause or reflection of behavioral change? In S. Rachman (Ed.), *Advances in behavior research and therapy* (Vol. 1, pp. 163–170). Oxford: Pergamon.

Bousfield, W. A. (1953). The occurrence of clustering in the recall of randomly arranged associates. *Journal of General Psychology, 49,* 229–240.

Bouton, M. E., Jones, D. L., McPhillips, S. A., & Swartzentruber, D. (1986). Potentiation and overshadowing in odor-aversion learning: Role of method of odor presentation, the distal-proximal cue distinction, and the conditionability of odor. *Learning and Motivation, 17,* 115–138.

Bower, G. H. (1981). Mood and memory. *American Psychologist, 36,* 129–148.

Bower, G. H., Fowler, H., & Trapold, M. A. (1959). Escape learning as a function of amount of shock reduction. *Journal of Experimental Psychology, 48,* 482–484.

Bower, G. H., & Hilgard, E. R. (1981). *Theories of learning* (5th ed.). Englewood Cliffs, N.J.: Prentice-Hall.

Bower, G. H., & Springston, F. (1970). Pauses as recording points in letter sequences. *Journal of Experimental Psychology, 83,* 421–430.

Bower, G. H., Starr, R., & Lazarovitz, L. (1965). Amount of response-produced change in the CS and avoidance learning. *Journal of Comparative and Physiological Psychology, 59,* 13–17.

Boyd, H., & Fabricius, E. (1965). Observations on the incidence of following of visual and auditory stimuli in naive mallard ducklings (*Anas platrhynchos*). *Behaviour, 25,* 1–15.

Brady, J. V. (1961). Motivational-emotional factors and intracranial self-stimulation. In D. E. Sheer (Ed.), *Electrical stimulation of the brain* (pp. 413–430). Austin: University of Texas Press.

Bramel, D., Taub, B., & Blum, B. (1968). An observer's reaction to the suffering of his enemy. *Journal of Personality and Social Psychology, 8,* 384–392.

Braud, W., Wepman, B., & Russo, D. (1969). Task and species generality of the "helplessness" phenomenon. *Psychonomic Science, 16,* 154–155.

Braveman, N. S. (1974). Poison-based avoidance learning with flavored or colored water in guinea pigs. *Learning and Motivation, 5,* 182–194.

Braveman, N. S. (1975). Formation of taste aversions in rats following prior exposure to sickness. *Learning and Motivation, 6,* 512–534.

Breitmeyer, B. B., & Ganz, L. (1976). Implication of sustained and transient channels for theories of visual pattern masking, saccadic suppression, and information processing. *Psychological Review, 83,* 1–36.

Breland, K., & Breland, M. (1961). The misbehavior of organisms. *American Psychologist, 61,* 681–684.

Breland, K., & Breland, M. (1966). *Animal Behavior.* New York: Macmillan.

Briggs, M. H., & Kitto, G. B. (1962). The molecular basis of memory. *Psychological Review, 69,* 537–541.

Bristol, M. M., & Sloane, H. N., Jr. (1974). Effects of contingency contracting on study rate and test performance. *Journal of Applied Behavior Analysis, 7,* 271–285.

Broadbent, D. E. (1958). *Perception and communication.* New York: Pergamon.

Brockner, J., & Rubin, Z. (1985). *Entrapment in escalating conflict.* New York: Springer-Verlag.

Brogden, W. J. (1939). Sensory pre-conditioning. *Journal of Experimental Psychology, 25,* 323–332.

Brooks, C. I. (1980). Effect of prior nonreward on subsequent incentive growth during brief acquisition. *Animal Learning and Behavior, 8,* 143–151.

Brown, J. L. (1975). *The evolution of behavior.* New York: Norton.

Brown, J. S. (1942). Factors determining conflict reactions in different discriminations. *Journal of Experimental Psychology, 31,* 272–292.

Brown, J. S., & Jacobs, A. (1949). The role of fear in the motivation and acquisition of responses. *Journal of Experimental Psychology, 39,* 747–759.

Brown, J. S., Martin, R. C., & Morrow, M. W. (1964). Self-punitive behavior in the rat: Facilitative effects of punishment on resistance to extinction. *Journal of Comparative and Physiological Psychology, 57,* 127–133.

Brown, P. L., & Jenkins, H. M. (1968). Autoshaping of the pigeon's key peck. *Journal of the Experimental Analysis of Behavior, 11,* 1–8.

Brown, R., Cazden, C., & Bellugi, U. (1969). The child's grammar from I to III. In J. P. Hill (Ed.), *Minnesota Symposium on Child Psychology* (Vol. 2, pp. 28–73). Minneapolis: University of Minnesota Press.

Brucke, E. (1874). *Lectures on physiology.* Vienna: University of Vienna.

Bruner, J. S. (1978). Learning the mother tongue. *Human Nature, 1,* 42–49.

Bruner, J. S., Goodnow, J. J., & Austin, G. A. (1956). *A study of thinking.* New York: Wiley.

Brush, F. R. (Ed.). (1970). *Aversive conditioning and learning.* New York: Academic.

Brush, F. R. (1971). Retention of aversively motivated behavior. In F. R. Brush (Ed.), *Aversive conditioning and learning.* (pp. 402–468). New York: Academic.

Bucher, B., & Fabricatore, J. (1970). Use of patient-administered shock to suppress hallucinations. *Behavior Therapy, 1,* 382–385.

Bugelski, B. R. (1968). Images as mediators in one-trial paired-associated learning: II. Self-timing in successive lists. *Journal of Experimental Psychology, 77,* 328–334.

Burgess, E. P. (1968). The modification of depressive behaviors. In R. D. Rubin & C. M. Franks (Eds.), *Advances in behavior therapy.* New York: Academic Press.

Burns, B. D. (1958). *The mammalian cerebral cortex.* London: Arnold.

Burns, R. A. (1976). Effects of sequences of sucrose reward magnitudes with short ITIs in rats. *Animal Learning and Behavior, 4,* 473–479.

Butler, R. A., & Harlow, H. F. (1954). Persistence of visual exploration in monkeys. *Journal of Comparative and Physiological Psychology, 47,* 257–263.

Butter, C. M., & Thomas, D. R. (1958). Secondary reinforcement as a function of the amount of primary reinforcement. *Journal of the Experimental Analysis of Behavior, 51,* 346–348.

Caggiula, A. R., & Szechtman, H. (1972). Hypothalamic stimulation: A biphasic influence on the copulation of the male rat. *Behavioral Biology, 7,* 591–598.

Caldwell, W. E., & Jones, H. B. (1954). Some positive results on a modified Tolman and Honziik insight maze. *Journal of Comparative and Physiological Psychology, 47,* 416–418.

Camp, D. S., Raymond, G. A., & Church. R. M. (1966). Response suppression as a function of the schedule of punishment. *Psychonomic Science, 5,* 23–24.

Camp, D. S., Raymond, G. A., & Church, R. M. (1967). Temporal relationship between response and punishment. *Journal of Experimental Psychology, 74,* 114–123.

Campbell, B. A., & Church, P. M. (1969). *Punishment and aversive behavior.* New York: Appleton-Century-Crofts.

Campbell, B. A., & Kraeling, D. (1953). Response strength as a function of drive level and amount of drive reduction. *Journal of Experimental Psychology, 45,* 97–101.

Cannon, D., Berman, R., Baker, T., & Atkinson, C. (1975). Effect of preconditioning unconditioned stimulus experience on learned taste aversions. *Journal of Experimental Psychology: Animal Behavior Processes, 104,* 270–284.

Cantor, M. B., & Wilson, J. F. (1984). Feeding the face: New directions in adjunctive behavior research. In F. R. Brush & J. B. Overmier (Eds.), *Affect, conditioning, and cognition* (pp. 299–314). Hillsdale, N.J.: Erlbaum.

Capaldi, E. J. (1964). Effect of N-length, number of different N-lengths and number of reinforcements on resistance to extinction. *Journal of Experimental Psychology, 68,* 230–239.

Capaldi, E. J. (1966). Partial reinforcement: A hypothesis of sequential effects. *Psychological Review, 73,* 459–479.

Capaldi, E. J. (1967). A sequential hypothesis of instrumental learning. In K. W. Spence & J. T. Spence (Eds.), *The psychology of learning and motivation* (Vol. 1, pp. 67–156). New York: Academic.

Capaldi, E. J. (1971). Memory and learning: A sequential viewpoint. In W. K. Honig & P. H. R. James (Eds.), *Animal memory* (pp. 115–154). New York: Academic.

Capaldi, E. J., Hart, D., & Stanley, L. R. (1963). Effect of intertrial reinforcement on the aftereffect of nonreinforcement and resistance to extinction. *Journal of Experimental Psychology, 65,* 70–74.

Capaldi, E. J., & Spivey, J. E. (1964). Stimulus consequences of reinforcement and nonreinforcement: Stimulus traces or memory. *Psychonomic Science, 1,* 403–404.

Capretta, P. J. (1961). An experimental modification of food preference in chickens. *Journal of Comparative and Physiological Psychology, 54,* 238–242.

Carew, T. J., Hawkins, R. D., & Kandel, E. R. (1983). Differential classical conditioning of a defensive withdrawal reflex in *Aplysia californica. Science, 219,* 397–420.

Carlson, N. R. (1981). *Physiology of behavior* (2d ed.). Boston: Allyn & Bacon.

Carlson, N. R. (1984). *Psychology: The science of behavior.* Boston: Allyn & Bacon.

Carlton, P. L. (1969). Brain-acetylcholine and inhibition. In J. T. Tapp (Ed.), *Reinforcement and behavior* (pp. 288–328). New York: Academic.

Carter, L. F. (1941). Intensity of conditioned stimulus and rate of conditioning. *Journal of Experimental Psychology, 28,* 481–490.

Catania, A. C., & Reynolds, G. S. (1968). A quantitative analysis of the responding maintained by interval schedules of reinforcement. *Journal of Experimental Analysis of Behavior, 11,* 327–383.

Cautela, J. R. (1977). The use of covert conditioning in modifying pain behavior. *Journal of Behavior Therapy and Experimental Psychiatry, 8,* 45–52.

Cermak, L. S., & Craik, F. I. M. (1979). *Levels of processing in human memory.* Hillsdale, N.J.: Erlbaum.

Channell, S., & Hall, G. (1981). Facilitation and retardation of discrimination learning after exposure to the stimuli. *Journal of the Experimental Analysis of Behavior, 7,* 437–446.

Chase, W. G., & Simon, H. A. (1973). The mind's eye in chess. In W. G. Chase (Ed.), *Visual information processing* (pp. 215–281). New York: Academic.

Cherek, D. R. (1982). Schedule-induced cigarette self-administration. *Pharmacology, Biochemistry, and Behavior, 17,* 523–527.

Cherry, E. C. (1953). Some experiments on the recognition of speech, with one and with two ears. *Journal of the Acoustical Society of America, 25,* 975–979.

Cheyne, J. A., Goyeche, J. R., & Walters, R. H. (1969). Attention, anxiety, and rules in resistance-to-deviation in children. *Journal of Experimental Child Psychology, 8,* 127–139.

Childress, A. R., Ehrman, R., McLellan, T. A., & O'Brien, C. P. (1986). Extinguishing conditioned responses during opiate dependence treatment. Turning laboratory findings into clinical procedures. *Journal of Substance Abuse Treatment, 3,* 33–40.

Chomsky, N. (1957). *Syntactic structures.* The Hague: Mouton.

Chomsky, N. (1965). *Aspects of the theory of syntax.* Cambridge, Mass.: M.I.T. Press.

Chomsky, N. (1968). *Language and mind.* New York: Harcourt Brace Jovanovich.

Chomsky, N. (1975). *Reflections on language.* New York: Pantheon.

Chorover, S. L., & Schiller, P. H. (1965). Short-term retrograde amnesia in rats. *Journal of Comparative and Physiological Psychology, 59,* 73–78.

Church, R. M. (1969). Response suppression. In B. A. Campbell & R. M. Church (Eds.), *Punishment and aversive behavior* (pp. 111–156). New York: Appleton-Century-Crofts.

Church, R. M., & Black, A. H. (1958). Latency of the conditioned heart rate as a function of the CS-UCS interval. *Journal of Comparative and Physiological Psychology, 51,* 478–482.

Church, R. M., Raymond, G. A., & Beauchamp, R. D. (1967). Response suppression as a function of intensity and duration of a punishment. *Journal of Comparative and Physiological Psychology, 63,* 30–44.

Cohen, P. S., & Looney, T. A. (1973). Schedule-induced mirror responding in the pigeon. *Journal of the Experimental Analysis of Behavior, 19,* 395–408.

Collias, N. E., & Collias, E. C. (1956). Some mechanisms of family integration in ducks. *Auk, 73,* 378–400.

Collier, G., Hirsch, E., & Hamlin, P. H. (1972). The ecological determinants of reinforcement in the rat. *Physiology & Behavior, 9,* 705–716.

Collins, A. M., & Loftus, E. F. (1975). A spreading activation theory of semantic processing. *Psychological Review, 82,* 407–428.

Collins, A. M., & Quillian, M. R. (1969). Retrieval time from semantic memory. *Journal of Verbal Learning and Verbal Behavior, 8,* 240–247.

Coltheart, M., Lea, C. D., & Thompson, K. (1974). In defense of iconic memory. *Quarterly Journal of Experimental Psychology, 26,* 633–641.

Colwill, R. C., & Rescorla, R. A. (1985). Instrumental conditioning remains sensitive to reinforcer devaluation after extensive training. *Journal of Experimental Psychology: Animal Behavior Processes, 11,* 520–536.

Conger, J. J. (1951). Effect of alcohol on conflict behavior in the albino rat. *Quarterly Journal of Studies of Alcohol, 12,* 1–29.

Conrad, C. (1972). Cognitive economy in semantic memory. *Journal of Experimental Psychology, 92,* 149–154.

Conrad, D. G. & Sidman, M. (1956). Sucrose concentration as reinforcement for lever pressing by monkeys. *Psychological Reports, 2,* 381–384.

Conrad, R. (1964). Acoustic confusions in immediate memory. *British Journal of Psychology, 55,* 75–84.

Conrad, R. (1971). The chronology of the development of covert speech in children. *Developmental Psychology, 5,* 398–405.

Coons, E. E., & Cruce, J. A. F. (1968). Lateral hypothalamus: Food and current intensity in maintaining self-stimulation of hunger. *Science, 159,* 1117–1119.

Corkin, S., Sullivan, E. V., Twitchell, T. E., & Grove, E. (1981). The amnesic patient H. M.: Clinical observations and test performance 28 years after operation. *Society of Neuroscience Abstracts, 7,* 235.

Coulter, X., Riccio, D. C., & Page, H. A. (1969). Effects of blocking an instrumental avoidance response: Facilitated extinction but persistance of "fear." *Journal of Comparative and Physiological Psychology, 68,* 377–381.

Craig, K. D., & Weinstein, M. S. (1965). Conditioning vicarious affective arousal. *Psychological Reports, 17,* 955–963.

Craig, R. L., & Siegel, P. S. (1980). Does negative affect beget positive effect? A test of opponent-process theory. *Bulletin of Psychonomic Society, 14,* 404–406.

Craik, F. I. M. (1979). Human memory. *Annual Review of Psychology, 30,* 63–102.

Craik, F. I. M., & Lockhart, R. S. (1972). Levels of processing: A framework for memory research. *Journal of Verbal Learning and Behavior, 11,* 671–684.

Craik, F. I. M., & Tulving, E. (1975). Depth of processing and the retention of words in episodic memory. *Journal of Experimental Psychology: General, 104,* 268–294.

Craik, F. I. M., & Watkins, M. J. (1973). The role of rehearsal in short-term memory. *Journal of Verbal Learning and Verbal Behavior, 12,* 599–607.

Creer, T. L., Chai, H., & Hoffman, A. (1977). A single application of an aversive stimulus to eliminate chronic cough. *Journal of Behavior Research and Experimental Psychiatry, 8,* 107–109.

Crespi, L. P. (1942). Quantitive variation of incentive and performance in the white rat. *American Journal of Psychology, 55,* 467–517.

Cronholm, B., & Molander, L. (1958). Influence of an interpolated ECS on retention of memory material. *University of Stockholm Psychological Laboratory Reports, 61.*

Crooks, J. L. (1967). Observational learning of fear in monkeys. Unpublished manuscript, University of Pennsylvania, Philadelphia.

Crovitz, H. F. (1971). The capacity of memory loci in artificial memory. *Psychonomic Science, 24,* 187–188.

Crowder, R. G., & Morton, J. (1969). Precategorical acoustic storage (PAS). *Perception and Psychophysics, 5,* 365–373.

Crowell, C. R., Hinson, R. E., & Siegel, S. (1981). The role of conditional drug responses in tolerance to the hypothermic effects of ethanol. *Psychopharmacology, 73,* 51–54.

Cruser, L., & Klein, S. B. (1984). The role of schedule-induced polydipsia on temporal discrimination learning. *Psychological Reports, 58,* 443–452.

Cunningham, C. E., & Linscheid, T. R. (1976). Elimination of chronic infant ruminating by electric shock. *Behavior Therapy, 1,* 231–234.

Daly, H. B. (1974). Reinforcing properties of escape from frustration aroused in various learning situations. In G. H. Bower (Ed.), *The psychology of learning and motivation* (Vol. 8, pp. 187–231). New York: Academic.

D'Amato, M. R. (1970). *Experimental psychology: Methodology, psychophysics, and learning.* New York: McGraw-Hill.

D'Amato, M. R. (1973). Delayed matching and short-term memory in monkeys. In G. H. Bower (Ed.), *The psychology of learning and motivation* (Vol. 7, pp. 227–269). New York: Academic.

D'Amato, M. R., & Fazzaro, J. (1966). Discriminated lever press avoidance learning as a function of type and intensity of shock. *Journal of Comparative and Physiological Psychology, 61,* 313–315.

D'Amato, M. R., Fazzaro, J., & Etkin, M. (1968). Anticipatory responding and avoidance discrimination as factors in avoidance conditioning. *Journal of Experimental Psychology, 77,* 41–47.

D'Amato, M. R., & Salmon, D. P. (1984). Cognitive processes in cebus monkeys. In H. L. Roitblat, R. G. Bever, & H. S. Terrace (Eds.), *Animal cognition,* (pp. 149–168). Hillsdale, N.J.: Erlbaum.

D'Amato, M. R., Salmon, D. P., & Colombo, M. (1985). Extent and limits of the matching concept in monkeys (*Cebus apella*). *Journal of Experimental Psychology: Animal Behavior Processes, 11,* 35–51.

D'Amato, M. R., & Schiff, E. (1964). Further studies of overlearning and position reversal learning. *Psychological Reports, 14,* 380–382.

Darwin, C. J., Turvey, M. T., & Crowder, R. G. (1972). An auditory analogue of the Sperling partial report procedure: Evidence for brief auditory storage. *Cognitive Psychology, 3,* 255–267.

Davidson, R. S. (1972). *Aversive modification of alcoholic behavior: Punishment of an alcohol-reinforced operant.* Unpublished manuscript, U.S. Veterans Administration Hospital, Miami, Florida.

Davis, J. M., Klerman, G., & Schildkraut, J. (1967). Drugs used in the treatment of depression. In L. Efron, J. O. Cole, D. Levine, & J. R. Wittenborn (Eds.), *Psychopharmacology: A review of progress* (pp. 719–747). Washington, D.C.: U.S. Clearinghouse of Mental Health Information.

Davis, M. (1974). Sensitization of the rat startle response by noise. *Journal of Comparative and Physiological Psychology, 87,* 571–581.

Davison, G. C. (1968). Systematic desensitization as a counterconditioning process. *Journal of Abnormal Psychology, 73,* 91–99.

Delgado, J. M. R., Roberts, W. W., & Miller, N. E. (1954). Learning motivated by electric stimulation of the brain. *American Journal of Physiology, 179,* 587–593.

Denny, M. R. (1971). Relaxation theory and experiments. In F. R. Brush (Ed.), *Aversive conditioning and learning* (pp. 235–297). New York: Academic.

Denny, M. R., & Weisman, R. G. (1964). Avoidance behavior as a function of the length of nonshock confinement. *Journal of Comparative and Physiological Psychology, 58,* 252–257.

Depue, R. A., & Evans, R. (1976). *The psychobiology of the depressive disorders: Implication for the effects of stress.* New York: Academic.

Deur, J. L., & Parke, R. D. (1968). Resistance to extinction and continuous punishment in humans as a function of partial reward and partial punishment. *Psychonomic Science, 13,* 91–92.

Dewey, J. (1886). *Psychology.* New York: Harper & Row.

Dews, P. B. (1962). The effect of multiples S^Δ periods on responding on a fixed-interval schedule. *Journal of Experimental Analysis of Behavior, 5,* 369–374.

Diamond, M. C., Linder, B., Johnson, R., Bennett, E. C., & Rosenzweig, M. R. (1975). Differences in occipital cortical synapses from environmentally enriched, improvished, and standard colony rats. *Journal of Neuroscience Research, 1,* 109–119.

Dickinson, A. (1976). Appetitive-aversive interactions: Facilitation of aversive conditioning by prior appetitive training in the rat. *Animal Learning and Behavior, 4,* 416–420.

Dickinson, A. (1980). *Contemporary animal learning theory.* Cambridge: Cambridge University Press.

Dickinson, A. (1989). Expectancy theory in animal conditioning. In S. B. Klein & R. R. Mowrer (Eds.), *Contemporary learning theories: Pavlovian conditioning and the status of traditional learning theory* (pp. 279–308). Hillsdale, N.J.: Erlbaum.

Dickinson, A., Colwill, R. C., & Pearce, J. M. (1980). Post-trial stimulation and the acquisition of conditioned suppression in the rat. *Quarterly Journal of Experimental Psychology, 32,* 149–158.

Dickinson, A., & Dawson, G. R. (1987). Pavlovian processes in the motivation control of instrumental performance. *Quarterly Journal of Experimental Psychology, 39B,* 201–213.

Dickinson, A., Hall, G., & Mackintosh, N. J. (1976). Surprise and the attenuation of blocking. *Journal of Experimental Psychology: Animal Behavior Processes, 2,* 313–322.

Dickinson, A., & Nicholas, D. J. (1983). Irrelevant incentive learning during instrumental conditioning: The role of drive-reinforcer and response-reinforcer relationships. *Quarterly Journal of Experimental Psychology, 35B,* 249–263.

Dodd, D. H., & Bradshaw, J. M. (1980). Leading questions and memory: Pragmatic constraints. *Journal of Verbal Learning and Verbal Behavior, 19,* 695–704.

Dodd, D. H., & White, R. M. (1980). *Cognition: Mental structures and processes.* Boston: Allyn & Bacon.

Domjan, M. (1976). Determinants of the enhancement of flavor-water intake by prior exposure. *Journal of Experimental Psychology: Animal Behavior Processes, 2,* 17–27.

Domjan, M. (1977). Selective suppression of drinking during a limited period following aversive drug treatment in rats. *Journal of Experimental Psychology: Animal Behavior Processes, 3,* 66–76.

Domjan, M., & Gemberling, G. A. (1980). Effects of expected vs. unexpected proximal US preexposure on taste-aversion learning. *Animal Learning and Behavior, 8,* 204–210.

Donegan, N. H., & Wagner, A. R. (1987). Conditioned diminution and facilitation of the UR: A sometimes opponent-process interpretation. In I. Gormezano, W. F. Prokasy, & R. F. Thompson (Eds.), *Classical conditioning III* (pp. 339–369). Hillsdale, N.J.: Lawrence Erlbaum Associates.

Drabman, R., & Spitalnik, R. (1973). Social isolation as a punishment procedure: A controlled study. *Journal of Experimental Child Psychology, 16,* 236–249.

Ducker, G., & Rensch, B. (1968). Verzogerung des Vergessens erlernter visuellen Aufgaben bei Fischen durch Dunkelhaltung. *Pfluegers Archiv fur die Gesamte Physiologie des Menschen und der Tiere, 301,* 1–6.

Du Nann, D. G., & Weber, S. J. (1976). Short- and long-term effects of contingency managed instruction on low, medium, and high GPA students. *Journal of Applied Behavior Analysis, 9,* 375–376.

Duncan, C. P. (1949). The retroactive effect of electroshock on learning. *Journal of Comparative and Physiological Psychology, 42,* 32–44.

Dunn, A. J. (1980). Neurochemistry of learning and memory: An evaluation of recent data. *Annual Review of Psychology, 31,* 343–390.

Durlach, P. J. (1989). Learning and performance in Pavlovian conditioning: Are failures of contiguity failures of learning or performance? In S. B. Klein & R. R. Mowrer (Eds.), *Contemporary learning theories: Pavlovian conditioning and the status of traditional learning theory* (pp. 19–69). Hillsdale, N.J.: Erlbaum.

Durlach, P. J., & Rescorla, R. A. (1980). Potentiation rather than overshadowing in flavor-aversion learning: An analysis in terms of within-compound associations. *Journal of Experimental Psychology: Animal Behavior Processes, 6,* 175–187.

Ebbinghaus, H. (1885). *Memory: A contribution to experimental psychology,* H. A. Ruger & C. E. Bussenius (Trans.). New York: Dover.

Efron, R. (1970). The relationship between the duration of a stimulus and the duration of a perception. *Neuropsychologia, 8,* 37–55.

Eibl-Eibesfeldt, I. (1961). The fighting behavior of animals. *Scientific American, 205,* 112–122.

Eibl-Eibesfeldt, I. (1970). *Ethology: The biology of behavior.* New York: Holt.

Eich, J. E. (1980). The cue-dependent nature of state-dependent retrieval. *Memory and Cognition, 8,* 157–173.

Eich, J. E. (1985). Levels of processing, encoding specificity elaboration, and CHARM. *Psychological Review, 92,* 1–38.

Eich, J. E., Weingartner, H., Stillman, R. C., & Gillin, J. C. (1975). State-dependent accessibility of retrieval cues in the retention of a categorized list. *Journal of Verbal Learning and Verbal Behavior, 14,* 408–417.

Eimas, P. D., & Corbit, J. D. (1973). Selective adaptation of linguistic feature detectors. *Cognitive Psychology, 4,* 99–109.

Eimas, P. D., Siqueland, E. R., Jusczyk, P., & Vigorito, J. (1971). Speech perception in infants. *Science, 171,* 303–306.

Ekstrand, B. R. (1967). Effect of sleep on memory. *Journal of Experimental Psychology, 75,* 64–72.

Ekstrand, B. R., Wallace, W. P., & Underwood, B. J. (1966). A frequency theory of verbal-discrimination learning. *Psychological Review, 73,* 566–578.

Elkins, R. L. (1973). Attenuation of drug-induced bait shyness to a palatable solution as an increasing function of its availability prior to conditioning. *Behavioral Biology, 9,* 221–226.

Elliot, L. L. (1967). Development of auditory narrow-band frequency contours. *Journal of the Acoustical Society of America, 42,* 143–153.

Ellis, H. C. (1987). Recent developments in human memory. In V. P. Makosky (Ed.), *The G. Stanley Hall lecture series.* Washington, D.C.: American Psychological Association.

Ellison, G. D. (1964). Differential salivary conditioning to traces. *Journal of Comparative and Physiological Psychology, 57,* 373–380.

El-Wakil, F. W. (1975). Unpublished master's thesis, University of Massachusetts, Amherst.

Emshoff, J. G., Redd, W. H., & Davidson, W. S. (1976). Generalization training and the transfer of prosocial behavior in delinquent adolescents. *Journal of Behavior Therapy and Experimental Psychiatry, 7,* 141–144.

Engberg, L. A., Hansen, G., Welker, R. L., & Thomas, D. R. (1973). Acquisition of keypecking via autoshaping as a function of prior experience: "Learned laziness"? *Science, 178,* 1002–1004.

Epstein, D. M. (1967). Toward a unified theory of anxiety. In B. A. Maher (Ed.), *Progress in experimental personality research* (Vol. 4). New York: Academic.

Epstein, R. (1981). On pigeons and people: A preliminary look at the Columban Simulation Project. *The Behavior Analyst, 4,* 43–55.

Eriksen, C. W., & Collins, J. F. (1967). Some temporal characteristics of visual pattern perception. *Journal of Experimental Psychology, 74,* 476–484.

Erlanger, H. S. (1974). Social differences in parents' use of physical punishment. In S. K. Steinmetz & M. A. Streus (Eds.). *Violence in the family*. (pp. 150–158). New York: Dodd, Mead.

Ervin, F. R, Mark, V. H., & Stevens, J. R. (1969). Behavioral and affective responses to brain stimulation in man. In J. Zubin and C. Shagass (Eds.), *Neurological aspects of psychopathology*. New York: Grune & Stratton.

Estes, W. K. (1944). An experimental study of punishment. *Psychological Monographs, 57* (Whole No. 263).

Estes, W. K. (1969). Outline of a theory of punishment. In B. A. Campbell & R. M. Church (Eds.), *Punishment and aversive behavior* (pp. 57–82). New York: Appleton-Century-Crofts.

Eysenck, M. W. (1978). Levels of processing: A critique. *British Journal of Psychology, 68*, 157–169.

Fabricius, E. (1951). Zur Ethologie Junger Anatiden. *Acta Zoologica Fennica, 68*, 1–175.

Fairweather, G. W., Sanders, D. H., Maynard, H., & Cressler, D. C. (1969). *Community life for the mortally ill: An alternative to institutional care*. Chicago: Aldine.

Falk, J. L. (1961). Production of polydipsia in normal rats by an intermittent food schedule. *Science, 133*, 195–196.

Falk, J. L. (1964). Studies on schedule-induced polydipsia. In M. J. Wayner (Ed.), *Thirst*. Oxford: Pergamon.

Falk, J. L. (1966). The motivational properties of schedule-induced polydipsia. *Journal of the Experimental Analysis of Behavior, 9*, 19–25.

Falk, J. L. (1967). Control of schedule-induced polydipsia: Type, size, and spacing of meals. *Journal of the Experimental Analysis of Behavior, 10*, 199–206.

Falk, J. L. (1969). Conditions producing psychogenic polydipsia in animals. *Annals of the New York Academy of Sciences, 157*, 569–593.

Fanselow, M. S., & Baackes, M. P. (1982). Conditioned fear-induced opiate analgesia on the formalin test: Evidence for two aversive motivational systems. *Learning and Motivation, 13*, 200–221.

Fanselow, M. S., & Bolles, R. C. (1979). Naloxone and shock-elicited freezing the the rat. *Journal of Comparative and Physiological Psychology, 93*, 736–744.

Fazzaro, J., & D'Amato, M. R. (1969). Resistance to extinction after varying amounts of nondiscriminative or cue-correlated escape training. *Journal of Comparative and Physiological Psychology, 68*, 373–376.

Feather, B. W. (1967). Human salivary conditioning: A methodological study. In G. A. Kimble (Ed.), *Foundations of conditioning and learning*. New York: Appleton-Century-Crofts.

Feeney, D. M. (1987). Human rights and animal welfare. *American Psychologist, 42*, 593–599.

Feigenbaum, E. A. (1970). Information processing and memory. In D. A. Norman (Ed.), *Models of human memory*. New York: Academic.

Felton, J., & Lyon, D. O. (1966). The post-reinforcement pause. *Journal of the Experimental Analysis of Behavior, 9*, 131–134.

Feltz, D. L. (1982). The analysis of the causal elements in Bandura's theory of self-efficacy and an anxiety-based model of avoidance behavior. *Journal of Personality and Social Psychology, 42*, 764–781.

Fenwick, S., Mikulka, P. J., & Klein, S. B. (1975). The effect of different levels of preexposure to sucrose on acquisition and extinction of conditioned aversion. *Behavioral Biology, 14*, 231–235.

Ferster, C. B., & Skinner, B. F. (1957). *Schedules of reinforcement.* New York: Appleton-Century-Crofts.

Flaherty, C. F. (1982). Incentive contrast: A review of behavioral changes following shifts in reward. *Animal Learning and Behavior, 10,* 409–440.

Flaherty, C. F. (1985). *Animal learning and cognition.* New York: Knopf.

Flaherty, C. F., & Davenport, J. W. (1972). Successive brightness discrimination in rats following regular versus random intermittent reinforcement. *Journal of Experimental Psychology, 96,* 1–9.

Flaherty, C. F., & Driscoll, C. (1980). Amobarbital sodium reduces successive gustatory contrast. *Psychopharmacology, 69,* 161–162.

Flakus, W. J., & Steinbrecher, B. C. (1964). Avoidance conditioning in the rabbit. *Psychological Reports, 14,* 140.

Flavell, J. H., Cooper, A., & Loiselle, R. H. (1958). Effect of the number of pre-utilization functions on functional fixedness in problem solving. *Psychological Reports, 4,* 343–350.

Flesher, D. (1941). L'amnesia refrogada dropo l'eltroshiek: Contributo allo studio della patogenesi della amnesia in genere. *Schweiz Archives Neurologia Psychiatry, 48,* 1–28.

Flood, J. F., Bennett, E. L., Orme, A. E., & Rosenzweig, M. R. (1975). Relation of memory formation to controlled amounts of brain protein synthesis. *Physiology and Behavior, 15,* 97–102.

Flood, J. F., Bennett, E. L., Rosenzweig, M. R., & Orme, A. E. (1973). The influence of duration of protein synthesis inhibition on memory. *Physiology and Behavior, 15,* 97–102.

Flory, R. K. (1969). Attack behavior as a function of minimum inter-food interval. *Journal of the Experimental Analysis of Behavior, 12,* 825–828.

Flory, R. K. (1971). The control of schedule-induced polydipsia: Frequency and magnitude of reinforcement. *Learning and Motivation, 2,* 215–227.

Flory, R. K., & Ellis, B. B. (1973). Schedule-induced aggression against a slide-image target. *Bulletin of the Psychonomic Society, 2,* 287–290.

Foder, J. A., Bever, T. G., & Garrett, M. F. (1974). *The psychology of language: An introduction to psycholinguistics and generative grammar.* New York: McGraw-Hill.

Forster, K. I. (1979). Levels of processing and the structure of the language processor. In W. E. Cooper & T. Walker (Eds.), *Sentence processing* (pp. 27–86). Hillsdale, N.J.: Erlbaum.

Fosco, F., & Geer, J. H. (1971). Effects of gaining control over aversive stimuli after differing amounts of no control. *Psychological Reports, 29,* 1153–1154.

Fowler, H., & Miller, N. E. (1963). Facilitation and inhibition of runway performance by hind- and forepaw shock of various intensities. *Journal of Comparative and Physiological Psychology, 56,* 801–805.

Fowler, H., & Trapold, M. A. (1962). Escape performance as a function of delay of reinforcement. *Journal of Experimental Psychology, 63,* 464–467.

Fox, M. W. (1969). Ontogeny of prey-killing behavior in canidae. *Behaviour, 35,* 259–272.

Franks, C. M., & Wilson, G. T. (1974). *Annual review of behavior therapy: Theory and practice* (Vol. 2). New York: Brunner/Mazel.

Freedman, P. E., Hennessy, J. W., & Groner, D. (1974). Effects of varying active/passive shock levels in shuttle box avoidance in rats. *Journal of Comparative and Physiological Psychology, 86,* 79–84.

Frey, P. W. (1969). Within- and between-session CS intensity performance effects in rabbit eyelid conditioning. *Psychonomic Science, 17,* 1–2.

Frey, P. W., & Butler, C. S. (1973). Rabbit eyelid conditioning as a function of unconditioned stimulus duration. *Journal of Comparative and Physiological Psychology, 85,* 289–294.

Frey, P. W., & Ross, L. E. (1968). Classical conditioning of the rabbit eyelid response as a function of interstimulus interval. *Journal of Comparative and Physiological Psychology, 65,* 246–250.

Frumkin, K., & Brookshire, K. H. (1969). Conditioned fear training and later avoidance learning in goldfish. *Psychonomic Science, 16,* 159–160.

Fuchs, C. Z., & Rehm, L. P. (1977). Self-control depression program. *Journal of Consulting and Clinical Psychology, 45,* 206–215.

Galbraith, D. A., Byrick, R. J., & Rutledge, J. T. (1970). An aversive conditioning approach to the inhibition of chronic vomiting. *Canadian Psychiatric Association Journal, 15,* 311–313.

Galef, B. G., & Sherry, D. F. (1973). Mother's milk: A medium for the transmission of cues reflecting the flavor of mother's diet. *Journal of Comparative and Physiological Psychology, 83,* 374–378.

Gallistel, C. R., Boytim, M., Gomita, Y., & Klebanoff, L. (1982). Does pinozide block the reinforcing effect of brain stimulation? *Pharmacology, Biochemistry and Behavior, 20,* 73–77.

Gamzu, E., & Williams, D. R. (1971). Classical conditioning of a complex skeletal act. *Science, 171,* 923–925.

Gantt, W. H. (1971). Experimental basis for neurotic behavior. In H. D. Kimmel (Ed.), *Experimental psychopathology: Recent research and theory* (pp. 33–48). New York: Academic.

Ganz, L. (1968). An analysis of generalization behavior in the stimulus deprived organism. In G. Newton & S. Levine (Eds.), *Early experience and behavior* (pp. 365–411). Springfield, Ill.: Charles C. Thomas.

Ganz, L., & Riesen, A. H. (1962). Stimulus generalization to hue in the dark-reared macaque. *Journal of Comparative and Physiological Psychology, 55,* 92–99.

Garb, J. J., & Stunkard, A. J. (1974). Taste aversions in man. *American Journal of Psychiatry, 131,* 1204–1207.

Garcia, J. (1989). Food for Tolman: Cognitions and cathexis in concert. In T. Archer & L. G. Nilsson (Eds.), *Aversion, avoidance and anxiety: Perspectives on aversively motivated behavior* (pp. 45–85). Hillsdale, N.J.: Erlbaum.

Garcia, J., Brett, L. P., & Rusiniak, K. W. (1989). Limits of Darwinian conditioning. In S. B. Klein & R. R. Mowrer (Eds.), *Contemporary learning theories: Instrumental conditioning theory and the impact of biological constraints on learning* (pp. 181–203). Hillsdale, N.J.: Erlbaum.

Garcia, J., Clark, J. C., & Hankins, W. G. (1973). Natural responses to scheduled rewards. In P. P. G. Bateson & P. H. Klopfer (Eds.), *Perspectives in ethology* (pp. 1–41). New York: Plenum.

Garcia, J., & Garcia y Robertson, R. (1985). Evolution of learning mechanisms. In B. L. Hammonds (Ed.), *Psychology and learning.* Washington, D.C.: American Psychological Association.

Garcia, J., Hankins, W. G., & Rusiniak, K. W. (1974). Behavioral regulation of the milieu interne in man and rat. *Science, 185,* 824–831.

Garcia, J., Kimeldorf, D. J., & Hunt, E. L. (1957). Spatial avoidance in the rat as a result of exposure to ionizing radiation. *British Journal of Radiology, 30,* 318–322.

Garcia, J., Kimeldorf, D. J., & Koelling, R. A. (1955). Conditioned aversion to saccharin resulting from exposure to gamma radiation. *Science, 122,* 157–158.

Garcia, J., & Koelling, R. A. (1966). Relation of cue to consequence in avoidance learning. *Psychonomic Science, 4,* 123–124.

Garcia, J., & Rusiniak, K. W. (1980). What the nose learns from the mouth. In D. Muller-Schwarze & R. M. Silverskin (Eds.), *Chemical senses.* New York: Plenum.

Gardner, B. J., & Gardner, R. A. (1971). Two-way communication with an infant chimpanzee. In A. M. Schrier & F. Stolnitz (Eds.), *Behavior of nonhuman primates: Modern research trends* (pp. 117–184). New York: Academic.

Gardner, B. J. & Gardner, R. A. (1980). Two comparative psychologists look at language acquisition. In K. E. Nelson (Ed.) *Children's language.* New York: Halsted.

Garner, W. R. (1953). An information analysis of absolute judgments of loudness. *Journal of Experimental Psychology, 46,* 373–380.

Gatchel, R. J., & Proctor, J. D. (1976). Physiological correlates of learned helplessness in man. *Journal of Abnormal Psychology, 85,* 27–34.

Gelfand, D. M., Hartmann, D. P., Lamb, A. K., Smith, C. L., Mahan, M. A., & Paul, S. C. (1974). The effects of adult models and described alternatives on children's choice of behavior management techniques. *Child Development, 45,* 585–593.

Geller, E. S., & Hahn, H. A. (1984). Promoting safety belt use at industrial sites: An effective program for blue collar employees. *Professional Psychology: Research and Practice, 15,* 553–564.

Gentry, G. D., Weiss, B., & Laties, V. G. (1983). The microanalysis of fixed-interval responding. *Journal of the Experimental Analysis of Behavior, 39,* 327–343.

Gentry, W. D., & Schaeffer, R. W. (1969). The effect of FR response requirement on aggressive behavior in rats. *Psychonomic Science, 14,* 236–238.

Gibbon, J., & Balsam, P. (1981). Spreading association in time. In C. M. Locurto, H. S. Terrace, & J. Gibbon (Eds.). *Autoshaping and conditioning theory* (pp. 219–253). New York: Academic.

Gibson, E. J. (1969). *Perceptual learning and development.* New York: Appleton.

Gibson, E. J., Walk, R. D., & Tighe, T. J. (1959). Enhancement and deprivation of visual stimulation during rearing as factors in visual discrimination learning. *Journal of Comparative and Physiological Psychology, 52,* 74–81.

Gilbert, R. M. (1974). Ubiquity of schedule-induced polydipsia. *Journal of the Experimental Analysis of Behavior, 21,* 277–284.

Giles, D. K., & Wolf, M. M. (1966). Toilet training in institutionalized, severe retardates: An application of operant behavior modification techniques. *American Journal of Mental Deficiency, 70,* 766–780.

Girodo, M. (1974). Yoga meditation and flooding in the treatment of anxiety neurosis. *Journal of Behavior Therapy and Experimental Psychiatry, 5,* 157–160.

Glass, A. L., & Holyoak, K. J. (1975). Alternative conceptions of semantic memory. *Cognition, 3,* 313–339.

Glass, A. L., & Holyoak, K. J. (1986). *Cognition.* New York: Random House.

Gleason, J. B., & Weintraub, S. (1978). Input language and the acquisition of communicative competence. In K. E. Nelson (Ed.), *Children's language* (Vol. 1, pp. 171–222). New York: Gardner.

Gleitman, H. (1971). Forgetting of long-term memories in animals. In W. K. Honig & P. H. R. James (Eds)., *Animal memory* (pp. 2–46). New York: Academic.

Gleitman, H. (1987). *Psychology* (3 ed.). New York: Norton.

Globus, A., Rosenzweig, M. R., Bennett, E. C., & Diamond, M. C. (1973). Effects of differential experience on dendritic spine counts in rat cerebral cortex. *Journal of Comparative and Physiological Psychology, 82,* 175–181.

Glueck, S., & Glueck, E. (1950). *Unraveling juvenile delinquency.* Cambridge, Mass.: Harvard University Press.

Gooden, D. R., & Baddeley, A. D. (1975). Context-dependent memory in two natural environments: On land and underwater. *British Journal of Psychology, 66,* 325–331.

Goodman, I. J., & Brown, J. L. (1966). Stimulation of positively and negatively reinforcing sites in the avian brain. *Life Sciences, 5,* 693–704.

Goodwin, D. W., Powell, B., Bremer, D., Hoine, H., & Stein, J. (1969). Alcohol and recall: State-dependent effects in man. *Science, 163,* 1358–1360.

Gordon, W. C. (1983). Malleability of memory in animals. In R. L. Mellgren (Ed.), *Animal cognition and behavior* (pp. 399–426). New York: North Holland.

Gordon, W. C., McCracken, K. M., Dess-Beech, N., & Mowrer, R. R. (1981). Mechanisms for the cueing phenomenon: The addition of the cueing context to the training memory. *Learning and Motivation, 12,* 196–211.

Gormezano, I. (1972). Investigations of defense and reward conditioning in the rabbit. In A. H. Black & W. F. Prokasy (Eds.), *Classical conditioning II: Current theory and research* (pp. 151–181). New York: Academic.

Gould, J. L. (1982). *Ethology: The mechanisms and evolution of behavior.* New York: Norton.

Granger, R. G., Porter, J. H., & Christoph, N. L. (1983). *Adjunctive behavior in children as a function of interreinforcement interval length.* Paper presented at Southeastern Psychological Association Convention, Atlanta, Georgia.

Grant, D. A., & Schneider, D. E. (1948). Intensity of the conditioned stimulus and strength of conditioning: I. The conditioned eyelid response to light. *Journal of Experimental Psychology, 38,* 690–696.

Grant, D. A., & Schneider, D. E. (1949). Intensity of the conditioned stimulus and strength of conditioning: II. The conditioned galvanic skin response to an auditory stimulus. *Journal of Experimental Psychology, 39,* 35–40.

Grant, D. S. (1975). Proactive interference in pigeon short-term memory. *Journal of Experimental Psychology: Animal Behavior Processes, 1,* 207–220.

Grant, D. S. (1976). Effect of sample presentation time on long delay matching in the pigeon. *Learning and Motivation, 7,* 580–590.

Grant, D. S. (1981). Short-term memory in the pigeon. In N. E. Spear & R. R. Miller (Eds.), *Information processing in animals: Memory mechanisms* (pp. 227–256). Hillsdale, N.J.: Erlbaum.

Grant, D. S., & Roberts, W. A. (1973). Trace interaction in pigeon short-term memory. *Journal of Experimental Psychology, 101,* 21–29.

Grant, D. S., & Roberts, W. A. (1976). Sources of retroactive inhibition in pigeon short-term memory. *Journal of Experimental Psychology: Animal Behavior Processes, 2,* 1–16.

Gratton, A. P., & Wise, R. A. (1988). Comparisons of connectivity and conduction velocities for medial forebrain bundle fibers subserving stimulation-induced feeding and brain stimulation reward. *Brain Research, 438,* 264–270.

Grau, J. W. (1987). The central representation of an aversive event maintains opioid and nonopioid forms of analgesia. *Behavioral Neuroscience, 101,* 272–288.

Gray, J. A. (1971). *The psychology of fear and stress*. New York: McGraw-Hill.

Green, K. F., & Churchill, P. A. (1970). An effect of flavors on strength of conditioned aversions. *Psychonomic Science, 21*, 19–20.

Greeno, J. G. (1974). Hobbits and orcs: Acquisition of a sequential concept. *Cognitive Psychology, 6*, 270–292.

Greiner, J. M., & Karoly, P. (1976). Effects of self-control training on study activity and academic performance: An analysis of self-monitoring, self-reward, and systematic planning components. *Journal of Counseling Psychology, 23*, 495–502.

Grice, G. R. (1948). The relation of secondary reinforcement to delayed reward in visual discrimination learning. *Journal of Experimental Psychology, 38*, 1–16.

Grice, G. R., & Hunter, J. J. (1964). Stimulus intensity effects depend upon the type of experimental design. *Psychological Review, 71*, 247–256.

Griffin, J. C., Locke, B. J., & Landers, W. F. (1975). Manipulation of potential punishment parameters in the treatment of self-injury. *Journal of Applied Behavior Analysis, 8*, 458.

Grossen, N. E., Kostensek, D. J., & Bolles, R. C. (1969). Effects of appetitive discriminative stimuli on avoidance behavior. *Journal of Experimental Psychology, 81*, 340–343.

Grossman, S. P. (1967). *A textbook of physiological psychology*. New York: Wiley.

Groves, P. M., Lee, D., & Thompson, R. F. (1969). Effects of stimulus frequency and intensity on habituation and sensitization in acute spinal lat. *Physiology and Behavior, 4*, 383–388.

Groves, P. M., & Thompson, R. F. (1970). Habituation: A dual-process theory. *Psychological Review, 77*, 419–450.

Grusec, J. E. (1972). Demand characteristics of the modeling experiment: Altruism as a function of age and aggression. *Journal of Personality and Social Psychology, 22*, 139–148.

Guthrie, E. R. (1934). Reward and punishment. *Psychological Review, 41*, 450–460.

Guthrie, E. R. (1935). *The psychology of learning*. New York: Harper.

Guthrie, E. R. (1942). Conditioning: A theory of learning in terms of stimulus, response, and association. In N. B. Henry (Ed.), *The forty-first year book of the National Society of Education: II. The psychology of learning* (pp. 17–60). Chicago: University of Chicago Press.

Guthrie, E. R. (1959). Association by contiguity. In S. Koch (Ed.), *Psychology: A study of a science* (Vol. 2, pp. 158–195). New York: McGraw-Hill.

Gutman, A., Sutterer, J. R., & Brush, R. (1975). Positive and negative behaviorial contrast in the rat. *Journal of the Experimental Analysis of Behavior, 23*, 377–384.

Guttman, N. (1953). Operant conditioning, extinction, and periodic reinforcement in relation to concentration of sucrose used as reinforcing agent. *Journal of Experimental Psychology, 46*, 213–224.

Guttman, N., & Kalish, H. I. (1956). Discriminability and stimulus generalization. *Journal of Experimental Psychology, 51*, 79–88.

Haber, A., & Kalish, H. I. (1963). Prediction of discrimination from generalization after variations in schedule of reinforcement. *Science, 142*, 412–413.

Haber, R. N. (1969). Eidetic images: with biographical sketches. *Scientific American, 220*, 36–44.

Haber, R. N., & Standing, L. G. (1969). Direct measures of short-term visual storage. *Quarterly Journal of Experimental Psychology, 21*, 43–45.

Hackmann, A., & McLean, C. A. (1975). A comparison of flooding and thought stopping in the treatment of obsessional neurosis. *Behavior Research and Therapy, 13*, 263–269.

Hake, D. F., Azrin, N. H., & Oxford, R. (1967). The effects of punishment intensity on squirrel monkeys. *Journal of the Experimental Analysis of Behavior, 10*, 95–107.

Halgren, C. R. (1974). Latent inhibition in rats: Associative or nonassociative? *Journal of Comparative and Physiological Psychology, 86*, 74–78.

Hall, G. (1979). Exposure learning in young and adult laboratory rats. *Animal Behavior, 27*, 586–591.

Hall, G., & Channell, S. (1985). Differential effects of contextual change on latent inhibition and on the habituation of an orienting response. *Journal of Experimental Psychology: Animal Behavior Processes, 11*, 470–481.

Hall, G., & Honey, R. (1989). Perceptual and associative learning. In S. B. Klein & R. R. Mowrer (Eds.), *Contemporary learning theories: Pavlovian conditioning and the status of traditional learning theory.* (pp. 117–147). Hillsdale, N. J.: Erlbaum.

Hall, G., & Pearce, J. M. (1979). Latent inhibition of a CS during CS-US pairings. *Journal of Experimental Psychology: Animal Behavior Processes, 5*, 31–42.

Hall, G., & Schachtman, T. R. (1987). Differential effects of a retention interval on latent inhibition and the habituation of an orienting response. *Animal Learning and Behavior, 15*, 76–82.

Hall, J. F. (1951). Studies in secondary reinforcement: I. Secondary reinforcement as a frequency of primary reinforcement. *Journal of Comparative and Physiological Psychology, 44*, 246–251.

Hall, J. F. (1966). *The psychology of learning.* Philadelphia: Lippincott.

Hall, J. F. (1976). *Classical conditioning and instrumental learning: A contemporary approach.* Philadelphia: Lippincott.

Hall, J. F. (1982). *An invitation to learning and memory.* Boston: Allyn & Bacon.

Halpern, T. & Poon, L. (1971). Human partial reinforcement extinction effects: An information-processing development from Capaldi's sequential theory. *Journal of Experimental Psychology, 89*, 207–227.

Hammen, C. L., & Krantz, S. (1976). Effect of success and failure on depressive cognitions. *Journal of Abnormal Psychology, 85*, 577–586.

Hammond, K., & Arkes, H. (1986). *Judgment and Decision Making.* New York: Cambridge University Press.

Hammond, L. J. (1966). Increased responding to CS- in differential CER. *Psychonomic Science, 5*, 337–338.

Hanratty, M. A., Liebert, R. M., Morris, L. W., & Fernandez, L. E. (1969). Imitation of film-mediated aggression against live and inanimate victims. *Proceedings of the 77th Annual Convention of the American Psychological Association*, 457–458.

Hanson, H. M. (1959). Effects of discrimination training on stimulus generalization. *Journal of Experimental Psychology, 58*, 321–334.

Harlow, H. F. (1971). *Learning to love.* San Francisco: Albion.

Harlow, H. F., & Suomi, S. J. (1970). Nature of love—Simplified. *American Psychologist, 25*, 161–168.

Harris, M. B. (1969). Self-directed program for weight control: A pilot study. *Journal of Abnormal Psychology, 74*, 264–270.

Harris, V. W., & Sherman, J. A. (1973). Use and analysis of the "Good Behavior Game" to reduce disruptive classroom behavior. *Journal of Applied Behavior Analysis, 6*, 405–417.

Hartman, T. F., & Grant, D. A. (1960). Effect of intermittent reinforcement on acquisition, extinction, and spontaneous recovery of the conditioned eyelid response. *Journal of Experimental Psychology, 60,* 89–96.

Hasher, L., & Griffin, M. (1978). Reconstruction and reproductive processes in memory. *Journal of Experimental Psychology: Human Learning and Memory, 4,* 318 –330.

Hawk, G., & Riccio, D. C. (1977). The effect of a conditioned fear inhibitor (CS−) during response prevention upon extinction of an avoidance response. *Behaviour Research and Therapy, 15,* 97–102.

Hawkins, R. D., Abrams, T. W., Carew, T. J., & Kandel, E. R. (1983). A cellular mechanism of classical conditioning in aplysia: Activity-dependent amplification of presynaptic facilitation. *Science, 219,* 400–405.

Haycock, J. W., van Buskirk, R., & McGaugh, J. L. (1977). Effects of catecholaminergic drugs upon memory storage processes in mice. *Behavioral Biology, 20,* 281–310.

Hayes, K.J., & Hayes, C. (1951). The intellectual development of a home-raised chimpanzee. *Proceedings of the American Philosophical Society, 95,* 105–109.

Hayes, J. R. (1978). *Cognitive psychology.* Homewood, Ill.: Dorsey.

Hayes, J. R. M. (1952). Memory span for several vocabularies as a function of vacabulary size. *Quarterly progress report.* Cambridge: Massachusetts Institute of Technology, Acoustics Laboratory.

Hayes, S. C., & Cone, J. D. (1977). Reducing residential electrical energy use: Payments, information, and feedback. *Journal of Applied Behavior Analysis, 10,* 425–435.

Hearst, E., & Jenkins, H. M. (1974). *Sign tracking: The stimulus-reinforcer relation and direct action.* Austin, Tex.: Monograph of the Psychonomic Society.

Heath, R. G. (1955). Correlations between levels of psychological awareness and physiological activity in the central nervous system. *Psychosomatic Medicine, 17,* 383–395.

Hebb, D. O. (1949). *The organization of behavior.* New York: Colley.

Herrnstein, R. J. (1961). Relative and absolute strength of response as a function of frequency of reinforcement. *Journal of the Experimental Analysis of Behavior, 4,* 267–272.

Herrnstein, R. J. (1979). Acquisition, generalization and discrimination reversal of a natural concept. *Journal of Experimental Psychology: Animal Behavior Processes, 5,* 116–129.

Herrnstein, R. J., & de Villiers, P. A. (1980). Fish as a natural category for people and pigeons. In G. H. Bower (Ed.), *Psychology of learning and motivation* (Vol. 14, pp. 60–97). New York: Academic.

Herrnstein, R. J., Loveland, D. H., & Cable, C. (1976). Natural concepts in pigeons. *Journal of Experimental Psychology: Animal Behavior Processes, 2,* 285–302.

Herrnstein, R. J., & Vaughn, W. (1980). Melioration and behavioral allocation. In J. E. R. Staddon (Ed.), *Limits to action: The allocation of individual behavior* (pp. 143–176). New York: Academic.

Hess, E. H. (1962). Ethology: An approach toward the complete analysis of behavior. In R. Brown, E. Galanter, E. H. Hess, & G. Mandler (Eds.), *New directions in psychology* (pp. 157–266). New York: Holt.

Hess, E. H. (1964). Imprinting in birds. *Science, 146,* 1128–1139.

Hess, E. H. (1973). *Imprinting.* Princeton, N.J.: Van Nostrand Reinhold.

Hetherington, E. M., & Ross, L. E. (1967). Discrimination learning by normal and retarded children under delay of reward and interpolated task conditions. *Child Development, 38,* 639–647.

Hetherington, E. M., Ross, L. E., & Pick, H. L. (1964). Delay of reward and learning in mentally retarded and normal children. *Child Development, 35,* 653–659.

Hilgard, E. R., & Marquis, D. G. (1940). *Conditioning and learning.* New York: Appleton-Century-Crofts.

Hill, W. F., & Spear, N. E. (1963). Extinction in a runway as a function of acquisition level and reinforcement percentage. *Journal of Experimental Psychology, 65,* 495–500.

Hill, W. F., & Wallace, W. P. (1967). Effects of magnitude and percentage of reward on subsequent patterns of runway speed. *Journal of Experimental Psychology, 73,* 544–548.

Hines, B., & Paolino, R. M. (1970). Retrograde amnesia: Production of skeletal but not cardiac response gradient by electroconvulsive shock. *Science, 169,* 1224–1226.

Hintzman, D. L., Block, R. A., & Inskeep, N. R. (1972). Memory for mode of input. *Journal of Verbal Learning and Verbal Behavior, 11,* 741–749.

Hiroto, D. S. (1974). Locus of control and learned helplessness. *Journal of Experimental Psychology, 102,* 187–193.

Hiroto, D. S., & Seligman, M. E. P. (1975). Generality of learned helplessness in man. *Journal of Personality and Social Psychology, 31,* 311–327.

Hoebel, B. G. (1969). Feeding and self-stimulation: Neural regulation of food and water intake. *Annals of the New York Academy of Sciences, 157,* 758–778.

Hoffman, H. S. (1968). The control of stress vocalization by an imprinting stimulus. *Behavior, 30,* 175–191.

Hoffman, H. S. (1969). Stimulus factors in conditioned suppression. In B. A. Campbell & R. M. Church (Eds.), *Punishment and aversive behavior* (pp. 185–234). New York: Appleton-Century-Crofts.

Hogan, J. A. (1989). Cause and function in the development of behavior systems. In E. M. Blass (Ed)., *Handbook of behavioral and neurobiology* (Vol. 8, pp. 129–174). New York: Plenum Press.

Hokanson, J. E. (1970). Psychophysiological evaluation of the catharsis hypothesis. In E. I. Megargee & J. E. Hokanson (Eds.), *The dynamics of aggression* (pp. 74–86). New York: Harper & Row.

Hokanson, J. E., & Burgess, M. (1962a). The effects of three types of aggression on vascular processes. *Journal of Abnormal and Social Psychology, 64,* 446–449.

Hokanson, J. E., & Burgess, M. (1962b). The effects of status, type of frustration, and aggression on vascular processes. *Journal of Abnormal and Social Psychology, 65,* 232–237.

Hokanson, J. E., Burgess, M., & Cohen, M. F. (1963). Effects of displaced aggression on systolic blood pressure. *Journal of Abnormal and Social Psychology, 67,* 214–218.

Hokanson, J. E., & Shelter, S. (1961). The effect of overt aggression on level of physiological arousal. *Journal of Abnormal and Social Psychology, 63,* 446–448.

Holder, H. D., & Garcia, J. (1987). Role of temporal order and odor intensity in taste-potentiated odor aversions. *Behavioral Neuroscience, 101,* 158–163.

Holland, P. C. (1983). Occasion-setting in Pavlovian feature discriminations. In M. L. Commons, R. J. Herrnstein, & A. R. Wagner (Eds.), *Quantitative analysis of behavior: Discrimination processes* (Vol. 4, pp. 182–206). New York: Ballinger.

Holland, P. C. (1986). Temporal determinants of occasion-setting in feature-positive discriminations. *Animal Learning and Behavior, 14,* 111–120.

Holland, P. C., & Rescorla, R. A. (1975). The effects of two ways of devaluing the unconditioned stimulus after first- and second-order appetitive conditioning. *Journal of Experimental Psychology: Animal Behavior Processes, 1,* 355–363.

Holmgren, B. (1964). Nivel de vigilia y relfecjos condicionados. *Boletin del Instituto de Investigaciones de la Actividad Nerviosa Superior (Havana), 1,* 33–50.

Homme, L. W., de Baca, P. C., Devine, J. V., Steinhorst, R., & Rickert, E. J. (1963). Use of the Premack principle in controlling the behavior of nursery school children. *Journal of the Experimental Analysis of Behavior, 6,* 544.

Horel, J. A. (1978). The neuroanatomy of amnesia: A critique of the hippocampal memory hypothesis. *Brain, 101,* 403–445.

Horel, J. A., & Misantone, L. G. (1974). The Kluver-Bucy syndrome produced by partial isolation of the temporal lobe. *Experimental Neurology, 42,* 101–112.

Horel, J. A., & Misantone, L. G. (1976). Visual discrimination impaired by cutting temporal lobe connections. *Science, 193,* 336–338.

Horner, R. D., & Keilitz, I. (1975). Training mentally retarded adolescents to brush their teeth. *Journal of Applied Behavior Analysis, 8,* 301–310.

Houston, J. P. (1967). Stimulus selection as influenced by degrees of learning, attention, prior associations, and experience with the stimulus components. *Journal of Experimental Psychology, 73,* 509–516.

Houston, J. P. (1986). *Fundamentals of learning and memory* (3d ed.). Orlando, Fla.: Harcourt Brace Jovanovich.

Hoveland, C. I. (1937). The generalization of conditioned responses: IV. The effects of varying amounts of reinforcement upon the degree of generalization of conditioned responses. *Journal of Experimental Psychology, 21,* 261–276.

Howard, D. V. (1983). *Cognitive psychology: Memory, language, and thought.* New York: Macmillan.

Hull, C. L. (1920). Quantitative aspects of the evolution of concepts: An experimental study. *Psychological Monographs, 28,* Whole No. 123.

Hull, C. L. (1943). *Principles of behavior.* New York: Appleton.

Hull, C. L. (1952). *A behavior system.* New Haven, Conn.: Yale University Press.

Hulse, S. H., Jr. (1958). Amount and percentage of reinforcement and duration of goal confinement in conditioning and extinction. *Journal of Experimental Psychology, 56,* 48–57.

Hulse, S. H., Jr., Fowler, H., & Honig, W. K. (Eds.) (1978). *Cognitive processes in animal behavior.* Hillsdale, N.J.: Erlbaum.

Hume, D. (1739). *A treatise of human nature: Being an attempt to introduce the experimental method of reasoning into moral subjects.* London: J. Noon.

Humphreys, L. G. (1939). Acquisition and extinction of verbal expectations in a situation analogous to conditioning. *Journal of Experimental Psychology, 25,* 294–301.

Hunt, R. R., & Mitchell, D. B. (1982). Independent effects of semantic and nonsemantic distinctiveness. *Journal of Experimental Psychology: Learning, Memory, and Cognition, 8,* 81–87.

Hunziker, J. C. (1972). *The use of participant modeling in the treatment of water phobias.* Unpublished master's thesis, Arizona State University, Tempe.

Huppert, F. A., & Piercy, M. (1979). Normal and abnormal forgetting in organic amnesia: Effect of locus of lesion. *Cortex, 15,* 385–390.

Hurwitz, H. M. B. (1964). Method for discrimitative avoidance training. *Science, 145,* 1070–1071.

Hussain, M. Z. (1971). Desensitization and flooding (implosion) in treatment of phobias. *American Journal of Psychiatry, 127,* 85–89.

Hutchinson, R. R., Azrin, N. H., & Hunt, G. M. (1968). Attack produced by intermittent reinforcement of a concurrent operant response. *Journal of the Experimental Analysis of Behavior, 11,* 498–495.

Hyden, H., & Egyhazi, E. (1964). Changes in RNA content and base composition in cortical neurons of rats in a learning experiment involving transfer of handedness. *Proceedings of the National Academy of Sciences, 52,* 1030–1035.

Hyson, R. L., Sickel, J. L., Kulkosky, P. J., & Riley, A. L. (1981). The insensitivity of schedule-induced polydipsia to conditioned taste aversions: Effect of amount consumed during conditioning. *Animal Learning and Behavior, 9,* 281–286.

Innis, N. K. (1979). Stimulus control of behavior during postreinforcement pause of FI schedules. *Animal Learning and Behavior, 7,* 203–210.

Ison, J. R., & Cook, P. E. (1964). Extinction performance as a function of incentive magnitude and number of acquisition trials. *Psychonomic Science, 7,* 203–210.

Jackson, R. L., Alexander, J. H, & Maier, S. F. (1980). Learned helplessness, inactivity, and associative deficits: Effects of inescapable shock on response choice escape learning. *Journal of Experimental Psychology: Animal Behavior Processes, 6,* 1–20.

Jacobson, E. (1938). *Progressive relaxation.* Chicago: University of Chicago Press.

Jacquet, Y. F. (1972). Schedule-induced licking during multiple schedules. *Journal of the Experimental Analysis of Behavior, 17,* 413–423.

James, C. T., & Greeno, J. G. (1967). Stimulus selection at different stages of paired-associate learning. *Journal of Experimental Psychology, 74,* 75–83.

James, W. A. (1890). *The principles of psychology* (Vols. I and II). New York: Holt.

Jarvik, M. E., Goldfarb, R., & Corley, J. L. (1969). Influence of interference on delayed matching in monkeys. *Journal of Experimental Psychology, 81,* 1–6.

Jaynes, J. (1956). Imprinting: The interaction of learned and innate behavior: I. Development and generalization. *Journal of Comparative and Physiological Psychology, 49,* 201–206.

Jenkins, H. M. (1977). Sensitivity of different response systems to stimulus-reinforcer and response-reinforcer relations. In H. Davis & H. M. B. Hurwitz (Eds.), *Operant-Pavlovian interactions* (pp. 47–62). Hillsdale, N.J.: Erlbaum.

Jenkins, H. M., Barnes, R. A., & Barrera, F. J. (1981). Why autoshaping depends on trial spacing. In C. M. Locurto, H. S. Terrace, & J. Gibbon (Eds.), *Autoshaping and conditioning theory* (pp. 255–284). New York: Academic.

Jenkins, H. M., & Harrison, R. H. (1960). Effect of discrimination training on auditory generalization. *Journal of Experimental Psychology, 59,* 246–273.

Jenkins, H. M., & Moore, B. R. (1973). The form of the autoshaped response with food or water reinforcers. *Journal of the Experimental Analysis of Behavior, 20,* 163–181.

Jenkins, J. G., & Dallenbach, K. M. (1924). Obliviscence during sleep and waking. *American Journal of Psychology, 35,* 605–612.

Jenkins, J. J., Mink, W. D., & Russell, W. A. (1958). Associative clustering as a function of verbal association strength. *Psychological Reports, 4,* 127–136.

Jenkins, W. O., McFann, H., & Clayton, F. L. (1950). A methodological study of extinction following aperiodic and continuous reinforcement. *Journal of Comparative and Physiological Psychology, 43,* 155–167.

Jensen, R. A., Martinez, J. L., Messing, R. B., Spiehler, V. R., Vasquez, B. J., Soumireu-Mourat, B., Liang, K. C., & McGaugh, J. L. (1978). Morphine and naloxone alter memory in rats. *Society for Neuroscience Abstracts, 4,* 260.

John, E. R. (1967). *Mechanisms of memory*. New York: Academic.

Johnson, E. E. (1952). The role of motivational strength in latent learning. *Journal of Comparative and Physiological Psychology, 45*, 526–530.

Johnson, N. F. (1968). Sequential verbal behavior. In T. R. Dixon & D. L. Horton (Eds.), *Verbal behavior and general behavior therapy* (pp. 421–450). Englewood Cliffs, N.J.: Prentice-Hall.

Johnston, T. D. (1981). Contrasting approaches to a theory of learning. *The Behavioral & Brain Sciences, 4*, 125–139.

Jones, M. C. (1924). The elimination of children's fears. *Journal of Experimental Psychology, 7*, 383–390.

Kalat, J. W., & Rozin, P. (1970). "Salience": A factor which can override temporal contiguity in taste-aversion learning. *Journal of Comparative and Physiological Psychology, 71*, 192–197.

Kalat, J. W., & Rozin, P. (1971). Role of interference in taste-aversion learning. *Journal of Comparative and Physiological Psychology, 77*, 53–58.

Kalat, J. W., & Rozin, P. (1973). "Learned safety" as a mechanism in long-delay learning in rats. *Journal of Comparative and Physiological Psychology, 83*, 198–207.

Kalish, H. I. (1969). Stimulus generalization. In M. H. Mary (Ed.), *Learning: processes*. London: Macmillan.

Kalish, H. I. (1981). *From behavioral science to behavior modification*. New York: McGraw-Hill.

Kallman, W. M., Hersen, M., & O'Toole, D. H. (1975). The use of social reinforcement in a case of conversion reaction. *Behavior Therapy, 6*, 411–413.

Kamin, L. J. (1954). Traumatic avoidance learning: The effects of CS-UCS interval with a trace-conditioning procedure. *Journal of Comparative and Physiological Psychology, 47*, 65–72.

Kamin, L. J. (1956). The effects of termination of the CS and avoidance of the US on avoidance learning. *Journal of Comparative and Physiological Psychology, 49*, 420–424.

Kamin, L. J. (1957). The retention of an incompletely learned avoidance response. *Journal of Comparative and Physiological Psychology, 50*, 457–460.

Kamin, L. J. (1959). The delay-of-punishment gradient. *Journal of Comparative and Physiological Psychology, 52*, 434–437.

Kamin, L. J. (1968). "Attention-like" processes in classical conditioning. In M. R. Jones (Ed.), *Miami symposium on the prediction of behavior: Aversive stimulation* (pp. 9–31). Miami: University of Miami Press.

Kamin, L. J. (1969). Predictability, surprise, attention, and conditioning. In B. A. Campbell & R. M. Church (Eds.), *Punishment and aversive behavior* (pp. 279–296). New York: Appleton-Century-Crofts.

Kamin, L. J., Brimer, C. J., & Black, A. H. (1963). Conditioned suppression as a monitor of fear of the CS in the course of avoidance-training. *Journal of Comparative and Physiological Psychology, 56*, 497–501.

Kamin, L. J., & Schaub, R. E. (1963). Effects of conditioned stimulus intensity on the conditioned emotional response. *Journal of Comparative and Physiological Psychology, 56*, 502–507.

Kanarek, R. B. (1974). *The energetics of meal patterns*. Unpublished doctoral dissertation, Rutgers—The State University, New Brunswick.

Kandel, E. R., & Schwartz, J. H. (1982). Molecular biology and learning: Modulation of transmitter release. *Science, 218*, 433–443.

Kaplan, M., Jackson, B., & Sparer, R. (1965). Escape behavior under continuous reinforcement as a function of aversive light intensity. *Journal of the Experimental Analysis of Behavior, 8,* 321–323.

Kaplan, P. S. (1984). The importance of relative temporal parameters in trace autoshaping: From excitation to inhibition. *Journal of Experimental Psychology: Animal Behavior Processes, 10,* 113–126.

Kaplan, P. S., & Hearst, E. (1982). Bridging temporal gaps between CS and US in autoshaping: Insertion of other stimuli before, during, and after CS. *Journal of Experimental Psychology: Animal Behavior Processes, 8,* 187–203.

Karsh, E. B. (1962). Effects of number of rewarded trials and intensity of punishment on running speed. *Journal of Comparative and Physiological Psychology, 55,* 44–51.

Katcher, A. H., Solomon, R. L., Turner, L. H., LoLordo, V. M., Overmeir, J. B., & Rescorla, R. A. (1969). Heart-rate and blood pressure responses to signaled and unsignaled shocks: Effects of cardiac sympathetomy. *Journal of Comparative and Physiological Psychology, 42,* 163–174.

Kaufman, E. L., Lord, M. W., Reese, T. W., & Volkmann, J. (1949). The discrimination of visual number. *American Journal of Psychology, 62,* 498–525.

Kaufman, M. A., & Bolles, R. C. (1981). A nonassociative aspect of overshadowing. *Bulletin of the Psychonomic Society, 18,* 318–320.

Kazdin, A. E. (1972). Response cost: The removal of conditioned reinforcers for therapeutic change. *Behavior Therapy, 3,* 533–546.

Kazdin, A. E. (1974a). Covert modeling, modeling similarity, and reduction of avoidance behavior. *Behavior Therapy, 5,* 325–340.

Kazdin, A. E. (1974b). Effects of covert modeling, multiple models, and model reinforcement on assertive behavior. *Behavior Therapy, 7,* 211–222.

Kazdin, A. E. (1978). *History of behavior modification: Experimental foundations of contemporary research.* Baltimore: University Park Press.

Keele, S. W., & Chase, W. G. (1967). Short-term visual storage. *Perception and Psychophysics, 2,* 383–385.

Kehoe, E. J., Gibbs, C. M., Garcia, A., & Gormezano, I. (1979). Associative transfer and stimulus selection in classical conditioning of the rabbit's nicitating membrane response to serial compound CS. *Journal of Experimental Psychology: Animal Behavior Processes, 5,* 1–19.

Keith-Lucas, T., & Guttman, N. (1975). Robust-single-trial delayed backward conditioning. *Journal of Comparative and Physiological Psychology, 88,* 468–476.

Keller, F. S., & Hull, L. M. (1936). Another "insight" experiment. *Journal of Genetic Psychology, 48,* 484–489.

Kellogg, W. N., & Kellogg, L. A. (1933). *The ape and the child.* New York: McGraw-Hill.

Kendler, H. H., & Gasser, W. P. (1948). Variables in spatial learning: I. Number of reinforcements during training. *Journal of Comparative and Physiological Psychology, 41,* 178–187.

Kenny, F. T., Solyom, L., & Solyom, C. (1973). Faradic disruption of obsessive ideation in the treatment of obsessive neurosis. *Behavior Therapy, 4,* 448–457.

Keppel, G. (1964). Facilitation in short- and long-term retention of paired associates following distributed practice in learning. *Journal of Verbal Learning and Verbal Behavior, 3,* 91–111.

Keppel, G. (1968). Retroactive and proactive inhibition. In T. R. Dixon & D. L. Horton (Eds.), *Verbal behavior and general behavior theory* (pp. 172–213). Englewood Cliffs, N.J.: Prentice-Hall.

Keppel, G., & Underwood, B. J. (1962). Proactive inhibition in short-term retention of single items. *Journal of Verbal Learning and Verbal Behavior, 1,* 153–161.

Kimble, G. A., & Reynolds, B. (1967). Eyelid conditioning as a function of the interval between conditioned and unconditioned stimuli. In G. A. Kimble (Ed.), *Foundations of conditioning and learning.* New York: Appleton-Century-Crofts.

Kimble, G. A. (1961). *Hilgard and Marguis' conditioning and learning* (2d ed.). New York: Appleton-Century.

Kimmel, H. D. (1965). Instrumental inhibitory factors in classical conditioning. In W. F. Prokasy (Ed.), *Classical conditioning: A symposium* (pp. 148–171). New York: Appleton-Century-Crofts.

King, G. D. (1974). Wheel running in the rat induced by a fixed-time presentation of water. *Animal Learning and Behavior, 2,* 325–328.

Kintsch, W. (1974). *The representation of meaning in memory.* Hillsdale, N.J.: Erlbaum.

Kintsch, W. (1977). On comprehending stories. In M. A. Just & P. A. Carpenter (Eds.), *Cognitive processes in comprehension* (pp. 33–62). Hillsdale, N.J.: Erlbaum.

Kintsch, W. (1980). Semantic memory: A tutorial. In T. D. Nickerson (Ed.), *Attention and performance VIII* (pp. 595–620). Hillsdale, N.J.: Erlbaum.

Kintsch, W., & Witte, R. S. (1962). Concurrent conditioning of bar-press and salivation responses. *Journal of Comparative and Physiological Psychology, 55,* 963–968.

Kirigin, K. A., Braukmann, C. J., Atwater, J. D., & Wolf, M. M., (1982). An evaluation of teaching-family (Achievement Place) group homes for juvenile defenders. *Journal of Applied Behavioral Analysis, 15,* 1–66.

Klein, D. C., & Seligman, M. E. P. (1976). Reversal of performance deficits and perceptual deficits in learned helplessness and depression. *Journal of Abnormal Psychology, 85,* 11–26.

Klein, M., & Kandel, E. R. (1978). Presynaptic modulation of voltage-dependent Ca2 + current: Mechanism for behavior sensitization in *Aplysia californica. Proceedings of the National Academy of Sciences (USA), 77,* 6912–6916.

Klein, S. B. (1972). Adrenal-pituitary influence in reaction of avoidance-learning memory in the rat after intermediate intervals. *Journal of Comparative and Physiological Psychology, 79,* 341–359.

Klein, S. B. (1982). *Motivation: Biosocial approaches.* New York: McGraw-Hill.

Klein, S. B., Domato, G. C., Hallstead, C., Stephens, I., & Mikulka, P. J. (1975). Acquisition of a conditioned aversion as a function of age and measurement technique. *Physiological Psychology, 3,* 379–384.

Klein, S. B., Freda, J. S., & Mikulka, P. J. (1985). The influence of a taste cue on an environmental aversion: Potentiation or overshadowing. *Psychological Record, 35,* 101–112.

Klein, S. B., McGee-Davis, T., Cohen, L., & Weston, D. (1984). Relative influence of cue predictiveness and salience on flavor aversion learning. *Learning and Motivation, 15,* 188–202.

Klein, S. B., & Spear, N. E. (1969). Influence of age on short-term retention of active-avoidance learning in rats. *Journal of Comparative and Physiological Psychology, 69,* 583–589.

Klein, S. B., & Spear, N. E. (1970a). Forgetting by the rat after intermediate intervals ("Kamin effect") as retrieval failure. *Journal of Comparative and Physiological Psychology, 71,* 165–170.

Klein, S. B., & Spear, N. E. (1970b). Reactivation of avoidance learning memory in the rats after intermediate retention intervals. *Journal of Comparative and Physiological Psychology, 72,* 498–504.

Klopfer, P. H. (1971). Imprinting: Determining its perceptual basis in ducklings. *Journal of Comparative and Physiological Psychology, 75,* 378–385.

Klopfer, P. H., Adams, D. K., & Klopfer, M. S. (1964). Maternal "imprinting" in goats. *National Academy of Science Proceedings, 52,* 911–914.

Knecht v. Gillman, 488 F.2d 1136 (8th Cir. 1973).

Knutson, J. F., & Kleinknecht, R. A. (1970). Attack during differential reinforcement of low rate of responding. *Psychonomic Science, 19,* 289–290.

Koegel, R. L., Firestone, P. B., Kramme, K. W., & Dunlap, G. (1974). Increasing spontaneous play by suppressing self-stimulation in autistic children. *Journal of Applied Behavior Analysis, 7,* 521–528.

Kohlenberg, R. J. (1970). The punishment of persistent vomiting: A case study. *Journal of Applied Behavior Analysis, 3,* 241–245.

Kohler, W. (1925). *The mentality of apes.* London: Routledge & Kegan Paul.

Kohler, W. (1939). Simple structural functions in the chimpanzee and the chicken. In W. D. Ellis (Ed.), *A source book of gestalt psychology* (pp. 217–227). New York: Harcourt Brace.

Kolers, P. A. (1976). Pattern-analyzing memory. *Science, 191,* 1280–1281.

Konarski, E. A., Jr. (1985). The use of response deprivation to increase the academic performance of EMR students. *The Behavior Therapist, 8,* 61.

Konarski, E. A., Jr., Johnson, M. R., Crowell, C. R., & Whitman, T. L. (1980). Response deprivation, reinforcement, and instrumental academic performance in an EMR classroom. *Behavior Therapy, 13,* 94–102.

Kovach, J. K., & Hess, E. H. (1963). Imprinting: Effects of painful stimulation upon the following response. *Journal of Comparative and Physiological Psychology, 56,* 461–464.

Krapft, J. E. (1967). *Differential ordering of stimulus presentation and semiautomated versus live treatment in the systematic desentization of snake phobia.* Unpublished doctoral dissertation, University of Missouri, Columbia.

Krechevsky, I. (1932). "Hypotheses" in rats. *Psychological Review, 39,* 516–532.

Kremer, E. F. (1971). Truly random and traditional control procedures in CER conditioning in the rat. *Journal of Comparative and Physiological Psychology, 76,* 441–448.

Kremer, E. F., Specht, T., & Allen, R. (1980). Attenuation of blocking with the omission of a delayed US. *Animal Learning and Behavior, 8,* 609–616.

Kubena, R. K., & Barry, H. (1969). Generalization by rats of alcohol and atropine stimulus characteristics to other drugs. *Psychopharmalogia, 15,* 196–206.

Kucharski, D., & Spear, N. E. (1985). Potentiation and overshadowing in preweanling and adult rats. *Journal of Experimental Psychology: Animal Behavior Processes, 11,* 15–34.

Kushner, M., & Sandler, J. (1966). Aversion therapy and the concept of punishment. *Behaviour Research and Therapy, 4,* 179–186.

Landauer, T. K. (1962). Rate of implicit speech. *Perceptual and Motor Skills, 15,* 646.

Lang, P. J. (1978). Self-efficacy theory: Thoughts on cognition and unification. In S. Rachman (Ed.), *Advances in behaviour research and therapy* (Vol. 1, pp. 187–192). Oxford: Pergamon.

Lang, P. J., & Melamed, B. G. (1969). Avoidance conditioning of an infant with chronic ruminative vomiting. *Journal of Abnormal Psychology, 74,* 1–8.

Langer, E. J. (1983). *The psychology of control.* Beverly Hills, Calif.: Sage.

Larew, M. B. (1986). *Inhibitory learning in Pavlovian backward conditioning procedures involving a small number of US-CS trials.* Unpublished doctoral dissertation, Yale University, New Haven, Conn.

Lashley, K. S. (1929). *Brain mechanisms and intelligence.* Chicago: University of Chicago Press.

Lashley, K. S. (1950). In search of the engram. *Symposia of the Society for Experimental Biology, 4,* 454–482.

Lashley, K. S., & Wade, M. (1946). The Pavlovian theory of generalization. *Psychological Review, 53,* 72–87.

Lasky, R. E., Syrdal-Lasky, A., & Klein, R. E. (1975). VOT discrimination by four- to six-and-a-half-month-old infants from Spanish environments. *Journal of Experimental Child Psychology, 20,* 215–225.

Lawrence, D. H., & DeRivera, J. (1954). Evidence for relational transposition. *Journal of Comparative and Physiological Psychology, 47,* 465–471.

Lawson, E. A. (1966). Decisions concerning the rejected channel. *Quarterly Journal of Experimental Psychology, 18,* 260–265.

Lazarus, A. A. (1971). *Behavior therapy and beyond.* New York: McGraw-Hill.

Le, A. D., Poulos, C. X., & Cappell, H. (1979). Conditioned tolerance to the hypothermic effect of ethyl alcohol. *Science, 206,* 1109–1110.

Lea, S. E. A. (1984). In what sense do pigeons learn concepts? In H. L. Roitblat, T. G. Bever, & H. S. Terrace (Eds.), *Animal cognition* (pp. 263–276). Hillsdale, N.J.: Erlbaum.

Leff, R. (1969). Effects of punishment intensity and consistency on the internalization of behavioral suppression in children. *Developmental Psychology, 1,* 345–356.

Lemieux, G., Davignon, A., & Genest, J. (1956). Depressive states during rauwolfia therapy for arterial hypertension. *Canadian Medical Association Journal, 74,* 522–526.

Lenneberg, E. H. (1967). *Biological foundations of language.* New York: Wiley.

Lenneberg, E. H. (1969). On explaining language. *Science, 164,* 635–643.

Lett, B. T. (1982). Taste potentiation in poison-avoidance learning. In R. Herrnstein (Ed.), *Harvard symposium on quantitative analysis of behavior* (Vol. 4). Hillsdale, N.J.: Erlbaum.

Leukel, F. A. (1957). A comparison of the effects of ECS and anesthesia on acquisition of the maze habit. *Journal of Comparative and Physiological Psychology, 50,* 300–306.

Levine, M. (1966). Hypothesis behavior by humans during discrimination learning. *Journal of Experimental Psychology, 71,* 331–338.

Levis, D. J. (1976). Learned helplessness: A reply and an alternative S-R interpretation. *Journal of Experimental Psychology: General, 105,* 47–65.

Levis, D. J. (1989). The case for a return to a two-factor theory of avoidance: The failure of non-fear interpretations. From S. B. Klein & R. R. Mowrer (Eds.), *Contemporary learning theories: Pavlovian conditioning and the status of traditional learning theory* (pp. 227–277). Hillsdale, N.J.: Erlbaum.

Levis, D. J., & Boyd, T. L. (1979). Symptom maintenance: An infrahuman analysis and extension of the conservation of anxiety principle. *Journal of Abnormal Psychology, 88*, 107–120.

Levitsky, D., & Collier, G. (1968). Schedule-induced wheel running. *Physiology and Behavior, 3*, 571–573.

Lewis, D. J. (1952). Partial reinforcement in the gambling situation. *Journal of Experimental Psychology, 43*, 447–450.

Lewis, D. J. (1959). A control for the direct manipulation of the fractional anticipatory goal response. *Psychological Reports, 5*, 753–756.

Lewis, D. J. (1960). Partial reinforcement: A selective review of the literature since 1950. *Psychological Bulletin, 57*, 1–28.

Lewis, D. J. (1969). Sources of experimental amnesia. *Psychological Review, 76*, 461–472.

Lewis, D. J. (1979). Psychobiology of active and inactive memory. *Psychological Bulletin, 86*, 1054–1083.

Lewis, D. J., & Duncan, C. P. (1956). Effect of different percentages of money reward on extinction of a lever-pulling response. *Journal of Experimental Psychology, 52*, 23–27.

Lewis, D. J., & Duncan, C. P. (1957). Expectation and resistance to extinction of a lever-pulling response as function of percentage of reinforcement and number of acquisition trials. *Journal of Experimental Psychology, 54*, 115–120.

Lewis, D. J., & Duncan, C. P. (1958). Expectation and resistance to extinction of a lever-pulling response as a function of percentage of reinforcement and amount of reward. *Journal of Experimental Psychology, 55*, 121–128.

Lewis, D. J., Smith, P. N., & McAllister, D. E. (1952). Retroactive facilitation and interference in performance on the modified two-hand coordinator. *Journal of Experimental Psychology, 44*, 44–50.

Liberman, A. M., Delattre, P., & Cooper, F. S. (1952). The role of perception stimulus-variables in the perception of the unvoiced stop consonants. *American Journal of Psychology, 65*, 497–516.

Liberman, R. P., & Raskin, D. E. (1971). Depression: A behavioral formulation. *Archives of General Psychiatry, 24*, 515–523.

Lick, J., & Bootzin, R. (1975). Expectancy factors in the treatment of fear: Methodological and theoretical issues. *Psychological Bulletin, 82*, 917–931.

Liebman, J. M., & Butcher, L. I. (1974). Comparative involvement of dopamine and noradrenaline in rate-free self-stimulation in substantia nigra, lateral hypothalamus and mesencephalic central gray. *Naunyn-Schmiedeberg's Archives of Pharmacology, 284*, 167–194.

Linden, D. R. (1974). The effect of intensity of intermittent punishment in acquisition on resistance to extinction of an approach response. *Animal Learning and Behavior, 2*, 9–12.

Lindsey, G., & Best, P. (1973). Overshadowing of the less salient of two novel fluids in a taste-aversion paradigm. *Physiological Psychology, 1*, 13–15.

Lockhart, R. A., & Steinbrecher, C. D. (1965). Temporal avoidance conditioning in the rabbit. *Psychonomic Science, 3*, 121–122.

Loftus, E. F. (1975). Leading questions and the eyewitness report. *Cognitive Psychology, 7*, 560–572.

Loftus, E. F. (1980). *Memory*. Reading, Mass.: Addison-Wesley.

Loftus, E. F., & Zanni, G. (1975). Eyewitness testimony: The influence of the wording of a question. *Bulletin of the Psychonomic Society, 5,* 86–88.

Logan, F. A. (1952). The role of delay of reinforcement in determining reaction potential. *Journal of Experimental Psychology, 43,* 393–399.

Logan, F. A. (1960). *Incentive.* New Haven: Yale University Press.

Logue, A. W. (1979). Taste aversion and the generality of the laws of learning. *Psychological Bulletin, 86,* 276–296.

Logue, A. W. (1985). Conditioned food aversion learning in humans. In N. S. Braveman & P. Bronstein (Eds.) Experimental assessment and clinical applications of conditioned food aversions. *Annals of the New York Academy of Sciences, 443,* 316–329.

LoLordo, V. M. (1979). Selective associations. In A. Dickinson & R. A. Boakes (Eds.), *Mechanisms of learning and motivation* (pp. 367–398). Hillsdale, N.J.: Erlbaum.

Lombardi, B. R., & Flaherty, C. F. (1978). Apparent disinhibition of successive but not of simultaneous negative contrast. *Animal Learning and Behavior, 6,* 30–42.

Long, D., & Allen, G. A. (1973). Relative effects of acoustic and semantic relatedness on clustering free recall. *Bulletin of the Psychonomic Society, 1,* 316–318.

Lorayne, H., & Lucas, J. (1974). *The memory book.* New York: Ballantine.

Lorenz, K. (1935). Der Kumpan in der Umwelt des Vogels. *Journal of Ornithology, 83,* 137–213, 289–413.

Lorenz, K. (1950). The comparative method of studying innate behavior patterns. In Society for Experimental Biology, Symposium No. 4, *Physiological mechanisms in animal behaviour* (pp. 221–268). New York: Academic.

Lorenz K. (1952). The past twelve years in the comparative study of behavior. In C. H. Schiller (Ed.), *Instinctive behavior* (pp. 288–317). New York: International Universities Press.

Lorenz, K. (1969). Innate bases of learning. In K. H. Pibram (Ed.), *On the biology of learning* (pp. 13–93). New York: Harcourt, Brace, & World.

Lorenz, K. (1970). Companions as factors in the bird's environment. In R. Martin (Trans.), *Studies in animal and human behaviour* (Vol. 1, pp. 101–258). Cambridge, Mass.: Harvard University Press.

Lorenz, K., & Tinbergen, N. (1938). Taxis und Instinkthandlung in der Eirollbewegung der Graigrans. *Zeitschrift fur Tierpsychologie, 2,* 1–29.

Lovaas, O. I., Koegel, R., Simmons, J. Q., & Long, J. S. (1973). Some generalization and follow-up measures on autistic children in behavior therapy. *Journal of Applied Behavior Analysis, 6,* 131–166.

Lovaas, O. I., & Simmons, J. Q. (1969). Manipulation of self-destruction in three retarded children. *Journal of Applied Behavior Analysis, 2,* 143–157.

Lovitt, T. C., Guppy, T. E., & Blattner, J. E. (1969). The use of free-time contingency with fourth graders to increase spelling accuracy. *Behaviour Research and Therapy, 7,* 151–156.

Lubow, R. E., & Moore, A. U. (1959). Latent inhibition: The effect of nonreinforced preexposure to the conditioned stimulus. *Journal of Comparative and Physiological Psychology, 52,* 415–419.

Luchin, A. S. (1942). Mechanization in problem solving. *Psychological Monographs, 54,* Whole No. 248.

Luthans, F., Paul, R., & Baker, D. (1981). An experimental analysis of the impact of contingent reinforcement of sales persons performance behavior. *Journal of Applied Psychology, 66,* 314–323.

Lynch, G. (1986). *Synapses, circuits, and the beginnings of memory.* Cambridge: MIT Press.

Lynch, G., & Baudry, M. (1984) The biochemistry of memory: A new and specific hypothesis. *Science, 224,* 1057–1063.

Maas, J. W., Dekirmenjian, H., & Fawett, J. (1971). Catecholamine metabolism, depression and stress. *Nature, 230,* 330–331.

MacCorquodale, K., & Meehl, P. E. (1954) Edward C. Tolman. In W. K. Estes et al. (Eds.), *Modern learning theory* (pp. 177–266). New York: Appleton.

MacKinnon, J. R. (1968). Competing responses in a differential magnitude of reward discrimination. *Psychonomic Science, 12,* 333–334.

Mackintosh, N. J. (1975). A theory of attention: Variations in the associability of stimuli with reinforcement. *Psychological Review, 82,* 276–298.

Mackintosh, N. J. (1983). *Conditioning and associative learning.* Oxford: Oxford University Press.

Mackintosh, N. J., Bygrave, D. J., & Picton, D. M. B. (1977). Locus of the effect of a surprising reinforcer in the attenuation of blocking. *Quarterly Journal of Experimental Psychology, 29,* 327–336.

Mackintosh, N. J., Dickinson, A., & Cotton, M. M. (1980). Surprise and blocking: Effects of the number of compound trials. *Animal Learning and Behavior, 8,* 387–391.

Mackworth, J. F. (1963). The duration of the visual image. *Canadian Journal of Psychology, 17,* 62–81.

MacPherson, E. M., Candee, B. L., & Hohman, R. J. (1974). A comparison of three methods for eliminating disruptive lunchroom behavior. *Journal of Applied Behavior Analysis, 7,* 287–297.

Maddux, J. E., & Stanley, M. A. (1986). Self-efficacy theory in contemporary psychology: An overview. *Journal of Social and Clinical Psychology, 4,* 249–255.

Madigan, R. J. (1978). Reinforcement context effects on fixed-interval responding. *Animal Learning and Behavior, 6,* 193–197.

Madsen, C. H., Madsen, C. K., Saudargas, R. A., Hammond, W. R., & Edgar, D. E. (1970). Classroom RAID (Rules, Approval, Ignore, Disapproval): A cooperative approach for professionals and volunteers. *Journal of School Psychology, 8,* 180.

Maier, N. R. F. (1931). Reasoning in humans: II. The solution of a problem and its appearance in consciousness. *Journal of Comparative Psychology, 12,* 181–194.

Maier, N. R. F. (1949). *Frustration: The study of behavior without a goal.* New York: McGraw-Hill.

Maier, N. R. F., Glazer, N. M., & Klee, J. B. (1940). Studies of abnormal behavior in the rat: III. The development of behavior fixations through frustration. *Journal of Experimental Psychology, 26,* 521–546.

Maier, N. R. F., & Klee, J. B. (1945). Studies of abnormal behavior in the rat: XVII. Guidance versus trial and error in the alteration of habits and fixations. *Journal of Psychology, 19,* 133–163.

Maier, S. F., & Seligman, M. E. P. (1976). Learned helplessness: Theory and evidence. *Journal of Experimental Psychology: General, 105,* 3–46.

Malamut, B. L., Saunders, R. C., & Mishkin, M. (1984). Monkeys with combined amygdalo-lesions succeed in object discriminations learning despite 24-hour interval. *Behavioral Neuroscience, 98,* 759–769.

Maleske, R. T., & Frey, P. W. (1979). Blocking of eyelid conditioning: Effect of changing the CS-UCS interval and introducing an intertrial stimulus. *Animal Learning and Behavior, 7,* 452–456.

Malleson, N. (1959). Panic and phobia. *Lancet, 1,* 225–227.

Malmo, R. B. (1965). Finger sweat prints in differentiation of low and high incentive. *Psychophysiology, 1,* 231–240.

Margules, D. L. (1969). Noradrenergic rather than serotonergic basis of reward in dorsal tegmentum. *Journal of Comparative and Physiological Psychology, 67,* 25–32.

Margules, D. L., & Stein, L. (1967). Neuroleptics versus tranquilizers: Evidence from animal behavior studies of mode and site of action. In H. Brill et al. (Eds.), *Neuropsychopharmacology* (pp. 108–120). Amsterdam: Elsevier.

Margules, D. L., & Stein, L. (1969). Cholinergic synapses of a periventricular punishment system in the medial hypothalamus. *American Journal of Physiology, 217,* 475–480.

Marshall, W. L., Boutilier, J., & Minnes, P. (1974). The modification of phobic behavior by covert reinforcement. *Behavior Therapy, 5,* 469–480.

Martin, L. K., & Riess, D. (1969). Effects of US intensity during previous discrete delay conditioning on conditioned acceleration during avoidance extinction. *Journal of Comparative and Physiological Psychology, 69,* 196–200.

Marx, J. L. (1980). Ape-language controversy flares up. *Science, 207,* 1330–1333.

Masterson, F. A. (1969). Escape from noise. *Psychological Reports, 24,* 484–486.

Matzel, L. D., Brown, A. M., & Miller, R. R. (1987). Associative effects of US pre-exposure: Modulation of conditioned responding by an excitatory training context. *Journal of Experimental Psychology: Animal Behavior Processes, 13,* 65–72.

Matzel, L. D., Schachtman, T. R., & Miller, R. R. (1985). Recovery of an overshadowed association achieved by extinction of the overshadowing stimulus. *Learning and Motivation, 16,* 398–412.

Mayer, J. (1953). Genetic, traumatic, and environmental factors in the etiology of obesity. *Psychological Review, 33,* 472–508.

Mazur, J. E., & Wagner, A. R. (1982). An episodic model of associative learning. In M. Commons, R. Herrnstein, & A. R. Wagner (Eds.), *Quantitative analyses of behavior: Acquisition* (Vol. 3, pp. 3–39). Cambridge, Mass.: Ballinger.

McAllister, W. R., McAllister, D. E., & Douglass, W. K. (1971). The inverse relationship between shock intensity and shuttle-box avoidance learning in rats. *Journal of Comparative and Physiological Psychology, 74,* 426–433.

McCalden, M., & Davis, C. (1972). *Report on priority lane experiment on the San Francisco–Oakland Bay Bridge.* Sacramento, Calif.: Department of Public Works.

McCarron, L. R. (1973). Psychophysiological discriminants of reactive depression. *Psychophysiology, 10,* 223–230.

McCord, W., McCord, J., & Zola, I. K. (1959). *Origins of crime: A new evaluation of the Cambridge-Somerville Youth Study.* New York: Columbia University Press.

McGaugh, J. L., & Landfield, P. W. (1970). Delayed development of amnesia following electroconvulsive shock. *Physiology and Behavior, 5,* 1109–1113.

McGeoch, J. A. (1932). Forgetting and the law of disuse. *Psychological Review, 39,* 352–370.

McGuigan, F. J. (1966). Covert oral behavior and auditory hallucinations. *Psychophysiology, 3,* 73–80.

McGuire, R. J., & Vallance, M. (1964). Aversion therapy by electric shock, a simple technique. *British Medical Journal, 1,* 151–152.

McLaughlin, T. F., & Malaby, J. (1972). Intrinsic reinforcers in a classroom token economy. *Journal of Applied Behavior Analysis, 5,* 263–270.

McNeill, D. (1966). Developmental psycholinguistics. In F. Smith & G. A. Miller (Eds.), *The genesis of language* (pp. 15–84). Cambridge, Mass.: MIT Press.

Meichenbaum, D. H. (1972). Examination of model characteristics in reducing avoidance behavior. *Journal of Behavior Therapy and Experimental Psychiatry, 3,* 225–227.

Mellgren, R. L. (1972). Positive and negative contrast effects using delayed reinforcement. *Learning and Motivation, 3,* 185–193.

Melton, A. W. (1963). Implications of short-term memory for a general theory of memory. *Journal of Verbal Learning and Verbal Behavior, 2,* 1–21.

Melton, A. W., & Irwin, J. M. (1940). The influence of degree of interpolated learning on retroactive inhibition and the overt transfer of specific responses. *American Journal of Psychology, 53,* 173–203.

Mendelson, J. (1966). The role of hunger in T-maze learning for food by rats. *Journal of Comparative and Physiological Psychology, 62,* 341–353.

Mendelson, J. (1967). Lateral hypothalamic stimulation in satiated rats: The rewarding effects of self-induced drinking. *Science, 157,* 1077–1979.

Mendelson, J., & Chorover, S. L. (1965). Lateral hypothalamic stimulation in satiated rats: T-maze learning for food. *Science, 149,* 559–561.

Menzel, E. W. (1978). Cognitive mapping in chimpanzees. In S. H. Hulse, H. Fowler, & W. K Honig (Eds.), *Cognitive processes in animal behavior* (pp. 375–422). Hillsdale, N.J.: Erlbaum.

Metalsky, G. I., Abramson, L. Y, Seligman, M. E. P., Semmel, A., & Peterson, C. (1982). Attributional styles and life events in the classroom: Vulnerability and invulnerability to depressive mood reactions. *Journal of Personality and Social Psychology, 43,* 612–617.

Meyer, D. E., & Schvaneveldt, R. W. (1971). Facilitation in recognizing pairs of words: Evidence of a dependence between retrieval operations. *Journal of Experimental Psychology, 90,* 227–234.

Meyer, V., Robertson, J., & Tatlovy, A. (1975). Home treatment of an obsessive-compulsive disorder by response prevention. *Journal of Behavior Therapy and Experimental Psychiatry, 6,* 37–38.

Mikulka, P. J., Leard, B., & Klein, S. B. (1977). The effect of illness (US) exposure as a source of interference with the acquisition and retention of a taste aversion. *Journal of Experimental Psychology: Animal Behavior Processes, 3,* 189–210.

Milby, J. B. (1971). Delay of shock-escape with and without stimulus change. *Psychological Reports, 29,* 315–318.

Miles, R. C. (1956). The relative effectiveness of secondary reinforcers throughout deprivation and habit-strength parameters. *Journal of Comparative and Physiological Psychology, 49,* 126–130.

Miller, G. A. (1956). The magical number seven, plus or minus two: Some limits on our capacity for processing information. *Psychology Review, 63,* 81–97.

Miller, G. A. (1965). Some preliminaries to psycholinguistics. *American Psychologist, 20,* 15–20.

Miller, H. R., & Nawas, M. M. (1970). Control of aversive stimulus termination in systematic desensitization. *Behavior Research and Therapy, 8,* 57–61.

Miller, N. E. (1941). The frustration-aggression hypothesis. *Psychological Review, 48,* 337–342.

Miller, N. E. (1948). Studies of fear as an acquirable drive: I. Fear as motivation and fear-reduction as reinforcement in learning of new responses. *Journal of Experimental Psychology, 38,* 89–101.

Miller, N. E. (1951). Comments on multiple-process conceptions of learning. *Psychological Review, 58,* 375–381.

Miller, N. E. (1985). The value of behavioral research on animals. *American Psychologist, 40,* 423–440.

Miller, N. E., & Coons, E. E. (1955). Conflict versus consolidation of memory to explain "retrograde amnesia" produced by ECS. *American Psychologist, 10,* 394.

Miller, R. R., & Matzel, L. D. (1989). Contingency and relative associative strength. In S. B. Klein & R. R. Mowrer (Eds.), *Contemporary learning theories: Pavlovian conditioning and the status of traditional learning theory* (pp. 61–84). Hillsdale, N. J.: Erlbaum.

Miller, R. R., & Schachtman, T. R. (1985). Conditioning context as an associative baseline: Implications for response generation and the nature of conditioned inhibition. In R. R. Miller & N. E. Spear (Eds.), *Information processing in animals: Conditioned inhibition* (pp. 51–88). Hillsdale, N.J.: Erlbaum.

Miller, R. R., Small, D., & Berk, A. M. (1975). Information content of rat scotophobin. *Behavioral Biology, 15,* 463–472.

Miller, R. R., & Springer, A. D. (1973). Amnesia, consolidation and retrieval. *Psychological Review, 80,* 69–79.

Miller, W. R., & Seligman, M. E. P. (1973). Depression and the perception of reinforcement. *Journal of Abnormal Psychology, 82,* 62–73.

Miller, W. R., & Seligman, M. E. P. (1975). Depression and learned helplessness in man. *Journal of Abnormal Psychology, 84,* 228–238.

Mills, C. B. (1980). Effects of context on reaction time to phonemes. *Journal of Verbal Learning and Verbal Behavior, 19,* 75–83.

Milner, B. (1970). Memory and the temporal regions of the brain. In K. H. Pribram & D. E. Broadbent (Eds.), *Biology of memory* (pp. 29–50). New York: Academic.

Milvy, P. (Ed.). (1977). *The marathon: Physiological, medical, epidemiological, and psychological studies* (Annals, Vol. 301). New York: New York Academy of Sciences.

Mineka, S. (1979). The role of fear in theories of avoidance learning, flooding, and extinction. *Psychological Bulletin, 86,* 985–1010.

Mineka, S., Davidson, M., Cook, M., & Keir, R. (1984). Observational conditioning of snake fear in rhesus monkeys. *Journal of Abnormal Psychology, 93,* 355–372.

Mineka, S., & Gino, A. (1979). Dissociative effects of different types and amounts of non-reinforced CS exposure on avoidance extinction and the CER. *Learning and Motivation, 10,* 141–160.

Misanin, J. R., Miller, R. R., & Lewis, D. J. (1968). Retrograde amnesia produced by electroconvulsive shock after reactivation of a consolidated memory trace. *Science, 160,* 554–555.

Mischel, W., & Grusec, J. E. (1966). Determinants of the rehearsal and transmission of neutral and aversive behaviors. *Journal of Personality and Social Psychology, 3,* 197–205.

Miyawaki, K., Strange, W., Verbugge, R. R., Liberman, A. M., Jenkins, J. J., & Fujimura, O. (1975). An effect of linguistic experience: The discrimination of [r] and [l] by native speakers of Japanese and English. *Perception and Psychophysics, 18,* 331–340.

Moltz, H. (1960). Imprinting: Empirical basis and theoretical significance. *Psychological Bulletin, 57,* 291–314.

Moltz, H. (1963). Imprinting: An epigenetic approach. *Psychological Review, 70,* 123–138.

Montague, W. E., Adams, J. A., & Kiess, H. O. (1966). Forgetting and natural language mediation. *Journal of Experimental Psychology, 72,* 829–833.

Monti, P. M., & Smith, N. F. (1976). Residual fear of the conditioned stimulus as a function of response prevention after avoidance or classical defensive conditioning in the rat. *Journal of Experimental Psychology: General, 105,* 148–162.

Moore, J. W. (1972). Stimulus control: Studies of auditory generalization in rabbits. In A. H. Black & W. F. Prokasy (Eds.), *Classical conditioning II* (pp. 206–230). New York: Appleton-Century-Crofts.

Moray, N. (1959). Attention in dichotic listening: Affective cues and the influence of instructions. *Quarterly Journal of Experimental Psychology, 11,* 56–60.

Moray, N., Bates, A., & Barnett, R. (1965). Experiments on the four-eared man. *Journal of the Acoustical Society of America, 38,* 196–201.

Morgane, J. P. (1961). Alterations in feeding and drinking of rats with lesions in the globi pallidi. *American Journal of Physiology, 201,* 420–428.

Morrison, G. R., & Collyer, R. (1974). Taste-mediated conditioned aversion to an exteroceptive stimulus following LiCl poisoning. *Journal of Comparative and Physiological Psychology, 86,* 51–55.

Morrison, S. D. (1976). Control of food intake in cancer cachexia: A challenge and a tool. *Physiology and Behavior, 17,* 705–714.

Moscovitch, A., & LoLordo, V. M. (1968). Role of safety in the Pavlovian backward fear conditioning procedure. *Journal of Comparative and Physiological Psychology, 66,* 673–678.

Moskowitz, B. A. (1978). The acquisition of language. *Scientific American, 239,* 92–108.

Mowrer, O. H. (1938). Preparatory set (Expectancy): A determinant in motivation and learning. *Psychological Review, 45,* 62–91.

Mowrer, O. H. (1939). A stimulus-response analysis and its role as a reinforcing agent. *Psychological Review, 46,* 553–565.

Mowrer, O. H. (1947). On the dual nature of learning—A reinterpretation of "conditioning" and "problem solving." *Harvard Educational Review, 17,* 102–148.

Mowrer, O. H. (1956). Two-factor learning theory reconsidered, with special reference to secondary reinforcement and the concept of habit. *Psychological Review, 63,* 114–128.

Mowrer, O. H. (1960). *Learning theory and behavior.* New York: Wiley.

Mowrer, R. R., & Gordon, W. C. (1983). Cueing in an "irrelevant" context. *Animal Learning and Behavior, 11,* 401–406.

Mowrer, R. R., & Klein, S. B. (1989). Traditional learning theory and the transition to contemporary learning theory. In S. B. Klein & R. R. Mowrer (Eds.), *Contemporary learning theories: Pavlovian conditioning and the status of traditional learning theory* (pp. 1–17). Hillsdale, N. J.: Erlbaum.

Moyer, K. E., & Korn, J. H. (1964). Effects of UCS intensity on the acquisition and extinction of an avoidance response. *Journal of Experimental Psychology, 67,* 352–359.

Moyer, K. E., & Korn, J. H. (1966). Effect of UCS intensity on the acquisition and extinction of a one-way avoidance response. *Psychonomic Science, 4,* 121–122.

Murdock, B. B., Jr. (1961). The retention of individual items. *Journal of Experimental Psychology, 62,* 618–625.

Murdock, B. B., Jr. (1962). The serial position effect of free recall. *Journal of Experimental Psychology, 64,* 482–488.

Nation, J. R., & Boyajian, L. G. (1981). Continuous before partial reinforcement. Resistance to extinction in humans. *American Journal of Psychology, 93,* 605–617.

Naus, M. J., & Halasz, F. G. (1979). Developmental perspectives on cognitive processing and semantic memory. In L. S. Cermak & F. I. M. Craik (Eds.), *Levels of processing in human memory* (pp. 259–288). Hillsdale, N.J.: Erlbaum.

Neeley, J. H., & Wagner, A. R. (1974). Attenuation of blocking with shifts in reward: The involvement of schedule-generated contextual cues. *Journal of Experimental Psychology, 102,* 751–763.

Neisser, U. (1967). *Cognitive psychology.* New York: Appleton-Century-Crofts.

Nelson v. *Heyne,* 491 F.2d 352 (1974).

Nevin, J. A. (1973). The maintenance of behavior. In J. A. Nevin (Ed.), *The study of behavior: Learning, motivation, emotion, and instinct* (pp. 201–236). Glenview, Ill.: Scott, Foresman.

Newport, E. L. (1977). Motherese: The speech of mothers to young children. In N. Castellan, D. P. Pisoni, & G. Potts (Eds.), *Cognitive theory* (Vol. 2). Hillsdale, N.J.: Erlbaum.

Nisbett, R. E., & Ross, L. (1980). *Human inference: Strategies and shortcomings of social judgment.* Englewood Cliffs, N.J.: Prentice-Hall.

Nissen, H. W. (1951). Analysis of a complex conditional reaction in chimpanzee. *Journal of Comparative and Physiological Psychology, 44,* 9–16.

Noble, C. E. (1966). S-O-R and the psychology of human learning. *Psychological Reports, 18,* 923–943.

Noble, M., & Harding, G. E. (1963). Conditioning of rhesus monkeys as a function of the interval between CS and US. *Journal of Comparative and Physiological Psychology, 56,* 220–224.

Norman, D. A. (1976). *Memory and attention* (2d ed.). New York: Wiley.

O'Hara, K., Johnson, C. M., & Beehr, T. A. (1985). Organizational behavioral management: A review of empirical research and recommendations for further investigations. *Academy of Management Review, 10,* 848–864.

O'Keefe, J., & Nadel, L. (1978). *The hippocampus as a cognitive map.* Oxford: Oxford University Press.

Olds, J. (1962). Hypothalamic substrates of reward. *Psychological Review, 42,* 554–604.

Olds, J., & Milner, P. (1954). Positive reinforcement produced by electrical stimulation of septal area and other regions of rat brain. *Journal of Comparative and Physiological Psychology, 47,* 419–427.

Olds, M. E. (1975). Effects of intraventricular 6-hydroxydopamine and replacement therapy with norepinephrine, dopamine and serotonin on self-stimulation in the diencephalic and mesencephalic regions in the rat brain. *Brain Research, 98,* 327–342.

Olton, D. S. (1978). Characteristics of spatial memory. In S. H. Hulse, H. Fowler, & W. K. Honig (Eds.), *Cognitive processes in animal behavior* (pp. 341–374). Hillsdale, N.J.: Erlbaum.

Olton, D. S. (1979). Mazes, maps and memory. *American Psychologist, 34,* 583–596.

Olton, D. S., Collison, C., & Werz, M.A. (1977). Spatial memory and radial arm maze performance of rats. *Learning and Motivation, 8,* 289–314.

Olton, D. S., & Samuelson, R. J. (1976). Remembrance of places passed: Spatial memory in rats. *Journal of Experimental Psychology: Animal Behavior Processes, 2,* 97–116.

Osborne, S. R. (1978). A quantitative analysis of the effects of amount of reinforcement on two response classes. *Journal of Experimental Psychology: Animal Behavior Processes, 4,* 297–317.

Overmier, J. B., & Seligman, M. E. P. (1967). Effects of inescapable shock upon subsequent escape and avoidance learning. *Journal of Comparative and Physiological Psychology, 63,* 28–33.

Overton, D. A. (1964). State dependent or "dissociated" learning produced with pentobarbital. *Journal of Comparative and Physiological Psychology, 57,* 3–12.

Overton, D. A. (1971). Discriminative control of behavior by drug states. In T. Thompson & R. Pickens (Eds.), *Stimulus properties of drugs* (pp. 87–110). New York: Appleton-Century-Crofts.

Padilla, A. M. (1973). Effects of prior and interpolated shock exposures on subsequent avoidance learning by goldfish. *Psychological Reports, 32,* 451–456.

Paivio, A. (1969). Mental imagery in associative learning and memory. *Psychological Review, 76,* 241–263.

Paivio, A. (1986). *Mental representations: A dual coding approach.* New York: Oxford University Press.

Paivio, A., Yuille, J. C., & Madigan, S. A. (1968). Concreteness, imagery, and meaningfulness values for 925 nouns. *Journal of Experimental Psychology Monograph Supplement, 76,* 1 (Pt. 2).

Paletta, M. S., & Wagner, A. R. (1986). Development of context-specific tolerance to morphine: Support for a dual-process interpretation. *Behavioral Neuroscience, 100,* 611–623.

Palmerino, C. C., Rusiniak, D. W., & Garcia, J. (1980). Flavor-illness aversions: The peculiar roles of odor and taste in memory for poison. *Science, 208,* 753–755.

Parke, R. D., & Deur, J. L. (1972). Schedule of punishment and inhibition of aggression in children. *Developmental Psychology, 7,* 266–269.

Parke, R. D., & Walters, R. H. (1967). Some factors determining the efficacy of punishment for inducing response inhibition. *Monograph of the Society for Research in Child Development, 32* (Whole No. 19).

Pate, J. L., & Rumbaugh, D. M. (1983). The language-like behavior of Lana Chimpanzee: Is it merely discrimination learning and paired-associate learning? *Animal Learning and Behavior, 11,* 134–138.

Patterson, F. G. (1978). Conversations with a gorilla. *National Geographic, 154,* 438–465.

Patterson, F. G. (1981). Ape language. *Science, 211,* 86–87.

Paul, G. L. (1969). Behavior modification research: Design and tactics. In C. M. Franks (Ed.), *Behavior therapy: Appraisal and status* (pp. 29–62). New York: McGraw-Hill.

Paul, G. P., & Lentz, R. J. (1977). *Psychosocial treatment of chronic mental patients: (Milieu vs. social learning programs).* Cambridge, Mass.: Harvard University Press.

Paulson, K., Rimm, D. C., Woodburn, L. T., & Rimm, S. A. (1977). A self-control approach to inefficient spending. *Journal of Consulting and Clinical Psychology, 45,* 433–435.

Pavlov, I. (1927). *Conditioned reflexes.* Oxford: Oxford University Press.

Pavlov, I. (1928). *Lectures on conditioned reflexes: The higher nervous activity of animals* (Vol. 1), H. Gantt (Trans.). London: Lawrence and Wishart.

Payne, J. W. (1976). Task complexity and contingent processing in decision making: An information search and protocol analysis. *Organizational Behavior and Human Performance, 16,* 366–387.

Pearce, J. M., Kaye, H., & Hall, G. (1982). Predictive accuracy and stimulus associability: Development of a model for Pavlovian learning. In M. L. Commons, R. J. Herrnstein, & A. R. Wagner (Eds.), *Quantitative analyses of behavior* (Vol. III, pp. 241–255). Cambridge, Mass.: Ballinger.

Pearce, J. M., Nicholas, D. J., & Dickinson, A. (1981). The potentiation effect during serial conditioning. *Quarterly Journal of Experimental Psychology, 33,* 159–179.

Penfield, W. W., & Mathieson, G. (1974). Memory: Autopsy findings and comments on the role of hippocampus in experiential recall. *Archives of Neurology (Chicago), 31,* 145–154.

Penfield, W. W., & Milner, B. (1958). Memory deficit produced by bilateral lesions in the hippocampal zone. *AMA Archives of Neurology and Psychiatry, 79,* 475–497.

Penney, R. K. (1967). Children's escape performance as a function of schedules of delay of reinforcement. *Journal of Experimental Psychology, 73,* 109–112.

Penney, R. K., & Kirwin, P. M. (1965). Differential adaptation of anxious and nonanxious children in instrumental escape conditioning. *Journal of Experimental Psychology, 70,* 539–549.

Perin, C. T. (1942). Behavior potentiality as a joint function of the amount of training and the degree of hunger at the time of extinction. *Journal of Experimental Psychology, 30,* 93–113.

Perin, C. T. (1943). A quantitative investigation of the delay-of-reinforcement gradient. *Journal of Experimental Psychology, 32,* 37–51.

Peterson, C., & Seligman, M. E. P. (1984). Causal explanations as a risk factor in depression: Theory and evidence. *Psychological Review, 91,* 347–374.

Peterson, L. R., & Peterson, M. J. (1959). Short-term retention of individual verbal items. *Journal of Experimental Psychology, 58,* 193–198.

Peterson, N. (1962). Effect of monochromatic rearing on the control of responding by wavelength. *Science, 136,* 774–775.

Peterson, R. F., & Peterson, L. R. (1968). The use of positive reinforcement in the control of self-destructive behavior in a retarded boy. *Journal of Experimental Child Psychology, 6,* 351–360.

Piliavin, I. M., Piliavin, J. A., & Rodin, J. (1975). Costs, diffusion, and the stigmatized victim. *Journal of Personality and Social Psychology, 32,* 429–438.

Piliavin, J. A., Dovidio, J. F., Gaertner, S. L., & Clark, R. D., III, (1981). Responsive bystanders: The process of intervention. In J. Grzelak & V. Derlega (Eds.), *Living with other people: Theory and research on cooperation and helping.* New York: Academic.

Plotnick, R., Mir, D., & Delgado, J. M. R. (1971). Aggression, noxiousness and brain stimulation in unrestrained rhesus monkeys. In B. E. Eleftheriou & J. P. Scott (Eds.), *The physiology of aggression and defeat.* New York: Plenum.

Plummer, S., Baer, D. M., & LeBlanc, J. M. (1977). Functional considerations in the use of procedural time out and an effective alternative. *Journal of Applied Behavior Analysis, 10,* 689–706.

Pollack, I. (1952). The information in elementary auditory displays. *Journal of the Acoustical Society of America, 24,* 745–749.

Pollack, I. (1953). The information in elementary auditory displays II. *Journal of the Acoustical Society of America, 25,* 765–769.

Poon, L. W. (1980). A system approach for the assessment and treatment of memory problems. In J. W. Ferguson & C. B. Taylor (Eds.), *The comprehensive handbook of behavioral medicine* (Vol. 1). New York: SP Medical and Scientific Books.

Postman, L. (1967). *Mechanisms of interference in forgetting.* Vice-presidential address given at the annual meeting of the American Association for Advancement of Science, New York.

Postman, L., & Phillips, L. (1965). Short-term temporal changes in free recall. *Quarterly Journal of Experimental Psychology, 17,* 132–138.

Postman, L., & Riley, D. A. (1959). Degree of learning and interserial interference in retention: A review of the literature and an experimental analysis. *University of California Publications in Psychology, 8,* 271–396.

Postman, L., Stark, K., & Fraser, J. (1968). Temporal changes in interference. *Journal of Verbal Learning and Verbal Behavior, 7,* 672–694.

Powell, J., & Azrin, N. (1968). The effects of shock as a punisher for cigarette smoking. *Journal of Applied Behavior Analysis, 1,* 63–71.

Powley, R. L. (1977). The ventromedial hypothalamic syndrome, satiety, and a cephalic phase hypothesis. *Psychological Review, 84,* 89–126.

Premack, A. J., & Premack, D. (1972). Teaching language to an ape. *Scientific American, 227,* 92–99.

Premack, D. (1959). Toward empirical behavior laws: I. Positive reinforcement. *Psychological Review, 66,* 219–233.

Premack, D. (1965). Reinforcement theory. In D. Levine, (Ed.), *Nebraska symposium on motivation* (pp. 123–180). Lincoln: University of Nebraska.

Premack, D. (1976). *Intelligence in ape and man.* Hillsdale, N.J.: Erlbaum.

Prescott, R. G. W. (1966). Estrous cycle in the rat: Effects on self-stimulation behavior. *Science, 152,* 796–797.

Prewitt, E. P. (1967). Number of preconditioning trials in sensory preconditioning using CER training. *Journal of Comparative and Physiological Psychology, 64,* 360–362.

Prochaska, J., Smith, N., Marzilli, R., Colby, J., & Donovan, W. (1974). Remote-control aversive stimulation in the treatment of head-banging in a retarded child. *Journal of Behavior Therapy and Experimental Psychiatry, 5,* 285–289.

Prokasy, W. F., Jr., Grant, D. A., & Myers, N. A. (1958). Eyelid conditioning as a function of unconditioned stimulus intensity and intertrial interval. *Journal of Experimental Psychology, 55,* 242–246.

Prokasy, W. F., Jr., & Hall, J. F. (1963). Primary stimulus generalization. *Psychological Review, 70,* 310–322.

Pubols, B. H., Jr. (1960). Incentive magnitude, learning and performance in animals. *Psychological Bulletin, 51,* 89–115.

Quartermain, D. (1976). The influence of drugs on learning and memory. In M. R. Rosenzweig & E. L. Bennet (Eds.), *Neural mechanisms of learning and memory* (pp. 508–518). Cambridge, Mass.: MIT Press.

Quartermain, D., Paolino, R. M., & Miller, N. E. (1965). A brief temporal gradient of retrograde amnesia independent of situational change. *Science, 149,* 1116–1118.

Rachlin, H., & Burkhard, B. (1978). The temporal triangle: Response substitution in instrumental conditioning. *Psychology Review, 85,* 22–47.

Rackham, D. (1971). *Conditioning of the pigeon's courtship and aggressive behavior.* Master's thesis, Dalhousie University, Halifax, Nova Scotia. Cited in E. Hearst & H. M. Jenkins. *Sign-tracking: The stimulus-reinforcer relation and directed action.* Austin, Tex.: The Psychonomic Society, 1974.

Randich, A., & LoLordo, V. M. (1979). Preconditioning exposure to the unconditioned stimulus affects the acquisition of a conditioned emotional response. *Learning and Motivation, 10,* 245–275.

Randich, A., & Ross, R. T. (1985). Contextual stimuli mediate the effects of pre- and postexposure to the unconditioned stimulus on conditioned suppression. In P. D. Balsam & A. Tomie (Eds.), *Context and learning* (pp. 105–132). Hillsdale, N.J.: Erlbaum.

Ransmeier, R. E. (1953). *The effects of convulsion, hypoxia, hypothermia, and anesthesia on retention in the master.* Unpublished doctoral dissertation, University of Chicago.

Rapport, M. D., & Bostow, D. E. (1976). The effects of access to special activities on the performance in four categories of academic tasks with third-grade students. *Journal of Applied Behavior Analysis, 9,* 372.

Rashotte, M. E., & Amsel, A. (1968). Transfer of slow-response rituals to extinction of a continuously rewarded response. *Journal of Comparative and Physiological Psychology, 66,* 432–433.

Razran, G. H. S. (1949). Stimulus generalization of conditioned responses. *Psychological Bulletin, 46,* 337–365.

Reber, A. S., Kassin, S. M., Lewis, S., & Cantor, B. (1980). On the relationship between implicit and explicit modes in the learning of a complex rule structure. *Journal of Experimental Psychology: Human Learning and Memory, 6,* 492–502.

Redd, W. H., Morris, E. K., & Martin, J. A. (1975). Effects of positive and negative adult-child interactions on children's social preference. *Journal of Behavior Therapy and Experimental Psychiatry, 19,* 153–164.

Rehm, L. P. (1977). A self-control model of depression. *Behavior Therapy, 8,* 787–804.

Reichle, J., Brubakken, D., & Tetrault, G. (1976). Eliminating perseverative speech by positive reinforcement and time-out in a psychotic child. *Journal of Behavior Therapy and Experimental Psychiatry, 1,* 179–183.

Reisinger, J. J. (1972). The treatment of "anxiety-depression" via positive reinforcement and response cost. *Journal of Applied Behavior Analysis, 5,* 125–130.

Reitman, W. R. (1965). *Cognition and thought: An information processing approach.* New York: Wiley.

Renner, K. E., & Tinsley, J. B. (1976). Self-punitive behavior. In G. Bower (Ed.), *The psychology of learning and motivation* (Vol. 10, pp. 156–198). New York: Academic.

Rensch, B., & Ducker, G. (1966). Verzogerung des Vergessens erlernter visuellen Aufgaben bei Tieren durch Chlorpromazin. *Pfluegers Archiv Fur die Gesamte Physiologie des Menschen und der Tiere, 289,* 200–214.

Rescorla, R. A. (1968). Probability of shock in presence and absence of CS in fear conditioning. *Journal of Comparative and Physiological Psychology, 66,* 1–5.

Rescorla, R. A. (1969). Pavlovian conditioned inhibition. *Psychological Bulletin, 72,* 77–94.

Rescorla, R. A. (1971). Summation and retardation tests of latent inhibition. *Journal of Comparative and Physiological Psychology, 75,* 77–81.

Rescorla, R. A. (1973). Effects of US habituation following conditioning. *Journal of Comparative and Physiological Psychology, 82,* 137–143.

Rescorla, R. A. (1974). Effect of inflation of the unconditioned stimulus value following conditioning. *Journal of Comparative and Physiological Psychology, 86,* 101–106.

Rescorla, R. A. (1978). Some implications of a cognitive perspective on Pavlovian conditioning. In S. H. Hulse, H. Fowler, & W. K. Honig (Eds.), *Cognitive processes in animal behavior* (pp. 15–50). Hillsdale, N.J.: Erlbaum.

Rescorla, R. A. (1981). Simultaneous associations. In P. Harzum & M. D. Zeiler (Eds.), *Predictability, correlation and contiguity* (pp. 47–80). New York: Wiley.

Rescorla, R. A. (1982). Effect of a stimulus intervening between CS and US in autoshaping. *Journal of Experimental Psychology: Animal Behavior Processes, 8,* 131–141.

Rescorla, R. A. (1985). Conditioned inhibition and facilitation. In R. R. Miller & N. E. Spear (Eds.), *Information processing in animals: Conditioned inhibition.* Hillsdale, N.J.: Erlbaum.

Rescorla, R. A., & Cunningham, C. L. (1978). Within-compound flavor associations. *Journal of Experimental Psychology: Animal Behavior Processes, 4,* 267–275.

Rescorla, R. A., & Durlach, P. J. (1981). Within-event learning in Pavlovian conditioning. In N. E. Spear & R. R. Miller (Eds.), *Information processing in animals: Memory mechanisms* (pp. 81–112). Hillsdale, N.J.: Erlbaum.

Rescorla, R. A., Durlach, P. J., & Grau, J. W. (1985). Contextual learning in Pavlovian conditioning. In P. D. Balsam & A. Tomie (Eds.), *Context and learning* (pp. 23–56). Hillsdale, N. J.: Erlbaum.

Rescorla, R. A., & Holland, P. C. (1982). Behavioral studies of associative learning in animals. *Annual Review of Psychology, 33,* 265–308.

Rescorla, R. A., & LoLordo, V. M. (1965). Inhibition of avoidance behavior. *Journal of Comparative and Physiological Psychology, 59,* 406–412.

Rescorla, R. A., & Skucy, J. C. (1969). Effect of response-independent reinforcers during extinction. *Journal of Comparative and Physiological Psychology, 67,* 381–389.

Rescorla, R. A., & Solomon, R. L. (1967). Two-process learning theory: Relations between Pavlovian conditioning and instrumental learning. *Psychological Review, 74,* 151–182.

Rescorla, R. A., & Wagner, A. R. (1972). A theory of Pavlovian conditioning: Variations in the effectiveness of reinforcement and non-reinforcement. In A. H. Black & W. F. Prokasy (Eds.), *Classical conditioning II* (pp. 64–99). New York: Appleton-Century-Crofts.

Revusky, S. (1971). The role of interference in association over a delay. In W. K. Honig & P. H. R. James (Eds.), *Animal memory* (pp. 155–214). New York: Academic.

Revusky, S. (1977). The concurrent interference approach to delay learning. In L. M. Barker, M. R. Best, & M. Domjan (Eds.), *Learning mechanisms in food selection* (pp. 319–363). Waco, Tex.: Baylor University Press.

Revusky, S., & Bedarf, E. W. (1967). Association of illness with prior ingestion of novel foods. *Science, 155,* 219–220.

Revusky, S., & Parker, L. A. (1976). Aversions to drinking out of a cup and to unflavored water produced by delayed sickness. *Journal of Experimental Psychology: Animal Behavior Processes, 2,* 342–353.

Reynolds, G. S. (1961a). Behavioral contrast. *Journal of the Experimental Analysis of Behavior, 4,* 57–71.

Reynolds, G. S. (1961b). Attention in the pigeon. *Journal of the Experimental Analysis of Behavior, 4,* 203–208.

Reynolds, G. S. (1961c). An analysis of interactions in a multiple schedule. *Journal of the Experimental Analysis of Behavior, 4,* 107–117.

Reynolds, W. F., & Pavlik, W. B. (1960). Running speed as a function of deprivation period and reward magnitude. *Journal of Comparative and Physiological Psychology, 53,* 615–618.

Riccio, D. C., & Haroutunian, V. (1977). Failure to learn in a taste aversion paradigm: Associative or performance deficit? *Bulletin of the Psychonomic Society, 10,* 219–222.

Richards, R. W., & Rilling, M. (1972). Aversive aspects of a fixed-interval schedule of food reinforcement. *Journal of the Experimental Analysis of Behavior, 71,* 405–411.

Ridgers, A., & Gray, J. A. (1973). Influence of amylobarbitone on operant depression and elation effects in the rat. *Pychopharmacologia, 32,* 265–270.

Riley, A. L., Lotter, E. C., & Kulkosky, P. J. (1979). The effects of conditioned taste aversions on the acquisition and maintenance of schedule-induced polydipsia. *Animal Learning and Behavior, 7,* 3–12.

Riley, A. L., & Wetherington, C. L. (1989). Schedule-induced polydipsia: Is the rat a small furry human? (An analysis of an animal model of alcoholism). In S. B. Klein &

R. R. Mowrer (Eds.), *Contemporary learning theories: Instrumental conditioning theory and the impact of biological constraints on learning* (pp. 205–233). Hillsdale, N.J.: Erlbaum.

Riley, A. L., Wetherington, C. L., Wachsman, A. M., Fishman, H. S., & Kautz, M. A. (1988). The effects of conditioned taste aversions on schedule-induced polydipsia: An analysis of the initiation and post-pellet temporal distribution of licking. *Animal Learning and Behavior, 16,* 292–298.

Rimm, D. C., & Mahoney, M. J. (1969). The application of reinforcement and participant modeling procedures in the treatment of snake-phobic behavior. *Behavior Research and Therapy, 7,* 369–376.

Rimm, D. C., & Masters, J. C. (1979). *Behavior therapy.* New York: Academic.

Rips, L. J., Shoben, E. J., & Smith, E. E. (1973). Semantic distance and the verification of semantic relationships. *Journal of Verbal Learning and Verbal Behavior, 12,* 1–20.

Risley, T. R. (1968). The effects and side effects of punishing the autistic behaviors of a deviant child. *Journal of Applied Behavior Analysis, 1,* 21–34.

Ritter, B. (1969). The use of contact desensitization, demonstration-plus-participation, and demonstration alone in the treatment of acrophobia. *Behavior Research and Therapy, 7,* 157–164.

Rizley, R. C. (1978). Depression and distortion in the attribution of causality. *Journal of Abnormal Psychology, 87,* 32–48.

Rizley, R. C., & Rescorla, R. A. (1972). Associations in higher order conditioning and sensory preconditioning. *Journal of Comparative and Physiological Psychology, 81,* 1–11.

Roberts, W. A., & Grant, D. S. (1978). An analysis of light-induced retroactive inhibition of pigeon short-term memory. *Journal of Experimental Psychology: Animal Behavior Processes, 4,* 219–236.

Robins, C. J. (1988). Attributions and depression. Why is the literature so inconsistent? *Journal of Personality and Social Psychology, 54,* 880–889.

Robinson, N. M., & Robinson, H. B. (1961). A method for the study of instrumental avoidance conditioning with children. *Journal of Comparative and Physiological Psychology, 54,* 20–23.

Roediger, H. L., III. (1980). Memory metaphors in cognitive psychology. *Memory and Cognition, 8,* 231–246.

Roitblat, H. L. (1980). Codes and coding processes in pigeon short-term memory. *Animal Learning and Behavior, 8,* 341–351.

Roitblat, H. L., Bever, T. G., & Terrace, H. S. (Eds.). (1984). *Animal cognition.* Hillsdale, N.J.: Erlbaum.

Rosch, E. (1973). On the internal structure of perceptual and semantic categories. In T. E. Moore (Ed.), *Cognitive development and the acquisition of language* (pp. 111–144). New York: Academic.

Rosch, E. (1975). Cognitive representations of semantic categories. *Journal of Experimental Psychology: General, 104,* 192–253.

Rosch, E. (1978). Principles of categorization. In E. Rosch & B. Lloyd (Eds.), *Cognition and categorization* (pp. 28–48). Hillsdale, N.J.: Erlbaum.

Rosch, E. & Mervis, C. B. (1978). Family resemblances: Studies in the internal structure of categories. *Cognitive Psychology, 7,* 573–605.

Rosellini, R. A., & Seligman, M. E. P. (1975). Learned helplessness and escape from frustration. *Journal of Experimental Psychology: Animal Behavior Processes, 1,* 149–158.

Rosenblatt, F. (1967). Recent work on theoretical models of biological memory. In J. Tou (Ed.), *Computer and information sciences* (Vol. 2). New York: Academic.

Rosenzweig, M. R. (1984). Experience, memory, and the brain. *American Psychologist, 39,* 365–376.

Rosenzweig, M. R., & Bennett, E. L. (Eds.). (1976). *Neural mechanisms of learning and memory.* Cambridge, Mass.: MIT Press.

Ross, L. E., Hetherington, M., & Wray, N. P. (1965). Delay of reward and the learning of a size problem by normal and retarded children. *Child Development, 36,* 509–517.

Ross, R. R. (1964). Positive and negative partial reinforcement effects carried through continuous reinforcement, changed motivation, and changed response. *Journal of Experimental Psychology, 68,* 492–592.

Roth, E. M., & Shoben, E. E. (1983). The effect of context on the structure of categories. *Cognitive Psychology, 15,* 346–379.

Roth, S., & Kubal, L. (1975). The effects of noncontingent reinforcement on tasks of differing importance: Facilitation and learned helplessness effects. *Journal of Personality and Social Psychology, 32,* 680–691.

Rotter, J. B. (1954). *Social learning and clinical psychology.* Englewood Cliffs, N.J.: Prentice-Hall.

Rotter, J. B. (1966). Generalized expectancies for internal versus external control of reinforcement. *Psychological Monographs, 80* (Whole No. 609).

Routtenberg, A., & Lindy, J. (1965). Effects of the availability of rewarding septal and hypothalamic stimulation on bar-pressing for food under conditions of deprivation. *Journal of Comparative and Physiological Psychology, 60,* 158–161.

Rovee-Collier, C. K., & Capatides, J. B. (1979). Positive behavioral contrast in 3-month-old infants on multiple conjugate reinforcement schedules. *Journal of the Experimental Analysis of Behavior, 32,* 15–27.

Rozin, P. (1977). The significance of learning mechanisms in food selection: Some biology, psychology, and sociology of science. In L. M. Barker, M. R. Best, & M. Domjan (Eds.), *Learning mechanisms in food selection* (pp. 557–589). Waco, Tex.: Baylor University Press.

Rozin, P., & Schull, J. (1987). The adaptive-evolutionary point of view in experimental psychology. In R. C. Atkinson, R. J. Herrnstein, G. Lindzey, & R. D. Luce (Eds.), *Handbook of experimental psychology* (pp. 503–546). New York: Wiley-Interscience.

Rudy, J. W., & Cheatle, M. D. (1977). Odor-aversion learning in neonatal rats. *Science, 198,* 845–846.

Rumbaugh, D. M., & Gill, R. V. (1976). The mastery of language-type skills by the chimpanzee (Pan). *Annals of the New York Academy of Sciences, 280,* 562–578.

Rumelhart, D. E., McClelland, J. L., & The PDP Research Group. (1986). *Parallel distributed processing: Explorations in the microstructure of cognition: Vol. 1. Foundations.* Cambridge, Mass.: Bradford Books/MIT Press.

Rundus, D. (1971). Analysis of rehearsal processes in free recall. *Journal of Experimental Psychology, 89,* 63–77.

Rundus, D., & Atkinson, R. C. (1970). Rehearsal processes in free recall: A procedure for direct observation. *Journal of Verbal Learning and Verbal Behavior, 9,* 99–105.

Runquist, W. N. (1957). Retention of verbal associates as function of strength. *Journal of Experimental Psychology, 54,* 369–375.

Rusiniak, K. W., Palmerino, C. C., & Garcia, J. (1982). Potentiation of odor by taste in rats: Tests of some nonassociative factors. *Journal of Comparative and Physiological Psychology, 96,* 775–780.

Russell, R. K., & Sipich, J. F. (1973). Cue-controlled relaxation in the treatment of test anxiety. *Journal of Behavior Therapy and Experimental Psychiatry, 4*, 47–49.

Samuel, A. L. (1963). Some studies in machine learning using the game of checkers. In E. A. Feigenbaum & J. Feldman (Eds.), *Computers and thought* (pp. 71–105). New York: McGraw-Hill.

Sand, L. I., & Biglan, A. (1974). Operant treatment of a case of recurrent abdominal pain in a 10-year-old boy. *Behavior Therapy, 5*, 677–681.

Sanger, D. J. (1986). Drug taking as adjunctive behavior. In S. R. Goldberg & I. P. Stolerman (Eds.), *Behavioral analysis of drug dependence* (pp. 123–160). New York: Academic.

Savage-Rumbaugh, E. S. (1986). *Ape language: From conditioned response to symbol.* New York: Columbia University Press.

Savage-Rumbaugh, E. S., Rumbaugh, D. M., & Boysen, S. (1980). Do apes use language? *American Scientist, 68*, 49–61.

Schaefer, H. H., & Martin, P. L. (1969). *Behavior therapy.* New York: McGraw-Hill.

Schaffer, H. R., & Emerson, P. E. (1964). The development of social attachments in infancy. *Monographs Social Research in Child Development, 29*, 1–77.

Schleidt, W. (1961). Reaktionen von Truthuhnern auf fliegende Rauvogel and Versuche zur Analyse inhrer AAM's. *Zeitschrift fur Tierpsychologie, 18*, 534–560.

Schneider, B. A. (1969). A two-state analysis of fixed-interval responding in the pigeon. *Journal of the Experimental Analysis of Behavior, 12*, 677–687.

Schneider, W., & Shiffrin, R. M. (1977). Controlled and automatic human information processing: I. Detection, search, and attention. *Psychological Review, 84*, 1–66.

Schooler, J. W., Gerhard, D., & Loftus, E. F. (1986). Qualities of the unreal. *Journal of Experimental Psychology: Learning, Memory, and Cognition, 12*, 171–181.

Schoonard, J., & Lawrence, D. H. (1962). Resistance to extinction as a function of the number of delay of reward trials. *Psychological Reports, 11*, 275–278.

Schoorman, F. D. (1988). Escalation bias in performance appraisals. An unintended consequence of supervisor participation in hiring decisions. *Journal of Applied Psychology, 73*, 58–62.

Schubot, E. D. (1966). *The influence of hypnotic and muscular relaxation in systematic desensitization.* Unpublished doctoral dissertation, Stanford University, California.

Schulman, A. H., Hale, E. B., & Graves, H. B. (1970). Visual stimulus characteristics of initial approach response in chicks *(Gallus domesticus). Animal Behavior, 18*, 461–466.

Schuster, C. R., & Woods, J. H. (1966). Schedule-induced polydipsia in the rhesus monkey. *Psychological Reports, 19*, 823–828.

Schuster, R., & Rachlin, H. (1968). Indifference between punishment and free shock: Evidence for the negative law of effect. *Journal of the Experimental Analysis of Behavior, 11*, 777–786.

Schwartz, B. (1989). *The psychology of learning and behavior* (3d ed.). New York: Norton.

Schweitzer, L., & Green, L. (1982). Reevaluation of things past: A test of the "retrospective hypothesis" using a CER procedure with rats. *Pavlovian Journal of Biological Science, 17*, 62–68.

Schwitzgebel, R. L., & Schwitzgebel, R. K. (1980). *Law and psychological practice.* New York: Wiley.

Scoville, W. B. (1954). The limbic lobe in man. *Journal of Neurosurgery, 11*, 64–66.

Scoville, W. B., & Milner, B. (1957). Loss of recent memory after bilateral hippocampal lesions. *Journal of Neurology, Neurosurgery and Psychiatry, 20,* 11–21.

Sears, R. R., Maccoby, E. E., & Levin, H. (1957). *Patterns of child rearing.* Evanston, Ill.: Row Peterson.

Seaver, W. B., & Patterson, A. H. (1976). Decreasing fuel-oil consumption through feedback and social commendation. *Journal of Applied Behavior Analysis, 9,* 147–152.

Seligman, M. E. P. (1970). On the generality of laws of learning. *Psychological Review, 77,* 406–418.

Seligman, M. E. P. (1975). *Helplessness: On depression, development, and death.* San Francisco: Freeman.

Seligman, M. E. P., & Campbell, B. A. (1965). Effects of intensity and duration of punishment on extinction of an avoidance response. *Journal of Comparative and Physiological Psychology, 59,* 295–297.

Seligman, M. E. P., & Johnston, J. C. (1973). A cognitive theory of avoidance learning. In F. J. McGuigan & D. B. Lumsden (Eds.), *Contemporary approaches to conditioning and learning* (pp. 69–110). Washington, D.C.: V. H. Winston.

Seligman, M. E. P., & Maier, S. F. (1967). Failure to escape traumatic shock. *Journal of Experimental Psychology, 74,* 1–9.

Seligman, M. E. P., Rosellini, R. A., & Kozak, M. (1975). Learned helplessness in the rat: Reversibility, time course, and immunization. *Journal of Comparative and Physiological Psychology, 88,* 542–547.

Seligman, M. E. P., & Schulman, P. (1986). Explanatory style as a predictor of productivity and quitting among life insurance agents. *Journal of Personality and Social Psychology, 50,* 832–838.

Sem-Jacobson, C. W. (1968). *Depth-electrographic stimulation of the human brain and behavior: From fourteen years of studies and treatment of Parkinson's disease and mental disorders with implanted electrodes.* Springfield, Ill.: Thomas.

Senkowski, P. C. (1978). Variables affecting the overtraining extinction effect in discrete-trial lever pressing. *Journal of Experimental Psychology: Animal Behavior Processes, 4,* 131–143.

Seward, J. P., & Humphrey, G. L. (1967). Avoidance learning as a function of pretraining in the cat. *Journal of Comparative and Physiological Psychology, 63,* 338–341.

Seyfarth, R. M., Cheney, D. L., & Marler, P. (1980). Monkey responses to three different alarm calls: Evidence of predator classification and semantic communication. *Science, 210,* 801–803.

Shanab, M. E., & Birnbaum, D. W. (1974). Durability of the partial reinforcement and partial delay of reinforcement extinction effects after minimal acquisition training. *Animal Learning and Behavior, 2,* 81–85.

Shanab, M. E., & Peterson, J. L. (1969). Polydipsia in the pigeon. *Psychonomic Science, 15,* 51–52.

Shanab, M. E., Sanders, R., & Premack, D. (1969). Positive contrast in the runway obtained with delay of reward. *Science, 164,* 724–725.

Sheffield, F. D. (1966). New evidence on the drive-induction theory of reinforcement. In R. N. Haber (Ed.), *Current research in motivation* (pp. 98–111). New York: Holt.

Sheffield, F. D., & Roby, T. B. (1950). Reward value of a non-nutritive sweet taste. *Journal of Comparative and Physiological Psychology, 43,* 471–481.

Sherman, A. D., Sacquitne, J. L., & Petty, F. (1982). Specificity of the learned helplessness model of depression. *Pharmacology, Biochemistry, and Behavior, 16,* 449–454.

Sherman, J. E. (1978). US inflation with trace and simultaneous fear conditioning. *Animal Learning and Behavior, 6,* 463–468.

Sherrington, C. S. (1906). *Integrative action of the nervous system.* New Haven, Conn.: Yale University Press.

Shettleworth, S. J. (1983). Memory in food hoarding birds. *Scientific American, 248,* 102–110.

Shettleworth, S. J., & Krebs, J. R. (1982). How marsh tits find their hoards: The roles of site preference and spatial memory. *Journal of Experimental Psychology: Animal Behavior Processes, 8,* 342–353.

Shiffrin, R. M., & Cook, J. R. (1978). Short-term forgetting of item and order information. *Journal of Verbal Learning and Verbal Behavior, 17,* 189–218.

Shiffrin, R. M., & Schneider, W. (1977). Controlled and automatic human information processing: II. Perceptual learning, automatic attending, and a general theory. *Psychological Review, 84,* 127–196.

Shimoff, E., Catania, A. C., & Matthews, B. A. (1981). Uninstructed human responding: Sensitivity of low-rate performance to schedule contingencies. *Journal of the Experimental Analysis of Behavior, 36,* 207–220.

Shipley, R. H. (1974). Extinction of conditioned fear in rats as a function of several parameters of CS exposure. *Journal of Comparative and Physiological Psychology, 87,* 699–707.

Sidman, M. (1953). Avoidance conditioning with brief shock and no exteroceptive warning signal. *Science, 118,* 157–158.

Sidman, M., & Stebbins, W. C. (1954). Satiation effects under fixed-ratio schedules of reinforcement. *Journal of Comparative and Physiological Psychology, 47,* 114–116.

Sidman, M., Stoddard, L. T., & Mohr, J. P. (1968). Some additional quantitative observations of immediate memory in a patient with bilateral hippocampal lesions. *Neuropsychologia, 6,* 245–254.

Siegel, S. (1969). Effect of CS habituation on eyelid conditioning. *Journal of Comparative and Physiological Psychology, 69,* 157–159.

Siegel, S. (1975). Evidence from rats that morphine tolerance is learned response. *Journal of Comparative and Physiological Psychology, 89,* 498–506.

Siegel, S. (1976). Morphine analgesic tolerance: Its situation specificity supports a Pavlovian conditioning model. *Science, 193,* 323–325.

Siegel, S. (1977). Morphine tolerance acquisition as an associative process. *Journal of Experimental Psychology: Animal Behavior Processes, 3,* 1–13.

Siegel, S. (1978). A Pavlovian conditioning analysis of morphine tolerance. In N. A. Krasnegor (Ed.), *Behavioral tolerance: Research and treatment implications* (NIDA Research Monograph No. 18). Washington, D.C.: U.S. Government Printing Office.

Siegel, S. (1979). The role of conditioning in drug tolerance and addiction. In J. D. Keehn (Ed.), *Psychopathology in animals: Research and clinical implications* (pp. 143–168). New York: Academic.

Siegel, S., & Andrews, J. M. (1962). Magnitude of reinforcement and choice behavior in children. *Journal of Experimental Psychology, 63,* 337–341.

Siegel, S., & Domjan, M. (1971). Backward conditioning as an inhibitory procedure. *Learning and Motivation, 2,* 1–11.

Siegel, S., Hinson, R. E., & Krank, M. D. (1978). The role of predrug signals in morphine analgesic tolerance: Support for a Pavlovian conditioning model of tolerance. *Journal of Experimental Psychology: Animal Behavior Processes, 4,* 188–196.

Siegel, S., Hinson, R. E., Krank, M. D., & McCully, J. (1982). Heroin "overdose" death: Contribution of drug-associated environmental cues. *Science, 216,* 436–437.

Siegel, S., Sherman, J. E., & Mitchell, D. (1980). Extinction of morphine analgesic tolerance. *Learning and Motivation, 11,* 289–301.

Signoret, J. L., & Lhermitte, F. (1976). The amnesic syndromes and the encoding process. In M. R. Rosenzweig & E. L. Bennett (Eds.), *Neural mechanisms of learning and memory* (pp. 67–75). Cambridge, Mass.: MIT Press.

Simon, H. A. (1973). The structure of ill-structured problems. *Artificial Intelligence, 4,* 181–202.

Simon, H. A. (1974). How big is a chunk? *Science, 183,* 482–488.

Simon, H. A. (1979). *Models of thought.* New Haven, Conn.: Yale University Press.

Skinner, B. F. (1938). *The behavior of organisms: An experimental analysis.* New York: Appleton-Century-Crofts.

Skinner, B. F. (1948). Superstition in the pigeon. *Journal of Experimental Psychology, 38,* 168–172.

Skinner, B. F. (1953). *Science and human behavior.* New York: Macmillan.

Skinner, B. F. (1957). *Verbal behavior.* New York: Appleton.

Slobin, D. I. (1966). Grammatical transformations and sentence comprehension in childhood and adulthood. *Journal of Verbal Learning and Verbal Behavior, 5,* 219–227.

Smith, E. E., Shoben, E. J., & Rips, L. J. (1974). Structure and process in semantic memory: A feature model of semantic decisions. *Psychological Review, 81,* 214–241.

Smith, M. C., Coleman, S. R., & Gormezano, I. (1969). Classical conditioning of the rabbit's nictatating membrane response at backward, simultaneous and forward CS-US intervals. *Journal of Comparative and Physiological Psychology, 69,* 226–231.

Smith, S. M. (1979). Remembering in and out of context. *Journal of Experimental Psychology: Human Learning and Memory, 5,* 460–471.

Smith, S. M. (1982). Enhancement of recall using multiple environmental contexts during learning. *Memory and Cognition, 19,* 405–412.

Smith, S. M., Glenberg, A, & Bjork, R. A. (1978). Environmental context and human memory. *Memory and Cognition, 6,* 342–353.

Smoke, K. L. (1933). Negative instances in concept learning. *Journal of Experimental Psychology, 16,* 583–588.

Snow, C. E. (1979). Mother's speech research: From input to interaction. In C. E. Snow & C. A. Ferguson (Eds.), *Talking to children: Language input and acquisition* (pp. 31–49). Cambridge: Cambridge University Press.

Snyder, S. H. (1974). Catecholamines as mediators of drug effects in schizophrenia. In F. O. Schmitt & F. G. Wordent (Eds.), *The neurosciences: Third study program.* Cambridge, Mass.: MIT Press.

Solnick, J. V., Rincover, A., & Peterson, C. R. (1977). Some determinants of the reinforcing and punishing effects of time-out. *Journal of Applied Behavior Analysis, 10,* 415–424.

Solomon, R. L. (1977). An opponent-process theory of motivation: IV. The affective dynamics of addiction. In J. D. Maser & M. E. P. Seligman (Eds.), *Psychopathology: Experimental models* (pp. 66–103). San Francisco: Freeman.

Solomon, R. L. (1980). The opponent-process theory of acquired motivation: The costs of pleasure and the benefits of pain. *American Psychologist, 35,* 691–712.

Solomon, R. L., & Corbit, J. D. (1974). An opponent process theory of motivation: Temporal dynamics of affect. *Psychological Review, 81,* 119–145.

Solomon, R. L., & Wynne, L. C. (1953). Traumatic avoidance learning: Acquisition in normal dogs. *Psychological Monographs, 67* (Whole No. 354).

Solomon, R. L., & Wynne, L. C. (1954). Traumatic avoidance learning: The principles of anxiety conservation and partial irreversibility. *Psychological Review, 61,* 353–385.

Spear, N. E. (1971). Forgetting as retrieval failure. In W. K. Honig & H. P. R. James (Eds.), *Animal memory* (pp. 47–114). New York: Academic.

Spear, N. E. (1973). Retrieval of memory in animals. *Psychological Review, 80,* 163–194.

Spear, N. E. (1978). *The processing of memories: Forgetting and retention.* Hillsdale, N.J.: Erlbaum.

Spear, N. E., Klein, S. B., & Riley, E. P. (1971). The Kamin effect as "state-dependent learning": Memory-retrieval failure in the rat. *Journal of Comparative and Physiological Psychology, 74,* 416–425.

Speers, M. J., Gillan, D. J., & Rescorla, R. A. (1980). Within-compound associations in a variety of compound conditioning procedures. *Learning and Motivation, 11,* 135–149.

Spence, K. W. (1936). The nature of discrimination learning in animals. *Psychological Review, 43,* 427–449.

Spence, K. W. (1937). The differential response in animals to stimuli varying within a single dimension. *Psychological Review, 44,* 430–444.

Spence, K. W. (1956). *Behavior theory and conditioning.* New Haven, Conn.: Yale University.

Sperling, G. (1960). The information available in brief visual presentations. *Psychological Monographs, 74* (Whole No. 498).

Sperling, G. (1963). A model for visual memory task. *Human Factors, 5,* 19–31.

Sperling, G. (1967). Successive approximations to a model for short-term money. *Acta Psychologia, 27,* 285–292.

Spinetta, J. J., & Rigler, D. (1972). The child-abusing parent: A psychological review. *Psychological Bulletin, 77,* 296–304.

Squire, L. R. (1986). Mechanisms of memory. *Science, 232,* 1612–1619.

Squire, L. R. (1987). *Memory and brain.* New York: Oxford University Press.

Staats, A. W., & Staats, C. K. (1958). Attitudes established by classical conditioning. *Journal of Abnormal and Social Psychology, 57,* 37–40.

Staats, C. K., & Staats, A. W. (1957). Meaning established by classical conditioning. *Journal of Experimental Psychology, 54,* 74–80.

Staddon, J. E. R. (1979). Operant behavior as adaption to constraint. *Journal of Experimental Psychology: General, 108,* 48–67.

Staddon, J. E. R. (1988). Quasi-dynamic choice models: Melioration and ratio-invariance. *Journal of the Experimental Analysis of Behavior, 49,* 303–320.

Staddon, J. E. R., & Ayres, S. L. (1975). Sequential and temporal properties of behavior induced by a schedule of periodic food delivery. *Behavior, 54,* 26–49.

Staddon, J. E. R., & Simmelhag, V. L. (1971). The "Superstition" experiment: A reexamination of its implications for the principles of adaptive behavior. *Psychological Review, 78,* 3–43.

Stapleton, J. V. (1975). Legal issues confronting behavior modification. *Behavioral Engineering, 2,* 35.

Stark, P., & Boyd, E. S. (1963). Effects of cholinergic drugs on hypothalamic self-stimulation response rates of dogs. *American Journal of Physiology, 205,* 745–748.

Starr, M. D. (1978). An opponent process theory of motivation: VI. Time and intensity variables in the development of separation-induced distress calling in ducklings. *Journal of Experimental Psychology: Animal Behavior Processes, 4,* 338–355.

Stein, L. (1969). Chemistry of purposive behavior. In J. T. Tapp (Ed.), *Reinforcement and behavior* (pp. 329–355). New York: Academic.

Stein, L., Belluzzi, J. D., & Wise, C. D. (1975). Memory enhanced by central administration of norepinephrine. *Brain Research, 84,* 329–335.

Stein, L., & Wise, C. D. (1969). Release of norepinephrine from the hypothalamus and amygdala by rewarding medial forebrain bundle stimulation and amphetamine. *Journal of Comparative and Physiological Psychology, 67,* 189–198.

Stein, L., & Wise, C. D. (1971). Possible etiology of schizophrenia: Progressive damage to the noradrenergic reward system of 6-hydroxydopamine. *Science, 1032–1036.*

Stein, L., & Wise, C. D. (1973). Amphetamine and noradrenergic reward pathways. In E. Usdin & S. H. Snyder (Eds.), *Frontiers in catecholamine research* (pp. 963–972). New York: Pergamon.

Steinbrecher, C. D., & Lockhart, R. A. (1966). Temporal avoidance conditioning in the cat. *Psychonomic Science, 5,* 441–442.

Stellar, J. R., Kelley, A. E., & Corbett, D. (1983). Effects of peripheral and central dopamine blockade on lateral hypothalamic self-stimulation: Evidence for both reward and motor deficits. *Pharmacology, Biochemistry, and Behavior, 18,* 433–442.

Stephens, C. E., Pear, J. J., Wray, L. D., & Jackson, G. C. (1975). Some effects of reinforcement schedules in teaching picture names to retarded children. *Journal of Applied Behavior Analysis, 8,* 435–447.

Stern, L. (1985). *The structures and strategies of human memory.* Homewood, Ill.: The Dorsey Press.

Steuer, F. B., Applefield, J. M., & Smith, R. (1971). Televised aggression and the interpersonal aggression of preschool children. *Journal of Experimental Child Psychology, 11,* 442–447.

Storms, L. H., Boroczi, G., & Broen, W. E., Jr. (1962). Punishment inhibits an instrumental response in hooded rats. *Science, 135,* 1133–1134.

Streeter, L. A., & Landauer, J. K. (1976). Effects of learning English as a second language on the acquisition of new phonetic contrast. *Journal of the Acoustical Society of America, 59,* 448–451.

Stuart, R. B. (1971). A three-dimensional program for the treatment of obesity. *Behavior Research and Therapy, 9,* 177–186.

Sutherland, N. S., & Mackintosh, N. J. (1971). *Mechanisms of animal discrimination learning.* New York: Academic.

Swanson, J. M., & Kinsbourne, M. (1979). State-dependent learning and retrieval: Methodological cautions against theoretical considerations. In J. F. Kihlstrom & F. J. Evans (Eds.), *Functional disorders of memory* (pp. 275–302). Hillsdale, N.J.: Erlbaum.

Sweeney, P. D., Anderson, K., & Bailey, S. (1986). Attributional style in depression: A meta-analytic review. *Journal of Personality and Social Psychology, 50,* 974–991.

Tait, R. W., Marquis, H. A., Williams, R., Weinstein, L., & Suboski, M. S. (1969). Extinction of sensory preconditioning using CER training. *Journal of Comparative and Physiological Psychology, 69,* 170–172.

Tait, R. W., & Saladin, M. E. (1986). Concurrent development of excitatory and inhibitory associations during backward conditioning. *Animal Learning and Behavior, 14,* 133–137.

Tanner, B. A., & Zeiler, M. (1975). Punishment of self-injurious behavior using aromatic ammonia as the aversive stimulus. *Journal of Applied Behavior Analysis, 8,* 53–57.

Tarpy, R. M., & Koster, E. D. (1970). Stimulus facilitation of delayed-reward learning in the rat. *Journal of Comparative and Physiological Psychology, 71,* 147–151.

Tarpy, R. M., & Mayer, R. E. (1978). *Foundations of learning and memory.* Glenview, Ill.: Scott, Foresman.

Tarpy, R. M., & Sawabini, F. L. (1974). Reinforcement delay: A selective review of the last decade. *Psychological Bulletin, 81,* 984–987.

Teitelbaum, P., & Epstein, A. N. (1962). The lateral hypothalamic syndrome: Recovery of feeding and drinking after lateral hypothalamic lesions. *Psychological Review, 69,* 74–90.

Tennen, H., & Eller, S. J. (1977). Attributional components of learned helplessness and facilitation. *Journal of Personality and Social Psychology, 35,* 265–271.

Terrace, H. S. (1963). Errorless discrimination learning in the pigeon: Effects of chlorpromazine and imipramine. *Science, 140,* 318–319.

Terrace, H. S. (1964). Wavelength generalization after discrimination learning with and without errors. *Science, 144,* 78–80.

Terrace, H. S. (1979). *Nim.* New York: Knopf.

Terrell, G., & Ware, R. (1961). Role of delay of reward in speed of size and form discrimination learning in childhood. *Child Development, 32,* 409–415.

Tharp, R. G., & Wetzel, R. J. (1969). *Behavior modification in the natural environment.* New York: Academic.

Theios, J., Lynch, A. D., & Lowe, W. F., Jr. (1966). Differential effects of shock intensity on one-way and shuttle avoidance conditioning. *Journal of Experimental Psychology, 72,* 294–299.

Thomas, E., & DeWald, L. (1977). Experimental neurosis: Neuropsychological analysis. In J. D. Maser & M. E. P. Seligman (Eds.), *Psychopathology: Experimental models* (pp. 214–231). San Francisco: Freeman.

Thompson, C. R., & Church, R. M. (1980). An explanation of the language of a chimpanzee. *Science, 208,* 313–314.

Thompson, R., & Dean, W. A. (1955). A further study on the retroactive effects of ECS. *Journal of Comparative and Physiological Psychology, 48,* 488–491.

Thompson, R. F., Clark, G. A., Donegan, N. H., Lavond, D. G., Lincoln, J. S., Madden, J., Mamounas, L. A., Mauk, M. D., McCormick, D. A., & Thompson, J. K. (1984). Neuronal substrates of learning and memory: A "multiple-trace" view. In G. Lynch, J. L. McGaugh, & N. M. Weinberger (Eds.), *Neurobiology of learning and memory* (pp. 137–164). New York: Guilford.

Thompson, R. F., Hicks, L. H., & Shvyrok, V. B. (1980). *Neural mechanisms of goal-directed behavior and learning.* New York: Academic.

Thompson, R. F., & Spencer, W. A. (1966). Habituation: A model phenomenon for the study of neural substrates of behavior. *Psychological Review, 73,* 16–43.

Thorndike, E. L. (1898). Animal intelligence: An experimental study of the associative processes in animals. *Psychological Review Monograph Supplement, 2,* 1–109.

Thorndike, E. L. (1932). *Fundamentals of learning.* New York: Teachers College, Columbia University.

Thune, L. E., & Underwood, B. J. (1943). Retroactive inhibition as a function of degree of interpolated learning. *Journal of Experimental Psychology, 32,* 185–200.

Tiffany, S. T., & Baker, T. B. (1981). Morphine tolerance in rats: Congruence with a Pavlovian paradigm. *Journal of Comparative and Physiological Psychology, 95,* 747–762.

Timberlake, W. (1983). The functional organization of appetitive behavior: Behavior systems and learning. In M. D. Zeiler & P. Harzem (Eds.), *Advances in analysis of behavior: Vol. 3. Biological factors in learning* (pp. 177–221). Chichester, England: Wiley.

Timberlake, W. (1984). A temporal limit on the effect of future food on current performance in an analogue of foraging and welfare. *Journal of Experimental Analysis of Behavior, 41,* 117–124.

Timberlake, W. (1986). Unpredicted food produces a mode of behavior that affects rats' subsequent reactions to a conditioned stimulus: A behavior-system approach to context blocking. *Animal Learning and Behavior, 14,* 276–286.

Timberlake, W., & Allison, J. (1974). Response deprivation: An empirical approach to instrumental performance. *Psychological Review, 81,* 146–164.

Timberlake, W., & Lucas, G. A. (1989). Behavior systems and learning: From misbehavior to general principles. In S. B. Klein & R. R. Mowrer (Eds.), *Contemporary learning theory: Instrumental conditioning theory and the impact of biological constraints on learning* (pp. 237–275). Hillsdale, N.J.: Erlbaum.

Timberlake, W., Wahl, G., & King, D. (1982). Stimulus and response contingencies in the misbehavior of rats. *Journal of Experimental Psychology: Animal Behavior Processes, 8,* 62–85.

Tinbergen, N. (1951). *The study of instinct.* Oxford: Clarendon.

Tinbergen, N., & Van Iersel, J. J. A. (1947). Displacement reactions in the three-spined stickleback. *Behavior, 1,* 56–63.

Tinsley, J. B., & Renner, K. E. (1975). Self-punitive behavior with changing percentages of reinforcement: The proper role of discrimination. *Learning and Motivation, 6,* 448–458.

Todd, G. E., & Cogan, D. C. (1978). Selected schedules of reinforcement in the black-tailed prairie dog *(Cynomys ludovicianus). Animal Learning and Behavior, 6,* 429–434.

Toister, R. P., Condron, C. J., Worley, L., & Arthur, D. (1975). Faradic therapy of chronic vomiting in infancy: A case study. *Journal of Behavior Therapy and Experimental Psychiatry, 6,* 55–59.

Tolman, E. C. (1932). *Purposive behavior in animals and men.* New York: Century.

Tolman, E. C. (1959). Principles of purposive behavior. In S. Koch (Ed.), *Psychology: A study of a science* (Vol. 2, pp. 92–157). New York: McGraw-Hill.

Tolman, E. C., & Honzik, C. H. (1930a). "Insight" in rats. *University of California Publications in Psychology, 4,* 215–232.

Tolman, E. C., & Honzik, C. H. (1930b). Degrees of hunger; reward and nonreward; and maze learning in rats. *University of California Publications in Psychology, 4,* 241–256.

Tolman, E. C., Ritchie, B. F., & Kalish, D. (1946). Studies of spatial learning: II. Place learning versus response learning. *Journal of Experimental Psychology, 36,* 221–229.

Tombaugh, T. N. (1966). Resistance to extinction as a function of the interaction between training and extinction delays. *Psychological Review, 19,* 791–798.

Tomie, A., Brooks, W., & Zito, B. (1989). Sign-tracking: The search for reward. In S. B. Klein & R. R. Mowrer (Eds.), *Contemporary learning theory: Pavlovian conditioning and the status of traditional learning theory* (pp. 191–223). Hillsdale, N.J.: Erlbaum.

Tomie, A., Murphy, A. L., & Fath, S. (1980). Retardation of autoshaping following unpredictable food: Effects of changing the context between pretraining and testing. *Learning and Motivation, 11,* 117–134.

Trabasso, T. R., & Bower, G. H. (1968). *Attention in learning: Theory and research.* New York: Wiley.

Tracy, W. K. (1970). Wavelength generalization and preference in monochromatically reared ducklings. *Journal of the Experimental Analysis of Behavior, 13,* 163–178.

Trapold, M. A., & Fowler, H. (1960). Instrumental escape performance as a function of the intensity of noxious stimulation. *Journal of Experimental Psychology, 60,* 323–326.

Trapold, M. A., & Winokur, S. (1967). Transfer from classical conditioning and extinction to acquisition, extinction, and stimulus generalization of a positively reinforced instrumental response. *Journal of Experimental Psychology, 73,* 517–525.

Traupmann, K. L. (1972). Drive, reward, and training parameters and the overlearning-extinction effect (OEE). *Learning and Motivation, 3,* 359–368.

Treisman, A. M. (1960). Contextual cues in selective listening. *Quarterly Journal of Experimental Psychology, 12,* 242–248.

Treisman, A. M., & Geffen, G. (1967). Selective attention: Perception or response? *Quarterly Journal of Experimental Psychology, 19,* 1–17.

Trenholme, I. A., & Baron, A. (1975). Intermediate and delayed punishment of human behavior by loss of reinforcement. *Learning and Motivation, 6,* 62–79.

Troland, L. T. (1928). *The fundamentals of human motivation.* New York: Van Nostrand.

Tulving, E. (1972). Episodic and semantic memory. In E. Tulving & W. Donaldson (Eds.), *Organization of memory* (pp. 381–403). New York: Academic.

Tulving, E. (1983). *Elements of episodic memory.* Oxford: Clarendon Press/Oxford University Press.

Tulving, E., & Donaldson, W. (1972). *Organization of memory.* New York: Academic.

Turvey, M. T. (1978). Visual processing and short-term memory. In W. K. Estes (Ed.), *Handbook of learning and cognitive processes* (Vol. 5, pp. 91–142). Hillsdale, N.J.: Erlbaum.

Ullmann, L. P., & Krasner, L. (1965). *Case studies in behavior modification.* New York: Holt, Rinehart & Winston.

Ulrich, R. E., Wolff, P. C., & Azrin, N. H. (1964). Shock as an elicitor of intra- and interspecies fighting behavior. *Animal Behavior, 12,* 14–15.

Underwood, B. J. (1945). The effect of successive interpolations on retroactive and proactive inhibition. *Psychological Monographs, 59* (Whole No. 273).

Underwood, B. J. (1951). Associative transfer in verbal learning as a function of response similarity and degree of first-list learning. *Journal of Experimental Psychology, 42,* 44–53.

Underwood, B. J. (1957). Interference and forgetting. *Psychological Review, 64,* 48–60.

Underwood, B. J. (1965). False recognition produced by implicit verbal response. *Journal of Experimental Psychology, 70,* 122–129.

Underwood, B. J. (1969). Attributes of memory. *Psychological Review, 76,* 559–573.

Underwood, B. J. (1977). *Temporal codes for memories: Issues and problems.* Hillsdale, N.J.: Erlbaum.

Underwood, B. J. (1983). *Attributes of memory.* Glenview, Ill.: Scott, Foresman.

Underwood, B. J., & Ekstrand, B. R. (1966). An analysis of some shortcomings in the interference theory of forgetting. *Psychological Review, 73,* 540–549.

Underwood, B. J., & Erlebacher, A. H. (1965). Studies of coding in verbal learning. *Psychological Monographs, 79* (Whole No. 606).

Underwood, B. J., & Freund, J. S. (1968). Effect of temporal separation of two tasks on proactive inhibition. *Journal of Experimental Psychology, 78,* 50–54.

Underwood, B. J., & Keppel, G. (1963). Coding processes in verbal learning. *Journal of Verbal Learning and Verbal Behavior, 1,* 250–257.

Underwood, B. J., & Postman, L. (1960). Extraexperimental sources of interference in forgetting. *Psychological Review, 67,* 73–95.

Ungar, G. (1976). Biochemistry of intelligence. *Research Communications in Psychology, Psychiatry and Behavior, 1,* 597–606.

Ungar, G., Galvan, L., & Clark, R. H. (1968). Chemical transfer of learned fear. *Nature, 217,* 1259–1261.

U.S. Department of Justice. Special Report: Drunk Driving, February 1988.

Vaccarino, F. J., Schiff, B. B., & Glickman, S. E. (1989). Biological view of reinforcement. In S. B. Klein & R. R. Mowrer (Eds.), *Contemporary learning theories: Instrumental conditioning and the impact of biological constraints on learning* (pp. 111–142). Hillsdale, N.J.: Erlbaum.

Valenstein, E. S. (1973). *Brain control.* New York: Wiley.

Valenstein, E. S., & Beer, B. (1964). Continuous opportunities for reinforcing brain stimulation. *Journal of Experimental Analysis of Behavior, 7,* 183–184.

Valenstein, E. S., Cox, V. C., & Kakolewski, J. W. (1969). The hypothalamus and motivated behavior. In J. T. Tapp (Ed.), *Reinforcement and behavior* (pp. 242–285). New York: Academic.

Vandercar, D. H., & Schneiderman, N. (1967). Interstimulus interval functions in different response systems during classical discrimination conditioning of rabbits. *Psychonomic Science, 9,* 9–10.

Vasta, R. (1975). Coverant control of self-evaluations through temporal cueing. *Journal of Behavior Therapy and Experimental Psychiatry, 7,* 35–37.

Verzeano, J., Laufer, M., Spear, S., & McDonald, S. (1970). The activity of neuronal networks in the thalamus of the monkey. In K. H. Pribram & D. E. Broadbent (Eds.), *Biology of memory* (pp. 239–271). New York: Academic.

Verzeano, M., & Negishi, K. (1960). Neuronal activity in cortical and thalamic networks. *Journal of General Physiology, 43,* Suppl., 177.

Voeks, V. W. (1954). Acquisition of S-R connections: A test of Hull's and Guthrie's theories. *Journal of Experimental Psychology, 47,* 137–147.

Vogel-Sprott, M., & Thurstone, E. (1968). Resistance to punishment and subsequent extinction of a response as a function of its reward history. *Psychological Reports, 22,* 631–637.

Wagner, A. R. (1969). Stimulus selection and a "modified continuity theory." In G. H. Bower & J. T. Spence (Eds.), *The psychology of learning and motivation* (Vol. 3, pp. 1–41). New York: Academic.

Wagner, A. R. (1981). SOP: A model of automatic memory processing in animal behavior. In N. E. Spear & R. R. Miller (Eds.), *Information processing in animals: Memory mechanisms* (pp. 5–47). Hillsdale, N.J.: Erlbaum.

Wagner, A. R., & Brandon, S. E. (1989). Evolution of a structured connectionist model of Pavlovian conditioning (AESOP). In S. B. Klein & R. R. Mowrer (Eds.) *Contemporary learning theories: Pavlovian conditioning and the status of traditional learning theory* (pp. 149–189). Hillsdale, N.J.: Erlbaum.

Wagner, A. R., Logan, F. A., Haberlandt, K., & Price, T. (1968). Stimulus selection in animal discrimination learning. *Journal of Experimental Psychology, 76,* 171–180.

Wahler, R. G., Winkel, G. H., Peterson, R. F., & Morrison, D. C. (1965). Mothers as behavior therapists for their own children. *Behaviour Research and Therapy, 3,* 113–124.

Walk, R. D., Gibson, E. J., Pick, H. L., Jr., & Tighe, T. J. (1959). The effectiveness of prolonged exposure to cutouts vs. painted patterns for facilitation of discrimination. *Journal of Comparative and Physiological Psychology, 52,* 519–521.

Walk, R. D., & Walters, C. P. (1973). Effect of visual deprivation on depth discrimination of hooded rats. *Journal of Comparative and Physiological Psychology, 85,* 559–563.

Wall, A. M., Walters, G. D., & England, R. S. (1972). The lickometer: A simple device for the analysis of licking as an operant. *Behavior Research Methods and Instrumentation, 4,* 320–322.

Wallace, M., Singer, G., Wayner, M. J., & Cook, P. (1975). Adjunctive behavior in humans during game playing. *Physiology and Behavior, 14,* 651–654.

Walters, G. C., & Grusec, J. F. (1977). *Punishment.* San Francisco: Freesman.

Walters, R. H. (1964). Delay of reinforcement gradients in children's learning. *Psychonomic Science, 1,* 307–308.

Wanner, E., & Maratsos, M. (1978). An ATN approach to comprehension. In M. Halle, J. Bresnan, & G. A. Miller (Eds.), *Linguistic theory and psychological reality* (pp. 119–161). Cambridge, Mass.: MIT Press.

Warner, L. H. (1932). An experimental search for the "conditioned response." *Journal of Genetic Psychology, 41,* 91–115.

Warrington, E. K., & Weiskrantz, L. (1968). A study of learning and retention in amnesic patients. *Neuropsychologia, 6,* 283–291.

Warrington, E. K., & Weiskrantz, L. (1970). Amnesic syndrome: Consolidation or retrieval? *Nature, 228,* 628–630.

Watkins, M. J. (1974). When is recall spectacularly higher than recognition. *Journal of Experimental Psychology, 102,* 161–163.

Watson, J. B. (1916). The place of the conditioned reflex in psychology. *Psychological Review, 23,* 89–116.

Watson, J. B., & Morgan, J. J. B. (1917). Emotional reactions and psychological experimentation. *American Journal of Psychology, 28,* 163–174.

Watson, J. B., & Raynor, R. (1920). Conditional emotional reactions. *Journal of Experimental Psychology, 3,* 1–14.

Waugh, N. C., & Norman, D. A. (1965). Primary memory. *Psychological Review, 72,* 89–104.

Weeks, R. A. (1975). Auditory location as an encoding dimension. *Journal of Experimental Psychology: Human Learning and Memory, 104,* 316–318.

Weidman, U. (1956). Some experiments on the following and the flocking reaction of mallard ducklings. *British Journal of Animal Behavior, 4,* 78–79.

Weinstock, S. (1958). Acquisition and extinction of a partially reinforced running response at a 24-hour intertrial interval. *Journal of Experimental Psychology, 56,* 151–158.

Weisberg, R., DiCamillo, M., & Phillips, D. (1979). Transferring old associations to new situations: A nonautomatic process. *Journal of Verbal Learning and Verbal Behavior, 17,* 219–228.

Weiskrantz, L., & Warrington, E. K. (1975). The problem of the amnesic syndrome in man and animals. In R. L. Isaacson & K. H. Pribram (Eds.), *The hippocampus* (pp. 411–428). New York: Plenum.

Weisman, R. G., & Litner, J. S. (1969). Positive conditioned reinforcement of Sidman avoidance behavior in rats. *Journal of Comparative and Physiological Psychology, 68,* 597–603.

Weisman, R. G., & Palmer, J. A. (1969). Factors influencing inhibitory stimulus control: Discrimination training and prior nondifferential reinforcement. *Journal of the Experimental Analysis of Behavior, 12,* 229–237.

Weiss, J. M., Glazer, H. I., & Pohorecky, L. A. (1976). Coping behavior and neurochemical changes: An alternative explanation for the original "learned helplessness" experiments. In G. Serban & A. King (Eds.), *Animal models in human psychobiology* (pp. 141–173). New York: Plenum.

Weiss, J. M., Stone, E. A., & Harrell, N. (1970). Coping behavior and brain norepinephrine in rats. *Journal of Comparative and Physiological Psychology, 72,* 153–160.

Wells, U. C., Forehand, R., Hickey, K., & Green, K. D. (1977). Effects of a procedure derived from the overcorrection principle on manipulated and nonmanipulated behavior. *Journal of Applied Behavior Analysis, 10,* 679–688.

Wessels, M. G. (1982). *Cognitive psychology.* New York: Harper & Row.

Westbrook, R. F., Homewood, J., Horn, K., & Clarke, J. C. (1983). Flavor-odor compound conditioning: Odor potentiation and flavor-attenuation. *Quarterly Journal of Experimental Psychology, 35B,* 13–33.

Wetherington, C. L. (1982). Is adjunctive behavior a third class of behavior? *Neuroscience and Biobehavioral Reviews, 6,* 329–350.

White, M. A. (1975). Natural rates of teacher approval and disapproval in the classroom. *Journal of Applied Behavior Analysis, 8,* 367–372.

Wickelgren, W. A. (1965). Acoustic similarity and retroactive interference in short-term memory. *Journal of Verbal Learning and Verbal Behavior, 4,* 53–61.

Wickelgren, W. A. (1974). *How to solve problems.* San Francisco: Freeman.

Wikler, A., & Pescor, F. T. (1967). Classical conditioning of a morphine abstinence phenomenon, reinforcement of opoid-drinking behavior and "relapse" in morphine-addicted rats. *Psychopharmacologia, 10,* 255–284.

Wilcott, R. C. (1953). A search for subthreshold conditioning at four different auditory frequencies. *Journal of Experimental Psychology, 46,* 271–277.

Wilcoxon, H. C., Dragoin, W. B., & Kral, P. A. (1971). Illness-induced aversions in rat and quail: Relative salience of visual and gustatory cues. *Science, 7,* 489–493.

Williams, D. C. (1959). The elimination of tantrum behavior by extinction procedures. *Journal of Abnormal and Social Psychology, 59,* 269.

Williams, M. (1950). The effects of experimentally induced needs upon retention. *Journal of Experimental Psychology, 40,* 139–151.

Williams, S. B. (1938). Resistance to extinction as a function of the number of reinforcements. *Journal of Experimental Psychology, 23,* 506–522.

Wingfield, A., & Byrnes, D. L. (1981). *The psychology of human memory.* New York: Academic.

Winston, H., Lindzey, G., & Connor, J. (1967). Albinism and avoidance learning in mice. *Journal of Comparative and Physiological Psychology, 63,* 77–81.

Wittrup, M., & Gordon, W. C. (1982). The alteration of a training memory through cueing. *American Journal of Psychology, 95,* 495–507.

Woddard, W. T. (1971). Classical respiratory conditioning in the fish: CS intensity. *American Journal of Psychology, 84,* 549–554.

Wolf, M. M., Hanley, E. L., King, L. A., Lachowicz, J., & Giles, D. K. (1970). The timergame: A variable interval contingency for the management of out-of-seat behavior. *Exceptional Children, 37,* 113–117.

Wolf, M. M., Risley, T., & Mees, H. L. (1964). Application of operant conditioning procedures to the behavior problems of an autistic child. *Behavior Research and Therapy, 1,* 305–312.

Wolpe, J. (1958). *Psychotherapy by reciprocal inhibition.* Stanford, Calif.: Stanford University Press.

Wolpe, J. (1976). *Theme and variations: A behavior therapy casebook.* Elmsford, N.Y.: Pergamon.

Wolpe, J. (1978). Self-efficacy theory and psychotherapeutic change: A square peg for a round hole. In S. Rachman (Ed.), *Advances in behavior research and therapy* (Vol. 1, pp. 231–236). Oxford: Pergamon.

Wood, F., Taylor, B., Penny, R., & Stump, D. (1980). Regional cerebral blood flow response to recognition memory versus semantic classification tasks. *Brain and Language, 9,* 113–122.

Wood, G., & Underwood, B. J. (1967). Implicit responses and conceptual similarity. *Journal of Verbal Learning and Verbal Behavior, 6,* 1–10.

Woodruff, G. (1979). Behavioral contrast and type of reward: Role of elicited response topography. *Animal Learning and Behavior, 7,* 339–346.

Woods, P. J., Davidson, E. H., & Peters, R. J. (1964). Instrumental escape conditioning in a water tank: Effects of variations in drive stimulus intensity and reinforcement magnitude. *Journal of Comparative and Physiological Psychology, 57,* 466–470.

Woodward, A. E., Jr., Bjork, R. A., & Jongeward, R. H., Jr. (1973). Recall and recognition as a function of primary rehearsal. *Journal of Verbal Learning and Verbal Behavior, 12,* 608–617.

Woodworth, R. S. (1918). *Dynamic psychology.* New York: Columbia University Press.

Wright v. *McMann,* 460 F.2d 126 (2d Cir. 1972).

Yule, W., Sacks, B., & Hersov, L. (1974). Successful flooding treatment of a noise phobia in an eleven-year-old. *Journal of Behavior Therapy and Experimental Psychiatry, 5,* 209–211.

Zaragoza, M. S., McCloskey, M., & Jamis, M. (1987). Misleading postevent information and recall of the original event: Further evidence against the memory impairment hypothesis. *Journal of Experimental Psychology: Learning, Memory, and Cognition, 13,* 36–44.

Zazdeh, L. A., Fu, K. S., Tanak, K., & Shimura, M. (Eds.). (1975). *Fuzzy sets and their applications to cognitive and decision processes.* New York: Academic.

Zeaman, D. (1949). Response latency as a function of the amount of reinforcement. *Journal of Experimental Psychology, 39,* 466–483.

Zechmeister, E. B. (1969). Orthographic distinctiveness. *Journal of Verbal Learning and Verbal Behavior, 8,* 754–761.

Zola-Morgan, S., & Squire, L. R. (1986). Memory impairment in monkeys following lesions limited to the hippocampus. *Behavioral Neuroscience, 100,* 155–160.

Zubin, J., & Barrera, S. E. (1941). Effect of electric convulsive therapy on memory. *Proceedings for the Society of Experimental Biology, 48,* 596–597.

AUTHOR INDEX

SUBJECT INDEX